Democracy
in the
United
States

ROBERT A. DAHL

Yale University

DEMOCRACY IN THE UNITED STATES: Promise and Performance

THIRD EDITION

Rand McNally
College Publishing Company

Chicago

RAND McNALLY POLITICAL SCIENCE SERIES

Credits for copyrighted material appear on p. 501.

76 77 78 10 9 8 7 6 5 4 3 2 1

To Kit
and his generation,
the inheritors

PREFACE TO THE THIRD EDITION

For many—perhaps most—readers this book will be a first encounter with a systematic and comprehensive analysis of the American political system. What such readers mainly seek, and rightly so, is to gain a better understanding of the political institutions and processes of the United States. With this goal in mind, I have sought to describe the major institutions and processes as objectively as I know how. But understanding requires not only description of *how* the elements operate but an explanation of *why.* I have therefore sought also to account for these institutions and processes, to explain why the various institutions and processes work the way they do.

Yet in my view readers are entitled to more than descriptions and explanations. In particular, American readers will often want to *appraise* the system, to judge how well the various institutions and processes function. I have therefore tried to assist and encourage the reader to develop a perspective from which to evaluate the performance of the political system, a perspective that may also serve as a guide in searching for better solutions. The perspective suggested here is solidly in the democratic tradition. But in my view it is more solidly based on experience and therefore less vulnerable to attack by critics of democracy than are the conventional views about democracy that many American readers may have accepted without critical examination. My intention, however, is not to persuade the reader to adopt any specific perspective but to consider more critically the grounds for his or her beliefs about democracy in the United States, and to begin developing elements of a political philosophy that will prove valid, useful, and open to growth throughout life.

In trying to achieve these goals in this third edition I have been enormously aided by the experience gained by Professor Douglas Shaw and his students at the University of Akron in using the previous edition. Professor Shaw's detailed comments and suggestions have helped me to clarify the exposition without indulging in oversimplification. I wish to express my appreciation to him and, thus, indirectly to his students. My thanks also go to James Austin, who helped me to bring the tables and charts up to date. Mrs. Nancy Hoskins managed to decipher my revised draft with exceptional skill and patience, often from a manuscript that would have driven a less resilient person to despair. Her secretarial skills and editorial assistance have greatly contributed to this edition, as they did to the last. Finally, I want to express my appreciation for the helpful editing of Ms. Charlotte Iglarsh of Rand McNally.

R.A.D.

TABLE OF CONTENTS

TABLES

FIGURES

INTRODUCTION

The United States approaches its two hundredth year of national existence governed by essentially the same Constitution that had been adopted within a few years after the Revolution ended (and thus older than any constitution prevailing in any other country). Had current circumstances been happier, an anniversary testifying to so much durability might have given rise to an exuberant and spontaneous national affirmation of the virtues of the American political system.

But the bicentennial year happened to follow a decade of unprecedented political strife. The severe conflicts that marked the decade began in the 1960s with unrest over the long-standing deprivation of the rights of blacks in the South. The flare-up of vast riots in the urban ghettos of the North spread to student uprisings in colleges and universities, and steadily swept over the country as opposition to the war in Vietnam intensified.[1] Hardly had the conflict over the Vietnam war begun to ebb than an event occurred that proved to be a minor episode in a much larger set of ominous happenings. In the early morning hours of June 17, 1972 the headquarters of the Democratic National Committee in the Watergate Hotel in the nation's capital were burglarized. Investigation led to a slow unraveling of extensive illegality centering in the White House; these findings led gradually to the near-certainty that the president would be impeached, convicted, and removed from office; and that near-certainty finally led to the president's precipitous resignation.[2]

---

1. See below, chapter 26.
2. See below, chapter 13.

It is not surprising that this decade of turmoil, deception, and misconduct weakened the confidence of many Americans in their political leaders and, what is more, in their political institutions.[3] Because Americans doubtless started from a higher plateau of faith in their political system than people in most other countries, there was more room for decline. In any event, the bicentennial did not find a great many people in a wildly celebratory mood.

A large, powerful, rich, complex, modern country like the United States is bound to have serious problems. Given these problems, the conflicts that are sure to arise, and the steadily rising level of education of the citizen body, it is likely that the old unthinking kind of faith has largely had its day and that many thoughtful Americans will continue to wonder about the adequacy of their political institutions.

The question that has to be confronted, as perhaps it has never been confronted before, is whether the American political system is satisfactory for the generations to come. If not, in what respects ought it to be changed? More specifically, has the presidency gone seriously awry, as a number of people have recently suggested? If so, in what ways? Should we Americans now be considering other alternatives? And what about Congress, that perennial target of criticism? Is it functioning as it should, or does it need significant changes, and if so, what should these be? What about the judicial system; state and local governments; the political parties?

Despite a prevalent illusion to the contrary, the best answers to questions like these are almost certainly not simple. Designing a constitution, or a significant change in an existing constitution, is a fearsomely complex enterprise fraught with unintended and unforeseeable consequences. Such great complexity in the nature of the problem ought to be a warning against hasty solutions, but difficulty in finding good solutions ought not to serve as an excuse for failing to confront the problem.

This book does not try to provide definite answers to the questions I have just raised. It does provide some of the basic understanding that would be necessary if we were to engage in an attempt to develop the best answers.

What we consider a satisfactory or adequate performance naturally depends on our criteria. In the case of Americans, our most fundamental criteria of performance are bound up with democratic ideas. Part One is therefore devoted to the task of clarifying the meaning of democracy, both as an ideal and as an achievement. In both theory and practice, democracy must necessarily take on a prime task: in order to obtain the benefits of cooperation, it must deal satisfactorily with

---

3. See below, chapter 10.

the existence of conflict. Human beings need one another; yet all recorded human experience demonstrates that human beings do not work in perfect harmony. Our actions conflict, and so we are driven apart from one another. As a consequence, political life carries with it the inescapable risk that conflict will lead to violence and domination, in which the winners rule over the losers. Democracy as an ideal seeks to meet this risk by insisting that a just government must be based upon the equality and consent of the citizens. These noble words are much overworked by Americans, but what do they actually mean in practice?

In Part One, we examine three answers. The standard answer learned in the schools is of course that the United States is a democracy, governed by the principle of majority rule. This is not, as we shall see, a wholly satisfactory answer. Having learned this answer in school and then discovering that the United States is certainly not a democracy in anything like the ideal sense, a great many people rush at once to the opposite conclusion—that it must therefore be dominated by a small ruling elite. The recent decade of disillusionment with American political institutions has led to a great upsurge in this perspective, which may be now fully as popular as the conventional school answer, if not more. Yet, even if it has important elements of truth, we shall see that there are difficulties in this all too easy response. What the American political system appears to be, like other systems we call democracies in everyday usage, is a complex combination of more or less democratic and nondemocratic elements. In this book such a political system is called a *polyarchy* in order to distinguish it from an ideal—or much more nearly ideal—democracy. If a polyarchy is not quite a democracy (and not quite a system of elite dominance, either), democratic ideals do nonetheless provide one with relevant standards of judgment for evaluating the performance of the country's institutions.

To look about the world as it is (and as it has always been) is to realize that democracy is by no means universally shared as an ideal; what is more, polyarchy exists in only a few dozen countries. These are a small minority of the countries in the world today and they contain only a minority of the people of the world. What special conditions, then, fostered a widespread belief in the democratic ideal in this country and thereby facilitated the development of polyarchy? Do these favorable conditions still exist, or have they so changed that democracy is no longer a wholly relevant ideal for Americans to hang on to? In Part Two, we examine the conditions that favored the emergence of polyarchy in the United States and the ways these conditions have changed.

If one concludes, as I do, that American conditions do not make the democratic ideal irrelevant as a standard of judgment or the institutions of polyarchy unworkable, the question remains whether the specific political institutions that Americans have evolved are still satisfactory today or are likely to be in the future. In Part Three, therefore, we look at the major institutions. In reflecting on their performance, it is important to understand how they have come to be the way they are. The Framers of the Constitution, of course, had a great deal to do with that. But the Framers are also important to our considerations because they had to deal with questions and alternative solutions that Americans have come to view as settled. For example, should the office of the Presidency be occupied by only one person—or several? In struggling to develop answers to questions of this kind, the Framers often had to grope in the obscurity of history, much of which was not strictly relevant. Although their foresight was remarkable, it is surely reasonable to ask whether our hindsight might not provide answers different from theirs. For example, does Congress *really* need two houses? If so, does it make sense to represent the fifty states equally, as in the Senate, or should both houses represent people? Although most Americans seem to be confident that equal state representation in the Senate is the only solution, James Madison, one of the greatest architects of the Constitution, argued (as we shall see) that equal representation of the States did not make much sense.

If the existence of conflict poses a crucial problem for all political systems, then the adequacy of a political system must also be judged by the ways in which it handles conflicts. In Part Four we shall investigate the factors that moderate or intensify political conflicts. We shall see that while the conditions of American political life ordinarily lead to comparatively moderate conflicts, in circumstances that seem to occur about once a generation conflicts are intensified, sometimes to the point of widespread unrest, serious violence, and uprisings. The 1960s were such a time.[4] On one occasion in our earlier history, as we all know, conflict led to such a sharp polarization of political forces that the political institutions could no longer cope successfully. A terrible and bloody civil war then erupted and left its mark on American life for a century. We shall try to understand the circumstances that can lead to such a tragic breakdown.[5]

If the institutions of polyarchy are to achieve the democratic ideals of political equality and consent, they must make it possible for citizens to act effectively to attain their goals. Ideally, the political institutions should provide citizens the opportunities to form intelligent judgments as to their needs and wants, to participate effectively in expressing those judgments, and to have their views weighed equally in the deci-

---

4. See below, chapter 26.
5. See below, chapter 27.

sions that control government policies in the final analysis. How then do Americans participate in political decisions and how can they act more effectively to secure their ends? The answer to this question is the substance of Part Five.

Finally, then, in the light of all these considerations, how are we to evaluate the performance of the American polyarchy? The answer is bound to reflect one's own judgments on many disputable questions of fact and value. In the last chapter, however, I shall set out a few of my own evaluations.

PART ONE

DEMOCRACY AS AN IDEAL
AND AS AN ACHIEVEMENT

1 CONFLICT AND COOPERATION

Like other forms of life on this planet, human beings confront a basic task: to deal satisfactorily with their conflicts and thereby secure the advantages of community and cooperation. Unlike other forms of life, human beings are endowed with a capacity to reflect on this task and to search for better solutions by conscious thought and deliberate choices.

The task of overcoming conflicts and achieving community and cooperation arises because human beings are unable and unwilling to live in complete isolation one from another. The advantages of cooperation and community life are so numerous and so obvious that they must have been evident to man from earliest times. By now, our ancestors have closed off the choice; for most of us the option of total isolation from a community is, realistically speaking, no longer open.

Nonetheless, however strongly human beings are driven to seek the company of one another, and despite thousands of years' practice, they have never discovered a way in which they can live together without conflict. Conflict exists when one individual wishes to follow a line of action that would make it difficult or impossible for someone else to pursue his own desires. Conflict seems to be an inescapable aspect of the community and hence of being human. Why conflict seems inescapable is a question that has troubled many people: philosophers, theologians, historians, social scientists, and doubtless a great many ordinary people. James Madison, who perhaps more than any other single delegate to the Constitutional Convention of 1787 gave shape to the American constitutional system, held that conflict was built into the very nature of men and women. Human beings have diverse abilities, he wrote in *The Federalist,* and these in turn produce diverse interests.

"As long as the reason of man continues fallible, and he is at liberty to exercise it," Madison wrote, "different opinions will be formed." Different opinions about religion, government, and other matters together with attachments to different leaders have "divided mankind into parties, inflamed them with mutual animosity, and rendered them much more disposed to vex and oppress each other than to cooperate for their common good." Thus, he concluded, "a landed interest, a manufacturing interest, a mercantile interest, a moneyed interest, with many lesser interests, grow up of necessity in civilized nations, and divide them into different classes, actuated by different sentiments and views."[1]

Whatever the explanation for conflict may be, and Madison's is but one among many, its existence is one of the prime facts of all community life. Yet if this were the only fact, then human life would truly fit the description by the English political philosopher, Thomas Hobbes, in his *Leviathan* (1651). Hobbes describes mankind in a state of nature—a condition without government—having little in the way of agriculture, industry, trade, knowledge, arts, letters or society. "And which is worst of all," he concluded in a famous sentence, to exist without government would mean "continual fear, and danger of violent death and the life of man, solitary, poor, nasty, brutish, and short."[2]

But life is not so dismal. A condition of totally unregulated conflict is, as Hobbes himself argued, obviously incompatible with community life. Along with the deep human need for living in communion with fellow human beings and alongside the inevitable conflicts that are generated whenever people try to live together, as far back into the past as one can pry, there have also been traces of a search for ways by which human beings can cooperate. Means have been sought for settling conflicts within a community without extensive violence and bloodshed, according to standards of justice held, at the very least, among those who enforce the rules. We cannot pause to probe the mystery; but the evidence is so great that we can safely accept it as a fact.

Thus our existence as social beings—social animals, if you prefer —is conditioned by a set of contradictory tendencies that, taken altogether, make us members of some political system:

1. Our need for human fellowship and the advantages of cooperation create communities.
2. But we are unable to live with others without conflict.
3. *Hence,* communities search for ways of adjusting conflicts so that cooperation and community life will be possible and tolerable.

---

1. Alexander Hamilton, John Jay, and James Madison, *The Federalist* (New York: Modern Library, n.d.), pp. 55–56. Madison's famous passages in *The Federalist,* too long to include here, are worth reading in full.

2. Thomas Hobbes, *Leviathan* (New York: Macmillan, 1947), p. 82.

The third stage is the turning point—from men and women as social animals to men and women as political animals. For if conflicts are to be settled, somewhere in the community there must be individuals or groups with enough authority or power to secure—if need be to compel—a settlement. Someone must make sure that the parties to a conflict abide by the judgment of the ruler, the will of God, existing rules, their own agreement, or law. At any rate, human communities do not seem ever to have existed without some such powers—without, that is, political institutions.

WHAT GOVERNMENT IS BEST?

To say that political institutions—governments—seem to be inevitable is not to say that they are always good. Unlike other animals, human beings can and do ask themselves whether things might not be better than they are. This concern for betterment stimulates some persons to search for standards by which to judge what is better. Thus when people become aware of their political institutions and the possibility of improving them, some begin to ask: What form of government is best?

No one knows when men first became conscious of their political institutions. We do know that for at least two thousand years before the first settlers came to America there had been in the Western world a distinct consciousness of political systems and an awareness of differences between them. During these twenty centuries people asked questions about politics, particularly during eras of great change and crisis when old systems confronted new ones. It is not a great step from becoming keenly aware that communities do have and probably must have governments—institutions for settling conflicts, enforcing rules, and perhaps even making rules—to the question, "What form of government is 'best'?" This question—like many other questions about politics—is likely to come to the fore in times of political disturbance and change; indeed it was one of the most important questions that confronted the Founders of the Republic who gathered in Philadelphia in 1787 to discuss constitutional problems.

Although they were very far from agreed on many questions, most of the Framers of the Constitution appear to have believed that they were forming "a more perfect union," as they asserted in the famous Preamble.

Nearly two centuries later, it is still as proper as it was then to ask what kind of political system would be best for the American people, and whether what has actually evolved in this country measures up satisfactorily to appropriate standards. That, in fact, is a central concern in this book.

Unfortunately, evaluating a political system is an enterprise of extraordinary difficulty. Consequently I would not want anyone to expect to find anything like a definitive answer here. Nonetheless, what follows are the questions I want to explore:

THE CENTRAL QUESTIONS

1. What standards or goals can we reasonably apply to the American political system? What obstacles to achieving these goals can we expect to arise?

To answer these questions is the task of Part One.

2. What special conditions in the United States favored the growth of democratic ideas and the institutions of polyarchy? Do these favorable circumstances still exist? (Part Two)

3. How did the key political institutions develop their present form, and how do they perform today? (Part Three)

4. How does the American political system deal with conflict? (Part Four)

5. Given the way the American political system operates, and the causes, how can citizens influence the conduct of the government? (Part Five)

6. How does the operation of the American political system measure up to the standards discussed in Part One? In the concluding chapter, I offer what is unavoidably a rather personal answer. It is hardly to be expected that every reader will agree with my appraisal. Even one who agrees that the descriptions and explanations offered in Parts Two, Three, and Four are essentially valid might arrive at a different judgment on the achievements of the American political system. Yet if we agree that the standards I am about to discuss are appropriate for judging the American polity, then it is less likely, I think, that we shall disagree widely in our appraisal.

2 TWO PRINCIPLES: EQUALITY AND CONSENT

Given the inevitability of conflict and the desirability of cooperation, what form of government is best? In particular, what kind of government is best for Americans?

Despite all the enormous changes affecting the American people and the world in which they live, the answer to this question that was most widely accepted by Americans during and after the American Revolution is still relevant today. This is the view that the government of a state is legitimate only if it derives its authority from the people. Behind the idea of government by the people lie beliefs in political equality and consent. We can see this view in the words that have become so much a part of the catechism of American schoolchildren as to be nearly devoid of specific meaning:

> We hold these truths to be self-evident, that all men are created equal, that they are endowed by their Creator with certain inalienable Rights, that among these are Life, Liberty and the pursuit of Happiness. —That to secure these rights, Governments are instituted among Men, deriving their just powers from the consent of the governed.

POLITICAL EQUALITY Even if the language of the Declaration is ambiguous, the principle is best understood not as a strictly factual proposition but as a moral or ethical assertion.[1] So interpreted, it does not imply that men are identical or equal in intelligence, strength, cunning, or many other respects. As a moral principle, its meaning might be summed up in this way: Human beings are entitled to be treated as if they were equal on all matters important to them. It is up to people who accept this moral principle to see to it that everyone has the minimal resources needed to make the principle workable in practice. Hence the common objection that men are not, in fact, equal by no means undermines the principle of political equality.

Nor is the objection fatal that no government—certainly none involving a large population—has ever managed to live up to the principle nor quite likely ever will. Ethical principles are intended as standards against which to judge achievement. We do not abandon standards of personal honesty, love, or justice merely because no one seems to be perfectly honest, loving, or just.

Why, you might ask, should one accept the principle of political equality? The authors of the Declaration did not try to prove its validity. They seem to have gotten by with the extravagant assertion that the principle is self-evident. It was convenient to assume so, for a consideration of the arguments for and against the principle of political equality would take us far beyond the limits of this book. Yet some of the reasons are worth mentioning here. Since they also relate to the idea of consent, we can treat the two ideas together.

CONSENT If political equality was often said to be 'self-evident,' Americans also fell into the habit quite early, as the Declaration shows, of asserting that the government of a state ought to rest on the consent of the people subject to it. Two years earlier, the First Continental Congress had already insisted

> That the inhabitants of the English colonies in North America, by the immutable laws of nature ... are entitled to life, liberty and property: and they have never ceded to any foreign power whatever, a right to dispose of either without their consent.

In their time, those were revolutionary words. The preamble of practically every state constitution adopted during the next several decades contained words to the general effect that the power of gov-

---

1. John Locke, who was a prime source of much of the political philosophy of the Founders, was explicit on this point: "Though I have said above ... 'That all men by nature are equal,' I cannot be supposed to understand all sorts of 'equality.' Age or virtue may give men a just precedency. Excellency of parts and merit may place others above the common level. Birth may subject some, and alliance or benefits others, to pay an observance to those to whom Nature, gratitude, or other respects, may have made it due; and yet all this consists with the equality which all men are in in respect of jurisdiction or dominion one over another, which was the equality I there spoke of as proper to the business in hand, being that equal right that every man hath to his natural freedom, without being subjected to the will or authority of any other man" (*Of Civil Government, Two Treatises* [London: J. M. Dent, 1924], p. 142).

ernment derives from the people and depends upon their consent. Such phrases, though not the ideas themselves, gradually became exhausted from sheer overwork. By now they come so easily to the lips of an American that few ever pause to ask *why* governments should or *how* they can rest on the consent of all.

Why Require Consent?

There are at least four reasons for insisting that governments ought, ideally, to derive their just powers from the consent of the governed.

First, government without consent is inconsistent with personal freedom. To the extent that I am compelled to obey rules that do not have my moral approval, I am not free. To be sure, personal freedom is an exacting demand; complete personal freedom is probably impossible to achieve. Nonetheless, one who believes in the value of individual freedom may reasonably hold that so far as possible no adult human being should ever be governed without his or her consent.

Second, government without consent can be an affront to human dignity and respect. We see this most vividly in extreme cases—the hapless victims in a concentration camp, who are subjected to the utmost humiliation, degradation, deprivation, and torture, losing thereby a part of their humanity.

Third, one might reason as follows: Certainly I do not want the government to act without *my* approval. But since I am not nor am I likely to be a dictator or a member of a ruling group, perhaps the safest way to ensure that the government will have *my* approval is to insist that it must have the approval of *everyone.* Reasoning from self-interest is not generally thought to be quite as noble as reasoning from general principles of freedom and dignity. Nonetheless we should rejoice, I believe, whenever freedom and dignity are supported by widespread self-interest; for nothing is quite so strong a buttress to social institutions as a firm foundation in self-interest.

Finally, one may insist on consent and equality because one thinks that governments "deriving their just powers from the consent of the governed" are more likely to be stable and durable. There are innumerable reasons why one may want stable government, including the fact that revolutions are very uncertain affairs. With a few exceptions, among which, happily, the American Revolution may be counted, those who start the first fires of a revolution are consumed in the holocaust. To control the course of a revolution is almost as difficult as to direct the path of a tornado. Whatever the reasons one may want stability in a government, it is reasonable to suppose that a government is less likely to create hostility, frustration, and resentment—sentiments that breed revolution—if it acts with the approval of its citizens than if it does not. Common sense and modern history both lend substance to this judgment. In the past century the most durable governments in the world have rested on widespread suffrage and other institutions for gaining consent.

PROBLEMS   To erect and maintain a political system that meets standards of political equality and consent to some reasonably satisfactory degree is an undertaking of very great difficulty. Let me mention five problems:

☐ Consent: How can *continuing* and not merely *past* consent be assured?
☐ Equality: How can gross inequalities be kept from undermining the principle of political equality?
☐ Conflict: How can a political system that is consistent with consent and political equality overcome conflicts?
☐ Competence: Can ordinary people govern themselves wisely?
☐ Effectiveness: Can they create and operate a government that is effective in solving the problems they want it to handle?

We turn to those questions in the next chapter.

3 FIVE QUESTIONS ABOUT EQUALITY AND CONSENT

1. ARE CONSENT AND POLITICAL EQUALITY TO BE CONTINUOUS?

Today the term *consent* has the flavor of the eighteenth century. It reminds us of the effort—successful, as it turned out—to destroy the legitimacy of monarchies by denying that they rested on the "consent of the people." In this perspective, you merely give or deny your consent to a person or government. To a particular government, you may perhaps give your consent once and for all.

Beyond this rather passive view, however, lies the notion that when certain decisions are made you ought to be able to express your deepest preferences, desires, or goals, and have them taken fully into account. If we also invoke the principle of political equality, your preferences as to the outcome ought to be weighed equally along with everyone else's: no more, no less; one person, one vote.

Considered as a continuing and active process, then, consent and political equality seem to require that full citizens must have unimpaired opportunities:

1. To figure out, discover, and formulate their goals: to find out what they really want.
2. By acting individually or in concert, to indicate their preferences to their fellow citizens and to the government.
3. To have their preferences weighted equally in the conduct of the government—that is, weighted with no discrimination because of *what* they want or *who* they happen to be.

How much lag or delay is reasonable between the time you formulate a goal and it is taken into account in decisions? Must institutions insure that your preferences are *immediately* taken into account? Is a year's delay reasonable? Two? Four? Longer? What about constitutional arrangements? Should not the system of government itself be more difficult to change than the specific policies of the government? If so, how difficult should it be to change or throw off a constitution?

For example, the fact that some people may have voted in the distant past to accept the Constitution of the United States is surely no reason why we, today, should feel bound to accept their verdict; particularly if we demand continuing 'consent' to the processes of government. Ideally, it seems, every new generation must be free to refuse its consent to the old rules and to make new ones. The Declaration of Independence contains these ringing phrases:

> That whenever any Form of Government becomes destructive of these ends [Life, Liberty, and the pursuit of Happiness], it is the Right of the People to alter or to abolish it, and to institute a new Government, laying its foundation on such principles and organizing its power in such form, as to them shall seem most likely to effect their Safety and Happiness.

Seventy years later, confronted by secession, and on the eve of war, in his inauguration speech, Lincoln reaffirmed the same principle:

> This country, with its institutions, belongs to the people who inhabit it. Whenever they grow weary of the existing government, they can exercise their constitutional right of amending it, or their revolutionary right to dismember or overthrow it.[1]

But "the people" is an ambiguous phrase. Do these famous words mean that whenever a majority is discontented with the government it should be free to change it? If they are not permitted to do so, then can we say that they have given their approval, in any realistic sense, to the processes of government? Yet if every majority were free to alter the rules of government, could a constitution be more binding than ordinary law? Is there no legitimate way by which groups smaller than a majority can receive guarantees that the rules they agree to abide by will be more or less permanent and will not change at the whim of the next legislature?

Questions like these lead directly to the problem of minority rights.

2. CAN SUFFICIENT EQUALITY BE MAINTAINED?

Political equality must surely be one of the most exacting demands ever placed on a government. Certainly it has never been attained in the United States, or anywhere else for that matter.

There are three persistent causes of political inequalities. *First,* some persons manage to acquire more political resources, influence, and power than others because of what appear to be *individual* charac-

---

1. Carl Sandburg, *Abraham Lincoln, The War Years,* vol. 1 (New York: Harcourt, Brace, 1939), p. 133.

teristics: matters of temperament, interests, skills, and specific endowments.

Second, independent of individual characteristics, *social* arrangements generally create some inequalities in political resources, influence, and power. Thus an enormous source of inequality in the United States has been racial discrimination against American Indians and Afro-Americans. So far as I am aware, no other country with continuing institutions of representative government (that claim to rest on equality and consent) has had such an appalling record of mistreatment of racial minorities. As we shall see, the tension between the effort to maintain a democratic republic and yet deny political equality to Afro-Americans has dominated political life in this country from the Constitutional Convention to the present day. Racial discrimination, however, is by no means the only source of unequal political resources. There are also large and persistent differences in education, income, wealth, access to communications, and so on.

Third, among any collection of people larger than a few thousand, not everyone can participate equally in all aspects of decision-making. Even if there were no other limitations, people rarely, if ever, have an unlimited amount of time to spend on making decisions. At a meeting of ten thousand people, only a tiny minority can have an opportunity to speak. Where citizens number in the millions, the opportunities must necessarily be even more restricted. In situations where everyone cannot be granted the right to participate fully, the principle of political equality itself dictates the need for a system of *representation.*

The criterion of equality might still be met if everyone could participate equally in choosing and influencing representatives, if the representatives were mere agents of their constituents, and if all were equal in influencing decisions. In practice these conditions are never wholly satisfied. For example, it appears to be very nearly impossible for a large collection of people to elect representatives who are nothing more than agents of their constituents. In practice, representatives invariably acquire an additional increment of power; they are not simply ordinary citizens expressing the collective will of their constituents. Among other causes are these: questions of policy are often highly complicated; citizens sometimes have no clear-cut views; if they do, they disagree among themselves; they often fail to keep in touch with their representatives; they find it hard to do much more than vote; they leave decisions pretty much to the person elected.

It is not surprising, as we shall see in the next chapter, that some critics contend that what is called a representative government is largely a front that conceals a *ruling elite.* The argument, to be sure, often gains support by confusing the undeniable existence of inequalities in political resources, influence, and power, with the existence of a ruling elite. Yet whatever the correct assessment may be, the existence of serious inequalities poses a problem for a system that claims to adhere to the principle of political equality.

3. CAN CONFLICTS BE HANDLED SATISFACTORILY?

Like any other government, a government by the people must somehow cope with the fundamental task of overcoming conflict. Early in the Constitutional Convention James Madison expressed a concern that must have been widely shared among the other delegates. Economic relationships, geographical location, religious feelings, even loyalties to particular leaders, could all lead to conflict. And what would restrain one faction in its struggles with another? Honesty? Reputation? Conscience? Religion? In Madison's view, all limits to faction that depend on the willingness of an individual or a group to exercise self-restraint are bound to be inadequate.[2]

Like most of the other delegates, Madison was more inclined to stress the dangers that could arise from a willful or tempestuous majority than from a minority. For he assumed that in a republic a majority could more easily have its own way. But he was not unmindful of the possibility that minority factions might also threaten a republic—if, for example, the minority happened to include the rich and those with military skills.[3]

The Dangers of Faction

Precisely what are the dangers of faction that preoccupied the Framers ? Curiously enough, none of the men at the Convention ever seems to have stated exactly what he had in mind. On this question even the clearest minds, like those of Madison and James Wilson of Pennsylvania, gave forth cloudy answers. When the delegates descended from vague generalities to concrete cases, the examples they chose generally involved attempts to bring about a less unequal distribution of property.[4] In fact, a careful reading of the record of debates suggests the cynical answer that when the delegates at the Constitutional Convention spoke of the dangers of faction they were usually thinking of attacks on property—their own.

With the aid of the experience that has accumulated since 1787, perhaps today we can see the problem of faction more clearly than the delegates to the Convention were able to do. We have learned some hard lessons. When someone says he opposes factions and parties,

---

2. See "Debates in the Federal Convention of 1787 as reported by James Madison," in *Documents Illustrative of the Formation of the Union of the American States*, selected, arranged, and indexed by Charles C. Tansill (Washington: Government Printing Office, 1927), p. 162 (hereafter cited as *Documents*).

3. *Ibid.*, p. 230.

4. For example, see Madison's comments, *Ibid.*, pp. 280–281.

what he usually means, it seems, is that he opposes every faction, every party, every interest—except his own. If one believes that policies proposed by others will deprive him of something he values, or if he so strongly believes his own policies are right that he would impose them on other people no matter what they prefer, he finds it easy to define what the others wish to do as tyranny and what he himself wishes to do as obvious justice.

Many of the concrete concerns of the Framers were, I believe, of this kind. To some extent, they elevated their own privileges into universal matters of abstract and universal right. Groups who might interfere with their privileges were, in their eyes, dangerous factions. In this respect they carried partisan attitudes into the Convention, yet were usually unaware that they did so. They were not necessarily cynical, merely human. (Does one have a right to expect more from men simply because they make a constitution?)

Yet it is too easy to jump to the conclusion that the fear of faction expressed by the Framers represented nothing more than sordid self-interest. Whatever their motives and biases may have been, whatever the extent to which they were influenced by their own economic positions and ideological perspectives, the problem they confronted was genuine, important, timely, persistent, and worthy of the concern they gave it. For the problem of faction is simply the mirror image of the problem of gaining consent—of governing with the consent of the governed. Goals of personal freedom, human dignity, enlightened self-interest, and political stability all justify a serious concern for gaining consent, and hence for keeping conflict within bounds, so that in the best of circumstances all citizens will feel that what they hold most dear is respected and protected by the government—while even in the worst of circumstances they will feel that the laws are at least tolerable, and do not encourage disloyalty, violence, or civil wars.

As practical men, the Framers were concerned lest conflicts get out of hand. Faction had contributed to the destruction of previous republics; faction was a worrisome fact of recent experience; and faction would be a standing danger to the new republic.[5]

The Inevitability of Conflict

Yet, being realists, the Framers also knew that conflict is inevitable. Conflict, as Madison said, is sown in the nature of humankind. An autocratic government might suppress the symptoms of conflict, as modern dictators have succeeded in doing; but even an autocracy cannot eliminate the causes. By establishing a republic in which citizens would enjoy a large measure of personal freedom, the Founders were bound to make it easy for conflict to erupt. How, then, was conflict to be man-

---

5. *Ibid.*, pp. 162–163.

aged? How could it be moderated so that it would not wreck the new republic? How could government be effectively carried on with something like the general consent of the people?

Since political philosophers, like architects, sometimes conceal their failures behind a handsome front, the unwary may conclude that the solution would be clear if one only understood the philosophers better. In this case, however, modesty may be misplaced. Although political philosophers have long wrestled with the problem, the disagreeable fact remains that they have not been able to prescribe a perfect solution except under certain highly improbable circumstances.

Solution: Agree on Policies

The obvious way out, of course, is to eliminate conflict. This happy solution is characteristic of many literary utopias, where social life is downright inhuman in its lack of conflict.

But if one concludes that complete agreement is a hopeless objective and not necessarily a very desirable one, then one must search elsewhere for a solution. Another way out is to search for specific policies that all citizens approve of, even though they may have initially disagreed with each other. Surely it is not absurd to suppose that conflict can sometimes be transformed into decisions that have the approval of everyone. Perhaps all of us have had experiences of this kind. This is particularly true when we try to arrive at decisions within a group in which everyone shares fundamental values, but may differ on specific questions.

The difficulty with all solutions along these lines is that decisions rarely do receive unanimous approval. Do I consent to decisions with which I disagree? Who is a better judge than I of what my 'will,' my policy, really is? Should anyone else have the authority to proclaim that a policy really has my consent? Although a distinction can be made between what I really believe is best and what I momentarily think or say is best, a good deal of experience suggests that to allow someone else to make this distinction for me is very dangerous.

A tyrant might insist, despite my denial, that he has my consent for all he does, because he knows better than I what I really want. When an individual says he disapproves of the policies of the government, even when these policies have the blessings of an enlightened dictator or an enlightened majority, the safest course in practice, I believe, is to assume that he knows his own mind. Otherwise, government by consent is likely to degenerate into a mere ritualistic formula.

Agree on a Process

Even if people cannot always agree on specific policies, however, an alternative solution is to gain their consent for a *process*. It is perfectly reasonable to me to say that I approve of the process by which certain kinds of decisions are made, even if I do not always like the specific results. Thus the consent of the governed may be interpreted to mean their approval of the processes by which decisions are arrived at and their willingness to abide by these decisions even when they seem wrong.

But what kind of a process shall I require? If I hold that no one can, as a general matter, know my goals and values better than I myself, then no doubt I will insist that the process of making decisions must provide me with a full opportunity to make my views known. Even if I am willing to leave details to experts, I do not want anyone else to have more power over the decision than I do. A solution along these lines might well appeal to me as the best attainable, given the inescapable conditions mentioned earlier. My need for human fellowship impels me to live in a society; I cannot live with others without sometimes disagreeing with them; therefore I must find some way to settle our conflicts that will appear fair to all of us.

One familiar process that is widely thought to meet these requirements is majority rule. In the next chapter we shall explore this solution, and some difficulties with it.

4. CAN THE PEOPLE GOVERN WISELY?

If the best government is one where all persons who are subject to a government's decisions must, somehow, give their active and express consent to those decisions, then clearly we will have—must have—rule by the people. Yet no government has ever tried to secure the active consent or participation of *all* the people. To take one example, persons under some rather arbitrary age like 18 or 21 are excluded everywhere from voting in elections. Why? Because they are assumed (by those beyond this threshold) to be, on the average, not yet competent enough to be allowed to participate in the government of the state.

Aha! one might say, isn't it possible that a lot of people over 18 or 21, or whatever age you may choose, are also incompetent to govern themselves? In fact, may not the people, taken as the general adult population, be incompetent to govern? If so, shouldn't the people *be* governed by those among them who are *best* qualified to govern?

The belief that the best government is necessarily one controlled by a small elite of the most qualified persons is ancient and powerful. One set of alternatives to rule by the people, then, consists of political arrangements that call for government by the minority, consisting of those best qualified to govern. The argument has never been more brilliantly nor more persuasively set out than it was over two thousand years ago in a work by a famous Greek philosopher critical of democracy in his own city, Athens. In *The Republic,* Plato argued that government should be in the hands of those best qualified to govern because of their exceptional virtues and knowledge. A crucial element in his argument is the assumption that the number of people properly qualified to govern is, in any community, almost certain to be a minority. The contrary view holds that everyone should govern since, ideally, no adult should be governed without his or her consent. It contends that political virtue and wisdom are not lodged exclusively in any identifiable group of persons. And it insists that if consent is to mean anything, every adult must be quite free to participate in all political decisions without fear or favor.

The debate between those who espouse these conflicting doctrines would not have endured so long if each viewpoint did not have a good deal to be said for it—and each runs into some rather serious problems.

Meritocracy, the aristocratic or elitist solution[6] is frequently used for governing other organizations, even by those who reject it for governing the state. Meritocracy is particularly common in organizations where superior skills are crucial to success and where, it is supposed, these superior skills can be more or less definitely defined and identified. The perennial appeal of the doctrine of meritocracy or aristocracy, then, is that it focuses directly on the problems of *fitness* to rule and stresses the importance of having good leadership, of giving authority to *skillful, wise,* and *virtuous* men or women. Leadership is a persistent problem in all political systems.

Yet it is one thing to govern a family, a ship, an army, a business firm, or a government bureau, and quite another to govern a community or a nation. As a matter of fact even in those institutions where 'aristocratic' solutions are supposed to work best, they have often produced notoriously incompetent leaders. Whatever may be the justification for the aristocratic solution for providing leadership in certain situations, there are four major objections to applying the aristocratic doctrine to the political system of an entire community:

First, the standards of skill, wisdom, and virtue required are unclear. Men of great learning are not always virtuous, and men of virtue are not always learned. After nearly twenty-five centuries, almost the only people who seem to be convinced of the advantages of being ruled by philosopher-kings are . . . a few philosophers. Though indispensable as advisers and occasionally skillful in politics, scholars, as a group, have not greatly impressed others with their competence as rulers. The skills of the businessman or military leader are highly spe-

---

6. Plato called his government *aristocracy,* meaning "rule by the best." Later that term came to be applied (in a way Plato never intended) to groups with hereditary privileges, such as the English or French aristocracy. Modern writers sometimes refer to *meritocracy,* or elite rule. Since there is no longer an agreed term meaning government by a minority consisting of the best qualified, I use the terms aristocracy, meritocracy, and elite rule more or less interchangeably in this book.

cialized, and very different from those required in government: Ulysses S. Grant, a great general, and Herbert Hoover, a great businessman, were not great presidents. In sum, it is easy to propose in academic circles that the skillful, wise, and virtuous should rule; but it is difficult to establish practical standards for identifying persons with superior skill, wisdom, and virtue in politics. There seems to be a very strong and very human tendency to solve the problem by defining skill, wisdom, and virtue in the image of one's own self, group, or class. Was it by chance that Plato, a philosopher, concluded that the best rulers would be contemplative men rather like himself?

Second, even if the standards were much clearer than they are, how are they to be applied? How are the rulers to be settled? In a mad scramble for power, the wise and virtuous are likely to be trampled to death. Popular election would turn the whole process upside down. Hereditary aristocracies have always been subject to the great gamble of genetics and early environment; there is no guarantee that the first-born son of a wise and virtuous father may not be a dullard, or a scoundrel, or both. One might propose that the rulers should be chosen by the wise and virtuous. But of course this only pushes the problem one stage farther back: Who is wise and virtuous enough to choose the wise and virtuous men who will choose the rulers?

Third, can a process designed to select only the wise and virtuous also insure that the leaders so chosen have widespread consent for their government? If it is said that surely the wise and virtuous would have general consent for their rule, then why not adopt the democratic solution and allow the people to choose their leaders? If, on the other hand, one objects that the people might not choose wise and virtuous leaders, then, since they are not the choice *of* and *by* the people, must they be imposed *on* the people? If so, would not the attempt to impose leaders on the people degenerate into a trial by battle in which the strongest, not the wisest and most virtuous, would win?

Finally, even if the skillful, wise, and virtuous could somehow be chosen as rulers, how can we be sure that they will not be corrupted by power? As we shall see when we consider the development of the American presidency, the dangers created by the mysterious alchemy of power are too familiar to be ignored.

For anyone convinced by these objections to meritocracy, the main alternative in the United States ever since colonial times has always been popular government. In the eyes of one who believes in equality and consent, no one group can be found with such clearly superior talent and virtue to entitle it to rule. With the proper conditions—and it is the job of one who advocates these goals to foster and maintain these conditions—practically everyone has sufficient knowledge and virtue to share, directly or indirectly, in the task of governing. In any case, even though I may lack technical knowledge as to the best or most efficient means, is anyone else likely to know better than I what end or goals are best for me?

Nonetheless, the problem is troublesome and real. Even if the ordinary citizen may be counted on, by and large, to know what ends are best for him, what about the excruciatingly difficult problems of means? For example, most of us could not possibly decide intelligently what pharmaceuticals should be sold freely, or prohibited, or issued only by prescription. Clearly, then, there are decisions that require me to *delegate* authority to others. One solution is to delegate some authority to elected representatives; but if I delegate, may I not end up with a kind of aristocracy of experts, or even false experts? As we shall see in the next chapter, some critics of representative government argue that this is exactly what happens.

5. WILL THE GOVERNMENT BE EFFECTIVE?

Can a government that tries to honor the ideas of consent and political equality be effective in dealing with the matters that the people regard as important?

Once again, the heart of the problem is the existence of disagreements over the ends for which a government should strive or the means most appropriate to achieving particular ends. A process that requires a search for policies that will satisfy everyone may be interminable. Because of the opposition of a minority, policies advocated by a substantial part of the people may be blocked for years or decades, or even indefinitely put off. Yet if minorities can be easily overridden, the government may be able to act with dispatch, but how effective will it be from the point of view of the minorities? It may not solve *their* problems. And what happens to *their* consent? Like the problem of conflict itself, the problem of governmental effectiveness is so intimately tied up with the solution of majority rule and alternatives to it that we must now turn to that solution and the problems it generates. But first let me summarize the argument so far.

SUMMARY

In the first two chapters, we saw that:

1. The benefits of human fellowship and cooperation impel human beings to seek ways of handling conflicts so that cooperation and community life will be possible and tolerable.

2. A conscious concern for this task generates the question: What government is best?

3. One answer, singularly important for Americans, is that the best government for a state is a government of the people based on political equality and the consent of all.

In this chapter we have seen that an attempt to establish and maintain a government that will satisfy the principles of equality and consent encounters five major problems: continuing consent, inequalities, conflict, competence, and governmental effectiveness. In the next three chapters, we shall examine three very general types of solutions.

4 MAJORITY-RULE DEMOCRACY AS A SOLUTION

Can a government be established and maintained that will surmount the challenges discussed in the last chapter and achieve rule by the people based on consent and political equality?

Probably the best known answer goes something like this: The requirements of consent can be satisfied if the citizens all approve of the principle of majority rule. By this principle all conflicts over the policies of government are settled, sooner or later, by a majority of citizens or voters—either directly in a public assembly or in a referendum, or indirectly through elected representatives. That this consent will be freely given, and not coerced, can be insured by legal and constitutional protection of basic rights to speak, write, publish, organize, oppose the government, vote, be a candidate, and the like. If these basic rights are protected for everyone, then political equality will also be attained.

There are, however, some problems concealed in this attractive answer. Let me mention a few.

WHAT PEOPLE? When one says he favors government by the people, the question immediately arises: what people? In practice, what we assume to be a *people* for purposes of self-government consists of a particular collection of human beings whose identity as a "people" or a nation has already been established, often by bitter controversy, violence, compulsion, and, as in the case of the American people, civil war.

Notice that by conceding to every human being claims to his or her consent and political equality you do not answer the question: what people? You simply require that an answer be found. For unless all the people of the world are to govern themselves in a single, unitary world state, the human species has to be separated into political communities within each of which self-government can take place.

When the term *democracy* was first used by the Greeks, they assumed that a "people" could not be more numerous or more diverse than the citizens of a small city-state. By the beginning of the nineteenth century, advocates of democracy pretty generally assumed that the citizens of a nation-state could constitute a "people." Yet the boundaries of nation-states are mainly products of struggle and violence. Do the persons incorporated within these boundaries, perhaps by force, necessarily form a "people"? If residents of a nation-state disagree as to whether they should form a single people or separate into two or more countries, are there general principles to which we may look for guidance? This much may be said: if there *are* general principles, they are obscure, difficult, controversial, and command so little agreement that when such issues arise, in practice force seems more likely to prevail than reasoned discussion and peaceful settlement.

Even if we were to agree that some particular collection of human beings—Americans, let us say—ought to constitute a single people for purposes of governing themselves according to the principles of consent and political equality, two further problems would remain. *First,* even the most ardent advocate of democracy does not intend that consent and political equality should apply literally to *all* the people. Full political equality will be denied to some part of the people, and their consent will be thought unnecessary, because they are held to be incompetent on grounds of immaturity. No one seriously contends that the suffrage should be extended to five-year-old children, for example. Thus "a majority of the people" really means, at most, "a majority of adults."

Second, suppose that a "people" such as the Americans, the Swiss, or the Canadians want to form themselves into a single self-governing unit for some purposes and at the same time into smaller units—states, provinces, cantons, cities, towns, etc.—for other purposes. If so, a majority of the people for some purposes must necessarily be different in size and composition from a majority for other purposes. In fact, a majority of adult citizens in the whole country may even be thought to have no right to overrule the majority of the smaller unit on some matters. We have now plunged deeply into the problem of *federal* states, to which it is difficult and sometimes impossible to apply simple democratic ideas formed on the model of the small city-state.

MAJORITY RULE VERSUS MINORITY RIGHTS The straightforward application of the principle that the majority should be sovereign on *all* questions of public significance is, as a practical matter, not likely to receive everyone's continuing approval—except under unusual circumstances. Continuing and universal approval of the principle of majority rule requires a high degree of consensus among all the citizens as to what the policies of government should be. While a citizen may make certain allowances for majority decisions that displease him, the more frequently one expects to be in a minority, the less likely one is to accept the principle of majority rule. The prospect of being in a minority can, perhaps, be accepted calmly so long as the issues are trivial. But the more important the issues, the more difficult it is to accept defeat by a hostile majority. The more I expect that majorities are going to insist on policies that conflict with my most cherished values, the more likely I am to oppose the principle of majority rule. Surely few people would be so loyal to the abstract principle as to approve of it even if they expected it to lead regularly to repugnant policies. At some point even the strongest adherent of majority rule will give up in despair. In a nation of convinced anti-Semites and religious bigots, a modern Jefferson might be compelled to oppose the principle of the sovereign majority.

It seems reasonable to conjecture that the more diverse the beliefs held among a body of people, the less likely it is that they will approve of the idea of making decisions by majority rule. To the extent that this conjecture is valid, it is a severe restriction on the principle of rule by a sovereign majority, particularly in societies with great diversity. For it seems entirely reasonable to hold that diversity of beliefs is likely to be greater the larger the number of citizens, the bigger the territory over which they are spread, and the greater the distinctions of race, ethnic group, regional culture, occupation, social class, income, property, and so on. Some advocates of rule by the sovereign majority have therefore argued, as did Rousseau, a French philosopher of the eighteenth century, that majority decisions would be acceptable only among very small bodies consisting of highly similar individuals. According to this view, nations, even as small as Norway and certainly as large as the United States, are unsuitable for rule by the people.

One possible way to maintain homogeneity would be to eliminate all dissenting minorities who would object to the decisions of a majority. In Athens the Ecclesia—the sovereign town meeting composed theoretically of all adult citizens—had the power of *ostracism,* by which it could banish an unpopular citizen from Athens for ten years. Rousseau evidently believed that unity would be maintained if dissident citizens had the right to emigrate—presumably to a more sympathetic community. Another possibility—painful to Americans—is secession. Yet all of these solutions entail serious practical and moral difficulties, particularly in the modern world. Emigration, for example, can be a staggering price to pay simply for being in a minority; must the price of one's beliefs depend solely on the numbers who happen to share them? Yet if emigration is purely optional, who would emigrate? Many dissenters would remain to deny the legitimacy of majority rule as it applies to them. Shall we then expel these dissenters in order to maintain consensus? To expel an individual from a community is not difficult; American communities have often done so, sometimes with the aid of tar and feathers. But to expel a significant minority that does not choose to depart in peace can mean civil war. It might be said that a discontented minority can be permitted to separate amicably by the simple expedient of redrawing the boundary lines and thus creating a new and independent state. But should every minority that wishes to do so be allowed to secede in full possession of the territory in which they happen to reside? Suppose this territory has been so integrated into the economy, transportation system, defenses, and sense of nationhood of the larger country that its loss would be a serious blow? Such forbearance and generosity are unlikely. In any case, what is to be the fate of a minority within a minority, as in the case of blacks in the South? And of minorities that are not geographically separated but intermixed, like Jehovah's Witnesses?

For Americans these questions are more than rhetorical; here, secession was proposed and rejected as a practical solution by a civil war. Lincoln's first inaugural address pierced the logic of secession:

> Plainly, the central idea of secession is the essence of anarchy. A majority held in restraint by constitutional checks and limitations, and always changing easily with deliberate changes of popular opinions and sentiments, is the only true sovereign of a free people. Whoever rejects it does, of necessity, fly to anarchy or to despotism. Unanimity is impossible; the rule of a minority, as a permanent arrangement, is wholly inadmissible; so that, rejecting the majority principle, anarchy or despotism in some form is all that is left.[1]

But even civil war did not finally settle the debate about the proper scope and limits of rule by majorities in the United States.

MAJORITY DECISIONS: HOW?   Even when a collection of people can agree to combine for purposes of self-government, and to construct their government faithfully according to the principles of consent, equality, and majority rule, *how* are they to do so?

Although the question raises a host of practical and theoretical problems, I wish to allude here only to one mentioned in the last chapter: representation. From ancient Greece to the American Revolution, advocates of democracy assumed that the people would be few in number. The principles of consent, political equality, and majority rule could thus be satisfied if the people directly governed themselves

---

1. Sandburg, *Abraham Lincoln, The War Years*, vol. 1 (New York: Harcourt, Brace, 1939), p. 132.

in an assembly open to all citizens. Here we have a key conclusion of all classical democratic theory. However, the greater the proportion of adults who are excluded from citizenship and, hence, from the right to participate in the assembly, and the greater the proportion of citizens who fail to exercise their rights to participate, the less persuasive is the classical solution. And the more numerous the people are, of course, the less valid the solution; for the more numerous the citizenry, the more the right to participate must be reduced simply to voting. When *full* participation—presenting proposals, discussion, advocacy, etc.— is necessarily confined to a few, equality requires that the few who govern should be *representative.* But representative how, and in what respects?

For example, if laws are made not by the people themselves but by their elected representatives, then is it not possible that laws passed by a majority of representatives may differ from the laws preferred by a majority of the people? Should this possibility be avoided at all costs? If so, how? There are a host of problems here, and no obviously right solutions.

Clearly, however, the *system of election* will have a bearing on the extent to which a majority of representatives correspond with the views of a majority of citizens. In practice, different countries have chosen significantly different kinds of election systems. Later on, we shall consider the effects of several main types of election systems. Meanwhile, the point to be kept in mind is that there seems to be no agreement as to what kind of system of election and representation is most nearly in accord with the principles of consent, equality, and majority rule.

POLITICAL EQUALITY AND INEQUALITY?

Finally, there is the problem posed in the last chapter. How, if at all, can sufficient equality be maintained? For if it is not, then political equality will become a mere formality.

For over two thousand years, from Aristotle to Rousseau and Jefferson in the eighteenth century, practically everyone who advocated popular rule also insisted on the need for a relatively even distribution of resources such as property. Yet to maintain enough equality in resources to insure genuine political equality has proved to be an exceptionally difficult problem. In fact, one view of political reality is that anything remotely approaching political equality is bound to be an illusion. This view forms the basis of the second general answer to our question, to which we turn in the next chapter.

SUMMARY

The solution of majority-rule democracy thus runs into serious theoretical and practical problems:

1. If individuals disagree as to whether they constitute a single people for purposes of self-government—as Americans disagreed in 1861—must the matter be settled finally by force, as Americans did? If not, must we grant to every minority the right to secede and establish its own government?

2. How can majority-rule democracy be applied in a federal system or in any other decentralized system in which certain territorial minorities are guaranteed certain rights to govern themselves? According to what principles are we to solve conflicts between the wishes of a majority of citizens in a state or province and a national majority?

3. More generally, how are minority rights to be secured, if not by placing restraints on the authority of majorities?

4. Since laws and policies will ordinarily be made by elected leaders and not by the assembled people, how can we insure that the leaders' decisions reflect majority preferences?

5. How, if at all, can sufficient equality of resources be maintained so that political equality is an actuality and not a mere formality?

5 RULE BY THE FEW AS A SOLUTION

Can a government be established and maintained that will achieve rule by the people based on consent and political equality? As we have just seen, the popular answer (majority-rule democracy) runs into some serious theoretical and practical problems. A second significant answer to our question is a straightforward *no.* Such a government, it is said, cannot be established; for no matter what the forms may be, in practice every political system is ruled by the few, not the many.

Unlike the argument for aristocracy or meritocracy, which asserts that a well-qualified minority *ought* to rule, this argument purports merely to describe what happens *in fact.* Advocates of meritocracy insist that rule by the people is undesirable. Spokespersons for the view that all governments are ruled by the few insist only that the people do not and probably cannot rule. If the people cannot rule, it is silly to discuss whether they *ought* to rule, just as it is silly to discuss whether they ought to be able to live without food and water. If rule by an elite —a system of "oligarchy"—is inevitable, the moral arguments for rule by the people are plainly irrelevant.

THEORIES OF RULE BY THE FEW Perhaps it is no accident that those who equate all politics with oligarchy[1] turn out to be observers whose initial enthusiasm for democ-

---

1. Strictly speaking, *oligarchy* means rule by the few, but it has also taken on the meaning of rule by the wealthy few, or rule by the few in their own selfish interests. Many modern writers also speak of rule by an elite, or elite rule. Strictly speaking, *elite* means a select, superior, or choice group, but today it is often used interchangeably with oligarchy. *Hegemony* or hegemonic rule emphasizes the preponderance or domination of the rulers over the subjects; it implies the absence of effective institutions by which subjects or citizens can control their rulers. In this and the next chapter I use all three terms as they seem appropriate.

racy in its purest form turns into disappointment and disgust when they discover how widely political reality departs from their democratic utopia.

Thus one critic of democracy argues for the inevitability of a ruling class:

> In all societies . . . two classes of people appear—a class that rules and a class that is ruled. The first class, always the less numerous, performs all political functions, monopolizes power and enjoys the advantages that power brings, whereas the second, the more numerous class, is directed and controlled by the first. . . .[2]

Another defines the elite as "the totality of qualities promoting the well-being and domination of a class in society." "This elite," he goes on to say, "exists in all societies and governs them even in cases where the regime in appearance is highly democratic."[3]

A third concludes that "the majority of human beings, in a condition of eternal tutelage, are predestined by tragic necessity to submit to the domination of a small minority, and must be content to constitute the pedestal of an oligarchy."[4] He sums up his theory in the "iron law of oligarchy":

> It is organization which gives birth to the domination of the elected over the electors, of the mandataries over the mandators, of the delegates over the delegators. *Who says organization says oligarchy.*[5] (Italics added).

Not everyone who equates "rule by the people" with rule by an elite is as pessimistic as these three theorists. Optimists believe that the ruling class may one day be forced to make way for rule by the people. Thus in *The Communist Manifesto* (1848), Karl Marx and Friedrich Engels asserted that "the history of all hitherto existing society is the history of class struggles." In the nineteenth century "the bourgeoisie has at last . . . conquered for itself, in the modern representative State, exclusive political sway. The executive of the modern State is but a committee for managing the common affairs of the whole bourgeoisie." Yet the increasingly more numerous proletariat would one day seize power "in the interest of the immense majority. The proletariat, the lowest stratum of our present society, cannot stir, cannot raise itself up, without the whole superincumbent strata of official society being sprung into the air."

The idea that representative institutions conceal a ruling elite has long been popular in the United States among observers disillusioned

---

2. Gaetano Mosca, *The Ruling Class*, trans. Hannah D. Kahn (New York: McGraw-Hill, 1939), p. 50.

3. *Vilfredo Pareto: Sociological Writings*, ed. S. E. Finer (New York: Praeger, 1966), p. 155.

4. Robert Michels, *Political Parties*, trans. Eden and Cedar Paul (New York: Collier Books, 1962), p. 354.

5. *Ibid.*, p. 15.

by the visible shortcomings of the American political system. Americans with unconventional and unpopular views who feel thwarted in their efforts to change 'the system' sometimes attribute their defeats to a half-hidden ruling class. Thus Socialists and Populists have thought the country to be run by Wall Street bankers. Many extreme conservatives believe that a small eastern 'liberal establishment' dominates communications, education, religion, finance, the Department of State, and, indeed, government generally. In recent years, the position of a dominant elite has often been assigned to 'the military-industrial complex.' In 1970, half the people in a national survey agreed with the statement that "the government is pretty much run by a few big interests looking out for themselves." Only 14 percent agreed that "it is run for the benefit of all the people."[6]

SOURCES OF OLIGARCHIC TENDENCIES

The view that in practice rule by the people means oligarchy draws a good deal of its strength from certain general characteristics of political life; for example, one of the writers quoted a moment ago seems to have been outraged to discover that his own Socialist party preached democracy but practiced oligarchy. How was it possible that parties dedicated to democratic ideals could be so undemocratic in their own internal government? His answer stressed a number of persistent sources for the tendency to oligarchy. These included:

☐ The need for organization, which in turn enhances the power of an organization's leaders.

☐ The impossibility of direct government among large numbers of persons, hence the need for representation, which increases the power of the representatives in comparison with the voters.

☐ Certain psychological tendencies among 'the masses': their desire to be led, gratitude toward their leaders, and a tendency to revere their leaders and magnify their virtues and capacities.

☐ Greater skills and competence of leaders, the inability of organizations to function without them, the incompetence of the mass of the people in most organizations.

☐ The financial power of the leaders, and their control over the organization's bureaucracy and technical services.

☐ Psychological changes in the leaders, particularly their increased sense of their own indispensability and their enhanced desire for power.[7]

---

6. Arthur H. Miller, "Political Issues and Trust in Government: 1964–1970," *The American Political Science Review,* 68:(Sept., 1974), 951–972, Table 1, 973.

7. Michels, *Political Parties.* Michels devotes a chapter to each of these sources and others.

Probably the strongest aspect of this theory—and as we shall see, its weakest, too—is its focus on persistent inequalities in power and influence that can be seen in every political system, including 'democratic' systems. Thus the theory fastens on a problem that, as we have already seen, is definite and serious.

CAUSES OF INEQUALITIES

In the last two chapters we saw that equality and consent are threatened by persistent inequalities. We noted that among the causes of political inequalities are social arrangements, individual characteristics, and in representative governments, the very process of representation itself. These factors in turn help to produce differences in political *resources, skills,* and *incentives.*

Resources

Political resources consist of all the means available to one for influencing the behavior of other people. In this country, political resources include access to money, hence wealth, income, and credit. They also include control over jobs; the ballot; popularity, friendships, reputation, and esteem in the eyes of others; knowledge or access to knowledge; control over mass media and other means of communication; and many other things.

One important political resource easily lost sight of is *time.* If you have no time left over from your other affairs to try to change the conduct of government, you are unlikely to be in a position to exercise much influence over it. Conversely, the more time you have available, the better your chances. Time is one of the most critical resources that professional politicians have. By hook or crook they manage to spend almost full time at the game of politics, while most of us devote only a few hours out of the year.

Still another resource which is unevenly distributed—inevitably so —is *officiality.* Constitutional rules, law, and practice allow officials to do things that ordinary citizens cannot. A major difference between the policeman and the man he arrests is that the office of the policeman entitles him to make arrests, using force if necessary. Official position invariably allocates to officials some resources that are denied to others: thus only judges can decide legal cases and only legislators can pass laws. By conferring officiality on the winner and denying it to the loser, elections award extra resources to the winner. In 1876, one electoral vote—a rather dubious one at that—was enough to confer the presidency on Rutherford B. Hayes rather than on Samuel J. Tilden. Even in that age of weak presidents, the presidency gave to Hayes important legal authority, such as the veto, that was denied to Tilden.

Allied to officiality as a resource, but not identical with it, is *legiti-*

mate authority: the widespread view that an individual or an office ought to be obeyed. Thus the president is powerful not only because of what the Constitution authorizes him to do but also because of what history and tradition authorize him to do.

Except perhaps for the ballot, and that only recently, all these resources are unequally distributed among adult American citizens. Hence it should not be too surprising if various citizens exert unequal influence on the conduct of government.

Skills

Even if two individuals had practically identical resources, they might, nonetheless, be unable to exercise equal influence over the conduct of government if one of them were politically more *skillful.* (Political skill might be considered, of course, as a special kind of resource, but it seems more illuminating to think of it as a capacity for using one's resources efficiently.) Although almost all political observers agree with the political philosopher Niccolò Machiavelli (1469–1527) that differences in political skills exist and are important, political skills, unlike military, entrepreneurial, artistic, and scientific skills, are hard to pin down and not well understood.

Incentives

Even if two individuals had identical resources and skills, one might exercise more influence over government than another simply because he or she *wanted* to influence the government and the other did not. If you do not care what the government is doing, you probably will not use your resources and skills to influence it; the more you care, the more of your resources you will be willing to invest and the harder you will try to acquire the necessary skills. Thus, your influence is partly dependent on your goals and estimates of the best strategies for obtaining them. We might call this third factor *incentives* for acquiring political skills and for employing resources to influence the conduct of government.

While some causes of political inequalities can be reduced or removed, others seem impossible to uproot. Can we ever get rid of all differences in political incentives? Should we even try to? Will differences in incentives not inevitably lead to differences in skills? Will not appointed and elected officials to whom authority is delegated inevitably have access to more political resources than do ordinary citizens?

Extreme advocates of the view that all political systems are dominated by a ruling group argue that so much inequality in resources, skills, and incentives is bound to persist as to make rule by the people impossible and rule by a particular class, stratum, or elite inevitable. However, to leap from the premise of inequality to the conclusion that all political systems are ruled by an elite entails some highly questionable assumptions.

A COMMON ERROR IN POLITICAL THINKING

In fact to equate all politics with oligarchy is to fall into the common error of dividing things into two mutually exclusive categories: good-bad, we-they, saints-sinners, Americans-foreigners, democracy-dictatorship. This is sometimes called the 'fallacy of dichotomous thinking.'

Most of us know that outside the domain of politics things can often be thought about as if they were located along a continuous line. Thinking in continuities is more flexible and more subtle than dichotomous thought. I think most of us would agree that it is not necessary, and is often unprofitable, to divide human beings, for example, into just two groups: tall-short, lean-fat, blond-brunette, healthy-sick, nice-vicious, etc. We all recognize that while it is convenient for some purposes to dichotomize, for others it is senseless. Imagine an insurance company that divided applicants for life insurance into young-old; a judicial system that knew only the categories guilty of murder or innocent; an educational system in which students were categorized as either idiots or geniuses!

Yet for many people it evidently seems reasonable to believe that if a country is not an ally, it is an enemy; if a political system is not a democracy, it is a dictatorship. And if the people do not rule, there must be a ruling elite.

The difficulty with two exclusive categories like these is that they often rob us of important distinctions. Even if the people do not rule, and political equality and consent are by no means fully achieved, are there not significant differences in political systems? Would it not make sense to say that while no country has a truly 'democratic' political system, some systems are *significantly more* democratic than others? An alternative interpretation, which answers in the affirmative, is the theory of polyarchy—a political system with important democratic elements which also contains some nondemocratic elements.

SUMMARY

1. An important line of thought argues that rule by the people is impossible and in practice every political system, whatever its forms, is ruled by an elite.

2. This line of argument draws strong support from the observable facts that (a) inequalities in power and influence seem to persist in all associations and societies despite their professed ideals, and (b) some of the causes of these inequalities seem extremely difficult, perhaps impossible, to remove.

3. However, the premise that inequalities in power and resources exist does not warrant the conclusion that a ruling class exists.

4. If we are to avoid the fallacy of dichotomous thinking, we need to consider the possibility that even if the people do not rule, and even though political equality and consent are by no means fully achieved, there may, nonetheless, be significant differences in the extent to which these goals are achieved in different political systems.

6 POLYARCHY AS A SOLUTION

Yet a third answer to the question of whether a government can be established and maintained that will achieve rule by the people based on consent and political equality holds that:

☐ All political systems fall considerably short of achieving these goals.
☐ However, some systems approach these goals considerably more than do others.
☐ These systems are not democracies in the ideal sense, yet they contain democratic components. Nor are they dominated by a united elite, yet elites and leaders play powerful parts.
☐ These systems, a mixture of elite rule and democracy, are called polyarchies.

Like democratic theories, the theory of polyarchy assumes that political systems can and should be distinguished and judged according to the extent to which they achieve rule by the people, political equality, and consent. Like elitist theories, the theory of polyarchy holds that all human organizations contain strong tendencies toward the development of inequalities and the emergence of powerful leaders. Yet while it incorporates these assumptions from both majority-rule and elitist theories the theory of polyarchy also offers an alternative interpretation of politics in 'democratic' systems.

DEMOCRACY: AN AMBIGUOUS TERM

So far I have usually managed to avoid using the term *democracy*. I have done so because no political term is more ambiguous, nor more productive of fruitless controversy. The term is not only ambiguous, it is thoroughly impregnated with connotations of goodness; practically everyone except outright advocates of meritocracy insists that democracy is good, that he or she, of course, advocates it—and that what he or she advocates is, naturally, true democracy.

One elementary source of ambiguity stems from the fact that our language permits democracy to be used both for (1) an ideal political system, which may not actually exist anywhere, and (2) a number of actual systems that do exist in our world of experience. Ever since the Greeks began presenting their ideas about politics more than two thousand years ago, a common practice among philosophers has been to set out the characteristics of an ideal, complete, or perfect polity, including a democratic polity. Simultaneous with this usage, actual systems have also been called democracies, even though they have always fallen far short of the ideal. Thus it is perfectly consistent with usage, and not logically contradictory, to say both that the United States *is* a democracy (actual) and that it is *not* a democracy (ideal).

While the language of the dictionary, politician, street, newspaper, TV commentator, and classroom fully authorize one to use the term *democracy* in both ways, to do so creates an enormous amount of confusion. It is amazing, indeed, how much controversy is produced by a difference in usage that every American must surely be aware of by the time he leaves high school. Yet while most of us calmly recognize that a ham in a meatmarket is not the same as a ham in a theater, and ordinarily find no difficulty in grasping which usage a speaker intends, the distinction between (ideal) democracy and (actual) democracies is a source of endless confusion and controversy, even, alas, among scholars. This is why the theory of polyarchy adopts a simple terminological distinction: the term *democracy* is reserved exclusively for an ideal state of affairs. Actual systems that appear to approach this ideal state of affairs more closely than other systems do, at least in some important respects, are called *polyarchies.* The theory of polyarchy assumes that all polyarchies fall short of democracy by a considerable and significant margin. Unlike some theories of elite rule, however, it offers grounds for believing that the gap can be narrowed. Yet unlike some theories of democracy, it does not say that unlimited extension of majority rule is the best or most feasible way of closing that gap. Moreover, it leaves open—as a practical problem to be solved pragmatically in specific circumstances—just how and how much the gap between democracy and polyarchy can actually be closed.

POLYARCHIES AS SYSTEMS ON A CONTINUUM   In order to avoid the fallacy of thinking that everything must fall into one of two exclusive categories, it is helpful to think about polyarchy as a collection of points along an imaginary line. Suppose we could measure the amount of 'democracy' in a political system. Suppose further that our measurements could be reduced to a single dimension stretching from ideal democracy at one end to its negation at the other. For convenience, call the negation of democracy autocracy.

Autocracy (—) _____ (+) Democracy

Now suppose that we measure the amount of 'democracy' in a set of political systems. These might be the political systems of two dozen different countries. When we locate these systems on our dimension, suppose we find that they cover a wide spread, thus:

Autocracy ·································· Democracy

Suppose we discover a fairly distinct cluster of countries lying closer than the others to the democratic end of the line. We shall then call these polyarchies. The countries near the autocratic extreme, we shall term *hegemonies* and the ones in between are *mixed systems.*

hegemonies   mixed systems   polyarchies

Autocracy ·································· Democracy

That is all very well as a mental exercise, you might say, but can we really do anything like this in practice? It appears that we can, though imperfectly.

THE CONDITIONS OF DEMOCRATIC GOVERNMENT RESTATED

In Chapter 3 we saw that if consent and political equality are to be active and continuing, every full citizen would have to possess unimpaired opportunities

☐ to formulate goals,
☐ to indicate his or her goals or preferences to other citizens and the government, and
☐ to have his or her preferences weighted equally with those of other citizens in the conduct of the government.

What would be required in order to insure these opportunities? Evidently a set of institutions:

1. In order to know what he wants, a citizen needs access to the best possible information. The worst situation would be one in which a single elite with interests and ambitions of its own controlled the major sources of information. At a minimum, then, it would be important to have access to alternative sources of information not under the control of any one elite.

2. To know what one wants and to indicate it to others, one needs the right to express oneself freely without fear of punishment, particularly by leaders.

3. In order to indicate one's preferences and have them taken into account in the conduct of government, one must be able to vote in elections.

4. To have one's preferences actually taken into account effectively, and weighted equally, elections must be free and honest, and also fair in the sense of adherence to the general principle of 'one man–one vote.'

5. To insure that elected leaders actually pay attention to one's preferences, it helps if leaders compete with one another for one's support, including one's vote.

6. In case no candidate is willing to advance one's ideas, one would need to be able to run for public office.

7. In order to explore one's preferences with others, to indicate them effectively, and to have them taken into account, one needs to be able to form and join organizations, including organizations formed for the purpose of competing in elections and advancing policies and programs in representative bodies.

8. Since all the previous requirements would come to naught if the officials who actually made the policies of government were unresponsive to elected officials and did not depend in any way on the outcome of elections, it is essential to have arrangements for insuring that government policies depend on votes and other expressions of preference by citizens. Thus the officials effectively determining policies must be dependent on the outcome of free and fair elections. These requirements are summarized in Table 6.1.

A SURVEY OF POLYARCHIES

To avoid the trap of thinking about these eight institutional guarantees in terms of only two exclusive categories, we might consider each one as we have just done with democracy. For each of the eight guarantees, let us imagine a line extending from complete attainment of the guarantee to its complete absence or negation. It would then be reasonable to expect that (1) while no country fully provides these guarantees, (2) countries vary significantly in the *extent* to which each of the guarantees is present.

Surprising as it may seem, political scientists have begun only recently to assemble and process the kinds of data needed to determine the extent to which guarantees like these are present. Nonetheless, it is possible to distinguish countries that provide these guarantees from countries that do not.

Thus in a recent study of political opposition, the eight institutional guarantees were assumed to indicate the extent to which opponents enjoyed opportunities to contest the conduct of the government. A number of indicators proved more or less satisfactory for measuring

Table 6.1
Some Conditions of
Democratic Government

To satisfy the principles of:	Every citizen must have unimpaired opportunities to:	In order for these opportunities to exist, the following institutional guarantees are required:
1. Consent 2. Political equality	1. Formulate preferences 2. Signify preferences 3. Have preferences weighted equally in the conduct of the government	1. Alternative sources of information 2. Freedom of expression 3. The right to vote 4. Free and fair elections 5. Competition among political leaders for votes and other support 6. The right to run for public office 7. Freedom to form and join organizations, including political parties 8. Institutions for making government policies depend on votes and other expressions of preference

the extent to which the institutional guarantees were present. It turned out, in fact, that the indicators could be satisfactory consolidated into a single, overall measure. This overall measure of the extent of opportunities available to political opposition to contest the conduct of the government was then joined with another dimension, the percent of adult citizens eligible to vote in national elections. The results are shown in Table 6.2.

The thirty countries in the upper-right corner of Table 6.2 represented the fullest attainment of the eight institutional guarantees in Table 6.1. They were, therefore, polyarchies in 1971. (The thirty countries are listed in alphabetical order in Table 6.3.) In these countries, over 90 percent of the adult citizens were eligible to vote in national elections, and the greatest opportunities existed for political opposition to contest the conduct of the government.

POLYARCHY AND MAJORITY-RULE DEMOCRACY

How do polyarchies deal with the difficulties in majority-rule democracy mentioned in Chapter 4?

What People?

As we have seen, democratic theory seems to provide no definite answer to the question: What constitutes a *people* for purposes of self-government? In practice, then, countries with polyarchic regimes use force, just as other regimes do, to repel threats to the integrity of the national territory. Consequently, as in other regimes, secession is, as

Table 6.2
Political Regimes in
114 Countries, 1975

		Extent of opportunities open to political oppositions to contest the conduct of government.[a]		
		Least	Medium	Greatest
Percent of adult citizens eligible to vote in national elections	Over 90%	18	16	30[b]
	20%–90%	1	4	—
	Under 20%	—	1	—
	No elections held	16	5	—
	Uncertain, transitional, etc.[c]	4	13	6
	Total (114)	39	39	36

[a] Based on the eight indicators of institutional guarantees listed in Table 6.1.

[b] The list contains five countries calling for special comment. *Ceylon* underwent a period of disorders culminating in the assassination of the prime minister in 1959, and a steady stream of charges by the government of attempted right-wing coups in the 1960s. In 1971 an uprising was put down by force. *Colombia*, after a decade of widespread violence from 1948 to 1958, managed relatively peaceful elections throughout the 1960s under a constitutional provision dividing membership in Congress equally between the two major parties. The provision required that the presidency alternate between the two major parties and that the membership of Congress be divided equally between them. The provision expired in 1974. In *Greece* polyarchy was established in 1974 after a period of military dictatorship. A constitution was still under discussion in 1975. In *India,* the Prime Minister in mid-1975 declared a state of national emergency, under which hundreds and possibly thousands of political opponents, including all the leaders of the opposition parties, were imprisoned, and a stringent censorship was imposed on the press. *Lebanon* underwent a violent conflict between conservative and radical political forces in 1975 in which thousands of lives were lost.

[c] Includes countries where a constitutional government or elections have been superseded or nullified at least once since 1960, the constitution has been suspended, a state of siege declared, or massive civil violence has occurred.

a practical matter, usually either impossible or extremely costly. (Colonies thought to lie outside the territory of the 'nation' may, of course, be granted independence.) To a considerable extent, then, large minorities are virtually 'compelled' to remain within the territorial limits of the nation. To make compulsory citizenship tolerable, great efforts are made to create and sustain a common sense of nationhood, so that minorities of all kinds will identify themselves with the nation. Hence secession or mass emigration are not usually thought of as practical alternatives.

Majority Rule versus Minority Rights

In practice, the effective scope of majority rule is limited in all polyarchies in at least three ways:

First, many matters of policy—religious beliefs and practices, for example—are effectively outside the legal authority of government. Sometimes, as in Britain, they are placed beyond the legal authority of government through understandings and agreements widely shared and respected. In many cases, as in the United States, these understandings and agreements are expressed in written constitutions that cannot be quickly or easily amended by a simple majority vote. Such a consti-

Table 6.3
Polyarchies, 1975

Fully inclusive polyarchies:	
1. Australia	16. Israel
2. Austria	17. Italy
3. Belgium	18. Jamaica
4. Canada	19. Japan
5. Ceylon*	20. Lebanon*
6. Colombia*	21. Luxembourg
7. Costa Rica	22. Netherlands
8. Denmark	23. New Zealand
9. Federal Republic of Germany	24. Norway
10. Finland	25. Sweden
11. France	26. Switzerland
12. Greece*	27. Trinidad and Tobago
13. Iceland	28. United Kingdom
14. India*	29. United States
15. Ireland	30. Venezuela

* See footnote b, Table 6.2

tution is regarded as peculiarly binding; and ordinary laws that run counter to the constitution will be invalid, or, at the very least, subject to special scrutiny.

Second, a great many questions of policy are placed in the hands of private, semipublic, and local governmental organizations such as churches, families, business firms, trade unions, towns, cities, provinces, and the like. These questions of policy, like those left to individuals, are also effectively beyond the reach of national majorities, the national legislature, or indeed any national policy-makers acting in their legal and official capacities. In fact, whenever uniform policies are likely to be costly, difficult, or troublesome, in polyarchies the tendency is to find ways by which these policies can be made by smaller groups of like-minded people who enjoy a high degree of legal independence.

Majority rule is also limited in a third way. Whenever a group of people believe that they are adversely affected by national policies or are about to be, they generally have extensive opportunities for presenting their case and for negotiations that may produce a more acceptable alternative. In some countries, many minorities may have enough power to delay, to obstruct, and even to veto the attempt to impose policies on them. Probably there are a few such minorities in every polyarchy.

Majority Decisions: How?

Although polyarchies restrict the scope of majority rule in the three ways just mentioned, there are significant variations in the extent to which a single party or a single unified coalition can acquire the authority to translate its proposals into government policy by winning a majority of votes in a national election. It may help to consider two hypothetical extremes.

At one extreme would be a system with *majority rule,* in which elections are *completely decisive.* Only two political parties compete in elections; the party that wins a majority of votes acquires a majority of seats in the legislative body; as a consequence it forms a cabinet which, together with its legislative majority, is able to convert the party's program into government policies. The opposition party may criticize the administration and hope to win its own majority in the next election; but until then it cannot prevent the majority party from governing as it pleases—within, to be sure, the three general kinds of limits mentioned above. Although this extreme type does not fully exist in any country, a few approach it much more closely than others. Britain represents one of the closest approximations.

At the other extreme would be a system requiring *unanimity,* in which elections are *not decisive.* Many parties compete in elections. No party wins a majority of votes or seats. Cabinets are formed from *all* the parties; thus the basic principle of the system is not majority rule, but unanimity. Nothing that is strenuously opposed by any significant minority can become government policy. Again, no country actually embodies this extreme type, but one of the countries that comes closest to it is Switzerland.

As we shall see in the next chapter, the political system of the United States seems to lie somewhere between the two extremes, but perhaps somewhat closer to Switzerland than to Britain.

Political Equality and Inequality

An essential difference between polyarchies and hegemonic regimes, as we have stressed, is the existence in polyarchies of effective institutional guarantees that protect the bulk of the population in the exercise of a broad range of elemental rights. For anyone who places a high value on these rights, the difference is decisive. I shall return to this point shortly.

Yet in spite of these institutional guarantees, differences in political resources, skills, and incentives produce in polyarchies, too, marked inequalities in influence. In this respect, polyarchies are a long way from the pure theory of majority-rule democracy, where all officials are mere agents of the people. For example, in a later chapter we shall see that the president of the United States is very far indeed from being merely the agent of the American people. In fact his extraordinary power and authority create a serious challenge to the future of the American political system.

Polyarchy, then, appears to be significantly different from majority-rule democracy. Is it significantly different from hegemonic rule by an elite?

COMPARISON OF POLYARCHY AND HEGEMONIC RULE BY AN ELITE

Differences

Polyarchy differs from hegemonic rule by an elite in at least three ways:

1. The extent of opposition permitted. As we have already seen, in polyarchies the barriers against opposition are much lower than in hegemonic regimes. In polyarchies, opponents can contest the conduct of the government by speaking out against it, publishing and distributing newspapers, pamphlets, brochures, magazines, books and other writings, holding meetings, organizing opposition parties, running candidates in elections, winning seats, and even displacing the incumbent administration. Although nonpolyarchies vary over a broad range, from brutally repressive autocracies to relatively tolerant mixed systems, in all of them the barriers to opposition are higher than in polyarchies. At the extreme, in fully hegemonic regimes, critics are denied all opportunities to contest the conduct of the government and opposition in any form is ruthlessly repressed.

2. The range of conflict and competition allowed. No political system, no matter how repressive, ever seems able to eliminate every vestige of competition and conflict among its leaders. But in highly hegemonic regimes, whether modern dictatorships or centralized monarchies of the seventeenth century, the range of permissible competition and conflict is extremely narrow, and much of that must be concealed from public view, so in such regimes competition is often reduced to little more than subordinates vying for the favors of the ruler. Woe to the subordinate who displeases the autocrat!

Whenever the barriers to opposition are lowered, leadership invariably splits into opposing cliques, factions, or parties competing for control of the government. Opposing cliques may have nothing nobler in mind than acquiring patronage, incomes, and wealth. Yet however narrow and selfish their aims may be, their infighting is often bitter, sometimes lethal. In their struggle to gain the upper hand, factions search for additional resources. Their need for resources often compels them to compromise with other factions. Thus coalitions of factions with similar but not identical interests develop within the governing stratum.

When institutional guarantees are extended to a point where the executive becomes dependent on winning a majority in the legislature, the legislator's vote becomes one of his resources. Factional leaders must now negotiate for these votes by offering something in return: flattery, recognition, offices, access, graft, policies. As the institutional guarantees are extended to broader and broader segments of the population outside the legislature, the same process repeats itself. To gain the support of voters, leaders of cliques, factions, or parties must now offer rewards to voters, whether flattery, recognition, offices, access, graft, or policies. These developments can be clearly seen in the slow transformation of many European centralized monarchies into narrow oligarchies, then into polyarchies.

3. Elections. The third and most visible difference between polyarchies and hegemonic rule is the periodic occurrence of local and national elections which are contested by competing political parties offering rewards to voters. Leaders actively seek to gain popular support and thus the right to hold office and participate in governing.

Perhaps no institution is more critical to the differentiation between polyarchies and nonpolyarchies than competitive elections. And perhaps no testimony to the importance of competitive elections is more impressive than the unbending resistance of ruling elites in hegemonic regimes to the introduction of fully protected national elections in which opposition parties would be effectively protected in their opportunities to compete for popular support. Even regimes that have reduced other barriers to opposition almost to the level of polyarchies are generally unwilling to cross this last, dangerous threshold to polyarchy. For once the threshold has been crossed, an elite's capacity to rule will almost certainly be drastically impaired—as no one knows better than a ruling elite protected from the threat of being displaced in an election.

Because elections open to contests by opposing political parties are bound to menace a ruling elite in a hegemonic system, the advocates of hegemony in one form or another typically deny the importance of elections and seek to show that elections actually permit an elite to dominate the country—the wrong ruling elite, of course. In order to substitute good rulers for bad, they are likely to argue, competitive elections must be suspended or abolished.

Do the Differences Matter?

Even if the institutional guarantees of polyarchy lower the barriers to opposition, produce conflict and competition among leaders, and make leaders dependent to some degree on winning the support of nonleaders in elections, it is reasonable to ask whether these differences really matter. One who believes in the theories of oligarchy described in the previous chapter might say that in the end, polyarchies and outright oligarchies are much the same in their essential consequences. The people do not rule, a critic might say, elites do.

Mosca's conclusion. Yet it is a highly revealing and often neglected fact that Gaetano Mosca, the father of modern elite theory, concluded in his later years that polyarchies were not only significantly different from dictatorships, they were also better.

Mosca, whose words on the inevitability of a ruling class were quoted in the last chapter (see page 35), lived long enough to witness the emergence of modern dictatorships, including Fascism in his native Italy. In 1923, when Mussolini had already come to power and was beginning to consolidate his Fascist dictatorship in Italy, Mosca brought out a revised and enlarged edition of the *Elements of Political Science,* in which, more than a quarter century earlier, he had advanced the theory of the ruling class. Mosca left no doubt where he now stood:

> If, . . . we take due account of the individual liberties that protect the citizen from possible arbitrary acts on the part of any or all of the powers of the state, especially of liberty of the press, which, along with liberty of parliamentary debate, serves to call public attention to all possible abuses on the part of those who govern, one readily sees the great superiority of the representative system.[1]

This was a remarkable concession. But the advance of Fascism was to wring from Mosca one more anguished declaration. For Mosca was not only a theorist; from 1908 onward he had also been a member of the Italian Parliament, first as a deputy, later as a senator. In 1925, Mussolini presented to the Italian Senate a bill that would strip the parliament of its right to initiate legislation and would make the prime minister independent of both king and parliament. As everyone knew, the bill symbolized the legalization of the dictatorship and the final end of the parliamentary regime. On Christmas Day, 1925, Mosca rose in the Senate to pronounce his obituary for parliamentary government:

> [He spoke, he said,] with a certain emotion because, let us be frank, we take part in the funeral rites of a form of government. I should not have thought possible that I would be the one to deliver the funeral oration on the parliamentary regime. . . . I, who have always taken a harsh attitude toward it, I am today obliged to lament its departure. . . . A form of government [he went on] can be judged only in one way: by comparing it with both its predecessor and successor. To speak of the latter would be premature. As to the predecessor: it was such that one may say in all sincerity: the parliamentary regime was better.[2]

SUMMARY   In this chapter we have briefly explored the theory of polyarchy, which incorporates certain aspects of both democratic and elitist theories, presents a critique of both, and offers an alternative way of understanding politics in different systems, particularly systems ordinarily called 'democratic.' The argument of the theory of polyarchy can be summarized as follows:

---

1. Mosca, *The Ruling Class*, pp. 474–475.
2. Gaetano Mosca, in *The Myth of the Ruling Class*, James Meisel (Ann Arbor: University of Michigan Press, 1958), pp. 225–226.

1. The theory of polyarchy assumes:

☐ A hypothetical line extending from pure or ideal democracy to its complete negation, autocracy. Democracy and autocracy are purely theoretical entities, not fully realized in the world of experience.

☐ At a minimum, in an ideal democracy consent and political equality would be active and continuing, not merely passive and intermittent.

☐ For consent and political equality to be active and continuing would, in turn, require that every full citizen have unimpaired opportunities to formulate and indicate his or her preferences and have them weighted equally in the conduct of the government.

☐ The existence of these opportunities requires at least eight kinds of institutional guarantees.

2. Political systems that provide these guarantees to a higher degree than other systems (even though incompletely) are called polyarchies.

3. Reasonably satisfactory (if imperfect) indicators for the presence of these eight guarantees make it possible to rank the systems of 114 countries. Thirty systems that provided the fullest opportunities for opposition in the late 1960s and had extended the suffrage to cover 90 percent of the adults are classified as polyarchies.

4. Polyarchies modify, amplify, or supplement the usual assumptions of majority-rule democracy in dealing with the problems of

☐ Who constitutes 'the people.'

☐ How and what rights are guaranteed to minorities.

☐ The extent to which electoral and other arrangements facilitate government by the representatives of majorities.

☐ Reducing inequalities.

5. Polyarchies differ from hegemonic rule by elites in

☐ The extent of opportunities available to opposition to contest the conduct of government.

☐ The amount of open conflict among political leaders and open competition for support of nonleaders, particularly by votes in elections.

☐ The periodic occurrence of local and national elections contested by competing political parties.

7 THE AMERICAN POLYARCHY: FIVE CHARACTERISTICS

Everyday language authorizes one to call the American political system a 'democracy,' as we saw in the last chapter. No matter what term is used in this book, doubtless most Americans will go on referring to their political system by that familiar term.

Yet it is perfectly clear, and will become clearer as we proceed, that in the United States—as in other countries called democracies—the political system departs markedly from the characteristics of an ideal democracy. This is not merely a matter of marginal differences, like a tiny blemish on a lovely face. It would be silly to contend, for example, that adult American citizens are even approximately equal in their influence on governmental decisions. The American polity contains an important element of democracy, but it is certainly not fully democratic.

In order not to blur the distinction between ideal and actual democracy, in this book the American system is called a polyarchy. For the United States is among thirty or so countries in which the eight institutional guarantees described in the last chapter exist more fully than in the remaining countries of the world.

Although by definition polyarchies have certain characteristics in common, they vary in their concrete institutions and practices. In fact, as political scientists have become more familiar with a larger number of polyarchies in recent years, they have discovered that polyarchy is a system with great individual variation. The unique history and conditions of each country tend to distinguish its polyarchy from the rest in its overall patterns.

Thus, although the American polyarchy by definition shares a number of characteristics with other polyarchies, it also differs from them in some ways. Taken altogether, its characteristics form a uniquely American pattern of polyarchy.

DISCRIMINATION AGAINST RACIAL MINORITIES

From colonial times onward, a distinct aspect of American life has been its harsh treatment of Indians and inhabitants of African racial stock. The presence of a black minority constituting about 10 percent of the population, who first lived here mainly as slaves and later as nominally free citizens, had a profound influence on the emergent characteristics of the American polity. I have called that polity a polyarchy. Yet until the late 1960s Southern blacks were excluded from all political life. In effect, the United States developed a kind of dual system, a polyarchy among whites and a hegemony over blacks. In this century Northern urban blacks gained access to political life. But it was not until after the passage of the Civil Rights Acts of 1964 and 1965 that the suppression of the blacks by Southern whites came to an end.

In the depth and extent of discrimination practiced against racial minorities, the United States appears to be unique among the polyarchies of the world. To be sure, its uniqueness in this respect is no doubt largely due to the fact that no other polyarchy contains such a large and distinguishable racial minority as blacks have formed in the United States. Whatever the explanations may be, the fact and its consequences are of primary concern here.

Consequently, just as the theme of racial discrimination runs like an ugly thread through the pattern of American history, so it constitutes an underlying theme in this book. Because racial discrimination has contributed mightily to the peculiar shape and character of the American polyarchy and to the pattern of its conflicts and compromises, we shall observe its effects again and again. Moreover, keep constantly in mind that a good deal of what follows applies to the American polyarchy and persons permitted to participate in it—whites, for the most part. It does not apply to those excluded from it, mainly blacks, nor to the hegemonic system used in the South (often with the tacit consent of the North) to deny influence to blacks.

EQUALITY: IDEAL VERSUS REALITY

Despite slavery and racial discrimination in the United States, the ideal of equality has always been unusually strong among Americans. Probably in no other country in the world has such a large proportion of the people professed a belief in both the desirability and the attainability of political and social equality over such a long period in their national history. In Chapter 9, we shall consider the pervasiveness of American beliefs in equality, and how they came about.

As we shall also see in that chapter, however, the realities of American life have always diverged in important ways from the ideal of equality. Racial discrimination is the most obvious contradiction. Yet even among white citizens the realities of political, social, and economic inequality have steadily conflicted with the American ideal of equality.

The contrast between the United States and the rest of the world may have caused Americans and foreign observers alike to underestimate the degree of inequality between whites. In the nineteenth century, inequalities of all kinds—political, social, economic, educational— were so much less between white Americans than between the citizens of any other country that inequality seemed to pose no great problem for democracy in the United States, at least among whites. Indeed, the emphasis was quite the other way: on the dangers to liberty of 'too much equality.'

But the transformation of the United States from an agricultural to an industrial society was in fact accompanied by the growth of many sharp disparities among white Americans—in social standing, wealth, income, education, knowledge, leisure time, and many other things. As we shall see, differences like these help to bring about significant differences in political activity and influence as well. There is evidence that these differences actually produce greater disparities in political participation among Americans than among the citizens of many European polyarchies.[1]

WIDE ACCEPTANCE OF AMERICAN INSTITUTIONS

Despite the very substantial gaps between the ideals and the realities of American life, the country's major institutions—slavery and racial discrimination to one side—have always been quite widely accepted by Americans. Throughout most of their history as an independent country, a high proportion of Americans seem to have accepted a belief in the desirability of democracy in general and their political system in particular. Few Americans, to say the very least, openly contest this belief. Even the economic and social institutions of the country have, over long periods of time, been less severely criticized and challenged than in many other countries. This widespread acceptance has had important consequences. For one thing, political movements openly hostile to the political system, or even to the prevailing social and economic institutions, have always encountered massive difficulties. Throughout the history of the United States, political life has been almost completely blanketed by parties, movements, programs, proposals, opinions, ideas, and an ideology directed toward a large mass of convergent 'moderate' voters. The history of radical movements, whether

1. Chapter 28, below.

of right or left, and of antisystem parties, as they are sometimes called, is a record of unrelieved failure to win control over the government. Even moderate democratic socialist parties have been unable to acquire much of a following, whereas in Europe they have usually played major roles.

Yet it would be a mistake—one both Americans and foreigners often make—to assume that this ideological convergence eliminates serious conflicts over the conduct of the government. The American Civil War should stand as a warning against glib interpretations.

In later chapters we shall see how a comparatively high degree of ideological convergence came about and what its limits are. How the confidence of Americans in their institutions declined during the turbulent period between President Kennedy's assassination in 1963 and President Nixon's resignation in 1974 is discussed in Chapter 10. We shall also see how convergence and divergence in beliefs affect political conflict.[2]

EXTREME PARTITIONING OF POLITICAL AUTHORITY

One of the most striking characteristics of the American polyarchy is the extent to which political authority is partitioned among a variety of actors, each somewhat independent of the others.

As we saw in the last chapter, polyarchies vary widely in the extent to which they allow the leaders of a party or coalition to acquire the authority to translate their proposals into government actions by winning a majority of votes in a national election. In Britain, elections have relatively decisive consequences for governmental decisions. In the United States, elections are less decisive. In this country it is difficult and rare for leaders of a single party or coalition to acquire the amount of authority that, for example, leaders of the majority party in the British House of Commons are ordinarily able to exercise over a fairly broad range of decisions. But in this country, as we shall see, the president can exercise, or at any rate in recent decades has exercised, a rather decisive authority over decisions involving military actions. A later chapter in this book (Chapter 13) will explore how the expansion of this power contributed to the crisis of the presidency, and the polyarchy itself, that developed in the 1960s and early 1970s. Outside this key area, however, the president and other leaders rarely form a coalition united enough to exercise decisive influence over a large variety of decisions.

The fact that elections are relatively less decisive and political authority more fragmented in the United States than in Britain and several other polyarchies can be attributed to two main sets of factors.

---

2. Part Four.

First, the *political institutions.* These were originally designed, not to make elections decisive or to facilitate the formation of a powerful majority coalition but with precisely the opposite purpose in mind: to prevent by a system of checks and balances the concentration of authority in any single set of government officials. As the institutions developed, they have largely fulfilled the original purpose of making it difficult for officials to operate as a cohesive governing coalition. In Parts Two and Three, we shall examine in more detail why the institutions were originally designed with this purpose in mind and how their development has achieved it.

Second, the normal *pattern of political conflict.* At the Constitutional Convention of 1787, James Madison predicted that if this country were large enough, the very diversity and variety of political interests and conflicts would create a barrier to the cohesion of national majorities. Madison has been proved substantially correct, at least for the United States. In Part Four we shall see how the normal pattern of differing viewpoints and conflict in the United States renders the task of forming a cohesive and powerful governing coalition extremely difficult (Chapter 24). We shall also see that the normal or usual pattern does not always hold. In the 1960s it did not prevent the emergence of severe conflict (Chapter 26). In the extreme instance it was displaced by a degree of polarization that helped to produce a civil war (Chapter 27).

INCREMENTALIST PERSPECTIVES ON POLITICAL ACTION

Most people who participate actively in political affairs in the United States appear to behave most of the time as if they were acting on three assumptions:

☐ That problems are more or less *divisible* or *independent,* not totally interrelated. The assumption is that you do not have to solve every important problem in order to solve one important problem.

☐ That problems can usually be dealt with satisfactorily by *incremental* or piecemeal adjustments of the existing state of affairs. The process of step-by-step adjustments can go on indefinitely.

☐ That satisfactory compromises can ordinarily be found that do not drastically damage the interests of anyone or at least of any 'important' group of participants. From this perspective it is usually thought to be both possible and desirable to limit the scope of conflict to the particular issue at hand, to cooperate with others in seeking solutions, and to accept compromise solutions.

These three assumptions are, of course, highly debatable. Many critics of American society deny one or more of them. Some argue that a number of evil consequences result directly from the inability or unwillingness of leaders, activists and the public to believe that most problems are really indivisible. Many important problems, they argue, cannot be dealt with satisfactorily by piecemeal changes. These issues cannot be solved without severely damaging some of the most fundamental interests of those who benefit from the status quo. Hence, any serious attempt to solve such problems necessarily entails severe, polarizing conflicts.

You might well decide, then, to reject one or more of the three assumptions listed above as a foundation for your own political strategies. Yet even if you adopt different assumptions, you would still need to take into account an important fact: for better or worse incrementalist perspectives have prevailed among most political activists in this country practically all the time and are therefore not likely to change abruptly.

What makes these perspectives even more difficult to change is that they probably result in part from the two characteristics of the American polyarchy just described:

1. An ideological coming-together, reflecting a wide acceptance by Americans of their institutions, makes it extraordinarily difficult (and, up to now, impossible) to gain a big public following for a movement that openly seeks comprehensive, radical, or revolutionary changes in a large number of American institutions. Also, most political activists hold views similar to the rest of the population on these matters. Consequently, political activists tend to believe that whatever problems the country confronts are not inherent in the fundamental character of the institutions themselves, but rather are specific, concrete, and separable from one another. Political activists who believe the existing system does not need to be profoundly transformed are likely to feel also that for this very reason satisfactory changes can be brought about by piecemeal alteration. And since, in this view, no basic institutions have to be destroyed to solve the problems confronting American society at any given time, no really fundamental interests are threatened. Hence it ought to be possible to narrow the scope of conflict to the particular problem, and to work out mutually acceptable solutions by cooperation and compromise.

2. Extreme partitioning of political authority creates seemingly insurmountable barriers to any movement that wants to use the government to bring about comprehensive, root-and-branch alterations in policies and institutions. As we shall see, partitioning creates innumerable strongholds where comparatively small groups can successfully resist attempts to bring about policies they regard as adverse to their interests. Partitioning encourages those who seek change to avoid attacking all these strongholds at once. Instead, they follow the tactics of divide-and-conquer, rejecting policies that could only succeed if the

fragmented and sprawling nationwide structure of political authority were coordinated as tautly as the moves of a professional football team or ballet group.

SUMMARY   Although by definition polyarchies have certain features in common, every polyarchy also seems to possess a combination of characteristics that to some degree distinguish it from others. The combination of characteristics that, taken together, tend to make the American polyarchy somewhat different from other polyarchies are:

1. A constant conflict has existed between our widely held belief in equality and the facts of American life.

2. American polyarchy has been shaped by a long history of severe discrimination against two racial minorities, American Indians and Afro-Americans. The South, in fact, developed a dual system: polyarchy among whites, hegemony over blacks.

3. American political, social, and economic institutions have tended to be rather widely accepted by Americans over rather long periods of time. Political movements highly critical of these institutions have rarely made much headway (as discussed in Part Two).

4. For at least two reasons, political authority is extremely partitioned:

☐ Because the political institutions were successfully designed to prevent concentration of authority (as discussed in Part Three).
☐ Because the normal pattern of conflict and differing viewpoints makes it difficult to form cohesive governing coalitions (as discussed in Part Four).

5. Partly because of the last two characteristics, most people who participate actively in political affairs in the United States seem to adopt incrementalist perspectives; that is, they seem to believe that problems are separable, can be dealt with satisfactorily by piecemeal adjustments, and can be solved by limiting the scope of conflict, cooperating with others in searching for solutions, and accepting compromises. Although incrementalist perspectives may be criticized as inadequate, they appear to be such an enduring characteristic of the American polyarchy that any person who wishes to bring about changes would have to take them into account in formulating his own strategies (as discussed in Part Five).

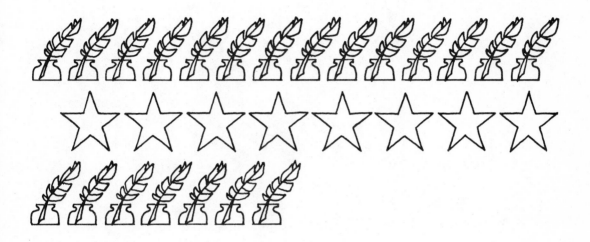

PART TWO

HOW AND WHY A POLYARCHY
EMERGED ON THE AMERICAN CONTINENT

8 THE FRAMERS AGREE TO A CONSTITUTION

In every polyarchy, contemporary political life is powerfully shaped by the arrangements and understandings that make up its constitution. With a few exceptions, Britain being the best known, these arrangements and understandings are to a great extent prescribed in a single written document held to be more binding and superior to ordinary law —a written constitution. In polyarchies with written constitutions, making and modifying the basic document are actions of singular importance.

To understand, then, how American political institutions came to be widely accepted and why the partitioning of authority is so marked in American political life, we must turn to certain key choices made at the Constitutional Convention of 1787.

As every American child learns in elementary school, the American Constitution, except for amendments, was formulated by fifty-five men gathered at a Constitutional Convention held in Philadelphia in 1787. Our school child may not realize, of course, that American political life is by no means governed entirely by that document. Political parties, for example, are nowhere mentioned in the Constitution. Nonetheless, the Constitution has probably contributed more than any other single factor to the special features, the peculiarities of form, substance, and process that differentiate the American from other polyarchies. Even if political parties go unmentioned in the Constitution, the American party system takes its shape from certain elements in the Constitution.

The Constitution proposed by the delegates to the Convention was both an end and a beginning. It was the culmination of a slow, steady, and gradual growth in America of institutions, practices, and ideas favorable to popular government. It was the beginning of a new period in which these institutions, practices, and ideas were to be tested and vigorously expanded.

The men at the Constitutional Convention did not create a polyarchy. They helped one to emerge. No small group can create popular government unless the people and their existing institutions are ripe for it. By 1787 Americans were ready for polyarchy. One is tempted to conjecture, that sooner or later, a polyarchy would surely have grown up. The men who worked in Philadelphia through the summer of 1787 did not—could not—give final shape to the American political system, nor even to its constitutional foundations. The shape of our system was bound to be influenced by social and economic conditions, by the beliefs and attitudes of other Americans, by events beyond the control of the handful of men in Independence Hall meeting week after week in the face of summer's heat and flaring tempers.

Yet, if it is easy to exaggerate the work of the Convention, it would be wrong to minimize its consequences. For the framework of government proposed by the men in Philadelphia, and in due course accepted by the states and the people, was a unique framework. Once it was put into effect, it was bound to influence the specific ways in which popular government would or could develop in the new United States. If the American political system today is different in some important respects from any other system, this is, at least in part, a result of the *particular* pattern of polyarchy that grew out of the beliefs, the proposals, the matters of agreement and conflict, the discussions, and the compromises of the Convention. As we shall see in Chapter 10, it is a result, too, of the fact that Americans of later generations continued to value, and hence to preserve, many of the major aspects of the pattern shaped at the Convention.

THE CONSTITUTIONAL CONVENTION

The Convention that was to draft the Constitution came into being in response to a resolution of Congress, which called for a convention of delegates appointed by the states to meet "for the sole and express purpose of revising the Articles of Confederation." The resolution scheduled the Convention to open in Philadelphia on the second Monday in May, 1787.

Twelve states thereupon appointed some sixty-five delegates to attend. Ten of these never showed up. Patrick Henry, selected as a delegate from Virginia, missed a second chance for fame by declining to appear. One state, Rhode Island, did not participate at all. Fearing a new constitution would concentrate too much authority in the national government—fears later confirmed by the document that emerged—Rhode Island refused to send a delegation.

The state delegations varied in size from New Hampshire's two to Pennsylvania's eight. The Pennsylvania delegation included Benjamin Franklin, who because of his advanced age played only a minor part in the proceedings, and two of the most active and important members of the Convention, James Wilson and Gouverneur Morris. Virginia's seven-man delegation was headed by George Washington, who was unanimously elected presiding officer of the Convention. It also included James Madison, who has often been called the chief architect of the Constitution. His fellow Virginian and future political ally, Thomas Jefferson, was abroad. He had succeeded Franklin as American minister to France, and could not be a delegate.

Of the fifty-five who came, some like Alexander Hamilton attended only a part of the time. About ten delegates appear to have dropped out along the way.

The Convention opened on May 14, 1787, in a simple but elegant building in Philadelphia (now known to millions of Americans as Constitution Hall). When only a small number of delegates showed up, the meeting quickly adjourned. On the 25th, when twenty-nine delegates had arrived from nine states, the Convention settled down to its work. The task continued through the heat of the summer. The public was barred. At their third meeting, the delegates adopted a rule of secrecy. Little news of the proceedings seems to have leaked to outsiders. On the last day of the Convention, Franklin was able to say that as to "the opinions I have had of its errors. . . . I have never whispered a syllable of them abroad. Within these walls they were born, and here they shall die." Elbridge Gerry of Massachusetts, perhaps because of a guilty conscience, thought Franklin's remarks were levelled at him.[1]

Under the impact of prolonged disagreements, eighteenth-century manners were sometimes strained. Yet the records indicate a remarkable civility in the speeches and an exceptionally high level of analysis.

Four months after they began, the delegates had completed their work. The final draft of the Constitution was at hand for those to sign who agreed with its basic principles. A last-minute proposal to increase the number of representatives in the House brought about a rare intervention by the presiding officer; George Washington briefly explained why he favored the change and it was unanimously approved.

---

1. Most of what we know about the debates is found in Madison's detailed, full, and apparently scrupulous "Notes of Debates," which he wrote down each day. He did not revise them until after he had retired from the presidency in 1817, and they were not finally published until 1840. The official record was little more than a list of votes taken. In addition to Madison, six other delegates kept notes less detailed than his. All of these notes are collected in Charles C. Tansill, ed., *Documents Illustrative of the Formation of the Union of the American States* (Washington, D.C.: Government Printing Office, 1927). The *Documents* retain the spelling, capitalization, and abbreviations of the author. I have used modern forms. Franklin's remarks are on p. 740, Gerry's on p. 744.

Saul K. Padover has arranged Madison's report on the debates according to topics (excluding some material) in *To Secure These Blessings* (New York: Washington Square Press, Ridge Press, 1962). This is the most convenient arrangement of the debates available.

Some members expressed doubts about the proposed Constitution but contended that it was the best that could be attained. They would, as one of them put it, "take it with all its faults." Others, however, confessed to deeper misgivings. A day earlier, George Mason of Virginia had made his last speech, saying that "this Constitution had been formed without the knowledge or idea of the people." The new government, he insisted, "would either end in monarchy, or a tyrannical aristocracy." He would not sign the document, he said, nor support it in Virginia. Now his colleague from Virginia, Edmund Randolph, also refused to sign. Too much power, he thought, had been given to the Congress.

Gerry of Massachusetts believed that conflict over the proposed Constitution would be so intense as to lead to civil war. He too would not sign. In the end, however, thirty-nine delegates did sign the proposed Constitution.[2]

For its ratification, the document now went to conventions called by the various states. Delaware ratified in December. By July, 1788, nine states had ratified—enough to put the Constitution into effect. Two others quickly followed. The last two dragged their feet. North Carolina delayed its ratification until the end of 1789. The one state that had resisted the Convention was the last to accept its work. In May, 1790, Rhode Island having, as it said, "maturely considered the Constitution for the United States of America . . . and having also seriously and deliberately considered the present situation of this State," proceeded to advance eighteen paragraphs interpreting the Constitution and to request twenty-one amendments. The honor of the state thus preserved, it ratified the Constitution in late May, 1790, almost three years to the day after the Convention had begun its work in Philadelphia.[3]

WERE THE FRAMERS CONSERVATIVES OR REVOLUTIONARIES?

The Constitutional Convention, curiously enough, has been described both as a revolutionary body and as a conservative one. There is truth in both views.

Until the year 1787, the entire history of mankind had never witnessed a single case of a successful and enduring representative republic over a large area. This was a fact of which every man at the Convention was well aware. If a delegate did not happen to know it when he arrived in Philadelphia, he learned it soon enough, for it was on the minds and lips of all the greater leaders of the Convention. Some

---

2. For the last two sessions of the Convention, see *Documents*, pp. 728–745.
3. For Rhode Island's statement, see *Documents*, 1052ff.

of the men who came to Philadelphia—most of them, as it turned out—had in view something that had never been done before. Rule by the people, though rare, was not new. But to expand representative government over a vast domain—that would be a new and revolutionary undertaking.

Although the Framers were uncertain as to how many people there were in the thirteen states, they evidently assumed that the total population was something between 2.5 and 3 million. One compilation used at the Convention counted 2.6 million whites and a half-million blacks. (These were conservative estimates: the federal census of 1790 showed a total population just under 4 million.) Already the number of free white male citizens was fifteen to twenty times as large as in Athens in the fifth century B.C. when the idea of democracy was first advanced. As Charles Pinckney of South Carolina pointed out in the early weeks of the Convention, "The United States include a territory of about 1500 miles in length, and in breadth about 400."[4] The state of New York alone was larger than the whole Greek mainland, larger than the entire Swiss Confederacy, larger than the Dutch Confederacy. And the men in Philadelphia took it for granted that in both population and territory the United States would expand—ultimately, perhaps, into a country of unbelievable vastness.

Revolutionaries Without Precedents

All the experience furnished by history seemed to foredoom an attempt to establish a national government on republican principles over such a great domain.

More than twenty centuries earlier, the citizens of many Greek city-states—especially Athens—participated in political decisions to an extent that probably has never existed since. Athenian politics was virtually a permanent town meeting. Yet the Greeks, for all their political genius, failed to create a federal system that would link one city with another in a representative republic. Indeed, they seem always to have held fast to their belief that citizenship was meaningless unless it provided for direct participation and control over political decisions. Their inability to develop a wider sense of citizenship and to create a larger state in which the perennial wars of Greek against Greek would be eliminated led in time to their subjugation, first by their Macedonian neighbors to the north, and then by the Romans.

More than any other people before them, and more than most since, the Romans learned the complex arts of managing a single government over a large area. The Republic of Rome endured for nearly

---

4. *Documents*, p. 805.

five centuries. The history of that Republic was as familiar to the men at the Convention as our own national history is to us, for their education had typically included a study of the classics; and they were always quick to cite Roman experience. They knew, then, that the Republic had been initially a city government, and that the Romans had been generous in extending the privileges of citizenship throughout the Italian peninsula, and that they had attempted (being a conservative people) to adapt the institutions of the city to the government of the new and greater Rome. Yet the Framers also knew that the Romans never did create an effective system of representation.

The Framers also knew that some of the cities of medieval Italy, like Florence, were republics. But Italy had never developed a national government; in *The Prince* (1513), Niccolò Machiavelli had concluded pessimistically that Italy was incapable of a republic and that only a vigorous and even tyrannical leader could ever bring peace and unity to Italy. Before the eighteenth century, the most extensive development of popular government had occurred among the rural cantons of Switzerland. Of all modern countries, only Switzerland can rightly claim to have had a lengthier experience with democratic institutions than the Unted States. In 1787, however, Switzerland was still a confederacy in which the cantons were sovereign states; their central 'national' assembly, the Diet, had virtually no power. If the men at the Convention had wanted such a confederacy, they need not have come to Philadelphia at all. The Articles of Confederation of 1781 already provided at least as much of a central government as the Swiss then enjoyed. Yet it was precisely because they were discontented in various degrees with the weak confederacy of the Articles that these Americans had assembled. The Swiss example, like Greece, told a good deal about the prospects of popular government on a small scale. But it did not provide a model for a representative republic in a new nation of several million people over a vast territory.

What the Framers proposed to do, then, had never been done before. More than that, a fair reading of a familiar body of historical experience would suggest that their efforts were more likely to fail than to succeed. You can have republican government in a canton, a city, or perhaps even a small state, historical experience seemed to say, but you cannot have it over a large area. Republics can link themselves into a confederacy with a weak central government; but if you want a strong central government you cannot have a republic. The Framers—with some fears, to be sure—rejected this dilemma. To avoid the greater risks of a weak confederacy, they proposed to establish the first great national republic. In this perspective, then, the Framers were indeed revolutionaries.

Conservatives?

Yet as revolutionaries they seem oddly out of place. They were, it is true, a youthful group. Nearly 40 percent were not over 40 years old, and three-quarters of them were under 50. Some of the most vigorous leaders at the Convention were surprisingly young. James Madison was 36, Gouverneur Morris was 35, Alexander Hamilton was 32, and Charles Pinckney of South Carolina was only 29.

Nonetheless, most of them had already had extensive and often even distinguished public careers. Many had acquired experience and reputation during the Revolutionary War. With few exceptions they were substantial and well-known figures in their states; some were respected throughout all thirteen states; and the fame of a few, like Franklin and Washington, extended to Europe. Most of them were moderately well-to-do: a few were exceedingly wealthy by the standards of the time. John Rutledge and Pierce Butler of South Carolina owned large plantations and could be counted on to defend the interests of the planting and slaveholding aristocracy of that state. Gouverneur Morris of Pennsylvania was a wealthy financier and a conservative aristocrat. Although Nathaniel Gorham of Massachusetts had started his business career as an apprentice to a merchant, by 1787 he was one of the leading businessmen in his state.

They were, then, a respectable group. Sixty percent of them were lawyers; nearly half, an incredibly high proportion for those times, were college graduates.

Although they may have seemed revolutionary to Europeans, in their American setting they were not so daring. To be sure, a national government constructed on republican principles was a new experiment for Americans and for the world, but by 1787 representative governments were already well established at the state level. The long period of colonial rule, extending over a century and a half, had given the people in the colonies considerable training in the skills required to operate a representative government. Despite the myths that have since grown up, the colonies had enjoyed an astounding measure of self-government. One house of a colonial legislature was invariably elected by the voters; the second house was sometimes appointed by the first; and in two states, Connecticut and Rhode Island, the governor was elected by the voters. Where the governor was appointed by the King, conflicts between governor and legislature contributed to the development of the art of managing representative institutions. Since the legislature usually controlled the purse strings and voted the governor's salary, even a royal governor could sometimes be outmaneuvered.

Just how many people were eligible to vote in colonial elections has been a matter of debate. For many years it was assumed that property requirements restricted the vote to a small and wealthy minority; but recent research indicates that in most of the colonies from one-half to three-quarters of the white adult males must have been eligible to vote in the years before the Revolution.[5] In Massachusetts, possibly as many as 95 percent of the adult males could vote.[6]

Counterrevolutionaries?

How did the delegates to the Convention look upon this strong tide of political equality? Some scholars have argued that the Constitution was the work of a small group of wealthy aristocrats who wished to stem the rapid advance of equality in the states by constructing a strong national government. Such a government, the argument ran, would protect the economic interests of large planters, speculators, financiers, merchants, and shippers from their natural enemies, the small farmers and the mechanics and artisans in the cities. Small farmers made up the overwhelming majority of the population of the United States, and urban workers, though still a small minority, nevertheless were a potential threat to the well-to-do.[7]

In recent years, however, this view of the Convention and its fruits has been subjected to extensive criticism. If the Framers were engaged in an anti-democratic counterrevolution, how did it happen that the Constitution was approved by eleven states within the following year? The answer had once been that a large part of the adult males were disfranchised by property requirements; hence the conventions held in the various states to approve or disapprove the Constitution were easily rigged by same aristocratic minority whose representatives had drafted the Constitution. But more recent evidence, as we have just seen, seems to indicate that suffrage was in fact rather widely held in most of the states. If the small farmers who comprised the overwhelming bulk of the population were opposed to the Constitution, they must have been very apathetic or confused, because they evidently did not turn out in large numbers to vote against it.

In the second place, in a surprisingly short time, the arrangements provided for in the Constitution seemed to have acquired very widespread approval among the general population. In fact, one of the most

---

5. Chilton Williamson, *American Suffrage from Property to Democracy, 1760–1860* (Princeton: Princeton University Press, 1960), ch. 2.

6. Robert E. Brown, *Middle-Class Democracy and the Revolution in Massachusetts, 1691–1780* (Ithaca: Cornell University Press, 1955), pp. 49–50.

7. The famous pioneering study in this vein was Charles Beard, *An Economic Interpretation of the Constitution* (New York: Macmillan, 1913). Many later historians adopted, expanded, or developed views implicitly contained in Beard's analysis. See, particularly, Merrill Jensen, *The Articles of Confederation* (Madison: University of Wisconsin Press, 1940), and his *The New Nation* (New York, Knopf, 1950). Beard was severely attacked by Robert E. Brown, *Charles Beard and the Constitution* (Princeton: Princeton University Press, 1956); and in turn defended by Lee Benson, *Turner & Beard, American Historical Writing Reconsidered* (New York: Free Press of Glencoe, 1960). A succinct and judicious evaluation of the debate is contained in Edmund S. Morgan, *The Birth of the Republic, 1763–89* (Chicago: University of Chicago Press, 1956).

influential people at the Convention, James Madison, was soon to become the main leader in Congress of the very forces—the small farmers —who, according to the theory, were defeated at the Convention by the aristocratic counterrevolution. Yet Madison, like Jefferson, was a staunch supporter of the Constitution, and there is no persuasive evidence that the small farmers were less so. In fact, it was not the small farmers or artisans who displayed the most opposition to the Constitution during the following generation, but a wealthy minority who distrusted democracy and disliked the power given to the people under the new republic.

Finally, on a number of key issues, including the issue of democracy versus aristocracy, the men at the Convention were not of one mind. Although most of them agreed on the need for a stronger central government, they disagreed—as we shall see—on the extent to which a strengthened central government should be under the influence of the people. If the framework of government they finally proposed showed what the Framers could agree on, it also reflected their disagreements and conflicts.

Pragmatic Reformers?

Indeed, as one reads Madison's reports of the debates at the Convention, one senses two rather different levels of debate. At one level there were practical problems of designing a system of government that would not only have the approval of the delegates and of the states but would work well enough to endure: Should there be one executive or three? How many representatives should there be in the legislative body? What specific powers should be given to Congress?

But underlying and greatly influencing the debates on practical matters, there were agreements and disagreements over political objectives that seemed to reflect more general political ideas and ideology. The rest of this chapter describes the principles on which they agreed. Chapter 9 discusses their disagreements, and the compromises they managed to work out.

AGREEMENTS: The Framers were agreed on three general principles: the need for a republic, the need to partition power and authority in order to preserve a republic, and the need to compromise if a republic were to be established and maintained.

THE NEED FOR A REPUBLIC It may seem so obvious as to need no stating that the Framers wanted to establish a form of government in which the executive and legislature would be chosen directly or indirectly by the citizens: that is, a republic. Yet there were those outside the Convention who were by no means convinced that the delegates truly intended to establish a republic. There were also those who opposed the very idea of a new constitution. Like the Rhode Islanders, they believed that a single republic could not exist on so grand a scale as the United States. In their view, thirteen republics were possible and desirable in America. But one large republic with a powerful central government was probably impossible, at least for long, and certainly undesirable.

Not everyone at the Convention agreed that a republic was the *best* form of government. Alexander Hamilton, for one, expressed unqualified admiration for the British monarchy and House of Lords. Yet like the other delegates, he knew that the overwhelming bulk of the American people would never put up with an effort to create a monarchy. Like many other delegates, he had doubts about the *feasibility* of republican government, but he was firmly committed nonetheless to the *objective* of creating a republican framework of government.

Thanks in part to the fact that the delegates, like the people at large, were substantially agreed on the need for a republic, Americans have never been divided over an issue that was to trouble a number of European countries. Alternatives like monarchy, or, in this century, dictatorship, have never gained enough public support to make them live options.

What *kind* of a republic Americans ought to have was something else again. On that question, as we shall see in the next chapter, the delegates were by no means agreed. Was it to be an aristocratic or a democratic republic? Should the government be controlled only by a part of the people, or by all the people? Like the specific arrangements for a chief executive, a legislature, and a judiciary, the question of an aristocratic versus a democratic republic was more controversial than the question of republican government itself.

THE NEED TO PARTITION AUTHORITY

The Framers were also agreed that a republic could not endure except on this condition: *Governmental power and authority must always be partitioned among several centers and never concentrated in a single center.* This assumption entered into practically everything approved at the Convention.

Instead of a single center of sovereign power, then, they had to insure the existence of multiple centers of power. None of these centers (whether representing a majority of the people or a minority) would be wholly sovereign. Although like their successors they agreed that the only legitimate sovereign is the people, they also agreed, and later generations of Americans seem to have concurred, that even the people ought never to be an absolute sovereign. Consequently no part of the people, such as a majority, in this view ought to be absolutely sovereign.

Reasons for the Assumption

There were several reasons why the delegates could readily agree on the assumption that the power of the government they proposed to establish must not be concentrated, but had to be partitioned among a number of different centers.

A practical reason. To begin with, probably every delegate assumed that any Constitution that concentrated power in the national government would be turned down by the states. Their task, as the delegates saw it, was to enlarge the powers of the national government; yet there was much opposition to a more powerful national government. The defenders of the Articles of Confederation would undoubtedly put up a very stiff fight against the new Constitution. To give unlimited powers to a majority of elected representatives was exactly equivalent to giving unlimited constitutional authority to the national government. But an unlimited national government in any form would surely be turned down in every state. The most that the Convention could do, therefore, would be to frame a national government with definitely *limited authority.*

Suspicion of power. In addition to this practical reason, there were others of a more philosophic cast. Whether democrats or aristocrats, the Convention delegates shared a hard-headed, unsentimental, skeptical view of the ability of human beings to withstand the temptations of power. They took it for granted that individuals are easily corrupted by power; to any person with great power, they might have said, self-restraint is a fragile dike. The best way to prevent the abuse of power, then, was not to trust in human character but to limit the legal authority allocated to any person and to set one power against another.

"Men love power," said Hamilton. "Give all power to the many, they will oppress the few. Give all power to the few, they will oppress the many. Both therefore ought to have power, that each may defend itself against the other."[8] "The rich," said Gouverneur Morris, a wealthy man himself, "will strive to establish their dominion and enslave the rest. They always did. They always will. The proper security against them is to form them into a separate interest. The two forces [the rich and the poor] will then control each other."[9] George Mason announced that "he went on a principle often advanced and in which he concurred,

---

8. *Ibid.,* pp. 217, 221.
9. *Ibid.,* p. 319.

that 'a majority when interested will oppress the minority.' "[10] Wilson, although unwavering in his advocacy of a democratic republic, warned:

> Despotism comes on mankind in different shapes, sometimes in an executive, sometimes in a military, one. Is there no danger of a legislative despotism? Theory and practice both proclaim it. If the legislative authority be not restrained, there can be neither liberty nor stability. . . . In a single house there is no check, but the inadequate one, of the virtue and good sense of those who compose it.[11]

Positive contributions. The Framers also tended to believe that in addition to serving as a check on despotism, the partitioning of authority would make some positive contributions. The existence of multiple centers of power, none of which would be wholly sovereign, would help (might indeed be necessary) to tame power, to secure the consent of all, and to settle conflicts peacefully:

☐ Because one center of power was set against another, power itself would be tamed, civilized, controlled, and limited to decent human purposes, while coercion, the most evil form of power, would be reduced to a minimum.

☐ Because even minorities would be provided with opportunities to veto solutions to which they strongly objected, the consent of all might be won in the long run.

☐ Because constant negotiations among different centers of power would be necessary in order to make decisions, citizens and leaders would perfect the previous art of dealing peacefully with their conflicts, not merely to the benefit of one partisan but to the mutual benefit of all the parties to a conflict.

Consequences of the Assumption

Agreement among the Framers on the need to partition the authority of the government enabled them to agree on other principles that seemed to follow from this assumption:

1. *The principle of limited authority.* Since the virtues and wisdom of men are not powerful enough to prevent their abusing their power, no person, official, or group—whether a minority or a majority—should ever be allowed to have unlimited legal authority. In other words, legal authority should always be strictly limited.

2. *The principle of balanced authority.* Purely legal or even constitutional restraints, standing by themselves, are sure to prove inadequate. Therefore, whenever authority is allocated by law or constitution to one official or body—whether representing a minority or

---

10. *Ibid.,* p. 587.
11. *Ibid.,* pp. 212–213.

a majority—that authority must be counterbalanced (to some degree) by allocating authority to some other official or body.

3. *The principle of offsetting social power.* Legal and constitutional arrangements will be subverted if some citizens or groups of citizens gain disproportionate opportunities for power in comparison with other citizens. Therefore, the potential power of one citizen or group must be offset by the potential power of other citizens.

Applications. From the first two principles it followed that the legal authority of the proposed national government should be carefully defined and limited, and that the authority allocated by the Constitution to one branch or body should be offset by authority allocated to another.

The Constitution reflects these two principles in a great variety of ways:

☐ It preserves the states as fixed elements in a federal system.
☐ It yields to the Congress specific, not unlimited legal powers (Article I, Section 8).
☐ It specifically denies to the Congress legal authority of some kinds (Article I, Section 9).
☐ It provides for a Congress consisting of two separate and rather independent branches, whose members have somewhat different qualifications and were, until 1913, chosen by different means (Article I, Sections 1, 2, 3).
☐ It forbids members of Congress from holding executive offices during the period for which they are elected, thus making it difficult for the president to influence them by appointing them to high offices in the Executive Branch (Article I, Section 6).
☐ It provides for a president elected for a fixed term independently of Congress and bars Congress from shortening his tenure (except by impeachment) and from increasing or decreasing his salary during his four-year term (Article II, Section 1).
☐ It assigns to the president definite but limited legal authority, including a veto of laws passed by Congress (Article II, Section 2).
☐ It provides for a Judicial Branch substantially independent of both president and Congress (Article III).
☐ It makes amendments to the Constitution difficult by requiring approval of two-thirds of the members of each house, and of three-fourths of the states (Article V).

Moreover, when in 1791 the Bill of Rights filled one of the great gaps in the Constitution, it amplified these principles by imposing further specific restraints on the Congress: It guaranteed a number of individual rights, and reemphasized (in the Tenth Amendment) the limited and federal character of the political system.

The third principle, offsetting social power, is more vague and more difficult to execute than the others. It draws strength less from the Constitution than from 'politics,' less from laws than from social and economic forces, less from officials than from citizens. The application of this principle, therefore, does not depend as much on what the Convention did as on what the country that existed outside the Convention has done; it depends less on the delegates than on the generations to come. Nevertheless the formulation of the principle goes back to the Convention, and specifically to Madison who, in a brilliant analysis during the second week of the Convention, sought to meet head-on the charge by the aristocratic faction that a democratic republic would open the door to oppression by the majority. Madison was familiar with some of the fears about the new republic that lurked in delegates' minds. There was the fear that republican liberties would allow for so much squabbling and conflict as to tear the country apart. Majorities would surely oppress minorities. This fear was compounded, he knew, by the enormous size of the American republic in comparison with all the city-states where republican government had hitherto existed.

Madison neatly turned the argument around. Far from being a disadvantage, he argued, the great size of the United States was a positive advantage. The American community would be divided into so great a number of different interests and partisan groups that a majority would never be able to unite for long on a program to oppress the minority.[12] The country's size and diversity were thus the best guarantees for the principle of offsetting social power.

The Assumption in Retrospect

In considering the importance in American political life of this belief in the need to partition power and authority, it is useful to keep four points in mind.

First, the impact of the belief stems not only from the thrust it gave to the decisions of the Framers but also from the fact that later generations of Americans have tended—although not always consciously—to adopt the same belief. They have also tended to accept as desirable the particular arrangements for, and the degree of, partitioned authority that help to distinguish the American political system from polyarchy in other countries.

Second, in applying their belief to the design of the Constitution, the Framers went much further in partitioning authority than those who later drafted the constitutions that govern today in many other polyarchies. A belief in the need for such an elaborate system of checks and balances is much less widely shared outside the United States than most Americans seem to be aware of.

---

12. *Ibid.,* p. 163.

Third, one reason the Framers went so far in applying their faith in the virtues of partitioned authority is that they faced a wholly novel task. In one sense they were conservatives, but in a longer perspective, they were revolutionaries. They confronted a new problem: in a large country, too large for the people to assemble, how, if at all, could you insure the sovereignty of the people and at the same time avoid tyranny? A few years after the Constitutional Convention, the French Revolution demonstrated what has been shown many times since: a solution is neither simple nor self-evident.

Fourth, the Framers may also have adopted an extreme pattern of partitioned authority because the doctrine itself is an incomplete guide to action. It is, in fact, more an orientation, perspective, or hunch than a political philosophy. Certainly it does not constitute a philosophy of democracy, a theory of polyarchy, or a complete strategy of decision-making.

It was, nonetheless, a perspective that crucially shaped their views on law, constitutional arrangements, and politics. And although it was not universally accepted, it was also a perspective shared by enough Americans to make the new Constitution not only acceptable, but workable.

THE NEED FOR COMPROMISE

The third principle that most of the delegates seemed to take for granted was that politics requires compromises. A constitution could not be brought into being without some compromises. And a republic could not endure among a people unwilling to settle their conflicts by compromise.

Had the Framers not seen some virtues in compromise, they would hardly have designed the Constitution as they did. For without the readiness to compromise, a framework of government based on the principle of partitioned authority would have been totally unworkable.

Compromises were essential to the workings of the Convention itself. Thus Madison and Wilson, who were among the most principled men at the Convention, were finally driven to accept equal state representation in the Senate despite their belief, which they never altered even in later years, that this feature of the Constitution could not be justified by any acceptable political principle except the principle that in politics compromise is sometimes more virtuous than purity.

Were men like Madison and Wilson right to have entered into a compromise that violated their principles? Should they have left the Convention in indignation, like John Lansing and Robert Yates of New York or Luther Martin of Maryland? Should they have refused to sign the document because they did not subscribe to everything in it, as George Mason, Edmund Randolph, and Elbridge Gerry did? Should they have refused to support it because, as some delegates concluded, the Constitution had been formed too secretly, with too little popular participation and consultation?

Questions like these are easy to answer if one has very weak principles of conduct—or very strong ones. To the person of weak principle, compromise is an easy path so long as one gains even a little in the bargain. To the person of rigid morality, the answer is equally obvious: it is better not to agree at all than to agree to an imperfect bargain.

But the problem is not just a personal affair, a matter of private morality. Since the way a political leader answers these questions may greatly affect the rest of us, the problem is also a public affair.

Lying between the simple extremes of unprincipled politics and rigid morality is a domain of action that has been called *the ethics of responsibility:* meaning by this term an attempt to weigh the consequences of each alternative as intelligently as possible, and then to choose the best available. Acting according to the ethics of responsibility, a political leader cannot enjoy the luxury of rejecting an imperfect compromise, even a highly imperfect compromise, so long as that compromise represents the best possible alternative presented by the world as it happens to be. Irresponsibility, in this view, consists not in making concessions, but in making unnecessary concessions; not in making imperfect bargains, but in failing to make the best possible bargains; not in adhering strictly to principles, but in holding rigidly to one principle at excessive cost to other principles. One may be irresponsible, then, not merely from a want of principles but also from a want of intelligence and knowledge of the real world. In the ethics of responsibility it is important not only to know what one wants but also to know exactly what one must do to get it, and what it will cost in other values as well as in money.

The Anglo-American political tradition has, at its best, accented the ethics of responsibility. If that tradition has rejected wholly unprincipled and unscrupulous politics as an aim unworthy of the political calling, it has also rejected fanaticism and rigidity as too simple for the complex world of political decision. If sheer opportunism is ignoble, rigid morality in politics is dangerous.

The men at the Convention were English (Wilson was a Scot) before they were American. Whatever else they were, they were not fanatics. Nor were they mere opportunists. They were above all realists, who knew or believed they knew the rough boundaries of the politically possible: yet they were principled realists who sought to achieve their aims with the imperfect materials at hand. When the committee appointed to examine a thorny question reported back to the Convention, Mason probably expressed the sentiments of most of the delegates when he said:

... There must be some accommodation on this point, ... however liable the report might be to objections, he thought it preferable to an appeal to the world by the different sides, as had been talked of by some gentlemen.... He would bury his bones in this city rather than expose his country to the Consequences of a dissolution of the Convention without any thing being done.[13]

That the ethics of responsibility provides no easy solutions is shown by the conduct of three prominent Virginia delegates. Despite grave reservations about the compromise that led to equal representation in the Senate, Madison signed the Constitution and vigorously supported its adoption. Edmund Randolph refused to sign. Yet upon concluding that the United States might well dissolve without the Constitution, he urged his fellow Virginians to adopt it. In spite of Mason's commitment to finding a mutually acceptable compromise, in the end he could neither sign the document to which he had contributed so much nor could he support its adoption. He returned to Virginia and opposed it.

Thus the Framers took for granted one of the key assumptions of the incrementalist, or step-by-step, perspective on political action: it is morally responsible to search for, and in American circumstances it is possible to discover, satisfactory compromises for specific problems, compromises that will not drastically damage the interests of any important group of participants. They also revealed something of the limits of compromise. Seventy-odd years later these limits were to be overrun on the issue of slavery. When the limits of compromise were breached, the Union that the Framers had helped to create dissolved into civil war.

In Part Four we shall try to understand how political conflict may go beyond the limits of peaceful compromise. Meanwhile, it is important to recognize that in acting according to the ethics of responsibility, and so combining principle with compromise, the delegates to the Convention bequeathed more than a constitution. In what they did there, and in what they did in public life in later years, they also helped to shape a way of entering into political decisions and evaluating political institutions that is as much a part of the American political system as the Constitution.

SUMMARY   1. The Framers were both revolutionary and conservative:

☐ They were revolutionary insofar as they attempted to establish a national government on republican principles over a great domain; for prior experience, conventional wisdom, and political science as-

---

13. *Ibid.*, pp. 329–330.

serted that a republic could exist only in a small unit, such as a city-state.

☐ In the American setting, however, they were for the most part building on existing institutions, practices, traditions, and already dominant social forces, rather than instituting radically new and unfamiliar political, social, or economic relationships.

2. Older interpretations that portrayed the Framers as a unified group of counterrevolutionaries who defeated the aspirations for democracy and equality of the overwhelming majority of the American people at the time—the small farmers—are rendered implausible because:

☐ Evidence that has become available since the older view was proposed shows that the suffrage was in fact rather widely dispersed in most states. Yet despite their opportunity to do so, voters did not turn out to vote down the proposed Constitution.

☐ In a very short time the Constitution seems to have acquired very wide approval among the general population, including particularly the small farmers. In fact, those who became the main leaders of the small farmers, like James Madison, helped to draft the Constitution and supported it strongly.

3. Although the Framers were by no means united on certain basic matters, they were generally agreed on:

☐ The need for a republic.

☐ The need to partition authority in order to maintain a republic.

☐ The need for compromise in order to establish and maintain a republic.

9 THE FRAMERS DISAGREE AND COMPROMISE

The Framers agreed on enough of the fundamentals to form a Constitution. The general principles they agreed on have become central elements in the way most Americans tend to think about the Constitution, law, and politics.

But they also disagreed on a number of crucial issues. It is highly instructive to examine those disagreements, for they posed some fundamental issues. And the compromises the Framers arrived at have had lasting consequences for American political life.

DISAGREEMENTS   Three of the crucial issues involved were these:

☐ Should the Constitution establish democracy or instead provide for some kind of meritocracy or aristocracy of talents?

☐ Who were the American people and how were they to govern themselves? As a confederacy of thirteen different peoples, as a single people, or both?

☐ If the principle of political equality were to be respected, did it imply equality among individuals or among political units?

The delegates to the Convention disagreed sharply on these matters. And disagreement on the answers to these questions did not end when the Framers completed the writing of the Constitution, nor when the Constitution was adopted by the states and put into effect. On the contrary, conflicting answers continued to reappear in American politics. Nearly all of the great conflicts that have wracked the country since 1787 have raised these questions anew. In fact, the differences in viewpoint expressed during the Convention continue to appear in American politics right down to the present day.

DEMOCRACY OR ARISTOCRACY?

Thanks to their rule of secrecy, the delegates were free to ventilate their opinions with unusual candor. They probably would not have spoken so frankly outside the closed doors of Independence Hall. Fortunately, then, the records of the Convention enable us to learn something about the real beliefs of the delegates. Secrecy was, no doubt, of particular value to those delegates who distrusted popular government and yearned for some kind of aristocratic republic in which the rich and the well-born would occupy a special place. These delegates might not have dared to admit in public what they were willing to affirm in private.

The Case for Aristocracy

The most articulate spokesmen for an aristocratic republic were Gouverneur Morris of Pennsylvania, Rufus King of Massachusetts, and of course Alexander Hamilton of New York. (Hamilton's influence was greatly reduced, however, by his extreme proposals and irregular attendance.) One of the delegates from Georgia, William Pierce, contributed little to the Convention but left a good deal to posterity, for he wrote some vivid sketches of the delegates, from which we learn that

> Mr. Gouverneur Morris is one of these geniuses in whom every species of talents combine to render him conspicuous and flourishing in public debate: —He winds through all the mazes of rhetoric, and throws around him such a glare that he charms, captivates, and leads away the senses of all who hear him. With an infinite stretch of fancy he brings to view things when he is engaged in deep argumentation, that render all the labor of reasoning easy and pleasing. But with all these powers he is fickle and inconstant, —never pursuing one train of thinking, —nor ever regular. He has gone through a very extensive course of reading, and is acquainted with all the sciences. No man has more wit, —nor can any one engage the attention more than Mr. Morris. He was bred to the law, but I am told he disliked the profession, and turned merchant. He is engaged in some great mercantile matters with his namesake Mr. Robert Morris. This Gentleman is about 38 years old, he has been unfortunate in losing one of his legs, and getting all the flesh taken off his right arm by a scald, when a youth.[1]

Morris's views on the Senate are a good example of his attitudes. Although he did not maintain a consistent position as to how the senators should be chosen, he was unwavering in his opinion of the proper role of the Senate:

> . . . It is confessed, on all hands, that the second branch ought to be a check on the first—for without its having this effect it is perfectly useless.

---

1. Charles C. Tansill, ed., *Documents Illustrative of the Formation of the Union of American States* (Washington, D.C.: Government Printing Office, 1927), pp. 101–102.

—The first branch, originating from the people, will ever be subject to *precipitancy, changeability,* and *excess.* Experience evinces the truth of this remark without having recourse to reading. This can only be checked by *ability* and *virtue* in the second branch. On your present system, can you suppose that one branch will possess it more than the others? The second branch ought to be composed of men of great and established property—*an aristocracy.* Men, who from pride will support consistency and permanency; and to make them completely independent, they must be chosen *for life,* or they will be a useless body. Such an aristocratic body will keep down the turbulency of democracy. But if you elect them for a shorter period, they will be only a name, and we had better be without them. Thus constituted, I hope they will show us the weight of aristocracy.[2]

Hamilton was a great admirer of the British Constitution as it existed (or rather as he believed it to exist) in the eighteenth century. "In his private opinion," Madison reports him as saying, "he had no scruple in declaring . . . that the British government was the best in the world: and that he doubted much whether any thing short of it would do in America."[3] Accordingly, Hamilton proposed to emulate the British system as closely as possible in designing a new construct for American government. An assembly elected by the people would take the place of the House of Commons. Corresponding to the House of Lords—"a most noble institution"—he proposed a Senate elected for life "or at least during good behaviour." The absence of a monarch was annoying. "As to the Executive, it seemed to be admitted that no good one could be established on republican principles. . . . The English model was the only good one on this subject. . . . Let the Executive also be for life."[4]

The Case for Popular Control

The most consistent spokesmen at the Convention in behalf of popular control were James Wilson of Pennsylvania, George Mason of Virginia, and James Madison.

Of these, Wilson seems to have had the deepest confidence in popular government and the most clear-cut vision of what a democratic republic should and would be. Wilson was a Scot, who had attended the University of St. Andrews before emigrating to America where he had taken up the practice of law. He was described by Pierce as follows:

Mr. Wilson ranks among the foremost in legal and political knowledge. He has joined to a fine genius all that can set him off and show him to advantage. He is well acquainted with man, and understands all the pas-

---

2. *Ibid.*, p. 838. The quotation is from the notes of Robert Yates, a delegate from New York.

3. *Ibid.*, p. 220.

4. *Ibid.*, pp. 221–222. In the plan Hamilton submitted on June 18, the Senate and the executive were to serve "during good behaviour," which ordinarily would mean for life (pp. 224–225). The notes kept by Yates of New York confirm Madison's account (see pp. 781–782), for various texts of Hamilton's plan of government, see pp. 979, 988.

sions that influence him. Government seems to have been his peculiar study, all the political institutions of the world he knows in detail, and can trace the causes and effects of every revolution from the earliest stages of the Grecian commonwealth down to the present time. No man is more clear, copious, and comprehensive than Mr. Wilson, yet he is no great orator. He draws attention not by the charm of his eloquence, but by the force of his reasoning. He is about 45 years old.[5]

Early in the Convention, Wilson announced that "he was for raising the federal pyramid to a considerable altitude, and for that reason wished to give it as broad a basis as possible. No government could long subsist without the confidence of the people. In a republican Government this confidence was peculiarly essential."[6] Wilson urged that not only the lower house but also the Senate and the president should be chosen by the people.[7]

Specific Issues

Wilson represented at best a small minority. At the other extreme, the ardent aristocrats were also a rather tiny group. Although decisions on specific questions were often influenced by considerations that had little to do with a delegate's preference for democracy or aristocracy, there were several issues on which the differences showed up most clearly. For example, should either the president or members of the Senate have a limited term or hold office for life or good behavior? Or, should the right to vote be constitutionally restricted to freeholders or property owners? On these issues, Wilson, Mason, and Madison took a democratic position, while on all three of them Morris favored the aristocratic view (Table 9.1).

A Compromise Solution

It falsifies history, then, to assume that the delegates at the Convention were in substantial agreement on the alternatives of a democratic republic versus an aristocratic republic. Clearly they were not. Yet it is also easy to exaggerate the extent of their differences. Although some delegates advocated a democratic republic and others an aristocratic republic, most of them were probably ranged somewhere between Wilson at one pole and Morris or Hamilton at the other. Madison was evidently near the midpoint of the Convention. He was as democratic as Wilson on some issues; but on others, such as limiting the suffrage to freeholders or advocating definite constitutional protections for wealth and property, he was conservative enough to maintain the confidence of pro-aristocratic delegates like Morris.

---

5. *Ibid.*, p. 101.
6. *Ibid.*, p. 126.
7. *Ibid.*, pp. 209–211.

Table 9.1
Three Issues in the
Constitutional Convention

	Limited Term for President	Limited Term for Senators	A Constitution without Restrictions on Suffrage
Wilson	Yes	Yes	Yes
Mason	Yes	Yes	Yes
Madison	Yes	Yes	Yes[a]
Hamilton	No	No	?[b]
G. Morris	No[c]	No	No[d]

[a] Madison's views are not entirely clear. On July 26 he opposed restricting the suffrage to freeholders. On August 7 he seemed to lean in that direction. See *Documents*, pp. 489, 935.

[b] Hamilton was absent during these discussions.

[c] At first Gouverneur Morris strongly supported a motion to give the executive tenure "during good behavior." "This is the way to get a good government," *ibid.*, p. 396. A week later, he seemed to have doubts, p. 447. But he generally opposed efforts to limit the term of the president, e.g., pp. 453, 458.

[d] Favored restricting the suffrage to freeholders, *ibid.*, pp. 489, 935.

A compromise solution was also facilitated by their general agreement on the need for a republic, described in the last chapter. Whatever some of the delegates may have thought of the competence of the people to rule, most believed that the new national government had to contain some important elements of popular government. Even Morris and Hamilton wanted one branch chosen by the people. To be sure, a few delegates went so far as to oppose the election of the lower house by the people; they wanted even this choice to be filtered through the state legislatures. But their views do not seem to have had much influence on the Convention.

The essence of the unspoken compromise they agreed on was simply to leave open the question of whether the new republic was to be an aristocracy or a democracy. That was to be decided by the future, by forces outside the control of the Framers. The Constitution left electoral procedures where they already were, under the control of the states. It specified that:

☐ Representatives were to be chosen by "the people of the several States." The voters ("electors") were to have whatever qualifications the state specified for elections to "the most numerous branch of the State Legislature" (Article I, Section 2).

☐ Senators were to be chosen by the legislature of each state. Hence, the Constitution laid down no requirements at all for voters (Article I, Section 3).

☐ The President was to be chosen by electors appointed by each state "in such manner as the legislature thereof may direct" (Article II, Section 1).

Conceivably, the states might have decided to limit the suffrage to a narrowly based wealthy class in each state. Alternatively, the states could extend the suffrage to most white males. The decision was not made by the Framers but by political activists in each state. For reasons we shall explore in the next chapter, American conditions all but insured that the decision would be against restricting political participation to a small upper class and in favor of extending it broadly. In this sense, the Constitution designed by the Framers did not *require* that the new Republic be democratic. Instead, the Constitution created the space within which a democratic republic could grow, if the conditions favored it—and they did.

A CONFEDERACY OR A NATIONAL REPUBLIC?

Were Americans in the process of becoming a single nation? Or were they thirteen separate nations? As one delegate observed about a month after the Framers got down to business, the Convention seemed to be hopelessly divided into

> Those on one side considering the states as districts of people composing one political society; those on the other considering them as so many political societies.[8]

Would Americans be served best by a new and vigorous national government—or by a confederation of state governments united by a relatively weak central government?

Nearly every delegate, to be sure, professed to be in favor of a federal system. But the word *federal* was no more than a label. The trouble was that they did not agree on what a 'federal' system was or should be. "Great latitude," Hamilton told the delegates, "therefore must be given to the signification of the term."[9]

The National Federalists

On the one side were a number of the most distinguished delegates at the Convention—Madison, Wilson, Hamilton, Gouverneur Morris—who wanted to create a strong national government. This group of delegates—one might call them National Federalists—had three distinct objects in mind. *First,* they sought a definite and considerable increase in the powers of the national government. Since practically everyone at the Convention agreed that the national government should be strengthened, the differences among the delegates on this score were a matter of degree. But matters of degree are extraordinarily important: after all, the difference between jumping into a hot bath, an icy lake, or a tub of boiling water is only a matter of degree.

Second, the National Federalists wanted a central government that had legal authority over individual citizens. To National Federalists, the

8. *Ibid.,* p. 297.
9. *Ibid.,* p. 216.

fatal flaw in the Articles of Confederation was that the Congress had no authority over individuals; Congress could act only through the states themselves. Clearly it is one thing to compel an individual to obey laws passed by the national government; but it is quite another to compel a state. The disobedience of individuals can generally be met by police, by courts, by fines and imprisonment; the disobedience of a state creates the terrifying choice of governmental impotence or civil war.

Third, the National Federalists wanted a national government that directly represented individual citizens and not simply the states. The central government, in their view, should be responsive to the citizens of the United States, not just to the states. To them, "the people" were the people of one United States, not thirteen different people in thirteen different states.

The State Federalists

Some of the delegates—the State Federalists, let us call them—were very strongly opposed to all these objectives of the National Federalists. Early in the proceedings, John Lansing of New York denounced the proposals of the National Federalists:

> I am clearly of opinion that I am not authorized to accede to a system which will annihilate the State governments. . . . Can we expect that *thirteen* States will surrender their governments up to a national plan?[10]

In fact, Lansing and his fellow New Yorker, Robert Yates, left the Convention not long after, protesting that state sovereignty would be destroyed under a national government.

Luther Martin of Maryland presented the most extensive case for State Federalism, ". . . that the general government was meant merely to preserve the state governments, not to govern individuals. . . . Its powers ought to be kept within narrow limits. . . . The States like individuals were in a state of nature equally sovereign and free."[11] "This," added Madison in one of his rare editorial comments, "was the substance of the residue of his discourse which was delivered with much diffuseness and considerable vehemence."[12] Like Lansing and Yates, Martin quit the Convention and fought bitterly in Maryland against the adoption of the Constitution.

Most of the delegates agreed with the State Federalists on two points. First, the states had to be preserved as constituent and important elements in a federal system. In this sense, almost everyone was

---

10. *Ibid.,* p. 787. This comment is found in the notes of delegate Yates, which were later transcribed by Lansing himself.

11. *Ibid.,* pp. 287–288.

12. *Ibid.,* p. 290.

a 'Federalist.' Hamilton, as usual, was a lonely exception; of all the National Federalists, he was the most extreme, for he was quite willing to see the states abolished.[13] But Hamilton's views found little support.

Second, there was the age-old conviction that a republic could not function over a large area. Madison had tried to blunt this point by arguing, as we have seen, that size was less a vice than a virtue. Yet the worry about size continued. "The largest states," Oliver Ellsworth of Connecticut observed, singling out Virginia and Massachusetts for special attention, "are the worst governed."[14] Although the delegates from these states denied the specific charge, the general point was admitted even by the most enthusiastic National Federalists.[15]

Nonetheless, the National Federalists were evidently much closer to the main body of the delegates than were the extreme State Federalists. National Federalism cut across the other principal splits and united men who disagreed on other questions. Thus, those who disagreed over the question of democracy versus aristocracy could unite behind the banner of National Federalism. The principle spokesmen for National Federalism were Wilson, Mason, and Madison, who supported a democratic republic, and Gouverneur Morris, Hamilton, and Rufus King of Massachusetts, who supported an aristocratic republic. National Federalism was not, as is sometimes supposed, exclusively an aristocratic doctrine: it was, and continued to be, advocated by those who believed in a democratic republic. Andrew Jackson and Abraham Lincoln did not have to invent National Federalism; they simply took it ready-made from the doctrines that prevailed at the Convention. The State Federalists, by contrast, were not only a minority at the Convention; if they were not then a minority in the nation, they were soon to become so, and they have remained a dissenting minority ever since.

Nor was the conflict between National Federalists and State Federalists, as is often thought, simply a mirror image of the contest between large states and small. New York, the fourth largest state, was represented not only by Hamilton, perhaps the most extreme National Federalist in the Convention, but also by Lansing and Yates, who were so extreme in their support for State Federalism that they left the Convention and opposed the Constitution. The fifth largest state, Maryland, sent both Luther Martin, an extreme State Federalist, and Daniel Carroll, a National Federalist. The three smallest states were Delaware,

---

13. See his discussion and his plan in *Documents*, pp. 215 ff., and his subsequent remark quoted in Madison's notes: "As *States*, he thought they ought to be abolished. But he admitted the necessity of leaving in them, subordinate jurisdictions" (*ibid.*, p. 238).

14. *Ibid.*, p. 276.

15. For example, see Hamilton's comments (*ibid.*, pp. 291–220), and those of James Wilson (*ibid.*, p. 274); Gouverneur Morris stated the prevailing view succinctly on July 19. "It has been a maxim in political science that republican government is not adapted to a large extent of country, because the energy of the executive magistracy can not reach the extreme parts of it. Our country is an extensive one." *Ibid.*, p. 408.

Rhode Island, and Georgia. Delaware, the smallest, was represented by (among others) George Read, who agreed with Hamilton that the states "must be done away."[16] Rhode Island, the second smallest, was a stronghold of State Federalism and sent no delegates. The third smallest, Georgia, sent William Pierce, a National Federalist.

Victory of the National Federalists

In the end, the National Federalists won a clear-cut victory. The Constitution contains all three of their principal objectives.

First, the new national government was endowed with a set of broad legal powers. Two of these, the power to tax and to regulate interstate commerce, were very comprehensive—or at least they could be so interpreted. The Congress, said the Constitution,

> ... shall have Power To lay and collect Taxes, Duties, Imports and Excises, to pay the Debts and provide for the common Defense and general Welfare of the United States. ...
> To regulate Commerce with foreign Nations, and among the several States, and with the Indian tribes (Article 1, Section 8).

As legislation of a later century was to show, these two powers were ample enough to permit extensive regulation of the economy. Under the first, for example, the production and sale of agricultural products would one day be so minutely controlled that a tobacco grower in North Carolina could not bring to market more than his allotted quota of tobacco. Under the second, even strikes by elevator operators in New York City would someday fall under the jurisdiction of the national government.

The new central government was given exclusive constitutional authority to coin money and issue currency. It could borrow money on its own credit. It could regulate bankruptcies. For all practical purposes, it had exclusive control over foreign relations, over the military establishment, over the declaration and conduct of war. It could establish a national judiciary with jurisdiction over all cases arising under the Constitution, laws of Congress, or treaties, and over a number of other matters as well. In a sweeping grant (as if to leave no doubts), the Congress was authorized "to make all laws which shall be necessary and proper for carrying into execution the foregoing powers, and all other powers vested by this Constitution in the government of the United States, or in any department or office thereof" (Article I, Section 8).

In the second place, all of these powers gave the national government legal authority over individual citizens. The president and the Congress would not have to work through the agency of state govern-

---

16. *Ibid.,* p. 299.

ments; they could deal directly with the individual citizens of the United States. To avoid all doubt on this crucial point, the Framers took pains to spell it out:

> This Constitution, and the laws of the United States which shall be made in pursuance thereof; and all treaties made, or which shall be made, under the authority of the United States, shall be the supreme law of the land; and the judges in every state shall be bound thereby, any thing in the Constitution or laws of any state to the contrary notwithstanding (Article VI).

Finally, the National Federalists insured that American citizens would be directly represented in the national government. They beat off all attempts to have the members of the lower house appointed by the state legislatures, and spelled out their victory in these words:

> The House of Representatives shall be composed of members chosen every second year by the people of the several states. . . . (Article I, Section 2).

The manner in which the president was to be chosen (as we shall see in Chapter 11) was one of the most difficult practical problems that confronted the delegates to the Convention. Though they changed their minds several times, in the end they decided that even the president would be chosen by the people of the United States, though in a manner that seemed somewhat more indirect to the delegates than it ever proved to be in practice (Article II, Section 1).

The states were represented, then, only in the Senate. After lengthy and often bitter controversy, it was finally agreed that the senators should be chosen by the state legislatures (Article I, Section 3). As it turned out, however, even this solution proved impractical, for it merely succeeded in converting the elections to the state legislatures into indirect senatorial elections. Nonetheless, this indirect selection remained until 1913, when the Seventeenth Amendment provided for the direct election of senators by the people.

EQUAL STATES OR EQUAL CITIZENS? Although the Declaration of Independence unambiguously affirmed the principle of political equality, the Convention delegates were far from united in accepting that principle or, insofar as they did accept it, the conclusions they drew from it. Does political equality mean—as most democratic theorists have affirmed—that individual citizens are to count equally in making decisions? Or does it mean that (as in the General Assembly of the United Nations) aggregates of citizens called states, not individuals, are to be assigned equal weights? Clearly, one contradicts the other if states vary in the number of citizens. For if individuals are weighted equally, then small states must have less weight than large; but if states are weighted equally, then a citizen of a large state will have less weight than a citizen of a small state.

More concretely, if there were to be a strong national government (as the National Federalists proposed), how should the various states share their control over the new government: Equally, as under the existing Articles? By wealth or taxes, as had sometimes been proposed? Or according to population? This question provoked the bitterest controversy at the Convention, and perhaps the most pointless.

The story of this famous conflict and the final compromise has been told many times. Right at the beginning, on May 29, Edmund Randolph of Virginia introduced a plan of government that favored National Federalism. This proposal, which quickly gained the name of the Virginia Plan, had the backing of the National Federalists. It had the advantage of a head start, and at once became the basis of nearly all the later work of the Convention. The second item in the Virginia Plan provided "that the rights of suffrage in the National Legislature ought to be proportioned to the quotas of contribution [i.e., taxes], or to the number of free inhabitants, as the one or the other rule may seem best in different cases."[17] On the basis of taxes, Virginia might have had sixteen representatives to one for Georgia.[18] On the basis of population, the disparity would have been less—about seven to one.[19] Naturally delegates from some of the small states objected. On June 15 they made their countermove through William Paterson of New Jersey, who presented a rival plan that would have left the existing system of equal state representation untouched.[20]

Although Paterson's New Jersey Plan was soon rejected, the conflict over representation remained to plague the Convention. At times, indeed, it looked as if the problem could not possibly be solved. The issue came up repeatedly; summer came on; tempers grew frayed; and delegates talked angrily of ending the Convention, going home, leaving the country with nothing but the old Articles of Confederation. There were even hints and veiled threats of disrupting the existing confederation. Some delegates from small states threatened their opponents from the large states by alluding to the possibility of foreign intervention. In a menacing outburst, Gunning Bedford of Delaware clashed with Rufus King of Massachusetts:

> Bedford: . . . We have been told with a dictatorial air that this is the last moment for a fair trial in favor of a good government. It will be the last

---

17. *Ibid.*, p. 116.

18. Based on a congressional recommendation for tax quotas in 1785. See Winton Solberg, *The Federal Convention and the Formation of the Union* (New York: Liberal Arts Press, 1958), p. 407.

19. The delegates used various population estimates, all differing by some margin from the subsequent census of 1790. Moreover, the question of whether slaves were to be counted would affect the representation of the Southern states. For population estimates, see *Ibid.*, Appendix II, pp. 407 ff.

20. *Documents*, pp. 204–207.

indeed if the propositions reported from the committee go forth to the people. I am under no apprehensions. The large states dare not dissolve the Confederation. If they do the small ones will find some foreign ally of more honor and good faith, who will take them by the hand and do them justice. . . .

King: . . . I can not sit down, without taking some notice of the language of the honorable gentleman from Delaware. It was not I that uttered . . . dictatorial language. This intemperance has marked the honorable gentleman himself. It was not I who with a vehemence unprecedented in this house, declared myself ready to turn my hopes from our common country, and court the protection of some foreign hand. This too was the language of the honorable member himself. I am grieved that such a thought has entered into his heart. I am more grieved that such an expression has dropped from his lips. The gentleman can only excuse it to himself on the score of passion. For myself whatever might be my distress, I would never court relief from a foreign power.[21]

Delegates from the large states in turn drew dismal pictures of the sad fate of small states if the United States were to dissolve. Both sides stood firm. A delegate from Delaware had reminded the Convention at the end of its first week that should there be any change from the existing system of representation—that, is, any departure from an equal weight for each state—"it might become their duty to retire from the Convention."[22] If the states were not given equal weight in the new government, Paterson of New Jersey warned, "New Jersey will never confederate. . . . She would be swallowed up. He [Paterson] had rather submit to a monarch, to a despot, than to such a fate. He would not only oppose the plan here but on his return home do everything in his power to defeat it there."[23] The other side seemed equally committed. It was his "firm belief," said Rufus King, "that Massachusetts would never be prevailed on to yield to an equality of votes" in the Senate.[24] Madison "entreated the gentlemen representing the small States to renounce a principle which was confessedly unjust, [and] which could never be admitted."[25]

Compromise

On June 29, the advocates of equal representation of states suffered their first defeat. On that day, by a vote of six states to four, the delegates rejected the principle of equal state representation in the lower house (Table 9.2). From this time forward, the question centered on the Senate. On July 2, over a proposal by Ellsworth of Connecticut that each state should have one vote in the Senate, the Convention

---

21. *Ibid.,* pp. 316–317. In the original, Madison puts these speeches in the third person.
22. *Ibid.,* p. 123.
23. *Ibid.,* p. 183.
24. *Ibid.,* p. 378.
25. *Ibid.,* p. 300.

Table 9.2
Votes at the
Convention on the Issue
of Equal Representation
for the States

States	In the House June 29	In the Senate July 2	July 7
Solid "Yes"			
Connecticut	Yes	Yes	Yes
New York	Yes	Yes	Yes
New Jersey	Yes	Yes	Yes
Delaware	Yes	Yes	Yes
Solid "No"			
Virginia	No	No	No
Pennsylvania	No	No	No
South Carolina	No	No	No
Waverers			
Maryland	Divided	Yes	Yes
North Carolina	No	No	Yes
Massachusetts	No	No	Divided
Georgia	No	Divided	Divided
Yes	4	5	6
No	6	5	3
Divided	1	1	2
	11 [a]	11 [a]	11 [a]

[a] Rhode Island sent no delegates. Those from New Hampshire arrived later.
Sources: *Documents*, pp. 303, 324, 340.

split in two. Five states supported Ellsworth's motion, five opposed it, and one was divided (Table 9.2). The Convention, split asunder, agreed to appoint a committee. The committee, consisting of one member from each state, reported back three days later with the recommendation "that in the 2nd branch each State shall have an equal vote."[26] On July 7 the decisive vote was taken on the committee report. Among the delegations that had fought against this principle, only Virginia, Pennsylvania, and South Carolina held firm to the last. North Carolina now swung to the other side. The vote of Massachusetts was lost because the delegates from Massachusetts were split. Georgia was also divided. Six states favored the compromise (Table 9.2). Thus, the issue was put to rest by a compromise that had little to be said for it except for one extremely important virtue: acceptability.

A Principle or a Bargain?

Though equal state representation has sometimes been hailed as a great constitutional principle, Hamilton's judgment of the controversy was not far off the mark: "The truth is," he said, with the cruel candor of youth that made him both feared and admired, "it is a contest for power, not for liberty."[27] Because the conflict was dramatic and dan-

---

26. *Ibid.*, p. 324.
27. *Ibid.*, p. 301.

gerous, and because it had the happy ending Americans firmly believe in, it has been given an importance by later generations out of all proportion to its real significance. The advocates of equal representation of the states were defending a principle that would soon be made obsolete.

Men like Madison and Wilson foresaw this with considerable clarity. "Can we forget for whom we are forming a government?" Wilson asked. "Is it for *men,* or for the imaginary beings called *States*?"[28] Madison asked:

> Was a combination to be apprehended from the mere circumstance of equality of size? Experience suggested no such danger. The journals of Congress did not present any peculiar association of these States in the votes recorded.... Experience rather taught a contrary lesson.... The States were divided into different interests not by their difference of size, but by other circumstances.[29]

Madison proved to be right. There has, in fact, never been a significant conflict between the citizens of small states and the citizens of large states. Or, to put it another way, there has been no important controversy in the United States that has not cut squarely across the people in both small states and large.

Nonetheless, equal representation of states in the Senate was firmly written into the Constitution (Article I, Section 3). And those delegates like Madison and Wilson who had so vigorously opposed a bad principle preferred compromise to a dissolution of the union. They swallowed their bitterness and accepted defeat. But they refused to concede that the outcome was anything more exalted than an unprincipled bargain that had to be accepted, not because it was just, but merely because the alternatives were still more unpleasant.

THE UNCOMPLETED AGENDA

As the years passed, the Constitution took an exalted place in the American creed alongside a faith in the virtues of democracy. The Framers came to be treated less as men than as gods. More than a century later, critics punctured the myth by showing that they were not gods but only men, and men with investments at that. It came to be intellectually fashionable to hold that the Framers really carried through a kind of aristocratic counterrevolution that somehow was converted, nonetheless, into a democratic republic as time wore on.

A more exact interpretation than either of these would surely be: The Framers could not create either a polyarchy or an oligarchy. Whatever their intentions were—and as we have seen, they did not agree on these—what they did was to create a framework of government. Once

---

28. *Ibid.,* p. 307.
29. *Ibid.,* pp. 292, 310.

this framework had been accepted, the government could become either a polyarchy or a kind of aristocratic or oligarchic republic. Which it was to be depended not on what any group of men could do in three or four months at a Convention in Philadelphia, but on what was to happen later, over years and decades and perhaps centuries, among Americans outside the Convention and among generations still unborn. And what these Americans then living and yet to be born would do, in turn depended on many factors—factors that no one at the Convention could control or even predict, some of which are even today little understood.

One thing is perfectly clear now, even if it was not so clear at the time: given the right conditions, the framework of government they had created could become a polyarchy.

SUMMARY   The Framers disagreed over:

☐ Democracy versus aristocracy.
☐ A national republic versus a confederacy.
☐ Whether political equality applied to individuals or to states.
   1. As to democracy versus aristocracy:
☐ They disagreed over whether the president and members of the Senate should have a limited term or hold office for life or good behavior. They also disagreed over whether the right to vote should be constitutionally restricted to freeholders or property-owners of some sort.
☐ However, they agreed on the need for an important element of popular participation in the national government.
☐ And by leaving the determination of the voting requirements to the state governments, in effect they allowed the decision as to a democratic versus an aristocratic republic to be made by political activists in the states.

   2. As to a confederacy versus a national republic, the National Federalists won a clear-cut victory.
   3. As to equal states or equal citizens, in order to have an acceptable document, those like Madison who held that the states should be represented entirely by population were finally compelled to compromise with those who held out for equality of state representation. The compromise was equal state representation in the Senate.
   4. The Framers themselves did not establish polyarchy. Their framework of government could have been adapted to polyarchy, as events were to prove, or had American conditions and dominant beliefs been less favorable to the development of polyarchy, to an aristocratic or oligarchic republic.

10 HOW AMERICAN CONDITIONS FAVORED POLYARCHY

In 1835, Harriet Martineau, an English writer visiting the United States, paid a call on James Madison, who was then 84 and within a year of his death. "Mr. Madison remarked to me," she wrote later, "that the United States had been 'useful in proving things before held impossible.' "[1]

This view of the American experience was not uncommon in the nineteenth century. It attracted foreigners like Miss Martineau to the United States in order to unravel the mystery.

> ... The experiment of the particular constitution of the United States may fail; but the great principle which, whether successfully or not, it strives to embody,—the capacity of mankind for self-government,—is established forever. It has, as Mr. Madison said, proved a thing previously held impossible.[2]

Today, polyarchy is no longer a novelty. Several dozen countries, as we have seen, operate under systems of polyarchic government. Some sixteen or seventeen of these countries have done so for more than half a century (excepting a few periods of foreign occupation in the first and second world wars).

Although polyarchy is not novel, it nonetheless remains comparatively uncommon. Only about one-fifth of the countries of the world have polyarchies, and in some of these countries polyarchy is new and shaky. Why polyarchy develops and endures in some countries and not in

---

1. Harriet Martineau, *Society in America*, ed. S. M. Lipset (Garden City: Anchor Books, 1962), p. 57.
2. *Ibid.*, p. 58.

others is a question that is still surrounded by a good deal of uncertainty and conjecture.

Polyarchy not only developed first in the United States, but it has proved highly durable there. Throughout the nineteenth century, Americans and foreigners were often fascinated—and sometimes repelled—by the existence of a 'democracy' in this country. Its mere presence seemed to offer visible proof that democracy in a large country was not a wholly utopian idea. Yet the proof generated a mystery: What was required for such an experiment to succeed? What was it about this country that created a congenial soil for the rapid evolution of this new political form? How was it that the Americans were able to prove "a thing previously held impossible"?

An important part of the answer lies in three general conditions that facilitated the rapid development of polyarchy. These were:

☐ A pervasive equality.
☐ A shared system of democratic beliefs.
☐ The constitutional framework.

Yet each of these favorable conditions had an unfavorable counterpart that could—and as it happened, would—create troublesome problems for the American polyarchy.

FIRST CONDITION: EQUALITIES   With few exceptions, Europeans who came to the United States during the first half of the nineteenth century were struck by the high degree of political, social, and economic equality among Americans. In 1832 a young, inquisitive, liberal French aristocrat, Alexis de Tocqueville, spent nine months travelling the length and breadth of the United States. On returning to France he wrote *Democracy in America,* a profound and sympathetic account that very quickly became one of the best known and most highly regarded books ever written about this country. The very kernel of Tocqueville's analysis of American democracy was the pervasiveness of equality. Some foreign visitors were charmed, some were offended, but all agreed that the prevailing level of equality was truly astounding.

Even when considered in the most cautious light, Tocqueville's conclusion appears to be correct: the world had never before witnessed so much equality of condition as existed in America. In everything that one says on this topic, of course, one is bound to except the Afro-Americans, particularly the great bulk who were slaves in the Southern states. This is no slight exception, but rather, as I indicated in Chapter 7, a basic feature that distinguishes polyarchy in America from polyarchy elsewhere. In addition, women were denied the suffrage, as they were to be almost everywhere until the twentieth century. It is well to keep in mind, then, that I speak at the moment only of the free white male population. Among these there was not only a fair approximation of universal suffrage, but evidently an amazing degree of social and economic equality as well. At the Convention, Charles Pinckney had portrayed Americans in words that were to be echoed two generations later by Tocqueville:

> ...Among [Americans] there are fewer distinctions of fortune and less of rank, than among the inhabitants of any other nation...Equality is...the leading feature of the United States.[3]

And Pinckney, like Tocqueville, pointed to the availability of land as the principle reason:

> ...this equality is likely to continue, because in a new country, possessing immense tracts of uncultivated lands, where every temptation is offered to emigration and where industry must be rewarded with competency, there will be few poor, and few dependent.[4]

If Pinckney's statement stood alone, we could count it as the kind of exaggerated rhetoric about equality that Americans seem to enjoy hearing themselves say to one another. But Pickney's observation in 1787 was also Tocqueville's in 1832. *Democracy in America* begins with:

> Among the novel objects that attracted my attention during my stay in the United States nothing struck me more forcibly than the general equality of condition among the people. I readily discovered the prodigious influence that this primary fact exercises on the whole course of society; it gives a peculiar direction to public opinion and a peculiar tenor to the laws; it imparts new maxims to the governing authority and peculiar habits to the governed. I soon perceived that the influence of this fact extends far beyond the political character and the laws of the country, and that it has no less effect on civil society than on government; it creates opinions, gives birth to new sentiments, founds novel customs, and modifies whatever it does not produce. The more I advanced in the study of American society, the more I perceived that this equality of condition is the fundamental fact from which all others seem to be derived and the central point at which all my observations constantly terminated.[5]

Economic equality. Unfortunately the kinds of statistical information one would need in order to make these observations more precise is largely lacking.[6] As we shall see below, Tocqueville underestimated the

---

3. Charles C. Tansill, ed., *Documents Illustrative of the Formation of the Union of American States* (Washington, D.C.: Government Printing Office, 1927), pp. 267, 270.

4. *Ibid.*, p. 267.

5. Alexis de Tocqueville, *Democracy in America*, 2 vols. (New York: Vintage Books, 1955), vol. I, p. 3. On this general point and its bearing on American development, see Louis Hartz, *The Liberal Tradition in America* (New York: Harcourt, Brace, 1955).

6. See, however, Ralph L. Andreano, "Trends and Variations in Economic Welfare in the United States before the Civil War," in *New Views on American Economic Development*, ed. R. L. Andreano (Cambridge: Schenkman, 1965), pp. 131–167.

degree of social and economic inequality in the cities. Yet one fact is beyond argument: during the first half-century of experience under the new Constitution, the United States was a country of farmers. Until 1840, seven out of ten workers were engaged in farming. In the two decades before the Civil War the proportion fell, but even in 1860, six out of every ten were in agriculture. Americans were, therefore, a rural people. In 1790, only 5 percent of the population lived in places with 2,500 inhabitants or more. In the 1830s, when Tocqueville and Harriet Martineau visited the United States, the proportion was about 10 percent. As late as 1860, it was only 20 percent.[7]

Unfortunately we can only guess at the distribution of property ownership among farmers. But observers agreed that among this vast farming population, property was, thanks to the availability of land, widely diffused. Tocqueville and Martineau found few rich and few poor, even though frontier families sometimes lived under the most miserable conditions, particularly during their first years. Because land was plentiful in relation to the population, labor was relatively scarce; society put a premium on a man's labor. In the towns and cities, wages were relatively high. In the countryside, sons of farmers found it possible to acquire their own farms. The European practice of keeping landed estates intact by passing them on to the eldest son was uncommon; even among the land-rich manorial proprietors of New York, Miss Martineau reported, the practice was disappearing.[8]

Equality extended in other directions, too. In a nation of farmers, there was no peasantry—not even any tradition of peasantry in the European sense. Large landed estates existed, to be sure, particularly in the South; but it was extremely difficult to keep free white farm labor from leaving. "The people of the United States," Miss Martineau observed, "choose to be proprietors of land, not tenants."[9] The large governmental establishments of the centralized European monarchies scarcely existed in the United States of 1831; in a population of over 13 million only 11,491 persons were employed by the federal government. Of these, nearly 9,000 were in the Post Office[10] and therefore dispersed throughout the country. The vast private corporations created by industrial capitalism had not yet arrived; the giant factories, the great financiers, the urban proletariat, the army of clerks and white-collar workers—these were still unknown. Nearly everyone, according to Tocqueville, had at least a modest education; though he encountered few great scholars in his travels, he also found few wholly uneducated

7. *Historical Statistics of the United States, Colonial Times to 1957*, prepared by the Bureau of the Census, with the cooperation of the Social Science Research Council (Washington, D.C.: U.S. Government Printing Office, 1960), p. 9, Series A 34–50; p. 72, Series D 36–45.

8. Martineau, *Society in America*, p. 264.

9. *Ibid.*, p. 179.

10. *Historical Statistics*, p. 710, Series Y 241–250.

people. In fact, though illiteracy was high among black slaves, among the whites it was exceedingly low for the time; between 1840 and 1860, the U.S. Census reported that among white people 20 years of age or over, only about one in ten could not read and write.[11]

Social equality. Europeans were frequently struck by the comparative weakness of social barriers among Americans. This was particularly so outside the Eastern cities, and most notably in the agricultural West. Even servants did not show the deference to which an Englishman or European was accustomed. Yet Martineau, perhaps too generously, insisted that "the manners of the Americans [in America] are the best I ever saw."[12] Indeed, among Americans then, as now, even family relationships were conducted with an astonishing amount of equality. The lack of strong parental domination, the tendency of parents to rely more on persuasion than severe punishment, and the free and easy ways of American children were as evident to Tocqueville and Martineau in the 1830s as they are to foreign visitors today. "For my own part," said Martineau, "I delight in the American children"; but (it is only fair to add) what she found charming, many others saw as insolence and lack of proper deference toward adults. Both Tocqueville and Martineau concluded that the family was a kind of miniature training ground in 'democratic' attitudes.

Beliefs in equality. Just as striking to the foreigner as all other aspects of equality was the extent to which Americans seemed to believe that equality was a virtue. No doubt there was a good deal of rhetoric, muddleheadedness, and hypocrisy in the widespread emphasis by Americans on the virtues of equality. But thoughtful foreigners like Tocqueville and Martineau held that the American belief in equality went far deeper than mere lip service. It seemed to them that Americans, taken in the large, believed that in essential value as a human being, one person was very much like another. In 1889, sixty years after Tocqueville and Martineau, an eminent British historian who served as ambassador to the United States, James Bryce, emphasized the same point in a happy metaphor:

> ...In America men hold others to be at bottom exactly the same as themselves. If a man is enormously rich...or if he is a great orator...or a great soldier...or a great writer...or a President, so much the better for him. He is an object of interest, perhaps of admiration, possibly even of reverence. But he is deemed to be still of the same flesh and blood as other men. The admiration felt for him may be a reason for going to

---

11. *Ibid.,* p. 206.
12. Martineau, *Society in America,* p. 272.

see him and longing to shake hands with him. But it is not a reason for bowing down to him, or addressing him in deferential terms, or treating him as if he was porcelain and yourself only earthenware.[13]

Qualification: Inequalities

Since so much of what has just been said about equality in agrarian America has long since passed into American mythology to provide us with gilt aplenty for our Golden Age, it might be unnecessary to emphasize the matter so strongly, except for one thing: Unlike many other American myths, this particular one seems to have considerable validity. And unless we realize how extensive was the equality of condition among Americans—to use the phrase of both Pinckney and Tocqueville —in the first half century or so after the Convention completed its labors, we shall not be able to understand why polyarchy took root so readily in this soil and survived through some hard times.

If, however, equality prevailed among Americans to a degree that had not been matched anywhere to that time, there were nonetheless important exceptions, and these the myth-makers usually forget to mention. Some of these exceptions were to threaten the system at its foundations; not even in our time have we seen the last of them.

Social status. First, even if social classes in the harsh European fashion were absent in America, rudimentary forms of social stratification did exist among the white population, most markedly in the old cities along the eastern seaboard and in the South. Martineau had some strong words to say about the snobbery she encountered among

> those who consider themselves the aristocracy of the United States: the wealthy and showy citizens of the Atlantic ports...I was told a great deal about "the first people in Boston": which is perhaps as aristocratic, vain and vulgar a city, as described by its own "first people," as any in the world.[14]

Were these rudimentary social classes merely a legacy of the past— or, worse, a foreshadowing of the future? Was equality only a fleeting aspect of American life? Would 'equality of condition' become more and more a myth, a dream about a vanished Golden Age? And would the new American aristocrats look with disdain on the political institutions of a democratic republic?

Business. To the extent that social equality reflected a general pervasive equality in property, wealth, and control over economic enterprise, it

---

13. James Bryce, *The American Commonwealth,* 2 vols. (London and New York: Macmillan, 1889), vol. II, p. 606.
14. Martineau, *Society in America,* p. 260.

rested upon a transitory phenomenon—the fact that Americans were predominantly a nation of farmers in a country where there was a vast supply of cheap land. But if Americans became a nation of businessmen and employees, what then? In 1800 about 10 percent of the people in the labor force were employees. By 1860 the number would grow to 60 percent. By 1960, 90 percent would be working for others.[15] What would happen when agrarian capitalism gave way to business capitalism? One answer was at least suggested by those parts of the United States where this had already occurred during the first half-century of the republic.

Urban business enterprise—commerce, banking, manufacturing—provided the second important source of inequalities. To be sure, business enterprise was still small; it was confined to a few cities. But it was exactly in the cities that the consequences were evident: disparities of wealth, the sharper delineation of social 'classes' and greater possibilities of political corruption. According to a recent estimate, in 1828 the wealthiest 4 percent of the population of New York City owned nearly half the wealth. Similar inequalities existed in Boston, Philadelphia, and probably other cities. The opulence of a wealthy few matched that of rich European aristocrats. And the disparities were increasing.[16]

Men like Jefferson and Madison often argued that the United States should, if possible, remain a nation of farmers and that business enterprise should not be encouraged; for they held that the equality of condition necessary to a democratic republic could not be maintained in a society that was based on business rather than on small farms. Was there any ground for the Jeffersonian dream of an agrarian democracy or for the fear that business enterprise and manufacturing would endanger democracy? Farmers are not necessarily more knowledgeable, upright, or more civic-minded than city dwellers, and a nation of landlords and peasants would surely be no Eden for lovers of democracy. Yet a country made up exclusively of small farmers is likely to be a country where equality prevails. The kernel of truth in the myth, then, was this: A nation of small farmers would almost automatically preserve a high degree of economic, social, and political equality. By contrast, the development of commerce, industry, manufacture, and banking on a large scale was bound to generate inequalities—in wealth, income, control over economic enterprise, social status, knowledge, skill, and, hence, in power too. Although Jefferson and Madison did not accurately foresee the shape of the future, they were right in their guess that the expansion of commerce and industry would create a serious obstacle to achieving a high degree of democracy in America.

15. Stanley Lebergott, "Labor Force Mobility and Employment," in R. L. Andreano, ed., *New Views on American Economic Development* (Cambridge, Mass.: Schenkman, 1965), pp. 362–376, at p. 369.

16. These findings, an important qualification of Tocqueville's thesis, which has generally been accepted uncritically by historians, are found in Edward Pessen, *Riches, Class, and Power Before the Civil War* (Lexington, Mass.: D. C. Heath, 1973), p. 33 and *passim*.

Table 10.1
Black Population in the
United States, 1800 to 1860

| | Total Population | Blacks | |
		Total	Slave
	(000)	(000)	(000)
1800	5,297	1,002	894
1810	7,224	1,378	1,191
1820	9,618	1,772	1,538
1830	12,901	2,328	2,009
1840	17,120	2,874	2,487
1850	23,261	3,639	3,205
1860	31,513	4,442	3,954

Source: *Historical Statistics,* p. 9, Series A 34–50; A 59–70. For 1800 and 1810, figures used for blacks are for all nonwhites.

Table 10.2
Black Population in the
South, 1800 to 1860

| | Total Population | Blacks | |
		Total	Slave
	(000)	(000)	(000)
1800	2,622	918	857
1810	3,461	1,268	1,160
1820	4,419	1,643	1,508
1830	5,707	2,162	1,980
1840	6,950	2,642	2,428
1850	8,983	3,352	3,117
1860	11,133	4,097	3,838

Source: *Historical Statistics,* p. 12, Series A 95–122.

In the cities of the eastern seaboard, it had already done so in their own day.

Blacks. The third exception to the prevalence of social, economic, and political equality was, as I have already said, the Afro-American. Whether free or slave, the prevailing practices of the white majority placed him in a position of social, economic, and political subordination. Yet blacks were no trifling minority; from 1800 to 1860 they were 15 to 20 percent of the population of the United States; in the South, one out of every three persons was a slave (Tables 10.1, 10.2).

In a society that preached equality and to a surprising extent practiced what it preached, slavery was a contradiction; and everyone knew it. It had been a sore point at the Constitutional Convention. Yet no one wanted to face the issue squarely, then or later, for everyone knew it was explosive. When Martineau entered the United States in 1834,

> ... There was an absolute and almost ominous silence in Congress about slavery. Almost every leading man told me in conversation that it was the grand question of all; that every member's mind was full of it; that nearly all other questions were much affected, or wholly determined by it; yet no one even alluded to it in public.[17]

17. Martineau, *Society in America,* pp. 78–79.

In 1836, the House of Representatives even went so far as to adopt a Gag Rule, as it came to be called, preventing the House from considering "all petitions, memorials, resolutions, propositions, or papers relating in any way or to any extent whatever to the subject of slavery or the abolition of slavery."[18]

The subjection of the blacks, a monument to inequality, cast a dark shadow over the prospects of democracy in America. For one thing, an ideology that justified slavery was difficult to reconcile with an ideology that made virtues of equality, liberty, and democracy. Yet the barefaced contradiction was too much to live with. There began, as a result, a strange effort to construct an ideology that justified both democracy and slavery, a task (carried on most enthusiastically but not exclusively in the South) that proved to be one long agony of tortured logic and denial of humanity to the Afro-American—whatever the cost to fact, reason, and sentiments of humanity.

Political participation. Another set of differences that contributed heavily to political inequality among Americans were differences in political skills and incentives. These are among the elemental causes of inequality mentioned in Chapter 5. In every political system, some citizens are much less interested and active in politics than others. Apathetic citizens disfranchise themselves; active citizens gain influence. Among Americans, as among other peoples, these differences are pronounced. We shall examine these differences in Chapter 28. There we shall see that only a small percentage of citizens give much time to politics; only a few are willing to make a career out of politics; and it is these few—the professional politicians—who exercise the greatest control over those vital instruments of polyarchy, the political parties.

Is this only a recent development? Were the early years of the republic a political Golden Age when citizens were far more interested, knowledgeable and active in politics than they are today? We do not have nearly enough of the right kinds of data to permit us to answer with confidence. The matter has recently become a subject of sharp controversy among scholars;[19] the dispute is too complex to enter into here. However, it seems to me reasonable to think that the kinds of factors associated today with differences in the degree one is interested

---

18. Richard B. Morris, *Encyclopedia of American History* (New York: Harper & Bros., 1953), p. 179.

19. A recent protagonist of the Golden Age theory is Walter Dean Burnham in "The Changing Shape of the American Political Universe," *American Political Science Review,* 59 (March, 1965), pp. 7–28. This article was attacked by Philip E. Converse in "Change in the American Electorate," in Angus Campbell and Converse, eds., *The Human Meaning of Social Change* (New York: Russell Sage, 1972), pp. 263–338. Burnham replied in "Theory and Voting Research: Some Reflections on Converse's 'Change in the American Electorate,'" *American Political Science Review,* 68 (September, 1974), pp. 1002–1023, which in turn was criticized in the same issue by Converse (pp. 1024–1027) and by Jerrold G. Rusk (pp. 1028–1049), who were answered in a "Rejoinder" by Burnham (pp. 1050–1057).

and participates in political life also operated in the nineteenth century. These factors include amount of education, type of occupation, income, and the strength of one's attachment to a political party. There is good reason for thinking that in the nineteenth century factors like these made for differences in political participation in the cities, and probably had some effect in the countryside as well. If so, they would have led to inequalities in influence over government. There is convincing evidence, in fact, that they did.[20]

SECOND CONDITION: IDEOLOGICAL AGREEMENT

For a polyarchy to survive, political equality is not enough. Political equals may quarrel: quarreling may bring civil strife. The policies of a majority may seem oppressive to a minority: the minority may revolt. Consent, you may remember, has a practical side: if the laws passed by the representatives of a majority fail to gain the tacit 'consent' of a large minority, a polyarchy is likely to be ripped apart.

In this case, too, destiny seemed to favor polyarchy in America. During the first half century under the new Constitution, there were powerful forces uniting Americans, forces strong enough to overcome tendencies toward disintegration. Among these was the rapid growth of a comparatively high degree of ideological agreement on a number of key aspects of their society.

Equality and democracy. Unfortunately, we have only weak evidence to go on; despite many learned attempts to do so, no one can say with much confidence what the content of these beliefs actually was. However, judging from contemporary descriptions, and particularly from Tocqueville, most Americans seemed to affirm the virtues of equality and democracy. Not all, to be sure, were equally fervent; nor was public utterance always the same as private belief; and practice did not necessarily correspond precisely with belief. Both Tocqueville and Martineau found skepticism and cynicism about democracy among the wealthy strata of the population. Nonetheless, no sharp ideological split between supporters and opponents developed, simply because the opponents were too few and too fearful of the opinions of the rest.

The Constitution. Americans also came to agree very quickly on the virtues of their constitutional system. The reverence of Americans for the Constitution, an attitude that has at different times puzzled, astonished, amused, and irritated foreign observers, evidently developed rapidly. Within an unbelievably short time, hardly more than a decade,

---

20. On the cities, Pessen, *Riches, Class, and Power,* presents some persuasive evidence in Part IV, "Influence and Power," pp. 249 ff.

Americans no longer debated seriously whether their constitutional system was good or bad; it appeared to be a postulate almost universally subscribed to that the American Constitution was a good one, if not in fact the best in the world. Americans ceased to be divided over questions of constitutional structure. There was, however, one aspect of the Constitution on which Americans did not wholly agree, and that was the full nature of the powers granted to the federal government. Yet even in this case the debate was not so much over the virtues of the Constitution, per se, as whether this or that interpretation of the Constitution was the correct one. Very early, therefore, a familiar semantic device appeared in American politics that continues down to the present time. To question the Constitution itself was taboo; one argued instead over what the Constitution 'really' meant. In this it was possible to isolate the Constitution itself from political debate.

Compromise. Not only Tocqueville but also the political practices of that time suggest that Americans also tended to agree on the virtues of political compromise. Tocqueville remarked on the self-restraint of Americans, on their reluctance not to push a good point too far.

Nationhood. With exceptional speed, Americans also developed a sense of nationhood. If it is difficult to be sure what the content of American beliefs is or has been, it is even harder to determine the exact nature of American national feeling. That such a nationalism exists is, however, beyond doubt, and evidently it came about surprisingly soon. Foreigners and Americans alike began to observe from the time of the Revolution onward that Americans seemed to feel themselves more and more to be a distinct people, a unique people, not Englishmen now, nor Canadians, nor Frenchmen, nor Mexicans, nor any other people but Americans. Americans soon gained a reputation among Europeans for being touchy about the virtues of the United States and even for having a sort of national vanity. Traveling abroad, blowhard Americans often alienated foreigners, as they have done ever since; while on this side of the Atlantic, the visitor who implied that the United States had any blemishes was likely to stir up a resentful counterattack.

Tocqueville's description. There is perhaps no more vivid description of this unity of beliefs than Tocqueville's summary:

> The observer who examines what is passing in the United States ... will readily discover that their inhabitants, though divided into twenty-four distinct sovereignties, [that is, the states,] still constitute a single people; and he may perhaps be led to think that the Anglo-American Union is more truly a united society than some nations of Europe which live under the same legislation and the same prince.

Although the Anglo-Americans have several religious sects, they all regard religion in the same manner. They are not always agreed upon the measures that are most conducive to good government, and they vary upon some of the forms of government which it is expedient to adopt; but they are unanimous upon the general principles that ought to rule human society. From Maine to the Floridas, and from the Missouri to the Atlantic Ocean, the people are held to be the source of all legitimate power. The same notions are entertained respecting liberty and equality, the liberty of the press, the right of association, the jury, and the responsibility of the agents of government. . . .

Not only are the Anglo-Americans united by these common opinions, but they are separated from all other nations by a feeling of pride. For the last fifty years no pains have been spared to convince the inhabitants of the United States that they are the only religious, enlightened, and free people. They perceive that, for the present, their own democratic institutions prosper, while those of other countries fail; hence they conceive a high opinion of their superiority and are not very remote from believing themselves to be a distinct species of mankind.[21]

The Persistence of Ideological Agreement

It is easy to exaggerate, as foreigners often have, the extent to which Americans agree. Americans do disagree, often bitterly. These disagreements sometimes lead to severe conflict. In one case they led to civil war.

Nonetheless, the early tendency toward a widely shared set of beliefs seems to have persisted throughout American history. If we put to one side for the moment some important changes brought about by the turbulent events from 1963–1974, the evidence from surveys indicates that:[22]

☐ It was very nearly impossible to find an American who said that he was opposed to democracy or favored some alternative—at least for the United States. On the contrary, nearly everyone professed to believe that democracy is the best form of government. [23]

☐ Although substantial numbers of citizens approved of proposals for

---

21. Tocqueville, *Democracy in America,* vol. I, pp. 409–410.

22. An exceptionally useful source for anyone interested in a profile of American political attitudes is Lloyd Free and Hadley Cantril, *The Political Beliefs of Americans: A Study of Public Opinion* (New Brunswick, N.J.: Rutgers University Press, 1967). The best summary of survey evidence on political attitudes of young people, with numerous citations to specific surveys, is Seymour Martin Lipset, "Youth and Politics," in *Contemporary Social Problems,* eds. R. K. Merton and Robert Nisbet (New York: Harcourt Brace Jovanovich, 1971), pp. 743–791. A useful comparison of college youth, noncollege youth, and adults is contained in Daniel Yankelovich, Inc., *Generations Apart,* a study conducted by Daniel Yankelovich, Inc., for the Columbia Broadcasting System (New York: Columbia Broadcasting System, 1969). Additional information can also be found in: Clyde Kluckhohn, "The Evolution of Contemporary American Values," *Daedalus,* 87, no. 2 (Spring, 1958), 78–109; Robert Lane, *Political Ideology, Why the American Common Man Believes What He Does* (New York: Free Press of Glencoe, 1962); Gabriel A. Almond and Sidney Verba, *The Civic Culture, Political Attitudes and Democracy in Five Nations* (Princeton, N.J.: Princeton University Press, 1963); Key, *Public Opinion;* Herbert McCloskey, "Consensus and Ideology in American Politics," *American Political Science Review,* 58, no. 2 (June, 1964), 361–382.

23. James W. Prothro and C. W. Grigg, "Fundamental Principles of Democracy: Bases of Agreement and Disagreement," *Journal of Politics,* 22 (Spring, 1960), 276–294.

specific constitutional changes, the broad elements of the system were widely endorsed.[24]

☐ There was substantial agreement that if defects existed in the laws and the Constitution they should be cured by traditional legal and political processes of change.[25]

☐ Most people continued to believe in the virtues of compromise.[26]

☐ Most Americans also continued to display complacency about their economic institutions. Proposals for extensive reconstruction did not enjoy much support.[27]

☐ Although a majority of Americans seemed willing to place themselves in the 'working class,' their sense of 'class' was obviously weak. The key word seems to be 'working,' not 'class.' Few believed that 'class lines' divide Americans into hostile camps.[28]

☐ Most Americans continued to profess a strong confidence in the possibilities of personal achievement. A great many continued to believe personal success was attainable by hard work and skill.[29]

---

24. Thus 61 percent said they would favor changing the terms of members of the House of Representatives from two years to four years; 24 percent were opposed; 15 percent expressed no opinion. There was little difference by region or party (American Institute of Public Opinion release, Jan. 14, 1966). 50 percent said they would favor limiting U.S. Senators to two 6-year terms; 38 percent were opposed; 12 percent had no opinion (AIPO release, Jan. 26, 1966). The evidence for wide support for the main elements in the Constitution is indirect; e.g., "Should the Constitution be made easier to amend?" 69 percent said "No" (AIPO, March 1, 1937, in Hadley Cantril, *Public Opinion 1935–1946* [Princeton, N.J.: Princeton University Press, 1951], p. 939). "Do you think the Constitution of the United States should ever be changed in any way?" 54 percent said "No"; 34 percent said "Yes"; 12 percent said "Don't Know" (NORC, Nov., 1943, *ibid.*).

25. One study provides as evidence for the point the percentages of "political influentials" (N = 3020) and "general electorate" (N = 1484) agreeing to the following statement: "There are times when it almost seems better for the people to take the law into their own hands than wait for the machinery of government to act." Political influentials–13 percent; general electorate–27 percent (McCloskey, "Consensus and Ideology," p. 365). In 1965 only 10 percent of a national sample said that they had "ever felt the urge to organize or join a public demonstration about something" (AIPO release, Nov. 17, 1965).

26. In 1969, the following percentages said they personally believed that "compromise is essential for progress": college youth–80 percent; noncollege youth–88 percent; parents of college youth–82 percent; parents of noncollege youth–85 percent (Yankelovich, *Generations Apart*, p. 5).

27. On business, see *Big Business from the Viewpoint of the Public*, Survey Research Center, Institute for Social Research (Ann Arbor: University of Michigan, 1951), pp. 18, 20, 26, 44, 56. In the midst of the Great Depression, responses to the question, "Should the government attempt to break up large business organizations?" were: 69 percent said "No" and 31 percent said "Yes" of those who had an opinion; 10 percent had no opinion (AIPO, July 19, 1937, in Cantril, *Public Opinion 1935–1946*, p. 345).

On government ownership, see *ibid.*, Polls 14 and 16, p. 345; Polls 53, 54, and 59, p. 349; and Poll 73, p. 351. The percentages of Americans who say they approve of labor unions has varied from 60 to 76 percent for three decades; Gallup figures are: 1936–72 percent; 1941–64 percent; 1953–75 percent; 1961–63 percent; 1965–71 percent. However, in recent years more people have said that the laws regulating labor unions were not strict enough than have said they were right or too strict (AIPO release, February 14, 1965). See also Free and Cantril, *Political Beliefs of Americans*, pp. 129–133.

28. See V. O. Key's analysis, "Occupation and Class," ch. 6 in *Public Opinion and American Democracy;* also Robert R. Alford, *Party and Society* (Chicago: Rand McNally, 1963), ch. 8.

29. The hypothesis that there has been a decline in the motivations for personal achievement is highly dubious. See the discussion in "A Changing American Character?" ch. 3, Seymour Martin Lipset, *The First New Nation: The United States in Historical and Comparative Perspective* (New York: Basic Books, 1963); the data cited in Key, *Public Opinion*, fn. 2, 4, p. 47, and fn. 5, p. 48; Fred I. Greenstein, "New Light on Changing American Values: A Forgotten Body of Survey Data," *Social Forces*, 42 (1964), 441–450; and Free and Cantril, *Political Beliefs of Americans*, pp. 114–115, 193–194.

☐ Thus Americans tended to express satisfaction rather than discontent with their lot. Most Americans claimed that life in the United States was the best they could attain anywhere in the world; few wanted to emigrate.[30] They expected that their own material conditions would improve, and that for their children life would be much better, provided there is no war.[31]

Qualifications: Differences in Depth and Distribution

How deeply these attitudes continue to run, how firmly they are held, and how they are shared among Americans are questions on which historical data shed almost no direct light; modern survey data provide only a little more. Survey data do, however, lend some support for the following assumptions:

1. If Americans are agreed on abstract general propositions about popular government, the Constitution, the virtues of individual liberty, and so on, an attempt to apply these generalities to concrete problems is likely to produce extensive disagreement.[32]
2. Statistically speaking, the more formal education one has, the more likely one is to express support for the general views just described. The greater one's income, the more likely one's support. Support also increases with the status or social prestige of one's occupation; it is higher among professional people, for example, than among skilled workers. Finally, the more active and involved a person is in political affairs, the more likely he or she is to support these views.[33] Generalizations about attitudes may not hold up with groups too small to have significant numbers in a sample—the very rich, for

---

30. The proportion has, however, increased markedly since the 1950s. In 1971 a Gallup survey asked respondents in nine countries: "If you were free to do so, would you like to go and settle in another country? What country?" Twelve percent of the American respondents said "Yes," with a preference for Australia, Canada, Britain, and Switzerland. This percentage, Gallup reported, was twice as large as in 1959 and three times what it was soon after World War II. It still remained lower than in any of the other countries, where the percentages who wanted to emigrate were: Britain, 41 percent; Uruguay (Montevideo only), 32 percent; West Germany, 27 percent; Greece, 22 percent; Finland, 19 percent; Sweden, 18 percent; Brazil (Sao Paulo, Rio), 17 percent; Netherlands, 16 percent (*The New York Times*, March 21, 1971, p. 27).

31. In 1965, white persons in a national survey said overwhelmingly that they were satisfied with their family income (69 percent); housing (77 percent); the work they did (87 percent); the education their children were getting (77 percent). Among nonwhites, however, the proportions who were dissatisfied were: on income—64 percent; housing—66 percent; on the work they did—38 percent; and on the education their children were getting—46 percent (AIPO release, September 1, 1965). See also William Buchanan and Hadley Cantril, *How Nations See Each Other* (Urbana: University of Illinois Press, 1953), p. 53; and Free and Cantril, *Political Beliefs of Americans*, p. 107.

32. The best evidence is found in Prothro and Grigg, "Fundamental Principles of Democracy"; McClosky, "Consensus and Ideology"; and Samuel A. Stouffer, *Communism, Conformity and Civil Liberties* (Garden City, N.Y.: Doubleday, 1955).

33. See the survey data reported and analyzed in Fred I. Greenstein, *The American Party System and the American People*, 2nd ed. (Englewood Cliffs, N.J.: Prentice-Hall, 1970), ch. 3, pp. 18–42; Seymour Martin Lipset, *Political Man* (Garden City, N.Y.: Doubleday, 1960), "Working Class Authoritarianism," ch. 4, pp. 97–130. See also Stouffer, *Communism, Conformity and Civil Liberties*.

example, or Wall Street brokers. Conceivably, support may fall off in these groups; we have no evidence one way or the other.

3. On all these matters there are dissentive minorities and sometimes they are quite large. Yet dissenters rarely reject the traditional democratic values of popular rule, political equality, and consent. On the contrary, they generally affirm these values; but they also tend to believe that American life and institutions have developed in ways inconsistent with democratic values, and demand changes which, they evidently believe, would move the country closer to attaining these values.

4. The connection between the word and the deed is rather uncertain. In particular, to express disagreement with widely prevailing views does not at all mean that one will actually do anything more to act out his dissent. Many—perhaps most—Americans who express disagreement do not, it seems, try to change the attitudes of others by discussion, or bring about changes by joining dissident political movements or trying to secure the nomination and election of candidates favorable to their views. The reasons for inaction include political apathy and indifference, lack of strong feeling, pessimism over the prospects of success, ignorance, and so on.[34]

Recent Changes

How much these attitudes have fluctuated over lengthy periods of time, or have undergone permanent change, it is impossible to say with the evidence available. However, there can be no doubt that the high confidence of Americans in their government and society declined under the impact of a decade of turbulence and political disaster.[35] The decade began in 1963 with the assassination of President Kennedy, followed in less than five years by the assassinations of Martin Luther King and Senator Robert Kennedy. There was rising unrest and demonstrations among blacks in the South and riots among blacks in the northern ghettoes. There were disturbances among college students and among a growing section of the public opposed to the Vietnam war. The decade saw the refusal of President Johnson to run for a second term; the forced resignation of Vice-President Agnew following charges of criminal misconduct; the Watergate investigation; and the impeachment process that culminated in the resignation of Richard Nixon. To compound difficulties, the period ended with abnormally high rates of both inflation and unemployment.

---

34. The evidence is indirect but strong. See Jack Citrin, "The Political Relevance of Trust in Government," *American Political Science Review*, 68 (September, 1974), pp. 973–988, at pp. 978–984; Herbert McCloskey, "Conservatism and Personality," *American Political Science Review*, 52 (March, 1958), 27–45; Lane, *Political Life*, Ch. 5, pp. 63–79, and Ch. 12, pp. 163–181; Campbell et al., *The American Voter*, Ch. 5, pp. 89–115.

35. See Chapters 13 and 26.

Table 10.3
Trust in Government,
1964–1970: How much
of the time do you think
you can trust the
government in Washington
to do what is right—
just about always, most
of the time, or only some
of the time?

	1964	1966	1968	1970
Always	14.0%	17.0%	7.5%	6.4%
Most of the time	62.0	48.0	53.4	47.1
Only some of the time[a]	22.0	31.0	37.0	44.2
Don't know	2.0	4.0[b]	2.1	2.3
Total	100.0%	100.0%	100.0%	100.0%
(N)[c]	(4658)	(1291)	(1557)	(1514)

[a] Indicates response interpreted as "cynical."

[b] Includes 1% coded "It depends."

[c] The sample size for each of the years applies to all five items. The 1964 N is weighted.

Source: Arthur H. Miller, "Political Issues and Trust in Government: 1964–1970," *The American Political Science Review,* 68 (September, 1974), pp. 951–972, Table 1.

Table 10.4
Trust in Government,
1964–1970: Would
you say the government for
the most part is run for
a few big interests
looking out for themselves
or that it is run for the
benefit of all the people?

	1964	1966	1968	1970
For benefit of all	64.0%	53.0%	51.8%	40.6%
Few big interests	29.0	34.0	39.2	49.6
Other; depends; both checked	4.0	6.0	4.6	5.0
Don't know	3.0	7.0	4.3	4.8
Total	100.0%	100.0%	100.0%	100.0%

Source: See Table 10.3.

Surveys in the first half of the 1970s revealed some of the changes. In 1973, around half of the people in one survey believed that there was "something deeply wrong in America today." Seventy-four percent agreed that "special interests get more from the government than the people do," 61 percent agreed with the statement that "what you think doesn't count very much any more." Large percentages also said they had less confidence in the government than five years earlier, citing as major reasons corruption, Watergate, the unresponsiveness of government, and government deception.[36]

A survey in 1964 had shown that 76 percent of the respondents thought they could trust the government in Washington to do what is right just about always or most of the time. By 1970, the figure had dropped to 54 percent, while the percentage who said they thought they could trust the government only some of the time had doubled— from 22 percent in 1964 to 44 percent in 1970 (Table 10.3). The percentage who said the government is run "by a few big interests looking out for themselves" rose in the same period from 29 percent to nearly 50 percent (Table 10.4). An index that combined these two items and three others to form an index of trust in government revealed a marked drop in the decade from 1964 to 1974 (Figure 10.1).

36. From the survey by Louis Harris and Associates in the report of the Subcommittee on Intergovernmental Relations of the Committee on Government Operations, United States Senate, *Confidence and Concern, Citizens View American Government, A Survey of Public Attitudes* (Washington, D.C.: Government Printing Office, 1973), pp. 212–223.

Figure 10.1
Trust in Government,
1958–1974

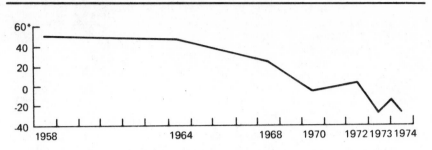

Source: Arthur H. Miller, "The Politics of Consumer Pessimism," *Economic Outlook, USA,* 2 (Spring, 1975), pp. 12–13, at p. 12.

* Larger numbers represent higher levels of trust in government.

The decline in confidence extended to specific institutions and processes of government. There were large increases in the percentages who felt that elections did not have much effect in making the government pay attention to what people think. Confidence in the responsiveness of political parties and of congressmen also declined.[37]

Persistence of Basic Beliefs

If a decade of tumult eroded some of the confidence of Americans in their government and society, it did not seem to undermine their basic preference for democracy and for the constitutional system as a whole. In 1972, only 14 percent said "I can't find much in our form of government to be proud of." The same percentage of Americans supported "a big change in our whole form of government." Fifty-five percent believed that the existing political system "should remain pretty much as it is."[38]

Basically, it appears, people were discontented with the performance of political leaders and institutions. They wanted it to measure up more to democratic ideals, to be more responsive to ordinary people like themselves and less responsive to "big interests." They were disappointed because their government was not as democratic as they had hoped or expected it would be. They were critical of the government's performance, not the democratic ideal by which they judged that performance. And even among college youth, where dissent was most strongly concentrated, preponderant majorities preferred the path of compromise and peaceful, nonviolent change.[39]

---

37. Arthur H. Miller, "Political Issues and Trust in Government," *American Political Science Review,* 68 (September, 1974), pp. 951–972, and "Rejoinder," *ibid.,* pp. 989–1001, Figure 1, p. 990.

38. Jack Citrin, "The Political Relevance of Trust in Government," p. 975.

39. Yankelovich, *Generations Apart,* pp. 23–24.

Factors Facilitating Ideological Agreement

How can one account for the rapid development of a similarity of beliefs and attitudes in the first half of the nineteenth century?

Homogeneity. The social and economic similarities of Americans, together with their common national origin and a common language undoubtedly helped a great deal: general ideas that appealed to one small farmer were very likely to have an appeal to another. Given a homogeneous population, similarities in beliefs were probably fostered also by physical isolation from Europe, by relatively firm boundaries to the east, north, and south, and by the existence of a unique political system that united Americans in a bold new experiment in self-government.

Conformism. Related to all these factors, there may be another, less flattering reason. A number of European observers, including Tocqueville and Martineau, were struck by the fear Americans displayed of seeming different from one another. To use the modern jargon, Americans often appeared to Europeans as strongly 'conformist' and 'other directed.' They worried about the opinions of their neighbors and were reluctant to express, or perhaps even to hold, unpopular views. Everyone seemed bent on converging around a middle point.

> ... The time will come [Harriet Martineau wrote of Americans] when they will be astonished to discover how they mar their own privileges by allowing themselves less liberty of speech and action than is enjoyed by the inhabitants of countries whose political servitude the Americans justly compassionate and despise. ... They may travel over the whole world, and find no society but their own which will submit to the restraint of perpetual caution, and reference to the opinions of others.[40]

Yet it is one thing to show how a certain unity of views arose, and quite another to explain how it continued to exist when the United States ceased to be a nation of small independent farmers. By 1880 workers in nonfarm occupations exceeded those in farming. Thereafter the farmers were an ever smaller minority; by 1957 less than one out of ten persons in the labor force was in agriculture, and of these only about half owned their own farms.[41]

Tradition. Probably the sheer inertia of an already venerable tradition helped the United States through periods of crisis. But the crises themselves may have helped even more. The resistance to change of the traditional attitudes must have increased as each great challenge to the

---

40. Martineau, *Society in America*, pp. 249–251.
41. *Historical Statistics*, Series D 1–12 and K 8–52.

liberal democratic, individualistic, success-oriented ideology was turned back. Each challenge offered the possibility of a rival ideology—aristocracy, slavocracy, socialism, or government by the wealthy few. Yet in each case these potential rivals for the minds of Americans were defeated; the older victorious ideology then became thoroughly intertwined with traditionalism. To attack the conventional ideas meant more and more to attack the whole course of American national history, to show that Americans had failed, long ago, to take the right path.

Yet these challenges might not have been successfully overcome if the "equality of condition" which Tocqueville had observed had vanished; if, in short, blatant contradictions had developed between the lives led by ordinary Americans and the aspirations offered in the dominant ideology. Increasing economic inequalities had accompanied industrialization, particularly in its early stages after the Civil War. Evidently, however, enough of the old "equality of condition" survived—if not in reality, at least in expectations—so that the old ideas won converts even among the very people who were worst off under industrial capitalism.[42]

Education. Two additional elements have helped to sustain the dominant traditional ideology in the twentieth century. One of these is the educational system, which from the primary grades through high school, and even in the universities, emphasizes the values and institutions expressed in the dominant liberal-democratic ideology. While the relationship between formal education and ideas is complex, especially with any specific person, one simple statistical fact stands out: in survey after survey of political attitudes and ideas among Americans, the amount of formal education appears as a highly significant variable. Indeed, education shows up as *the* most significant variable, even when the effects of socioeconomic status and occupation are cancelled out. As we have already observed (and this is the important point) the greater one's formal education, the more likely one is to endorse the key proposition in the prevailing ideology.

A Persistent Ambiguity: Majority Rule

However successful the Framers may have been in resolving many of the practical problems they confronted, they were unable to agree on

---

42. Comparative studies of rates of social mobility are still too few for confident conclusions. S. M. Lipset and Reinhard Bendix argue that "the overall pattern of social mobility appears to be much the same in industrial societies of various Western countries" in *Social Mobility in Industrial Society* (Los Angeles: University of California Press, 1960), p. 13. In the light of later studies this view appears to be doubtful. Perhaps the most that one can say at this point is that social mobility is or has been relatively high in the United States, as compared with such European countries as Britain and the Netherlands, in some but not in all respects. See S. M. Miller, "Comparative Social Mobility: A Trend Report," *Current Sociology,* 9, no. 1 (1960), 1–5; Thomas Fox and S. M. Miller, "Occupational Stratification and Mobility," in *Comparing Nations,* eds. Richard L. Merritt and Stein Rokkan (New Haven, Conn.: Yale University Press, 1966), pp. 217–237.

the appropriate place of the majority principle. This fact, and the extensive partitioning of the public authority resulting from their work, helped to create an important source of ambiguity that Americans have never resolved. It is not too much to say that *the great body of Americans has never agreed on any single, definite, widely understood rule for final, authoritative, legitimate decision-making in government.*

Neither the Constitution, constitutional doctrine, nor American ideology have ever treated all political institutions, national and federal, as components of an ordered hierarchy in which some constitutional units are always subordinate to others. Constitutionally speaking, the president does not dominate Congress; nor, on the other hand, is the president a mere agent of Congress; the Senate is not constitutionally superior to the House, nor are Congress and the president to the judiciary, nor are the governors and state legislatures to the president and Congress.

Nor do Americans agree on a principle of majority rule that would provide a way for ordering these institutions into a single lawful hierarchy. Majority rule? But which majority? How large? Operating in what institution? By what means? And anyway, what of minority rights? Given varying interpretations of political legitimacy possible within the American tradition, the extent to which a particular principle or institution is upheld often depends on whose interests are being threatened. When the principle of majority rule is invoked to support 'national' majorities (for example, as revealed in presidential and congressional elections), it is also used to support local, state, or regional majorities. This conflict over the legitimacy of 'national' versus 'local' majorities, as we saw in the last chapter, goes all the way back to the Constitutional Convention.

The American doctrine of partitioned authority holds that majorities lose their legitimacy if they infringe on natural rights or other absolute standards of political right or justice. Because there is always much dispute as to what these natural rights or absolute standards are and how far they extend, the boundary between majority rule and individual rights has been continually disputed throughout America's national history. Nonetheless, the doctrine that the right of a majority to govern is properly restricted by 'unalterable' rights is not widely challenged among Americans.

Since earliest times, doctrines of unalterable rights and of states' rights have been both invoked by defeated minorities to challenge the legitimacy or constitutionality of laws enacted or proposed by the president and Congress. Attacks on national law in the name of individual or states' rights or both were expressed in the Virginia and Kentucky Resolutions of 1789–99, the declaration of the Hartford Convention in 1814, the South Carolina Resolutions in 1828, the "Exposition and Protest" accompanying them, the Ordinance of Nullification in 1832, and

South Carolina's "Declaration of the Cause of Secession" in December, 1860. These principles were revived in the South from 1954 onward as the doctrine of 'interposition' to justify resistance to the Supreme Court's decisions on integration.

Specific institutions are admired or criticized by different groups at different times depending on the particular interests at stake; but the doctrine of partitioned authority itself is rarely rejected outright. In the 1930s, liberals attacked the Supreme Court and defended majority rule; in the 1950s and 1960s, the prestige of the Court among liberals had never been higher. During the early years of the New Deal, conservatives saw the Court as a bastion of freedom; in the 1950s some of them came to view it as rather tyrannical. During the New Deal and the Fair Deal, liberal Democrats frequently extolled the virtues (and political legitimacy) of a strong president; with the election of a Republican president in 1952 they began to discover new virtues in Congress; that theme was quickly muted after 1960, with the election of a Democratic president and revived again after Mr. Nixon's victory in 1968. Many conservatives insist that "power must be kept close to the people"; they praise the legitimacy of 'states' rights'; but in the 1950s and 1960s many conservatives also opposed attempts to bring power 'closer to the people' by reapportioning state legislatures or protecting the rights of blacks to vote in the South.

To be sure, there is the belief in the final legitimacy of rule by the people; that "this country, with its institutions, belongs to the people who inhabit it," as Lincoln said. "Whenever they shall grow weary of the existing government, they can exercise their constitutional right of amending it, or their revolutionary right to dismember or overthrow it." Yet 'the people' have not chosen to amend the Constitution in order to establish a single hierarchy of authority in our political institutions. Quite the contrary: 'the people' have never shown the slightest interest in any of the schemes for doing so that are propounded by eager constitution-makers. Moreover, a *majority* of the people is not constitutionally sovereign even in amending the Constitution, unless that majority happens also to constitute a majority in three-fourths of the states. Indeed, in at least one respect—representation in the Senate—a unanimity of opinion in three-fourths of the states does not make 'the people' constitutionally sovereign even in its power to amend the Constitution; for the final words of Article V of the Constitution read: ". . . no State, without its Consent, shall be deprived of its equal Suffrage in the Senate."

To anyone searching for a single principle of legitimate decision-making, it is of little value to say that 'the people' may exercise "their revolutionary right to dismember or overthrow" the political institutions. Perhaps if Americans agree on a single principle, it would be this: unanimity, though unattainable, is best; institutions must therefore be so contrived that they will compel a constant search for the highest attainable degree of consent. But this leaves a vast area of decision-making open to conflict.

THIRD CONDITION: THE CONSTITUTIONAL FRAMEWORK

So powerful were the two conditions discussed so far that it is difficult to imagine that polyarchy would not have developed in the United States. Seen in this light, the contribution of the Constitutional framework looks pretty unimportant.

Such a view no doubt runs counter to what I take to be a belief common among Americans: that "it was the Framers who created democracy in America." As we have just seen, however, the Constitutional Convention created an instrument of government that could have been adapted to either a relatively aristocratic republic—a meritocracy—or a more democratic republic—a polyarchy. The direction in which the new system was to develop was not wholly within the control of any constitutional convention. In recent times, we have relearned the ancient lesson that a constitution is a frail barrier along the path of an aspiring dictator who has a large and disciplined following.

Proper constitutional agreements are, obviously, necessary conditions for a polyarchy. Polyarchy cannot exist if there are no elections, no legislatures, no legal rights to speak freely about politics, no courts to enforce these rights. But it is equally obvious that constitutional arrangements are not sufficient to insure polyarchy. For there must also be suitable social and economic conditions, and appropriate beliefs among the citizens. Thanks to greater experience with polyarchic government, the task of drafting a constitution for a polyarchy is, nowadays, very much easier than it was in 1789. But it is as difficult as ever to insure the proper socioeconomic conditions and set of beliefs.

Consider two problems: *first,* the problem of power. In order for a satisfactory approximation of democracy to exist, power over government must not be distributed too unequally among the citizens. One of the most important contributions to the wide diffusion of power over government is broad suffrage. But standing alone, even universal suffrage is insufficient, for legal equality in the voting booth can be nullified by inequalities outside. Imagine an agricultural society, for example, where a tiny group of people owns all the land; where these people control the police, the military, the newspapers, the radio; and where the great bulk of the population consists of uneducated agricultural laborers dependent for their livelihood on the few landowners. Is it likely that the introduction of universal suffrage and a wide variety of constitutional guarantees would, by themselves, produce a durable polyarchy?

Second, there is the problem of unity and diversity, of consensus and conflict. Even if power were equally distributed, a polyarchy might nonetheless be destroyed by internal dissension. A minority, outvoted, might grow to prefer dictatorship to the prospect of obeying laws passed and enforced by the representatives of a hostile majority.

As we have seen, for reasons with which the Framers had very little to do, conditions in the United States were unusually favorable for a solution to both these problems. In fact, then, what produced polyarchy in America was not so much the American Revolution and the Constitutional Convention as the underlying forces that facilitated a second, silent revolution. These were the forces that made for pervasive equality and widespread acceptance of American institutions.

In less favorable circumstances, the American experience might only have added new evidence that a "thing previously held impossible" was indeed impossible. For the Constitution might easily have been adapted to an aristocratic system of government. The Framers, as we saw, left the alternatives open. It was the second, silent revolution that settled the matter.

Most notably, as we saw in the last chapter, the Constitution left open the question of how broad the suffrage was to be. Conceivably, then, the states might have limited the franchise to a wealthy few. That was, after all the situation in Britain, where only about 5 percent of the total population over 20 years of age could vote in 1831. After Britain was shaken by a protracted political crisis over the successful battle to enlarge the suffrage in 1832, the percentage over 20 who could vote was still only 7 percent.[43]

In the United States, however, the suffrage was already fairly widely diffused in most of the states in 1787, and in subsequent decades it was expanded, not contracted. The causes for this expansion were complex. They include, of course, the two conditions just described—equality and democratic beliefs. These insured that the framework of government designed by the Framers would have to prove itself capable of adapting to the impulse toward democratization or else be cast aside.

Yet in downgrading the contribution of the Constitution to the process of democratization, it is important to keep in mind that the framework was not, in fact, cast aside. It did not need to be. For even if the Constitution did not itself *guarantee* a broadly based republic, it was quite capable of *adapting* to such a republic. Moreover, by requiring that the national government rest on elections and by making that government relatively powerful and important, it practically insured that demands for broad participation would exist; by guaranteeing fundamental liberties in the Bill of Rights, the Constitution made it likely that these demands would be expressed, heard, organized, channeled.

---

43. Dolf Sternberger and Bernhard Vogel, eds., *Die Wahl Der Parlamente*, 2 vols. (Berlin: Walter de Gruyter and Co., 1969), vol. 1, *Europa*, p. 632.

Thus, because it was flexible enough to adapt to the pressures for democratization, the constitutional framework also gained acceptability. Thereby it contributed to the thrust toward ideological agreement and the widespread acceptance of American institutions.

SUMMARY   How was it that Americans were able to prove "a thing previously held impossible"? This chapter examined three conditions favorable to polyarchy. Yet each was qualified in a way that would leave a legacy of unsolved problems:

1. The conditions of American life fostered equality and equalitarian attitudes to a degree that astounded observers like Tocqueville. Yet the United States also contained sources of inequalities. The most extreme inequalities stemmed from slavery and racial discrimination, but other sources included social status, business enterprise, and differences in political skills and incentives.

2. Aided by their experiences and environment, Americans rapidly converged toward a shared belief in a democratic ideology and in the major American institutions. Yet this outward agreement conceals many differences in the depth and content of the belief. It also leaves at least one key matter, the proper place of majority rule, persistently ambiguous.

3. The constitutional framework was perhaps the least important condition for the emergence of polyarchy in the United States. Nonetheless, although it left open the issues of aristocracy versus democracy, at the same time it made the national government important and its offices and policies worth contesting; it provided for elections to the main offices; and it guaranteed a set of basic liberties in the Bill of Rights. In so doing it created a constitutional framework that could be democratized as demands arose, and could stimulate and protect these demands. In addition, the adaptability of the framework to democratization helped to make political institutions widely acceptable to the American people. Thus the constitutional framework contributed to the sharing of beliefs that, as was suggested in Chapter 7, has tended to be one of the pronounced characteristics of American polyarchy.

Yet here, too, there is a legacy of unsolved problems. For the extreme partitioning of authority and the ideas supporting it that are so basic a part of the American polyarchy have created certain persistent problems for the operation of polyarchy in the United States—including, as we just saw, a continuing unresolved ambiguity about the legitimate limits of majority rule itself.

Two sets of factors contribute to the extreme partitioning of authority in the United States: political institutions and patterns of division and conflict. In the next part of this book we shall see how the first of these, the political institutions, contribute to the system of partitioned authority.

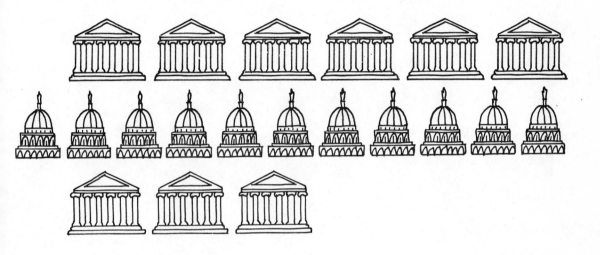

PART THREE

THE MAJOR INSTITUTIONS:
DESIGN AND PERFORMANCE

11 THE PRESIDENCY: DESIGN

For many a fervent proponent of democracy, it is awkward to admit that a 'democratic' system needs leaders. The admission seems to imply that the people are not wholly capable of governing themselves. Yet every political system with more than a handful of citizens has to provide for governmental ·functions that the whole people are unable or unwilling to perform individually or collectively. One such function is to work out specific proposals of policies that the government should adopt. Another is to insure that these policies are properly executed. A third is to undertake emergency actions, especially on matters of war and foreign affairs. Still another is to perform certain kinds of symbolic functions—as symbolic head of the state for internal and for international purposes and as spokesman for and representative of unity. These functions are carried on in polyarchies (as in other systems) by political leaders.

In American life, far and away the most important political leader is, of course, the president. As a contribution to the art of politics, the American presidency is unique. The institution was not at the outset a copy of anything else; nor, despite a number of attempts, has it been successfully copied elsewhere.

AT THE CONVENTION: THE ABSENCE OF MODELS

To understand the presidency it is instructive to put ourselves briefly in the shoes of the delegates to the Convention. These men were both too practical and too versed in political experience to doubt that some functions of leadership had to be performed in the political system for which they were designing a constitution. They knew they had to design the office of 'national executive,' 'executive magistracy,' 'magistrate,' or 'executive,' as they referred to it at various times.

Yet how were they to create an 'executive magistrate' who would perform whatever functions the other institutions could not properly execute and who at the same time would not be a political monstrosity? In 1787, the problem was far more baffling than it would be today, because the alternatives we are familiar with today were unknown. A popularly elected president was a novelty; the chief alternative solution, a prime minister chosen by a parliament, had not yet emerged in its modern form even in Britain.

Every problem was unsolved, every proposal debatable, every solution risky. Answers necessarily had to be highly speculative.

SIX QUESTIONS
IN SEARCH
OF ANSWERS

How Many?

It is true that earlier republics furnished some experience, but republican executives had generally consisted of several men, each of whom served as a check on the others. This was the famous solution of the Roman Republic. Although the plural executive is designed to solve one problem, it creates another. The plural executive may help to prevent any single person from gaining too much power; yet where one executive checks another, decisions may be paralyzed. That system must, therefore, avoid great emergencies, particularly those requiring decisive action in international affairs and war; or else, as in the Roman Republic, it must have some provision for a temporary 'dictator' armed with emergency powers.

Because of these disadvantages, the plural executive is rarely used in polyarchies. Switzerland has employed it most successfully—but Switzerland is small, maintains a vigorous neutrality, remains free of alliances and international organizations, and avoids war.

The idea of a plural executive had little support at the Convention. Edmund Randolph of Virginia

> strenuously opposed a unity in the executive magistracy. He regarded it as the fetus of monarchy. . . . He could not see why the great requisites for the executive department, vigor, despatch and responsibility could not be found in three men, as well as in one man.[1]

But Randolph won few converts. After all, the Articles of Confederation had followed the pattern of the ancient republics; the only executive provided for in the Articles was a committee appointed by Congress, "to sit in the recess of congress, to be denominated 'A

---

1. Charles C. Tansill, ed., *Documents Illustrative of the Formation of the Union of the American States* (Washington, D.C.: Government Printing Office, 1927), p. 132.

Committee of the States,' and to consist of one delegate from each state." Not even Randolph wanted to duplicate that feeble system in the new Constitution. In their own constitutions, the states (except for Pennsylvania) had settled, nominally, for a single executive—though often he was so hedged around by a legislative council that the executive was in fact plural.

Whatever the reasons, the proposal for a single executive was agreed to in the early days of the convention. It was almost the only question having to do with the presidency on which the Convention, having once made a decision, did not later change its mind.[2]

How Long?

In the absence of an appropriate model for a republican executive, the most visible alternative was the form that all members of the Convention knew best: a hereditary monarchy. Yet it was precisely because this solution was barred to them by their own beliefs and the attitudes of the country— "... there was not a one-thousandth part of our fellow citizens who were not against every approach toward monarchy," said Elbridge Gerry of Massachusetts—that there existed the vacuum they had to fill. To Alexander Hamilton—if we can rely on Madison's notes—a republic was inherently a second-best form of government because, unlike a monarchy, it could provide no good solution to the problem of the executive. He concluded:

> ... That we ought to go as far in order to attain stability and permanency, as republican principles will admit. Let one branch of the legislature hold their places for life or at least during good behaviour. Let the executive also be for life.[3]

One weak spot of Hamilton's argument was, as everyone knew, the simple matter of genes and the accidents of human personality. A great king may have a son less suited to kingship than his own jester. A king famed for his justice may beget a tyrant. To a king of intelligence, vision, courage, and resolution, the mysteries of genes and childrearing may produce an heir who is shortsighted, irresponsible, weak, and irresolute. Writing some years later, Jefferson reflected on the monarchs of Europe:

> While in Europe, I often amused myself with contemplating the characters of the then reigning sovereigns. . . . Louis XVI was a fool, of my own knowledge. . . . The King of Spain was a fool, and of Naples the same. They passed their lives in hunting, and despatched two couriers a

---

2. No one except Randolph spoke against the single executive. Three states—New York, Delaware, and Maryland—voted against it on the decisive vote of June 4. Virginia voted for it, although the delegation was split down the middle: Madison, Washington, and two others favored the single executive; Randolph, George Mason, and John Blair opposed it (*Documents*, p. 132).

3. *Ibid.*, pp. 221–222.

week, one thousand miles, to let each other know what game they had killed the preceding days. The King of Sardinia was a fool. All these were Bourbons. The queen of Portugal, a Braganza, was an idiot by nature. And so was the King of Denmark. Their sons, as regents, exercised the powers of government. The King of Prussia, successor to the great Frederick, was a mere hog in body as well as in mind. Gustavus of Sweden, and Joseph of Austria, were really crazy, and George of England, you know, was in a straight waistcoat. There remained, then, none but old Catherine, who had been too lately picked up to have lost her common sense. . . . These animals had become without mind and powerless; and so will every hereditary monarch be after a few generations. . . . And so endeth the book of Kings, from all of whom the Lord deliver us.[4]

The Americans had thrown off one hereditary monarch; it was obvious to all—including Hamilton—that they would not tolerate another.

An executive for life might solve some of these problems; but such a system would create others. To give a person a lifetime in which to accumulate power is dangerous. A lifetime tenure might even be enough to establish a dynasty. Sickness, senility, insanity have turned good leaders into evil ones; yet an executive appointed for life might not yield power gladly and might have too much power to be dispossessed without violence. The Roman emperors were the obvious model: they had held office for life. Yet while some of them were undoubtedly great leaders and ruled during times of great prosperity and peace, many were brutal tyrants.

An executive chosen for life had no support at the Convention. Even Hamilton, when he got down to his specific proposals, called for an appointment not explicitly for life, but "during good behavior." When James McClurg (a delegate from Virginia whose role at the Convention was brief and unimportant) moved that the executive hold office "during good behavior," the idea won little acclaim. That distinguished advocate of an aristocratic republic, Gouverneur Morris, briefly endorsed it but changed his mind a few days later.[5] Madison tactfully suggested that "respect for the mover entitled his proposition to a fair hearing and discussion."[6] George Mason remarked:

> . . . He considered an Executive during good behavior as a softer name only for an Executive for life. And that the next would be an easy step to hereditary monarchy.[7]

The proposal was turned down by a close vote—four states in favor,

4. *Thomas Jefferson On Democracy*, selected and arranged by Saul K. Padover (New York: Penguin Books, 1946), p. 26.
5. See *Documents*, pp. 396, 447.
6. *Ibid.*, p. 398.
7. *Ibid.*

six against—which, according to Madison, grossly exaggerated the actual support the proposal had enjoyed at the Convention.[8]

While this proposal was disposed of fairly easily, the Convention twisted and turned like a sleeper tormented by a bad dream as it tried to decide just what term would be proper. On July 24, the Convention had a particularly trying day: Luther Martin proposed a term of eleven years; Gerry suggested fifteen; King, twenty years—"the medium life of princes"; Davie, eight years. After that day's work, the Convention adjourned without having decided anything at all.

The log of votes in the Convention on the length of term of the president reveals the uncertainty of the delegates:

June 1: Seven-year term, *passed,* 5 states to 4.

June 2: Ineligible for reelection after seven years, *passed,* 7–2.

July 19: Seven-year term, *defeated,* 5–3.

Six-year term, *passed,* 9–1.

Ineligibility for a second term, *defeated,* 8–2.

July 26: Seven-year term, with ineligibility for reelection, *passed,* 7–3.

Sept. 6: Seven year term, *defeated,* 8–3.

Six-year term, *defeated,* 9–2.

Four-year term, *passed,* 10–1.

How Chosen?

But having settled on a four-year term, how was the executive to be chosen? On this question the Convention could never quite make up its mind. Almost to the end, it would move toward a solution and then, on second thought, reverse itself in favor of some different alternative. On no question was experience so uncertain a guide. If ultimately the Convention invented the popularly elected presidency, it would be excessively charitable to say that the delegates in Philadelphia foresaw what they were doing.

The most obvious solution in 1787 was the election of the executive by the legislature. This was the essence of the cabinet system that was evolving in Britain. Yet, in 1787, that evolution was far from complete. Neither in Britain nor in this country did anyone quite realize how much the prime minister was shifting from the agent of the king to the representative of a parliamentary majority. When one spoke of the British executive in 1787 one still meant the king, not the prime minister.

In the American states, too, under new or revised state constitutions, the governor was generally chosen by the legislature. Yet the experience of the various states suggested some of the disadvantages of that solution: If the executive were elected by the legislature, what

---

8. He wrote in his Notes that "The avowed friends of an Executive, 'during good behaviour' were not more than three or four, nor is it certain they would finally have adhered to such a tenure." *Ibid.,* p. 399, fn.

was to prevent him from becoming a mere creature of that body? To some of the men at the Convention, this was exactly what was needed. Thus Roger Sherman of Connecticut

> ...was for the appointment by the legislature, and for making him [the executive] absolutely dependent on that body, as it was the will of that which was to be executed. An independence of the executive on the supreme Legislature, was in his opinion the very essence of tyranny if there was any such thing.[9]

Was Sherman thinking of his own state—one of the few in which the governor was popularly elected?

The main reason given by those who opposed election by the Congress was a fear that the executive would be too weak. The chief spokesman for an aristocratic republic, Gouverneur Morris, joined with the spokesmen for the democratic republic, Madison and Wilson, in opposing election by the Congress. But to find an alternative was infinitely more difficult. If the executive were elected by the people, as Wilson proposed, would he not then be too dependent on the whims of popular majorities? And could the people possibly know enough to make a wise choice?

Thus the argument went on. Every possible solution seemed fatally flawed. Should the president be chosen by the Congress? by the Senate only? by the people? by the state governors? by the state legislatures? by electors chosen by the people? As Madison wearily concluded in late July, "there are objections against every mode that has been, or perhaps can be proposed."[10]

The United States came within a hair's breadth of adopting a kind of parliamentary system. The Virginia plan had proposed that the executive be chosen by the national legislature. On July 17 this mode won unanimous approval. It won another trial vote, 6–3, on July 26. As late as August 24 the Convention voted against an attempt to substitute election by the people or by electors for choice by the legislature. Yet when a committee reported out on September 4—two weeks before the end of the Convention—it suggested the 'electoral college' solution which was embodied in Article II of the Constitution. No one altogether knows what happened in the interval; perhaps many delegates who had voted earlier for election by the legislature were so unsure of their grounds, so weary of the dispute, and so fearful of further haggling and possible deadlock that they eargerly accepted the compromise suggested by the committee.

Whatever the reasons, all who struggle today with the task of in-

---

9. *Ibid.,* p. 134.
10. *Ibid.,* p. 449.

Table 11.1 Agony over the Presidency: Proposals at the Convention for Choosing the President	The National Legislature (Congress)	President to be chosen by		The People	State Governors
		Presidential Electors chosen by			
		The People	State Legislatures		
June 2	Virginia Plan (discussed)	Defeated 8–2			
June 9					Defeated 9–0
July 17	Passed unanimously		Defeated 8–2	Defeated 9–1	
July 19			Passed 6–3 (Mass. divided)		
July 24	Passed 7–4				
July 26	Passed 6–3 (referred to Committee of Detail)				
Aug. 6	Proposed by Committee of Detail				
Aug. 24		Defeated 6–5		Defeated 9–2	

Sept. 4   Committee of Eleven, to which this and other sections had been referred, proposed essentials of present Constitution: "Each State shall appoint in such manner as its legislature may direct a number of electors equal to the whole number of Senators and members of the House of Representatives to which the State may be entitled in the Legislature [Congress]."

Sept. 6   This proposal adopted, 9–2.

Sept. 17   Constitution signed.   Convention adjourns.

venting new political institutions may be comforted by the record of the Convention's torment (see Table 11.1).

How Removed?

Although the Framers spent a great deal of time over the problem of how the president was to be chosen, they spent very little time over the question of how he was to be removed. A few delegates insisted that he ought not to be removable at all. Franklin remarked that removal by impeachment was preferable to removal by assassination. After a brief discussion, the Convention tentatively decided that the president was "to be removable on impeachment and conviction for malpractice or neglect of duty."

What body was to be in charge of removal? The delegates readily agreed that the president was to be impeached by the House of Representatives. They borrowed the concept of impeachment from Britain, where *impeachment* was distinguished from *conviction*. Impeachment was—and is—equivalent to a grand jury's finding of sufficient grounds for guilt to warrant a trial of the accused. The controversial question was where the trial of the president should take place after the House voted in favor of impeachment. Some delegates wanted the trial to take place in the Supreme Court. For a time this view prevailed. But other delegates objected that the justices of the Supreme Court, being dependent on the president for their appointments, would not have enough independence of judgment. The delegates finally voted in favor of trial by the Senate.

The grounds for impeachment were at various times in the debates specified as treason, bribery, malpractice and neglect of duty. The last two did not survive, and no one quite knows how the ambiguous phrase "or other high crimes and misdemeanors" finally crept into the final draft.

The upshot is, then, that

☐ The House has sole power of impeachment (Article I, Section 2); an ordinary majority is sufficient.
☐ The Senate has sole power to try all impeachments. Moreover, "when the President of the United States is tried, the Chief Justice shall preside: And no person shall be convicted without the concurrence of two-thirds of the members present" (Article I, Section 3). "The President, Vice-President, and all civil officers of the United States, shall be removed from office on impeachment for, and conviction of, treason, bribery, or other high crimes and misdemeanors" (Article II, Section 4).[11]

The power of removing the president by a process of impeachment and conviction has only been brought into play twice. The first time was the impeachment of President Andrew Johnson by a substantial majority in the House. He was acquitted by one vote less than the necessary two-thirds in the Senate. The second time, the process would unquestionably have resulted, as we shall see in Chapter 13, in Richard Nixon's conviction and removal from office in 1974. But on the eve of the proceedings by the House, Nixon resigned and thus averted what otherwise would have culminated in his conviction.

What Powers and Functions?

In providing for the powers and functions of the president the Framers were the least comprehensive and left the most to future developments. As a glance at Article II will show, only one-third of the article is devoted to the powers of the president. In fact, the grand edifice of the American presidency, the most powerful popularly elected office in the world, rests, in a narrowly legalistic sense, on barely three hun-

11. Charles L. Black, Jr., *Impeachment, A Handbook* (New Haven: Yale University Press, 1974) presents an excellent brief discussion of impeachment by a well-known constitutional lawyer.

dred words in the Constitution. What is more, of a dozen 'powers' granted in those three hundred words, only half are of really critical importance:

☐ The president is vested with "the executive power."
☐ "He shall take care that the laws be faithfully executed."
☐ He is commander in chief of the armed forces.
☐ He is vested with certain powers of appointment.
☐ "He shall have power, by and with the advice and consent of the Senate, to make treaties. . . . He shall receive ambassadors and other public ministers."
☐ In addition, Article I gives him a veto over legislation. A two-thirds vote in each house is required to override his veto. (Art. I, Sec. 7).

From a mere reading of these phrases in the Constitution it would be impossible to derive anything like an adequate understanding of the powers of an American president. As we shall see in the next two chapters, the development of that edifice was more the work of those who occupied it than of those who originally designed it.

A Separate Head of State?

The Framers failed to grapple with the problem of what to do with the ceremonial and symbolic functions of the "head of state." The role of a head of state calls for ceremony, ritual, pageantry, symbolic displays of national pride, unity, and allegiance to the country and its past. If the Framers thought such functions unimportant, they were proved to be wrong.

In a number of European countries that were to develop into polyarchies long after the American Constitutional Convention, a hereditary monarch with virtually no executive authority or political power has been maintained for these purposes. Interestingly, this solution has been adopted (as much by accident as by deliberate design) in countries where democratic ideas and the institutions of polyarchy are just as strongly supported as in the United States: Britain, Denmark, the Netherlands, Norway, and Sweden. In those polyarchies without a hereditary monarch, most have a separate official—a president or governor general—as ceremonial head while the prime minister is the actual chief executive.

This arrangement has enabled many of these countries to avoid a problem that has come to plague the American presidency. By focusing sentiments of national pride, loyalty, awe, and deference on the monarchy, they have deflected these feelings away from the chief executive. As a result, the chief executive tends to be viewed as human, fallible, down-to-earth, and not invested with the majesty of office appropriate to the monarch.[12]

In deciding that a single executive elected for a specific term was to be vested with "the executive power" and the right to "receive ambassadors and other public ministers," the Framers of the American Constitution in effect endowed the president with the ceremonial and symbolic functions of head of state. They seem not to have considered the possibility of splitting off this role. Instead, they seem to have assumed without reflection that the president must be chief executive *and* symbolic head of state. Several consequences have followed from their solution.

☐ To the burden of his political and executive duties, the president must also add the obligations of ceremony and ritual that fall to the head of state in any large and powerful country.

☐ Roles that are at times confusing and conflicting are united in a single office. The president's role as symbolic head of state and spokesman for the nation as a whole, especially in times of urgency, conflicts with his role as partisan political leader and advocate of specific policies. Moreover, presidents characteristically take advantage of their role as head of state to enhance their political influence.

☐ Thus as we shall see in Chapter 13, the Framers unwittingly contributed to the recent evolution of the "Imperial Presidency."

☐ The character and moral qualities of the president, and to some extent those of the president's family and associates, take on great importance. The president is not simply the nation's top political leader, but is also the nation's single most visible and influential moral leader. Unfortunately, many of the qualities that seem to be required for a politician to win the presidency are inconsistent with the president's role as a model of morality.

THE UNFINISHED BUSINESS

Most modern polyarchies have rejected the Framers' solution; they have preferred the parliamentary system. In this system the chief executive is chosen by and is dependent on the confidence of the national legislature, and a hereditary monarch, president, or governor general is symbolic head of state. The difficulty foreseen by the critics of an executive chosen by the Congress—his weakness—has come to pass in some countries and not in others. In Britain, the prime minister gradually emerged as a powerful leader who could count on the disciplined majority that chose him in parliament. In the twentieth century few British

---

12. See Fred I. Greenstein and Sidney Tarrow, *Political Orientations of Children: The Use of a Semi-Projective Technique in Three Nations* (Beverly Hills, Calif.: Sage Publications, 1970).

cabinets have ever fallen through a vote of *no confidence;* the prime minister is nearly as secure in his five-year tenure as the president is in his four-year term. A number of other polyarchies have followed a similar path. However, in France under the Third Republic (1870–1940) and the Fourth (1946–58), the worst fears of men like Wilson and Madison were vindicated: the cabinet, dependent on parliament, was its creature; governments fell with the appalling frequency—about every seven months on the average during the Fourth Republic. The Fifth Republic (1958–) granted great executive authority to its first president, General Charles de Gaulle, and in 1962 a constitutional amendment providing for the direct popular election of the president was approved by nearly two-thirds of the voters in a national referendum. A number of other countries that chose the parliamentary-cabinet system have had an experience similar to that of France. Some have had both experiences. In Sweden during the nineteen-year period from 1917–36, there were eleven governments; yet, since 1936, Swedish cabinets have been remarkably stable and have carried through comprehensive reforms.

If the Convention had adhered to the Virginia plan and thereby left the choice of the executive to the Congress, would the United States have developed a stable and powerful executive like the British prime minister—or a weak and unstable executive like that of France under the Third and Fourth Republic? It is difficult to say.

But, instead of speculating on that subject, let us take stock of what the Convention did and did not do. The Convention

☐ Provided unity in the office of chief executive.
☐ Insured that the president would (short of impeachment or death) remain in office for a fixed four-year term. Thus there would ordinarily be continuity and stability in the executive office at least for four years.
☐ Provided the president with an electoral base, a constituency, independent of the Congress.
☐ Armed the president (Article II) with constitutional powers not dependent on the Congress, the president's electors, the people, or the states. Hence, both in election and in powers, the president could be to some degree independent of congressional majorities and of popular opinion.
☐ And placed no limit on the number of times a president could be reelected. (The Twenty-second Amendment, providing that "no person shall be elected to the office of the President more than twice" was not enacted until 1951.)

On the other hand, the Convention

☐ Could not foresee how the election of the president by the method they chose at the ultimate hour would actually work. Would presidential electors tend to speak for aristocracy, and thus choose a person who would be a brake on the Congress and the people? Or would they themselves be agents of popular majorities and choose presidents who appealed to the populace rather than to elite groups?

☐ Did not provide for a method by which conflicts between the president and the other branches might be resolved, other than by the cumbersome and unlikely process of impeachment or, somehow, through elections. Conflict between executive and legislature was, in the eyes of most of the delegates to the Convention, not wholly undesirable; conflict was the essence of the rationale for partitioning of power. But would conflict between president and Congress lead to unproductive stalemate?

☐ Could not know how weak or powerful the president's office they had created would become in actual practice. Would the president be sufficiently independent to keep from being a mere weak creature of the Congress? Conversely, might he become powerful enough to overweigh the 'balances' in the system? Was the president, despite all the efforts they had made to prevent it, a potential tyrant? Would he be too powerful—or not powerful enough?

SUMMARY   1. Although the presidency is the main center of political leadership in the American polyarchy, it is less the result of a carefully thought-out design than of the continued elaborate growth of an institution very loosely prescribed by the Constitution.

2. Handicapped by the absence of relevant models, after a display of great confusion and uncertainty the Framers managed to reach agreement on answers to five basic questions about the office of the chief executive: How many? How long? How chosen? How removed? Should there be a separate head of state?

3. The answers to three other basic questions had to await future developments:

☐ How powerful would the office become, and on what kinds of questions?

☐ How dependent would the president actually be on the votes of the people?

☐ How would conflicts between president and Congress be dealt with?

These questions remained to be answered by the presidents themselves, and by the political forces of which they were a part.

12 | THE PRESIDENCY: EVOLUTION AND PERFORMANCE

The evolution of the presidency is the story of a cumulative increase in the role—or, better, the roles—that the president is expected to play in the American political system, and, more recently, in the world. Every 'great' president has left the office somewhat altered and enlarged. The presidency is like a family dwelling that each new generation alters and enlarges. Confronted by some new need, a president adds on a new room, a new wing; what began as a modest dwelling has become a mansion; every president may not use every room, but the rooms are available in case of need.

THE CONTRIBUTIONS OF THE PRESIDENTS

Head of State: Washington

Washington's greatest legacy to future presidents was, perhaps, in creating and acting out superbly the symbolic roles that presidents have generally played ever since. He served as head of state for official, semiofficial, and popular functions; as a key spokesman for national unity; and as a symbol of the obligation imposed on all officials, on all Americans, to obey the Constitution and to behave according to the spirit of constitutionalism. In playing the role of constitutional monarch to a republic, Washington was assisted both by his beliefs and by his practices. For he appears to have believed that the president could and should be free of partisan attachments. Yet he himself was a staunch Federalist who was prone to see 'the spirit of party' in others, but not in his own administration. "He is to be blamed," a modern critic has written, "not for allying himself with a party, but for not knowing that he had done so, and for denouncing those opposed to his party as opposed to the government. He was most in the grip of party feeling at the time when he was being represented as being above it."[1]

His practices helped rescue Washington's image of himself as above partisanship. For in Alexander Hamilton, his secretary of the treasury, Washington had a lieutenant who came as close as any American cabinet member ever has to being a prime minister to the president. It was Hamilton who discharged many of the political duties that later presidents discharged themselves, and it was therefore Hamilton, not Washington, who became the prime target of the emerging opposition. It was Hamilton who developed the administration's major policies; Hamilton who struggled to build a durable presidential coalition; Hamilton who mobilized the Congress on behalf of presidential policies.

Party Leader: Jefferson

Under Jefferson, these two roles—constitutional monarch and prime minister, chief magistrate and party leader, president of the country and head of a faction within the country—were fused.

If every president since Jefferson has played the role of party leader, none has ever performed it with more consummate skill. Before he became president, and as an important instrument in gaining the presidency, Jefferson and his staunch ally Madison had forged the political party, which in due time was to be called the Democratic-Republican, and finally the Democratic party, as a nationwide organization with many of the features of modern parties.[2] As president, Jefferson perfected the instrument he had helped to construct. He was perhaps as professional a party leader as has ever occupied the White House.[3]

Yet if Jefferson saw himself as a spokesman both for the nation as a whole and for the majority (and the party) that elected him, he accepted the fact that he must work in and through the Congress, the only legitimate representative of the popular will. In this respect, Jefferson reflected the traditional republican doctrine expressed by the delegates to the Constitutional Convention. This view—it has been called the Whig view—holds that the true representative of the people is the legislature; the task of the executive is to 'execute' the commands of the legislative body. In persisting as long as it did in its original decision to have the chief executive elected by Congress, the Convention was to some extent reflecting this deeply ingrained respect for the representativeness of the legislative body. When Roger Sherman an-

1. Joseph Charles, *The Origins of the American Party System* (New York: Harper Torchbooks, 1961), p. 44.

2. Charles, *Origins of the American Party System;* and Noble E. Cunningham, Jr., *The Jeffersonian Republicans in Power, Party Operations 1810–1899* (Chapel Hill: University of North Carolina Press, 1963).

3. For his activities, see Cunningham, *Jeffersonian Republicans in Power, passim.*

nounced that "an independence of the executive on the supreme legislature was in his opinion the very essence of tyranny," he spoke for a powerful tradition. Not even Jefferson claimed that the president might be as representative of the popular will or of a national majority as the Congress.

Spokesman for National Majorities: Jackson

It was Jackson who proclaimed this role for the president and thereby justified his use of the veto against congressional majorities. Jackson and his followers formulated a revolutionary new concept of the democratic executive: because in the American system, the national leader elected by and responsible to the people was the only official elected by votes cast over the whole nation, he was therefore the most legitimate representative and could speak, as no other official could, for the majority of the nation.

As a result of gradual change in the method of electing the president, Jackson had, in fact, rather better grounds for claiming to be the elected spokesman of the nation than Jefferson had. You will recall that the Constitution directs that "each state shall appoint, *in such manner as the legislature thereof may direct,* a number of electors" who, in turn, choose the president (Article II, italics added). At first, in most states the legislatures themselves chose the presidential electors; when Jefferson was named president in 1800, the electors were chosen by the state legislatures in ten of the sixteen states. By 1828, however, only two states out of twenty-four (Delaware and South Carolina) still followed the old practice, and when Jackson was reelected in 1832 the only state in which electors were chosen by the legislature was South Carolina—which, incidentally, stubbornly persisted in this outdated practice until 1860.[4] Thus by Jackson's time the electoral college was already becoming a quaint but for the most part reliable way of designating the choice for president. Consequently, in Jackson's view, if there were a clash between president and Congress, the president had as much—if not more—right to speak for the people of the country, or a majority of them, as the Congress.

In accusing him of breaking tradition, Jackson's enemies were correct, even if their language was characteristically intemperate. Chancellor Kent, the distinguished Federalist jurist of New York, wrote in 1834:

> I look upon Jackson as a detestable, ignorant, reckless, vain and malignant tyrant. . . . This American elective monarchy frightens me. The ex-

---

4. For methods of electing presidential electors, 1788–1836, see *Historical Statistics of the United States, Colonial Times to 1957,* Bureau of the Census (Washington, D.C.: U.S. Government Printing Office, 1960), p. 681.

periment, with its foundations laid on universal suffrage and our unfettered press, is of too violent a nature for our excitable people. . . .[5]

His views were echoed by one of Jackson's major political rivals, Henry Clay:

We are in the midst of a revolution hitherto bloodless, but tending rapidly towards a total change of the pure republican character of the government, and to the concentration of all power in the hands of one man.[6]

If the passages seem familiar, even hackneyed, it may be because every strong president since Jackson has provoked similar expressions. Jackson's opponents chose to call themselves Whigs in order to emphasize their adherence to the traditional view that the legislature was the supreme representative agency in a republic. They professed to seek a restoration of Jeffersonian Democratic-Republicanism. In 1840, a Whig newspaper thundered:

If ever there was a genuine republican party in the country it is that party which General Harrison now worthily leads and leads to victory. What are its objects and ends? To restore the Constitution, the charter of public liberty, to authority, to reduce the more the monarch's power of the President of the United States.[7]

Yet, though the Whig view of the presidency lingered on, and echoes of it are heard occasionally even now, it was Jackson's enlarged conception that has generally prevailed in practice. Jackson's own accomplishments as president were mainly negative; his success depended almost entirely on his use of the executive power and the veto to negate congressional policies rather than on leadership in creating new legislation; yet during his two terms in office he added a spacious new wing to the presidency. His conception of the role of president as a national leader with his own independent basis of legitimacy in a popular majority has won the support of all our most famous presidents; it has come to be widely accepted among political leaders and the public; and it has even shaped the development of our other elected chief executives at the state and municipal level, the governors and mayors.

Jackson's presidency foreshadowed Lincoln's. When, in 1832, a special convention called by the state legislature of South Carolina adopted an ordinance nullifying the tariff acts of 1828 and 1832, and the state legislature passed laws to enforce this Ordinance of Nullification, Jackson issued a proclamation to the people of South Carolina that described nullification as an "impractical absurdity." He asserted the supremacy of the sovereign and indivisible federal government over the

---

5. From the modern classic on the presidency: Edward S. Corwin, *The President, Offices, and Powers* (New York: New York University Press, 1948), p. 21.

6. *Ibid.*, p. 22.

7. Quoted in Wilfred E. Binkley, *President and Congress* (New York: Knopf, 1947), p. 88.

states and denied the right of any state either to disobey federal laws or to leave the Union. Jackson asked for and received from Congress the authority to enforce revenue laws by military force. But force proved to be unnecessary. The crisis was resolved by a compromise on the tariff and the questions at issue were postponed, to be confronted by Lincoln when he assumed office in 1861.

National Leader in Crisis: Lincoln

It was Lincoln who carried to the outermost boundaries the president's role as leader in times of national emergency. Two thousand years earlier the Roman Republic had provided for a short-term dictator to cope with great emergencies. At the Constitutional Convention, which was much concerned, as we have seen, with the danger of creating a tyrant, no one seems to have proposed a grant of 'emergency powers' to the executive. Constitution-makers in other countries were later to fill that gap by various devices, not all of them successful. American presidents have coped, not by changing the letter of the Constitution but by adding invisible text between the lines.

Lincoln, to be sure, was not the first president to be confronted by a crisis. But his predecessors had confronted only minor crises compared with the breakup of the United States. History decreed that it would be Lincoln who should stretch the Constitution to its very limits— or, to be candid, beyond them. Earlier, as a Whig, Lincoln had espoused the narrow Whig doctrine on the presidency; yet Lincoln's first inaugural address was no Whig statement: it could have been delivered by Jackson:

> ...I hold that, in contemplation of universal law and of the Constitution, the Union of these States is perpetual.... It follows from these views that no State upon its own mere motion can lawfully get out of the Union; that resolves and ordinances to that effect are legally void; and that acts of violence...against the authority of the United States are insurrectionary or revolutionary.
>
> I therefore consider that, in view of the Constitution and the laws, the Union is unbroken and to the extent of my ability I shall take care, as the Constitution itself expressly enjoins upon me, that the laws of the Union be faithfully executed in all the states. Doing this I deem to be only a simple duty on my part; and I shall perform it, so far as practicable, unless my *rightful masters, the American people,* shall...direct to the contrary.
>
> The chief magistrate *derives all his authority from the people.*... His duty is to administer the present government, as it came to his hands, and to transmit it, unimpaired by him, to his successor.[8]

Lincoln's view that the president "derives all his authority from the people" created, for him, a source of authority even more exalted than

---

8. The address is quoted in full in Sandburg, *Abraham Lincoln, The War Years,* vol. I, pp. 125–135, emphasis added.

the Constitution or the Congress; and his view that 'the Union' was 'perpetual' no doubt justified, to him, violations of the Constitution and disregard for congressional sentiment. "Was it possible to lose the nation," he asked in 1864, "and yet to preserve the Constitution?"

Acting to preserve the Union and the Constitution (so he argued) Lincoln developed a power and authority in the presidency hitherto undreamed of and not witnessed again for a century.[9] Among other actions, he suspended the writ of *habeas corpus,* a power the Constitution assigned to the Congress. He spent public money in pursuit of war aims without congressional authorization or appropriation. Calling upon "the power in me vested as Commander in Chief of the Army and Navy," he emancipated the slaves in the Southern states. Acting under that same 'war power', he developed and began to administer his own program of reconstruction in the defeated South. Moreover, as one historian has written, "Lincoln understood his Constitution. He knew, in many cases, just how he was transgressing and his infractions were consequently deliberate."[10]

Perhaps few presidents have had less of the tyrant in their nature than Lincoln, as much charity, and as little will to dominate for the mere sake of domination. It is these qualities of the man himself, the mixture of great strength with great self-restraint, the compound of resolution and forbearance, that have helped to make him an all but mythical prototype of the great popular leader. And it is because of this, and the cruel choices he faced, that it is less than charitable to be harsh about his methods.

MODERN DEVELOPMENTS

Crisis Leader

If, after Lincoln's death, Congress and the Whig view of the presidency reasserted themselves, the role of emergency 'dictator' that Lincoln had created could not be wholly forgotten. Lincoln had acted mainly under two clauses of the Constitution: "The President shall be Commander in Chief of the Army and Navy of the United States . . ." and "he shall take care that the laws be faithfully executed." During the two world wars; the cold war that followed World War II; the Korean war (1950–52); during the Cuban missile crisis of 1962 when the confrontation between the United States and the Soviet Union brought the world to the very gates of the inferno; and through the escalation and de-escalation of the Vietnam war—Presidents Wilson, Franklin Roosevelt, Truman, Eisenhower, Kennedy, Johnson, Nixon, and Ford all drew heavily on these constitutional sources. Congress added other powers

9. See Arthur M. Schlesinger, Jr., *The Imperial Presidency* (Boston: Houghton Mifflin, 1973), pp. 58–64.
10. Binkley, *President and Congress,* p. 127.

by delegating through normal statutory law wide discretionary authority to the president, usually, but not always, for a fixed period. The president's 'war power' is indeed a mighty arsenal.

Foreign Affairs

To the enormous role of the president as emergency head of the country in war, the requirements for survival in the modern world have added yet another role of great scope: the nation's leader in foreign affairs. Starting from a rather modest base in the Constitution,[11] the president has become the dominant figure in foreign policy. Woodrow Wilson first developed the role in its modern form, although his performance ended in failure. He foresaw (four years before he became president, when the matter was still cloudy) that control over foreign policy would give the president enormous power as the United States moved from the wings to the center of the world stage.[12] After the outbreak of World War I, Wilson virtually took control of foreign policy into his own hands, so much so that what was to have been his greatest triumph, the Peace Treaty and the League of Nations Covenant, became his greatest defeat at the hands of a hostile Senate. From 1938 onward, as World War II drew near, Franklin Roosevelt more and more dominated the foreign relations of the United States. Every president since then has had to give a major part of his attention to foreign affairs; Congress, the courts, and the country have long since shown by word and deed that they expect the initiative on foreign policy to lie with the chief executive.

Policy Initiation

In this century the president has come to play still another role: the president, not the Congress, now ordinarily initiates legislation, and presidents now normally bring their skills, resources, and prestige to bear on the Congress in order to secure congressional support for their policies. They are often unsuccessful. Yet it is doubtful whether either the Congress or the electorate would now be content with a chief executive who adhered faithfully to the Whig view frequently heard in the nineteenth century; the view summed up by Lincoln, for example, when he was a Whig congressman: "Were I President, I should desire the legislation of the country to rest with Congress, uninfluenced in its

---

11. Article II, Section 1. "The executive power shall be vested in a president of the United States of America. . . ." Section 2. "The president . . . shall have power, by and with the advice and consent of the Senate, to make treaties, provided two thirds of the senators present concur; and he shall nominate, and by and with the advice and consent of the Senate, shall appoint ambassadors, other public ministers and consuls. . . ." Section 3. "He shall . . . receive ambassadors and other public ministers. . . ."

12. Woodrow Wilson, *Constitutional Government in the United States* (New York: Columbia University Press, 1908), pp. 77–78.

origin or progress, and undisturbed by the veto unless in very special and clear cases."[13] Although Lincoln did not practice what he preached, in the last half of the nineteenth century his successors generally followed the Whig ideal rather than Lincoln's. Theodore Roosevelt, however, took a much bolder role in legislation. Woodrow Wilson formulated a view of the president's role in policy-making that, if daring at one time, has become conventional in this century: "The Constitution bids him speak, and times of stress and change must more and more thrust upon him the attitude of originator of policies."[14]

Later, as governor of New Jersey, Wilson said: ". . . a new role, which to many persons seems a little less than unconstitutional, is thrust upon our executives. The people are impatient of a president or a governor who will not formulate a policy and insist upon its adoption."[15] As president, Wilson lived up to his conception; no president since Jefferson worked so closely with his party in Congress nor was more effective in gaining congressional support for his policies: tariff reform, the Federal Reserve Act, the Federal Trade Commission Act, the Clayton Anti-Trust Act.[16]

Wilson's successors, particularly Franklin Roosevelt, Truman, Kennedy, and Johnson, took for granted that they, not Congress, must originate legislation and must use every means at their disposal to secure its adoption by Congress. Thus in securing passage of most of the New Deal legislation, the weightiest influence was that of Franklin Roosevelt.[17] Although even as late as the New Deal, congressmen occasionally spoke as if the president's role in legislation was a seizure of their own legitimate authority, objections of this kind have grown less and less vocal. The death knell of the Whig view may have been sounded when Republican congressional leaders complained of President Eisenhower's failure to present them promptly with a full legislative program.

Administrative Head

The most recent role in the now vast presidential repertory is the responsibility as head—if sometimes only nominal head—of the extensive administrative structure that has developed for handling national affairs in this century. In 1901, the federal government had some 231,000 civilian employees. By 1930 the number had reached 590,000. Under

13. Corwin, *The President, Offices, and Powers,* p. 381, fn. 60.

14. Wilson, *Constitutional Government,* p. 73.

15. Quoted in Arthur W. Macmahon, "Woodrow Wilson: Political Leader and Administrator," in *The Philosophy and Policies of Woodrow Wilson,* ed. Earl Latham (Chicago: University of Chicago Press, 1958), p. 100.

16. Lester V. Chandler, "Wilson's Monetary Reform," John Perry Miller, "Woodrow Wilson's Contribution to Antitrust Policy," and Richard P. Longaker, "Woodrow Wilson and the Presidency," in Latham, *Philosophy and Policies of Woodrow Wilson.*

17. See the tabulation in Lawrence H. Chamberlain, *The President, Congress and Legislation* (New York: Columbia University Press, 1946), p. 450. See also Chamberlain's comments, pp. 18–19.

the impact of the New Deal and then World War II, civilian federal employment swelled to a total of 3.7 million in 1944, from which it receded to something over 2 million in the years that followed. Controlling this enormous establishment and meeting the constitutional obligation "to take care that the laws be faithfully executed" is a complex and time-consuming presidential task. Cabinet officers, bureau chiefs, commission heads are powerful people; and it is difficult indeed for the occupant in the White House to keep track even in a general way of what they are doing, or to secure their compliance with his own policies. Each president brings to this all but impossible task his own techniques and style. None discharges it without failures.

As administrative head, the president has access to certain resources that he may use to do more than enforce the laws in a neutral fashion. The president's influence on the conduct of the administrative agencies—the bureaucracy—is also a *political* resource that can be used to manipulate public opinion, to gain campaign contributions, or to promote administration policies, the interests of friends and allies, the president's own re-election, and the election of other candidates, including a successor. Thus most administrations see to it that government expenditures go up in election years—and they go up more during presidential election years than during the midterm Congressional elections.[18] The aim, obviously, is to give the public a taste of heightened prosperity, and thus influence the election.

The president also has access to agencies that might be used to reward friends and punish enemies in more specific ways: investigative agencies like the Federal Bureau of Investigation and the Central Intelligence Agency; or the Internal Revenue Service, which inspects tax returns and punishes violators; or the Department of Justice, which prosecutes alleged lawbreakers; and innumerable agencies that award contracts, hire and fire employees, and spend money in other ways. In 1971, in preparation for President Nixon's re-election campaign the following year, a White House political aide listed some "Basic Types of Patronage" that could be used to secure the president's re-election. (Table 12.1)

Thus an unscrupulous president might use the administrative resources of the office to build something very much like an old style city political machine, which uses contracts, patronage, police coercion, and graft to destroy the opposition and insure full domination of political life by the boss. The difference—and it is a great one—is that while the old-style machine has been confined to a single city, or occasionally a single state, the president's machine would be nationwide. That very aim, as we shall see in the next chapter, was adopted by

18. Edward R. Tufte, "The Political Manipulation of the Economy: Influence of the Electoral Cycle on Macroeconomic Performance and Policy" (unpublished manuscript).

Table 12.1
View from the
White House, 1971

The Basic Types of Patronage	
1. Jobs	full-time, part time, retainers, consultantships, etc.
2. Revenue	
Contracts	federal government as purchaser—GSA
Grants	do-good programs—EDA, Model Cities, NSF research, etc.
Subsidies	needy industries—airlines, etc.
Bank Deposits	all federal accounts
Social Need Program	direct benefit to citizens, i.e., Social Security, welfare, etc.
Public Works Projects	
3. Execution of Federal Law	resides mainly in Department of Justice whose interpretive power touches every vested interest.
4. Information and Public Relations Capacity	a professional (?) public relations office in each department and agency constitutes an enormous public information apparatus.
5. Travel	domestic transportation can be provided by law, foreign travel, international conferences, etc. are available.

Source: The Senate Watergate Report, *The Final Report of the Senate Select Committee on Presidential Campaign Activities* (the Ervin Committee), Vol. 1 (New York: Dell, 1974), p. 326.

many of the people involved in the re-election of President Nixon in 1972. It is true that the effort led to his downfall, and might do so for any other president. But one cannot be so sure of the outcome next time—if there is a next time.

A SUCCESS?   Thus the elastic framework created for the presidency has been filled out and expanded by the presidents. Today the presidency is a result of the forces that have played upon that office: the initial impetus received from the Convention, the men who have held the office, the situations and times in which they have acted, and the responses of other leaders and of ordinary citizens.

Undeniably, what has emerged is one of the most influential offices in the world; considering the place of the United States in international affairs, it is no mere exaggeration to suggest that the American president today is, taken all around, the most important popularly elected official in human history.

But how successful is the presidency as an office in a polyarchy with aspirations toward democracy? To answer this question would require us to place the presidency in the perspective of other important elements in the American political system. Description of the elements that bear heavily upon his power and his actions, particularly the Congress, the courts, elections, political parties, federalism, local governments awaits later chapters. It is convenient and perhaps even necessary for clarity that we examine each of these major institutions separately; but, like examining the organs of the human body one by one, we might end with little sense of how they operate as a system. Nonetheless, it is not too soon to deal briefly with two questions that pertain to the success of the presidency as the chief magistrate of a polyarchy. First, given all the roles that the Constitution, the presidents themselves, and historical developments have thrust upon the president, is the office now too great for one person? If so, what if anything can be done about it? Second, does the office give the incumbent too much power measured by democratic standards—or not enough measured by the demands heaped upon him?

CONFLICTING DEMANDS

All the roles that have accumulated in the repertory of the president impose a burden that is appallingly difficult to discharge, and perhaps impossible to discharge well. A friendly critic can easily find serious deficiencies in the performance of all our twentieth-century presidents. The presidency may have become a testing ground where failure is now the normal outcome. What human being *could* fulfill the awesome obligations of that great office?

The difficulty is that the different roles of the president create conflicting demands that cannot be met except by a truly superhuman performance. Thus the president's responsibilities as symbolic head of state and moral model for the country are likely to conflict with his role as master politician, and particularly with the requirements needed to be a successful leader of his party and initiator of policy. Any person who fights his way to the presidency by means of the brutal efforts required to win nomination and election, and who then successfully exploits the resources of his office to guide his policies through Congress and gain the support he needs in the country, is not altogether likely to have (or at least, *seem* to have) the moral qualities required to symbolize the country's highest traditions of morality.

Perhaps no modern president was either more comfortable or successful as symbolic head of state than Dwight Eisenhower; yet he left the initiation of policies mainly to Congress, which was controlled during most of his presidency by the opposition party. Lyndon Johnson, who was superbly skillful as Senate majority leader during Eisenhower's administration, performed wretchedly as symbolic head of state when he himself became president.

There are other conflicts. A president may, like Johnson, possess a sure grasp of domestic issues, gained over half a lifetime in Congress; and yet, like Johnson, he may have only a weak understanding of foreign affairs.

Proposals are often made for sloughing off some of these roles. Thus it has been suggested that the president might give up his symbolic roles: his duties as head of state. But where are these duties to be lodged? As we have seen, a number of polyarchies solve the problem, at least in part, with a hereditary monarchy or an elected head of state who serves as a figurehead. Thus Britain, Sweden, Norway, Denmark, Holland, and Belgium have all retained their royal families for ceremonial purposes. Australia, Canada, and New Zealand each have a governor general. Switzerland, Germany, Austria, Italy, and India have a ceremonial president. These solutions have worked well. Yet a constitutional monarch is as unacceptable to Americans as it was in 1787. As for the other alternatives, if a special ceremonial office were to be created after nearly two centuries under the presidential system, it would probably not work in practice. The president's symbolic role is too important to him politically to make him willing to yield its advantages to a figurehead. Would he not, in fact, fight such a constitutional amendment tooth and nail? Moreover, what head of state, ambassador, member of Congress, or plain citizen would sit with a figurehead if he or she could meet with the real center of authority?

If the symbolic role of the office cannot be lodged elsewhere, what of the administrative role? It is sometimes suggested that the vice-presidency be turned into a kind of administrative chief of staff. But the president's burdens arise less from administrative details than from all the decisions that cannot be delegated without abdicating his responsibilities. A vice-president who took over the responsibility for presidential decisions would in effect be another president; surely, few presidents would tolerate such a rival. As for delegating work to subordinates, the president already has a White House staff of more than a thousand employees. He can, if he wishes, create a chief of staff, as Eisenhower did with Sherman Adams. But the danger here is that the president may become too much the captive of his chief of staff; most presidents are unwilling—rightly, I think—to allow one subordinate such a monopoly over access to them.

It has been suggested that the president make greater use of the Cabinet. Yet it is not clear how this would help. Cabinet officers are appointed for many reasons; they do not necessarily have great administrative skills; they may not always agree with the president on policy; indeed one task of the president, and no easy one, is to make sure that department heads follow his policies. The Cabinet is, in any case, a large and unwieldy collection.

Critics sometimes yearn for a president who would be 'above politics.' He could thus give up his role as party leader by yielding this presumably unworthy task to unworthy politicians. This seems to have been, at times, Eisenhower's view of the presidency: "... in the general derogatory sense you can say that, of course, I do not like politics."[19]

---

19. Richard E. Neustadt, *Presidential Power, the Politics of Leadership* (New York: Wiley, 1960), p. 166.

Yet the result of not liking 'politics' was that Eisenhower did not work at the job of party leader, and this in turn resulted, as it would for any president, in a considerable diminution of his authority with Congress.[20] A president who wants to persuade Congress to adopt his program will, above all, execute the role of party leader, as Jefferson, McKinley, Wilson, the two Roosevelts, Truman, Kennedy, and Johnson all did.

The presidency, then, is unquestionably too great for any human being. No president can ever measure up to its obligations.[21]

It can be said that no one is really qualified to be president of the United States, least of all now in the last part of the twentieth century. Yet in this period of history, could anyone assume this position who did not believe that it is the world's most important public office or did not sense, with at least a touch of awe, the rich traditions of an office that is intertwined with the history of the nation?

TOO MUCH POWER?   The presidency has evolved into "the vital place of action in the system," as Woodrow Wilson described it.[22] But in the process has the country come to depend dangerously on presidential power for doing good—which may also be power for doing evil? Is the president too powerful? Or sometimes not powerful enough?

Four points are important in searching for an answer to these questions:

First, an answer ought to transcend partisanship, but it usually does not.

Second, given roughly the same opportunities and resources available to different presidents, there have been and doubtless will continue to be large variations in the extent they use their resources to acquire power.

Third, there are great variations in the president's power with respect to different kinds of issues, particularly domestic matters as compared with foreign and military affairs.

Fourth, the expansion of presidential power that transformed the office into the 'imperial presidency' was reversed in 1974 with the resignation of Richard Nixon. Although some of the causes of that expansion are probably irreversible, a number of special factors need not

20. For a concrete example, see the description of the congressional battle over renewing the Reciprocal Trade Act in 1955 in Raymond A. Bauer, Ithiel de Sola Pool, and Lewis A. Dexter, *American Business and Public Policy, The Politics of Foreign Trade* (New York: Atherton Press, 1963), ch. 5.

21. In previous editions, I also emphasized the excessive demands of the office in terms of time and energy—the *workload* of the presidency. Two recent accounts by White House insiders have persuaded me that this aspect of the presidential burden has been exaggerated. Both George Reedy, who was press secretary and special assistant to Johnson, and William Safire, who was a White House speech writer for Nixon, flatly reject the view that the president is 'overworked' in the ordinary sense. See George Reedy, *The Twilight of the Presidency* (New York: World Publishing Co., 1970), ch. 2, pp. 16 ff., and William Safire, *Before the Fall* (Garden City, N.Y.: Doubleday, 1975).

22. Wilson, *Constitutional Government,* p. 73.

necessarily recur. There is hope, then, that the presidency may be restored to a better constitutional balance.

Is There a Nonpartisan Answer?

Answers to the question of whether the president has too much power are usually strongly influenced by one's partisan attitudes. During Franklin Roosevelt's presidency, conservative Republicans, who fought his policies, contended that the president had too much power; to liberal Democrats sympathetic with his policies, he had too little power. During Richard Nixon's presidency, the viewpoints were generally reversed. In the next chapter we shall see how the fact that partisans condone an expansion in the power of *their* kind of president contributed to the rise of the imperial presidency.

Yet a purely partisan answer is hardly adequate. Presumably in the future as in the past there will be Democratic presidents and Republican presidents, liberal presidents and conservative presidents. Like the constitutional system as a whole, the presidency ought to be impartial in design. It should serve one party as well as another. Conversely, it ought to give no special advantages to any party or to any partisan policy or perspective.

This is more easily said, of course, than accomplished in practice.

Variations among Presidents

Throughout the history of the presidency, there have been many fluctuations in the extent to which presidents initiate policies and secure their adoption and enforcement by the national government. Lincoln, as we have seen, all but single-handedly determined policies relating to the war and the South. On Lincoln's death a reaction against executive power set in, and from Grant's inauguration in 1869 until McKinley entered the White House in 1897, the presidency was eclipsed by Congress. McKinley's presidency may be regarded as the beginning of a continuing increase in presidential control over policy making. This increase in presidential power has been marked, however, by significant fluctuations caused both by the man and the circumstances. In emergencies such as the Great Depression and particularly in wartime, presidents have inevitably expanded their unhampered control over policy. The man himself—his skills, energy, style, and goals—also makes a difference. A student of the presidency has compared Franklin Roosevelt and Dwight Eisenhower:

> ... Roosevelt's methods were the product of his insights, his incentives, and his confidence. No president in this century has had a sharper sense of personal power, a sense of what it is and where it comes from; none has had more hunger for it, few have had more use for it, and only one or two could match his faith in his own competence to use it. Perception and

desire and self-confidence, combined, produced their own reward. No modern president has been more nearly master in the White House.

... With Eisenhower, seemingly, the case is quite opposite.... Through Eisenhower's first six years his power sense was blunt in almost the degree that F.D.R.'s was sharp. As late as 1958 he had not quite got over "shocked surprise" that orders did not carry themselves out. Apparently he could not quite absorb the notion that effective power had to be extracted out of other men's self-interest; neither did he quite absorb the notion that nobody else's interest could be wholly like his own. And he seems to have been unaware of all his natural advantages in turning different interests toward his own.[23]

A president who is reluctant to develop the potential power of the office, or does not know how to, is obviously likely to be less influential than one who both wants and knows how to increase and retain presidential authority.

Variations in Power on Different Issues

Even strong, energetic, and skillful presidents vary in the amount of influence they exert on different matters. Obviously the president's power depends on the extent to which others are in a position to exercise control over him or the matters he deals with. To put the point in a way that will now be familiar to the reader: the more that authority on a given matter is partitioned among other individuals, offices, and institutions outside his control, the less the president's power will be. In general, the president is most severely limited when:

☐ Presidential constitutional authority is clearly restricted.
☐ The president is not thought to be the only person who can legitimately deal with the matter at hand.
☐ No emergency is thought to exist.
☐ Public opinion is well-defined, highly structured, and not responsive to the president.
☐ Well-organized groups outside the Executive Branch regularly participate in the kind of decision at hand.

Conversely, the president's own control over a decision is greatest when:

☐ Presidential constitutional authority is broad and ill-defined.
☐ The president is thought to have a special legitimacy in dealing with the matter.
☐ An emergency is thought to exist.
☐ Public opinion is weak, unstructured, and highly responsive to the president.
☐ Few, if any, well-organized groups outside the Executive Branch regularly participate.

---

23. Neustadt, *Presidential Power*, pp. 161, 163–164.

Decisions vary in the extent to which these factors are present. However, domestic policies often fall most clearly into the first category, while foreign and military policies sometimes fall into the second.

Domestic policies. On most questions of domestic policy and sometimes on foreign policy, the president is hedged in by the Congress, the Supreme Court, his own officials, his party leaders, public opinion, the national communications media, and the prospect of coming elections, both presidential and congressional. Observers who look at the presidency from a distance can easily underestimate how much these factors limit the president's range of action. For decades, the Congress rejected presidential proposals on civil rights and medical care. Within three months after President Truman ordered the government to seize the steel industry during the Korean war, the Supreme Court held his action unconstitutional, and the steel mills had to be returned at once to private hands. To pick another example from the experience of a strong executive with a leaning toward decisive action, Truman dallied month after month before relieving General MacArthur of his command in Korea for failure to execute orders. For not only was MacArthur a distinguished general with a following in Congress and the country, but also, as Truman said later, MacArthur "was a commander in the field. You pick your man, you've got to back him up."[24] A president may have to discard or modify a policy because of negative responses from farmers, doctors, an ethnic group, a region, union leaders, or an industry. For the publics that comprise 'public opinion' have influence by means of congressional and presidential elections.

In fact, in recent decades most presidents have been severely mauled by Congress sooner or later. Even Franklin Roosevelt was stymied on domestic reform from 1938 onward by a congressional coalition of Republicans and Southern Democrats. Neither Harry Truman nor John F. Kennedy was able to get much legislation past the Congress. Richard Nixon suffered the unprecedented humiliation of having two of his candidates for the Supreme Court turned down by the Senate and some of his key legislative programs defeated, emasculated, or modified. More recently, Gerald Ford could not persuade Congress to adopt key elements in his energy program.

Thus election to the office of the presidency by no means carries with it the authority to carry out the policies that the successful candidate promised to execute during his campaign. Even if the president has a stronger claim to speak for a national majority than anyone else in the United States, the system of partitioned power means that his

24. *Ibid.*, p. 146. The incident is described and analyzed in considerable detail in Neustadt's book.

claim is not ordinarily backed up with the political resources to make it good.

Foreign affairs. Some questions of foreign policy are rather like matters of domestic policy. Thus most presidential requests for foreign aid have been cut by the Congress, often severely, despite the best efforts of the White House to retain the full amounts requested. It is true, nonetheless, that certain kinds of foreign policy issues have come closest to the situation of wide presidential discretion just described as crisis leadership. Roosevelt's conduct of World War II, Truman's decision to enter Korea, Kennedy's decisions on the Bay of Pigs and the Cuban missile crisis, Johnson's escalation and Nixon's de-escalation of the war in Vietnam, and Nixon's attempted rapprochement with China were all cases where a president was able to exercise enormous discretionary power.

For these and many other issues of foreign policy, all the factors listed above are on the President's side. Thus the constitutional provisions making the president commander-in-chief and leader on foreign policy have come to provide a superabundance of unchallengable legal authority. In addition, from Lincoln's time onward, the presidency accumulated a special legitimacy on these matters: people expected the president to take the lead. Moreover, whenever a widespread sense of emergency existed, potential opposition was hesitant and easily squelched by suggestions that it was unpatriotic or incompetent to act in these domains; public opinion was unstructured and easily swayed; the country was thought to be in danger or at least in need of a decisive military response; hence all loyal citizens were expected to rally behind the president; in crisis the people must trust their leaders, and so on. Finally, in these circumstances, well-organized groups capable of giving advice and participating in decisions were almost exclusively located in the Defense Department, the State Department, and the White House itself. When it was caught in a seeming emergency, the Senate Foreign Relations Committee would be inclined to back away. The large number of organized interest groups that would have leaped into action at the first sign of movement on such issues as taxation, labor relations, agricultural subsidies, tariffs and quotas, and many other domestic subjects simply did not exist.

The early opponents of the war in Vietnam confronted just such a situation. The political processes that usually operate in domestic affairs to provide a well-organized and articulate minority with some leverage on policy somewhere in the Executive Branch, Congress, or the Court were simply not operating in decisions on Vietnam. For some years opponents of the war, though more numerous than, say, farmers, had far less influence on policy than farm lobbies. They lacked well-established organizations with ready access to Congress and the executive, were often short on the political skills necessary to develop political access and a permanent organization, were cut off from the leadership of both major parties, and were unable to persuade the courts to intervene. Their inability to use conventional means effectively is undoubtedly one reason why antiwar groups so often relied on the technique of mass demonstrations.

End of the Imperial Presidency?

To judge whether the president has acquired too much power, at least on a number of critical matters, we must examine the historic peak of uncontrolled presidential power reached under Richard Nixon. Had the presidency remained as it came to be during his tenure, the answer to our question could hardly be in doubt. Were the excesses of that period merely a deviation from the norm, or did they reflect the effects of long-run, more enduring factors? We turn to this question in the next chapter.

SUMMARY   1. Presidents have filled out the loose design of the office prescribed in the Constitution, and in doing so have enlarged the presidency by defining a number of roles the president can and indeed is expected to play.

2. These include the responsibilities and powers as symbolic head of state, party leader, spokesman for national majorities, national leader in times of crisis, chief of foreign affairs, policy initiator, and administrative head.

3. Among the problems of the presidency for which no clear solutions have so far emerged are:

□ The conflicting demands on the office, which may well have become too great for any person to satisfy.
□ The *power* of the office. On the one hand the president's power tends to be highly circumscribed on domestic matters, where power is extensively partitioned. On certain foreign-military decisions, on the other hand, presidential power is often of vast scope.

13 THE CRISIS OF THE IMPERIAL PRESIDENCY

The evolution of the presidency placed within the control of a single person all the roles described in the last chapter—head of state, party leader, spokesman for national majorities, national leader in times of domestic crisis or turbulence, national leader in foreign affairs, commander-in-chief of the nation's military forces, chief initiator of policy, head of the federal administration. These roles provided the president with vast political resources and extraordinary opportunities for making crucial decisions. Particularly on foreign and military matters, these decisions would encounter few checks by other centers of power. Further, the presidential office developed a potential for punishing critics and opponents, distributing favors to friends and supporters, extracting large campaign funds from businesses seeking favorable public policies, wilfully and knowingly violating the laws and Constitution, conducting in secret matters of great consequence for the country, and by these and other means influencing the election to the office itself.

This was the 'imperial presidency.'' Although it reached its apex under Richard Nixon, the imperial presidency had a long history and numerous causes. Some of these causes were transitory and declined in importance with Nixon's downfall in 1974 as a result of the Watergate episode. But other causes were more enduring.

---

1. The term imperial presidency comes from the book of that title by Arthur Schlesinger, Jr. (Boston: Houghton Mifflin, 1973). Schlesinger's treatment of the historical development of the authority and practices of the imperial presidency is the best available.

GROUNDSWELL
TOWARD
IMPEACHING
A PRESIDENT

What was Watergate?

At 2:30 A.M. on June 17, 1972, five men were arrested for breaking into the offices of the Democratic National Committee in the Watergate —an apartment, hotel, shopping, and office complex in Washington, D.C. This was the beginning of "Watergate." More than two years later, on August 8, 1974, after a chain reaction triggered off by the break-in had brought the country to the verge of impeaching and convicting a president, Richard Nixon resigned to forestall his removal from office by Congress.[2]

"What was Watergate? Why was Watergate? Is there an antidote that will prevent future Watergates? If so, what is that antidote?" These were the questions posed by a distinguished senior member of the United States Senate in a report to the Senate in 1974. These are the questions we shall explore in this chapter. Questions like these had led to the formation in 1973 of the Senate Select Committee on Presidential Campaign Activities (known as the Ervin committee) to seek out the answers.[3] The answers brought about the resignation of Richard Nixon and important changes in the conduct of the presidency. It is still unclear, however, whether the events preceding and following Nixon's resignation produced "an antidote that will prevent future Watergates." To understand why we remain uncertain over the effectiveness of the antidote, we need to understand the answers to the first two questions: What was Watergate? Why was Watergate?

The Watergate break-in was first treated mostly as a semicomic episode of little importance. However, Carl Bernstein, 28, and Bob Woodward, 29, two young reporters for the Washington *Post,* who had been assigned to the story of the break-in, had insisted on following out several unexplained aspects. Tireless investigations over many months on their part uncovered a trail that led from Watergate to the

---

2. This section has drawn on the following sources: *Impeachment of Richard M. Nixon, President of the United States, Report of the Committee on the Judiciary, House of Representatives,* August 20, 1974, completely reprinted by the New York Times, *The Final Report of the Committee of the Judiciary, House of Representatives* (New York: Bantam Books, 1975), paperback. (Cited below as *Final Report.*)

The Final Report of the Select Committee on Presidential Campaign Activities, [the Ervin committee], *United States Senate, June 1974,* completely reprinted as *The Senate Watergate Report,* 2 vols. (New York: Dell, 1974), Vol. 1. (Cited below as *Senate Watergate Report.*)

Watergate: Chronology of a Crisis, 2 vols. (Washington, D.C.: Congressional Quarterly, 1974). This was published in 1975 in a one volume edition with another 400 pages of material. *Presidency, 1974* (Washington, D.C.: Congressional Quarterly, 1975).

Jonathan Schell, *The Time of Illusion,* published in *The New Yorker Magazine,* Parts I–VI, June 2, 6, 16, 23, and 30, and July 7, 1975.

Carl Bernstein and Bob Woodward, *All the President's Men* (New York: Warner Paperback Library, 1975).

Theodore H. White, *Breach of Faith, The Fall of Richard Nixon* (New York: Atheneum, 1975).

William Safire, *Before the Fall, An Inside View of the Pre-Watergate White House* (New York: Doubleday and Co., 1975).

A detailed "Chronology of Watergate-Related Events" by Linda Amster will be found in the *New York Times, The White House Transcripts* (New York: Bantam Books, 1974), pp. 813–877. It ends on May 2, 1974, three months before Nixon's resignation.

3. *Senate Watergate Report,* p. 7.

White House.[4] Their work, together with investigative reporting by the *New York Times,* the *Los Angeles Times,* and *Time* magazine, changed "the Watergate caper" from campaign comedy to a portentous national drama. Had it not been for the work of a number of dedicated newspaper reporters and the willingness of their editors to back them up, quite possibly none of these inquiries would ever have taken place.

What then *was* the answer to Senator Ervin's first question? What *was* Watergate?

Viewed in narrow perspective, Watergate was an incident in which a group of men, acting in behalf of the Committee to Re-Elect the President (CRP), broke a law and violated the legal rights of others. Fearing that if CRP's responsibility were known the president's chances for re-election might be damaged, the President conspired with his chief officials, including the attorney general of the United States, to conceal CRP's role. In this he was initially successful. At the time of the election in November 1972, only the conspirators themselves knew of his involvement. Few voters even suspected it. He was overwhelmingly re-elected.

A broader answer to Senator Ervin's question, however, would be that at its zenith under President Nixon the imperial presidency had reached proportions that were morally, politically, legally, and constitutionally intolerable. The office was in danger of being transformed into a grotesque elective monarchy with a scope and power beyond anything the Framers had ever intended—though it was not unlike what some had feared might happen and yet had hoped to prevent by their system of partitioned power.

Foreign Affairs

Like his predecessor Lyndon Johnson, President Nixon ran the war in Vietnam with little effective control by Congress, even less by public opinion, and none by the judiciary. The imperial presidency had grown to the point where the power to declare and to wage war was for all practical purposes in the hands of the president. He could decide on his own whether to withdraw troops, when, and how many. He could decide when to bomb North Vietnam and when to stop bombing, when and on what terms to negotiate with the North Vietnamese, when to break off peace negotiations, when to resume them. After a moderately conciliatory and apparently peace-seeking policy in the months prior to his reelection in November 1972, in mid-December he authorized the heaviest bombing of the war. Two weeks later, he abruptly called it off.

So complete was the president's control over the conduct of the war that he often deceived Congress and the public as to what was

---

4. The details of their investigations are described in Bernstein and Woodward, *All the President's Men.*

happening. Sometimes the deception was so great that his critics appeared to be fighting with phantoms created by their own imaginations.

This was illustrated by the bizarre fourteen-month 'secret' bombing of Cambodia. Cambodia was a neutral country, badly torn by its own internal conflicts. Because North Vietnamese troops made use of Cambodian territory, however, in March 1969, only three months after taking office, Nixon authorized the military to begin air strikes against Cambodia. At his insistence, the operation was undertaken in the utmost secrecy. Operational reports prepared after each mission were falsified to indicate that bombing targets were in Vietnam, not Cambodia. From the beginning of the operation in March 1969 until May 1970, heavy bombers in 3700 sorties dropped a total of over 100,000 tons of bombs on Cambodia. Throughout this fourteen-month period, the President continued to assure the country that Cambodia had never been attacked by either Americans or South Vietnamese forces. This, of course, was completely false. Although a few congressmen were privately informed, administration voices continued to deny the bombing in their testimony before congressional committees. It was not until July 1973, that the Secretary of Defense confirmed the bombing to the Senate Armed Forces Committee.[5]

Nixon's clandestine bombing of Cambodia ultimately contributed in two ways to the groundswell of Congressional and public opinion for impeachment.

Unconstitutionality of the secret bombing. As evidence for the bombing and the attempt to conceal it began to rise to the surface, a considerable number of people in Congress, in the communications media, and among the general public came to believe that the president had violated the Constitution. Among other provisions he had violated was the exclusive authority of Congress to declare war. He had, after all, declared and waged war against Cambodia—and denied that he was doing so!

Illegal wiretapping. Several months after the clandestine bombing began, the *New York Times* managed to discover what was going on and published an account. Pretty clearly, someone in the administration had leaked the secret to the *Times.* To discover the source of the leak, the president, his chief aide, H. R. Haldeman, Attorney General John Mitchell, and Secretary of State Henry Kissinger inaugurated a process of illegal wiretapping of the telephones of a number of government officials and newspapermen. Two years later, when the *New York*

5. *Final Report,* pp. 311–314, 401–407.

Times began publishing a secret Pentagon history of the Vietnam war (The Pentagon Papers),[6] the President again resorted to wire-tapping. He established an investigative unit within the White House (called the Plumbers—to plug the leaks) which also engaged in wiretapping and other illegal activities. These actions, and the attempts to conceal and deny them, ultimately formed an important part of the evidence for impeachment.[7]

The Cambodian invasion. The President was overreaching the bounds of his proper authority in ways that were not yet known and which, when revealed, would contribute to his downfall. But in late April, 1970, he suddenly displayed a seemingly limitless power over foreign policy in a dramatic public action. On the night of April 30, the President went on the air to inform a nation grown weary with the war that he had decided to send American troops into Cambodia—to knock out the enemy and supplies that fourteen months of still unacknowledged bombing had not destroyed. The decision was taken without any prior Congressional consultation. A wave of antiwar demonstrations swept the country. Many universities closed down entirely. "Civil disorders greater than anything previously seen in the United States in the twentieth century spread throughout the country."[8] At Kent State University, four students engaged in an antiwar demonstration were shot and killed by National Guardsmen called out by the governor. The invasion of Cambodia proved futile; no significant enemy forces or supplies were encountered. Within two months, the invasion was called off.[9]

Thus the Cambodian bombing and invasion added evidence to the view that in foreign affairs, the presidency was—to use a common expression of the day—out of control. Cambodia contributed to the growing belief that a better constitutional balance between president, Congress, the Courts, and the public somehow had to be found.

Domestic actions. Although the president showed that he was beyond effective constitutional control in his conduct of foreign affairs, it was

---

6. *New York Times, The Pentagon Papers* (New York: Bantam Books, 1971).

7. *Final Report,* pp. 212–248. For the reactions of one White House speech writer to being wiretapped, see Safire, *Before the Fall,* pp. 166 ff. A source in the White House that Bernstein and Woodward labeled 'Deep Throat' described the growing White House willingness to engage in illegal wiretapping this way: "In 1969, the first targets of aggressive wiretapping were the reporters and those in the administration who were suspected of disloyalty. Then the emphasis was shifted to the radical political opposition during the antiwar protests. When it got near election time, it was only natural to tap the Democrats. The arrests in the Watergate sent everybody off the edge because the break-in could uncover the whole program." Bernstein and Woodward, *All the President's Men,* p. 299.

8. Schell, *New Yorker,* June 9, p. 84.

9. "They had not found a Communist headquarters, nor had they encountered the enemy on a large scale. As it turned out, the enemy . . . had withdrawn deeper into Cambodia. . . . (T)he most momentous military result of the invasion had turned out to be a takeover of some two-thirds of Cambodia by the insurgent forces." *Ibid.,* p. 88.

not there but in actions directed toward American citizens at home that he finally created the grounds on which he was checked in his expansion of the imperial presidency.

Although the ramifications of Watergate in the broadest sense are too extensive to be adequately summarized here, two central aspects of Watergate bear so directly on the nature of the imperial presidency that they require a brief if incomplete discussion.

First, in its broader meaning Watergate represented an attempt to use the presidency to build a national political machine that by means both legal and illegal would reward friends, punish enemies, deceive the public, alter public opinion, and thus convert the election of a president into a plebiscite voted on by an electorate manipulated from the White House. Second, Watergate represented an attempt to use the powers and resources of the presidency to insure the secrecy of this effort and thus to conceal it wholly from scrutiny by Congress, the judiciary, and the public. This was the 'cover-up.'

Toward a National Political Machine

The break-in at the Democratic National Committee headquarters in the Watergate came about as a part of a comprehensive effort to use all the powers available to the White House to secure the re-election of the president. Most presidents, of course, assiduously seek their re-election. Had President Nixon merely used some of the resources of the presidency to secure his own re-election, he would have done only what most of his predecessors had done. But taken in their totality, the efforts he sponsored went far beyond what had ever been done by any previous chief executive. The investigations of the Ervin Committee in the Senate and the Judiciary Committee in the House of Representatives, which is charged with initiating the impeachment process, established that among other things Nixon and his close associates were responsible for:

Carrying out a political intelligence plan involving illegal acts. The object was to gain information about the private lives and political plans of the president's political opponents by means that included the illegal use of electronic surveillance. The Watergate break-in was in pursuance of this plan.[10]

Carrying out a political enemies project involving the improper and illegal use of the Internal Revenue Service. At the request of top presidential aides H. R. Haldeman and John Ehrlichman, the president's legal counsel, John Dean, prepared a memorandum entitled "Dealing with our political enemies."

---

10. *Final Report,* pp. 39–58.

> This memorandum [he wrote] addresses the matter of how we can maxi-
> mize the fact of our incumbency in dealing with persons known to be
> active in their opposition to our administration. Stated a bit more bluntly—
> how we can use the available federal machinery to screw our political
> enemies.[11]

In pursuance of this project, the administration sought to use the Internal Revenue Service to gain confidential information that could be
used to discredit opponents or to harass them with IRS investigations
and audits. (In fairness it should be said that the IRS generally resisted
this effort. Whether it could have overcome the pressure from the
White House much longer is, however, doubtful.)[12]

Illegally using federal investigative agencies for political purposes.
"Another technique of the White House staff," the Ervin committee reported, "was to obtain derogatory information about individuals from
investigative agencies such as the FBI and to disseminate the information to the press by way of selective 'leaks'."[13]

Generating misleading expressions of public opinion. In a number
of ways, the White House sought to create a false sense of public opinion. Thus letter-writing campaigns were stimulated "designed to give
the impression . . . of a broad base of support for positions advocated
by President Nixon. . . . Letters were prepared, except for signatures,
by [an employee of the Republican National Committee] and then distributed to volunteers in Washington and throughout the country who
signed the letters and then sent them in as personal letters to the ad-
dresses designated by the R[epublican] N[ational] C[ommittee]."[14] "Independent citizen's committees" were also created to place advertise-
ments in newspapers.[15] Although these actions were not illegal, they

---

11. *Senate Watergate Report*, p. 211.

12. These efforts are detailed in the *Senate Watergate Report*, pp. 210–228, and the *Final
Report*, pp. 207–211. An earlier effort to discredit George Wallace for President Nixon's political
purposes is described in the *Final Report*, pp. 205–206.

13. *Senate Watergate Report*, p. 228. For president's use of the Secret Service, see p. 233.

14. *Senate Watergate Report*, pp. 236–237.

15. *Ibid.*, 241–246.
Bernstein and Woodward in *All the President's Men* report the following remarks from
'a well-placed CRP official.' "Remember the decision to mine Haiphong [Harbor in North Viet-
nam] about five months before the election? Some of us felt that that decision could make or
break the president. We spent $8,400 on false telegrams and ads to stir up phony support for
the President's decision. Money was used to pay for telegrams to the White House to tell the
President what a great move it was, so that [Ronald] Ziegler [press secretary to the president]
could announce that the telegram support was running some large percentage in support of
the president. Money also went to pay for a phony ad in the *New York Times*."
"Notice," the man from CRP said, "it is signed by about ten supposedly independent
people, leaving the impression that citizens are . . . willing to fork over several thousand dollars
of their money to express their opinion. Not so. The ad was paid for by CRP. . . ." pp. 293–294.
The CRP also rigged a poll by the local Metromedia television station asking viewers
whether they agreed or disagreed with the president on the mining of Haiphong harbor. An
employee described it as follows: "Everyone [at CRP] had to fill out fifteen postcards. Ten people
worked for days buying different kinds of stamps and getting different handwriting to fake the
responses. . . . Thousands of newspapers were bought from the newsstands and the ballots were
clipped out and mailed in." (Bernstein & Woodward, *All the President's Men*, pp. 293–295.)
Not surprisingly, the poll showed 'public opinion' in favor of the president's action.

were deliberately deceptive and went well beyond the practices of previous presidential candidates.

Disseminating false and misleading information to discredit Nixon's political opponents. Presumably in order to discredit Senator Robert Kennedy and perhaps any other Democratic presidential candidate, one of the Plumbers forged an 'official' cable to demonstrate, as he put it, that under President Kennedy "a Catholic U.S. administration had in fact conspired in the assassination of [President Diem of Vietnam] a Catholic chief of state in another country.[16]

In preparation for the forthcoming presidential campaign, in mid-1971 Haldeman approved the hiring with campaign funds of one Donald Segretti. Directed by presidential aides, Segretti organized a 'dirty tricks' operation to discredit Nixon's political opponents. At that time, Senator Edmund Muskie, the Democratic front-runner, was thought to be the strongest threat to Nixon's re-election. Public opinion polls showed Senator Muskie leading both President Nixon and Governor George Wallace in a three-way race. Special efforts were therefore made to bring Muskie into disrepute in order to prevent him from winning in the state Democratic primaries and gaining the nomination.[17] Some of the actions probably did serve their purpose.[18] Muskie's campaign for the nomination entered into a decline, and the candidate preferred by the White House as the weakest opponent, George McGovern, was in fact nominated.

Adopting and carrying out a plan to use the financial resources of the federal government, both legally and illegally, to swing the presidential election. In the spring of 1972, a proposal delicately called "Increasing the Responsiveness of the Executive Branch" was approved by Haldeman. Although other presidents had also made use of the government's enormous array of jobs, contracts, and other expenditures for political purposes, probably no previous effort had ever been so extensive, systematic, and carefully thought out, or executed with

---

16. *Senate Watergate Report,* pp. 204–205.

17. As one example, a counterfeit letter on Muskie stationery was mailed to supporters of Democratic contender Senator Henry Jackson. The letter contained allegations of sexual improprieties involving Jackson and also Senator Hubert Humphrey, another Democratic contender. The action violated a section of the United States code prohibiting the distribution of unsigned political literature. (In September 1973, Segretti was sentenced to six months in prison after pleading guilty to three counts.) Harassment of Muskie by such means was extensive. Among other things CRP financed a write-in campaign in the New Hampshire primary to siphon votes away from Muskie. *Ibid.,* pp. 249–311.

18. In particular, Muskie was damaged by a spurious 'Canuck Letter' in which he appeared to insult French Canadians. The letter appeared in an anti-Muskie newspaper in New Hampshire, where Americans of French Canadian origin comprise a significant share of the voters. This incident may have contributed to his emotional response to the same newspaper's unfavorable story about Muskie's wife. He was reported to have broken down and cried. According to Bernstein and Woodward, "There was no dispute among Muskie's backers, his opponents and the press that the incident had a disastrous effect on his campaign. It shattered the calm, cool, reasoned image that was basic to Muskie's voter appeal, and focussed the last-minute attention of New Hampshire voters on the alleged slur against the French-Canadians who would be a formidable minority of voters in the Democratic primary." *All the President's Men,* pp. 132–133. See also *Senate Watergate Report,* pp. 308–311.

such deliberation. The plan reveals in sharp perspective the kinds of economic resources the imperial presidency had at its disposal for creating a kind of elective monarchy. The aim, the document said, was to "politicize the bureaucracy" and to "politicize the Executive Branch." As usual, secrecy was the rule: "Naturally, steps would be taken (1) to insure that information about the program itself and the departmental plans would not be leaked and (2) keep the president and the White House disassociated with the program in the event of a leak."[19]

Thus to insure his re-election President Nixon sponsored a series of activities which, taken together, would over time have created a formidable political machine. Indeed, these various plans might have turned the imperial presidency into a kind of elective monarchy that would, for all practical purposes, bar all effective competition for the office. In the short run they probably helped to swell Nixon's overwhelming vote in the election of 1972. In the longer run, however, they contributed to Nixon's downfall.

FALL OF THE PRESIDENT

The evidence of Nixon's wrongdoing was steadily mounting. The Ervin Committee in the Senate, often following leads given by the press, had dug deep. The Judiciary Committee of the House was relentlessly digging even deeper. Nor was Congress the only source of official investigations into Watergate.

The Judicial Branch

The federal judicial system was also at work. Over a two-year period, investigations by a federal grand jury had brought numerous indictments of persons involved both in Watergate and in the subsequent attempt by the administration to conceal its own involvement. The five men indicted for breaking into Democratic National Headquarters and two others who had conspired with them had been brought to trial, convicted, and sent to prison. Fifteen other persons had been indicted, most of them from the president's staff. They included three of President Nixon's closest associates: Nixon's first Attorney General, John Mitchell, and the president's two top aides in the White House, H. R. Haldeman and John D. Ehrlichman. Seven had already pleaded guilty.

The Executive Branch

What is more, while the White House was attempting by every means available to conceal its involvement, another part of the Execu-

---

19. The plan is described in the *Senate Watergate Report*, pp. 329 ff. The quotations above are on pp. 334 and 332.

tive Branch was investigating and prosecuting Watergate conspirators. Nixon's second Attorney General had resigned because of his close association with some of the indicted men, including his predecessor, John Mitchell. It was commonly thought in Washington that the Department of Justice had not been pursuing the Watergate affair with the utmost vigor, and almost from the beginning a demand had arisen for a special prosecutor to be appointed. Apparently to stave off the rising public disbelief in recurrent denials that the president himself was implicated in what came to be called the cover-up, Nixon had appointed as his third Attorney General a lawyer and public servant of unquestioned probity, Elliot Richardson. At the Senate hearings on his confirmation, Richardson had agreed to appoint a special prosecutor in the Justice Department to handle the Watergate investigation. He duly appointed a distinguished Harvard Law School professor, Archibald Cox, who aggressively ferreted out evidence and insisted on access to the White House documents. Although Cox's relentless pursuit of evidence led to his firing (see further discussion on pp. 163–164), his replacement, Leon Jaworski, continued the search.

The Cover-up Expands and Fails

By conspiring to conceal the involvement of his associates in Watergate, the president himself had violated the law. Moreover, the holder of the one national office charged by the Constitution with the responsibility to "take care that the laws be faithfully executed" was himself involved in an effort to conceal lawbreaking. This Watergate cover-up rapidly dwarfed the initial episode in importance. As the various investigations closed in, the cover-up had to be continually expanded. In time, the President was involved in a vast effort to violate the laws and the Constitution.

It was mainly the growing effort to conceal the illegal actions of the president and his associates that led finally to the adoption by the Judiciary Committee of the House of Representatives of three articles of impeachment. What turned the tide in favor of impeachment, in Congress and in the country, were Nixon's own actions and mainly his own words.

Had he not tape-recorded his actions in his own words, and had these words not become known, it is altogether possible that the move to impeach him could not have succeeded.

Nixon and his closest White House associates believed that the media, the intellectuals, the universities, the whole 'establishment,' as he and his associates often called it, were his enemies. It was 'us' against 'them.' 'They' were bound to distort his place in history. To prevent this, Nixon and Haldeman were determined to leave a detailed record of Nixon's presidency. Some day Nixon and other sympathetic biographers would show his accomplishments in their proper perspective. Following this line of thought, Nixon and Haldeman had tape-recording equipment installed in the White House in 1971. The President is reported to have "mentioned to Haldeman in 1972 that it would be a good idea to get started 'cleaning up' the tapes, and Haldeman had said no, there was plenty of time."[20]

In testimony before the Senate Watergate Committee in mid-1973 a former White House aide revealed the existence of the tapes. Immediately a struggle began to secure their release. Claiming 'executive privilege' (see further discussion on pp. 164–165), Nixon refused to release the tapes and other presidential papers, turning down two subpoenas from the Ervin committee. A third came from the government's special prosecutor, Archibald Cox, who was engaged in preparing evidence of criminal misconduct for the federal grand jury investigating the ramifications of Watergate. When the President rejected the subpoena from the special prosecutor, Cox went to Federal District Court Judge John J. Sirica. In August, 1973, Judge Sirica ordered the President to turn over to him the tapes of nine conversations relating to Watergate in order to decide whether they should then be turned over to the special prosecutor. When Nixon again refused, a U.S. Court of Appeals upheld Sirica.

The Saturday Night Massacre. A profound constitutional confrontation between the president and the judiciary was in the making, with the president on one side and the judiciary and Congress on the other. Nixon now took an action that was to constitute a major turning point toward impeachment.

First he ordered Cox, the special prosecutor, "as an employee of the executive branch to make no further attempts by the judicial process to obtain tapes, notes, or memoranda of presidential conversations." Cox announced that he would go back into court to obtain compliance with the court's order. The President ordered his third attorney general, Elliot Richardson, to fire Cox. Richardson refused. "At stake, in the final analysis," he said, "is the very integrity of the governmental processes I came to the Department of Justice to help restore." Thereupon he resigned. A presidential aide then called on Deputy Attorney General William Ruckelshaus to fire Cox. He also refused and promptly resigned. Finally a newly appointed solicitor general, who now automatically became acting attorney general, was ordered to fire Cox. He did so.

These events of Saturday, October 20, 1973, revealed at a press

---

20. This account of the origins of the tapes and Haldeman's failure to "clean them up" is from Safire, *Before the Fall*, p. 292. See also pp. 272–277, and 307–315.

conference that evening, came to be known as the Saturday Night Massacre. The action galvanized the country. Mail and telegrams, much of it favoring impeachment, flowed into congressional offices in greater volume than at any time in living memory. Hitherto impeachment had scarcely been considered a serious alternative; now it was discussed everywhere. On Tuesday, October 23, shortly after Congress returned from a brief recess, members of the House began introducing resolutions calling for the impeachment of the president. These went for consideration to the House Judiciary Committee. Astounded by what an aide called the 'firestorm' he had created, Nixon now reversed himself. On the day Congress resumed, the President's counsel announced to Judge Sirica that the president would comply with the order of the Court; the president would yield the nine tapes.

Although the president continued to fight a rear-guard action over relinquishing tapes, in March 1974 he did yield a number of tapes to the House Judiciary Committee. But the Committee insisted on others. At the end of April the president went on national television and with a neatly piled stack of transcripts beside him announced that he was releasing edited transcripts of forty-six taped conversations subpoenaed by the Judiciary Committee. Despite unexplained silences, erasures, garbling, and omissions, the transcripts confirmed what the Judiciary Committee was learning from a mountain of other testimony and documents. But because of crucial gaps in the transcripts, the Judiciary Committee then subpeonaed the tapes themselves, including a number not among the edited transcripts released by the President. The president thereupon defied the Committee's subpoena.[21]

Committee Vote and Presidential Resignation

On July 24, 1974, the Supreme Court, without a single dissent, rejected Nixon's claim of 'executive privilege' to withhold requested tapes from the special Watergate prosecutor; the President, however, gave no indication that he was about to obey the Court.

On that same day, the House Judiciary Committee also began its formal debate, broadcast to the public, on three articles of impeachment. Referring to the Watergate break-in, Article I charged:

> Subsequent thereto, Richard M. Nixon, using the powers of his high office, engaged personally and through his subordinates and agents, in a course of conduct or plan designed to delay, impede, and obstruct the investigation of such unlawful entry; to cover up, conceal and protect those responsible; and to conceal the existence and scope of other unlawful covert activities.

---

21. The struggle over the tapes up to his April 30 televised address is summarized in "The Tapes: A Nine-Month Battle for Disclosure," in *Watergate: Chronology of a Crisis*, vol. 2, p. 337. The rest of the dispute is described in *Presidency, 1974*, pp. 4–8.

After describing in nine numbered paragraphs "the means used to implement this course of conduct," the Article concluded:

> In all of this, Richard M. Nixon has acted in a manner contrary to his trust as President and subversive of constitutional government, to the great prejudice of the cause of law and justice, and to the manifest injury of the people of the United States.
>
> Wherefore Richard M. Nixon, by such conduct, warrants impeachment and trial, and removal from office.

Article II charged him with

> violating the constitutional rights of citizens, impairing the due and proper administration of justice and the conduct of lawful inquiries, or contravening the laws governing agencies of the executive branch and the purposes of those agencies.

The Article cited his illegal use of the Internal Revenue Service, FBI, CIA, and his interference with the Department of Justice.

Article III cited his most recent refusals to produce "papers and things (tapes)" subpoenaed by the Committee for the purpost of arriving at the evidence bearing on the impeachment question.

Article I was adopted by a vote of 27 to 11, Article II by 28 to 10, and Article III by 21 to 17. A solid phalanx of ten Republican members rejected all three articles. But the climax of the great national drama was still to come.

Seeing that a vote in the House to impeach was now a foregone conclusion, particularly in view of the president's continued refusal to yield up all of the tapes, the White House on August 5, announced that the president was releasing the crucial tapes. Nixon's own words on the tapes broke the dam. They unambiguously implicated him in the cover-up. The solid Republican phalanx dissolved overnight as the members of the Committee who had voted against Article I now stated publicly that they would support it.

Beyond all doubt the House would have speedily voted to impeach and the Senate to convict President Nixon. In the light of the now unanimous recommendation by the Committee, it was obvious that votes in the House and Senate would approach unanimity. A few days later Nixon resigned and Vice-President Gerald Ford assumed the office.

"Our long national nightmare is over," said Ford. "Our Constitution works. Our great republic is a government of laws and not of men."

One must certainly hope that this is true. Whether the gross constitutional imbalance reflected in Watergate—using that term in its broadest sense—has been corrected depends, however, on the answers to Senator Ervin's remaining questions: *Why* was Watergate? Is there an antidote that will prevent future Watergates? If so, what is that antidote? How we answer these questions will depend on our assessment of the factors that helped to create the imperial presidency. As noted earlier, some of these factors were transitory, and may have vanished with the fall of Richard Nixon. Others were of a more enduring nature. As they preceded Nixon, so they remain even after his fall.

ENDURING CAUSES   To begin with, by deciding in favor of a single executive, the Framers gave the president a number of comparative advantages that are well understood in a great variety of organizations: greater capacity for unity, decisiveness, speed, coherence, consistency, coordination, and secrecy.

Mystique of the Mandate

To these advantages the office also adds the special aura, or mystique, of the so-called 'presidential mandate'. Andrew Jackson's claim to be the best and only true spokesman for national majorities foreshadowed the growing acceptance of this myth of the mandate. In claiming a mandate, the president asserts that by virtue of his election he represents the will of the people and therefore has both a right and an obligation to put his policies into effect by any means constitutionally available. Over against this spacious prerogative, the mandate of an individual senator or representative is small indeed. The veneration for the office of president, the unique visibility of its incumbent, the fact that any president is more widely known than anyone else in the country, the greater impersonality of Congress as an institution, the inability of Congress to develop alternative leaders of great visibility and influence, all combine to strengthen the special attitude toward the president.

Presidents are not unwilling, of course, to exploit this mystique whenever they can. The greater their popularity, presumably the stronger the mandate, and conversely. Because his popular vote in 1960 barely exceeded Nixon's, President Kennedy, like a monarch whose title rests on dubious ancestry, felt he could not lay much of a claim to a popular mandate; he looked to a larger victory in the next election to endow him with that element of popular majesty. After Lyndon Johnson had crushed Barry Goldwater in the election of 1964, he was in a position to call upon the mystique of the mandate to justify his policies. President Nixon's even more overwhelming victory in 1972 gave him grounds for claiming an equally overwhelming mandate.

The myth of the mandate is widely held. It seems largely impervious to the fact that presidential elections reflect a complex mixture of sentiments, beliefs, and preferences that hardly make for a clear-cut referendum on policies. That the mystique survived Nixon's downfall is suggested by a comment made ten months later by George Reedy, a one-time White House aide to President Johnson and a keen observer of the office. Speaking of President Ford, he said, "He does not have that ultimate sanctification of an election.... Having the mystical consent of the people to be their President is almost like being anointed with oil."[22]

United States as a World Power

Neither Nixon's fall nor the debacle of Vietnam altered the fact that the United States is a major world power. The advantages of the president as head of state, commander-in-chief, and executive in charge of foreign and military affairs remained, as do the comparative disadvantages of the Congress. In his first test of presidential discretion on military intervention abroad—the landing of Marines to rescue the *Mayaguez* crew in Cambodian waters—President Ford acted with only minimal and belated Congressional consultation. His conduct was followed by a notable absence of congressional criticism, a solid round of applause from congressional leaders and newspaper editors, and a rise in his public popularity.

Constitutional Doctrine

Although the Constitution does not assign much specific authority to the President (in the way it does to Congress), at least one specific grant, the veto, gives him very substantial power with respect to legislation.[23] The vagueness of the Constitution on other matters has done little to impede the growth of presidential power. Quite the contrary; drawing upon a few cryptic sentences in the Constitution, the Supreme Court has vindicated presidential claims to broad discretionary authority. The justices may of course change their minds, and by doing so they may change constitutional doctrine, but until they do (or the Constitution is amended) the President will retain broad authority on some very important matters.

Thus the Court has defined very generous boundaries to the president's control over foreign relations. In an important case in 1936 the Court drew a distinction between the limited authority conferred by the Constitution on the president in domestic matters, and the 'inherent' authority of the president in foreign affairs, which the Court said is not restricted by the Constitution.[24] Consequently, Congress can delegate to the President a degree of discretionary authority in foreign affairs

---

22. Quoted in the *New York Times*, June 23, 1975, p. 20.

23. One effort to put the relative constitutional power over legislation of Senate, House, and President into quantitative terms led to the conclusion that "the power indices for the three bodies are in the proportion 5:5:2. The indices for a *single* congressman; a *single* senator, and the President are in the proportion 2:9:350." L. S. Shapley and Martin Shubik, "A Method for Evaluating the Distribution of Power in a Committee System," reprinted in Roderick Bell, David V. Edwards, and R. Harrison Wagner, eds., *Political Power, A Reader in Theory and Research* (New York: The Free Press, 1969), 209–213, at p. 211.

24. U.S. v. Curtiss-Wright Corporation et al., 299 U.S. 304 (1936).

that might not be permissible in domestic matters.[25] How broad the President's inherent authority over foreign affairs may be, the Court left unclear; nor did it clarify how far the Congress could go in restricting that 'inherent' authority. Although the opinion was later criticized on this and other grounds, it reflected the tendency of the Court to look sympathetically on a president's claim to discretionary authority in foreign affairs, particularly in the absence of explicit limits imposed by an act of Congress.[26]

Joined to the president's authority over foreign affairs is the 'executive power' ("The executive power shall be vested in a president . . ."), the obligation to "take care that the laws be faithfully executed," and the authority as "commander-in-chief of the army and navy of the United States and of the militia of the several States, when called into the actual services of the United States." Together, these constitute vague but by now substantial constitutional buttresses for presidential discretionary authority. The exact limits remain unclear. Thus when a strike was threatened against the steel industry in the midst of the Korean War in 1952, President Truman seized the country's steel plants in order to avert the strike. He did so with no statutory authority. When the steel companies contested his seizure, his counsel argued that the president's authority derived from his position as bearer of the executive power, commander-in-chief, and officer responsible for the execution of the laws. By a vote of 6 to 3, the Court denied the legality of the steel seizure.[27] The majority was divided, however, as to whether Truman's constitutional theory was wrong (as one justice maintained) or whether existing Congressional legislation (the Taft–Hartley Act governing labor-management relations) had by implication forbidden the drastic action Truman had taken to settle the dispute. One constitutional authority has said of the Court's opinion (denying Truman's constitutional claim) that it "is historic and unworkable."

> If there had been no congressional utterance on the matter, and if none could be procured, it is quite plain that this strike had nevertheless to be avoided in some fashion. There were many precedents, in and out of the Court, for the President's acting on his own regarding matters on which Congress also might act.[28]

---

25. *Ibid.*

26. One critic has written of the case: "It remained for our time to furnish a powerful impetus to presidential expansionism in the shape of some ill-considered dicta in *United States* v. *Curtiss-Wright Export Corp.* . . . Despite searching criticism, Curtiss-Wright has become the foundation of subsequent decisions and has all too frequently been cited for an omnipresent presidential power over foreign relations." In Raoul Berger, *Executive Privilege: A Constitutional Myth* (Cambridge, Mass.: Harvard University Press, 1974), pp. 100–101.

27. Youngstown Sheet and Tube v. Sawyer, 343 U.S. 579 (1952).

28. Charles L. Black, Jr., *Perspectives in Constitutional Law* (Englewood Cliffs, N.J.: Prentice-Hall, 1970), p. 62.

In this instance, then, the Court did intervene to restrain the President. It is important to keep in mind, however, that even though President Truman justified his actions by reference to the Korean War, what he did was assumed to be something quite extraordinary—a move that a president would rarely if ever be likely to make again. In addition, his action exclusively involved Americans on American soil. Even so, as we have seen, the opinions of the justices left the bounds of presidential authority uncertain.

Sometimes, even where the plain words of the Constitution clearly indicate that the president has exceeded his constitutional authority, the judiciary chooses not to restrain the president. Thus, throughout the entire Vietnam war, federal courts were repeatedly invited to consider whether it was unconstitutional for the president to conduct a war in the absence of a congressional declaration of war. The words of the Constitution itself seem clearly to prohibit him from doing so, and a reading of the debates as recorded by James Madison reinforces this interpretation.[29] Some federal courts nonetheless held the war legal on the ground that by its various acts, such as appropriations, Congress *had* given its approval to the war. When one bold U.S. District Court judge declared the bombing of Cambodia in 1973 contrary to explicit and unambiguous congressional enactments, and thereupon issued an injunction against further bombing, his decision was promptly overruled. The Second Circuit Court, to which the matter was immediately appealed, issued a stay that prevented the injunction from being applied, pending reconsideration of the case by a higher court. On further appeal, the Supreme Court took a similar position. The Second Circuit Court, which now reviewed the case on its merits, decided to adopt a familiar practice of the judiciary when it confronts cases too explosive politically for it to dispose of with safety: it held that the question was 'political,' involving issues best left to the president and Congress to decide, and not within the competence of the courts to adjudicate.

The courts have also been reluctant to move in too closely on presidential claims that 'executive privilege' enables a president to refuse to Congress or courts access to information that the chief executive believes must be kept secret for reasons of national security, foreign affairs, or the needs of the office. As he did with many of his other claims to presidential authority, President Nixon finally pressed the doctrine of executive privilege beyond acceptable limits in his efforts

---

29. The language first proposed gave Congress the power to *make* war. On a motion by Madison and Gerry the language was changed to *declare* war, thus "leaving to the Executive the power to repel sudden attacks." Arguments for vesting the power in the Senate (Pinkney) and in the President (Butler) were rejected. *Documents Illustrative of the Formation of the Union of the American States,* Charles C. Tansill, ed. (Washington, D.C.: Government Printing Office, 1927), pp. 561–563.

to keep the famous tapes of his conversations with White House intimates from being made public. As noted in the earlier discussion of the Judicial Branch, Federal District Court Judge John J. Sirica held that the tapes were necessary for a grand jury inquiry into the Watergate conspiracy, and issued a subpoena. The subpoena for the tapes was upheld by the Court of Appeals in a decision that sought to distinguish between legitimate and exaggerated claims to confidentiality.[30] Nixon's demand for secrecy was particularly flagrant, since its effect—presumably also its intent—would have been to deny a federal grand jury evidence bearing directly on criminal wrongdoing by members of Nixon's White House staff. Even if in this extraordinary case the judiciary rejected a claim to executive privilege, the Courts can probably be counted on to respect the claim whenever the president makes a reasonable showing that the consequence might indeed impair the effectiveness of the office.

Absence of Alternative Sources of Leadership

For all these reasons, no other institution has been able to offer much competition for the president's various roles. As a rival, the Supreme Court is obviously disqualified. And the Congress, a recurrent source of hope for those who wish to whittle down the presidency from its superhuman proportions, has not been a strong source of alternative leadership, at least in this century. Central to the concerns of most senators and representatives are the voters of the particular state or district from which they are elected. Obviously no member can claim simply by virtue of election to House or Senate to be as qualified as the president to serve as head of state, party leader, national leader in domestic or foreign crises, or head of the executive-administrative bureaucracy. Unlike the president, no member of Congress can claim that his or her election is a mandate from the whole country. Although a good case can be made that as a body Congress is, in its own way, fully as representative of the country as the president, and might often be more so, 435 members of Congress and 100 senators do not speak with a single voice. To be sure, congressional leaders who were backed by majorities in House and Senate might make a convincing claim to speak for Congress and so to speak for the country as much as does the president. Characteristically, however, congressional leadership is highly fragmented. The particularistic interests of the members, combined with all the special advantages of the president that have been mentioned, have thus made it impossible in this century for congressional leaders to rival the president.

---

30. Raoul Berger, in *Executive Privilege*, pp. 100–101, fn. 6, vigorously attacks the "constitutional myth" of executive privilege. His "Epilogue" discusses the decision on the White House tapes, pp. 348–372.

After President Nixon resigned, the succession of his vice-president, Gerald Ford, who had been a congressman for many years and was well-liked by his colleagues, created hopes that Congress would now successfully assert its claims. But these hopes have remained largely unfulfilled.

Conclusion

Thus even before the events in Nixon's presidency associated with Watergate, impeachment, and resignation had occurred, the presidency had acquired the features of an office that was uncomfortably close to the British monarchy in the eighteenth century:

> Despite the numerous limitations placed upon the royal power since 1660, the king remained the dominant figure in political life. The Constitution endowed the monarch, as chief executive, with control of government patronage and national policy, a share in one or both of which is ever the goal of the aspiring politician. He who would secure place, honour, pension, or other favor must go to Court. He who would influence the great decisions of state must first convince his Majesty. It should be said, however, that in neither of these areas was royal power absolute.... Though the Constitution made no distinction between royal policy and national policy, the king could not carry out decisions strenuously disapproved by a parliamentary majority and devoid of the necessary financial support. On the other hand, to obtain a favour or to implement a design opposed by the monarch was extremely difficult. Nothing but heavy pressure from external circumstances could ordinarily force the king to act against his will. If not absolute, therefore, royal control of policy and patronage was at once so extensive in its scope, so pervasive in its influence, and so concentrated in the king's person that politics inevitably revolved about the throne.[31]

SPECIAL FACTORS   In addition to these more or less enduring causes, a number of special factors also contributed to the growth of the imperial presidency.

Wide Support Since the 1930s

For one thing, the idea of strong presidential leadership gained a large and solid corps of influential advocates who were dazzled by the presidency of Franklin D. Roosevelt. This view gained its most enthusiastic support among liberal Democrats who believed that only a strong Rooseveltian leader could bring about the reforms they felt were necessary.

It is hardly surprising that beliefs about the relationships and rela-

---

31. Archibald S. Foord, *His Majesty's Opposition 1714–1830* (Oxford: Oxford University Press, 1964), pp. 16–17. That the imperial presidency was discernible before the Watergate revelations is suggested by the fact that this analogy appeared in the 1971 edition of this book. And in his excellent book on the presidency in 1970, George Reedy, reflecting his experiences as an aide to President Johnson, wrote eloquently of "The American Monarchy." (*Twilight of the Presidency* [New York: World Book Publishing Co., 1970], Ch. 1 and *passim*.)

tive authority of president, Congress and Supreme Court are strongly influenced by partisan and ideological considerations. For example, when the Supreme Court struck down New Deal legislation in the 1930s, liberals attacked and conservatives defended the Court and its powers. In the 1950s and 1960s, however, when the Court, under the leadership of Chief Justice Warren, made decisions much favored by liberals they became its strongest defenders; conservatives, meanwhile, turned critics.

Much the same thing occurs with views about the president and Congress. Franklin D. Roosevelt and the New Deal converted Democratic liberals into enthusiastic exponents of presidential power; they often saw Congress as much too powerful and obstructive—a stronghold of petty, parochial, reactionary privilege. Conservative Republicans, on the other hand, were more favorable to Congress. They were critical of presidential power and appreciative of Congress' tendency to modify or reject presidential programs of a reformist kind—medical care, for example.

Between Roosevelt and Johnson, the liberal Democratic view gained many adherents. Eminent historians, political scientists, and constitutional lawyers—who, it happened, were generally also liberal Democrats—found "no support in law or in history" for efforts to scale down the president's authority.[32] With a trusted Republican president in the White House, during the two terms of Dwight Eisenhower, (1953–1961) Republicans began moving closer to the prevalent Democratic view. Democrats, who continued to count on taking over the White House in the near future, remained loyal to their conception of a strong president. Thus both liberal Democrats and conservative Republicans often united around the ideal of strong, vigorous national leadership by a president with extensive discretion to act decisively, particularly in foreign and military affairs. Perhaps no one pushed the doctrine further than the Republican candidate for President in 1964, an avowed conservative.

> The Constitution, [Senator Goldwater said] gives the president, not the Congress, the primary war-making powers. . . . There is no question that the President can take military action at any time he feels danger for the country, or, stretching a point, for its position in the world.[33]

Congressional leaders and the media added their voices to the growing consensus. Thus in expanding the imperial presidency both Johnson

---

32. The remark was made by Henry Steele Commager, the eminent historian, referring to a resolution introduced by two conservative Republicans in Congress seeking to prevent President Truman from sending additional American Army divisions to Europe without congressional authorization. Commager's view was shared by Arthur Schlesinger, Jr., who wryly reports what he came to regard as his own transgressions, in *The Imperial Presidency*, p. 139.

33. *Ibid.*, p. 170.

and Nixon were able to capitalize upon a conception of the presidency that was already well established. They regarded Congress with some disdain as a troublesome, complaining, obstructive, and unworthy hindrance to presidential freedom of action. In this, they simply drew upon a common view, cultivated by advocates of a strong presidency who were unwitting and finally regretful accomplices in the construction of the imperial presidency.

The full flowering of the imperial presidency during the Vietnam war, the role of Congress in bringing Nixon to the verge of impeachment, the shocking revelations in the process, his resignation and replacement by a man who had not been elected to the office by the people—these brought about a dramatic shift in attitudes toward presidential authority and the relations between president, Congress, and the courts. Many advocates of expanded presidential power were revolted and frightened by the monstrous office they had helped to create. Many liberals were now much more supportive of congressional authority; many conservatives reverted to their traditional mistrust of executive power. Although both the support for Congress and mistrust of presidential power would doubtless moderate with time, it seems likely that a more long-lasting consequence of the collapse of the imperial presidency is a certain persistent wariness about presidential power—a keen caution, incidentally, not unlike that of the Framers themselves.

Successful Assertion of Presidential Claims

Partly as cause and partly as effect of the wide support that presidential authority came to have, presidents from FDR onward were able to assert successfully claims to discretion that might in other circumstances have been rejected by Court, Congress, influential leaders, or even the electorate. Thus when the North Korean army invaded South Korea in June, 1950, President Truman, without consulting congressional leaders, decided to commit American air and sea forces to the support of South Korea. Two days later he invited leaders from both parties to the White House and informed them of his decision. Neither they, nor Congress as a body, objected. When in the space of a few more days, Truman enlarged the American commitment by dispatching ground forces to engage in what proved to be a large and costly war, he acted again without involving the Congress in his decision. On the advice of his Secretary of State, in fact, he chose not to ask for a congressional joint resolution endorsing his actions but to rely instead on the authority given him by the Constitution as president and commander-in-chief. The Congress never contested his claim, even though popular support for the war waned, and with it his own popularity. The Korean war was ended as it was begun—through an exercise of presidential discretion by Truman's successor, President Eisenhower.

A decade later, Eisenhower and then Kennedy, acting in complete secrecy, supported and planned an invasion of Cuba by Cuban nationals. That it was a complete fiasco gave Kennedy doubts about the wisdom of generals, and might have fostered constructive doubts about presidential discretion. But these were stilled by the great Cuban missile crisis of 1962, which Kennedy dealt with exclusively by consultation within the executive branch. The seeming coolness and toughness of Kennedy's decisions, the withdrawal of the Russians from their risky adventure, and the worldwide relief that nuclear holocaust had been averted, turned the handling of the crisis into an apparently irrefutable argument for presidential discretion in the nuclear age. The precedents were already well-established when President Johnson sent 22,000 American troops into the Dominican Republic in the spring of 1965 without congressional authorization. So the exercise of presidential discretion to fight a war in Southeast Asia did not require much that was new in constitutional theory and practice.

With each of these episodes, the president successfully asserted not only a right to act without congressional authorization, or even consultation, but also a right to make decisions in secret. The right to some degree of secrecy in making certain kinds of military decisions and in the conduct of delicate international negotiations has been universally asserted and generally acknowledged. 'Executive privilege' based upon these claims was hard to contest. Yet secrecy could be, and as evidence was later conclusively to show, was abused. It could be used merely to conceal mistakes or unpopular, even illegal, actions. With the flourishing of discontent in the 1960s,[34] secrecy was also successfully claimed and used in order to investigate—and at times harass—dissidents.

Thus the White House gradually turned into a place where crucial decisions, perhaps involving foreign and military affairs, or perhaps not, were taken in secrecy. Accountability suffered, for a president could not be held accountable to Congress, the public, and the courts, if neither the Congress, the public, nor the courts knew what those decisions were.

Decline of Internal Opposition

The imperial presidency was crowned under Johnson and to an even greater extent under Nixon by a withering away of effective opposition within the president's circle of advisers. Past presidents had deliberately kept open a variety of conflicting channels of communication, or at least made themselves available to diverse sources of advice. As

---

34. See Chapter 26, below.

majority leader in the Senate, Lyndon Johnson himself was a master at consultation, negotiation, and compromising diverse points of view. Under the impact of Vietnam, however, his style became increasingly closed. One after another, critics of his Vietnam policies either left his administration or fell silent.

> ... During the planning on Vietnam, during the time he had been, as a new President, faced with this most terrible dilemma, he had been cautious and reflective. ... But when things went badly, he did not respond that well, and he did not, to the men around him, seem so reasonable. There would be a steady exodus from the White House during 1966 and 1967 of many of the men, both hawks and doves, who had tried to reason with him and tried to affect him on Vietnam. ... He began to sulk, he was not so open, not so accessible, and it was not so easy to talk with him about the problems and difficulties involved in Vietnam. [Secretary of Defense] McNamara's success was in direct proportion to his optimism; as he became more pessimistic the President became reluctant to see him alone. Johnson ... was, sadly, open-minded when things went well, and increasingly close-minded when things went poorly, as they were now about to do.[35]

Later, testifying before a Senate Committee examining executive privilege, one of Johnson's key aides, George Reedy, testified that "discussions around the President ... were 'really monologues in which one man is getting reflections of what he sends out.' "[36]

President Nixon moved along a similar path. A loner by nature, who saw politics in a paranoid 'us-against-them' fashion, Nixon organized his White House staff in a way that had the effect of cutting him off from contacts with persons who might have given him conflicting advice, criticism, contrary views, or new information.[37] Like Johnson, as the crisis of his presidency deepened, Nixon retreated more and more into isolation.

Secrecy

Yet if the presidency moved toward a kind of elective monarchy— a plebiscitary chief executive, in more modern language—the fact that in order to acquire and regain office a president must win elections does impose some limits on his discretionary power. After all, the

---

35. David Halberstam, *The Best and the Brightest* (New York: Random House, 1972), pp. 622–623.

36. Quoted in Schlesinger, *Imperial Presidency*, p. 186.

37. A comparatively sympathetic insider's account of the Nixon White House will be found in William Safire, *Before the Fall*, Part IV, Ch. 5, "Loners Stick Together" and Ch. 6, "Nixon's Haldeman," pp. 272–294. Safire holds that although some symptoms of "groupthink" as described by the psychologist Irving Janis did not apply to Nixon's White House, some did. Thus of the characteristic of groupthink that there is "direct pressure on any member who expresses strong arguments against any of the group stereotypes, illusions or commitments making clear that this type of dissent is contrary to what is expected of all loyal members," Safire comments: "When I objected to the torrent of interviews given by the President in early 1971, arguing that it made him look like a sudden convert to publicity, I was ostracized for three months." pp. 273–274.

Figure 13.1
Watergate and the Decline of Nixon's Popularity

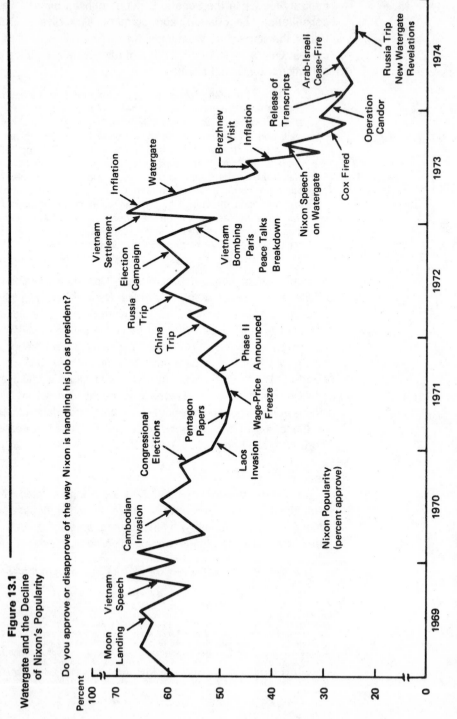

Do you approve or disapprove of the way Nixon is handling his job as president?

Source: Gallup Opinion Index, Report No. 111 (September, 1974), p. 12.

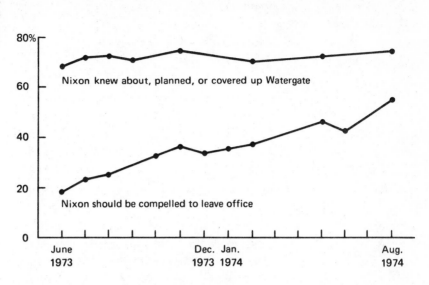

Source: Gallup Opinion Index, Surveys on Watergate, June 1973–August 1974.

essence of Watergate both in its narrow and broader meanings was *secrecy*. As Nixon and his associates obviously knew, the imperial presidency could not long withstand public scrutiny.

Presidents are, of course, very far from being merely agents of public opinion. They have never been so. Unquestionably, they influence it, even manipulate it; and by manipulating public opinion they may win their own re-election—as Nixon sought to do, and to some extent may have succeeded in doing. Yet when a president's actions can be known to the public, when the veil of secrecy is torn aside and discussion, debate, contest, and critical scrutiny take place, a president loses an important part of his capacity for manipulating public opinion for his own purposes.

Most presidents steadily lose public support while in office. Johnson's standing declined so disastrously that he chose not to run a second time. With the Watergate revelations, Nixon's public standing declined (Figure 13.1). The public soon came to believe that Nixon was implicated and a majority then hesitantly concluded that he must leave office (Figure 13.2). As Americans learned the wholly unfamiliar mechanics of impeachment and the nature of the charges, a majority of them moved toward support of impeachment and conviction (Table 13.1).

In the best of circumstances, the conduct of foreign relations will

Table 13.1
Support for
Nixon's Impeachment

Question A: "Now let me ask you first of all, if you think there is enough evidence of possible wrongdoing in the case of President Nixon to bring him to trial before the Senate?"

Question B: "Just from the way you feel now, do you think his actions are serious enough to warrant his being removed from the Presidency?"

	A. Impeachment			B. Removed from office		
	Yes	No	No Opinion	Yes	No	No Opinion
August, 1974	65%	23%	12%	57%	31%	12%
July, 1974	51	30	19	46	38	16
June, 1974	50	32	18	44	41	15
May, 1974	51	31	18	48	37	15
April, 1974	52	33	15	46	42	12

Source: *Gallup Opinion Index*, Report No. 111 (September, 1974), p. 8.

pose special problems for a polyarchy. But what was singularly dangerous about the growth of the imperial presidency under Nixon was the use of presidential power to do illegally and in secret what could never have withstood public scrutiny. Obviously public opinion cannot serve as a check on the president if the public does not know what the president is doing. The public cannot know if Congress does not know. In the final analysis, then, if the drift toward an elective monarchy is to be permanently and not merely temporarily reversed, we must look as much to Congress as to the occupant of the White House.

SUMMARY

1. Placing within the control of a single person all the presidential roles described in Chapter 12 made possible the imperial presidency, which reached its apex under President Nixon with Watergate.

2. In its narrower sense, what has come to be called "Watergate" refers to an illegal break-in sponsored by Nixon's associates, and his subsequent attempt, in violation of law and constitutional obligations, to cover up this illegal action.

3. In its broader sense, "Watergate" refers to the growth of the imperial presidency under Nixon to a point where the office was in danger of being transformed into an elective monarchy or plebiscitary chief executive with powers, often exercised secretly, beyond anything the Framers ever intended and incompatible with the maintenance of a polyarchy. This growth was exhibited in

☐ Foreign affairs, notably in the fourteen-month secret bombing of Cambodia.
☐ Domestic actions, notably in the covert attempt to create a national political machine, and in the secret cover-up of Watergate.

4. When President Nixon's secret, illegal, and unconstitutional actions were revealed, the Congress, supported by public opinion, moved toward a certain, nearly unanimous, decision to impeach and convict, and thus to remove him from office. To avoid being removed in this way, Nixon resigned.

5. Among the enduring causes for the growth of the imperial presidency are:

☐ The comparative advantages of the single executive.
☐ The mystique of the presidential mandate.
☐ The position of the United States as a world power.
☐ Constitutional doctrine, particularly as to the 'war powers' of the president.
☐ The absence of alternative sources of leadership, notably the Congress.

6. Among causes for the growth of the imperial presidency that may prove to be special and transitory were:

☐ Wide support since the 1930s for the idea of a 'strong' president.
☐ The successful assertion on repeated occasions of presidential claims to broad discretionary powers.
☐ The decline of internal opposition within the administrations of both Johnson and Nixon.
☐ The successful use of secrecy to conceal the nature and significance of important presidential actions.

14 CONGRESS AS REPRESENTATIVE: THE DESIGN

If the president has become the main source of drive, energy, and leadership in the American political system, what functions does the Congress perform?

THE CONGRESS AND THE CONVENTION: AGREEMENTS

The design of the Congress presented the Convention not only with some of its easiest problems but also with a few of its thorniest ones. That there must be a legislative body was a matter beyond debate. It must consist of two houses. One of these must represent 'the people.' The national legislature must have power to make national law. This body would be the chief if not, in fact, the exclusive source of national law, other than the Constitution itself. It would serve as a check on the president. These propositions were not seriously contested.

The minimum functions of the Congress were three: to make national laws, to represent 'the people,' and to check and control the power of the chief executive. These functions were obviously interrelated. Given the political ideas prevalent in the United States and among the Convention delegates the only legitimate source of new laws, other than amendments to the Constitution, would be the legislature. Most of the delegates doubtless took it for granted that policy-making would consist almost entirely of law-making, that proposals for new laws would originate in the legislature, which would examine these proposals, act on them and, if it so decided, give them the necessary stamp of legality. To make policy was to make law; to make law was to legislate; and only a legislature could legislate.

Essentially, legitimacy was conferred on a legislature in the law-making process because of its representative character. The legislature was to represent, to stand for, to serve on behalf of the citizens of the United States.

That the Congress should (and would) also serve as a check on the chief executive followed from the general principle of partitioning power by pitting one part of government against another: "by so contriving the interior structure of the government as that its several constituent parts may, by their mutual relations, be the means of keeping each other in their proper places," as the authors of *The Federalist* were to put it.[1]

While the delegates no doubt took this checking role of the Congress for granted, they said surprisingly little about it at the Convention. In the light of later developments, this is a curious omission. It may be accounted for in two ways. *First,* the delegates saw the legislature as the most dynamic and most dangerous branch; hence they were preoccupied—one might almost say obsessed—with the problem of building adequate restraints on that body. When they spoke of the relations between chief executive and Congress, their concern was invariably with the role of executive as a check on the Congress, not the other way around.

Second, as we saw in Chapter 11, throughout most of the Convention it appeared that the president was going to be elected by the Congress. This in itself, it was assumed, would provide a powerful check by legislature on executive; hence the delegates may have assumed that further discussion of the adequacy of Congress's power to check the president was unnecessary. Indeed, the problem, in their eyes, was quite the opposite; if Congress elected the president, would this not give the legislature too much control over the executive, and, conversely, the executive too little independence of the legislature? In the end, as we know, they solved this problem by creating an executive elected independently of the Congress.

DISAGREEMENTS   Yet if the delegates to the Constitutional Convention were evidently in substantial agreement that the national legislature they proposed to create would, at a minimum, make national laws, represent the people of the United States, and help control the chief executive, they did not agree on other matters. Nor could the delegates to the Convention accurately foresee the shape of future problems as the United States developed into a great nation and then a world power.

Of the questions left unsettled by the Convention, two are particularly important.

---

1. Hamilton et al., *The Federalist* (New York: Modern Library, n.d.), No. 51, p. 336.

☐ *First,* even if it be assumed that Congress is to 'represent the people' in some sense, should it represent each citizen equally, or should some minorities or 'interests' be given extra protection by means of extra weight in the national legislature?

☐ *Second,* if the Congress is to make laws and to check the executive, how far should its control over policy and appointments extend?

I propose to explore the first of these questions in this chapter, and the second in Chapter 16.

MAJORITIES IN THE HOUSE, MINORITIES IN THE SENATE

Like everyone else who has ever seriously examined the problems of 'representing the people,' the Convention delegates were confronted by some exceedingly difficult questions. Their compromises helped to shape the American political tradition, but their conflicting viewpoints persist within that tradition down to the present day.

The House: Representing Majorities

The House of Representatives, as Roger Sherman of Connecticut suggested it be named, presented only minor difficulties. Although there was scattered opposition to the idea that one house of Congress was to be elected by the people, the proposal passed early and easily and was never subsequently contested. Yet it seems to have been widely assumed at the Convention that the House of Representatives would be the driving force in the system. It was thought that the people's representatives would be turbulent and insistent; they would represent majorities and would be indifferent to the rights of minorities. The people would be the winds driving the ship of state and their representatives would be the sails, swelling with every gust. Gouverneur Morris evidently reflected the dominant view when he remarked that "the first branch, originating from the people, will ever be subject to *precipitancy, changeability, and excess.*"[2]

Given their agreement on the need to partition power, particularly the power of a majority and its representatives, it followed that the 'popular branch' (like every other branch) must be hedged in by constraints: by the Constitution itself, the president, the courts, the states, and, not least, the other house of Congress.

The Senate: Protecting Minorities

In the composition of the other house, the Convention faced one of its most difficult problems. It arrived at a compromise solution that a

---

2. *Documents Illustrative of the Formation of the Union of American States,* Charles C. Tansill, ed. (Washington, D.C.: Government Printing Office, 1927), p. 838. The quotation is from the notes of Robert Yates; Madison recorded substantially the same words, p. 319.

majority of the delegates probably opposed in principle but had to accept out of expediency. The problem had two sides, one intellectual and the other political. Although the second has been much emphasized, the first has been almost ignored. Yet it goes to the heart of a problem still debated in the United States.

The intellectual problem turns on this question: Is it possible to protect minorities by giving them a larger share of representatives in a legislature than they would be entitled to simply by their numbers, without at the same time creating a potential injustice to other minorities or to majorities? The Convention wrestled with this problem, as Americans have ever since; but it cannot be said that the Framers came up with an intellectually defensible solution.

Morris' solution. Gouverneur Morris, as might be expected, saw the question as a straightforward one of protecting the rich minority from the 'people' and vice versa. What qualities, he asked, are necessary in the second branch of the Congress if it is to check the excesses of the people's representatives:

> ... *Abilities* and *virtue,* are equally necessary in both branches. Something more then is now wanted. 1. the checking branch must have a personal interest in checking the other branch, one interest must be opposed to another interest. Vices as they exist, must be turned against each other. 2. It must have great personal property, it must have the aristocratic spirit; it must love to lord it through pride. . . . 3. It should be independent. . . . To make it independent, it should be for life. . . . By thus combining and setting apart, the aristocratic interest, the popular interest will be combined against it. There will be a mutual check and mutual security. 4. An independence for life, involves the necessary permanency. . . .[3]

In this blunt view of the inherent conflict of social classes, 'the rich' versus 'the rest,' 'the aristocratic interest' versus 'the popular interest,' Morris may have overstated his case, but he undoubtedly reflected a common view.

Madison's solution. In a masterly analysis marked by his customary moderation, Madison espoused a similar point of view; but he rejected Morris' solution. Madison pointed out that legislature must not only protect the people against their rulers; it must also protect them against their own transient impulses or a want of information as to their true interests. Without such protection, the people could produce harm to themselves or to the fundamental rights or interests of a minority. The essential question was how to guard against the danger that a coalition of interests large enough to comprise a majority would oppress the

---

3. *Ibid.,* pp. 319–320.

minority. And how was this to be done on 'republican principles'—in a republic where, after all, the legislature was to be elected by the people?[4]

Madison posed the problem clearly. Because the popular branch might act out of impulse, ignorance, or interest "to commit injustice on the minority," the second branch must be so constituted as to "aid on such emergencies, the preponderance of justice by throwing its weight into that scale."[5]

But how was the second branch to be made up? Here was the nub of the difficulty. If the second branch were elected by the people (as James Wilson, the most persistent advocate of a democratic republic, proposed), then it would represent the same interests as the other house and would hardly serve as a check on it. Elbridge Gerry of Massachusetts, worried by the fact that farmers vastly outnumbered businessmen, observed: "To draw both branches from the people will leave no security to the latter [commercial] interest; the people being chiefly composed of the landed interest, and erroneously supposing that the other interests are adverse to it."[6] What interests were the senators supposed to represent? Why should *these* particular interests be given special weight? And how were senators to be chosen to represent these interests? Although the first two questions were logically prior, debate turned almost entirely on the last question. Yet it is the first two that were—and are—most troublesome.

WHICH MINORITIES? Should a legislature represent interests or individuals? It cannot do both. For if interests are to be given equal representation, then individuals must be denied equal representation. There is no way out of this dilemma. And why should some interests be given more power than others? It might be argued that unless a certain interest were given extra numbers in the legislature, it would be unjustly treated by a legislative majority. (This was the essence of Morris' and Madison's argument.) Yet, in this solution to the problem of majority 'tyranny,' there are two exceedingly serious difficulties.

First, since almost any minority might be unjustly treated by a majority, it would seem to follow that *every* minority should be overrepresented—doctors, lawyers, college professors, businessmen, trade unionists, cotton farmers, wheat farmers, tobacco farmers, Catholics, Jews, Negroes, 'Wasps' (White Anglo-Saxon Protestants). We quickly arrive at an absurdity. Morris and Madison were rescued from this absurdity because of the simplicity of prevailing conceptions of the inter-

---

4. *Ibid.,* pp. 279–281.
5. *Ibid.,* p. 281.
6. *Ibid.,* p. 170.

ests of the country in 1787. Charles Cotesworth Pinckney suggested that "the people of the U.S. may be divided into three classes—*professional men . . .; commercial men . . .; the landed interest. . . ."*[7] This simple scheme was reasonable in 1787; it would be unacceptable today.

Second, if an interest is given special weight, what is to prevent it from using its added power unjustly toward the majority? If a minority has enough representation to prevent a majority from acting unjustly toward it, it will also have enough representation to prevent a majority from acting justly. Are we to suppose that minorities invariably act justly, and majorities never? Neither Morris nor Madison made such an untenable assumption. If, as Morris said, the rich always have and always will "strive to establish their dominion and enslave the rest," what would happen if the rich were given enough power to veto the actions of a majority that wanted to enact, say, a progressive income tax? Would the rich not use their power in naked self-interest to prevent themselves from being taxed more heavily than others? Or suppose that the rich are mistreating their employees: Is a legislative majority to be prevented from passing laws regulating employer-employee relations, simply because the rich are opposed?

The Permanent Interests?

In conceiving of the representation of interests in different houses, men like Morris were reverting, probably without being aware of it, to a medieval concept of a parliament that represented the estates of the realm. In Britain there was the House of Lords for church and aristocracy, the House of Commons for the commoners—though in actual practice in 1787 only a tiny percentage of adult males could vote in elections to that House. Within two years, the king of France was to summon the Estates-General, an outdated assemblage that had not met since 1614, which consisted of the First Estate, or lower clergy, the Second Estate or nobility, and the Third Estate or the 'people.' But the Third Estate lost no time in facilitating a revolution that forever ended the Estates-General in France.

The problem of the Convention was that while some delegates may have conceived of a legislature as somehow representing 'interests' in different chambers, in the United States the various 'permanent' interests could not be as easily identified for constitutional purposes as the medieval estates. The Americans, after all, consisted almost entirely of small farmers plus a handful of merchants and artisans. There was no titled aristocracy, as in Britain, no churchly estate, as in France and Sweden. When one got right down to the heart of the matter, by European standards Americans were all commoners. Consequently, although

---

7. *Ibid.,* pp. 271–272.

the familiar distinction between the House of Lords and the House of Commons unquestionably influenced the thinking of the Convention about a second chamber, an American version of the House of Lords had to be . . . another House of Commons.

The concrete proposals presented to the Convention were, therefore, tame. Some delegates may have thought that property qualifications could be made higher for senators; but the point was not pressed, and in the end no property qualifications were set by the Convention for any public office. Some delegates may have envisioned special property qualifications for those who elected the senators, yet no such requirement was laid down. Note that in the speech of Madison's quoted above, the only specific proposals he makes for insuring the kind of Senate he had in mind is that senators be elected for a long term—nine years—at a relatively advanced age. As it turned out, their term is for six years and the 'advanced' age is 30—six years younger than Madison himself when he made the speech.

What happened, then, to the idea of representing interests? Probably two things. *First,* however attractive the idea might have seemed abstractly, concrete proposals to overrepresent the rich—this was the only interest that anyone seemed to have in mind—were bound to end in obvious absurdities, fatal unpopularity, or both. In the America of 1787, the rich were not a traditional and legitimate aristocracy; they were never to become so. Even in England, by 1787 it is doubtful whether the peerage could have gained by force or persuasion the special place in the British constitutional system it had inherited from the past. More than a century would elapse before the ancient power of the peerage over legislation would, for all practical purposes, finally be eliminated.

Second, the whole question of the composition of the Senate was abruptly changed from the problem of representing a special economic or class interest, as Morris and Madison had posed it, to the problem of representing a very different sort of interest: that of the smaller states.

States?

Madison and Morris fiercely opposed equal representation in the Senate for the smaller states and fought for representation according to population. It soon became clear however that their solution might well wreck the whole scheme for a new Constitution; they were, in a sense, defeated by their own arguments. Having argued that the Senate should protect the minority interest against the majority interest, how were they to meet the arguments of delegates who contended that the smaller states, as an outnumbered minority, needed special protection from the more populous states? "Besides the Aristocratic and other interests, which ought to have the means of defending themselves," William Johnson of Connecticut reasoned, "the States have their interests as such, and are equally entitled to like means."[8]

Wilson, the unswerving democrat (and happily for him, a delegate from a large state), encountered no difficulty in disposing of Johnson's argument on abstract democratic principles.

> ...Such an equality will enable the minority to control in all cases whatsoever, the sentiments and interests of the majority.... It would be in the power then of less than ⅓ to overrule ⅔ whenever a question should happen to divide the states in that manner. Can we forget for whom we are forming a government? Is it for *men,* or for the imaginary beings called *States?*[9]

But Madison found it more difficult to counter the small-state argument with a straightforward appeal to the principle of political equality among all citizens; because only a few days earlier, as we have just seen, he had asserted the desirability of using the Senate to give minorities special protection from majorities. He therefore combined an appeal to the majority principle with a pragmatic argument that there was in fact no small-state interest different from the interests of the large states.[10]

This argument could equally well be turned against the position Madison himself had taken four days earlier in defense of minority rights against a majority. Perhaps it is for this reason that from this day forward he spoke for representation by population in the Senate, and not as one fearful of majorities.

In the end, as we know, the small states won. They did not win because they ever persuaded the great architects of the Constitution—like Madison and Morris, and least of all Wilson—that the small-state position was just. For these men never were converted. As so often happens in political affairs, the small states won simply because of their bargaining power. To Madison, Morris, and Wilson, better a Constitution that granted equal representation to states in the Senate than no Constitution at all. The bargain was struck. It has held ever since.

SUMMARY   1. In designing the Constitution, the Framers assumed that the House of Representatives, being popularly elected, would speak for popular majorities.

2. Given their commitment to partitioning power, they insisted that the House, like all the other institutions of government, must be hedged in by constraints, lest majorities become tyrannical.

---

8. *Ibid.,* p. 297.
9. *Ibid.,* p. 307.
10. *Ibid.,* pp. 310–311.

3. The Senate, on the other hand, was to be a bulwark for the protection of minorities.

4. Although there was general agreement that the Senate should represent different 'interests' from the House, there was vast disagreement over the application of this principle.

☐ Some delegates to the Convention thought that the Senate should protect the interests of the rich minority against the encroachments of popular majorities.

☐ These delegates were influenced by a medieval conception of a parliament that represented the 'estates' of the realm.

☐ Other delegates, including many from the smaller states, saw the Senate purely and simply as a protection for the interests of the smaller states.

☐ A number of delegates, reasoning from the principle of partitioning power, agreed that the Senate should represent interests different from the House but were at a loss to define what these interests ought to be.

5. Because of the threat by the delegates from the small states to reject a Constitution without equal state representation in the Senate, their demand was finally accepted. Though many delegates from larger states felt that equal representation of the states was bad in principle, they compromised simply in order to make the Constitution acceptable to all the states.

15 CONGRESS AS REPRESENTATIVE: PERFORMANCE

If the House was intended to represent the people and the Senate the states, to what extent has Congress fulfilled these expectations? Indeed, what, or whom, does Congress represent?

To answer these questions is no simple matter. It will help to distinguish between two aspects of representation. *First,* different citizens may be unequally represented because the boundaries of legislative constituencies—states in the case of senators, and congressional districts in the case of congressmen—operate so as to overrepresent some parts of the electorate and to underrepresent others. *Second,* as we saw in Chapter 5, different citizens may be unequally influential with respect to their representatives because they have different political incentives, skills, or resources: money, information, friendship, access, social standing, and the like.

THE SENATE: PROTECTOR OF WHICH MINORITIES?

Small States?

Consider the first of these problems. In the Senate the people of the smaller states are of course overrepresented and the people of the larger states are underrepresented; that, after all, was precisely the point of the compromise. Yet the degree of over- and underrepresentation has increased since 1787. According to the Census of 1790, the free population of Virginia was eight times larger than that of Delaware. In 1960, the population of New York was almost seventy-five times that of Alaska; the population of California fifty-five times that of Nevada. As Table 15.1 shows, in the period 1968–72, twenty-five states with 17 percent of the electorate furnished half the senators, while the eight largest

Table 15.1
Advantage and
Disadvantage in the
Senate: 1968–1972

State	State Electorate (000)	Percentages of Total Electorate	Cumulative Percentage	Index of Advantage[a]
1. Vermont	71	.10%	.10%	19.05
2. Alaska	96	.14	.24	14.09
3. Wyoming	142	.21	.45	9.53
4. Nevada	148	.22	.67	9.14
5. North Dakota	220*	.33	1.00	6.15
6. Delaware	230	.34	1.34	5.88
7. Hawaii	241*	.36	1.70	5.61
8. South Dakota	306	.45	2.15	4.42
9. Idaho	310	.46	2.61	4.36
10. Montana	315	.47	3.08	4.29
11. New Hampshire	324*	.48	3.56	4.17
12. Utah	374*	.55	4.11	3.62
13. New Mexico	378	.56	4.67	3.58
14. Arizona	408*	.60	5.27	3.32
15. Rhode Island	413	.61	5.88	3.27
16. Maine	421	.62	6.50	3.21
17. Nebraska	569	.84	7.34	2.38
18. Arkansas	635	.94	8.28	2.13
19. Mississippi	646	.96	9.24	2.09
20. South Carolina	672	.99	10.23	2.01
21. West Virginia	732	1.08	11.31	1.85
22. Kansas	872	1.29	12.60	1.55
23. Oregon	921	1.36	13.96	1.47
24. Colorado	926	1.37	15.33	1.46
25. Maryland	956*	1.41	16.74	1.41
26. Oklahoma	1005	1.49	18.23	1.35
27. Kentucky	1038	1.53	19.76	1.30
28. Alabama	1051	1.55	21.31	1.29
29. Washington	1067*	1.58	22.89	1.27
30. Louisiana	1085	1.60	24.49	1.25
31. Connecticut	1089*	1.61	26.10	1.24
32. Tennessee	1164	1.72	27.82	1.16
33. Georgia	1179	1.74	29.56	1.15
34. Iowa	1203	1.78	31.34	1.12
35. Missouri	1284*	1.90	33.24	1.05
36. Wisconsin	1339*	1.98	35.22	1.01
37. Virginia	1396	2.06	37.28	.97
38. North Carolina	1473	2.18	39.46	.92
39. Florida	1675*	2.47	41.93	.81
40. Minnesota	1732	2.56	44.49	.78
41. Indiana	1738*	2.57	47.06	.78
42. Massachusetts	2371	3.56	50.62	.57
43. New Jersey	2792	4.13	54.75	.48
44. Ohio	3151*	4.66	59.41	.43
45. Michigan	3407	5.03	64.44	.40
46. Texas	3414	5.04	69.48	.40
47. Pennsylvania	3644*	5.39	74.87	.37
48. Illinois	4608	6.81	81.68	.29
49. New York	5905*	8.73	90.41	.23
50. California	6492*	9.59	100.00	.21

50 percent of the Senate

50 percent of the electorate

Total electorate: 67,628,000. Mean State Electorate: 1,352,560.

$$* \text{ Index of advantage} = \frac{\text{mean state electorate}}{\text{actual state electorate}} = \frac{1,352,560}{\text{actual state electorate}}$$

* 1968

Source: U.S. Bureau of the Census, *Statistical Abstract 1974*, Table 686, p. 427.

states with more than half the electorate had only sixteen senators out of one hundred.

Yet Madison's judgment has been confirmed. The great conflicts have not been between large states and small states. Although there have been many lines of political conflict in the United States, differences between large states and small states have surely been the least important of these. The tariff, slavery, civil rights, monetary and fiscal problems, taxation, regulation of business, welfare programs, foreign and military policies—none has produced conflicts between large states and small states. It would be difficult to demonstrate, therefore, that the small states have *needed* their extra influence in the Senate in order to protect themselves against the large states.

Other Minorities?

If the Senate has not had to protect the small states, has it, however, served to protect other minorities? If so, are these particular minorities entitled to special protection? Although the problem is a thorny one, the answer to the first question is probably yes; the answer to the second is, I believe, very much more debatable. Three preliminary observations are in order.[1]

First, the argument for equal representation of states in the Senate frequently seems to rest upon a false psychological equation; small states are equated with small interests and small interests with small or defenseless persons. Our humanitarian desires to protect relatively defenseless persons from aggression by more powerful individuals are thereby invoked on behalf of small states. But states consist of people; and it is the interests of people we are concerned with. What we need to know, therefore, is what sorts of people are benefited or handicapped by equal representation in the Senate.

I assume that we do not wish to endorse the principle that all small interest groups must have a veto on policy. For then we could never specify any situations short of unanimity in which a lawmaking majority should be permitted to act. And thus we would make it impossible not merely to operate under republican principles, but to govern at all. The first to exercise their vetoes might be the gangsters, the murderers, the thieves—in short, the criminal population. The rest of us would not be far behind: capitalists, laborers, farmers, even college professors, the exploiters and the exploited, the social and the antisocial, the sweatshop operator, the labor racketeer, the income tax evader, and a thousand other groups, would exercise their veto on public policy.

Second, we must also avoid the fallacy of assuming that if the Senate represents or overrepresents some minorities situated in certain geographical areas in the United States, it necessarily represents *all*

1. The following discussion is adapted from Robert A. Dahl, *A Preface to Democratic Theory* (Chicago: University of Chicago Press, 1956), pp. 113–118.

minorities situated in those areas. This is clearly false. There are minorities within minorities. The dominant regional group may be represented in the Senate while the subordinate regional minority is excluded. Hence a Senate veto may merely preserve or extend the control of the dominant regional group over the subordinate minority. For example, blacks in the South and migrant farm laborers of the West are clearly not the minorities who have benefited from equal representation in the Senate. Moreover, even in a situation of full political equality, a regional minority protected by equal representation of geographical units in a legislative body would be a majority in its own area; and the defeated minority in that region would be unprotected by equal representation. Actually, even if the minority in the region consisted of individuals with preferences like those of the majority in the whole electorate, equal representation by geographical areas would, paradoxically, strip this regional minority of protection in all cases where positive government action was required to prevent the regional majority from tyrannizing over it.

Third, equal representation by geographical units overrepresents some minorities concentrated in sparsely populated areas but underrepresents those concentrated in heavily populated areas. Moreover, to the extent that a minority is not geographically concentrated, it receives no protection as such from equal state representation. In a society in which all minorities were distributed in equal proportions among the voters of every state, no minority would receive any protection per se from equal state representation. Why, then, this special tenderness toward minorities concentrated geographically in sparse areas?

In sum:

☐ The only minorities protected by equal state representation as such are geographical minorities concentrated in sparse areas.

☐ But some of the minorities in these areas are left unprotected; indeed, representatives of the dominant group may actually use their overrepresentation in the Senate to bar action intended to guard the unprotected.

☐ Minorities in heavily populated areas are underrepresented in a system of equal state representation.

☐ The conclusion seems inevitable that the benefits and disadvantages flowing from equal state representation in the Senate are allocated in an entirely arbitrary fashion and cannot be shown to follow from any general principle.

**THE HOUSE:
REPRESENTATIVES
OF THE MAJORITY?**

What then of the House? How has it represented the people, or a majority of the people?

There is lurking in these innocent questions an implicit assumption that we know what it means for a member of Congress to 'represent the people.' The fact is, however, that the notion is shot through with problems. Should a representative seek to represent the people of his or her district, or the people of the United States? A majority only, or majorities and minorities? Opening up a classic debate, should the representative try to act as a *trustee,* "a free agent [who] follows what he considers right or just—his convictions or principles, the dictates of his conscience," or a *delegate* of his constituents who seeks to discover and follow his constituents' views.[2] These are matters on which there has been enormous debate, and it would take us too far afield to explore the issues here.[3]

Yet it seems clear that if the principles of political equality and consent are to have any concrete meaning at all, voters should be able to select representatives who will reflect their views or values in legislative decisions. Certainly it would be incompatible with political equality and consent if the decisions of the legislature did not embody the basic preferences of a majority of the people but instead the preferences of some minority, whether that minority be the elected legislators themselves, other officials, or interest groups. In this day and age, even representatives, who look upon themselves as trustees for the best interests of the voters in their districts, and not simply as their agents or delegates, would have to agree that the voters ought to replace them in the next election if, upon reflection, they were to conclude that their representative had not acted in accordance with their best interests. As we have already seen, the Framers themselves assumed pretty much without argument that the House would reflect the preferences of a majority of the people.

Standards of Performance

Starting from this simple assumption, what standards can we use to judge the performance of the House of Representatives? Many people, including some of the justices of the Supreme Court, evidently believe that the principles of political equality and consent would best be met if the House of Representatives met the following requirements:

1. *One person, one vote:* The country must be divided into districts of approximately equal population (or voters).
2. *Single member districts with plurality elections:* Each district must elect one and only one representative. The candidate who gains the most votes (in American parlance, a plurality) should win the seat.

---

2. Heinz Eulau, John C. Wahlke, William Buchanan, and Leroy C. Ferguson, "The Role of Representative: Some Empirical Observations on the Theory of Edmund Burke," *American Political Science Review,* 53 (September, 1959), 742–756, at pp. 749–750.

3. See Hanna Fenichel Pitkin, *The Concept of Representation* (Los Angeles: University of California Press, 1967). See also Hanna Fenichel Pitkin, ed., *Representation* (New York: Atherton Press, 1969); and J. Roland Pennock and John W. Chapman, eds., *Representation (Nomos X)* (New York: Atherton Press, 1968).

3. *Popular control:* When a representative votes on legislative matters, thanks to elections his or her vote should pretty generally, and certainly over the long run, correspond with the views of a majority of the people (or voters) in the district.
4. *Legislative majority rule:* The House should make its decisions by majority vote of its members.

It may come as a blow to one who adheres to these standards to discover that the House of Representatives has not regularly conformed with these principles; what is more, even if it did, it would not necessarily insure political equality, majority rule, and minority representation.

ONE PERSON, ONE VOTE   The Constitution, you may recall, does not require that House members be elected by districts; it leaves "the Times, Places and Manner of holding Elections for . . . Representatives" to the state legislatures (Article I, Section 4). In practice the states have been divided by the state legislatures into a number of districts equal, normally, to the number of representatives. Moreover, the same system exists for state legislatures themselves: the state legislators are also elected in districts. Now the obvious consequence of this arrangement is that with changes in population in the states, the heavy hand of history may produce growing disparity between the number of citizens in one district and another. This is what happened to the House of Representatives.

Originally, as we have seen, most of the population of the United States lived in rural areas. As the urban dwellers increased and finally outnumbered the rural population, the number of representatives they were granted in the state legislatures failed to increase at the same rate. The explanation is simple. Reapportionment was up to the state legislators. Any reapportionment could only reduce the proportion of legislators elected by the rural population. The existing state legislatures were already controlled or strongly influenced by representatives drawn from rural districts. Quite naturally, therefore, the rural representatives who dominated the state legislatures were unwilling to pass bills providing for the reduction of their own power through reapportionment. Hence the House of Representatives came to overrepresent the rural and small-town areas at the expense first of the cities and later of the suburbs. What this overrepresentation of the rural and small-town areas meant in practice was that the House somewhat overrepresented what might loosely be called 'conservative' and 'small-town' attitudes.

Paradoxically, while population changes were making the House less responsive to cities and suburban areas, the same changes were making the Senate more so. For few states lacked one or more big cities and extensive suburban areas; in every state, the rural and small-town population shrank. By 1950, 80 percent of the people in the Northeast lived in urban areas; in the West 70 percent; in the North Central region, 64 percent; and in the least urbanized region, the South, just under half.[4] Consequently, while a great many senators had to be sensitive to the concerns of their urban voters, a substantial number of members of the House could safely ignore the cities and the suburbs.[5]

On the whole, then, far from being a turbulent forum for the people, "ever subject to precipitancy, changeability, and excess," the House had become a slightly more conservative institution than the Senate or the presidency. Its members were more inclined to share the views of farmers and small-town folk than those of the working classes in the cities or the white-collar workers and executives in the suburbs; more likely to think nostalgically of a United States that had disappeared some generations ago than to press vigorously for solutions to problems of the urban America that now existed.

On a number of occasions, citizens in various states appealed to the Supreme Court to remedy the inequalities in representation in state legislatures and in the House of Representatives. But, until 1962, the Court steadily refused to intervene, on the ground that inequitable representation was not a judicial matter but was a 'political question' that could only be remedied by the appropriate political bodies.[6] Because the legislative majorities that controlled these bodies would only decrease their own power by reapportionment, naturally they refused to approve of laws or constitutional amendments that would have remedied the situation. Consequently the position of the Court meant, in effect, that nothing could be done. Beginning in 1962, however, the Court reversed its traditional position in a series of historic decisions that laid down the requirement of 'one man, one vote' not only for both houses of all state legislatures but for the United States House of Representatives itself.[7] In the ensuing years, reapportionment by state legislatures and courts brought the House ever closer to districts of equal population.

SINGLE-MEMBER DISTRICTS WITH PLURALITY ELECTIONS   Will apportioning the House into districts with equal populations—the principle of one person, one vote—insure political equality and majority rule? Not necessarily. For even if every representative were to speak for his constituents' views (a problem we shall examine in a

---

4. M. Gendell and H. L. Zetterberg, eds., *A Sociological Almanac for the United States* (New York: Bedminster Press, 1961), Table 86, p. 83.

5. See Lewis A. Froman, Jr., *Congressmen and their Constituencies* (Chicago: Rand McNally, 1963), "Why the Senate Is More Liberal than the House," ch. 6.

6. See, for example, *Colegrove* v. *Green*, 328 U.S. 549 (1946).

7. The leading decisions were *Baker* v. *Carr*, 369 U.S. 186 (1962), *Wesberry* v. *Sanders*, 376 U.S. 1 (1946), and *Reynolds* v. *Sims* 377 U.S. 533 (1964). For a further discussion, see Robert A. Goldwin, ed., *Representation and Misrepresentation* (Chicago: Rand McNally, 1968).

Figure 15.1
Votes and Seats in Single-
Member Districts of a
Hypothetical Legislature

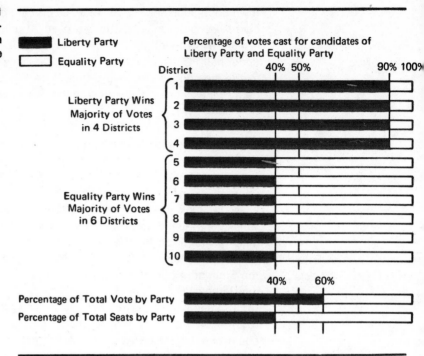

Figure 15.1
Votes and Seats in Single-
Member Districts of a
Hypothetical Legislature

Liberty Party
Equality Party

Percentage of votes cast for candidates of
Liberty Party and Equality Party

Liberty Party Wins
Majority of Votes
in 4 Districts

Equality Party Wins
Majority of Votes
in 6 Districts

Percentage of Total Vote by Party
Percentage of Total Seats by Party

moment), *single-member districts with plurality elections neither insure
majority rule nor minority representation.*

An extreme example will readily show why such a system cannot
insure majority rule. For the sake of simplicity, let us assume that a
legislature has one hundred representatives elected from a voting population of one million, divided into ten equal districts, each with one
hundred thousand voters. Suppose that 60 percent of the voters cast
their ballots for candidates of the Liberty Party and 40 percent for candidates of the Equality Party. Imagine further that the partisans of Liberty
are heavily concentrated in four districts, while the partisans of Equality
are somewhat more dispersed among six. The partisans of Liberty,
though a decisive majority of voters, would win only a minority of seats,
while the partisans of Equality, though only a minority of voters, would
win a decisive majority of seats (Figure 15.1).

Yet if single-member districts with plurality elections do not insure
majority rule, neither do they guarantee minority representation. Suppose that instead of being concentrated, the partisans of Liberty were
evenly dispersed over all ten districts. Since 60 percent of the voters
in every district would vote for the party of Liberty, it would win 100
percent of the seats. You will notice that a party with a bare 51 percent

of the voters could win 100 percent of the seats and thereby deny any representation to 49 percent of the voters! The distortion grows even worse when there are more than two parties. Suppose three parties split the vote 34 percent–33 percent–33 percent. Then the party with 34 percent of the vote *could* win every seat—even though two-thirds of the voters had cast their ballots for another candidate, and might prefer either of the losers to the winner. As the number of parties increases, so of course does the potential of this system for absurdity.

Because the single-member district with plurality elections cannot insure either majority rule or minority representation, a number of polyarchies (including such sturdy examples as Switzerland, the Netherlands, and all of the Scandinavian countries) have rejected this solution and have instead adopted systems of proportional representation (PR). PR schemes are designed to insure a close correspondence between the percentage of votes cast for the candidates of a given party and the percentages of seats the party wins. Many Americans oppose PR because of fears that PR would produce a multiplicity of parties—as, indeed, it probably would. We shall return to this point in later chapters. For most Americans, however, the single-member district is probably little more than an article of faith. Even the eminent justices of the Supreme Court failed to note that with single-member districts and plurality elections, merely to establish districts of equal size does not really guarantee 'one man, one vote.' For as our examples have shown, voters who are in the majority can receive a disproportionately larger payoff in seats than voters who are in the minority. It is arguable, then, that the principle of one person, one vote logically requires the introduction of PR. Incidentally, it is worth noting that nothing in the Constitution definitely prescribes single-member districts nor prohibits states from choosing representatives under a PR system.

POPULAR CONTROL   Achieving satisfactory electoral arrangements may prove to be far easier than insuring that representatives reflect the views of constituents. For this is less a problem of mechanics than of information and incentives.

Three Conditions

Suppose for the moment that electoral arrangements provided satisfactorily for one person, one vote and distributed seats to majorities and minorities in ways we regard as fair. What further conditions would be required to insure that a representative's vote on legislative issues corresponds pretty closely with the views of a majority of his or her constituents? To simplify the matter, let us push to one side the special (and serious) problem created by nonvoting, and assume that most of

Figure 15.2
Paths to Popular Control

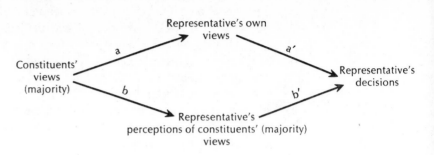

the electorate does vote. Then the following conditions would appear to offer a strong guarantee of popular control over elected representatives:

1. *Voter awareness.* Voters are aware of the positions that candidates take on issues. Thus when incumbents run for re-election, their constituents are aware of their past voting records.
2. *Appropriate choice.* Armed with this knowledge, constituents vote in favor of the candidate whose policies are closest to their own.
3. *Corresponding policy decisions.* When he or she acts on matters before the House, the representative adopts positions that correspond with the views of a majority of constituents because:
   a. The representative seeks to act according to their views (a delegate) *and* is aware of how a majority of the voters stand; or
   b. The representative seeks to act according to his or her own views (a trustee) *but* as a result of condition 2 these views coincide with those of a majority of voters.

These two paths are shown in Figure 15.2.

It would be unreasonable to expect that these conditions would be fully met in a representative system in a large country. Yet a study of voters and representatives during 1958–60 resulted in disturbing evidence that these conditions are very far indeed from being achieved in the United States.[8] Because this study, which broke new ground, has not yet been repeated, its findings should be regarded as somewhat tentative. Yet they fit too well with other surveys to be dismissed as wildly atypical.

8. Donald E. Stokes and Warren E. Miller, with the facilities of the Survey Research Center, University of Michigan, surveyed voters in 116 randomly selected congressional districts and interviewed the incumbent congressmen and major party candidates for the House from the same districts. Their findings have been published in Angus Campbell, Philip E. Converse, Warren E. Miller, and Donald E. Stokes, *Elections and the Political Order* (New York: Wiley, 1966), chs. 11 and 16; and in an article by Warren E. Miller, "Majority Rule and the Representative System of Government," in *Mass Politics*, eds. Erik Allart and Stein Rokkan (New York: Free Press, 1970), ch. 10.

Some Disturbing Evidence

Voter awareness. Only a small minority of voters seem to be aware of the positions that candidates for the House of Representatives take on issues. Here are some findings:

☐ Of the people who lived in districts where the House seat was contested in 1958, 59 percent—well over half—said that they had neither read nor heard anything about either candidate for Congress, and less than one in five felt that they knew something about both candidates.

☐ Of people who went to the polls, 46 percent conceded that they did so without having read or heard anything about either candidate.

☐ A candidate who already occupies the office and is running for reelection—the incumbent candidate—is by far the better known. In districts where the incumbent was opposed for reelection in 1958, 39 percent of the respondents knew something about the member of Congress. Only about 20 percent said they knew anything at all about his or her opponent.

☐ Even voters who say they know something about a candidate appear to know almost nothing of his or her policies or party programs. The popular image of a member of Congress is almost barren of policy content. References to current legislative issues comprised not more than a thirtieth part of what the constituents had to say about their representatives.

☐ The information of constituents aware of their representative consisted mainly of diffuse value judgments: good man, experienced, knows the problems, has done a good job, and the like. Beyond this the representative's image consisted of a mixed bag of impressions, some of them wildly improbable, about ethnicity, the attractiveness of family, specific services to the district, and other facts in the candidate's background.[9]

Appropriate choice. Given the fact that most voters lack the requisite information, they do not ordinarily base their vote on a judgment of the candidates' policies. Instead, they vote predominantly on the basis of party loyalty:

---

9. All these propositions are direct quotations or paraphrases from Campbell et al., *Elections and the Political Order,* pp. 204–207. However, a 1970 Gallup Survey adds further confirmation. The relevant questions and percentages were: "Do you happen to know the name of the present representative in Congress from your district?" "Yes," 53 percent; "No," 47 percent. "Do you know how your representative voted on any major bills this year?" "Yes," 21 percent; "No," 75 percent; "Don't know," 4 percent. "Is your representative a Democrat or a Republican?" "Don't know," 38 percent. "Has your representative done anything for the district that you definitely know about?" "Yes," 19 percent; "No," 76 percent; "Don't know," 5 percent. "Has your representative done any favors for you?" "Yes," 4 percent; "No," 96 percent. "How much thought have you given to the coming November election . . . quite a lot or only a little?" "Quite a lot," 25 percent; "Some," 18 percent; "Little," 42 percent; "None," 15 percent (Gallup Opinion Index No. 64, October, 1970, pp. 9–14).

☐ In 1958 only one vote in twenty was cast by persons without any sort of party loyalty. And among those who did identify themselves with a party, only one in ten voted against their party. As a result, something like 84 percent of the ballots that year were cast by voters who voted their usual party line.

☐ Traditional party voting is seldom connected with current legislative issues. In saying what they liked and disliked about the parties, only about 15 percent of the comments of party loyalists dealt with current issues of public policy.

☐ Moreover, only about half the voters actually knew which party had controlled the Congress during the two years prior to the election.[10]

Corresponding policy decisions. The extent to which the positions adopted by representatives correspond with the views of their constituents varies a good deal from one issue to another. The correspondence is moderately high in the areas of some key issues, negligible in others. It was found that:

☐ The way representatives voted was influenced both by their own views (*a'* in Figure 15.2) and by their perceptions of the opinions in their districts (*b'* in Figure 15.2). Indeed, together these two factors strongly influenced the decisions in all three issue areas.

☐ Representatives felt that their chances of re-election depended quite substantially on their personal record and standing.

☐ The correspondence between the views of constituents and the way representatives voted was quite high on civil rights, lower on social welfare measures, and nonexistent or even negative on foreign policy.[11]

Sources of Variation in Constituent Control

Why this variation? The answer lies in the variation in the influence exerted on a member of Congress on different matters and at different times.

Going back for a moment to Figure 15.2, we can readily see how each of the links, from constituent attitudes to the representative's vote on roll calls, may be weakened or broken by the impact of other forces.

Constituent influences. From the evidence we have just been examining, it is apparent that links *a* and *b* are often weak and sometimes virtually nonexistent. Consider the link at *a*, for example. Given the relative lack of prominence given to issues and policies in the mind of average voters when voting for their representatives, it is hardly surprising

10. Campbell et al., *Elections and the Political Order*, pp. 197–199.

11. *Ibid.*, pp. 206, 362–366; and Miller, "Majority Rule and the Representative System," pp. 300–301.

that they often cast their ballots for a candidate whose views happen to be quite different from their own. It turned out, in fact, that of the three issue areas examined in the study mentioned previously, only on civil rights did the representative's own attitude correlate strongly with his or her constituents' attitudes. And much of this correlation is accounted for by Southern representatives who, like their constituents, sharply opposed legislative proposals on civil rights.

All the factors that would weaken the link at *a* also weaken it at *b*. It might be difficult even for a pollster with a sophisticated survey to sort out majority attitudes on a great many policy questions. The representative, of course, is no pollster, and 'surveys' such as a member of Congress might take are usually unsystematic and prone to error.

In the real world, communication between constituents and members of Congress is a highly uncertain matter. It is bound to be so in a large country, as one can easily see by performing a simple mental experiment: If every adult in an average congressional district tried to gain the attention of his or her representative for half an hour, and if the representative were to devote ten hours a day the year round to nothing but communicating with constitutents, it would take a quarter of a century to hear all of them!

The fact is, of course, that most people do not communicate with their representative at all. In a typical year, probably something under 15 percent of the population ever write or talk to a member of Congress or any other public official in order to give their opinions on a public issue. The minority of citizens who do try to influence Congress do not necessarily represent majority opinion. It has been found again and again that certain factors are associated with higher levels of political activity of any kind, and these would apply to efforts to influence members of Congress.

There is still another element of great importance. People who happen to be aroused about an issue because their goals, values, prestige, esteem, income, ethnic loyalties, or other interests are involved, are, it is obvious, much more likely to influence a member of Congress than people who are not aroused. Moreover, because of uncertainties in communication, their activity may make their numbers and resources seem greater than they are.[12]

---

12. Bauer, Pool, and Dexter, *American Business and Public Policy*, p. 211. See also Lewis A. Dexter, "The Representative and His District," ch. 8, in *The Sociology and Politics of Congress* (Chicago: Rand McNally, 1970). This is a revised version of an article originally appearing in *Human Organization*, 16 (Spring, 1957). Part 2 of *Sociology and Politics of Congress* discusses the issue of what congressmen attend to at considerably greater length. From the converse standpoint, the issues involved are discussed in greater depth in Lewis A. Dexter, *How Organizations Are Represented in Washington* (Indianapolis: Bobbs-Merrill, 1969), especially "When the Job Is Chiefly Lobbying," ch. 4; and "Helping and Seeking Help on Capitol Hill," ch. 5; pp. 55–101. Bauer, Pool, and Dexter found, for example, that businessmen who favored tariff protection were more likely to write their representatives in 1954–1955 than those who favored tariff reductions; thus, although public sentiment favored a liberal trade policy by about three to one, to members of Congress who surveyed their mail it might have looked as if the public actually favored protectionist policies by two to one.

Given all these difficulties in knowing what a majority of his or her constituents wants, how does a member of Congress arrive at judgments about their views? A perceptive observer of Congress suggests:

A congressman's conception of his district confirms itself, to a considerable extent, and may constitute a sort of self-fulfilling prophecy.

A congressman hears most often from those who agree with him.

Some men automatically interpret what they hear to support their own viewpoint.

In more general terms, what congressmen hear and how they interpret what they hear depends on who they are.

For any particular congressman, his interpretation results from his being the particular kind of person he is and is reputed to be.

A congressman's reputation among those who might want to influence him determines in large measure what actually is said to him.

Some communications tend to be unclear in their meaning. A good deal of so-called lobbying by constituents tends to be nothing more than a social visit and a general discussion.

What the congressman listens to is partly accidental.

'Pressure' is how you see it. What you call pressure, or what you feel to be pressure, depends on how thick your skin is.

Opportunism is also where you see it. Few congressmen attribute their friends' decisions or their own to opportunism.[13]

Other influences. But, of course, the attitudes of constituents are by no means the only influences to which representatives respond. They are, in fact, the object of a number of different efforts to influence their behavior, including the way they vote on roll calls. The main sources of direct influence are indicated in Figure 15.3. Thus just as the president's power varies with the strength of other factors, so does that of the member of Congress. With some crucial modifications, we may say about the member of Congress what was said about the president in Chapter 12: In general, a representative is most severely limited when the constitutional authority of Congress is clearly restricted; when Congress deals with a problem on which it has no unique legitimacy; when an emergency requiring executive action is thought to exist; when public opinion is well-defined, highly structured, and not responsive to the member of Congress; and when well-organized groups outside the representative's own committees regularly participate in the kind of decision at hand. Conversely, a representative is most free to act independently when the constitutional authority of Congress is broad; the Congress has special legitimacy to act; no emergency is thought to exist; public opinion is weak, unstructured, and highly responsive to the member of Congress; and when few if any well-organized groups outside the representative's own committees regularly participate.

---

13. These statements are taken from Dexter, "The Representative and His District," pp. 151–175.

Figure 15.3
Influences
on a
Representative's
Vote on a Roll Call

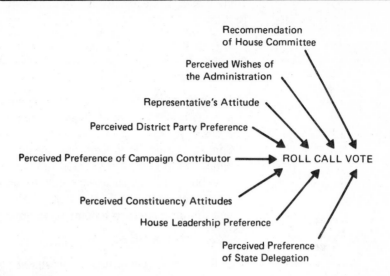

Recommendation
of House Committee

Perceived Wishes of
the Administration

Representative's Attitude

Perceived District Party Preference

Perceived Preference of Campaign Contributor ——▶ ROLL CALL VOTE

Perceived Constituency Attitudes

House Leadership Preference

Perceived Preference
of State Delegation

Source: Allart and Rokkan, *Mass Politics,* p. 292.

Each of these factors varies a good deal. Thus on foreign policy, the attitudes of constituents are typically very general, unstructured, and relatively responsive (particularly in emergencies) to the president. So a "number of Congressmen are disposed to follow the administration's advice, whatever they or their districts think."[14] Consequently there is often little or no relation on foreign policy issues between the attitudes (if any) of a majority of constituents and the position a member of Congress takes on these matters—even though the representative may confidently believe that the position taken expresses the attitudes of the district's voters. At the other end of the spectrum, on such questions as busing school children for racial integration, public opinion is likely to be much more articulate, definite, visible, organized, and angry. If public opinion also happens to fall predominantly on one side—as with the issue of school busing in districts that are heavily white—the representative becomes almost exclusively an agent of the voters in the district. If he or she does not go along with majority sentiment, the voters will, for once, be aware of it, and are more than likely to cast their ballots for the opposing candidate.

SUMMARY   Congress has not altogether fulfilled the expectations of the Framers that the Senate would protect the interests of minorities, particularly the

---

14. Campbell et al., *Elections ana the Political Order*, p. 362.

small states, while the House would reflect the desires of popular majorities.

1. In the Senate, by and large, the major political conflicts have not been between the small and large states. As to other minorities, it appears that:

☐ The only minorities protected by equal state representation as such are geographical minorities concentrated in sparsely populated areas.
☐ Some minorities in these areas are unprotected and vulnerable.
☐ Minorities in heavily populated areas are underrepresented.
☐ The benefits and disadvantages to various minorities from equal state representation in the Senate seem to be allocated arbitrarily and do not appear to follow any general principle.

2. In the House:

☐ Only in recent years has enforcement by the Supreme Court of the principle of one person, one vote led to districts of approximately equal population.
☐ Yet the method of choosing representatives from single-member districts by means of plurality elections insures neither majority rule nor minority representation.
☐ Popular control over the House, it appears from recent if somewhat tentative evidence, is further handicapped because:
  1. Most constituents are unaware of the positions that candidates for the House take on issues.
  2. Partly as a result, most voters do not base their vote on a judgment of the candidates' policies.
  3. As a result of the first two factors and others, the extent to which the positions on issues taken by members of Congress correspond with their constituents' views varies a good deal from one issue area to another. One study showed relatively high correspondence on civil rights and virtually none on foreign affairs.

16 CONGRESS AS POLICY MAKER: PERFORMANCE

In the ways their governments arrive at national policies, polyarchies vary over a much greater range than is commonly supposed. No other polyarchy makes its policies by processes quite like those typically used in the United States. A visitor from Britain or Sweden familiar only with government policy making in his own country would very likely be confused and puzzled by American policy making. He might be aghast as well.

The Congress contributes substantially to the distinctiveness of policy making in the United States. In no other polyarchy does the national legislature have quite the same functions and power in policy determination as the Congress. To say that the Congress is different is not, of course, to say that it is better or worse than other legislative bodies, judged by democratic standards or other criteria.

Taken together, three features tend to distinguish the role of Congress in policy making from the role of parliaments in most other polyarchies:

☐ *Shared power and cooperation:* On a great many decisions the president and each house of Congress have very considerable influence, yet ordinarily none of the three has enough influence to prevail completely against the determined opposition of the others. Hence their cooperation is required.

☐ *Antagonism and conflict:* Yet there is ordinarily a certain amount of antagonism and conflict between the president and the Congress and between House and Senate.

☐ *No decisive procedure:* Unlike many other polyarchies, there is no established procedure for putting an end to these conflicts and bringing about a state of harmony. No single process, such as a national election, is truly *decisive* in granting any participant, party, or coalition the authority needed to carry out its policies.

SHARED POWER AND COOPERATION The president and each of the houses of Congress have substantial resources for bringing influence to bear on making national policies. As we saw in Chapters 12 and 13, on some types of important decisions, the president has, at times, all but escaped the control of Congress. Yet over the whole domain of policy such unlimited presidential discretion is comparatively rare. Indeed, it may prove to be a phase in the shifting balance between presidential and congressional influence on policy-making that has always been an aspect of their relationship. Some of these swings are short run, from one term or president to the next. Some are long run. At the extreme phases of these long-run shifts, the president or Congress may be dominant. Yet these extreme phases seem incapable of persisting, for both president and Congress have too many resources that are rooted in the Constitution and in other general features of the American system. These resources may lie dormant in the extreme phases, but they do not vanish.

Historical Fluctuations

As we have seen, the high point of presidential power in the nineteenth century was reached under Lincoln in his attempt to prevent the dissolution of the Union. But with the conclusion of the Civil War, Congress vigorously reasserted its authority. The control of the president over policy and appointments began to recede immediately after Lincoln's death. The "Whig" view, as it has been called, of the ascendancy of Congress over the president was pushed to its outermost limits by the radical Republicans who dominated the House of Representatives under the leadership of Thaddeus Stevens.[1] In order to tie the hands of the president, in 1867 the Congress passed (over President Andrew Johnson's veto) a Tenure of Office Act that was designed to prevent the president from removing officials (including Cabinet officers) without the consent of the Senate. Johnson, who rightly believed that the act was unconstitutional, chose to defy Congress and dismissed Secretary of War Stanton, who was openly disloyal to him. The House then voted 126 to 47 to impeach the president. Johnson escaped conviction in the Senate by only one vote.

Peak of congressional influence. Although Andrew Johnson escaped conviction, the Congress nonetheless became the center of energy in

---

1. See Fawn M. Brodie, *Thaddeus Stevens, Scourge of the South* (New York: Norton, 1959), pp. 324 ff.

the system. Under President Grant, control over both policies and appointments fell exclusively into the hands of Congress; the president became little more than a figurehead. " ... The predominant and controlling force, the centre and source of all motive and of all regulative power," observed a young historian and political scientist named Woodrow Wilson in 1885, "is Congress."[2]

Congress's monopoly of control was exercised chiefly through its innumerable committees; actual control was lodged with the committee chairman—each lord of his own domain—and with leaders elected in the party caucus. Most notable was the Speaker of the House, who toward the end of the century became a personage as important as the president—and a good deal more powerful with respect to legislation.

President after president yielded control over policy without a murmur. The Whig view was gospel to the presidents themselves. This was the age of industrial growth, new fortunes, and the worship of business success. There was a widespread faith in the virtues of an uncontrolled economy, particularly in the Republican party, which controlled the White House throughout most of this period. The ascendant political forces of the day had no broad program of legislation or reform to enact. Vigorous government was considered a danger. A weak president controlled by a Congress concerned more with patronage than with broad legislative programs provided a political system perfectly adapted to the purposes of business, so long as corruption did not interfere with profits or alienate the growing middle classes.[3]

Resurgence of the presidency. The resurgence of the presidency from the low point reached under Grant was gradual. It may seem unbelievable today, but the greatest battles between president and Congress during this period resulted from the attempts of Presidents Hayes, Garfield, and Cleveland to regain from the Senate control over their own Cabinet appointments, an effort in which each succeeded only after considerable effort. But none of these men had the slightest intention of asserting control over policy, which they took for granted was entirely in the domain of the Congress.[4] It was only at the turn of the century, with William McKinley and Theodore Roosevelt, that greater control over policy came to be lodged in the White House.

Thus the power of Congress over policy and appointments has declined since its peak in the period after the Civil War. In the twentieth

2. Woodrow Wilson, *Congressional Government: A Study in American Politics* (New York: Meridian Books, 1956), p. 31.

3. See E. E. Schattschneider, "United States: The Functional Approach to Party Government," in *Modern Political Parties,* ed. S. Neumann (Chicago: University of Chicago Press, 1956), pp. 194–218, especially at p. 197.

4. The principal battles over appointments are described in Binkley, *President and Congress,* ch. 7, pp. 145–167.

century not only has the president broken the monopoly of Congress over policy—and, of course, over appointments—but, as we have seen, he has also largely taken command over the initiation of new policies.

Resurgence of Congress? As the imperial presidency began to totter on the brink of collapse in 1973 and 1974, the Congress began to reassert itself. In 1973 it passéd a bill intended to restrict to sixty days the authority of the president to deploy military forces in foreign combat without further congressional approval. When Nixon vetoed the measure, both houses voted to override his veto. In 1974, Congress passed legislation designed to provide it for the first time with an alternative to the president's budget. After Nixon's resignation and replacement by Ford, there were other signs that Congress intended to take greater initiative in future. President Ford on his part, made no effort to reestablish the imperial presidency.

It seems wholly unlikely, however, that a president will ever again be as weak in relation to Congress as presidents were in the post–Civil War period. In the longer run, the enduring factors favoring presidential power will lead to a successful reassertion of presidential authority. Yet unless the experiences described in Chapter 13 are wholly forgotten, there is a good chance that presidential authority will not again increase nor Congressional authority decline to their relative positions at the height of the imperial presidency.

In comparing the power of Congress today with that of the nineteenth century, it is important to keep in mind that Congress is now a far more active institution. It is far better equipped to deal with complex matters of public policy, and far more deeply involved in an incredible range of important issues than it ever was or could be in the nineteenth century. What has happened is this: in the post–Civil War period, during a time when the doctrine of complete government noninterference marched triumphant and the foreign policy of the United States limited the country to a role of neutrality and isolation, there was, in plain fact, very little policy for either president or Congress to initiate and to enact. But, in the twentieth century, government regulation and control, welfare programs, foreign affairs, military policy, and the taxation and spending measures required for all these purposes have produced a veritable 'policy explosion.' If Congress were to do no more than to consider the principal measures submitted to it by the chief executive, it would have plenty to do; yet the Congress does considerably more.

In this sense, then, the power of Congress has grown: the decisions Congress makes by modifying, passing, or rejecting measures affect all of us to an incomparably greater extent today than in the nineteenth century. If the Congress had not met after 1868 and had left behind a dutiful caretaker president to enforce existing laws, neither the United States nor the world would have been much different several decades later from what, in fact, they were. But the United States of the 1970s could not possibly exist legally on the statutes of the 1920s.

In sum, in the post–Civil War period, Congress enjoyed a monopoly control over policies mostly of trivial importance; whereas today, even if its influence in some key decisions has been small, as we saw in Chapters 12 and 13, on the whole it is true that Congress shares with the president control over policies of profound consequence.

Congress as Policy Maker Today

Input and output. In recent decades the input and output of laws requiring congressional action has become staggering. In the First Congress, one hundred forty-four measures were introduced. Throughout the first twenty-five years of the nineteenth century, the number of measures introduced climbed steadily from one Congress to the next. Nor did the upward trend stop after the initial phase. The number of measures introduced reached its highest point with the Sixty-first Congress (1909–11) when over forty-four thousand measures were introduced. Many of these were 'private bills'; claims for property damage or personal injury by government agents; matters of immigration, citizenship, or deportation of specific individuals; correction of individual military and naval records; private land bills, and the like. Changes in congressional rules (involving, among other things, delegation of many such decisions to executive officials) have since reduced the number of these private bills. In the second quarter of the twentieth century the number of private measures introduced in each Congress varied from a low point of something over eight thousand in the middle of World War II to a high point of nearly twenty-five thousand during the Seventy-first Congress (1929–31).

The output of public measures has not kept pace with this enormous input. The First Congress passed a total of one hundred eight public bills. The output of the Congress gradually increased until about 1930, when it seems to have stabilized at a number varying between one hundred and one thousand public measures passed in each Congress.[5]

Congress remains, both formally and actually, a key organ in making laws. In many other democracies the parliament has become a rubber stamp for the cabinet, or at least a body with a dutiful majority that can be relied on to pass without resistance the measures submitted to it by the cabinet. By comparison, the American Congress is far too independent of the president, and the American political parties have far too

---

5. These figures will be found in *Historical Statistics of the United States: Colonial Times to 1957*, Bureau of the Census (Washington, D.C.: U.S. Government Printing Office, 1960), pp. 689–690.

many dissimilar interests to make this possible here except in rare circumstances. It is true that when Franklin Roosevelt took office in the bleakest days of the Great Depression, he found a Congress eager to do his bidding. "The first months of the New Deal," the leading historian of that period has written, "were to an astonishing degree an adventure in unanimity."[6] Yet the honeymoon, the famous Hundred Days, did not last even through the crisis of the Depression. After 1933, Congress gradually recovered self-confidence; and in 1937 Northern Republicans and Southern Democrats forged an alliance that brought the period of New Deal reform to a virtual end. Again, from 1963 to 1965, President Lyndon Johnson matched Roosevelt's 1933–37 record for new legislation. Thanks in part to Johnson's exceptional skills with Congress and in part to the overwhelming Democratic majorities resulting from the 1964 elections (the largest since 1938 in the House and since 1942 in the Senate), one major bill after another passed Congress. But by 1966 Congress was again displaying a more independent spirit.

If the Congress continues, then, to be a formidable participant in making laws, certain developments have nonetheless greatly modified its role.

Initiative. First, as we saw in Chapter 12, in this century much of the initiative in legislation has shifted to or is now shared with the chief executive. A good deal of the content and substance of the legislation with which Congress deals consists of policies in which the president takes the lead. Although important legislation is still formulated in Congress, a substantial part of its work consists of modifying or rejecting policy proposals emanating from the Executive Branch.[7]

Variations. Second, as we have also seen, the relative importance of president and Congress in policymaking is not, and probably cannot be, static. It varies with the circumstances and with the kinds of policies at stake (Figure 16.1). Although the Congress, despite its reputation to the contrary, sometimes acts with exceptional dispatch, legislatures have never proved as suitable as executives for handling emergency actions. Like all legislatures, Congress is most handicapped in times of crisis and in dealing with military and foreign affairs. On questions where time and secrecy are not of the essence, Congress is much stronger—for example, on legislation having to do with domestic affairs or with aspects of foreign affairs where the need for speed or circum-

---

6. Arthur M. Schlesinger, Jr., *The Coming of the New Deal* (Cambridge, Mass.: Houghton Mifflin, 1959), p. 423.

7. For a careful study of the distribution of legislative responsibility on thirteen major bills in the Eighty-ninth Congress (1965–1966) during the presidency of Lyndon Johnson see David Price, *Who Makes the Laws?* (Cambridge, Mass.: Schenkman Publishing Co., 1972), pp. 290–291 and *passim.*

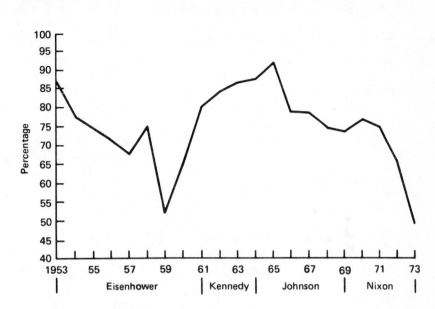

Figure 16.1
Presidential Success on
Votes, 1953–1973*

Source: Congressional Quarterly, "Nixon, the Fifth Year of His Presidency," 1974, p. 58.
*Percentages based on votes on which presidents took a position.

spection is not paramount: policies with respect to agriculture, labor, business, taxation, immigration, appropriations, and the like. Finally, on all questions having to do with the distribution of benefits or deprivations, Congress tends to play an important part; even during World War II, when it was a matter of deciding how the burdens of war were to be distributed among different groups of Americans, Congress played a preeminent role.[8]

Presidential decisions. In the third place, it must always be kept in mind that laws, these days, are only one part of policy. Many of the most important decisions, particularly in foreign and military affairs, do not require legislation, at least not directly. Sometimes, too, even where legislation is required, the chief executive has, for all practical purposes, already committed the Congress and the country; in these cases Congress may modify but it cannot easily reverse the basic commitment that has been entered into. Thus Congress could play only a passive role in our entry into the Korean war, the increasing U.S. presence in

8. See Roland Young, *Congressional Politics in the Second World War* (New York: Columbia University Press, 1956).

Vietnam from 1956 onward, and the suspension of nuclear testing by the executive.

Other forms of influence. Fourth, Congress participates in policymaking in many ways other than by making laws. Its informal participation, usually by consultation between president and congressional leaders, is traditional and important. Many actions technically within presidential discretion, frequently including actions on foreign and military affairs, are taken by the president only after he consults with congressional leaders to find out whether he will have adequate support for the decision he proposes to make. If he does not, he may back down. To give an example: In 1954, when the fall of the French fortress of Dienbienphu in Indochina was imminent, a defeat that France foresaw as her complete collapse in Southeast Asia, President Eisenhower, Secretary of State Dulles, and the chairman of the Joint Chiefs of Staff, Admiral Radford, advocated aiding the French with an air strike by Navy and Air Force planes. In a secret meeting, under questioning from congressional leaders, including then Majority Leader of the Senate Lyndon Johnson, it became apparent that congressional leaders were reluctant to support the action unless the administration could find allies abroad, particularly Britain. But Britain, too, was reluctant; and in the end the plan was abandoned. Even in this case, in the view of one observer, the president could probably have won congressional support "provided he had asked for it forcefully and explained the facts and their relation to the national interest of the United States." But he did not, and his soundings of congressional opinion evidently did prevent immediate intervention in support of the French.[9] Sometimes the Congress tries to tie the president's hands publicly by passing a resolution, as in the series of resolutions from 1951 to 1961 in which one or both houses declared, in most cases unanimously, their opposition to admitting Communist China to the U.N. Sometimes, on the other hand, when it suits his purposes, the president openly asks for an expression of congressional approval. President Lyndon Johnson obtained a joint resolution indicating congressional support for actions during a crisis that he announced took place in the Gulf of Tonkin, off North Vietnam, in August, 1964. To the discomfiture of some members of Congress, the president later used this resolution as evidence of congressional authorization for his policy of bombing North Vietnam, increasing the number of American troops, and escalating American participation in other ways.

Congressional committees also share with the president a substan-

---

9. See Chalmers M. Roberts, "The Day We Didn't Go to War," *The Reporter*, September 14, 1954, 31–35, reprinted in *Legislative Politics USA*, T. J. Lowie, ed. (Boston: Little, Brown, 1962), pp. 240–248. The quotation is at p. 248.

tial measure of influence over the administrative agencies.[10] Indeed, probably no national legislature in any other polyarchy has greater influence over bureaucracy, and most have far less. Committees acquire and maintain this influence because they control appropriations and legislation wanted by the agencies. Committee influence over administration is exercised chiefly by means of hearings, both public and off-the-record, and by investigations. Like the president, a congressional committee can often influence policies informally without actually spelling out their demands in a law. This is accomplished by day-to-day contacts between committee staff and people in the executive agencies, on-site visits, inspection tours, informal briefings, and the like. It is important to keep in mind, too, that while presidents, cabinet members, heads of departments, and even bureau chiefs come and go, many ranking members on congressional committees remain in Congress a very long time. During these years they acquire a great deal of knowledge and often develop a proprietary interest in the agencies that fall within the jurisdiction of their committee.

Finally, Congress participates in policy making in an important indirect way, by serving as a source of information to the public—and sometimes to the Executive Branch. Congressional debates and discussions, particularly on the floor of the Senate, and the hearings conducted by congressional committees produce a steady flow of reports and news about existing and proposed policies. A committee hearing in which witnesses are heard over weeks, months, and even years is often a vital instrument in calling public attention to an issue and winning support for or against some proposal. Although it is impossible to assess the exact weight such hearings have had, it would be a mistake to underestimate their importance by looking only for effects on *general* public opinion; for often what committee hearings do is to change, solidify, or mobilize the opinions of *specific* publics whose influence is critical to a particular piece of legislation—cotton farmers, the leaders of the AFL-CIO, an ethnic group, bankers, the elderly.

ANTAGONISM AND CONFLICT   Yet if president and Congress must ordinarily share in the process of making decisions, they do not ordinarily do so harmoniously.

Different Interests

Aside from jealousies and antagonisms that have their origins in personalities and institutional loyalties, conflict also stems from the fact

---

10. For an excellent description of the workings of the committees see Richard F. Fenno, Jr., *Congressmen in Committees* (Boston: Little, Brown, 1973).

that the president, the Senate, and the House each reflects, and in a sense represents, a different assortment of interests. An individual or organization with good access to a powerful committee chairman in the Senate, for example, may have little access to the chairman of the equivalent committee in the House, and perhaps none at all to the White House or influential agencies in the Executive Branch.

Each also has to keep a different set of constituents in mind. Elected politicians often misperceive the views of the electorate. As we saw in the last chapter members of Congress often do. Nevertheless they give a great deal of thought to the actions they think will win or lose favor among their constituents. In fact, the desire to be re-elected is so central in the ambitions of so many members of Congress that a substantial part of their activities and of the organization and processes of the Congress can best be explained as by-products of the members' electoral needs and desires.[11]

A hasty view of the matter might lead one to suppose that since the president, the Senate, and the House are all chosen by the same American electorate it must follow that each has essentially the same general set of constituents in mind. Yet this is not the case.

Different Electorates

To begin with, it is not strictly true to say that the electorates in presidential and congressional elections are identical. Voting turnout in congressional elections in off years is ordinarily about 25 percent less than the turnout in presidential elections. Moreover, the off-year electorate is not just a smaller cross-section of the electorate in presidential years. As we shall see in Chapter 21, in midterm congressional elections, voters are more likely to vote strictly according to their party loyalties. In addition, of course, changes in mood, temper, and issues may occur in the two-year interval between presidential and midterm elections. Often voters become somewhat disenchanted with the president, and, therefore, they turn against his party. The net effect, often, is to produce majorities in House or Senate at odds with one another or with the President on key issues. Although the prospect of conflict is most evident when midterm elections give the opposition party a majority in one or both houses, conflict is normal even when the president and a majority of members of each house are of the same party. We shall explore these shifts in the electorate in more detail in Chapter 21, but the important point to keep in mind here is that midterm elections enhance the possibility of conflict between the president and the two houses of Congress.

---

11. This is the thesis of one of the best recent works on Congress: David R. Mayhew, *Congress, The Electoral Connection* (New Haven, Conn.: Yale University Press, 1974).

Different Constituencies

An even more important source of conflict, perhaps, is the fact that even in presidential years the national electorate is carved up into different constituencies for the president, senators, and congressmen. These differences influence their perceptions and calculations as to the key groups that need to be appeased in one way or another. Their calculations of the needs, interests, attitudes, pressures, and future responses of those they represent—calculations clouded with a good deal of uncertainty and misinformation—almost inevitably lead to different conclusions when made by a majority of 436 representatives, a majority of 100 senators, or the president. These differences in judging what their constituents want or oppose contribute to the conflict.

NO DECISIVE PROCEDURE   What most sharply distinguishes policy making in the United States from the process existing in most other polyarchies is the absence of any established procedure for eliminating conflicts between the president and the two houses. In some (though by no means all) polyarchies a particular process is *decisive* with respect to policy making. An institution or process is decisive if, by winning a victory, a political party or coalition will have all the authority it needs to carry out its policies during a limited term of office. In some polyarchies, *elections* are relatively decisive. In some, the *formation of the cabinet* is somewhat decisive. In others, there is no decisive procedure; the United States is one of these.

Contrasts

Britain. By contrast with the United States, British elections for seats in the House of Commons are relatively decisive. By winning a majority of seats, a party is in a position to select the prime minister. The prime minister in turn chooses his cabinet. Because British political parties are highly unified the prime minister and his cabinet, being the actual leaders of the victorious party, can confidently assume that their majority in the House of Commons will support the party's basic policies. In the highly unlikely event that an important proposal by the cabinet was rejected by the House, the cabinet would resign and new elections would be held. In practice, however, this almost never happens; party discipline is strong enough to insure a majority of votes for all key policies proposed by the cabinet. The opposition party, knowing that it cannot defeat the cabinet on any major issue, concentrates on winning public opinion to its programs and candidates so that it can achieve a future parliamentary majority. Parliament itself is not, then, a site for genuine encounters so much as it is a forum from which to influence the next election. Parliamentary debate is not intended to persuade Parliament as much as the public—and hence to affect future elections. Negotiations by the opposition to enter the cabinet would, on the whole, be futile, and everyone knows it.

Other polyarchies. In some polyarchies where elections are a good deal less decisive than in Britain, the formation of the cabinet is relatively decisive. The Scandinavian countries serve as examples. There, when a party or several parties with a majority of seats in the parliament enter into a coalition and constitute a cabinet, the policies they have agreed on stand a very good chance of being enacted. The parties in the coalition usually have a majority of the parliament, and their members are unified and disciplined in their voting. Since the parties are particularly reluctant to upset the applecart by voting against the coalition program and thus bringing about the downfall of the cabinet, the cabinet can generally count on getting a majority of votes for its policies.

The United States

In some polyarchies, however, neither elections nor cabinet formation are really very decisive. In fact, no single process may be truly decisive. This is the case in the United States. A president who has just won a majority of popular and electoral votes after campaigning in behalf of his platform may be quite unable to persuade Congress to enact the policies he proposes. Nor is there likely to be a disciplined majority in Congress capable of carrying through its own program. Even when voters elect a president and majorities in both houses of Congress all from the same party, the elections are likely to be far more indecisive than in Britain. Well-informed political commentators, for example, will speculate as to just how much of the president's program or the party's platform will actually be adopted by Congress. For in the United States policy making typically involves a vast amount of negotiation and compromise, and, even so, great risk that proposals advanced by the president or congressional leaders will be significantly modified or even defeated outright. Thus there is no established procedure for eliminating the conflicts between the president and the houses of Congress. In parliamentary systems where the cabinet must have the confidence of a majority of the parliament (or the lower house), conflict between cabinet and parliament would ordinarily be resolved by the resignation of the cabinet. Either a new cabinet would be formed or new elections would be called. But of course no such mechanisms exist in the United States.

The Framers' commitment to partitioning power, as we saw, prevented them from devising a system in which the executive would be wholly dependent on the Congress, much less on the lower house. Nor were they able to see as clearly as we can today that the British parliamentary system was moving away from the separation of powers that had been described and praised by Montesquieu, the great French political theorist of the eighteenth century, whose work was a veritable bible for many of the founding fathers.

Would a Parliamentary System Be Better?

It is intriguing to speculate how the American polyarchy would function under a parliamentary system, or with arrangements that would permit the calling of elections in case of continuing deadlock. These have been seriously proposed at various times. Despite their complaints, however, Americans have been unwilling to entertain seriously the notion that the Constitution needs altering in any fundamental way. Aside from the uncritical assumption of many ordinary citizens that American constitutional arrangements are the best in the world, scholars are aware of how difficult it is to predict what will happen when institutions that operate well in one country are transplanted to another. The parliamentary system seems to operate most successfully in relatively homogeneous countries with unified parties and a national structure that is unitary, as in Britain or the Scandinavian countries, rather than federal, as in the United States. Where these conditions are lacking, the parliamentary system often produces weak and ineffectual coalition governments or elaborate systems for handling conflict that are not demonstrably superior to the interminable negotiation, bargaining, and compromise that characterize the American polyarchy. Nonetheless, Americans might improve their policy making processes if they were more experimental about their political and constitutional arrangements than they have been since 1787.

SUMMARY   Taken together, three features tend to make the role of Congress in policy making rather different from that of national legislative bodies in most other polyarchies:

1. Because Congress and the president share power over policy-making, they must cooperate. Although there are short-run and long-run swings in the relative influence of the one or the other, both possess independent resources of power.

2. There is ordinarily a certain amount of antagonism and conflict between the president and Congress or between the House and the Senate.

3. Unlike many other polyarchies, there is no established procedure for putting an end to these conflicts and bringing about a state of harmony, as in some parliamentary systems where either elections or cabinet formation tend to be decisive. Proposals for introducing some such arrangements in the United States have never made much headway, partly because of the exceptional, if often unthinking, reverence most Americans display toward their Constitution, and partly because the consequences are hard to predict.

17 THE SUPREME COURT AND JUDICIAL REVIEW: DESIGN AND DEVELOPMENT

The Supreme Court is not an elected body; it is, indeed, intentionally insulated from electoral politics. Yet it has the authority, which Americans call *judicial review,* to strike down legislation enacted by elected representatives. Whether it be a federal law approved by the Congress and the president, a state law approved by a state legislature and governor, or a municipal ordinance approved by, let us say, city council and mayor, it is subject to judicial review. Is this not a distinctly undemocratic element in the American polyarchy? If so, should it be permitted to exist?

The problem would not arise if Americans had self-consciously chosen to construct an aristocratic republic or meritocracy. For an aristocratic republic might very well have given a Supreme Court the power to nullify laws passed by the representatives of the people. A Supreme Court so armed could shield aristocratic power from popular attack. But because Americans created a polyarchy where democratic principles of political equality and consent are the main grounds of legitimacy for political institutions, the extraordinary position of the Supreme Court in the American political system has ever been a source of controversy.

The authority for judicial review is based on two general kinds of arguments. The first is that judicial review is implied by the Constitution, which is itself accepted as legitimate; or at the very least, that judicial review rests on a long-standing tradition that for all practical purposes incorporates it into the constitutional system. This argument might be called the traditional constitutionality of judicial review. It is a very strong argument, and to most Americans concerned with the question, it seems to be convincing.

However, this argument does not tell us whether judicial review is compatible with *democracy.* The second general argument for judicial review does try to answer this question: It holds that judicial review is implied by the principles of democratic government. As we shall see, this argument, though more relevant to our question, is much weaker than the first.

THE UNCERTAIN DESIGN OF THE FRAMERS

The traditional constitutionality of judicial review must start with the intentions of the Framers of the Constitution, for if they had never intended judicial review, it would be unreasonable (in the absence of an amendment) to argue that it is implied by the terms of the Constitution! Unfortunately, what the Framers intended the Supreme Court to be is a highly debated question; even more unfortunately, judging from the records of the Convention, the delegates scarcely discussed the functions of the proposed Court. Most relevant to the question of judicial review was a highly controversial provision (ultimately rejected) in the Virginia plan. That provision and the brief but sharp skirmishes it produced are interesting for what they reveal about the intentions, or lack of them, of the founding fathers.

The Virginia Plan

The proposal in question—it was the eighth in the series of resolutions that historians have called the Virginia plan, introduced on May 29 by Edmund Randolph of Virginia—provided for a Council of Revision to consist of the president "and a convenient number of the national judiciary." This Council was to have a veto on laws passed by Congress or by a state legislature. Although the proposal did not say so explicitly, discussion among the delegates reveals their clear understanding that the Council's veto was to be used much as the president has come to use his veto: to block 'bad' laws, even though these might not be unconstitutional. Under Randolph's proposal, the Congress could overcome the Council's veto simply by passing the measure a second time. As to state laws, the plan evidently intended to provide that a state legislature could overcome the veto by passing a measure a second time with a larger than ordinary majority in each house of the state legislature; the exact number or proportion was left blank in Randolph's proposal.

Like the Constitution itself, the Virginia plan said not one word about the power of judicial review as we know it: that is, the power to decide on the constitutionality of laws. In fact, many delegates distinguished sharply between the power of the courts to declare acts

Table 17.1
Should the federal judiciary have the authority to declare legislation by Congress or a state legislature invalid on the ground that the law is:

	Bad policy ?	Unconstitutional ?
Option 1	No	No
Option 2	Yes	Yes
Option 3	Yes	No
Option 4	No	Yes

of Congress or the state legislatures *unconstitutional,* and the proposed Council of Revision which was for the purpose of inhibiting 'bad' but not necessarily unconstitutional legislation.

We can probably perceive a bit more clearly now than did the delegates the options they were implicitly confronting. These are presented schematically in Table 17.1. Option 1 was supported by one of the important men of the Convention, John Dickinson of Delaware.[1] Option 2 was supported by four of the most influential members of the Convention—James Wilson and Gouverneur Morris of Pennsylvania and James Madison and George Mason of Virginia. They were in favor of giving the judiciary not only the power to declare laws unconstitutional but also a veto power over policy by means of the Council of Revision.[2] Not surprisingly, no one advocated Option 3, an alternative that seems rather illogical on the face of it. Some delegates supported Option 4, including Luther Martin of Maryland, a State Federalist, and Elbridge Gerry of Massachusetts, a National Federalist.[3]

The proposal for a Council of Revision was vigorously defended by Wilson, Gouverneur Morris, and Madison, but it was rejected three times by the delegates, the last time, virtually without debate, by a decisive vote of 8–3.[4]

The Framers' Intentions

What conclusions as to the intentions of the Framers can we draw from their debates?

First, as we noted above, the record of the debates leaves their intentions unclear. Probably a great many delegates did not have very precise intentions with respect to the powers of the judiciary.

Second, it is a reasonable inference that a majority of the delegates accepted the notion that the federal courts would rule on the constitutionality of state and federal laws involved in cases before them; that is, a majority probably accepted either Option 2 or Option 4. Some

1. *Documents Illustrative of the Formation of the Union of American States,* Charles C. Tansill, ed. (Washington, D.C.: Government Printing Office, 1927), p. 549.
2. *Ibid.,* pp. 422–428.
3. *Ibid.,* p. 147.
4. *Ibid.,* pp. 152, 429, 548.

additional, though by no means conclusive, evidence is provided by the straightforward stand announced in *The Federalist* No. 78—written, ironically, by Hamilton, who had taken no part in the debates on the judiciary:

> ...By a limited Constitution, I understand one which contains certain specified exceptions to the legislative authority; such, for instance, as that it shall pass no bills of attainder, no *ex-post-facto* laws, and the like. Limitations of this kind can be preserved in practice no other way than through the medium of courts of justice, whose duty it must be to declare all acts contrary to the manifest tenor of the Constitution void. Without this, all the reservations of particular rights or privileges would amount to nothing.[5]

Third, it is also a reasonable inference that a majority of delegates rejected the notion that judges should participate in policy making. That is, a majority probably rejected Option 2. It was for exactly this reason, it appears, that the Council of Revision was turned down three times. Ever since the Convention, defenders of judicial review have generally assumed that judicial review is authorized only on questions of constitutionality and not on questions of policy. This is the explicit position of the Supreme Court itself. As we shall see in the next chapter, however, the Court *has* from time to time decided on matters of policy.

JOHN MARSHALL'S BOLD DESIGN

In the light of these observations, it is difficult to sustain the view that when Chief Justice John Marshall enunciated the doctrine of judicial review in the famous case of *Marbury* v. *Madison*[6] on February 24, 1803, he usurped powers that the Framers had intended to deny to the federal judiciary.

The case had arisen in a contest that ranged the Chief Justice on the one side and the president on the other. The confrontation was acutely partisan in its overtones. Marshall was a Federalist who had been appointed to his position by the recent Federalist president, John Adams. His opponent, President Thomas Jefferson, was a Democratic-Republican who had defeated Adams in the bitter election of 1800. During the last days of his presidency, Adams had appointed a number of fellow Federalists to various positions as judges or justices of the peace. Some of them, however, had not received their official appoint-

---

5. Hamilton et al., *The Federalist* (New York: Modern Library, n.d.), p. 505. *The Federalist* (or *The Federalist Papers*) consisted of anonymous essays published in 1787 and 1788 that explained the proposed Constitution. They were written by Hamilton, Madison, and John Jay (an eminent New Yorker, later first Chief Justice of the Supreme Court) and were enormously influential. They are frequently used as sources on the intentions of the Framers.

6. 1 Cranch 1937 (1803). Reams have been filled about this famous case and concerning judicial review. A detailed history of the case itself has been written by a Supreme Court justice Mr. Justice Harold Burton, "The Cornerstone of Constitutional Law: The Extraordinary Case of Marbury v. Madison," *American Bar Association Journal,* 36 (October 1950), 805–883.

ment papers or commissions. These were resting on the desk of the Secretary of State, who refused to forward them. The Secretary of State was none other than the great architect of the Constitution, James Madison, now a coleader with Jefferson of the Democratic-Republican Party. Madison had refused to deliver the commission to a Federalist named Marbury that would appoint him a justice of the peace in the District of Columbia. Marbury sued Madison under an act of Congress that empowered the Supreme Court to issue to executive officers a writ of mandamus compelling them to attend to their duties. The Constitution nowhere mentions the right to issue a writ of mandamus as a part of the Court's authority.

In a case completely embroiled in partisan conflicts, Marshall managed both to claim power for the federal judiciary (which was still strongly dominated by Federalists) and to avoid an outright and possibly damaging confrontation with Jefferson: He held that the act of Congress under which Marbury sought a writ of mandamus was unconstitutional. Marshall's argument adhered closely to the reasoning of Hamilton in *The Federalist* No. 78, which was in line, as we have seen, with what one can reasonably infer to have been the dominant view at the Convention.

The argument presented by Chief Justice Marshall was succinct and persuasive:

1. The Constitution is the supreme law of the land, binding on all branches of the government—legislative, executive, judicial.
2. The Constitution deliberately establishes a government with limited powers.
3. Consequently "an act of the legislature, repugnant to the constitution, is void." If this were not true, then the government would be unlimited; and the Constitution would be an absurdity.
4. "It is emphatically the province and duty of the judicial department to say what the law is."
5. "So if a law be in opposition to the constitution ... the court must determine which of these conflicting rules governs the case. This is of the very essence of judicial duty."
6. "If, then, the courts are to regard the constitution, and the constitution is superior to any ordinary act of the legislature, the constitution and not such ordinary act, must govern the case to which they both apply."
7. Hence if a law is repugnant to the Constitution, when that law comes before a court, the judges are duty bound to declare that law void in order to uphold the supremacy of the Constitution.[7]

7. *Marbury* v. *Madison*, 1 Cranch 1937 (1803).

Marshall's opinion has the majestic finality of a proof of a theorem in elementary Euclidian geometry. It has been quoted and paraphrased thousands of times in defense of judicial review by judges, lawyers, historians, political scientists, and others. Since Marshall's time, the Supreme Court has used the power of judicial review on more than eighty occasions to strike down federal legislation. It has used the power many more times—no one has ever calculated how many—to hold state laws unconstitutional. The Court's actions have invariably been met with protest. Yet more often than not, critics protest a particular decision rather than the general principle of judicial review. And the bitterest critics of the Court in one decade are often the Court's boldest defenders in the next.

Thus the principle of judicial review is firmly anchored simultaneously in tradition and in a highly compelling rational-legal appeal to the supremacy of the Constitution.

There remains, nonetheless, the nagging question of democracy.

JUDICIAL REVIEW AND DEMOCRATIC PRINCIPLES

Does the power of judicial review entail a nondemocratic, an aristocratic, even an oligarchic principle of government? The defenders and critics of judicial review have wrestled with this question ever since *Marbury* v. *Madison*. Jefferson may have had *Marbury* v. *Madison* in mind when in his old age he wrote to a friend that "the judiciary in the United States is the subtle corps of sappers and miners constantly working underground to undermine the foundations of our confederated republic. . . . A judiciary independent of a king or executive alone is a good thing; but independence of the will of the nation is a solecism [an incongruity], at least in a republican government."[8]

A Dialogue

The controversy can perhaps be summarized best in an imaginary dialogue between a critic and an advocate of judicial review:

Critic: I'm quite willing to concede that a tradition of constitutionality may convey a measure of legitimacy to judicial review. I say, though, that judicial review is definitely an undemocratic element in the American polyarchy. After all, most of the people in eighteenth-century Britain no doubt regarded their constitutional system—kings, lords, and all—as legitimate. Yet you would not argue, I'm sure, that eighteenth-century Britain was a democracy. Aristocracies, monarchies, even dic-

---

8. Letter to Thomas Ritchie, December 25, 1820, in Paul Leicester Ford, ed., *The Writings of Thomas Jefferson* (New York: G. P. Putnam's Sons, 1899), pp. 170–171, quoted in John R. Schmidhauser, ed., *Constitutional Law in the Political Process* (Chicago: Rand McNally, 1963), pp. 145–146.

tatorships, I suppose, might acquire legitimacy in the eyes of the people they rule; yet they wouldn't be democratic. In different times and places, all sorts of political institutions have acquired a certain degree of legitimacy; yet I wouldn't want many of these institutions in this country. I wonder if judicial review hasn't generated a conflict between two different principles of legitimacy accepted by Americans—a conflict between our traditions of constitutionality and our supposed commitment to democracy. Our commitment to democracy logically requires us to uphold the principles of political equality and consent. Yet it is patently absurd to say that the Supreme Court reinforces these principles when it strikes down laws supported by a majority of the people's representatives in Congress and by the one nationally elected official we have, the president. What I say, then, is this: judicial review may be good or it may be bad, but it is obviously not democratic.

Advocate: I disagree. I agree with Alexander Hamilton and John Marshall: ours is a *limited* government. Our democratic ideal is definitely not majority-rule democracy but a *limited* democracy with partitioned power. Judicial review is a key element in the partitioning of power. I don't contend, as Marshall did, that judicial review is inherent in a written constitution; I know as well as you do that a number of other polyarchies that were not in existence when Marshall wrote his famous opinion now have written constitutions, and yet don't give their courts the power of judicial review. I say, however, that the *limited* character of our government is an absolutely essential characteristic. If it were stripped of its constitutional limitations, ours would be a totally different system. What's more, we Americans continue to believe strongly in limited government; and judicial review helps to preserve limited government by protecting the Constitution from violations by state governments, by the federal government, or by particular parts of the federal government, such as the Congress. This is why Americans overwhelmingly believe in judicial review. Do you argue that democracy requires *unlimited* government?

Critic: You misunderstand me. Of course I know that we possess a written Constitution. I realize that someone has to interpret the meaning of what's written in that Constitution. I can see that in the course of events cases come to the courts that depend on what the Constitution means. So, in deciding the cases before them, the courts must interpret the Constitution. Let me remind you, however, that the United States is not the only country in the world with a written constitution. In fact, most polyarchies have a written constitution. Yet many of them don't have judicial review—and I think it's fair to say that not one has a supreme court as powerful as ours.

Advocate: I don't quite see how we could function *without* judicial review.

Critic: What are you afraid of—the American people? If the American people wanted unlimited government, do you really think that a few individuals on our Supreme Court could prevent it? Why, the voters would elect a president and a Congress who would impeach and convict the justices one day and appoint new ones the next! Limited government exists in this country not because the Supreme Court wants it but because, as you said yourself, we Americans want it. And limited government will cease the day Americans cease to want it, no matter what nine judges on a court may say or do! So long as the bulk of the American people want limited government, they will elect representatives to Congress and the presidency who adhere to this commitment. If Americans should stop wanting limited government, they will elect revolutionaries committed to unlimited government, and our Constitution will be as dead as the Articles of Confederation. So here's my answer: The best protection for limited government in a polyarchy, in fact the only protection, consists of the people and their elected representatives. What I'm saying is this: Polyarchy depends on the self-restraint of the people. If they don't exercise self-restraint, they won't have a polyarchy and no court can keep it for them! If they *do* exercise self-restraint, then they don't *need* to have judicial review.

Advocate: What you say is all very well in the abstract. But remember, ours is also a federal system. Suppose a state government violates the Constitution—for example, by depriving some of its citizens of their right to assemble or to speak freely? A majority of the voters in the United States might oppose the state action, but even if they knew about it—which they probably wouldn't—what could they do?

Critic: I admit that federalism complicates matters. I've noticed that most federal polyarchies do have some form of judicial review. I'm quite willing to endorse the principle, on purely democratic grounds, that national majorities should prevail over state majorities. Even so, I don't see why you couldn't adopt the Swiss pattern; the federal judiciary could review the constitutionality of state laws but not of federal laws.

Advocate: If you need judicial review in order to keep the states from invading the powers of the federal government, doesn't the logic of your argument cut the other way, too? What if the *federal* government invades the powers of the *states?*

Critic: That might once have been a forceful argument. But isn't it true that today the federal government can constitutionally regulate almost anything through its powers over taxation and interstate commerce? If the federal government *doesn't* regulate everything, that's only because the president and Congress don't want to do so. You see, restraints do depend on the people and their elected representatives, *not* on the courts.

Advocate: You ignore the possibility that a demagogic president or a large congressional majority, or both together, might pass laws that would deprive some particular minority of important constitutional rights.

Critic: Don't we have periodic elections? If we Americans really believed in these rights, we would vote out such a Congress at the next election. If we didn't, I don't see how the Supreme Court could maintain our rights, at least in the long run.

Advocate: In the *long* run, no. But do we have to forget about the *short* run? A majority of voters, or a majority of their representatives, might act under the temporary pressures of impulse, passion, hysteria, crisis. Politicians might not be steadily antilibertarian; yet they might be temporarily so. In such cases the Court could void laws passed during short-run periods of folly.

Critic: Isn't this really the heart of the matter? You assume that a majority of Americans and their elected representatives can't always be trusted to act within the spirit of limited government. You believe that when they're misguided, the Supreme Court can maintain the essential conditions of a libertarian polyarchy by nullifying federal laws contrary to a Constitution designed for limited government. That's not such a bad argument. But what about these two problems? First, will the Supreme Court really stand up against a majority in order to protect some embattled minority that is threatened by a federal law, or won't it be moved by much the same passions and prejudices as the majority of people and their representatives? Second, even assuming now that the Court does stand against majorities, will it uphold general and abstract principles of right or justice, or won't it instead strike down laws it disapproves on grounds of *policy?* Judges are human. I like to remind people of what Jefferson said in 1820: "Our judges are as honest as other men, and not more so. They have, with others, the same passions for party, for power, and the privilege of their corps."[9] Even when judges aren't swayed by the same passions and prejudices as a majority, they may be moved by the passions and prejudices of a particular minority. If they use judicial review and the claim of 'constitutionality' simply to impose their own views about good and bad laws, haven't they contrived to evolve into exactly the kind of body that your Constitutional Convention thought it was preventing?

Advocate: Well, we both seem to agree on one thing anyway: Americans seem to want judicial review. But if what you say is true and they can sweep it aside when they don't want it, how in the world can you argue that there is anything undemocratic about judicial review?

9. Letter to Jarvis in 1820, quoted in *Thomas Jefferson on Democracy,* by Saul K. Padover (New York: Penguin Books, 1946), p. 64.

Theory and Experience

Our imaginary dialogue suggests several lines of thought.

To begin with, from the perspective of democratic principles, it is *federal* legislation, not state or municipal law, that sets the greatest challenge to the legitimacy of judicial review. It is reasonable to argue, at any rate, that in order to make their rule effective, the people of the *United States* might properly establish a supreme court with authority to negate state and municipal laws contrary to the national laws and Constitution. Orthodox majority-rule democracy would surely make it legitimate for the people of a country to insure that the preferences of *national* majorities prevailed over those of minorities, even if these minorities happened to be a majority of a state or a locality. Because federal legislation creates the problem, we concentrate mainly on that aspect here.

Democratic theory unclear. However, our dialogue also suggests that democratic theory provides no absolutely decisive argument as to the legitimacy of judicial review of federal legislation, that is, of laws passed by Congress and ordinarily not only signed but actively sponsored by the president. In the American polyarchy, judicial review seems to furnish a neat paradox:

☐ Because a nonelected body exercises final authority to nullify legislation enacted by the elected representatives of the people, judicial review seems to run flatly counter to the principles of consent and political equality.

☐ Yet if a large majority of Americans adhere to the ideal of limited—not majority-rule—democracy and support the Court's authority as an element in a system of partitioned power, the abolition of judicial review would appear to make the overall design of the system less, not more, responsive to the preferences of the citizen body.

Comparative experience. Nonetheless, if theory provides no crystal-clear answers, experience shows that judicial review is not inherent in polyarchy. Judicial review does not exist in most polyarchies. Probably in none is the authority of the highest court as broad as that exercised by the Supreme Court of the United States.

It follows, therefore, that adequate protection for the basic rights and institutional guarantees of polyarchies does not *necessarily* require the existence of judicial review. In fact, some countries with extraordinarily high levels of security for the rights of individuals and groups, such as Britain and the Scandinavian countries, have not granted their judiciary the power to nullify acts of their parliaments.

Two Alternative Possibilities

The extent to which the exercise of judicial review supports or conflicts with democratic principles would depend significantly on the *particular purposes* for which it was used. We can imagine two extreme possibilities:

☐ *The Court as a privileged interest group.* Judicial review might simply permit members of the Supreme Court and groups whose views they happen to reflect to impose on the country their own preferences, biases, views, and ideological commitments. These views might have nothing to do with, or even run flatly counter to, democratic goals such as political equality and consent.

☐ *The Court as protector of the national polyarchy.* The exercise of judicial review might help to reinforce the principles of political equality and consent and thereby strengthen polyarchy. Thus the Judicial Branch would insure that legislatures, executives, administrators, and lower courts adhered to the principle of political equality in their decisions, decision-making processes, and modes of representation, etc. In addition, the Court might support the principle of consent by guaranteeing that basic political rights of minorities would not be overridden through actions by lawmaking majorities, administrators, or lower courts.

A people committed to democratic ideals would surely reject the first kind of performance. Yet they might support the second in order to make sure that if they were to lapse momentarily from what they regarded as their deepest principles, the judiciary would nonetheless insure that these principles were upheld.

SUMMARY 1. Because judicial review does not appear to be implied in the principles of consent and political equality, its existence in the American polyarchy has always been a source of controversy and unresolved problems.

2. The legitimacy of judicial review in the American polyarchy rests heavily on tradition. Yet at the Constitutional Convention itself, the Framers appear to have been uncertain in their views as to the authority of the Supreme Court. It seems reasonable to conclude from their debates that a majority rejected the idea that judges should participate in *policy making* but accepted the notion that federal courts would rule on the *constitutionality* of state and federal laws in cases brought before them.

3. It was Chief Justice John Marshall who in *Marbury* v. *Madison* definitely established the existence and the rationale for judicial review.

That decisive precedent and Marshall's arguments have come to form the heart of the traditional belief in the legitimacy of judicial review.

4. Yet the traditional arguments do not answer the question whether the power of judicial review is consistent with the principles of political equality and consent—whether, in short, judicial review is a distinctly undemocratic element in the American polyarchy.

5. An exploration of this question reveals that the answer must depend to some extent on the actual performance of the Court—whether it has used its power to protect or advance particular views and interests, or to uphold the principles of political equality and consent.

18 THE SUPREME COURT AND JUDICIAL REVIEW: PERFORMANCE

THE WORK OF THE COURT

How then has the Supreme Court actually used its extraordinary authority? More than a hundred thousand cases are filed each year in federal courts. Of these, nearly five thousand finally reach the Supreme Court.[1] Most of these the Court disposes of by means of briefly stated decisions (often a single sentence), based solely on the record sent up from lower courts. The nine justices of the highest court hear argument on less than two thousand cases. Most of these involve some questions of constitutional interpretation.

Many of these cases are also highly partisan, highly 'political' issues. Sometimes they involve highly controversial political issues of great immediacy and urgency, such as the cases mentioned in Chapter 13: Truman's seizure of the steel industry during the Korean War, or attempts by opponents of the Vietnam war to have federal courts declare the president's war actions unconstitutional, or Judge Sirica's decision in the Watergate investigations that President Nixon was obliged to turn over to the Court some of the famous White House tapes.

Even where the need for a decision is less urgent, the cases argued before the Court will often represent a battle in a larger conflict over the policies or conduct of national, state, or local governments.

---

1. The number has been growing at a staggering rate. In 1953 it was only 1,463. These figures are from the handiest recent compendium on the work of the Court: *Congressional Quarterly,* "The Supreme Court, Justice and the Law" (Washington, D.C.: Congressional Quarterly, 1974), p. 74. Among other things, this volume of the Congressional Quarterly lists all the acts of Congress held unconstitutional by the Supreme Court from the Judiciary Act of 1789, overturned in *Marbury* v. *Madison* in 1803, to a 1971 amendment to the Food Stamp Act of 1964 held unconstitutional in 1973. As of this last decision, some ninety-seven acts had been held unconstitutional (pp. 113–118). Pp. 33–55 list a glossary of common legal terms. A glance through these cases conveys a good idea of the Court's most significant work. See also Chief Justice Warren E. Burger, "Reducing the Load of 'Nine Mortal Men,'" *The New York Times,* August 14, 1975.

This was the situation, it will be recalled, in the historic case of *Marbury* v. *Madison* described in the last chapter. Most of the issues on which the country is deeply and often passionately divided now find their way to the Court. In recent years the Court has ruled on racial discrimination, school and neighborhood integration, school busing, abortion, government aid to parochial schools, obscenity, government secrecy, reapportionment, capital punishment, wiretapping, inequities in financing public education . . .

Ordinarily all nine justices participate in decisions. (Occasionally the number is less because of a vacancy or because a justice is ill or disqualifies himself for some reason.) The majority principle prevails. Crucial decisions on the constitutionality of congressional acts are sometimes made by votes of five to four and fairly often by six to three. In effect, then, what is constitutional or unconstitutional can change if one or two justices join the dissenters or if they leave the Court by retirement or death and are replaced by justices with a different outlook.

It is therefore reasonable to wonder how much the views of a justice on the *constitutionality* of an act of Congress may be influenced by his views about its desirability as a matter of *policy.*

THE RECORD   An examination of the cases in which the Supreme Court has held *federal* legislation unconstitutional leads to a number of observations.

The Uncertain Line Between Policy and Constitutionality

Both of the basic arguments for judicial review discussed in the last chapter—the traditional constitutionality of judicial review and the Court as protector of the national polyarchy—assume that it is possible to make a reasonably clear distinction between decisions about *policy* and decisions about *constitutionality.* Yet the boundary has proved a difficult one for the Court to delineate and abide by. Since the Court's claim to legitimacy rests on the validity of this distinction, it is always at pains to insist that its decisions are made purely on constitutional grounds and have nothing to do with the views the justices may hold on matters of public policy. The record, however, suggests otherwise. In an earlier day it was perhaps easier to believe that the Constitution is so clear and certain rights are so natural and self-evident that their fundamental validity is as much a matter of definite knowledge, at least to all reasonable creatures, as the color of a ripe cherry. But today we know that the line between abstract right and policy is extremely hard to draw. A court can and does make policy decisions by going outside established 'legal' criteria found in precedent, statute, and Constitution. In this respect the Supreme Court occupies a most peculiar position, for it is characteristic of the Court that from time to time its members decide cases where constitutional criteria are not adequate in any realistic sense to the task. A distinguished legal scholar who was a member of the Court, the late Mr. Justice Frankfurter, once described the business of the Supreme Court in these words:

> It is essentially accurate to say that the Court's preoccupation today is with the application of rather fundamental aspirations and what Judge Learned Hand calls "moods," embodied in provisions like the due process clauses, which were designed not to be precise and positive directions for rules of action. The judicial process in applying them involves a judgment . . . that is, on the views of the direct representatives of the people in meeting the needs of society, on the views of presidents and governors, and by their construction of the will of legislatures the Court breathes life, feeble or strong, into the inert pages of the Constitution and the statute books.[2]

Very often, then, the cases before the Court involve alternatives about which there is severe disagreement in the society, as in the case of segregation or economic regulation. The very setting of the case is, then, 'political.' Moreover, these are usually cases where competent students of constitutional law, including the learned justices of the Supreme Court themselves, disagree; where the words of the Constitution are general, vague, ambiguous, or not clearly applicable; where precedent may be found on both sides; and where experts differ in predicting the consequences of the various alternatives or the degree of probability that the possible consequences will actually follow.

If the Court were assumed to be a 'political' institution, no particular problems would arise. It would be taken for granted that the members of the Court would resolve questions of fact and value by introducing assumptions derived from their own beliefs or those of influential clienteles and constituents. However, since both of the main arguments for judicial review require the assumption that the Court is not a political institution but exclusively a legal one, to accept the Court as a political institution would solve one set of problems at the price of creating another. Nonetheless, if the nature of the cases arriving before the Court is sometimes of the kind I have described, then the Court cannot act strictly as a legal institution. That is to say, it must choose among controversial alternatives of public policy by appealing to at least some standard of acceptability on questions of fact and value that cannot be found in or deduced from precedent, statute, and Constitution.

Court versus Congress and President: Minor Victories

A second conclusion to emerge from the record is that the Court frequently loses its battles with the president and Congress on matters of *major* policy, particularly if successive presidents and Congresses

---

2. Justice Felix Frankfurter, "The Supreme Court in the Mirror of Justices," *University of Pennsylvania Law Review,* 105 (April 1957), 781–796, at p. 793.

continue to support the policy the Court has called unconstitutional. The Court wins skirmishes; in a long war it may win a battle; it does not often win continuing wars with Congress.

Court versus past Congresses. More than half the decisions in holding federal acts unconstitutional were decided by the Supreme Court more than four years after the legislation was enacted. Thus the Court frequently does not confront *current* legislative majorities so much as past majorities.

Court versus current Congresses. Where the Court confronts the major policies of a current president and Congress, it nearly always loses. In about two-thirds of the cases involving major policies of current lawmaking majorities, the Court's decision has, in effect, been reversed by congressional action—often simply by rewriting the law. Dramatic evidence is provided by twelve decisions in which a Supreme Court controlled by a conservative majority declared various aspects of FDR's New Deal program unconstitutional. Of these, four involved trivial or minor policies. One involved a major New Deal policy contrivance, the NRA; it seems fair to say, however, that President Roosevelt and his advisers were relieved by the Court's decision regarding a policy that they had come to find increasingly embarrassing. In view of the tenacity with which FDR held to his major program, there can hardly be any doubt that, had he wanted to pursue the policy objective involved in the NRA codes, as he did for example with the labor provisions, he would not have been stopped by the Court's special theory of the Constitution. As to the seven other cases, whatever some of the eminent justices might have thought during their fleeting moments of glory, they did not succeed in interposing a barrier to the achievement of the objectives of the legislation; and in a few years most of the constitutional dogma on which they rested their opposition to the New Deal had been unceremoniously swept under the rug.

Court versus Congress and President: Major Delays

Nonetheless, although the Court loses most of its battles against a *persistent* president and Congress, on some matters of public policy its influence is consequential. Thus it has delayed policies for more than a decade and even more than a generation. What is more, if the views that finally prevailed on the Court are correct, then its lengthy obstruction had no proper constitutional basis to begin with. For example:

Workmen's compensation. A congressional act requiring employers to compensate longshoremen and harbor workers injured on the job was invalidated by the Supreme Court in 1920. In 1922, Congress passed a new law which was, in its turn, knocked down by the Court in 1924. In 1927 Congress passed a third law, which was finally upheld in 1932. Thus the Court delayed workmen's compensation for twelve years.

Child labor. Two child labor cases represent the most effective battle ever waged by the Court against legislative policy makers. The original legislation outlawing child labor, based on the commerce clause, was passed in 1916 as part of President Wilson's New Freedom program. In 1918 the Supreme Court held the law unconstitutional by a vote of five to four. Congress moved at once to circumvent the decision by means of the tax power, but in 1922 the Court blocked that approach. In 1924, Congress returned to the fray with a constitutional amendment. The amendment was rapidly endorsed by a number of state legislatures, but then began to meet so much resistance in the states remaining that the enterprise miscarried. In 1938, under President Franklin Roosevelt, new legislation was passed—twenty-two years after the first. A Court with a New Deal majority finally accepted child labor legislation in 1941 and thereby brought to an end a battle that had lasted a full quarter-century.

Court versus Congress and President: Setting the Agenda

The Court through its decisions (and the grounds for these decisions, set out in the written opinions of the justices) also influences national policy in another way. It determines to some extent what kinds of issues will be considered by the president, Congress, and other political leaders and activists at the national, state, or local levels, some of the terms on which these issues will be discussed and debated, and the scope of the permissible alternatives. In this way it helps set the national agenda, so to speak.

Racial integration in the public schools is an example. By its famous decision in 1954 declaring that racially segregated schools are unconstitutional and "inherently unequal," the Supreme Court brought school desegregation and, finally, the whole area of civil rights into the forefront as pressing national issues.[3]

Court versus President and Congress: Protector of Minority Rights?

Based on its record since the 1950s one might suppose that the Court has had a splendid history of protecting the fundamental rights

3. *Brown v. Board of Education of Topeka,* 347 U.S. 483 (1954). This emphasis on the Court's role in agenda setting I owe to an article by Jonathan D. Casper, "The Supreme Court and National Policy-Making," *The American Political Science Review* (forthcoming).

of otherwise defenseless minorities against encroachment by the president and Congress. In this view of the Court's role we would expect to find a considerable number of important cases in which the justices have declared unconstitutional laws passed by Congress, or orders by the president, on the ground that they impaired the rights of citizens granted by the first ten amendments (the Bill of Rights).

Looking over the annals of the Court, however, two conclusions are strikingly evident. *First,* most of the cases in which the Court has defended the rights of unpopular minorities against majorities are quite recent. They mainly occurred between 1954 and 1968, during a period of 'judicial activism,' as it has been called, when the Court was presided over by Chief Justice Earl Warren. *Second,* even then, most of these cases involved state or local laws, not acts of Congress. An inspection of the historical records shows:

1. There have been only a handful of cases, all since 1964, in which the Court has held a provision of *federal* law to be unconstitutional—as contrary to the fundamental liberties of religion, speech, press, and assembly guaranteed by the First Amendment. Two cases involved federal legislation directed toward alleged Communists. In two others, parts of certain federal acts were held to violate rights of antiwar protesters.[4]

2. In about ten cases prior to 1964, the Court has held congressional acts unconstitutional because they violated other provisions of the Bill of Rights. An inspection of the issues in all the earlier cases indicates that the lawmakers and the Court were not very far apart. Moreover, the issues were mainly of such a minor sort that it is doubtful whether the fundamental conditions of liberty in this country were altered by more than a hair's breadth as a result.

3. Over against these decisions we must put the substantial number of cases in which the Court used the protections of the Bill of Rights, or the constitutional amendments enacted after the Civil War to protect the rights of the newly freed blacks, not to uphold the weak against the strong but quite the reverse: to preserve the rights and liberties of a relatively privileged group at the expense of the rights and liberties of a submerged group. The victors in these cases were chiefly slaveholders at the expense of slaves, whites at the expense of non-whites, and property holders at the expense of wage earners and other groups.[5] For example, in the Civil Rights cases (1883) the Court upheld white supremacy and segregation by *striking down* a federal statute in-

4. For brief summaries, see *Congressional Quarterly,* "The Supreme Court," pp. 113–118, Nos. 75, 80, 87, 92, and 93.
5. *Ibid.,* Nos. 5, 10, 13, 16, 17, 19, and 28. For an exception to this dismal record, see No. 24.

tended to guarantee "the full and equal enjoyment of accommodations . . . of inns, public conveyances . . ., theatres, and other places of public amusement."

These cases, unlike some of the relatively unimportant ones previously discussed, all involved liberties of genuinely fundamental importance, where an opposite policy would have meant basic shifts in the distribution of rights, liberties, and opportunities in the United States. Moreover, the policies sustained by the Court's action have since been repudiated in every civilized nation of the Western world, including our own.

4. In a dozen or more cases since 1964, however, the Court *has* struck down provisions of federal laws directed against unpopular minorities. Beginning in 1964 the Court all but singlehandedly dismantled the Subversive Activities Control Act of 1950, which was explicitly directed against Communists. The Court also struck down laws denying certain of the constitutional rights of other unpopular groups, such as welfare clients, gamblers, and drug dealers.[6]

Protector of National Polyarchy Against State and Local Attacks

As was suggested in the last chapter, the problem of judicial review from a democratic perspective arises in its most acute form with respect to *federal* legislation, not state and local actions. In the domain of state and local actions the record of the Court, although uneven over its whole history, has come increasingly closer in this century to the model of protector of the national polyarchy. In innumerable cases it has declared unconstitutional state or local laws, practices, and actions held to infringe on fundamental rights guaranteed by the Constitution.[7] It has also markedly enlarged the scope of those rights.[8] After the failure of a last-ditch conservative Court effort to halt the New Deal, the Court has since provided a constitutional foundation for the vast new national powers employed by all subsequent administrations in behalf of their

---

6. The rights most commonly violated are the guarantees of the Fifth Amendment against self-incrimination ("No person . . . shall be compelled in any criminal case to be a witness against himself") and the right to due process (". . . nor be deprived of life, liberty, or property, without due process of law."). For the cases involving Communists, see *ibid.*, Nos. 74–77 and 80; welfare clients, Nos. 84 and 96 (food stamps); gamblers, Nos. 82 and 91; drug dealers, Nos. 85 (marijuana) and 88 (cocaine).

7. For example, in *Julian Bond* v. *James "Sloppy" Floyd* (1966) a unanimous Court held that Julian Bond's exclusion from the Georgia House because of his statements against the war in Vietnam violated the First Amendment. In *Bachellar* v. *State of Maryland* a unanimous Court held that where it was impossible to determine whether convictions for disorderly conduct in blocking a public sidewalk resulted from the unpopular views of the defendants (they were arrested during a demonstration against the war in Vietnam), the convictions violated the First Amendment and must be reversed.

8. For example, in *Goldberg* v. *Kelly* (1970) by a vote of five to three the Court held that a welfare recipient was denied due process under the Fourteenth Amendment because his public assistance payments were terminated with no opportunity for him to have a hearing. In *Pickering* v. *Board of Education* (1968) the Court unanimously held that a public school teacher may not be dismissed for criticizing the school board unless the criticism is knowingly or recklessly false.

programs. And, as we saw in Chapter 15, the Court has imposed the principle of one person, one vote on unwilling legislative bodies.

THE COURT AS A POLITICAL INSTITUTION

How can we explain the behavior of the Court over the long run? Why does it have such a spotty record as protector of the national polyarchy? Why did it move more sharply in this direction during the "Warren Court" (1954–1968)? And why particularly against incursions by state and local governments? A large part of the answer lies in the fact that the Supreme Court is inescapably a participant in the larger political process of the American polyarchy.

Part of the Dominant Coalition

National politics in the United States, as in other stable polyarchies, is dominated by relatively cohesive alliances that endure for long periods of time. Recall the Jeffersonian alliance, the Jacksonian, the extraordinarily long-lived Republican dominance of the post–Civil War years, and the New Deal alliance shaped by Franklin Roosevelt. Each is marked by a break with past policies, a period of intense struggle, followed by consolidation, and finally decay and disintegration of the alliance.

Except for short-lived transitional periods during which the old alliance is disintegrating and the new one is struggling to take control of political institutions, the Supreme Court is inevitably a part of the dominant national alliance. It becomes so for an exceedingly simple reason: the eminent justices of the United States Supreme Court are mortal. They grow old. Sooner or later they retire or die. As they leave the Court new justices acceptable to the current coalition take their place.

Over the whole history of the Court, one new justice has been appointed on the average of every twenty-three months. Thus a president can expect to appoint two new justices during one term of office; and if this were not enough to tip the balance on a normally divided Court, the president would be almost certain to succeed in two terms. For example, Roosevelt made nine appointments; Truman, four; Eisenhower, five; Kennedy in his brief tenure, two; Johnson, two; Nixon, four. Presidents are not famous for appointing justices hostile to their own views on public policy; nor could they expect to secure confirmation of an individual whose stance on key questions was flagrantly at odds with that of the dominant majority in the Senate. When Nixon violated this assumption in 1970 by his attempt to appoint first Clement Haynsworth and then G. Harrold Carswell, he was twice defeated. Typically, justices are persons who, prior to appointment, have engaged in public life and have committed themselves publicly on the great questions of the day.

As Mr. Justice Frankfurter once pointed out, a surprisingly large proportion of the justices, particularly of the great justices who have left their stamp upon the decisions of the Court, have had little or no prior judicial experience. Nor have the justices—certainly not the great justices—been timid souls with a passion for anonymity. Indeed, it is not too much to say that if justices were appointed primarily for their 'judicial' qualities without regard to their basic attitudes on fundamental questions of public policy, the Court could not play the influential role in the American political system that it does in reality.

It is reasonable to conclude, then, that the prevailing policy views on the Court will never be out of line for very long with the prevailing policy views among the lawmaking majorities of the United States. And it would be most unrealistic to suppose that the Court would, for more than a few years at most, stand against any major alternatives sought by a lawmaking majority. President Franklin D. Roosevelt's difficulties with the Court when it steadily struck down his early New Deal legislation, were truly exceptional. Roosevelt had unusually bad luck; he had to wait four years for his first appointment; the odds against this long interval are about five to one. With average luck, his battle with the Court would never have occurred; even as it was, although his 'court-packing' proposal to increase the number of justices did formally fail, by the end of his second term in 1940 Roosevelt had appointed five new justices, and he gained three more the following year.

As an element in the leadership of the dominant alliance, the Court tends to support the major policies of the alliance. Acting solely by itself with no support from the president and Congress, the Court is almost powerless to determine the course of national policy.

The Supreme Court is not, however, simply an *agent* of the alliance. It is an essential part of the political leadership and possesses some bases of power of its own, the most important of which is the unique standing attributed to its interpretations of the Constitution. The Court would jeopardize this standing if it were flagrantly to oppose the major policies of the dominant alliance; such a course of action, as we have seen, is one in which the Court will not normally be tempted to engage.

It follows that within the somewhat narrow limits set by the basic policy goals of the dominant alliance, the Court *can* sometimes make national policy. Its discretion, then, is not unlike that of a powerful committee chairman in Congress who cannot, generally speaking, nullify the basic policies substantially agreed on by the rest of the dominant leadership, but who can, within these limits, often determine important questions of timing, effectiveness, and subordinate policy. Thus the Court is least effective against a current lawmaking majority—and evidently least inclined to act.[9] It is most effective when it sets the bounds of policy for officials, agencies, state governments, or even regions, a task that has come to occupy a very large part of the Court's business.

The main objective of presidential leadership is to build a stable and dominant aggregation of minorities with a high probability of winning the presidency and one or both houses of Congress. Ordinarily the main contribution of the Court is to confer legality and constitutionality on the fundamental policies of the successful coalition.

But if this were the only function of the Supreme Court, would it have acquired the standing it has among Americans? In fact, at its best —and the Court is not always at its best—it does more than merely provide legality and constitutionality to the actions of the national coalition. The Supreme Court sometimes serves as a guide and even a pioneer in arriving at different standards of fair play and individual right than have resulted, or are likely to result, from the interplay of the other political forces. This is done by the way the Court interprets and modifies national laws, perhaps but not necessarily by holding them unconstitutional. Thus in recent years, as we have seen, the Court has modified by interpretation or declared unconstitutional provisions of federal law restricting the rights of unpopular and even widely detested minorities —military deserters, Communists, and alleged bootleggers, for example. The judges, after all, inherit an ancient tradition and an acknowledged role in setting higher standards of justice and right than the majority of citizens or their representatives might otherwise demand. For reasons we have already examined, if the standards of justice propounded by the Court are to prevail, they cannot be too remote from general standards of fairness and individual right among Americans. At the same time, most Americans are too attached to the Court to want it stripped of its power, although they may—and do—protest its decisions, or even call for the impeachment of a particular justice whose decisions some of them detest.

There are times, too, when the other political forces are too divided to arrive at decisions on certain key questions. At very great risk, the Court can intervene in such cases; and sometimes it may even succeed in establishing policy where the president and Congress are unable to do so. Probably in such cases it can succeed only if its action conforms to a widespread set of explicit or implicit norms held by the political leadership: norms that are not strong enough or are not distributed in such a way as to insure the existence of an effective lawmaking majority, but are nonetheless sufficiently powerful to prevent any successful attack on the legitimacy and power of the Court. This is probably the

---

9. See Richard Funston, "The Supreme Court and Critical Elections," *American Political Science Review* 69 (September 1975), 795–811.

explanation for the relatively successful work of the Court in enlarging the freedom of blacks to vote, in its famous school integration decisions, and in the reapportionment cases. Even in these instances, the ends sought could not have been obtained by the Court itself. They required action by other policymakers: the president, Congress, state governors, and legislators, and municipal governments. It was, after all, not the decisions of the Court but the passage and enforcement of the Civil Rights Acts of 1964 and 1965 that opened up the electoral process to Southern blacks. School integration, so optimistically promised by the Court's decision in 1954, was still unachieved a generation later.

Yet the Court does even more than this. Considered as a political system, polyarchy is a set of basic procedures for arriving at decisions. The operation of these procedures presupposes the existence of certain rights, obligations, liberties, and restraints; in short, certain patterns of behavior. The existence of these patterns of behavior in turn presupposes widespread agreement (particularly among the politically active and influential segments of the population) on the validity and propriety of the behavior. Although its record is by no means lacking in serious blemishes, at its best the Court helps to gain acceptability, not simply for the particular policies of the dominant political alliance, but for the basic patterns of behavior required for the operation of a polyarchy.

Yet in order to *confer* acceptability, the Court must itself *possess* acceptability. To the extent that the acceptability of every political institution in the American polyarchy depends finally on its consistency with democratic principle, the acceptability of judicial review and the Court's exercise of that power must stem from the presumption that the Court is ultimately subject to popular control. The more the Court exercises self-restraint and the less it challenges the policies of lawmaking majorities, the less the need or the impulse to subject it to popular controls. The more active the Court is in contesting the policies of lawmaking majorities, the more visible becomes the slender basis of its legitimacy according to democratic standards, and the greater the efforts will be to bring the Court's policies into conformity with those enacted by lawmaking majorities.

If the persistent temper of a dominant coalition is to use the Court as a privileged interest group or a protector of privileged interest groups, no Court can long persist as protector of the national polyarchy. By yielding—and aging, retirement, and death make yielding inevitable—the Court may gain the confidence and respect of the coalition's leaders in the White House and Congress. Yet it will lose the confidence and respect of those who seek to justify its authority on democratic principles. And at the next swing of the political pendulum, the Court may well find that it has impaired its own authority.

Where the dominant coalition is prepared to allow or even encourage the Court to act as defender of the national polyarchy, the Court will gain in whatever acceptability it can draw from democratic principles. Yet in such periods, as in the others, the Court will rarely find it necessary to nullify any major policies of the dominant political coalition. Even as defender of the national polyarchy, then, its victories against the president and Congress are likely to be rare and transitory. Thus in this role—and it it is hard to find grounds for its acceptability in any other—it will serve mainly as an arbiter in the federal system, protecting the fundamental requisites of polyarchy against inroads by minorities in states and localities. Although it has not always played this role well, and at times not even at all, it has probably performed better in recent decades than throughout most of its previous history.

In the end, however, we must not lose sight of the fact that the Court's power of judicial review over *national* legislation is, at best, an exceedingly weak guarantee of polyarchy in the United States. At its worst, the Court's power of judicial review has no claim to legitimacy according to democratic criteria.

SUMMARY   An examination of the performance of the Supreme Court in the actual cases in which it has declared federal laws unconstitutional indicates that:

1. The line between decisions about the wisdom of policy and decisions about constitutionality has been a difficult one for the Court to discover and abide by.

2. The Court has rarely succeeded in using judicial review to prevent the president and Congress from pursuing any major policies on which they agree.

3. However, in some instances the Court has directly influenced national policies in two ways: *First,* it delayed reforms for a decade or more. These include such matters as workmen's compensation and the abolition of child labor, which the Court finally accepted as constitutionally valid. *Second,* its decisions help to set the national agenda—to determine the nature of the issues considered by political leaders.

4. Until recently, the Court has not made a significant contribution as protector of the rights of otherwise weak or defenseless minorities against encroachment by the federal government.

5. However, through judicial review the Court has made an important contribution, particularly in recent decades, as protector of the national polyarchy against encroachment by state and local governments.

These aspects of the Court's performance are largely to be explained as follows:

1. Since members of the Court are mortal, they retire or die and are replaced by new appointees.

2. In making appointments, the president and Senate pay attention not only to the constitutional views of the prospective appointees but also to the implications of their views or record for matters of public policy.

3. Thus if a coalition persists for some time in controlling the presidency and Congress, it is certain to gain a majority of members of the Court who are sympathetic with the general policy views and goals of the dominant coalition.

4. The extent to which the Court is, at the one extreme, a privileged interest group or, at the other, a defender of the national polyarchy depends, then, largely on the mood, temper, and outlook of the dominant forces in the presidency and the Congress.

5. For this reason, the Court's power of judicial review over national legislation appears to be a rather weak guarantee of polyarchy.

19 STATE AND LOCAL GOVERNMENTS: CONTRIBUTIONS TO POLYARCHY

Although the national government is only one of many governments that Americans support, it is the largest, most inclusive, and most powerful of all the governments within the United States. The national government receives from most Americans a greater share of their loyalty, obedience, affection, and taxes than any other government. It is without much question the dominant government in the American polyarchy.

The national government is one of more than eighty thousand governments of all kinds existing within the boundaries of the United States. Of these, more than a fourth are school districts. Even if we ignore special districts for schools and other specialized functions and consider only general territorial governments, the states, counties, municipalities, townships, and towns have numbered altogether close to thirty-eight thousand for the last thirty or forty years (Table 19.1).

These territorial governments below the national level are of bewildering variety and complexity. The governments of the fifty states constitute a vast field in themselves. The thousands of towns and cities create a political tapestry even more complex. It has been estimated, to take one example, that the metropolitan area around New York City alone includes 1,467 'distinct political entities.'[1] *Governing New York City,*[2] a monumental study (as befits the largest city in the country) amounts to over eight hundred pages.

What contributions do territorial governments below the national level make to the American polyarchy? If one tries to imagine how the

---

1. Robert C. Wood, *1400 Governments* (Garden City: Doubleday Anchor, 1964).

2. Wallace Sayre and Herbert Kaufman, *Governing New York City* (New York: Russell Sage Foundation, 1960).

Table 19.1
Number and Type of
Government Units in the
United States, Selected
Years, 1942–1972

Unit of Government	1942	1957	Number 1962	1967	1972	Change 1942–1972
U.S. Government	1	1	1	1	1	0
States	48	48	50	50	50	+2
Counties	3050	3047	3043	3049	3044	−6
Municipalities	16220	17183	17997	18048	18517	+2297
Towns and Townships	18919	17198	17144	17105	16991	−1928
School Districts	108579	50446	34678	21782	15781	−92798
Special Districts	8299	14405	18323	21264	23885	+15586
Total	155116	102328	91236	81299	78269	−76847

Source: U.S. Department of Commerce, Bureau of the Census, *1972 Census of Governments*, No. 4 Historical Statistics.

American political system might operate without them, four possible contributions suggest themselves:

1. By reducing the workload of the national government, they make polyarchy at the national level more manageable.
2. By permitting diversity in problem-solving and by localizing or 'denationalizing' issues, they sometimes reduce conflicts at the national level and thus make polyarchy more viable.
3. By providing numerous more or less independent or autonomous centers of power throughout the system, they further increase the partition of power.
4. By facilitating self-government at local levels, they greatly expand the opportunities for learning and practicing the ways of polyarchal government in the United States.

MAKING NATIONAL POLYARCHY MORE MANAGEABLE

Alternatives

The imagination boggles in the attempt to conceive of the United States as a polyarchy which operates nationally by means of elected leaders and competitive political parties, but which is governed locally through a centralized bureaucracy, federally appointed and controlled, that would administer tasks now carried on by thirty-eight thousand territorial governments. After all, most self-governing nations are no larger than our larger states.

Complete centralization. How would a completely centralized system actually function in the United States? On the one hand, the system might be centralized not only in law but *in fact* as well. In this case, would not the power of the chief executive and the insensitivity of the national bureaucracy to local variation crush local diversity? What is more, the burdens on national policy makers—the president, the Congress, the courts, the administrative agencies—would be frightful; to superimpose these new tasks on their present duties (which, we have seen, are already enormous) would surely create a workload well beyond their capacities to handle.

De facto decentralization. National policymakers might meet such an impossible workload by either neglecting their duties or delegating decisions to other officials. To the extent that national officials delegated decisions to other officials who were closer to the local scene, the system might become centralized in law but decentralized in fact. National uniformity would doubtless be too rigid and oppressive to remain tolerable for long. National officials would develop strong but informal local ties. Local pressures would be felt. The wise administrator would learn to adapt his policies to local circumstances. Sooner or later, American citizens might conclude that law should conform more closely to fact. In short: If local governments did not exist, they would quickly be invented.

De facto centralization. It might be objected, however, that there is a third alternative, and that this alternative has actually come to pass in the United States: a system decentralized in constitutional and legal form but centralized in fact. It is often said that the rapidly increasing role of the national government has deprived local territorial governments of their earlier functions; 'the demise of local government' is as common a theme in the United States as 'the rise of the executive' and 'the decline of Congress.'

The Expansion of Local Governments

The degree of centralization or decentralization of an organization has so far proved all but impossible to measure. Hence, one cannot meet the argument directly by producing satisfactory evidence on the amount of change in degree of centralization in the political system of the United States over the past half century. But a fairly large number of different indicators do reveal that the role of local governments in American life has actually *expanded* in this century. Evidently what has happened is that all our territorial governments—national, state, and local—have increased their functions. Whether it be national, state, or local, every government carries out more tasks today than it did a few generations ago.

For example, the expenditures, revenues, and functions of the state and local governments have steadily grown in recent decades. True, since the high period of the New Deal in 1936, federal expenditures have risen faster than those of the state and local governments. But the lion's share of federal outlays has been consumed by national defense,

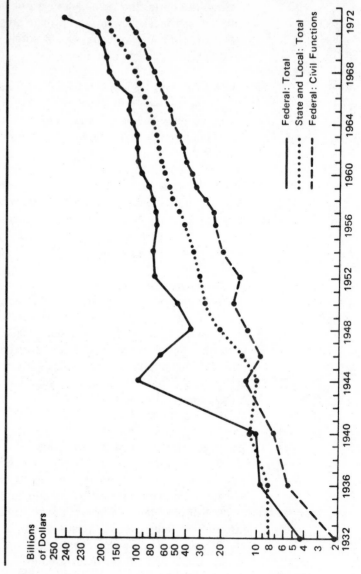

Figure 19.1
Federal, State, and Local
Expenditures, 1932–1972

Source: Department of Commerce, Bureau of the Census, *1972 Census of Governments*, No. 4 Historical Statistics, pp. 36–40.

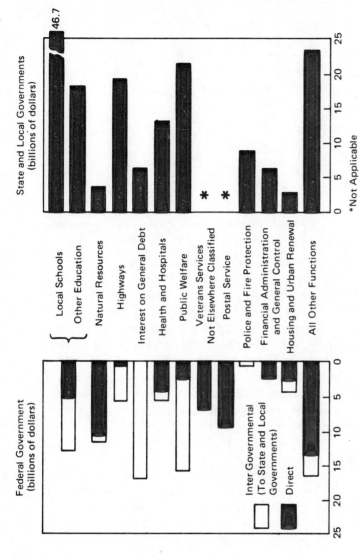

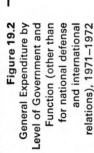

Figure 19.2
General Expenditure by
Level of Government and
Function (other than
for national defense
and international
relations), 1971–1972

Source: Department of Commerce, Bureau of the Census, *1972 Census of Governments*, No. 5 Graphic Summary, p. 28.

Year	GNP (billions)	Expenditure as Percentage of GNP		
		Federal	State-Local	Total
1902	$ 21.6	1.1	4.7	5.8
1927	96.3	1.5	7.5	9.0
1938	85.2	5.9	10.3	16.2
1948	259.4	3.4	6.8	10.2
1963	583.9	3.7	11.1	14.8
1967	793.5	3.6	11.8	15.4
1968	864.2	3.4	11.9	15.3
1969	930.3	3.5	12.5	16.0
1970	977.1	3.7	13.4	17.1
1971	1055.5	4.1	14.3	18.4
1972	1155.2	4.2	14.6	18.8

Sources: Figures for 1902–63, James A. Maxwell, *Financing State and Local Governments* (Washington: The Brookings Institution, 1965), Appendix Table A-3; for 1967–1972, *1972 Census of Governments*, Vol. 6, No. 4, Historical Statistics, pp. 35–40. GNP figures for 1968–1972 are from *Statistical Abstract 1974*, p. 373. (Intergovernmental payments are charged to the level of government making final disbursement.)

international relations, space programs, veterans' services, and interest on the public debt. If we eliminate these items, we discover that the difference virtually disappears; since the 1930s, state and local expenditures have climbed at about the same rates as federal expenditures for strictly civil functions (Figure 19.1). 'Obsolete' state and local governments spend far more than the federal government for education, highways, health and hospitals, and public welfare (Figure 19.2). Revenues from strictly state and local sources—that is, excluding all federal grants—were fourteen times greater in 1972 than in 1940 (Figure 19.3). Of about fourteen million civilians employed by government in 1972, approximately one in five were federal employees, more than one in five were state employees, and the rest were employed by local governments (Figure 19.4).

Far from having lost functions, then, the local governments have been gaining new ones. There is no record that state and local governments spent any funds at all for housing development until 1938, when they spent 3 million dollars. In 1963 they spent 446 million dollars. The state and local governments are a major factor in the national economy. In 1972 their expenditures for civil functions were equivalent to nearly 15 percent of the gross national product, compared with 4 percent for the federal government (Table 19.2).

There are then no valid grounds for doubting that both in fact and in law the local territorial governments of the United States assume a huge burden, which, in their absence, would have to be discharged somehow by federal officials. It seems reasonable to conclude that in a country as vast and as complex as the United States, local governments are necessary simply (if for no other reason) in order to achieve a level

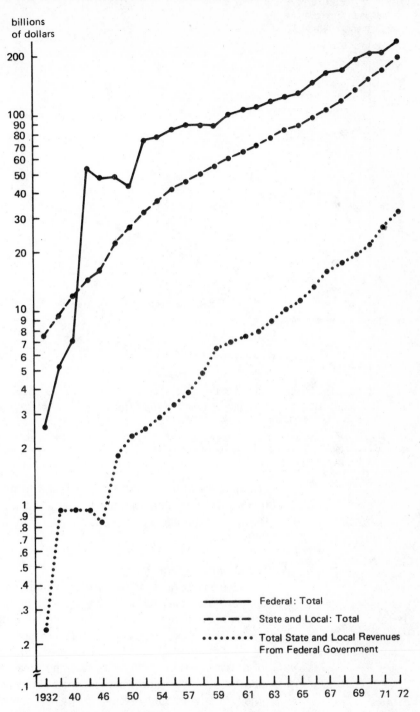

Figure 19.3
Federal, State, and Local
Revenues, 1932–1972

billions
of dollars

Federal: Total

State and Local: Total

Total State and Local Revenues
From Federal Government

Source: Department of Commerce, Bureau of the Census, *1972 Census of Governments*, No. 4 Historical Statistics, pp. 36–40.

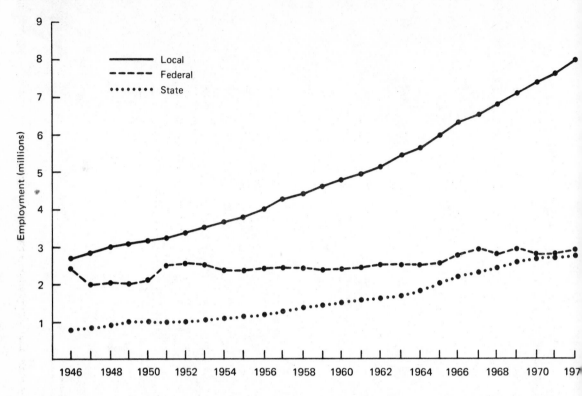

Figure 19.4
Trends in Government
Employment, 1946–1972

Employment (millions)

Legend:
— Local
--- Federal
···· State

1946 1948 1950 1952 1954 1956 1958 1960 1962 1964 1966 1968 1970 197

Source: Department of Commerce, Bureau of the Census, *1972 Census of Governments*, No. 4 Historical Statistics, p. 59.

of efficiency in government high enough to make polyarchy at the national level tolerable. Without the local governments, national governmental institutions would probably go under from the sheer weight of their burdens.

The Criterion of Efficiency

One might nonetheless wonder whether local governments in the United States operate above some minimum level of tolerability. They may provide enough efficiency to keep the system stumbling along, but are they anything like as efficient as they should be?

Unfortunately, dear though it be to advocates of governmental reform, the criterion of efficiency does not take one very far. Efficiency is measured by the ratio between costs and gains, or 'inputs' and 'outputs.' What we count as costs or gains, inputs or outputs, depends on what we value and how much we value it. Consequently, to one who believes strongly in the values of democracy, the efficiency of state and local governments must be measured in large part by comparing their costs, using the term in a very broad sense indeed, against their contributions by democratic standards of performance. This is necessarily a highly subjective judgment.

It seems perfectly reasonable to ask how well state and local governments perform the various tasks assigned to them by law. Are they efficient administrative units in the narrow sense that they economize, cut costs, act with expertness and dispatch? The question seems reasonable, but it is nonetheless almost impossible to answer. One must first ask a counterquestion: With what are we to compare them? If we compare state and local governments with some theoretical ideal, it would be easy to show that like every other human institution they fall very far short of ideal achievement. But we know this much in advance. We can scarcely compare state and local governments with private firms, because neither the inputs nor the outputs of state and local governments are sufficiently like those of private enterprise to make comparisons valid. How can we compare the relative efficiency of the New York Police Department in controlling crime and traffic with the efficiency of General Motors in producing and marketing automobiles? There seems to be little possibility of a useful or even a meaningful comparison; even those intrepid spirits who would contend that General Motors is the more efficient of the two organizations would not propose, I imagine, to turn the police force of New York City over to General Motors.[3]

Can we compare the administrative efficiency of state and local governments with that of federal agencies? Here again we run into formidable problems because of the differences in outputs—the services performed. In any case, an adverse comparison would be highly misleading if it led one to conclude that the federal government would perform local functions more 'efficiently,' in the restricted sense, than do the local governments themselves.[4] For we need to know what would happen to the present level of efficiency of federal agencies if the federal government were to take on all the additional tasks now performed at local levels.

Perhaps the only way out of this dilemma is to compare similar local units with one another. Yet given the enormous variety of local governments, even this is a much more formidable enterprise than it might seem.

---

3. Two economists, Frank Levy and Edwin M. Truman, have pointed out the pitfalls in comparing an organization producing economic goods with one producing government goods in their "Toward a Rational Theory of Decentralization: Another View," *American Political Science Review,* 65 (March, 1971), 172–179.

4. From this point forward the term *local governments* means state and local, except where the context clearly implies the more restricted meaning of a city, town, county, etc. There is no generally accepted word to cover both state and local; local, therefore, will have to do the work of two.

Thus, despite its surface appeal, the criterion of efficiency does not take one very far. For appraising governments, 'efficiency' is a concept either too slippery to be meaningful or too precise to be applicable. However, three observations may nevertheless be permissible. *First,* American state and local governments have generally lagged behind the federal government in introducing reforms thought to contribute to administrative efficiency. Reforms on which state and local governments have lagged include the development of a nonpartisan and expert civil service, an executive budget, a single chief executive with substantial hierarchical control over administrative agencies, an adequate specialized staff for the chief executive, and so on. Corruption seems to occur more frequently, and on a larger scale, in local units than in the federal government. Pay scales are lower, both at the start and at the end of one's career.

Second, there are enormous variations among the different units of local government. By almost any objective test, the best local governments are as efficient as any unit found in the federal government; the worst are appalling. Between the best and the worst, there is a whole universe of types. No one can ever judge the quality of local government in the United States by his experience with one or two units.

Third, whatever weight one may give to the democratic contributions of local governments (we shall proceed to that matter next), it is obvious that the American polyarchy would be a very different system without the presence of local governments that enjoy a great measure of autonomy.

REDUCING CONFLICTS   If one cannot speak with much confidence about the efficiency of local governments as administrative units, one can say more about their efficiency as instruments of polyarchy. To begin with, how does the existence of thirty-eight thousand local territorial governments affect the course and severity of political conflicts?

The contributions of local government are, I think, two. Local governments make it possible for different groups of citizens to arrive at different solutions to problems. And they reduce the strain on the national political system by keeping many questions out of the national arena.

The Possibility of Diverse Solutions

A great and inescapable defect exists in any system of rule by majorities: On all questions in which the policy of a minority conflicts with the policy preferred by a majority, neither can prevail without frustrating the desires of the other. In this respect decisions by governments— whether democratic or not—are different from decisions in a perfectly free market operating according to standard text book theory. The citizen is not equivalent to the consumer. In a model 'free' market it does not matter that in my role as consumer I prefer buying books to phonograph records, while you prefer records to books. Within broad legal limits, we may both spend our incomes as we please, and the market will respond. In the market, differences among individuals in tastes and values need not lead to conflict among them.

Why not, then, substitute the market for the government? The most important reason is that there are a great many matters that the mechanisms of the marketplace are ill-equipped to handle—including the ultimate question of what should and what should not be left to the market. If I as a citizen wish to raise taxes and spend more money in order to construct new schools, and if you prefer lower taxes and no new schools, we cannot both get what we want. We cannot, that is, if we are in exactly the same political system. But if you and the people who think like you are in one political system, while I and other like-minded people are in another, we can perhaps both have what we want. In this way we could both be free to go our own different ways; both our governments might enjoy the full consent of all their citizens. Here is the kernel of truth in Rousseau's belief that small autonomous democracies consisting of like-minded citizens offer the greatest promise of freedom and self-government.[5]

Denationalizing Conflict

Local governments permit Americans to take or to keep many questions out of the great arena of national politics, and therefore out of a strictly 'either/or' kind of conflict. They make it possible for Americans to deal with many problems in different ways, ways presumably more in harmony with local tastes and values than any national solution could possibly be. To this extent, the presence of a vast network of local governments with a good deal of autonomy has probably reduced by a considerable margin the severity of conflict that a wholly national system would run into. By denationalizing many conflicts, local governments can reduce the strain on national political institutions. The importance of taking conflicts out of the national context can hardly be overestimated, particularly in a large country like the United States where there is great diversity in resources and local problems.

Limits. Yet the experience of the United States with the question of the role of black people in American life also suggests some limits on the process of localizing conflicts.[6] For some sixty years after the Constitu-

---

5. See Chapter 4, above.
6. This conflict is discussed in more detail in Chapter 27.

tional Convention, conflict over slavery was reduced by denationalizing the issue. All the famous compromises of the pre–Civil War period were agreements to narrow the question of slavery to a regional level. Within little more than a decade after the end of the Civil War, too, the issue of the place of the freed slaves was denationalized: for another sixty years or more national conflict on this issue was avoided. When the question of the place of blacks in American life did become nationalized, as it did in the 1850s and again a century later in the late 1940s and 1950s, that question turned into one of the most explosive issues in American politics. In the first case, nationalizing the conflict led directly to civil war; in the second, to violence and federal troops, demonstrations, and passage of Civil Rights Acts in the 1950s and 1960s.

Local injustice. This experience reveals some of the limits to the process of denationalizing conflicts. It is quite one thing to allow various groups of like-minded people to follow their own desires; but it is quite another to remove a dispute from the national arena in order to hand it over to local despots, as Americans did in the case of blacks for all except a few decades in our national history.

The case of blacks is, admittedly, an extreme one, and it is worth keeping that fact in mind. It is an extreme case partly because as both slaves and freedmen, the blacks lacked allies, at least in substantial numbers, outside the South. Members of a minority who feel oppressed in their localities would ordinarily search for allies in the national political arena. And they would count on their allies to keep the dispute alive in the Congress and in presidential elections—in short, to prevent the conflict from becoming fully denationalized. Today, Southern blacks have allies outside the South—and, for that matter, some in the South itself; consequently it would be impossible to denationalize that conflict today.

Unwillingness. In some disputes, then, the parties simply will not allow the issue to be cast out of national politics. This is a second limit to the process of denationalizing conflicts. The more interwoven the fabric of society, the less likely it is that different localities will be permitted to go their different ways—at least if these ways are very different from one another. The Kansas-Nebraska Act of 1854 was intended by Senator Stephen Douglas to put an end to the rising conflict over whether slavery was to be legal in new states carved out of the Western territories. He hoped to denationalize the dispute by letting the settlers in each new state decide the matter for themselves. Yet his bill was no sooner law than the political forces of the North and West began to realign themselves. For, while it had been possible to keep the issue of slavery more or less out of national politics, it proved impossible to prevent the question of slavery in the territories from turning quickly into a controversy between national political leaders.

With these reservations in mind, it is nonetheless true that the existence of local governments possessing a considerable measure of autonomy does permit extensive variations among communities in the way they carry on their activities. There are differences in the variety and range of functions. But perhaps more common are differences in levels of expenditure, in emphasis, in administrative and political styles, in the sorts, of people who hold office, and in their attitudes. Educational facilities, public health, unemployment compensation, hospital care, city planning, community redevelopment, and dozens of other activities vary enormously in quality and quantity from state to state and even from locality to locality. The differences are mainly a function of the resources available; but not entirely. For example, in 1961, state expenditures for public schools were in rough proportion to state income per capita in twenty-seven states, but markedly high in relation to income in eleven states, and markedly low in ten states.[7] Or, to take another example from the field of education, in New England private schools at all levels have played a much more significant role than they do in the Middle West, where resources have been poured almost exclusively into public education.

American local governments have, then, permitted an important measure of local variety and differences. In so doing, doubtless they have reduced the strain on national institutions. People are able to work out many of their problems in their states and localities, finding solutions that would lead to interminable debate and conflict if they were imposed uniformly throughout the United States. Even though the most pressing questions of the day cannot be denationalized, the existence of local autonomy helps to free the national arena for precisely these 'national' issues.

PARTITIONING POWER

Liberty, Equality, and Democracy

How, if at all, can liberty and democracy be maintained in a society of equals? Americans, who usually take the answer for granted, are often surprised to discover that this is one of the oldest problems in political theory. It was a question for Aristotle, the Greek philosopher four centuries before Christ. Two thousand years later, it was a central problem for the profound French observer Alexis de Tocqueville in his analysis of the United States in the 1830s.

Why is there a problem at all, one might ask. Perhaps we can best

---

7. Herbert Jacob and Kenneth N. Vines, eds., *Politics In the United States, A Comparative Analysis* (Boston: Little, Brown, 1965), p. 354, Table 1.

answer this question by noting the contrary, even paradoxical, aspect of equality as it was seen by Tocqueville. To Tocqueville, an increasing equality was not only inevitable in America and Europe, it was also a necessary condition for democracy. At the same time, Tocqueville, like Aristotle, believed that extensive political, economic, and social equalities created a natural political environment for the tyrant. Thus he formulated a dilemma for democrats: a necessary condition for democracy is also a condition that facilitates despotism. The whole of his two-volume *Democracy in America* can be read as an exploration of the circumstances by which tyranny might be avoided and liberal democracy preserved in a society of equals.

The fear of despotism. The problem, as Tocqueville saw it, was this: In a society of equals, there are no intermediate institutions or classes powerful enough to prevent the rise of a despot. Having eliminated aristocracy, a society of equals needs institutions to perform the political function he attributed, perhaps overgenerously, to a well-established aristocracy—some force to stand in the way of the aspiring despot. In a nation of equals, no individual is strong enough to stop the despot; and citizens are incapable of acting as a body except through leaders. Even should citizens want to oppose the despot (Tocqueville thought that they probably would not), in the absence of an intermediate layer of leaders they would be powerless. Tocqueville painted a haunting picture of that peculiar tyranny in which democracy might one day culminate. It would be the tyranny of an equal people united under a popular leader, the special tyranny that was appropriate to democracy because it would thrive on the very equality so indispensable to democracy.

> I seek to trace the novel features under which despotism may appear in the world. The first thing that strikes the observation is an innumerable multitude of men, all equal and alike, incessantly endeavoring to procure the petty and paltry pleasures with which they glut their lives. Each of them, living apart, is as a stranger to the fate of all the rest; his children and his private friends constitute to him the whole of mankind. As for the rest of his fellow citizens, he is close to them, but does not see them; he touches them, but does not feel them; he exists only in himself and for himself alone; and if his kindred still remain to him, he may be said at any rate to have lost his country.
>
> Above this race of men stands an immense and tutelary power, which takes upon itself alone to secure their gratifications and to watch over their fate. That power is absolute, minute, regular, provident, and mild. It would be like the authority of a parent if, like that authority, its object was to prepare men for manhood; but it seeks, on the contrary, to keep them in perpetual childhood: it is well content that the people should rejoice, provided they think of nothing but rejoicing. For their happiness such a government willingly labors, but it chooses to be the sole agent and the

only arbiter of that happiness; it provides for their security, foresees and supplies their necessities, facilitates their pleasures, manages their principal concerns, directs their industry, regulates the descent of property, and subdivides their inheritances: what remains, but to spare them all the care of thinking and all the trouble of living?

Thus it every day renders the exercise of the free agency of man less useful and less frequent; it circumscribes the will within a narrower range and gradually robs a man of all these uses of himself. The principle of equality has prepared men for these things; it has predisposed men to endure them and often to look on them as benefits.

After having thus successively taken each member of the community in its powerful grasp and fashioned him at will, the supreme power then extends its arm over the whole community. It covers the surface of society with a network of small complicated rules, minute and uniform, through which the most original minds and the most energetic characters cannot penetrate, to rise above the crowd. The will of man is not shattered, but softened, bent, and guided; men are seldom forced by it to act, but they are constantly restrained from acting. Such a power does not destroy, but it prevents existence; it does not tyrannize, but it compresses, enervates, extinguishes, and stupefies a people, till each nation is reduced to nothing better than a flock of timid and industrious animals, of which the government is the shepherd.[8]

The hope of preserving freedom. In spite of his melancholic vision of the possible fate of democratic societies, Tocqueville was hopeful about the United States—precisely because Americans had not made impotent the intermediate institutions, the democratic alternatives to aristocracy. Indeed, Americans had not only conserved and strengthened certain old institutions, they had even created some new ones. In the power, autonomy, and self-consciousness of the legal profession, in the freedom of the press, in a variety of private associations, political and nonpolitical, Americans had, he thought, developed their substitutes for the political functions of an aristocracy as an offset to tyranny. Constitutional arrangements themselves had added even more barriers to halt the eager tyrant. Among these constitutionally created barriers were, naturally, the federal system and the tradition of local self-government.

How Local Governments Help

From our present perspective, what can we say about Tocqueville's judgment? Do state and local governments help to tame our political leaders?

Training. The first and most obvious contribution of local representative institutions is to provide a training ground for political leaders. Here

---

8. Alexis de Tocqueville, *Democracy in America,* 2 vols. (New York: Vintage Books, 1955), vol. 2, pp. 336–337.

Table 19.3
U.S. Presidents,
1900–75: Previous
Elective Offices

	State Legislature	Governor	Congress House	Senate	Vice-President
McKinley		★	★		
T. Roosevelt	★	★			
Taft					
Wilson		★			
Harding	★			★	
Coolidge	★	★			★
Hoover					
F. D. Roosevelt	★	★			
Truman				★	★
Eisenhower					
Kennedy			★	★	
L. Johnson			★	★	★
Nixon			★	★	★
Ford			★		a

a Ford was appointed Vice-President under the provisions of the Twenty-fifth Amendment.

they learn the political arts required in a polyarchy. In the terminology of contemporary political science, local institutions carry on the functions of political socialization and recruitment. The enormous number and variety of governments in the United States, many of them with elective offices and many involved in some way with party or factional politics, provide a vast political school that turns out a sizable stratum of subleaders with at least modest political skills. Many of the national political leaders are drawn from this pool of men and women trained in local and state politics; it is this pool, too, that often furnishes the local leaders in moments of emergency—when, for example, a possible unjust local regulation threatens to become a reality and citizens feel the need to act.[9]

Thus, of the fourteen men who served as president in this century, all except three—Taft, Hoover, and Eisenhower—had previously held elective political office. Of the ten with experience in an elective office, six had held office as governor or member of the state legislature (Table 19.3). A large proportion of congressional leaders have also been state officeholders, usually holding elective office. Just as being senator or governor is the best public position from which to win the presidency, so, too, the Senate itself recruits a large share of its membership from the House and from state or local officeholders (Table 19.4).

Most state governors first learn their craft in state and local politics. Out of almost one thousand governors elected in the United States from 1870 to 1950, slightly over half had previously been in the state

9. For example, see William K. Muir, Jr., *Defending "The Hill" Against Metal Houses*, ICP case series, no. 26 (University, Ala.: University of Alabama Press, 1955); and Robert A. Dahl, *Who Governs? Democracy and Power in an American City* (New Haven, Conn.: Yale University Press, 1961), pp. 192 ff.

Table 19.4
Previous Offices held by
U.S. Senators, 1959–71

	Percent of Senators who had held following offices
State legislator	32%
United States representative	30
Law enforcement	24
State governor	17
Local office	14
Administrative offices, governmental	13
Statewide elective office	12
Congressional staff	3

Sources: *Congressional Directory* (Washington, D.C.: Government Printing Office, 1971); *Who's Who in American Politics,* 3rd ed. (New York: R. R. Bowker, 1971). Total number of senators included, 152. This excludes the judiciary because of the difficulty in determining whether the office is elective or appointive.

legislature, a fifth had held local elective office, and nearly a fifth had held some statewide elective office.[10]

A base for opposition. The state and local governments also help to provide a secure base to which opposition may retire when it has suffered defeat elsewhere, in order to sally forth and challenge its opponents at the next election. If the two major parties are highly competitive at the national level, perhaps the weaker competition and even the numerous local one-party monopolies are the price to be paid. In the thirty-six year period from McKinley's election in 1896 to Franklin Roosevelt's election in 1932, the Democratic party enjoyed only eight years in the White House; it had a majority in the Senate during only six years. Yet, thanks to a secure fortress in the South and massive strength in northern cities like New York, Boston, and Chicago, it remained a formidable party at every election. The Democratic party was thus able to organize the national campaign in 1932 that brought Roosevelt into office for the first of his four terms. The Republicans recovered from the devastation of Roosevelt's landslide victory in 1936 because their state and local party strongholds were never completely overrun. By 1938 they were, in coalition with Southern Democrats, powerful enough to bring further New Deal reforms to a halt. Within individual states the situation is often much the same: the party or faction that controls the state house encounters its toughest opposition in the big cities.

Partitioning of power. Finally, the state and local governments have helped to partition power. In the United States, as we have seen, basic constitutional arrangements partition the power of national officials. The

10. Joseph A. Schlesinger, *How They Became Governor* (East Lansing, Mich.: Governmental Research Bureau, 1957), p. 11. See also his *Ambition and Politics: Political Careers in the United States* (Chicago: Rand McNally, 1966).

state and local governments have undoubtedly contributed to the extreme partitioning of power characteristic of the American polyarchy. State and local governments also have provided a number of centers of power whose autonomy is strongly protected by constitutional and political traditions. A governor of a state or the mayor of a large city may not be the political equal of a president (at least not often), but he is not a subordinate who can be appointed or discharged at the president's pleasure. Here, then, is a part of the intermediate stratum of leadership that Tocqueville looked to as a barrier to tyranny.

State and local governments have contributed something further to the partitioning of power. They have increased the options available to citizens. Citizens who find one group of leaders unsympathetic to their wishes can often turn to another group that influences a different level or sector of government. Thus a group that finds its needs ignored at the local level may turn to the state or to the federal government; the system also works the other way around. In its earlier years, for example, the American labor movement, often blocked in its efforts to win national legislation, turned to state governments to lead the way in the regulation of the working day, workmen's compensation, employment of women and children, and unemployment compensation. In recent decades, it has more often concentrated its efforts for positive gains on the national government, where it is assured of more sympathetic attention than in many of the states. At the state level, the labor movement has grown more concerned with occasional negative actions—such as blocking laws limiting the right to strike.

FACILITATING SELF-GOVERNMENT: THE DARKER SIDE

To what extent do local government's elections help citizens to participate in decisions and to elect leaders responsive to their wishes?

As with the criterion of efficiency, the problem posed by this question is to find a suitable yardstick with which to compare local governments.

There can be no question that, like the national government, local governments fall very far short of ideal democracy. But perhaps a more useful comparison is with the national government, since both sets of governments exist within the same general political culture and society. In two respects, local politics in the United States seems to operate at lower levels of performance than national politics.

Less Two-Party Competition

First, competition between political parties is weaker at local levels than at the national level. The extent of two-party competition, in fact, is roughly correlated with the size of the political unit: it declines from the national arena to statewide contests for U.S. senator, governor, and other statewide elective offices, and declines again from statewide elections to contests in smaller units—congressional districts, cities, and towns. Though we do not have the data one would need to confirm the hunch, there is every reason to suppose that two-party competition is rarest of all in the smallest units: wards, city and town council districts, state legislative districts, and the like. To overstate the point: effective contests for office and votes in a larger area do not result from effective electoral contests between the parties in the smaller areas; they are produced by parties that are highly unequal in strength in the smaller units. The smaller the area, evidently, the more difficult it is for the opposition to challenge the incumbents by presenting a rival slate of candidates.

The principle that the smaller the area the less the chances of two-party competition is quite evident from the data. Nationally, the Democratic and Republican parties are highly competitive. The presidency is contested vigorously in great nationwide campaigns; the outcome is always to some extent in doubt; over the years the presidency shifts back and forth from one party to the other. The Congress, too, is the site of considerable party competition. Neither party can take for granted that it will control either the presidency or the Congress after the next election.

In many states, though by no means all, party competition is a good deal weaker than it is in the national arena. For example, between 1914 and 1954, in six states of the Old South the Republicans did not win a single election for governor, United States senator, or presidential electors. During the same period, the Democrats won no elections in the Northern state of Vermont. In five more Southern states and one Northern state (Maine), the second party did not win more than one election out of every ten. In another nine states, the second party won fewer than one election out of four.[11]

Using elections for governor and for the members of each house of the legislature from 1946 to 1963, a study published in 1965 classified the party systems of the fifty states as follows:

One-party Democratic: 8 states.
Modified one-party Democratic: 9 states.
Two party: 25 states.
Modified one-party Republican: 8 states.
One-party Republican: no states.[12]

11. The data are from Austin Ranney and Willmoore Kendall, *Democracy and the American Party System* (New York: Harcourt, 1956), Tables 2, 3, and 4, pp. 162–164. In 1956 Ranney and Kendall classified twenty-six states as two-party systems, ten as one-party states, and twelve as modified one-party states. Another classification will be found in Joseph A. Schlesinger, "A Two-Dimensional Scheme for Classifying the States According to Degree of Inter-Party Competition," *American Political Science Review*, 49 (December 1955), 1120–1128.

12. Austin Ranney, "Parties in State Politics," in Jacob and Vines, *Politics in the United States*, pp. 64–65.

Figure 19.5
Party Competition in the
Twelve Most Populous
States: House Candidates,
1970; Senate Candidates,
1966–1970

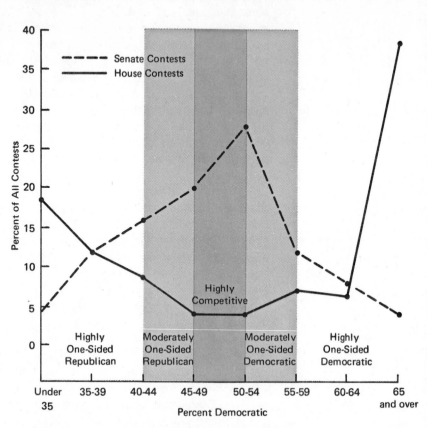

States include California, Florida, Illinois, Indiana, Massachusetts, Michigan, New Jersey, New York, North Carolina, Ohio, Pennsylvania, and Texas.

Not only is competition greater in the national arena than in statewide contests, it is also greater in statewide elections than in smaller units. Similarly, elections for U.S. senator are more closely contested than elections for the House of Representatives. Figure 19.5 shows this dramatically. In 1970, in the twelve most populous states, the Republican and Democratic candidates split the vote in the 45–55 percent range in less than 9 percent of the contests for House seats. In senatorial elections from 1966 to 1970, 48 percent of the contests fell into this highly competitive range.

In the towns, cities, counties, and state legislative districts, party competition is probably even weaker. Unfortunately, we lack good data with which to test this guess. But we do know that in a very high proportion of American cities elections are required by law to be non-

Region	Number of Cities 25,000 and Over	Percentage Nonpartisan
West	143	91.4
Plains	59	88.4
Border	42	78.5
Mountain	31	77.5
Great Lakes	187	68.5
South	152	63.1
New England	85	56.5
Middle Atlantic	134	13.4

Source: 1970 Census Tracts, Preliminary Estimates, and *Municipal Yearbook, 1968.*

Regions are defined: *West:* Alaska, California, Hawaii, Oregon, Washington; *Plains:* Colorado, Iowa, Kansas, Nebraska, North Dakota, Oklahoma, South Dakota, Wyoming; *Border:* Kentucky, Missouri, Tennessee, West Virginia; *Mountain:* Arizona, Idaho, Montana, Nevada, New Mexico, Utah; *Great Lakes:* Illinois, Indiana, Michigan, Minnesota, Ohio, Wisconsin; *South:* Alabama, Arkansas, Florida, Georgia, Louisiana, Mississippi, North Carolina, South Carolina, Texas, Virginia; *New England:* Connecticut, Maine, Massachusetts, New Hampshire, Rhode Island, Vermont; *Middle Atlantic:* Delaware, Maryland, New Jersey, New York, Pennsylvania.

partisan: the name of a political party cannot appear on the ballot. Everywhere except the Middle Atlantic states, most cities over twenty-five thousand require nonpartisan elections for local offices (Table 19.5). Even in cities where elections are formally and actually contested by both parties, the second party is often weak and rarely if ever wins the mayor's office or a majority of council members.

All this does not mean, of course, that in these states and cities there is no active competition for public office; there is. Where the second party is weak, competition often takes place *within* the dominant party. Yet even when intraparty conflict is sharp, it must necessarily occur not between highly organized parties but between individuals or loose factions. To be sure, in some one-party states, as in Louisiana over an extended period, two rival factions within the same party may perform many of the functions of political parties.[13] In general, however, the absence of sharp competition for office by organized political parties seems to accentuate the significance of personal qualities and to diminish emphasis on policies.[14]

Less Citizen Participation

If local governments fall somewhat short of the national government in the extent to which two or more organized parties compete vigorously to win elections and gain control over the policy making machinery of government, they also seem to elicit less participation by

13. Allan P. Sindler, "Bifactional Rivalry as an Alternative to Two-Party Competition in Louisiana," *American Political Science Review*, 49 (September 1955), 641–662; and *Huey Long's Louisiana* (Baltimore: Johns Hopkins Press, 1956).

14. Sindler, "Bifactional Rivalry"; see also the classic statement in V. O. Key, Jr., *Southern Politics* (New York: Knopf, 1949). A good statement of the findings may be found in Fred I. Greenstein, *The American Party System and the American People*, 2nd ed. (Englewood Cliffs, N.J.: Prentice-Hall, 1970), pp. 66–70.

Table 19.6

Percentage of Population
of Voting Age Who Vote
in City and
National Elections

Presidential election, 1960[a]	63.8%
House of Representatives, 1960[a]	59.4
Elections for city officials, 1961–2[b]	46.5
Concurrent with state or national elections	43.5
Not concurrent	31.2

Sources: (a) *Congress and the Nation, A Review of Government and Politics* (2 vols.) (Washington, D.C.: Congressional Quarterly Service, 1965–1969), vol. 2, p. 438; (b) Robert A. Alford and Eugene C. Lee, "Voting Turn-out in American Cities," *American Political Science Review*, 62 (September, 1968) 796–813; Table 1, p. 803. The data are for 80 percent of the cities above 25,000 population in 1960.

citizens than the national government. In this respect, the local governments have disappointed the hopes of democratic theorists like Jefferson who believed that the true centers of American democracy would be the local governments. These would attend to the everyday problems of most interest and importance to the citizen, and, lying within easy reach, would be the most responsive and responsible instruments of self-government.

In elections. So far as one can judge from available data, citizens are less active in state and local elections than in national elections. Although the evidence is by no means all one-sided, one fact is clear: presidential elections attract a larger number of voters (and probably much more attention) than most elections to state and local offices. Only one-half to two-thirds as many citizens turn out for city elections as for national elections (Table 19.6). However, since all contests, including those for the House and Senate in midterm elections, fare badly in comparison with the presidential contest, participation in state[15] and local elections is not too much lower than participation in off-year congressional elections.

The myth of a Golden Age. It is sometimes thought that participation in local governments was much higher in the good old days; that lower participation is entirely a modern phenomenon, resulting from the increased importance of national affairs. But such scattered evidence as we have does not seem to sustain this belief in a Golden Age of local democracy.[16] For example, data on voting in New Haven, Connecticut, from 1820 to recent times show conclusively that the proportion of citizens who have voted in elections for mayor has always been less than those who have voted in presidential contests (Figure 19.6).

It is difficult to say how common this pattern was in the nineteenth

15. Lester W. Milbrath, "Political Participation in the States," in Jacob and Vines, *Politics in the United States,* states that "turnout in state elections is closely comparable to turnout in representative elections. If the state or representative election occurs in a non-presidential year, the turnout is likely to be significantly lower" (p. 37).

16. See Chapter 10, footnote 19.

Figure 19.6
New Haven, Connecticut:
Percentage of Eligible
Voters Voting in
Presidential and Mayoralty
Elections, 1860–1950

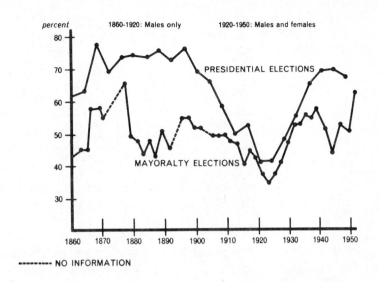

percent   1860-1920: Males only   1920-1950: Males and females

PRESIDENTIAL ELECTIONS

MAYORALTY ELECTIONS

- - - - - - NO INFORMATION

Source: Robert A. Dahl, *Who Governs? Democracy and Power in an American City* (New Haven, Connecticut: Yale University Press, 1961), p. 277.

century. Turnout in state and national elections in the first half of the nineteenth century showed considerable variation from state to state. In Connecticut, turnout was invariably higher for national than for state elections; yet in the neighboring New England states, gubernatorial elections produced the higher turnout. New York and New Jersey were like Connecticut; in Virginia, as elsewhere in the Old South, turnout was higher in state elections than in national elections.[17]

Thus the evidence points to several conclusions, mainly negative. It is not true, as an enthusiastic follower of Jefferson might hold, that the smaller a political unit is, the more its citizens will participate in political affairs. To the extent that voting is a fair measure of participation, that hypothesis is definitely not borne out today. Although there was probably greater variation in patterns of electoral participation in the first part of the nineteenth century than there is now, the hypothesis was not confirmed by experience even then. Nor is it true that participation in state and local elections has fallen off as these units have grown in size and as the role of the national government has expanded.

In short, local territorial governments in the United States are not,

17. See Richard P. McCormick, *The Second American Party System, Party Formation in the Jacksonian Era* (Chapel Hill: University of North Carolina Press, 1966), pp. 99, 123, 133, 186, 248, and *passim.*

Table 19.7
How Closely Governmental
Affairs are Followed
at Four Levels

Level of Governmental Affairs	Rank of How Closely Followed				Total[a]	N
	First	Second	Third	Fourth		
International	20%	16%	22%	42%	100%	983
National	32	31	26	10	99	983
State	17	33	27	22	99	983
Local	30	20	25	25	100	983
Total[a]	99%	100%	100%	99%		
N	983	983	983	983		

[a] Total percentages do not equal 100% due to rounding.
Source: Jennings and Zeigler, "The Salience of American State Politics," p. 525.

and evidently never have been, distinctive sites for high levels of civic participation.

FACILITATING SELF-GOVERNMENT: THE BRIGHTER SIDE

There is no blinking the fact that by democratic standards local governments—like the national polyarchy—are highly defective. Yet, to right the balance, one needs to consider what polyarchy would be like in the United States if representative governments did not exist in the states and localities. While one might argue persuasively that the best alternative to what we have now is more self-government, it would be hard to make a good case that, from a democratic point of view, we would be better off with less.

It may be worth asking, then, how the local governments in the United States compare with the national government as institutions of self-government. Are they markedly worse? Although a precise answer is impossible, the evidence does support three propositions which we shall consider next:

First, citizens seem to be about as *concerned* with local affairs as with national and international affairs.

Second, except by comparison with voting in presidential elections, citizens *participate* as much in local as in national politics, if not more.

Third, they probably have greater *confidence* in their capacity to act effectively at local levels.

Concern

The degree of interest expressed by Americans in state and local affairs compares favorably with their level of interest in national affairs. Some excellent evidence on this point is furnished by an analysis of data from surveys made during the elections of 1966 and 1968.[18] After

18. M. Kent Jennings and Harmon Zeigler, "The Salience of American State Politics," *American Political Science Review,* 64 (June, 1970), 523–535. Incidentally, these findings correct a view I had advanced earlier that "the average American is bound to be much less concerned about the affairs of his state than of his city or country" in Robert A. Dahl, "The City in the Future of Democracy," *American Political Science Review,* 61 (December 1967), 968.

weeding out 17 percent of the respondents who indicated that they paid hardly any attention at all to government and public affairs, the 1966 survey (Table 19.7) found that:

☐ About as many people give their attention to local affairs as to national affairs. Thirty percent say they follow local affairs more closely than national or international affairs, compared with 32 percent who follow national affairs more closely, and 20 percent for international affairs.
☐ State affairs rank fourth (17 percent), just behind international affairs. However, 50 percent rank state affairs either first or second. In the 1968 survey 37 percent said they paid a great deal of attention to state politics, and another 51 percent said they gave it some attention.
☐ Evidently some citizens tend to give special attention to state and local affairs, others to national and international affairs. Both groups are about the same size.

Concern for local politics should hardly be surprising, since many of the problems that people regard as urgent and important require some action by local governments: education, crime, poverty, welfare, public health, racial discrimination, housing, parking, streets and highways, to name a few. A national survey conducted in 1973 showed that about four out of ten Americans thought that local and state governments "affected their lives personally" a great deal. (Table 19.8). Although this was less than the percentage who thought the federal government affected them a great deal (63 percent)—a not unrealistic judgment—it was nonetheless a substantial ground for being concerned with state and local governments.[19]

Participation
The relatively lower turnout in local elections than in presidential elections does not prove that Americans are less active in local affairs. For one thing, the presidential contest is unique. Even if voters are as

---

19. A survey in the 1950s asking how much impact national and local government had on daily life showed much less difference between the two levels:

	National Government	Local Government
Great effect	41%	35%
Some effect	44	53
No effect	11	10
Other, don't know, etc.	4	2
	100%	100%
Total number of cases	970	970

Source: Gabriel Almond and Sidney Verba, *The Civic Culture, Political Attitude and Democracy in Five Nations* (Princeton, N.J.: Princeton University Press, 1963), pp. 80–81. The difference between the two surveys may be a result of the slight differences in the questions, or, as seems likely, the increased visibility of national politics through the 1960s and 1970s.

	Local percent	State percent	Federal percent
A great deal	38	39	63
Only somewhat	33	38	21
Hardly at all	26	19	13
Not sure	3	4	3

Table 19.8 Degree to Which Government "affects people's lives personally" (1973)

Source: Louis Harris and Associates for the Subcommittee on Intergovernmental Relations of the Committee on Government Operations, United States Senate, *Confidence and Concern, Citizens View American Government* (Washington, D.C.: Government Printing Office, 1973), pp. 278, 281–282, 284, 287–288, 290, 292–293. (Note: Several of the headings on these pages are misleading.)

involved in local affairs as in national affairs, as the evidence suggests may be the case, the lower frequency of sharp two-party competition would probably reduce the turnout at elections, partly because the contest itself would be less exciting, partly because the parties would work less vigorously to get out the vote. Moreover, voting is only one form of participation; some of the other ways of participating in politics are more easily carried on at the local than at the national level: getting in touch with one's council member about a torn-up street is a good deal easier than getting in touch with one's representative or senator or the president about inflation.

Even if local governments fall far short of potential and ideal, they do provide channels through which citizens may express their views on local matters when they have an urge to do so. In the 1973 survey, 24 percent of the respondents reported that they had gone to their local government to get something done, compared with 13 percent who had gone to the state government, and only 11 percent who got in touch with the federal government. Interestingly, however, among those who had, the percentage who had found state or local government helpful was slightly less than those who had a favorable response from the federal government (Table 19.9).

Citizen Effectiveness

Evidence does suggest that Americans look on their local governments as more accessible, more manageable, and more responsive than the federal government. An exhaustive study of the political attitudes of fifteen lower-middle-class citizens in an Eastern city found:

> ... The fact is that these men were pretty discouraged by the idea of *doing* something about any big problems....
>
> Eastport's common men find themselves politically impotent on most important specific issues, do not petition or write letters with any frequency, are dubious of the wisdom of the electorate on these issues, see elections as only partially successful instruments for imparting instructions to candidates, find themselves often confused by the complexity of public affairs, and tend to think of elected officials as better judges of policy than they themselves are.[20]

20. Robert Lane, *Political Ideology, Why the American Common Man Believes What He Does* (New York: Free Press of Glencoe, 1962), pp. 164–165.

	Percentage who have gone	Of those who have gone, percentage who		
		Found government helpful	Were highly satisfied	Were not satisfied at all
Local government	24	64	39	35
State government	13	66	39	34
Federal government	11	73	46	24

Source: Louis Harris, *Confidence and Concern.*

	National and International	Local Issues
Very well	7%	21%
Moderately well	38	44
Not so well	37	23
Not at all	14	10
Depends, other, don't know, etc.	4	2
	100%	100%
Total number of cases	970	970

Source: Almond and Verba survey, unpublished data.

Yet far from being alienated, most of these fifteen men felt that they were politically important. How, the study asks,

> ...do they come to have this sense of political importance? One reason is that many of them have political connections and for local matters they *have* influence, can get close to somebody who may pretend to more authority than he has but who conveys to his circle of acquaintances the sense that they are in communication with important people when they speak to him.[21]

There are also other reasons, of course; but this sense of accessibility and responsiveness may be an important one. The national survey taken in the 1950s (footnote 17, above) tends to confirm the hunch that the closeness, accessibility, and comprehensibility of local government enhance the confidence of citizens that they *can do something* about local affairs. Almost two out of three respondents agreed and only a third disagreed with the statement that "politics and government are so complicated that the average man cannot really understand what is going on." Yet the number who said that they understood "local issues in this town or part of the country" very well was three times as large as the number who said they understood "the important national and international issues facing the country" very well. In fact, over half the respondents said that they did not understand national and international issues at all or not so well, compared with only a third who felt this way about local issues (Table 19.10).

21. *Ibid.*, p. 165.

Table 19.11
"If you make an effort to
change a proposed law or
regulation you considered
very unjust or harmful,
how likely is it that you
would succeed?"

	Local regulation	National law
Very likely or moderately likely	28%	11%
Somewhat unlikely	15	18
Not at all likely, impossible	25	36
Likely only if others joined in	25	24
Other, don't know	6	9
	100%	100%
Total number of cases	970	970

Source: Almond and Verba survey, unpublished data.

Nor is it only a matter of being able to grasp local issues better; citizens also seem to think that they can act more effectively at the local level. To be sure, not many ever do act at either the local or national level. In fact, seven out of ten respondents in this survey said they had never tried to influence a local decision, while eight out of ten said they had never tried to influence the Congress. Yet many were confident that, if the need arose, they would act and might even be successful. What did they think they could do, they were asked, if a law or regulation which they considered "very unjust or harmful" were being considered by the local government or by Congress? The number who said that it was very likely or moderately likely that they would do something about the law or regulation was slightly larger in the case of a local law (49 percent) than for a national law (42 percent). The number who said that it was not at all likely that they would do something about an unjust law or regulation was a little less for local laws (27 percent) than for national laws (33 percent). The percentages who expected that they could be successful in their efforts were somewhat higher in the case of the local law (Table 19.11).

DECLINE IN CONFIDENCE

The years of turbulence dating approximately from the assassination of President Kennedy in 1963 until the resignation of President Nixon in 1974 weakened the confidence of many Americans in their government.[22] On the whole, however, local governments fared less badly than the national government—which is hardly surprising, since the crucial events mainly involved national, not state and local politics. In the 1973 survey, the number who said they had less confidence in government than they had five years earlier was about twice as great for the federal government (57 percent) as for state (26 percent) or local governments (36 percent). Moreover, while few wanted power taken away from local

22. These changes in attitude are described in Chapter 11 under Qualifications. The events are discussed in Chapter 13 and Chapter 29.

	Local government	State government	Federal government
Made stronger	61%	59%	32%
Power taken away	8	11	42
Kept as is	23	22	17
Not sure	8	8	9

Source: Louis Harris, *Confidence and Concern.*

or state governments and most wanted these governments to be stronger, there was now much more suspicion of the power of the federal government (Table 19.12).

SUMMARY   The thousands of governments in the United States below the level of the national government, particularly the fifty states and the municipal governments, contribute to the operation of the American polyarchy in four ways:

1. They make polyarchy more manageable at the national level by reducing the workload of the national government.

2. They reduce conflicts at the national level and thus help to make polyarchy at the national level more viable because:

□ They allow for the possibility of diverse solutions to problems and thus reduce the pressure for uniformity imposed by national majorities.

□ They permit some potential conflicts to be taken out of the arena of national politics to be handled at local levels. However, this process is subject to two defects: it may permit injustices, as in the case of Southern blacks; and for this or other reasons, the parties to the conflict may not allow an issue to be removed from national politics.

3. They create numerous more or less independent and autonomous centers of power. As a result:

□ They provide a training ground for political leaders to acquire the arts of governing in a polyarchy.

□ They help provide the opposition party with a base when it is defeated elsewhere.

□ They help to partition power.

4. They help to enlarge the domain of self-government by increasing the opportunities available for citizens to participate in government. Although the achievements of local governments are mixed when compared to national government, the findings nonetheless indicate that they play an important role:

- In comparison with the national government, at local levels there is less party competition, and less participation in elections.
- However, evidence indicates that citizens are as much concerned with local as with national and international affairs.
- The easier accessibility of local governments makes it easier for citizens to get in touch with officials.
- Citizens feel they can grasp local issues better and can be more effective in dealing with them.

20 POLITICAL PARTIES: THE UNFORESEEN ELEMENT

In recasting classical ideas about direct democracy into forms suitable for a representative system, nothing was more self-evident than the need for an elected legislature. In the nineteenth century, many Americans came to believe further that an elected chief executive might also contribute an important element of 'democratic' representation. In this country that view has been pretty widely accepted from the Jacksonian period onward. Fitting the Supreme Court into a 'democratic' framework, as we saw in Chapters 18 and 19, has been infinitely more difficult; perhaps Americans are more ready to interpret judicial review as a 'democratic' device than a scrupulous attention to theory and practice would permit.

These major political institutions of American polyarchy, all prescribed in outline by the Constitution, appear to have considerably stronger claims to legitimacy than another institution which, though central to the operation of polyarchy, was unanticipated by the Framers and is nowhere mentioned in the Constitution: the system of political parties. Political parties have been among the most visible and important elements in the American polyarchy for a century and three-quarters, yet many Americans continue to doubt their desirability as democratic institutions. Even in 1964, before all the recent events that were to weaken the confidence of Americans in their political institutions, two out of three Americans believed that elections are highly important in making the government responsive to the people. But only four out of ten conceded as much for political parties (Table 20.1). Nearly seven out of ten persons in a 1966 Wisconsin survey agreed with the proposition that "More often than not, the political parties create

Table 20.1
U.S. Citizens' Views on the Relative Importance of Parties and Elections in Making Government Responsive, 1964 and 1972

Make the government pay attention:	(Percent)			
	Elections[a]		Parties[b]	
	1964	1972	1964	1972
A good deal	65%	57%	40%	28%
Some	25	35	39	52
Not much	6	8	13	19
Don't know	4	—	7	—
Total %	100%	100%	99%	99%
N =	(1450)	(1601)	(1450)	(1566)

[a] "How much do you feel that having elections makes the government pay attention to what the people think?"

[b] "How much do you feel that political parties help to make the government pay attention to what the people think?"

Sources: For 1964, Jack Dennis, "Support for the Institution of Elections by the Mass Public," *American Political Science Review*, 64 (September 1970), 831, Table 7. The survey data were obtained from the 1964 Election Study by the University of Michigan Research Center. For 1972, Arthur H. Miller, "Rejoinder," *American Political Science Review*, 68 (September 1974), 989–1001. I have computed the percentages from Table 1, p. 991.

Table 20.2
Distribution of Response on Party System Support Items, Wisconsin, 1966

Items	Percent							
	Strongly Agree	Agree	Partly Agree–Partly Disagree	Disagree	Strongly Disagree	Don't Know	Not Ascertained	Total Percent[a]
"More often than not, the political parties create conflicts where none really exists."	9%	60	11	13	—[b]	6	1	100%
"It would be better if, in all elections, no party labels were put on the ballot."	4	30	8	50	6	3	—[b]	101%
"The parties do more to confuse the issues than to provide a clear choice on them."	6	48	23	18	1	3	1	100%
"Our system of government would work a lot more efficiently if we could get rid of conflicts between the parties altogether."	8	35	11	33	8	3	2	100%
"The conflicts and controversies between the parties hurt our country more than they help it."	4	37	17	36	3	3	1	101%

[a] Some rows do not add to 100% due to errors of rounding. N = 607.

[b] Less than 1%.

Source: *Ibid.*, Table 6.

conflict where none really exists" (Table 20.2). Even more revealing: over 40 percent believed that party conflict was more harmful than helpful and the country would be better off without it. The decline in confidence that took place in the decade from 1964–1974 eroded support for political parties even further. By 1972, only 28 percent of a national sample now thought parties helped a good deal to make government pay attention to what people think (Table 20.1).[1]

In contrast to these popular views of parties, most contemporary democratic theorists insist that party competition and conflict are essential processes for increasing popular control in a large system. As we shall see in the discussion of early development of parties, given the institutional guarantees of polyarchy, parties are inevitable; from a democratic perspective, they are also thought to be desirable.

Why was it, then, that the Framers failed to perceive the importance of parties? How did political parties come about? What contributions *do* they make? Why is it that democratic theorists believe parties are desirable, whereas so many citizens doubt their legitimacy?

DISTRUST OF PARTIES

The kinds of criticisms of political parties made by Wisconsin respondents in Table 20.2 have been around in one form or another for a very long time. Parties are seen as creating artificial conflicts rather than helping to solve genuine conflicts, and as promoting the narrow, selfish interests of politicians rather than the general welfare. The view accepted by a substantial minority of Wisconsin adults, that parties are harmful to the country and we ought to get rid of them, has an ancient history. It was, in fact, the accepted view until the time of the American Constitutional Convention.

Framers' Lack of Foresight

The three great milestones in the development of democratic institutions are: the right to participate in governmental decisions by casting a vote; a system of representation; and the right of an organized opposition to appeal for votes against the government in elections and in parliament. The last is, in a highly developed form, so wholly modern that there are people now living who were born before it had appeared in most of Western Europe.

Throughout recorded history, it seems, stable institutions providing legal, orderly, peaceful modes of political opposition have been rare. If peaceful antagonism between factions is uncommon, peaceful competition among organized, permanent political parties is an even rarer

---

1. See also Jack Dennis, "Trends in Public Support for the American Party System," *British Journal of Political Science*, 5 (1975), 187–230.

historical phenomenon. Legal party opposition is, in fact, a recent unplanned invention that has been confined for the most part to a handful of countries. Even more recent are organized political parties that compete peacefully in elections for the votes of the great bulk of the adult population able to exercise the franchise under nearly universal suffrage. Universal suffrage and long-lasting mass parties are, with few exceptions, products of the twentieth century. A hundred years ago they did not exist outside the United States.

Because some conflict of views seems to be unavoidable in human affairs, political societies have always had to deal somehow with the fact of opposition. Nevertheless, that there might legitimately exist an organized group within the political system to oppose, criticize, and if possible oust the leading officials of government was until recently an unfamiliar and generally unacceptable notion. When the delegates at the American Constitutional Convention of 1787 expressed their fear of "factions" as the undoing of republics, they spoke the traditional view.[2]

Previous experience. The most long-lived republic in history, the aristocratic republic of Venice, explicitly forbade the formation of enduring political organizations. It sought to provide sufficient checks and balances among officials to prevent arbitrary decisions and to insure a large measure of consensus for the laws; thus organized opposition was seen as unnecessary and a danger to the stability of the republic. Not all the ancient and medieval republics went quite so far as Venice. Factions, coalitions, and alliances of one kind or another existed in and outside of the popular assemblies of Athens, and in the late Roman Republic political alliances sought votes both for candidates and for laws in various popular assemblies. But evidently these groups were never highly organized, had no permanent structure, and even lacked definite names. Moreover, sooner or later, factions typically settled their differences by bloodshed.

The system of managing the major political conflicts of a society by allowing one or more opposition parties to compete with the governing parties for votes in elections and in parliament is not only modern, then; surely it is also one of the greatest and most unexpected social discoveries that man has ever stumbled onto. Up until two centuries ago, no one had accurately foreseen it. In Britain, to be sure, during the eighteenth century, rival groups had formed in Parliament, to which the names Whig and Tory were often applied. But

> ... Whigs and Tories did not constitute political parties as they came to be
> in the late nineteenth and twentieth centuries. Those labels were often

---

2. This section is adapted from the preface to Robert A. Dahl, *Political Oppositions in Western Democracies* (New Haven, Conn.: Yale University Press, 1966).

adopted by, or foisted upon, men who had little in common and few or no
real ties. In 1714 and for many years thereafter, the basic political unit was
the group or connexion, often called a party, formed under the leadership
of a successful politician.[3]

In the parliament of Sweden during what came to be known as the Era
of Liberty from 1718 to 1772, parliamentary factions "strongly reminis-
cent of the parallel groupings of Whigs and Tories in eighteenth century Britain" also developed.[4]

But these factional groups in Britain and Sweden were a long way
from modern parties. There is little reason to suppose that in the late
eighteenth century American political leaders knew anything about the
Swedish system. As for Britain, the significance of the Whig and Tory
factions in Parliament was quite unclear at the time; it was only much
later that, looking backward, one could perceive in them the barest beginnings of a party system that has continued to develop and to change
down to the present day.

Older usage of party. The word *party* itself did not have quite the same
meaning to Washington, Madison, and Jefferson that it has today. Political party has come to signify an institution, a durable, organized force
that outlasts the particular individuals who adhere to it at any moment.
But when American political leaders used the term in the late eighteenth
century—as they did more and more frequently from the Constitutional
Convention onward—they did not seem to have had in mind an organized institution, the way we do today; parties did not yet *exist* as organized institutions. Rather, the founding fathers had in mind a more or
less cohesive *current of political opinion,* a general agreement on some
public issue by a group of people. Terms like *party, faction, interest,
sect, division,* or *group* were used more or less interchangeably.[5]

Thus it is not surprising that the Framers had no explicit place for
political parties in their grand design. They could hardly have foreseen
organized political parties as we know them any better than they could
have foreseen the internal combustion engine and the automobile. In a
strict sense political parties had not yet been *invented.*

---

3. Archibald S. Foord, *His Majesty's Opposition* (New York: Oxford University Press, 1964),
p. 20. See also Sir Ivor Jennings, *Party Politics,* vol. II: *The Growth of Parties* (London: Cambridge University Press, 1961), pp. 24 ff.; Sir Lewis Namier, ed., *The Structure of Politics at the
Accession of George III* (New York: St. Martin's Press, 1961), "The Electoral Structure of England," ch. 2.

4. Dankwart A. Rustow, *The Politics of Compromise* (Princeton, N.J.: Princeton University
Press, 1955), pp. 11–12.

5. See for example Madison's "A Candid State of Parties" published in the Philadelphia
National Gazette in 1792, reprinted in Noble E. Cunningham, Jr., *Making of the American Party
System 1789 to 1809* (Englewood Cliffs, N.J.: Prentice-Hall, 1965). Speaking of the time of the
Revolution, Madison says that "those who espoused the cause of independence and those who
adhered to the British claims, formed the parties of the first period." A moment later, he begins
to speak of divisions: "The Federal Constitution . . . gave birth to the second and most interesting division of the people . . . those who embraced the constitution . . . those who opposed the
constitution. . . . This state of parties was terminated . . . in 1788" (pp. 10–11).

As noted above, the Framers shared the prevailing view that parties, factions, and partisan conflict had been the undoing of both republics and monarchies. Many of them would have agreed with a New York jurist who wrote in 1794 that "In examining the history of nations, we discover examples of the pernicious tendency of faction." To prove his point he conjured up "the mortal conflict which existed between the houses of York and Lancaster," the disputes in France between Catholics and Huguenots, the fall of Athens and the decline of the Roman Republic.[6]

In 1787 and in the early years of the American republic it was difficult to distinguish ordinary, everyday political conflict involving factions and parties, as we are familiar with it today, from civil disorder, uprisings, breakdown, and internal wars.

Initial hostility to parties. No one, I imagine, thought that political conflict could be avoided entirely. But some important leaders seem to have believed that *persistent* deep differences of opinion could be avoided; perhaps those in political life and the public would come fresh to each question, ready to examine it with an open mind unclouded by attachments to any lasting faction or party. Leaders who held this view attacked "the spirit of party" for its evil effects, as Washington did in his Farewell Address. When parties began to be organized, terrible results were predicted: "Party spirit is the demon which engendered the factions that have destroyed most free governments," thundered the distinguished Senator Hillhouse of Connecticut in a Senate speech in 1808. "Regular, organized parties only, extending from the Northern to the Southern extremity of the United States, and from the Atlantic to the utmost western limits, threaten to shake this Union to its center."[7] This view, ironically, was often—though not always—espoused by Federalists, who, so it appeared, did not object to the existence of their own party but only to that of their opponents' party, organized by Jefferson and Madison.

Federalist leaders sought to curb the party of opposition; and it takes no great exercise of the imagination to conceive that the issue of a democratic versus an aristocratic republic hung in the balance during the years from 1794 to 1800. In 1794, when farmers in western Pennsylvania refused to pay a tax on their homemade whisky and rose up in a small display of defiance that took the name of the Whisky Insurrection, President Washington himself took the occasion to attack the Democratic Societies. (These were newly formed political clubs with Jeffersonian views.) He described them

---

6. William Wyche, "Party Spirit," in *The Making of the American Party System*, p. 13.
7. Cunningham, *Making of the American Party System*, p. 25.

as centers of sedition and resistance to government and requested the Senate and House to follow his lead. The Senate complied, but in the House Madison argued eloquently that it was unconstitutional for Congress to censure the clubs. Their members were simply exercising their right of free speech.[8]

As Madison put it in a letter to Monroe:

The game was to connect the democratic societies with the odium of the insurrection, to connect the republicans in Congress with those societies, to put the president ostensibly at the head of the other party, in opposition to both.[9]

The Alien and Sedition Acts passed by the Federalists in 1798 were animated by a similar hostility to criticism by opposition; enforcement became a partisan matter. The Acts placed heavy penalties on criticism of the government and its leaders; the Sedition Act in particular was used to bludgeon the opposition. Twenty-five persons were prosecuted under the act, and ten of them, all Democratic-Republican editors and printers, were convicted.[10]

As it turned out—fortunately for the future of the American polyarchy—the actions of the Federalists did nothing to prevent and much to inflame the spirit of party they found so odious; consequently they, along with the leading Democratic-Republicans, must be counted among the true, if unwitting, architects of modern parties.[11] It was because of the views of Federalists—and because it was the Democratic-Republicans, after all, who were being jailed for opposition—that Jefferson and Madison were so deeply alarmed by the Alien and Sedition Acts, which they saw as not only unconstitutional but also a despotic threat to republican government. They registered the strength of their objection by the Kentucky Resolution (drafted by Jefferson) and the Virginia Resolution (drafted by Madison) which denounced the Acts as unconstitutional.

Growing acceptance. Fortunately, the time of the Federalists was running out; the tide of republicanism was running in. When that tide swept Jefferson into office as president in the election of 1800, he pardoned the Democratic-Republican editors and printers still in prison. The de-

---

8. Page Smith, *John Adams,* 2 vols. (Garden City, N.Y.: Doubleday, 1962), vol. 2, p. 865.

9. Quoted in Noble E. Cunningham, Jr., *The Jeffersonian Republicans, The Formation of Party Organization 1789–1801* (Chapel Hill: University of North Carolina Press, 1957), p. 66.

10. Richard B. Morris, *Encyclopedia of American History* (New York: Harper, 1953), p. 129.

11. Jefferson's political party was usually referred to as Republican. This is the name by which most present-day historians also refer to it. Occasionally in Jefferson's time his followers also referred to themselves as Democratic-Republicans. In 1828 the supporters of Andrew Jackson for president presented themselves as the true heirs of Jefferson and took the name Democratic-Republican. Although that remained the official name for many years, the party quickly came to be called simply the Democratic Party. The party known today as Republican was not formed until 1854. To minimize confusion with the later Republican Party, I refer to Jefferson's party as Democratic-Republican.

testable Sedition Acts expired the day before he took the oath of office, and he allowed the Alien Act to expire the following year. Thus the doctrine that political parties were constitutionally protected, an uncertain and even contested doctrine during the last decade of the old century, came to rest on firmer ground during the first decade of the new.

Unlike many of their Federalist opponents, Jefferson and Madison held that opposing and persistent divisions in opinion—parties in this sense—were inevitable in a free republic, even if, in some circumstances, their clashing ambitions might endanger the existence of the republic. In 1813, after four years away from Washington and the White House, Jefferson wrote his old friend John Adams that

> men have differed in opinion, and been divided into parties by these opinions from the first origin of society; and in all governments where they have been permitted freely to think and to speak. The same political parties which now agitate the U.S. have existed through all time. . . . To me then it appears that . . . these will continue through all future time: that every one takes his side in favor of the many, or of the few, according to his constitution, and the circumstances in which he is placed.[12]

EARLY DEVELOPMENT OF PARTIES

Are Parties Inevitable in Polyarchies?

The fact that rival parties now exist in every polyarchy and not in a single dictatorship hints at the possibility that parties may be inevitable in any organization that accepts democratic principles. To leap to this conclusion would be going too far if we refer to small democratic organizations with a high degree of consensus. But at the national level the operation of rival parties seems to be linked inescapably with the main institutional guarantees of polyarchy, whether the nation be as small as Iceland or as huge as the United States.

To begin with, the kinds of liberties and institutional guarantees that define polyarchy—freedom of speech, press, and assembly, for example—are the factors that make parties possible; or to put it in a slightly different way, it would be next to impossible both to prohibit all political parties and to allow full freedom of speech, press, and assembly. Stern and prolonged application of the Sedition Act might have curbed parties, but only by curbing freedom of speech, press, and peaceful assembly.

The possibility of parties does not, however, mean that they are *inevitable.* What carves the actual out of the possible is in this case the ceaseless striving of political leaders for victory: their never-ending effort to win elections and marshal legislative majorities in support of particular persons, policies, or programs. The instrument invented in the United States between 1789 and about 1809 for winning elections

12. Cunningham, *Making of the American Party System,* pp. 19–20.

and marshaling legislative majorities was the political party. If necessity is the mother of invention, then given the goals and ambitions of those in government and the existing stock of knowledge, techniques, and institutions, the political party was as certain to be invented as the cotton gin, the steam engine, and interchangeable machine parts.

So whatever the intentions of the Framers may have been, their Constitution, if it were kept to, made political parties not only possible but inevitable. With the Bill of Rights the Constitution made parties *possible;* once given the Bill of Rights, the institutions of representation and election designed in Articles I and II made parties *inevitable.*

Birth of Parties

We can see the parties struggling to be born in the early springtime of the new republic. In this country as elsewhere, parties were not spontaneous growths: they were created by the interaction of leaders and responsive followers. To be sure, in 1793 there was across the country a sudden and seemingly spontaneous flowering of popular associations that called themselves Democratic or Republican societies. These associations were uniformly on the side of what were coming to be called Democratic-Republicans in distinction to Federalists. Yet as a historian has observed, they were partisans of the Democratic-Republican interest, but they were not a party. They did not nominate candidates, manage election campaigns, or seek to control legislatures.[13] They also lacked another characteristic of parties—durability. Within three years most of these societies had vanished.

So it was not in these associations that the germ of party first appeared but, as in Britain and Sweden, in the national legislature. For, whatever Washington might have hoped, we can observe men like Hamilton, Madison, and Jefferson struggling to invent the political party.[14] The first Congress left few traces of party voting.[15] But Hamilton's economic program stimulated sharp opposition, led by Jefferson and Madison, that was to consolidate itself more and more fully in the succeeding Congresses. Probably nothing did more to promote this consolidation than the opposition in Congress in 1795 to a treaty with Britain (Jay's Treaty) that critics claimed gave up too much to Britain in return for too little. The Democratic-Republicans, as the congressional followers of Madison and Jefferson had begun to call themselves, held a closed party meeting, or caucus, the first in congressional history, to determine wheth-

---

13. Cunningham, *Jeffersonian Republicans, Formation of Party Organization,* p. 64.

14. See *ibid.,* and also Noble E. Cunningham, Jr., *Jeffersonian Republicans in Power, Party Operations 1801–1809* (Chapel Hill: University of North Carolina Press, 1963); and Cunningham, *Making of the American Party System;* Joseph Charles, *Origins of the American Party System* (New York: Harper, 1961); William N. Chambers, *Political Parties in a New Nation, The American Experience 1776–1809* (New York: Oxford University Press, 1963); Manning J. Dauer, *The Adams Federalists* (Baltimore: Johns Hopkins Press, 1953).

15. Cunningham, *Jeffersonian Republicans, Formation of Party Organization,* p. 7.

er they would vote for the appropriations required to put the treaty into effect.[16] Under the stimulus of leadership, organization, and antagonism, both Federalists and Democratic-Republicans became increasingly cohesive. When Jefferson became president, he had little difficulty in converting both the Democratic-Republican party and the party caucus into efficient instruments for marshaling the votes of the Democratic-Republican majorities in the Congress.

Institutional Development

The institutions that have been used ever since to mobilize party support in Congress were well developed by the end of Jefferson's two terms in office: the caucus of the party faithful to determine the party line; the election of a partisan rather than a neutral Speaker of the House by the majority party; the development of recognized party leaders; close collaboration between the president and his party leaders in the Congress; and the shrewd use of patronage by the president to solidify support.

Meanwhile, need had mothered additional party institutions. There was, above all, the problem of presidential nominations. It was as obvious to Hamilton, Madison, Jefferson, and their peers as it is to us that unless they could marshal their forces in behalf of a single candidate, their opponents might win.[17] In 1796, both parties used an informal (and secret) congressional party caucus to gain agreement on the presidential candidate; thereafter, the device was regularly and openly used until 1824, when it fell into decay. (The present system of national nominating conventions began in 1831 with the new Anti-Masonic party, and in 1832 with the Jacksonian Democrats.)

Yet, unlike the factions and foreshadowing of parties in the eighteenth-century parliaments of Britain and Sweden, early parties in the United States confronted still other needs. And these needs added the elements that made the parliamentary, or legislative, party recognizably modern. That is to say, it is modern in the sense that the Model-T Ford, primitive though it may appear alongside one of the chrome-plated monsters of the present day, nonetheless symbolizes the begin-

16. *Ibid.*, p. 82.

17. In the case of the presidency the problem was further complicated because as the Constitution then stood party leaders had to insure that their candidate for the vice-presidency received fewer votes than their presidential candidate. As one might imagine this provided splendid opportunities for intrigue, as in 1796 when Hamilton conspired to secure *more* votes for the Federalist vice-presidential candidate, Pinckney, than for the presidential candidate, Adams. In the end the maneuver failed, but Jefferson, the presidential candidate of the Democratic-Republicans, received the second largest number of electoral votes after Adams, and thus became vice-president under Adams. In 1800, the Democratic-Republicans failed to arrange properly for votes to be thrown away; as a result the Democratic-Republican candidates for president and vice-president, Jefferson and Burr, ended in a tie. That was broken by Congress only after a lengthy crisis. The Constitutional defect, which by now was apparent to all, was eliminated in 1804 by the Twelfth Amendment.

ning of a radically new era in transportation. These needs were created because the United States was already a republic with broadly based suffrage, voters who had to be mobilized, won, persuaded, held firm. Thus party organization was obviously needed, not only in the Congress but throughout the country: to make nominations for countless public offices from U.S. senator to dog-catcher; to skirmish in a variety of elected legislative bodies; to carry on the never-ending series of electoral campaigns; to mobilize voters. To intelligent and ambitious politicians who not only clearly perceived but enthusiastically embraced the institutions of a democratic republic—as many old Federalists were unable or unwilling to do—these needs were obvious. The means were perhaps less obvious but by no means obscure to the eager and discerning eye. And so by the end of Jefferson's two terms in office, the major parts of the modern machinery of the American party system had been invented.

Some of the instructions issued in 1805 to party workers by Alexander Wolcott, the Connecticut "State-manager" (as he signed himself) of the Democratic-Republican party, would still be appropriate today:

> ...I ask you...to appoint in each town of your county, an active, influential, republican manager....
> The duties of a Town-manager will be,
> 1st. To appoint a district manager in each district or section of his town, obtaining from each an assurance that he will faithfully do his duty,
> 2d. To copy from the list of his town the names of all male inhabitants, who are taxed,
> 3d. To call together his district managers, and with their assistance to ascertain,
> 1st. The whole number of males, who are taxed [i.e., eligible to become voters],
> 2d. How many of the whole number are freemen [i.e., voters],
> 3d. How many of the freemen [voters] are decided republicans,
> 4th. How many ——— decided federalists,
> 5th. How many ——— doubtful,
> 6th. How many republicans who are not freemen, but who may be qualified [to vote] at the next proxies.

Wolcott went on with further instructions that would cheer the heart of any party leader today.[18]

Where the Democratic-Republicans moved with amazing speed to construct the required machinery, the Federalists held back; their organization never came close to matching that of their opponents. A lingering preference for an aristocratic republic seems to have blinded them to their true place in a more democratic republic. It clouded their under-

---

18. The document is in Cunningham, *Making of the American Party System*, pp. 115–118.

standing of their real prospects, and thus perhaps contributed to their neglect of party machinery. In any case, this neglect was probably one cause of their decline.[19]

As Federalism began to disappear and the Democratic-Republicans commanded ever wider support, the machinery of party was allowed to decay. But it never was totally lost, nor was the memory of it. During Jackson's presidency, there was no need to invent the political party a second time. Party machinery was quickly rebuilt, and it has endured ever since.

Formation and Development of a Two-Party System

A two-party system virtually vanished as the Federalists died out in the 1820s. During and after Jackson's presidency in the 1830s, a new two-party system emerged. In fact, under this "second American party system," as one writer has called it, "the two new parties were balanced and competitive in every region. For a very brief period—between 1840 and 1852—the nation, for the only time in its history, had two parties that were both truly national in scope."[20] This period saw the development of two highly competitive political parties bearing most of the characteristics American parties have exhibited ever since. These were the Whigs, who were loosely related to the Federalists, and the Jacksonian Democrats, who claimed to be the true descendants of the party of Jefferson and Madison. However, the strength of party organization and voting support in each state varied in the succeeding years. Probably not until recently have both parties been as highly organized and well balanced across the country as they were during the period between 1840 and 1852.

The Whigs disintegrated in the 1850s. The new Republican party, founded in 1854 (not to be confused with the Jeffersonian forerunners of the present Democratic party), became a strictly non-Southern party, which it has remained till very recently. And the one-party Democratic South was created in the wake of the Civil War. All of these developments led to a decline in two-party competition that endured for nearly a century. Since about 1946, however, there again has been rising competition between the two parties, with the Democrats increasing in strength in upper New England and the Midwest, and the Republicans growing throughout the South.

SUMMARY   1. Modern democratic theory assigns a central role to conflict and competition among rival political parties. Yet the centrality of parties was

---

19. Shaw Livermore, Jr., *The Twilight of Federalism, The Disintegration of the Federalist Party 1815–1830* (Princeton: Princeton University Press, 1962), pp. 8–9, 29–30.

20. McCormick, *The Second American Party System*, p. 14.

not foreseen by the Framers of the Constitution and even today many Americans question the legitimacy of party conflict.

2. The Framers' lack of provision for political parties might be explained by

☐ Their fear of the destructive effects of faction.
☐ The absence of organized political parties in earlier republics and their primitive development in eighteenth-century Britain.

3. Whatever their specific intentions, however, the Constitution made political parties both *possible* and *inevitable*. The Bill of Rights guaranteed the legality of parties, and thus insured their possibility. Given the possibility, the need to win elections and marshal legislative majorities made parties inevitable.

4. After an initial period of Federalist hostility to parties and organized opposition culminating in the Alien and Sedition Acts in 1798, the victory of the Democratic-Republican party, organized and led by Jefferson and Madison, secured the acceptability of political parties in the American polyarchy.

5. In order to gain the votes in Congress and among the electorate needed to approve and support its policies, the Democratic-Republican party began to develop most of the features that have characterized political parties in the American polyarchy ever since.

6. However, the system of two well-organized national parties dates from the "second American party system" of 1840–1852.

21 EIGHT CHARACTERISTICS OF THE AMERICAN PARTY SYSTEM

The party systems of modern polyarchies are of great variety and complexity. Because the party system of each country is a particular combination of characteristics, every country can make a passable claim to the uniqueness of its party system. Among the polyarchies of the present day, multi-party systems are the most numerous; yet even they differ greatly. Only a few countries have followed the British two-party model; Britain herself does not always adhere to it, for sometimes a third party plays a critical role in British politics. The American version of the two-party model has not yet been precisely copied in any other polyarchy.

Although one of the two contemporary parties did not emerge until the 1850s, as we saw in the last chapter the American party system took pretty much of its present shape before the end of Jackson's presidency. What makes that party system distinctive is its combination of eight characteristics.

A TWO-PARTY SYSTEM
The first and most obvious characteristic of the American party system is the fact that national elective offices—the presidency and the Congress—are monopolized by two parties. In no other large polyarchy (and only a few smaller ones) do third parties have so slight a representation in national politics as in the United States. Since 1860 every presidential election has been won by either a Democrat or a Republican; in only four presidential elections during that period has a third party ever carried a single state, and only once gained as much as a quarter of the popular vote (Table 21.1). In American politics, rapid growth in third-party votes is a sure sign of an unusual state of affairs.

Year	Party	Percentage of total votes cast
1832	Anti-Mason	8.0
1848	Free Soil	10.1
1856	American	21.4
1860	Breckinridge Democratic	18.2
	Constitutional Union	12.6
1892	Populist	8.5
1912	Theodore Roosevelt Progressive[a]	27.4
	Socialist	6.0
1924	La Follette Progressive	16.6
1968	American Independent (Wallace)	13.5

[a] The vote for the Republican party was 23.2 percent, making the vote of the short-lived Progressive party the second highest of the election.

Source: Daniel A. Mazmanian, *Third Parties in Presidential Elections* (Washington, D.C.: The Brookings Institution, 1974), p. 5.

For example, a surge of support for a third party occurred in 1860 when the opposition to Lincoln was divided among three candidates; in 1892 when the Populist party was the vehicle of widespread discontent among farmers and urban workers; in 1912 when Theodore Roosevelt split the Republican party; in 1948 when the States' Rights party fought another losing skirmish in the long battle for white supremacy; and in 1968 when widespread unrest and discontent with Democratic and Republican leadership helped Governor George Wallace of Alabama capture over 13 percent of the presidential vote. Since 1862, one of the two major parties has always had a clear majority of seats in the House; in the Senate, independents or third-party members have prevented a clear majority during a total of ten years. The numbers of seats held by third-party members is almost always extremely low (Table 21.2).

Why Only Two Major Parties?

In Chapter 20 I offered some reasons why more than one party is likely to exist in a polyarchy. But if the most frequent pattern is for polyarchies to have more than two important parties, why are there only two major parties in the United States?

Patterns of consensus and cleavage. One part of the explanation is to be found in the patterns of consensus and cleavage that ordinarily (though not always, as we shall see) characterize American political life.[1] In earlier chapters we saw how a considerable measure of ideo-

---

1. Political scientists often refer to political *cleavages*, meaning differences between persons that tend to create, or are prominently associated with, conflicts. Among the most frequent lines of cleavage are differences in race, ethnic origins, religion, region, economic position, ideology, etc.

Table 21.2
Third Party Seats Won
in Elections to Congress,
1862–1970

Seats	Elections	
	House	Senate
None	21	27
One	7	15
2–5	21	11
6–10	9	1
11–15	4	1
16–20	2	0
More than 20	0	0
Total elections	51	51

Source: *Congress and the Nation, A Review of Government and Politics,* 2 vols. (Washington, D.C.: Congressional Quarterly Service, 1965–1969) vol. 2, p. 26.

logical agreement developed in the United States. As a result, comparatively few Americans disagree sharply on many essential matters that in other polyarchies help to create large followings for separate parties—separate Catholic parties in Italy and the Netherlands, for example, or separate Protestant parties in the Netherlands, or farmers' parties in the Scandinavian countries, or separate working-class parties throughout Europe. In addition, the normal pattern of cross-cutting cleavages, which we shall examine in Chapter 24, facilitates the existence of two fairly comprehensive catch-all parties that manage to find a place for practically every active interest.

Electoral mechanics. Second, electoral mechanics have an impact. It hardly seems open to question that the introduction of any of the common systems of proportional representation for the election of representatives to Congress would encourage splits in the major parties and serious competition from additional parties. Systems of proportional representation under which a party's share of seats in the legislative body is approximately equal to its share of votes in the country are used in most European polyarchies and contribute to (even if they do not completely explain) the existence of three or more sizable parties.

In the United States, congressmen and senators, like members of parliament in Britain, are elected in districts (or states) under the principle of winner-take-all. Notice how the two systems—proportional representation (PR) and winner-take-all—bear on the calculations of voters and politicians. Under PR, voters and politicians can be sure that the proportion of seats won by a party will be very nearly the same as the party's nationwide share of votes. Consequently, under PR, voters know that they will not throw away their vote by voting for a minority party; and leaders of minority parties do not have much of an incentive to consolidate with other parties in order to win elections. Under the winner-take-all system, on the other hand, the share of seats a party wins ordinarily varies a good deal from its share of votes. It is easy to see why: if the voters for all the parties were spread evenly throughout the country, the largest party would win *all* the seats. Fortunately, party support is, in fact, unevenly distributed around the country; a second party can therefore win victories in districts or regions where its votes are heavily concentrated. But the general effect—let us call it the snow-balling effect—is to reward the winning party with a larger share of seats than votes, and to penalize the second party by awarding it a share of seats smaller than its share of votes.

Thus in a two-party system where one representative is elected from each district under the winner-take-all principle (as in elections to our House of Representatives) a gain of one percent in the votes for Party *A* will result in a gain of *more* than 1 percent in the seats won by that party. And of course a loss of 1 percent in votes will mean a loss of *more* than 1 percent in seats won. By way of illustration, let us suppose that in elections to the House of Representatives, when each of the parties wins 50 percent of the votes, each also wins 50 percent of the House seats. But suppose that when a party wins 51 percent of the votes it wins 52 percent of the House seats; when it wins 52 percent of the votes, it wins 54 percent of the seats, and so on. Thus for each 1 percent a party wins in votes, it gains an additional 2 percent in seats. This proportion is called the *swing ratio*. In our example, the swing ratio is 2. Meanwhile, of course, the share of the losing party would have gone down by the same proportion: when it wins 49 percent of the votes it gains only 48 percent of the seats, with 48 percent of the vote, 46 percent of the seats, and so on. As the vote diverges from 50 percent, the advantage for the majority party in seats and the corresponding penalty for the minority party both increase. Thus if the votes were 65 percent to 35 percent, the seats would be 80 percent to 20 percent.

Calculations show that in elections to the House of Representatives from 1900 to 1970, the swing ratio was a little over 2 (2.09).[2] Thus the snowballing effect of the electoral mechanics has tended to reinforce the two-party system by giving extra seats to the majority party, reducing the seats of the minority party, and making it very close to impossible for a third party to gain a significant number of representatives.

For a third party, the effects of the winner-take-all system are devastating. Although a small percentage of Americans vote for third-party candidates in nearly every election, they often gain no seats at all and never win anything like a proportionate number (Figure 21.1). In the

2. Edward R. Tufte, "The Relationship between Seats and Votes in Two-Party Systems," *American Political Science Review*, 67 (June 1973), 540–554. Tufte introduces and defines swing ratio on p. 542. Estimates of swing ratios are in Table 1, p. 543 and Table 6, p. 550.

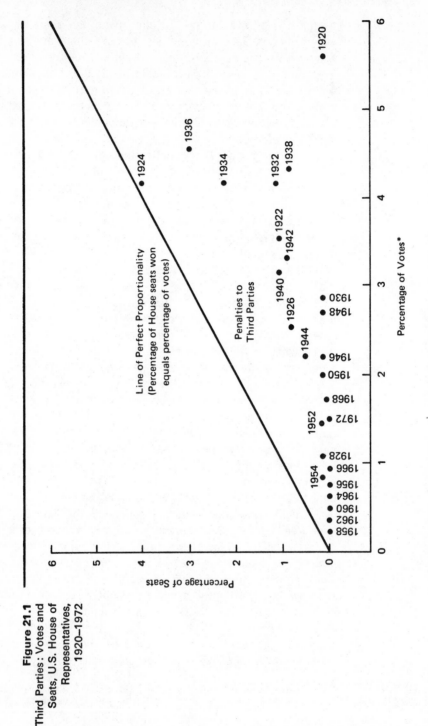

Figure 21.1
Third Parties: Votes and Seats, U.S. House of Representatives, 1920–1972

*Reporting of third-party votes is subject to considerable error. Different sources frequently disagree on totals.
Sources: 1920 to 1956: U.S. Bureau of the Census, *Historical Statistics of the United States, Colonial Times to 1957;* 1956 to 1962: *Congressional District Data Book* (Washington, D.C.: Government Printing Office, 1963); 1964 to 1972: *Statistical Abstract of the United States,* 1974.

election of 1920, for example, the third-party candidates for the House won 1.4 million votes, or 5.6 percent of the total, and acquired exactly one seat out of 435, or slightly more than one-fifth of 1 percent!

The same principle operates in Senate elections. So, too, in presidential elections; because all the electoral votes of a state go to the presidential candidate with the largest share of popular votes in that state, the snowballing effect in presidential elections is even more visible. Because the presidency is the most strategic post in the entire political system, and because it is completely indivisible, in a presidential contest the winner does indeed take all and leaves no crumbs to the loser. Consider what happens, then, in a three-way presidential election like that of 1912. Taft and Theodore Roosevelt split the Republicans almost down the middle. Taft won 23 percent of the popular votes but only 1.5 percent of the electoral votes! Theodore Roosevelt won 27 percent of the popular votes and only 16.5 percent of the electoral votes. The victor, Democrat Woodrow Wilson, gained 82 percent of the electoral votes by winning forty out of forty-eight states—yet he had only 42 percent, less than a majority, of the popular votes!

To a politician, the instructions contained in this kind of election are unambiguous: If you want to win a presidential election, don't split your party; don't back a third party; concentrate instead on building up the largest possible coalition of interests, no matter how dissimilar the parts, in support of the candidate of one of the two major parties.

Party loyalties. A third reason why two parties, not three or more, monopolize national politics is the force of habit and tradition. The two parties have been dominant for a century; the invariable fate of third parties is to be overwhelmingly defeated and often to disappear after one election. Many people acquire their basic political positions and loyalties early, when they are still strongly under the influence of parents and family. This is true also of attitudes toward the parties; hence, party loyalties tend to be transmitted from parents to children. The mere fact then that the Republican and Democratic parties monopolize votes during one generation makes it very much easier for them to monopolize votes during the next generation. To break out of a minority position on the other hand, a third party must overcome the enormous inertia of habit.

VARIABILITY OF EFFECTIVE COMPETITION   The second characteristic of the American system is that the degree of effective competition between the two parties varies greatly throughout the country and, in general, declines with the size of the unit. We noted in Chapter 19 that many towns and cities lack effective two-party competition either because party support is overwhelmingly one-sided or because the functions of parties have been curtailed by nonpartisan elections—or both. Party competition is likely to be closer at the state level, as we saw; yet only about half the states can be regarded as having two-party systems. At the national level, however, the parties compete on a more even basis. To be sure, during long periods, one of the two parties may win the presidency much more often than the other: the Republicans from 1896 to 1932, the Democrats from 1932 to 1952. But measured by the proportion of congressional seats and votes in presidential and congressional elections, neither party manages to hold a big lead for very long.

As we saw in the last chapter, the degree of party competition varies over time as well as locale. Since the mid-1950s, there have been two somewhat contradictory trends. On the one hand, in presidential elections the parties have become more competitive throughout the country, particularly as the century-long dominance of the South by the Democrats began to disintegrate. For example, Virginia, which only once since the Civil War had voted for a Republican candidate (in 1928), voted Republican in five out of six presidential elections between 1952 and 1972. In the same twenty-year period, Louisiana, which had an unbroken record of Democratic support following the Civil War, voted twice for a Democratic candidate, three times for a Republican, and once for a third-party candidate, George Wallace.

At the same time, however, there has been a decline in the effectiveness of party competition for seats in the House. In the late 1950s, the margin of victory of the front-runner was less than 5 percent in about 20 percent of the House districts. By 1970, in only 13 percent of the districts was the margin under 5 percent. For reasons that are still debated by political scientists, members of the House who run for reelection—the incumbents—appear to have a growing advantage over their challengers.[3]

DIFFUSION AND DECENTRALIZATION OF CONTROL

Third, control over nominations and the policies of the parties is spread throughout several political levels. In many cases it is decentralized to state and local organizations. This is not to say that the parties are democratically controlled, for they are not; but control is not as tightly centralized in the hands of a single set of leaders as in many parties in other polyarchies.

Even in the presidential nominating convention, one of the few methods by which American national parties act collectively, control is generally diffuse. Except for the party of a president at the end of his

---

3. *Ibid.,* p. 550. See also David R. Mayhew, "Congressional Representation: Theory and Practice in Drawing the Districts," in *Reapportionment in the 1970s,* Nelson W. Polsby, ed. (Berkeley: University of California Press, 1971), pp. 249–290.

first term—when normally the president dominates the convention that nominates him—control over a convention is usually spread so thin and the outcome is so uncertain that millions of Americans, including the best-informed ones in the midst of the convention, continue to speculate about the outcome of the winning ballot. Senatorial nominations are decentralized to state organizations; nominations of congressmen to state and district organizations. Control over nominations of state and local officials is, of course, highly decentralized. And within states and localities, control is still further diffused by the direct primary.

Much the same diffusion and decentralization applies to policies. The incumbent president can largely determine presidential policy, and that, as we have seen, is a good deal. But control over the policies and votes of his party colleagues in Congress is comparatively modest— and is negligible in the states and localities.

Causes

Why is control over party nominations and policies much more diffused and decentralized in the United States than in some of the important parties in other democracies?

Federalism. The most potent factor is probably the sheer force of federalism. Federalism insures that the states and localities are in a great many respects autonomous, independent of direct control by national officials. Strong state and local political organizations can be built without federal patronage and can survive electoral defeat at the national level; the innumerable nominations for state and local office, the never-ending cycle of state and local elections make it very much easier for those on the spot to exert control than for national officials to do so. In addition, most of the laws controlling nominations, elections, party organization, and party finance, all highly strategic matters for party leaders, are passed and enforced by state governments.

Urban machines. Another factor of considerable historical importance is the weight that urban machines have had within the two parties, particularly the Democratic party.

Attitudes. Traditional American political attitudes, as we have seen, seem to endorse diffusion and decentralization of power in all of our political institutions; it should not be too surprising if these attitudes carry over into the political parties. Among Americans, centralized parties seem to lack the accepted status that they have in countries like Britain and Sweden, with ancient and strong traditions of hierarchy and centralization.

Institutionalism. Finally, the past weighs heavily on the future simply because decentralization of party control is thoroughly institutionalized. A party leader who sought to centralize control over nominations and policy would be throwing out a clear-cut challenge to thousands of other party leaders whose power would thereby be diminished. Since few people yield power cheerfully, any national leader who sought to gain more control over a party would stir up fierce opposition from state and local leaders in the entrenched strongholds of party power throughout the length and breadth of the country. The individual power of these local leaders is not great on the national scene; but united, they would be an awesome force. Knowing in advance that the most likely outcome would be their own disastrous defeat, national leaders never lay down the challenge.

LOW COHESION   *Fourth,* the same factors that operate to prevent centralization of control in the parties also inhibit the development of parties that are highly united in support of particular policies. The most visible evidence of unity in a party is the extent to which members of a party vote the same way on bills and other measures in a legislature. If all the members of a party in a legislature always voted the same way, a party would of course display complete unity. In a two-party system, if each of the parties were perfectly unified, then on every legislative question over which the parties disagreed all the members of one party would vote one way while all the members of the other party would vote against them. Such total party unity is unusual, but in some countries the parties are much closer to complete unity than in the United States. For example, in this century British parties display far greater unity in voting in the House of Commons than do our parties in the Congress (specifically the House).

High cohesion in the national legislature is not uncommon among the larger parties in many other polyarchies. To this extent the relatively low cohesiveness displayed by American parties is something of an exception, and—despite the beliefs of many Americans—not inherent in a 'democratic' political system.

A word of caution is needed, however. Party unity is very far from being a negligible factor in the Congress. None of the other lines of cleavage in Congress—metropolitan-rural, North-South, liberal-conservative—seem to predict as well as party the way members will divide over a number of different issues and sessions. Thus the author of one statistical study of the question concluded that

> quantitative analysis of roll call votes shows, contrary to majority opinion, that significant differences exist between our major parties. While it is true that American discipline falls short of that achieved in some European

democracies, and is less effective than party discipline in the McKinley era in the United States, evidence of great party influence can still be found. Party pressure seems to be more effective than any other pressure on Congressional voting, and is discernible on nearly nine-tenths of the roll calls examined.[4]

And in some state legislatures—Connecticut, for example—the parties are about as cohesive as in any European parliament.[5]

IDEOLOGICAL SIMILARITY AND ISSUE CONFLICT

Fifth, although the parties frequently differ on specific issues, they are not markedly different in their basic perspectives: the fundamental values they assert, what they prescribe as the proper institutions for Americans, their conception of the potentialities and promise of American life, and so on. In short, they do not advocate sharply conflicting *ideologies.* In this respect the major parties of the United States differ from those in a number of European countries. In those polyarchies the spectrum of parties with a significant electoral following may run from communists or socialists on the left, through liberal democrats and Christian (usually Catholic) Democrats in the center, to conservative and even more or less fascist parties on the right.

The fact that the two major parties in the United States do not differ so markedly in their explicit ideologies as parties do in many European countries does not mean, as is sometimes said, that American parties advocate no ideology at all. They do. But both Republicans and Democrats in the United States advocate much the same ideology. Both parties express a commitment to democracy, to the Constitution, and to the key social and economic institutions of American life: privately owned business firms, universal free public education, separation of church and state, religious toleration, and the like. To a European accustomed to the sound and fury of clashing ideologies, American party battles seem tame and uninteresting.

Differences in Rhetoric

In this case likeness is not identity, however. To a Buddhist the differences between Baptists and Episcopalians might seem negligible— but they are not so negligible to Baptists and Episcopalians. Although Republicans and Democrats profess to worship the same gods and endorse the same commandments, the rhetoric employed by the leaders of the two parties tends to have differing emphases. These differences in emphasis vary over time. To generalize from recent decades, one might say that where Democratic rhetoric emphasizes the equality of

---

4. Julius Turner, *Party and Constituency: Pressure on Congress* (Baltimore: Johns Hopkins Press, 1951), p. 23.

5. See Duane Lockard, *New England State Politics* (Princeton: Princeton University Press, 1959), p. 279.

Americans in dignity, respect, and rights, Republican rhetoric emphasizes their liberties and differences in capacities. Where Democratic
rhetoric extols the accomplishments of the federal government, Republican rhetoric extols the benefits of action through state and local governments. Where Democratic rhetoric emphasizes the virtues and possibilities of public action through government, Republican rhetoric
emphasizes the virtues of business enterprise. Where 'regulation of
business' is often portrayed as desirable in Democratic rhetoric it is
more often portrayed as evil in Republican rhetoric. Where Democratic
rhetoric declaims the needs and aspirations of the less well off—the
poor, the underprivileged, the culturally deprived, the aged—Republican rhetoric declaims the needs and aspirations of the solid and successful strata. (Both, of course, unendingly praise the virtues of the
average man, the middle class, the middle-of-the-road, the taxpayer,
the American way.)

Similarities in Ideology

Despite differences like these in shading and emphasis, the ideological commitments of leaders in both parties are usually so much
alike that, in many campaigns, opponents find it tempting to distinguish
themselves ideologically from one another by gross exaggerations, car-
icatures, and downright falsehoods. Because it provided a firmer basis
than usual for ideological distinctions, the 1964 presidential campaign
was something of a departure from the norm. The Republican candidate, Senator Barry Goldwater, unashamedly professed an extremely
'conservative' ideology that was intended to be, and was, at odds with
the 'liberal' or 'liberal-conservative' ideology that most Republican and
Democratic leaders had espoused for several decades. Even so the
senator's 'conservatism' was scarcely distinguishable from the prevailing ideology of both parties in the nineteenth century; and 'conservatives' found it difficult to formulate a coherent expression of abstract
ideology that did not simply restate platitudes long since incorporated
into the rhetoric of both parties.

Differences in Policies

The most marked difference between the parties is not in their
ideologies but in their programs and policies. The differences are often
much greater than a mere examination of rhetoric would lead one to
expect—greater sometimes, in fact, than the difference between European parties that substitute rhetoric for concrete programs. It is very
far from being the case that the parties adopt identical platforms at
their national conventions. And although American parties are not as
cohesive as parties often are in other countries, on many issues Democrats and Republicans divide quite sharply. The content of party conflict
changes from one historical period to the next; but in every generation

Figure 21.2
Presidential Support
Scores, 1961–1974*

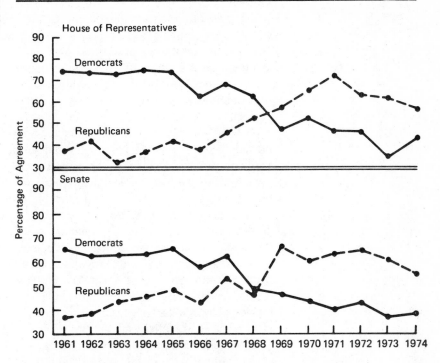

* Support scores for Nixon and Ford in 1974 are averaged.

Source: Presidential Support Scores from the Congressional Quarterly Service. Number of roll calls used to determine presidential support scores were: for House: 1961, 65; 1963, 71; 1964, 52; 1965, 112; 1966, 103; 1967, 127; 1968, 103; 1969, 47; 1970, 65; 1971, 57; 1972, 37; 1973, 125; 1974, 107. For Senate: 1961, 124; 1962, 125; 1963, 115; 1964, 97; 1965, 162; 1966, 125; 1967, 165; 1968, 164; 1969, 72; 1970, 91; 1971, 82; 1972, 46; 1973, 185; 1974, 151.

there are persistently divisive issues that distinguish Democrats and Republicans.[6]

When the president lines up on one side and the leaders of the opposition party on the other, the chances are particularly good that a high proportion of Democrats will vote one way and Republicans another. From 1961 to 1968, for example, the Democrats in the House and Senate gave much more support to the measures of the Democratic administration than did the Republicans. After the election of a Republican president in 1968, naturally Republicans in the House and Senate gave the president more support than the Democrats (Figure 21.2).

---

6. For example, in a study of the four sessions of 1921, 1931, 1937, and 1944, it was found that Democrats and Republicans in the House disagreed markedly on measures pertaining to tariff; patronage; government (as opposed to private) action on electric power, crop insurance, and other matters; the size of the federal bureaucracy; public works; social, welfare, and labor matters; and farm policy. The difference between the percentage of Democrats and the percentage of Republicans who voted for a given measure on a roll call was on the average more than 50 percent. On tariff measures, the average difference was almost 80 percent (Turner, *Party and Constituency*, pp. 36–38).

Causes

The explanation for this combination of ideological similarity and conflict over issues goes to the very heart of the American political system. An overwhelming proportion of American voters do not sharply divide on beliefs that in other countries generate followings for ideologically divergent parties. A party that preaches anti-democratic doctrines, revolutionary aims, hostility to the Constitution or constitutional processes, religious, racial, or ethnic conflict, the repression or favoring of a particular religion, or nationalization of the means of production at best appeals to a small part of the electorate. Thus, since the major parties direct their appeal to the great bulk of the electorate, they cannot diverge very much ideologically. For reasons we have already explored, the effect of the election machinery is to reduce even further the prospect of success for an ideologically divergent party. Hence, paradoxically, party conflict in campaigns, elections, and policy-making constantly reinforces the prevailing ideology and weakens the impact of political movements with rival ideologies. A similarity of ideological perspectives among most Americans has insured the success of ideologically similar parties; and the domination of American politics by ideologically similar parties has in turn reinforced the similarity of ideological perspectives among the American people.

Yet, because these ideological perspectives are not identical but vary in strength, emphasis, and to some extent even in content, they do allow for considerable—at times extensive—divergence on matters of policy. The strategy of the parties, then, is to seek support among voters not only by proclaiming their own ideological purity and the horrendous deviation of the other party from ideological orthodoxy, but also by advocating policies they expect to appeal to voters. But, it might be asked, if both parties want to win the largest number of votes, why don't they both advocate the same policies? Often, of course, they do. But there are several important reasons why they do not. For one thing, politicians lack perfect information about voters' attitudes; in the absence of perfect information there is considerable uncertainty as to what strategy will have the greatest appeal and will maximize votes in the coming election. Like other people, politicians fill in areas of ignorance by making guesses. And the hunches of politicians are shaped by politicians' own experiences, prejudices, wishes, and fantasies; by the views of people on whom they depend for information and advice; by their conceptions of what their most loyal and deserving supporters actually want; and even by their views as to what is 'best for the country.'

DIFFERENCES IN PARTY FOLLOWINGS The sixth characteristic of American parties has a double aspect: (1) With few exceptions, each of the parties draws votes in significant numbers from every stratum of the population; but (2) many strata consistently vote more heavily for one party than the other. In general, then, neither party has a monopoly of the votes within any category of Americans. Yet the hard core of undeviating supporters for each party is located in different strata. Nothing is static, of course, including the composition of party followings. But the hard core of each party is particularly slow to change.

Following a massive shift in party support during the Great Depression and the New Deal in the 1930s, a rather stable pattern emerged. The groups most favorable to the Republicans were people of higher incomes and social status with college educations and professional and managerial occupations, people in medium-sized towns and cities, and Protestants. Groups most favorable to the Democrats were people of lower incomes and social status with grade-school and high-school education, working in skilled or unskilled manual occupations, trade-union members and their families, residents of metropolitan areas, Catholics, and blacks.

During the 1960s, however, this pattern began to break up. The breakup was probably in part a result of the political disorientation and alienation that occurred during the decade of intense conflict from 1964 to 1974.[7] It may also be a result of certain long-run changes in American society, such as the modernization of the South and the rapid increase in the proportion of college-educated voters. Whatever the explanation, Republican candidates gained and Democratic candidates lost support among white blue-collar workers, Catholics, and Southern white Protestants. These groups were the very core of the New Deal Democratic coalition that had developed under the leadership of President Franklin D. Roosevelt. At the same time, Democratic candidates gained and Republicans lost among certain groups of higher social and economic status that had been the traditional stronghold of Republicanism; those included professional people, the college-educated, and white persons under 30 from the upper social and economic groups[8] (Figure 21.3).

Democrats use rhetoric and advocate policies designed to appeal to their followers in working-class occupations and the big cities; Republicans use rhetoric and advocate policies designed to appeal to their followers in the business community and small towns. When the Democrats place more emphasis on equality and the virtues of the underprivileged, and Republicans on opportunity and the virtues of the more privileged, they are appealing to their respective hard cores of loyal followers. Yet neither party wishes to ignore potential votes in other social strata; hence each party designs its rhetoric and its pro-

7. See Chapter 13 and Chapter 26.

8. Everett Carl Ladd, Jr. with Charles D. Hadley, *Transformation of the American Party System: Political Coalitions from the New Deal to the 1970s* (New York: Norton, 1975), p. 226 ff. See also Everett Carl Ladd, Jr. and Charles D. Hadley, *Political Parties and Political Issues: Patterns in Differentiation Since the New Deal* (Beverly Hills, Cal.: Sage Publications, 1973).

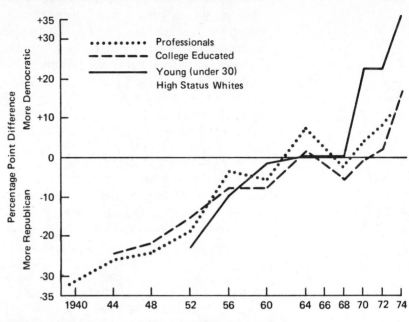

Figure 21.3
Democratic Gains Among Three High-Status Groups

Source: Ladd, *Transformation of the American Party System*, p. 255.

gram not only to retain the loyalty and enthusiasm of its hard core of zealous adherents but at the same time to win over less-committed voters in all the major categories of the population.

DURABILITY The seventh characteristic of American parties is their extraordinary durability. With no bending of historical fact, the life of the Democratic party can be traced as far back as President Jackson in 1830. Indeed, as we noted in the last chapter, a good claim can be made that the present party is the direct institutional descendant of Jefferson's party. The Republican party has contested every national election since 1856. The two parties have thus dominated national politics for a century. No other party system in the world is so old.[9]

Why have American parties endured so long? First, by diligently seeking to advance and protect the interests of the social groups from which they draw their most dependable support, the parties retain a hard core of loyal followers even in greatest adversity. These social groups endure; their loyalty helps the parties to endure. For the Democrats, the two low points in this century were the presidential elections

9. In Britain, the Conservatives trace their lineage back to the late eighteenth-century Tories led by the younger Pitt; the Liberals to the Whigs led by Charles James Fox; but the Labour party dates back only to 1905.

of 1920, when they received 34 percent of the popular votes, and 1924, when their share dropped to 29 percent. The low points for the Republicans were 1936 (36.5 percent) and 1964 (38.5 percent). Thanks to their hard core of loyalists, neither party has ever come close to being wiped out.

Second, with an extraordinary number of people, party loyalties are acquired early in life, under the influence of family and friends, and thereafter remain unaltered except under the impact of a major shock like the Great Depression. Third, the parties have been skillful enough to adjust their programs and even their rhetoric to changing times and popular attitudes, though ever since the 1930s the Republicans have found it difficult to adapt to the transformations brought on by the Depression and the New Deal. Combined with all of these factors, the electoral mechanics and the ideological cohesion of the great bulk of the electorate have, as we saw earlier, made it exceptionally difficult—in fact, impossible so far—for a third party to win over enough voters to displace either of the two major parties.

Yet despite the extraordinary durability of the two major parties and the historic inability of third parties to make much headway in the American polyarchy, the turbulence that marked American political life from the mid-1960s onward was, as we saw in Chapter 10, accompanied by a measure of disenchantment with both the parties. The strength of party loyalties grew weaker. The proportion of independents, who claimed no attachment to either party, rose. Percentages declined of those who had always voted for the presidential candidate of only one party, and who voted a straight ticket for the national, state, and local candidates of only one party.[10]

VARIABILITY IN PARTY SUPPORT　The changes in the parties since the 1960s discussed above point to one other characteristic of American parties. This is probably the most obvious and in some ways the most important characteristic of all: the effectiveness of each of the parties in winning loyalty and support varies markedly over time. The history of American parties shows that the electoral fortunes of a party may change very rapidly. No politician is likely to forget this lesson. As a consequence the typical party politician works zealously to discover what voters want, and then tries to shape the political strategies of his or her party in order to win their votes on election day.

In a loose way American national elections—or, more precisely, a brief series of several elections—can be classified into two broad cat-

---

10. Gerald Pomper, *Voters' Choice, Varieties of American Electoral Behavior* (New York: Dodd, Mead, 1975), p. 20 ff; *ISR Newsletter* (Institute for Social Research, University of Michigan), 1, no. 13 (Winter 1972), pp. 5–7; Walter DeVries and V. Lance Tarrance, *The Ticket-Splitter: A New Force in American Politics* (Grand Rapids, Mich.: William B. Eerdmans Publishing Co., 1972), pp. 19–38.

egories: elections that pretty much repeat the patterns of popular division and support of preceding elections (or are only a one-time transitory departure from them); and those in which a major and rather long-lasting shift or realignment in party support takes place.

The first, sometimes called *reinforcing,* or *maintaining* elections, are normal; *realigning* elections are abnormal. Maintaining elections seem to occur during periods of moderate conflict; realigning elections are more likely during periods of severe conflict. The most important sets of realigning elections in American history were probably these: 1796 and 1800, 1856 and 1860, 1932 and 1936. The presidential elections of 1968 and 1972 may have reflected, and also helped to bring about, a realignment of the two parties.[11]

Maintaining Elections

In maintaining elections, pre-existing party loyalties predominate. The great bulk of the electorate consists of people who identify themselves with one of the two major parties. Between elections and during the campaigns their party loyalties are not severely strained. They perceive no serious conflict between their habitual loyalty to a party, and the candidates, policies, programs, and actions of that party. Their loyalty and the absence of highly divisive issues within the party tend in fact to soften or eliminate their perceptions of differences between themselves and their party.

Maintaining elections, then, are stabilizing elections. They reflect and even reinforce party loyalties and perpetuate pre-existing voting patterns in the electorate with only small changes. In a series of maintaining elections, the parties may be quite evenly matched or one party may have a significant advantage. In the first situation, a small change in the electorate may reduce the previous majority to a minority. All the national elections from 1874 to 1894 were maintaining elections, but the elections were remarkably close. In 1880, the Republican presidential candidate (Garfield) won with a plurality less than 40,000 votes; in 1884, the Democrat (Cleveland) won with a plurality less than 30,000 votes. In eight out of the ten congressional elections, the Democrats gained a majority in the House; in only two elections did they gain a majority in the Senate.

Where one party acquires a significant advantage, as the Republi-

---

11. Recent works on historical party changes and realignments are James L. Sundquist, *Dynamics of the American Party System* (Washington, D.C.: The Brookings Institution, 1973). Walter Dean Burnham, *Critical Elections and the Mainspring of American Politics* (New York: W. W. Norton, 1970). Earlier discussions are V. O. Key, Jr., "A Theory of Critical Elections," *Journal of Politics,* 17 (February 1955), 3–18; Campbell et al., *The American Voter* (New York: Wiley, 1964), pp. 531 ff.; Angus Campbell, "Voters and Elections: Past and Present," *Journal of Politics,* 26 (November 1964), 745–757; Angus Campbell, "Surge and Decline: A Study of Electoral Change," "A Classification of the Presidential Elections," and Campbell et al., "Stability and Change in 1960. A Reinstating Election," ch. 5, pp. 78–95, all in Campbell et al., *Elections and the Political Order.*

cans did from 1896 to 1932, the other party loses more or less regularly. Until there is a major realignment in voters' loyalties, the minority party is likely to win the presidency only if (1) there is a split in the majority party, as in 1912 when Wilson won the presidency with 42 percent of the popular vote, or (2) if they have the good fortune to nominate a candidate of extraordinary popularity, like General Eisenhower in 1952 and 1956, who manages to win votes for *himself* even though he cannot win voters for his *party.*

Changes: long-run versus short-run. As these examples suggest, even during a long series of maintaining elections, political attitudes and loyalties are never completely frozen. Even maintaining elections may reflect changes of four kinds:

☐ Slow, *long-run shifts* may occur *throughout* practically the *entire electorate,* as in the period 1896–1928 when there seems to have been a long-run shift toward the Republicans throughout the North, or from 1936 to 1964 when a massive glacial shift toward the Democrats took place.

☐ Superimposed on these gradual shifts in the electorate as a whole, *long-run changes* also take place *within specific groups* at much slower or faster rates; for example from 1936 to 1964, the proportion of blacks voting Democratic increased much more rapidly than that among any other group.

☐ *Short-run fluctuations* usually occur from presidential to midterm congressional elections; typically there is a drop-off in the percentage of the vote cast for candidates of the president's party.

☐ *Short-run surges* may also occur in presidential elections, as in 1952 and 1956 when, despite the long-run increase in the percentage of voters who identified themselves with the Democrats, General Eisenhower nonetheless won enormous personal victories.

Explanation of short-run fluctuations. A number of explanations have been offered for the drop-off in support of congressional candidates of the president's party at the midterm elections. At one time, before the advent of survey data, the most popular explanation was that midterm elections were a kind of referendum on the president. Data from surveys, however, ran against this explanation. The drop was then attributed to differences in the make-up of the smaller midterm electorate as against the larger turnout in presidential election years. That the midterm turnout invariably declines is not open to question (Figure 21.4), and it is also true that the division of votes between Democratic and Republican candidates is more stable in congressional contests than in the presidential race (Figure 21.5). But whatever may have been the

Figure 21.4
Turnout in Presidential
and House of
Representatives Elections,
1952–1972

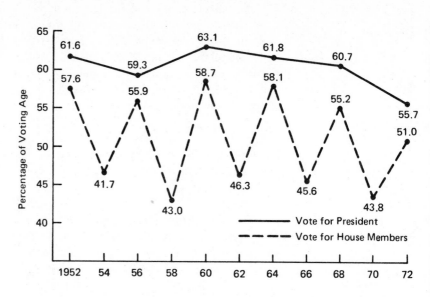

Source: Arseneau and Wolfinger, "Voting Behavior."

case in the 1950s, recent research shows that in the 1960s and 1970s
the electorate in mid-term congressional elections, though smaller, has
not been markedly different in composition from the voters who turn
out in presidential election years.[12]

The explanation for the wider fluctuations in support for presidential candidates shown in Figure 21.5 is to be found not in differences in
the composition of the electorate but in the amount of information
voters have about candidates. Most voters know something about the
presidential candidates, and they have feelings and attitudes about the
candidates. By contrast, a great many voters do not know who their
representative in Congress is; fewer know how he or she has voted;
and even fewer know anything at all about the opposing candidate. In
this situation the most significant cue when one enters the polling booth
is the party. Hence in congressional elections voters tend to vote a
straight party line.[13]

By itself, however, this difference in information does not explain

12. From Robert B. Arseneau and Raymond E. Wolfinger, "Voting Behavior in Congressional Elections," a paper presented at the 1973 Annual Meeting of the American Political
Science Association, New Orleans, Sept. 4–8.
13. *Ibid.*

Figure 21.5
Democratic Percentage
of the Popular Vote for
President and U.S. House
of Representatives,
1960–1974

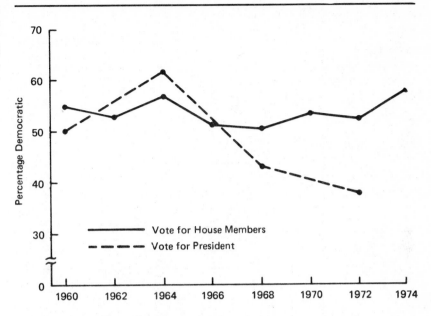

Source: Ladd, *Transformation of the American Party System*, p. 258.

the drop-off in support for congressional candidates of the president's party. The best explanation now available represents an almost complete turnaround back to the notion of congressional midterm elections as a kind of referendum on the president. Given the fact that voters do not know much about Congress or their own representative (many cannot correctly identify which party had the majority of seats in the preceding Congress), they take their cue from how well they think the president is doing. If he is doing badly—and he is nearly always doing less well than his supporters expected when they voted for him—they are more likely to vote for congressional candidates from the other party.

It has been shown, in fact, that the magnitude of the midterm loss in votes can be explained in large part by two factors. One is the degree of change in the popularity of the president. As I have just suggested, most presidents do decline in popularity after a brief honeymoon period following their election (Figure 21.6). This spells trouble for their party and its congressional candidates when they come up for election in the middle of the president's term. The second factor is the performance of the economy during the year before the midterm elections. If the economic situation is deteriorating, voters tend to hold the president and his party responsible. In midterm elections, they are more

Figure 21.6
Presidential Popularity

Do you approve of the way President——is handling his job as president?
(by four-month periods: Jan.-April; May-Aug.; Sept.-Dec.)*

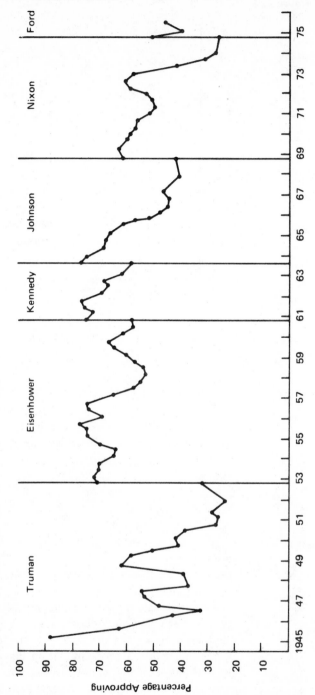

* Truman 1951 data (Feb., April, Nov.); 1952 (Oct.)
Sources: Truman and Eisenhower data from "The Polls—Presidential Popularity," *Public Opinion Quarterly*, 15 (1961), 135–137. Kennedy data from Hazel Gaudet Erskine, "The Polls: Kennedy As President," *Public Opinion Quarterly*, 27 (1964), 334–335. Johnson data through 1965 from *Gallup Opinion Index*, Report No. 6, November, 1965, p. 3. Johnson data from 1965 through 1968 from *Gallup Opinion Index*, Report No. 55, January, 1970, pp. 14–16. Nixon data from *Gallup Opinion Index*, Report No. 111, Sept., 1974, p. 12. Ford data from *Gallup Opinion Index*, Report No. 120, June, 1975, p. 3.

likely to support congressional candidates of the opposition party.[14]

A series of maintaining elections can be likened to a rather stable sand dune on the edge of the ocean in the absence of great storms. Occasional winds change the shape of the dune somewhat. A steady wind from one direction may gradually displace the center of the entire dune to the left or to the right. Not all parts of the dune change at the same rate. Nonetheless, its shape and position remain substantially unchanged from one year to the next.

Realigning Elections

A series of elections in which the parties become realigned is better symbolized by a sand dune subject to the pressure of a storm.[15] Disorganized by the turbulence, its structure momentarily destroyed, it undergoes violent changes in form and position. After the storm, one who had long regarded it with affection might find it impossible to recognize the old dune.

In a series of realigning elections, then, the party loyalties of a great mass of voters are first torn loose and then reattached either to a new party or to the opposite party. After a series of realigning elections has run its course, party alignments are decisively different. The balance of support may be tilted significantly away from one party toward another. A party may even be destroyed. Severe political conflicts precede and accompany realigning elections. In times of severe conflict, the issues of politics are too visible to enable many voters to remain loyal to a party that holds a position in the conflict markedly different from their own.

Examples. During the 1790s the parties were first realigned—though if we consider that the parties were still in their infancy, perhaps it would be more appropriate to say that they were *aligned.* In any case, conflicts disrupted the coalition that had framed the Constitution and weakened the Federalists. These conflicts crystallized so much support for the Democratic-Republicans that after their victory in 1800 they were never to be defeated by the Federalists.

---

14. This explanation is advanced by Edward R. Tufte, "Determinants of the Outcome of Midterm Congressional Elections," *American Political Science Review,* 69 (September, 1975), 812–826. For his two variables, Tufte used (1) a Gallup Poll question on whether respondents approve or disapprove of the way the president is doing his job, and (2) the amount of change in real disposable income per capita between the year of the midterm election and the previous year. These two comparatively simple variables predicted a high proportion of the change in votes for the candidates of the president's party for the House of Representatives in midterm elections from 1938 to 1972.

15. Important studies of 'critical' or 'realigning' elections are Sundquist, *Dynamics of the Party System,* and Burnham, *Critical Elections.* Everett Carl Ladd, Jr., in *Transformations of the Party System,* argues that to focus on the elections is to direct attention "to the wrong class of objects. . . . The election is but one current in the sweeping tide of sociopolitical change." See also the controversy between Burnham and two critics, Philip E. Converse and Jerrold G. Rusk, "Political Change in America," *American Political Science Review,* 68 (September, 1974), 1002–1057.

The 1850s also saw a period of realignment. The Whigs disintegrated in the North. Northern Whigs, Free Soilers, and even many northern and border-state Democrats turned toward the Republican party. Reconstruction temporarily created Republican governments in the South, but as quickly as it was permitted to do so the South became the Democratic Solid South; and it remained so until the 1950s and 1960s.

The 1880s and 1890s saw another major realignment. From 1876 to 1892, the Democrats and Republicans had been running neck-and-neck in presidential races. In four of these elections, the Democratic candidate had outpolled the Republican in popular votes; in the fifth (1880), the Republican, Garfield, had won with a margin of less than 10,000 votes over his Democratic rival—a difference of less than ½ of 1 percent of the total popular vote! In the late 1880s, discontent among farmers fanned into flame the most important third-party movement since the rise of the Republicans: the People's party. In 1896, Populists and Democrats jointly endorsed William Jennings Bryan as their candidate for president. But the Republicans, led by William McKinley, turned back the agrarian challenge. For the first time since 1872, the Republican candidate won a majority of popular votes. The Middle West, where the Democrats had developed strength, became a Republican stronghold. No Democratic candidate again won a majority of popular votes until Franklin Roosevelt's election of 1932; and except in 1912 and 1916, Democratic candidates lost by huge margins. From 1900 to 1932, the Democrats polled fewer votes than the Republicans in all congressional elections save three. Not once did they win a majority of all popular votes.

Party realignment also occurred during the 1930s. The elections of that decade marked a shift away from the Republican party toward the Democrats that continued for the next thirty years. In the nine presidential elections from 1932 to 1964, the Republicans won only twice—with General Eisenhower in 1952 and 1956. In that thirty-four year period, Republicans had majorities in the House of Representatives for only four years. The extent to which deeper underlying tides were running against the Republican party was strikingly visible in the midst of its greatest triumph, the 'surge' election of 1956 in which General Eisenhower was swept into office by an overwhelming majority; for the second time since the election of 1876, the party that won the presidency did not win a majority of seats in the House.

Nonetheless, Eisenhower's election foreshadowed another period of major realignment. Although the Democrats steadily won majorities in Congress, they rarely won the presidency. Of the six presidential elections from 1952 to 1972, they won only two—one of these (1960) by only a few thousand votes. As we saw earlier, the New Deal Democratic coalition put together by Franklin D. Roosevelt began to disintegrate.

Table 21.3
"In politics as of today,
do you consider yourself
a Republican, Democrat,
or Independent?"
1940–1974

	Democrat	Republican	Independent
1940	42%	38%	20%
1950	45	33	22
1960	47	30	23
1964	53	25	22
1965	50	27	23
1966	48	27	25
1967 (Feb)	46	27	27
1968 (June)	46	27	27
1969 (July)	44	29	27
1970 (Oct)	45	29	26
1971 (June)	44	25	31
1972 (June)	43	28	29
1973 (May)	43	24	33
1974 (July)	44	23	33

Source: *Gallup Opinion Index,* Report No. 109, July, 1974.

The party now tended to become a coalition of 'top' and 'bottom,' of the better educated, higher occupational groups at one extreme, and the blacks and poor at the other.[16] Unlike previous periods, however, their rivals failed to gain. The number of Republican partisans continued to decline (Table 21.3). More and more voters were 'up for grabs' during presidential elections. As a result, there were gigantic surges in the presidential vote: in 1964, Lyndon Johnson, a Democrat, gained an unprecedented 61.1 percent of the votes. In 1972, it was Nixon, a Republican, who now won 61 percent of the vote. The Democrats shrank to 38 percent, their worst defeat in fifty years.

SUMMARY   The following combination of characteristics distinguishes the American party system from that in other polyarchies:

1. National elective offices—the presidency and the Congress—have been overwhelmingly monopolized by only two parties. Factors that tend to limit competing parties to two in the American polyarchy are:

☐ The normal pattern of moderately high consensus and cross-cutting divisions.
☐ The impact of a winner-take-all electoral system.
☐ The persistence of party loyalties.

2. The degree of effective competition between the two parties varies greatly throughout the country and, in general, declines with the size of the unit. It varies over time as well.

---

16. See Ladd, *Transformations of the Party System,* and Pomper, *Voters' Choice.*

3. Control over nominations and policies is spread throughout all political levels. In many cases control is decentralized to state and local organizations. The principal causes of diffused and decentralized control are federalism, urban machines, American beliefs about partitioning power, and institutionalization.

4. Comparatively speaking, American parties are much less united in their support of particular policies than are parties in many other polyarchies.

5. Moreover, although the parties frequently differ on specific issues, they are much less different in ideology than are parties in most polyarchies.

6. With few exceptions each party draws votes in significant numbers from every level of the population. Many groups, however, consistently vote more heavily for one party than the other.

7. The two major parties have been of exceptional durability. They are, in fact, among some of the oldest political institutions existing anywhere. Recently, nonetheless, some observers have been raising doubts as to their continued survival.

8. The extent to which each party has been effective in winning loyalty and support has varied a great deal over time. Even during periods that leave the bare advantage with one of the parties, there are significant short-run fluctuations. In addition, from time to time major realignments take place when party loyalties are massively disrupted and large numbers of voters shift from one party to the other, thus shifting the longer-run balance of advantage to different coalitions of forces. Such a period of realignment began in the 1960s and may result in substantial though as yet unclear alterations in the traditional two-party system.

22 THE PERFORMANCE OF POLITICAL PARTIES: CONTRIBUTIONS TO POLYARCHY

In the light of long experience, not only in the United States but in all other polyarchies, there is no longer much ground for doubting that political parties make substantial contributions to the operation of a polyarchy—at any rate to a polyarchy in a large country. To most advocates of democracy who reflect on the problem, the positive contributions of parties far outweigh their negative aspects. But in many polyarchies, including the United States, the negative aspects stimulate a lively interest in the possibility of reforming the parties or the party system.

The principal contributions of parties, it might be suggested, are three:

☐ They facilitate popular control over elected officials.
☐ They help voters to make more rational choices.
☐ They help in the peaceful management of conflicts.

Yet each of these propositions must be qualified. To explore adequately the contributions and defects of parties, even American parties, would require a volume in itself. The articles, essays, and books that appraise political parties and advance or criticize proposals for reform would form a sizeable library.

A brief discussion can nonetheless open up some of the major questions.

PARTIES AND POPULAR CONTROL
One of the strongest claims made for political parties is that they assist the electorate in gaining some degree of control over elected officials and, thus, over the decisions of government.

Contributions

Bringing together individual preferences. For one thing, they carry on much of the organizing that makes a large-scale system of elections, representation, and legislation workable. The ambitions that induce party politicians to carry on these organizing tasks may repel democratic purists who would prefer motives closer to those invoked in the noble rhetoric with which men and women, good and bad, usually cloak their deepest purposes. Yet, whatever one may think of the motives of party politicians, they perform some functions that are essential if polyarchy is to remain effective: nominations, for example. In the absence of concerted effort, an election in which a candidate satisfactory to a majority *might* have emerged victorious may be won instead by a candidate who is satisfactory only to a minority. Surely it is no virtue if a majority of like-minded voters are presented with three satisfactory candidates to run against a fourth candidate they agree is worse; for if they distribute their votes over the three they like, the fourth may win even though he or she be the most objectionable. Once like-minded voters see that it is worthwhile to organize themselves around a single candidate they have already begun to form a party.

Organizing opposition. The organization furnished by party is particularly necessary if an opposition is to exist. The dominant forces have somewhat less need of party organization; a president might, for example, operate with a sort of nonparty coalition. This is no doubt why party machinery fell into decay when opposition temporarily became merely an exercise in futility during the long death agonies of the Federalists and before the reappearance of new divisions around which an opposition could form. When there was no opposition, there were no effective parties. One could also put it the other way round. When there is no party, there is not likely to be an effective opposition. To displace the incumbents, who have the resources of government at hand, an opposition needs to organize, focus its forces, keep up the pressure, draw in every possible ally—all of which spells party. It is, thus, no accident that in Europe it was usually the Labour or Socialist opposition parties that first developed modern party organization—during the lengthy period they dwelt in opposition before assuming office.

Preventing one-party dominance. Then, too, the sheer efficiency of party organization for winning political victories means that a single party, unchecked by another, would be a danger in a republic. One party needs to be counterbalanced by another. The citizens of a republic might well resolve: Let there either be no parties, or at least two parties, but never only one party. For if there is only one party, those among us who disagree with it will surely be outweighed, even though we be more numerous than our opponents. Since we cannot prevent at least one party from forming, lest by doing so we destroy our republican liberties, let there always be two parties or more. In this way we shall insure another kind of separation of powers and create additional checks and balances to sustain our liberties.

Pooling the resources of the many. A fourth way in which parties assist popular control is to enable the many to pool their resources to offset the advantages of the few. This is doubtless one reason why Federalists looked upon parties with less enthusiasm than did Democratic-Republicans. The chief resources of the many are their numbers and their votes; unorganized and leaderless they are no match for smaller numbers with wealth, skills, information, and informal organizational networks. Even when parties are internally oligarchic, as they generally are, a party competing for the votes of the otherwise unorganized many gives them more power than they would have if there were no parties at all.

Tendencies toward Internal Oligarchy

Despite these contributions, parties have been subjected to a barrage of criticism on the ground that they are internally undemocratic and are ruled by oligarchies.[1] The charge is in considerable measure true. That the nominations and policies of political parties tend to be controlled by leaders, rather than the rank and file of members or registered supporters, seems undeniable. There is, as we saw, more decentralization and diffusion of control in the two American parties than in many European parties; even so, both the Democratic and Republican parties would be more accurately described as coalitions of oligarchies than as democratic organizations.

Nominations: from caucus to convention. Given the democratic ideology prevailing among Americans, it was to be expected that efforts would be made to 'democratize' control over nominations in American parties; these efforts have diffused power, but they have not by any means turned the parties into 'democratic' systems. As we saw, presidential candidates were first nominated by the Federalist and Democratic-Republican caucuses in Congress. While the caucus continued to be used for several decades for presidential and vice-presidential nominations, an alternative system began to develop for nominating

---

1. Among the most famous and most influential criticisms of this kind were those of Moisei Ostrogorski, *Democracy and the Organization of Political Parties,* edited and abridged by S. M. Lipset, 2 vols. (Garden City, N.Y.: Anchor Books, 1964), first published in 1902; and Robert Michels, *Political Parties* (New York: Collier Books, 1962), first published in 1915. For an appraisal of Ostrogorski, see Austin Ranney, *The Doctrine of Responsible Party Government* (Urbana: University of Illinois Press, 1962). For a critique of Michels, see John D. May, "Democracy, Organization, Michels," *American Political Science Review,* 59 (June 1965), 417–429.

candidates to other offices, national, state, and local. This was the nominating *convention,* which, being a representative system, seemed more appropriate than the caucus to the spirit of democracy. The caucus fell into even worse repute because it sometimes dramatized for all to see the fact that nominations were made by narrow unrepresentative groups. One such episode, in 1824, killed the congressional caucus as a device for nominating presidential candidates.

The obvious solution called for by democratic principles was to have a party's presidential candidate chosen by a representative assembly, itself consisting of delegates elected by the party's followers. This was the origin of the presidential nominating convention. The first appearance of a presidential nominating convention took place in September, 1831, when the short-lived Anti-Masonic party nominated candidates for president and vice-president at a convention in Baltimore. Henry Clay's National Republicans (soon to become the Whigs) followed suit in December, also in Baltimore. Jackson's followers, the Democratic-Republicans, met in the same city in May, 1832, to nominate Jackson and Van Buren.[2] Ever since then, the national convention has been used for nominating presidential and vice-presidential candidates.

Although national nominating conventions are representative in form, probably no one who knows how they work would argue that they are very democratic. At most, the convention is a contest among coalitions of state and local party leaders. Because representative techniques seemed to have failed, advocates of democratic control over nominations turned to direct democracy: party members or supporters would themselves choose the candidate of their party. This was the direct primary.

Direct primary. Toward the end of the last century the convention began to be displaced by the direct primary, which is now almost universally employed for party nominations to executive offices other than the presidency and the vice-presidency. Yet even the direct primary has not democratized the parties—in part, of course, simply because most people do not participate in crucial day-to-day decisions or, for that matter, even in the primaries.[3]

Internal Control and Responsiveness to Voters

Although the conventional American view is that parties would perform better if they were internally democratic, the question is by no

---

2. These events are described in Ostrogorski, *Democracy and the Organization of Political Parties,* vol. 2, *The United States,* pp. 17–39.

3. In examining fifteen non-Southern states over the period 1932–1952, the late V. O. Key discovered that "in three out of four primaries . . . the total Democratic primary vote plus the total Republican primary vote did not exceed 35 percent of the number of citizens 21 years of age or over. . . . At the extreme of high participation in only one out of twelve primaries did more than 50 percent of the potential vote turn up at the polls." V. O. Key, Jr., *American State Politics: An Introduction* (New York: Knopf, 1956), p. 134.

means as simple as the standard view suggests. Our starting point must be the functions we want parties to perform, and to perform well. If one of these is to facilitate popular control over elected officials—as it surely is—then it does not follow that this result is to be obtained only, or even best, by internal party democracy.

An analogy may help to clarify the point. Political parties are sometimes likened to business firms competing for customers—the customers being in this case the voters. And just as business firms are driven by competition to satisfy consumers, even if they are *internally* not governed by consumers in the way that a consumers' cooperative is, so, it is sometimes argued, competitive parties will fulfill all of the essential functions of democratic control listed earlier, even though each party is internally controlled by its leaders. If the main function of competing parties is to insure that the views of voters are translated into government policies, then it is less important that parties be internally democratic than that they be responsive to the views of the voters.[4]

Would greater internal democracy insure that the parties would be more responsive to the voters? If we take presidential nominations as the most crucial test case, the answer is not as clear as one might hope. One difficulty is that no matter what the party rules provide in the way of opportunities to participate, the experience of nearly 150 years indicates that *in practice* nominations are made by a comparatively small number of political activists who are highly motivated and exceptionally active in the nominating process. These activists are, roughly speaking, of two kinds. One is the familiar party 'regular,' party leaders who over a considerable period of time occupy positions of influence in the party and regularly devote a large share of their time, energy, and resources to party activities. The others are the 'irregulars,' insurgents and amateurs who become active in behalf of a particular cause or candidate. Having been drawn into a campaign, some of the irregulars may later become regulars, but many drop out after the campaign is over, or bide their time until another attractive cause or candidate comes along.

The difficulty is that neither the regulars nor insurgents necessarily represent the opinions of voters—whether we mean voters in general or the hard core of the party's electorate who identify themselves with the party and usually support its presidential candidates. What happens when those who control a party (whether they are regulars or insurgents) fail to represent the views of the voters? The answer seems obvious: their candidate is probably defeated in the elections.

Both parties furnish recent evidence on this point. By the late

---

4. An interesting and important theoretical analysis on this subject is found in Anthony Downs, *An Economic Theory of Democracy* (New York: Harper & Brothers, 1957).

1950s the Republican leaders, big and small around the country, who exercised dominant influence over nominations and policy, no longer represented their Republican followers, nor—and this is even more important—did they represent the great bulk of the voters, Republicans or Democrats. In fact, Democratic leaders were actually *closer* in their views to rank-and-file Republicans than were the Republican leaders.[5] Not surprisingly, voters continued their steady shift in allegiance toward the Democratic party. Then, in 1964, the most ideologically conservative activists in the Republican party, a group of insurgents whose views probably represented only a minority among Republican voters and an even smaller minority in the electorate as a whole, seized control of the nominating convention from the Republican 'establishment,' nominated Senator Goldwater, and suffered one of the three or four worst defeats in the entire history of the party.[6]

The Goldwater insurgency in the Republican Party was duplicated in the Democratic party by the nomination of George McGovern in 1972. McGovern was an insurgent candidate who gathered around him an enthusiastic corps of activists, most of whom were irregulars without prior political experience. His candidacy was probably aided somewhat—though not decisively—by a change in party rules intended to make the Democratic convention more representative of hitherto underrepresented groups—specifically blacks, women, and youth. The McGovern forces won a majority of delegates elected in the primaries and then went on to victory in the Democratic convention. In the election, McGovern suffered the worst defeat of any Democratic candidate in fifty years.

The delegates to the Democratic convention, it turned out, were highly unrepresentative of Democratic supporters. And of all the groups at the convention, the insurgent McGovern delegates deviated most from the views of rank-and-file Democrats. The women delegates chosen under the new rules were not at all representative of rank-and-file Democratic women, nor the youth of rank-and-file young people. Even the black delegates were rather unrepresentative of attitudes among the black population at large, and among black Democratic supporters. Ironically, in 1972, the delegates to the Republican convention were

---

5. Herbert McClosky, Paul J. Hoffman, and Rosemary O'Hara, "Issue Conflict and Consensus among Party Leaders and Followers," *American Political Science Review,* 54 (June, 1960), 406–427, Table 1, p. 410, and *passim.*

6. For an analysis, see P. E. Converse, A. R. Clausen, and W. E. Miller, "Electoral Myth and Reality: The 1964 Election," *American Political Science Review,* 59 (June, 1965), 321–336. The percentages of the total popular vote received by the Republican presidential candidate in their four great defeats were: 1964, Senator Goldwater, 38.5; 1936, Alfred M. Landon, 36.5; 1912, William H. Taft, 23.2; and 1856, John C. Fremont, 33.1. In 1912 Theodore Roosevelt, the Progressive candidate, received 34.9 percent of the votes, many of them from Republicans; Woodrow Wilson, the Democratic candidate, received only 41.9 percent of the votes.

much closer to the views of rank-and-file Democrats in the country at large than were the delegates to the Democratic convention.[7]

The lesson seems fairly clear: When the policies of party leaders get too far out of line with those desired by the voters, support for the party will erode, and the party is likely to get beaten in elections.

In sum: The main contribution that parties make to popular control is to be found less in their internal operations than in their external effects—in competing for votes, organizing elections and legislatures, strengthening the opposition, providing offsetting checks to one another, and helping the many to overcome the otherwise superior resources of the few.

PARTIES AND RATIONALITY

Popular control, however, is of little value if voters are simply duped by party leaders or mindlessly vote for their parties without weighing the candidates and the issues. It might be argued that even if parties do help the electorate gain some degree of control over elected officials, the control of the voters is a sham because it is irrational. Do parties reduce the irrationality of politics—or do they actually increase it?

It would be absurd to attribute to political parties all the forms of irrational and nonrational behavior that have ever been commonplace in human affairs and that exist in political systems of all sorts. The relevant question is whether parties change the amount and kinds of 'irrational' behavior from what would exist in the absence of parties.

Unhappily, the question is all but unanswerable. 'Levels' or 'amounts' of irrationality are terms that can only be used figuratively. No one has been able to measure changes in 'the amount of rationality' in political systems. The most extreme cases of collective irrationality in modern times have occurred in dictatorships, where whole populations have fallen under the absolute domination of paranoid leaders like Stalin and Hitler. By comparison, stable polyarchies appear to be models of rational action. The question is, then, whether polyarchies would be more—or less—rational without competing parties.

One could theorize endlessly in response to this question without arriving at a conclusive answer. Let me therefore confine my conjecturing to two aspects that everyone would agree *do* characterize political parties: (1) Parties present to voters a very small number of alternatives out of the total number theoretically available. This effect is particularly strong in a two-party system with single-member districts; for at elec-

---

7. The observations in this and preceding paragraphs on the 1972 Democratic convention are based on Jeane Kirkpatrick, "Representation in American Political Conventions: The Case of 1972," *British Journal of Political Studies* (July, 1975), and Dennis G. Sullivan, Jeffrey L. Pressman, Benjamin I. Page, and John J. Lyons, *The Politics of Representation: The Democratic Convention 1972* (New York: St. Martin's Press, 1974).

tions the voter is usually confronted with only two rival candidates. (2) Each party develops a core of followers whose loyalty is fortified by nonrational factors like sentiment, pride, jealousy, combativeness, gamesmanship, and habit.

Reducing Alternatives

Consider the first point. A voter presented with two rival candidates, might prefer neither of them so much as a third possible candidate who failed to win a nomination by either party. Similarly, on some matter of policy a voter may like the policy proposed by both parties less than some other alternative neither party is willing to advance. Reasoning along these lines, one might conclude that multi-party systems would offer voters a more rational choice than two-party systems. Yet, if four parties are better than two, are eight parties better than four? And sixteen parties better than eight? Or, for that matter, why not a separate candidate for every point of view held by any citizen in the country? But suppose the voter were confronted with a choice among twenty parties and twenty candidates. Might he not then reason as follows: These are too many alternatives; I cannot possibly appraise them all. Anyway, what do I gain if the candidate I vote for wins? If there are twenty parties in the parliament, my representative and all the others will have to make many compromises by the time they reach the final decision. How do I know what compromises they will make? It would be much better if most of the compromises had been made already, so that I could then choose between two possible coalitions, knowing roughly the direction in which each would go if it won a majority of seats . . . .

Evidence does, in fact, suggest that the need to choose among a large number of parties is, for all except a small minority of voters, highly confusing and may lead, as in France, to discrediting the whole party system.[8]

Such reasoning might cause a voter to swing between two poles. At one pole, accepting the need for eliminating alternatives in order to arrive at a decision, the voter would enjoy the advantage of being confronted at elections by only two major alternatives. At the other pole, accepting the need to have one's favorite alternative presented in order to have full freedom of choice, the voter would enjoy the advantage of being confronted at elections by a wide array of alternatives. Carried to an extreme, the first would result in a plebiscite, like several under the French Fifth Republic, where the only choices were to vote 'yes' or 'no' to a simple proposition. In this case, the voter might feel badly cheated

8. Philip Converse and Georges Dupeux, "Politicization of the Electorate in France and the United States," in Campbell et al., *Elections and the Political Order*, ch. 14, especially pp. 277–278.

and powerless because the choices were too narrow. The second solution, carried to the other extreme, would result in an array of choices so great that no voter could possibly estimate the effect of his or her vote on the ultimate outcome of the election and the ensuing parliamentary bargaining. In this case, one might feel badly cheated and powerless because the choices were far too many.

The fact remains, then, that whenever a diversity of viewpoints and desired alternatives exists among the citizens of a polyarchy, the citizens must, sooner or later, by one process or another, reject all but one alternative (even if the final choice is, in effect, the null alternative of inaction). There is no escaping this process; it is the essence of 'rationality'; the only question is where and how it takes place. Much of the process of winnowing out alternatives could take place *before* an election, or *in* the election itself, or in negotiations *after* the election. All party systems do some winnowing *before* an election, making the election itself more decisive by reducing the alternatives, thus leaving less winnowing to be done *after* the election by bargaining and negotiation among members of different parties. The contrast is most marked between the British two-party system and a multiparty system like that of Italy. The American party system, like the multiparty systems of the Scandinavian countries or the Netherlands stands somewhere in between.

The notion, then, that parties increase irrationality in making choices by reducing the alternatives is based upon too simple a picture of the processes by which collective political decisions can be made. All such processes necessarily involve a drastic reduction in the alternatives. Although the question is obviously exceedingly complex, it seems much more reasonable to conclude that on the whole the parties play a beneficial role in this process.

Consequences of Party Loyalty

Consider now the second aspect of parties, the fact that they develop a core of followers loyal to the point of blind, nonrational support. The more the parties succeed in their efforts, it might be said, the more the weight of reason in politics is bound to decline. Parties may be the backbone of polyarchy, but all bone and no brain makes for a dull system. Does party loyalty impair the rationality of voters?

There are four markedly divergent answers.

Spontaneous combination. The first and oldest is the simple solution presented in one of the earliest systematic analyses of British and American parties, that by Moisei Ostrogorski in 1902.[9] It consisted of

---

9. Ostrogorski, *Democracy and the Organization of Political Parties.* For a discussion, see Ranney, *The Doctrine of Responsible Party Government,* p. 115.

discarding the use of *permanent* parties . . . and in restoring and reserving to party its essential character of a combination of citizens *formed specially for a particular political issue.* . . . [A] party holding its members, once they have joined it, in a viselike grasp would give place to combinations forming and reforming spontaneously, according to the changing problems of life and the play of opinions brought about thereby. Citizens who part company on one question would join forces in another.[10]

This solution, however, has not been adopted in any polyarchy. The advantages of permanent organizations are so great that Ostrogorski's spontaneous combinations would be too readily defeated—and are. Thus, in this country as in every other polyarchy his specific solution has been decisively rejected in favor of permanent parties. A second view, seemingly more in keeping with reality, became much more widely accepted.

The rational independent. This is the view that while the great bulk of the voters are party loyalists who act not so much in pursuit of rational aims as from nonrational loyalties, a considerable body of independents stands outside the two parties. It is the votes of these independents, the argument runs, that essentially determine elections. And independents, it is said, are relatively rational and reflective: it is they who give genuine consideration to the candidates and programs of the two parties and then make their choices. Consequently, so long as the number of these thoughtful independents is sufficiently large and the number of loyalists on each side is less than a majority, the independents determine the outcome. Hence party competition places the decisive voice in elections exactly where it belongs, with the more thoughtful, judicious, and reflective citizens committed to neither party. Unlike the first appraisal, this view is on the whole favorable to the role of parties: they are useful, at any rate, as long as they do not gain so many partisans that they no longer need to contest for the votes of the independents.

The irrational voter. Alas for this optimistic view, it was based almost exclusively on data available within easy reach of the armchair. Beginning with the presidential election of 1940, social scientists used the new techniques of opinion surveys in a series of studies that have revolutionized our knowledge about American voters. From these studies, based upon lengthy and carefully analyzed interviews with a scientifically selected sample of the electorate, a new picture emerged—based for the first time, it seemed, on hard fact. In this new group portrait, the face of the rational voter is all but invisible. Social scientists learned what was plausible enough all along: people who were most interested and most informed about politics were also likely to be the most parti-

---

10. Ostrogorski, *Democracy and the Organization of Political Parties*, vol. 2, p. 356.

san. The least partisan voters were likely to be uninterested and uninformed about issues, personalities, and other aspects of a campaign. Unfortunately for the older portrayal of the independent as the ideal voter, it now became clear that the less partisan or more 'independent' of party loyalties a voter was, the less likely he or she was to be interested in politics, to be informed about candidates and issues, or to go to the polls. The portrait of the voter painted by these studies was, then, rather gloomy. On the one hand, it appeared, most voters were party loyalists who voted less out of an intelligent concern for policy than from sheer loyalty, habit, and inertia. On the other hand, the reflective independent, once honored for his contribution, scarcely existed in real life. A voter who was not interested enough in politics to be partisan was unlikely to be interested enough to make an intelligent judgment on the election.

In the light of the evidence from these recent studies, campaigns and elections began to seem rather meaningless. The overwhelming number of interested voters, these surveys revealed, made up their minds even before a campaign started. In fact, the more interested voters were, the more likely they were to make up their minds even before the candidates were nominated! To be sure, some voters were open-minded. Those who had 'open' minds during the campaign and did not decide how they would vote until the polling days drew near were very likely to have minds so open, it seems, as to be downright vacant. An election, looked at in the bleakest light shed by the data, seemed to be little more than sound and fury, signifying nothing . . . a tale told by an idiot.

The sometimes rational voter. Combined with a measure of healthy skepticism common among social scientists, the hard facts of election studies helped to give wide credence to this perspective among those engaged in studying elections. Yet there is some reason for thinking that, as is often the case, a plausible view had been pushed too far. Later research has tended to show that on matters they feel are important to them, a substantial number of voters discriminate competently between parties and presidential candidates.[11] Voters are par-

---

11. Thus David E. Repass concluded from an analysis of the issues in the 1960 and 1964 elections, as the public saw them, that "by and large the voting public has at least a few substantive issues in mind at the time of an election, and the voters seem to be acting more responsibly than had previously been thought. . . . We have shown that the public is in large measure concerned about specific issues, and that these cognitions have considerable impact on electoral choice" ("Issue Salience and Party Choice," *American Political Science Review*, 65 [June 1971], 389–400). From the analysis of responses of a random sample of registered voters in Hawaii in the 1968 presidential campaign, Michael J. Shapiro concludes that "for our sample and with respect to our referent population of voters, voting choices are rational" ("Rational Political Man: A Synthesis of Economic and Social-Psychological Perspectives," *American Political Science Review*, 63 [December 1969], 1106–1119). Less direct but relevant evidence is also contained in William H. Riker and William James Zavoina, "Rational Behavior in Politics: Evidence from a Three Person Game," *American Political Science Review*, 64 (March 1970), 48–60.

ticularly sensitive to objective changes in economic conditions. Thus when elections are preceded by a period of economic decline, voters will give their support to congressional candidates of the party in opposition to the president. Since the president has, at least since the 1930s, taken major responsibility for developing programs to avoid deep recessions and inflation, this response by voters reflects a fairly sensible judgment. One study of presidential popularity from Harry Truman to Lyndon Johnson, as reflected in Gallup polls, found that "an economy in slump harms a president's popularity, but an economy which is improving does not seem to help his rating."[12]

PARTIES AND CONFLICT

What of the possible third contribution of American parties, the contribution they make to the peaceful management of political conflicts? Do they not actually intensify conflict—as many Americans believe—and, at times, endanger the prospect for a peaceful settlement of disputes?

The answer to these questions is somewhat obscure. As we shall see in the next part of this book, the extent to which party competition softens or inflames conflicts doubtless depends on the prevailing pattern of cleavages. Because patterns of cleavage and conflict form a large and complex topic that bears heavily on the operation of the American polyarchy, we turn our attention to these matters in the next part of this book.

SUMMARY

The possible contributions of political parties to polyarchy are generally thought to be three:

1. Political parties facilitate popular control over governmental leaders by:

☐ Combining individual preferences into one policy or position.
☐ Organizing oppositions.
☐ Preventing one-party dominance.
☐ Pooling the resources of the many to offset the advantages of the few.

Internally, however, political parties show strong tendencies toward oligarchic leadership. Attempts to democratize the process of nominations, at first by replacing the caucus with the convention and later by replacing or supplementing conventions with direct primaries, have not fully offset the tendency to internal oligarchy.

---

12. John E. Mueller, "Presidential Popularity from Truman to Johnson," *American Political Science Review*, 64 (March 1970), 18–34. On the effects of economic fluctuations on congressional elections, see Edward R. Tufte, "Determinants of the Outcomes of Midterm Congressional Elections," *American Political Science Review*, 69 (September, 1975), 812–826. Although one study shows that economic upturns also help the congressional candidates of the incumbent party (Gerald H. Kramer, "Short-term Fluctuations in U.S. Voting Behavior, 1896–1964," *The American Political Science Review*, 65 [March 1971], 131–143), a more recent study finds that while downturns lead to penalties, upturns do not produce gains. (Howard S. Bloom & H. Douglas Price, "Voter Response to Short-Run Economic Conditions: The Asymmetric Effect of Prosperity and Recession," *American Political Science Review*, 69 [December 1975]).

Nonetheless, the responsiveness of government in a polyarchy is affected more by the extent to which the parties are competitive with one another than by their internal organization.

2. Parties may facilitate more rational choices among voters. The extent to which parties enhance rationality is, however, confused by two different tendencies:

☐ On the one hand, by combining individual preferences, political parties help to reduce the number of alternatives confronting those who participate in decisions, including the voters. In reducing alternatives, the parties contribute to an essential requirement of rational action.

☐ On the other hand, parties become objects of irrational loyalties, affections, and hostilities that often appear to cloud the judgment of voters when they are confronted by alternative candidates or issues.

Because of the effects of seemingly blind partisan loyalties, the effect of parties on voter rationality is a subject of dispute.

☐ An early study contended that parties interfere with rational choice and should be replaced by "combinations forming and reforming spontaneously." However, no polyarchy operates with free-forming organizations rather than parties.

☐ For many years it was popular to hold that even if party loyalists behave irrationally, elections are ordinarily decided by relatively rational independent or nonpartisan voters. However, systematic surveys conducted over several decades showed that voters without partisan attachments were, on the whole, more poorly informed and more prone to irrational political judgments than were partisan voters.

☐ These findings led to a third view, common among social scientists who had immersed themselves in the depressing findings of surveys, that voting is not a very rational act. In this view, most voters are partisans who vote from loyalty, habit, and inertia; while the voter who lacks partisan loyalties is likely to be indifferent and poorly informed.

☐ More recently, however, evidence has been adduced to suggest that substantial numbers of voters are at least moderately rational in their voting decisions. It has been found that voters tend to support the congressional candidates of the incumbent president's party when the economy is rising, and turn to the candidates of the opposing party during periods of economic decline.

3. Political parties may help in the peaceful management of conflicts. However, the extent to which the parties diminish or aggravate conflicts very likely depends on the prevailing pattern of cleavages, which will be examined in the next section.

PART FOUR

CONFLICT AND CONCILIATION
IN THE AMERICAN POLYARCHY

23

CONFLICT
AND CONCILIATION

CHANGE: INCREMENTAL, COMPREHENSIVE, REVOLUTIONARY

One of the commonest characteristics of utopian writings is that nothing ever changes in these ideal political systems. Yet it is a central fact of life that no living system is ever static. What is true of living organisms is also true of systems consisting of live human beings—economic systems, social systems, political systems.

Since change is ongoing and universal, one can examine it from a thousand different perspectives and classify it in a thousand different ways. Let us focus our attention on *political* change and the *sources* or causes of political change.

Two Key Aspects of Political Change

Political change may be distinguished as to location and magnitude.

Location. As to location, change may take place in:

1. The operating *structure* of government, as when a polyarchy replaces an oligarchy, a dictatorship replaces a polyarchy, a presidential system replaces a parliamentary system, or direct election of senators replaces election by state legislatures.
2. The *policies* adopted and enforced by the government, as when Congress passed civil rights acts in 1964 and 1965, or Medicare in 1965.
3. The *relative influence* of different strata and groups on the policies and decisions of government, as after the election of 1800 when

small farmers and southern planters clearly gained greater influence while New England commercial interests lost.[1]

Magnitude. Political change may be small or great with respect to each of these locations or dimensions.[2] For the sake of simplicity, however, let me reduce change to three magnitudes.

1. Incremental, or marginal, when
   a. The operating *structure* is unaltered, except perhaps in matters of detail.
   b. Changes in *policies* are gradual rather than sweeping innovations or reversals of established policies. And,
   c. These changes result from negotiating and bargaining among spokesmen for groups whose *relative influence* remains more or less stable or subject only to gradual changes.
2. Comprehensive, when
   a. The operating *structure* is unaltered, except in matters of detail.
   b. Sweeping innovations or decisive reversals of established *policies* occur. And,
   c. These policy changes result from significant shifts in the *relative influence* of different groups.
3. Revolutionary, when comprehensive change in *policies* and *relative influence* (2b and 2c) is also combined with profound alterations in the operating *structure* of government. Broadly used in this way, the term applies only to the location and magnitude of change and implies nothing as to the means by which changes are brought about. In this broad usage, then, revolutionary change may be peaceful or violent.[3]

Political Change in the United States

As we saw in Chapter 1, most Americans seem to favor *incremental or piecemeal change.* In any case, incremental change is the normal pattern in American political life. Although it often seems depressingly slow and is rejected by revolutionaries as inadequate, a few examples will show how much can be achieved by means of a series of small but

---

1. A change may also take place in the social, ethnic, religious, psychological, or other significant characteristics of political leaders, as when blacks gained public office in the South during Reconstruction, and again following the Civil Rights Acts of 1964 and 1965. Because change in the characteristics of political leaders is often only a means of bringing about the other kinds of changes, in what follows I propose to ignore this kind of political change, important as it is, and concentrate on the others.

2. The reader who enjoys playing with classification—a somewhat barren enterprise to which social scientists are strongly addicted—may wish to construct the eight possible combinations of 'small' versus 'large' changes in structures, policies, and group influence.

3. A stricter usage emphasizes the attempt to bring about revolutionary changes by 'revolutionary' means; i.e., overthrowing the existing government by force. When we examine alternative strategies for bringing about changes in the conduct of the government in Chapter 29, the term will be used in this narrower sense.

steady changes. Anything that grows at the rate of 3 percent a year will double in size about every twenty-three years; at 5 percent a year it will double in fourteen years. The United States achieved its extraordinarily high gross national product by growing at a rate of about 3⅔ percent a year from the 1840s onwards. The population increased from 17 million in 1840 to more than 200 million in 1970 by growing at an average rate of about 2 percent a year. Gross national product per capita during this period grew at the rate of about 1⅔ percent a year, personal consumption at about 1¾ percent a year. The world population explosion that has caused so much concern in recent years is produced by annual increments of only 2 to 4 percent. The highest rate of growth in per capita gross national product in the 1950s in any industrial country, Communist or non-Communist, was less than 7 percent. The average annual increase in the population of cities over 20,000 in the United States from 1920 to 1950 was less than one-fifth of 1 percent. If output per man-hour in the United States increases by 5 percent annually, in fifty years each worker would produce eleven times as much as he does now.[4]

Incremental change, then, can be a powerful means for transforming a society—and has been so in the United States. However, *comprehensive changes* also occur at times; in fact, comprehensive changes are, as we shall see in later chapters, associated with some of the most dramatic events in American political history.

What of *revolutionary* political changes? The war between the American colonies and Britain is properly called a revolution, for it resulted in a profound change in the structure of government, in the relative influence of Americans and British officials, and in the policies pursued by the government. Making and adopting the Constitution might also be regarded as revolutionary in the sense employed here, even though that revolution, unlike the preceding one, was free of violence. For the Constitution clearly represented a decisive change in governmental structure; the policies of the new government, particularly Hamilton's economic policies, were sweeping innovations; and (the point is more debatable) the new government was associated, even if briefly, with a significant increase in the influence of men of commerce and finance. The Hartford Convention in 1814 and the South Carolina legislature in 1832 (discussed in Chapter 27) might be said to have *sought* revolutionary change, unsuccessfully. The Civil War was one

4. The data on which the calculations in the paragraph are based were drawn from the following sources: Bruce M. Russett, ed., *World Handbook of Political and Social Indicators* (New Haven: Yale University Press, 1964), Tables 1, 7, 10, 45; Hearings Before the Joint Economic Committee, Congress of the United States, April 7–10, 1959, Part 2, Table 1, p. 271; Abram Bergson and Simon Kuznets, *Economic Trends in the Soviet Union* (Cambridge, Mass., Harvard University Press, 1963), Tables 8.2, 8.3, and 8.4, pp. 337–340; *Congress and the Nation*, vol. 1, p. 1532; Louis J. Walinsky, "Keynes Isn't Enough," *The New Republic*, 154 (April 16, 1966), 14–16.

part revolution, one part the failure of a revolution. The secessionists failed to revolutionize the structure of government by seceding and establishing an independent confederacy. Yet if the North defeated the South's revolution, Lincoln and the Republicans represented a decisive shift of influence away from southern planters to free farmers, commerce, industry, and northern labor; and the legislation and constitutional amendments enacted during and after the Civil War constituted sweeping, indeed revolutionary, shifts in long-established policies. The challenge of the Confederacy was, however, the last large-scale appeal to a revolutionary change of regime that has been made in American politics; since that time, proposals for revolutionary change have been the exclusive monopoly of tiny political movements.

SOURCES OF POLITICAL CHANGE

Why do political changes come about? What generates the forces that lead to political changes?

To seek satisfactory answers to these questions would take us far beyond the confines of this book and into a domain where knowledge is rather speculative. Processes of change are obviously of critical importance to understanding the past, acting in the present, and shaping the future; they have been much studied, yet they are not at all well understood.

Changes in Technology

It is possible to distinguish some of the important factors that trigger political changes. One is technological change. A new technique, instrument, or machine is introduced. Because it outperforms the old, practical people acting from practical motives replace the old with the new. As the new technique spreads, it alters opportunities, advantages, handicaps, relations among individuals, groups, regions. There are changes in access to resources of power, changes in perspective, ideas, ideologies, changes in demands, changes in patterns of conflict and agreement. And so political change occurs.

The introduction of gunpowder into Europe ended the military superiority of the mounted knight in armor; it heralded the day of the musket and foot soldier. And so it helped to bring feudalism to an end. The mariner's compass vastly expanded the possibilities of navigation; it facilitated the discovery of the New World and the creation of overseas empires; it was to one of these that Englishmen fled and created a new social, economic, and political order. Eli Whitney's invention of the cotton gin, as every American schoolchild is taught, made cotton a highly profitable crop; the profitability of cotton stimulated the spread of slavery and the domination of the South by a planter class. Thus, in the endless, complex, and little-understood chain of causes of which Whitney's invention is an early link, there is also the Civil War, the Ku Klux Klan, the "separate but equal" doctrine, its overthrow by the Supreme Court decision of 1954, and the Civil Rights Acts of 1964 and 1965.

Changes in Social and Economic Institutions

Changes in social and economic institutions may also bring on political changes. And institutional changes may of course be triggered by technological changes; the relationships are extraordinarily complex. The modern, privately owned, limited-liability business corporation was an institutional change that swept away most other forms of business in the nineteenth century. The competitive price system and the free market were institutional innovations of the late eighteenth and early nineteenth centuries. They responded to, but they also generated, technological changes; they created a new business class, a new middle class, a new urban working class, and a new set of problems, conflicts, and political changes that have not come to an end. In England, the same dense network of causes, one historian has argued, connects an innovation in 1795 by well-meaning justices of the peace trying to cope with rural unemployment and poverty to the triumph of the ideas of Adam Smith, the scrapping of all governmental controls over the price of labor, land, goods, and capital, and thence, in reaction and self-defense, to English socialism and the welfare state.[5] Why did the United States become a land of small free farmers in the nineteenth century, while Brazil did not? Both had a great supply of land. But the Englishmen who settled America did not bring feudal institutions here, whereas the Portuguese and Spanish in Latin America did.

Changes in Ideas and Beliefs

Ideas and beliefs, too, bring about political change. Simple mechanistic interpretations of history treat ideas in the minds of men as mere reflections of technology and institutions. Ideas are not, certainly, completely independent; but neither are technology and institutions. The relationships are too complex to try to sort out here. Yet ideas, beliefs, perspectives, and ideologies do change, and it is obvious that these changes often precipitate political changes. As Tocqueville pointed out in his introduction to *Democracy in America*, equality had been spreading throughout Europe long before the Americans founded their republic. Equality was spreading—inevitably, so it seemed to him—as an idea and as a fact. If a growing equality in the actual conditions of life helps to sustain the idea of equality, may not the idea of equality help to sustain the fact of equality? Or, to take a more specific example, arguments over the virtues and vices of balanced budgets—an issue over which a

---

5. Karl Polanyi, *The Great Transformation* (New York: Rinehart & Co., 1944).

number of Americans have displayed considerable passion—are above all a question of ideas and beliefs. Differences in ideas about these matters have consistently led to conflict between academic economists and conservative bankers.

Interaction of Change

Ideas, institutions, and techniques are intertwined in ways too complex to unravel. During Andrew Jackson's great conflicts over the Bank of the United States, why did none of the protagonists give serious consideration to a solution that would probably be one of the first to occur to a presidential adviser or a member of Congress today: a government regulatory commission to keep the Bank in check? In large part, it seems, because the regulatory commission as an institution had really not yet been invented and its possibilities were not yet understood. The perceptions, ideas, and ideology, if you will, that have developed with the growth of the regulatory state of the twentieth century were for all practical purposes not present in 1830. Jackson did not reject the idea of a regulatory commission in the sense that a critic of regulation might reject it today; nor could he have adopted the idea of a regulatory commission. For he simply did not perceive the idea as we do today, nor did anyone else in his time.

Thus perspectives change, social and economic institutions change, technology changes. And these changes trigger political changes. But government and politics are not necessarily mere by-products of changes. Government policy may trigger changes in ideas, in social and economic institutions, in technology. The policies and practices of the New Deal surely helped to change the perspectives of Americans about the proper role of government. It was government action that created a new institution in the Tennessee Valley Authority. It was government action that produced the institutions of modern Social Security (action in this country was long antedated by the innovation in Europe). And it was government action that led directly to the most awesome technological innovation in history, the unleashing of nuclear power.

THE DEPTH OF CHANGE AND CONFLICT

When one reads about some great revolution, one is inclined to suppose that sooner or later everyone in the society was, surely, drawn into the orbit of the revolution. Yet it might be far more realistic to assume—as some theorists have—that rapid historical changes and political conflicts of all kinds, even great revolutions, directly involve only the tiniest and most visible minorities, the activists and the political, social, economic, cultural, and religious elites. Probably the truth lies somewhere between these extreme views. Unfortunately it is impossible to specify precisely where the truth does lie, for our knowledge is severely limited. The unhappy fact is that until the late 1930's, when systematic opinion surveys first began to be used, no means existed for measuring the spread of views and opinions in a population. Hence, historical generalizations about the way opinions were distributed among Americans (or any other population) before about 1936 must be treated with great caution.

What is striking from modern evidence, however, is how many Americans there are to whom political life is totally foreign. About one fifth of American adults are for all practical purposes apolitical. Politics is so remote from their lives as to lack much meaning: they rarely vote or otherwise participate in politics, and their views on political matters are uninformed and shallow. These people constitute what might be called the apolitical levels. They seem to constitute a significant proportion of every citizen body in all historical periods. And there is not much doubt that in the United States the apolitical strata have always constituted a sizeable group.

It is highly reasonable to suppose, then, that during all periods of American history the 'burning issues of the day,' the 'great debates,' the 'fierce conflicts' of politics have scarcely engaged the attention of the apolitical strata at all; perhaps a fifth to a half of the adults have always been so wholly involved in the events of their daily lives—worries over jobs, income, health, family, and friends—that they have barely followed what later generations regard as great historical events. Ordinary voters who do at least bother to vote are no doubt more engaged. But it is the minority of politically active citizens who are highly active politically—and most of all the tiny minority of leaders—who have always been most fully engaged in political conflicts. No matter how important historians might regard it today, to most Americans in 1854, the passage of the Kansas-Nebraska Act was doubtless very much less interesting and important than the marriage of a daughter, a son moving west, a death in the family, the baby's croup, the bad harvest, the local scandal.

But of course when the leaders and the politically active citizens fail to resolve their differences, as they did in 1860, the cost in lives is levied on the whole people.

CONFLICT:
MODERATE
AND SEVERE
Just as communities arise because of people's need for human fellowship and the advantages of cooperation, so also, as we saw in Chapter 1, human beings are unable to live together without conflict. Hence, communities search for ways of adjusting conflicts so that cooperation and community life will be possible and tolerable. In its institutions and practices, polyarchy provides one such way of dealing with conflict. As

we saw in Chapter 2, it is a solution that has been strongly shaped by attempts to satisfy the democratic criteria of political equality and consent.

A crucially important aspect of polyarchy, then, is that political conflict is singularly visible. It is not driven underground. It is protected, institutionalized, even cherished.

In this respect, political life in a polyarchy is far different from the drab political scene usually described in utopian writings. Utopias are invariably unflawed by conflicts. Most of them are pervaded by the deathly stillness of the graveyard. So, too, in modern dictatorships the official ideology often proclaims that the regime has achieved a utopian social harmony demonstrated by the absence of political conflict. Modern authoritarian regimes thus deny legitimacy and legality to internal conflicts. The leaders of such regimes use the vast coercive resources of their political, social, and economic system to drive social conflicts underground—and often, quite literally, their opponents as well.

To be a confident citizen of a polyarchy thus requires a certain toughness and robust assurance in the face of public conflict that subjects of a dictatorial regime need not possess. Now it is true that conflict can be dangerous to a political system. And citizens take a certain gamble when they opt for a polyarchy. For the citizens of a polyarchy may react to severe political conflict in ways that endanger or destroy the survival of their political system: by violence, by suppressing one's opponents, civil war, secession, disloyalty, even by widespread demoralization, apathy, and indifference.

Yet to say that severe political conflict is undesirable is not to say that all political conflict is undesirable. So long as people have different views and the liberty to express their views, conflicts will exist. To condemn all political conflict as evil is to condemn diversity and liberty as evils. If you believe that some diversity is inevitable, and that liberty is desirable, then you must hold, logically, that political conflict is not only inevitable but desirable.

This is therefore the dilemma: In a polyarchy moderate political conflict is both inevitable and desirable. Yet severe political conflict is undesirable, for it endangers *any* political system. A polyarchy can escape from this dilemma only if conflict is somehow kept within bounds. But how is this possible? How can conflict, like atomic energy, be tamed and put to peaceful purposes?

Indicators of Severe Conflict

It is not easy to say precisely what one means by the severity or intensity of a conflict, but the essential standard appears to be this: Within a particular political system the more the people on each side see the other side as enemies to be destroyed by whatever measures may be necessary, the more severe the conflict. Evidence that a conflict is increasing in severity would therefore be an increasing harshness of language, in which one's opponents were portrayed as implacable enemies to be annihilated; an increasing stress on or actual employment of violence against opponents; or an increasing use of means to victory that previously were regarded as impermissible, illegitimate, perhaps even illegal or unconstitutional.

Factors Affecting the Severity of Conflict

What circumstances, then, are likely to lend moderation to a dispute or, conversely, to inflame it into a conflict of great severity?

The stakes. To begin with the most obvious point, how severe a conflict is depends on how much is at stake. The more at stake, the harder a question is to settle.

Mutual benefits or zero-sum game. But how severe a conflict is also depends on whether the people engaged in the dispute can discover mutually beneficial solutions. The ideal outcome, naturally, would be one in which all the contestants were not only better off than before but better off than under any alternative solution. To be sure, if solutions of this kind were common, conflict would rarely occur. Nonetheless, there is a clear difference between two types of disputes. In one type, no contestants can come out ahead except by making others worse off ("If you win, I lose," or what mathematicians call a "zero-sum game"). In another kind of dispute there is a solution with mutual benefits under which no one will be worse off than before, and some may even be better off. If two people are faced with a deal in which every dollar gained by A will make B worse off than he or she is now, neither of them has much incentive to negotiate. If the best solution for both is identical—if each stands to gain most by one solution—then negotiation is hardly necessary. If, on the other hand, A's best solution is different from B's, but there appear to be compromise solutions under which one or both might be better off than they are now and neither would be worse off, both have every reason to negotiate in order to arrive at a mutually acceptable decision.

The worst possible conflict, then, is one involving very high stakes and no solutions other than the mutually incompatible kind, "If you win, I lose." Consequently, conflicts involving two mutually incompatible ways of life among different citizens are bound to place an exceedingly serious strain on a polyarchy. Here the term *way of life* means the rights, privileges, and human relationships a group most highly prizes

Figure 23.1
Agreement Piles up
Heavily on One Side:
The J Curve

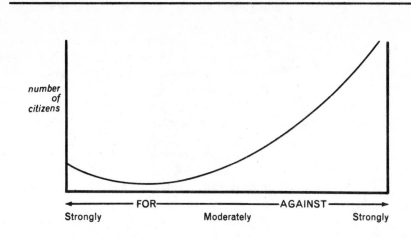

number
of
citizens

◄——————FOR——————————————AGAINST——————►
Strongly   Moderately   Strongly

—their families and friends, economic position, social standing, respect, religious beliefs, and political powers. Any group that sees its
way of life at stake in a dispute will, obviously, be reluctant to compromise. If the whole society is divided and if no compromise is possible
—if the conflict is over two completely incompatible ways of life—then
any political system is likely to break down. There are no cases, I think,
in which a polyarchy has managed to settle conflicts of this kind peacefully.

So far we have been concerned with the characteristics of the
conflict itself. But the severity of a conflict also depends on the people
who are engaged in it, particularly their numbers and their location in
the political system.

Numbers. In a polyarchy, elections mean that sheer numbers are often
important. Hence how severe a conflict is depends in part on how many
citizens hold similar views, or views that differ only slightly, and how
many hold extreme views. The greater the relative number of citizens
who hold extreme (and opposing) views, the greater the danger that a
conflict will be disruptive. Conversely, the greater the proportion of
citizens who hold views that differ only slightly—that is, moderate views
—the less the danger. In a stable polyarchy, the great bulk of citizens
will, presumably, more or less agree on many questions. In some cases,
the agreement would pile up so heavily on one side of an issue that the
matter would cease to produce much controversy. A graph of such a
distribution would assume the shape that statisticians, for obvious rea-

Figure 23.2
Disagreement Is Moderate:
The Bell-Shaped Curve

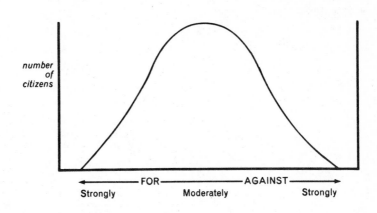

sons, call a J curve[6] (Figure 23.1). A vast number of questions that might be of abstract interest to philosophers, moralists, theologians, or others who specialize in posing difficult and troublesome questions are, in any stable political system, irrelevant to politics because practically everyone is agreed and no one can stir up much of a controversy. If a controversy does arise because of the persistence of a tiny dissenting minority, in a polyarchy the chances are overwhelming that it will soon be settled in a way that corresponds with the view of the preponderant majority.

Sometimes people may disagree and yet hold moderate opinions. A distribution of this kind, which is called a bell-shaped curve, is illustrated in Figure 23.2. When a conflict of views takes this shape, the chances are that it will be solved rather easily. Polyarchies with two major parties manage conflicts of this kind with special ease, because both parties tend to converge toward the center. Since an overwhelming number of voters are clustered at the center, and only a few at the extremes, the two major parties not only *may* ignore the extremes with impunity, they *must* do so if they want to win elections. The cost of

6. For theory and data bearing on the discussion in this section, see particularly Key, *Public Opinion and American Democracy* (New York: Knopf, 1961), ch. 2; and Dahl, *Political Oppositions in Western Democracies* (New Haven, Conn.: Yale University Press, 1966). Discussions of relationships between the behavior of political parties and various distributions of political opinions may be found in Downs, *An Economic Interpretation of Democracy* (New York: Harper, 1957) and Gerald Garvey "The Theory of Party Equilibrium," *American Political Science Review,* 60 (March 1966), 29–38. A useful critique of some of the assumptions involved will be found in Donald E. Stokes "Spatial Models of Party Competition," in Campbell et al., *Elections and the Political Order* (New York: Wiley, 1966), ch. 9.

Figure 23.3
Disagreement Is Severe
and Extreme: The U Curve

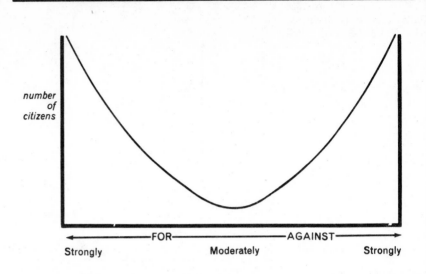

making an appeal to voters with extreme attitudes is to lose the much more numerous support of the moderates near the center.

In cases of the first two kinds, where opinion is strongly one-sided or overwhelmingly moderate, the conflict is not likely to be severe. If the extremes predominate, however, conflicts of great severity are likely (Figure 23.3). Whenever extreme opinions grow at the expense of moderate opinions or one-sided agreement, obviously conflict becomes much more dangerous, for it is much harder to find a basis for mutually profitable compromises. Moreover, in these circumstances the political parties find it profitable to adapt their appeals to the views of citizens at the extremes. While extreme parties flourish, center parties grow weak. Sooner or later, one of the extreme parties or coalitions is likely to begin considering ways by which it may suppress or destroy the other, and violence is on the way.

Location. The severity of conflict depends, however, not only on the sheer numbers of people who hold divergent views, but also on their positions in the political system. *Officials and other political leaders* may be more moderate or more extreme in their views than ordinary citizens. Thus leaders may exaggerate or minimize the deep differences of opinion among the general population. The more they minimize cleavages, the less severe the political conflict; the more they emphasize and exaggerate differences of opinion, the more severe the conflict

Figure 23.4
Moderation Among
Leaders, Extremism Among
Ordinary Citizens

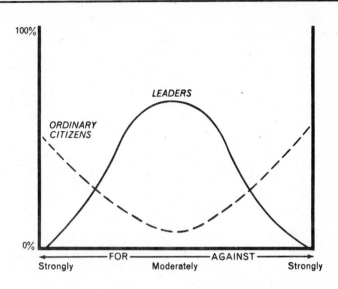

is likely to be. In Figure 23.4, leadership opinion is moderate, while rank-and-file opinion is sharply divided. In Figure 23.5, the situation is reversed; ordinary citizens are not as badly split as leaders. We would expect a situation like that suggested by the latter figure to produce more severe political conflict and greater danger to a republic than the situation represented by Figure 23.4.

In a polyarchy, what could produce differences between the attitudes of ordinary citizens and the attitudes of political leaders? If political leaders were chosen at random from the general population, then significant differences would be most unlikely. But the selection of political leaders is, as we know, very far from a random process. Even in a polyarchy, some kinds of people are more likely to gain public office and power than others.

Citizens who are the most interested and active in politics are more likely to rise to the top than citizens who find politics uninteresting or otherwise unattractive. People who are interested and active in politics often differ in important respects from people who are less interested, less active, less effective—in short less influential. In the United States, for example, citizens who are most interested and active in politics and most confident that they can be effective tend also to have more education, higher incomes, and jobs of higher status. If the more active, interested, and influential strata of citizens tend to differ from the rest of the population in education, income, and occupations, is it not likely that

Figure 23.5
Extremism Among Leaders
Moderation Among
Ordinary Citizens

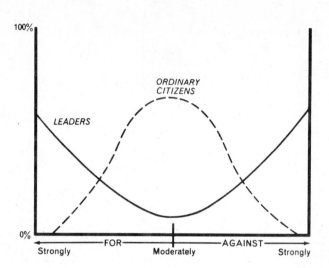

they will also differ in political views? Hence, instead of mirroring the political views of the rest of the population, leaders might be either more moderate or more antagonistic, and this may increase or decrease the severity of the conflict.

The way in which attitudes are distributed *geographically* is also relevant, particularly in countries where legislators are not chosen under some system of proportional representation. If a country is divided into election districts or states in which the office goes to the candidate with the most votes, and all other candidates with fewer votes are defeated, the intensity of a political conflict may depend on where different views are located in the country. An opposition minority that is concentrated in a particular region will find it easier to gain representation in the legislature than one that is dispersed more or less evenly throughout the nation. Moreover, even without extra representation because of the election system, a regional minority is in a relatively strong position to keep its views alive, to command conformity to its views within the region, to punish dissenters, and to portray their opponents as outsiders, aliens, foreigners.

Patterns of cleavage. The special effects of regionalism on conflict call attention to a broader observation—namely, that the severity of a conflict depends on the way in which one conflict is related to another. A society offers a number of different lines along which cleavages in a conflict can take place; differences in geography, ethnic identification, religion, and economic position, for example, all present potential lines of cleavage in conflicts. If all the cleavages occur along the same lines, if the same people hold opposing positions in one dispute after another, then the severity of conflicts is likely to increase. The man on the other side is not just an opponent; he soon becomes an enemy. But if (as Madison foresaw) the cleavages occur along different lines, if the same persons are sometimes opponents and sometimes allies, then conflicts are likely to be less severe. If you know that some of your present opponents were allies in the past and may be needed as allies again in the future, you have some reason to search for a solution to the dispute at hand that will satisfy both sides. The people on the other side may be your opponents today; but they are not your enemies, and tomorrow they may be your allies.

A few purely hypothetical illustrations will help to clarify the significance of the different patterns of cleavage that will be discussed in the next three chapters. Imagine that American opinion is divided over two issues, abortion and a comprehensive national health program. Assume, too, that Americans are divided pretty sharply by social and economic status into an upper and a lower class. Suppose that all the members of the upper class are in favor of abortion and against a national health program, while all the members of the lower class are against abortion and in favor of national health. This would represent a concentration around two opposites, or complete polarization (Panel [a] in Figure 23.6).

In this situation, one would expect to find two antagonistic camps, each supporting one of two major political parties. These two parties would be completely divided from one another both along class lines and in policies—probably, too, in general ideological outlook. The situation would look rather like that depicted earlier in Figure 23.3. In Chapter 27 we shall see how something roughly like this came about in the United States in the 1850s. We know what the outcome of that polarization was: civil war.

Now instead of this grim picture of impending civil war, let us imagine that half of each social class are in favor of abortion and half are opposed. Suppose further that of those who are in favor of abortion, half are in favor of national health care and half are opposed; those who oppose abortion are divided over national health care in the same way. Instead of polarizing Americans into two mutually exclusive camps, the crosscutting effect of these cleavages would be to fragment people into eight groups: four upper-class groups and four lower-class groups (Panel [b] in Figure 23.6).

Figure 23.6
Three Hypothetical
Examples of Possible
Patterns of Cleavage
on Two Issues

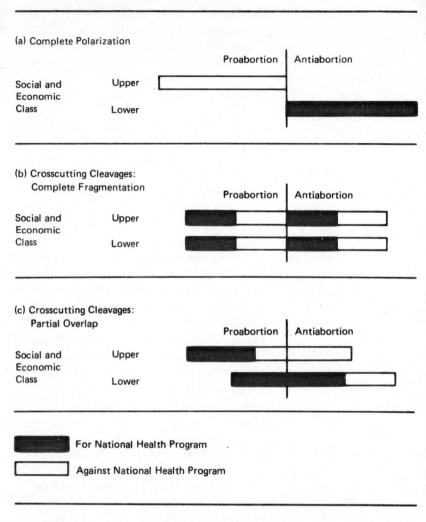

(a) Complete Polarization

Proabortion | Antiabortion

Social and Economic Class — Upper

Lower

(b) Crosscutting Cleavages:
Complete Fragmentation

Proabortion | Antiabortion

Social and Economic Class — Upper

Lower

(c) Crosscutting Cleavages:
Partial Overlap

Proabortion | Antiabortion

Social and Economic Class — Upper

Lower

For National Health Program

Against National Health Program

In this situation, it would be difficult to contain the conflict within only two parties, and if these differences were accompanied by strong feelings of antagonism, the two parties would certainly fragment further. For example, if Democrats adopted a platform against abortion and in favor of national health care, they would repel that half of the upper and lower classes who favor abortion. They would also lose an additional quarter in each class opposed to a national health program. Thus four parties would be likely to appear. If class antagonisms were also strong, eight parties might appear! For example, one internally consistent party might draw support exclusively from members of the upper class who are in favor of both abortion and national health care. Another party might draw support exclusively from upper-class citizens who are in favor of abortion and against national health care. And so on.

A third possibility is that the opinion splits would cut across one another in such a way as to make two parties possible without polarization (Panel (c) in Figure 23.6). For example, if less significance were attached to the abortion issue than to medical care, Democratic party leaders might find it possible to play down the issue of abortion and build a coalition in favor of a national medical care program. They could draw from both classes, though they would gain more from the lower class than the upper. Republican leaders, finding the abortion issue equally divisive, might also succeed in playing it down, and they might then put together a coalition against a national medical program. Their support would also come from both classes, but more heavily from among the upper classes.

As we shall see in the next chapter, conflicts in American politics much of the time look something like this third pattern of overlapping or crosscutting cleavages.

Political institutions. There is still one more factor to consider. Political institutions themselves may aggravate conflicts, or make it easier to settle them. It is striking how the British parliament in the late seventeenth and during the eighteenth century became an institution for settling disputes that up until then—and in most other countries afterward—threatened the regime itself. This development within Parliament does not wholly explain, of course, why Britain has not had a civil war since the seventeenth century; a fuller answer would require, among other things, an explanation of the path of parliamentary development itself. Nonetheless, the presence in Britain since the end of the seventeenth century of an institution that elaborated a set of conventions, devices, practices, and mechanisms for settling disputes has surely helped Britain to make changes and to negotiate internal conflicts peacefully for the past three hundred years.

It would take no great imagination to conceive of political institutions that would have the opposite effect, that would intensify rather than reduce conflict. Suppose, for example, that the American Constitution automatically awarded the presidency and a majority on the Supreme Court to the party with the most numerous votes in an election, and awarded Congress to the party with the next largest number of votes. Conflict would then be built squarely into the constitutional system. (Because, as we have seen, the Framers deliberately sought to build conflict into the constitutional structure, the effects of their design on political conflicts in the United States will be discussed later.)

Although the extent to which political institutions intensify or soften conflicts is a highly complex matter, one might hope to distinguish political mechanisms according to three characteristics: whether they (1) facilitate gaining *consent* through negotiation, (2) facilitate making *decisions* with or without much consent, or (3) facilitate both *consent and decisions.*

A system that required extensive consent but made it difficult to reach a decision—for example, a system in which all decisions had to be made by unanimous vote—would so greatly prolong negotiations and impede decisions that the prospect of mounting a revolution in order to get something done might become increasingly attractive. On the other hand, in a system where it was easy for leaders to make decisions without seeking the consent of others, minor questions could be settled with dispatch. But when ordinary citizens seriously disagreed with one another or with their leaders in such a system, decisions could be imposed without their consent; to secure obedience many citizens would have to be coerced by the government. By embittering and alienating the citizens who were coerced, such a system might ripen disputes into resistance and revolution. Thus a system that could somehow facilitate both negotiation of consent and arriving at decisions might serve best to keep conflicts from becoming so severe as to generate a revolution.

CONFLICT: A SUMMARY Let me now draw together the threads of this discussion of conflict in a summary that will be helpful in understanding the next three chapters.

The intensity or severity of a political conflict in a polyarchy is indicated by the extent to which people on each side see the other as an enemy to be destroyed; political disagreements become severe when there is an increase in the threat or actual use of violence, suppression of opponents, civil war, secession, disloyalty, or a marked increase in demoralization, apathy, indifference, or alienation.

The intensity or severity of a political conflict depends on at least four sets of factors:

1. How much is at stake.
   a. The more at stake, the more severe a conflict is likely to be.
   b. A 'zero-sum' conflict in which compromise is difficult or impossible because no contestant can possibly be made better off except by making other contestants worse off is likely to be more severe than a conflict in which there is a possibility of mutual benefits—a compromise in which no contestant need be worse off than before, and some may be better off.

	Conflict is more likely to be	
Table 23.1	Moderate if:	Severe if:
Factors that Moderate or Intensify Political Conflicts		

	Moderate if:	Severe if:
1. Political views and attitudes are	convergent	divergent
2. The stakes involved are	low	high
a. Compromise	will yield mutual benefits	is difficult or impossible
b. Ways of life are	not endangered	endangered
3. Lines of cleavage are	crosscutting	cumulative
4. Political institutions provide		
a. Negotiations for consent but no provision for arriving at decisions	no	yes
b. Decisions without consent	no	yes
c. Agreed processes for negotiating consent and arriving at decisions	yes	no

   c. Conflicts involving incompatible 'ways of life' are bound to be particularly severe.

2. The way in which politically relevant attitudes are distributed among citizens and leaders.
   a. The greater the number of citizens who hold extreme (and opposing) views, the more severe a conflict is likely to be. Conversely, the greater the number who hold moderate views, the less severe a conflict is likely to be.
   b. The more extreme the views of political leaders and activists in comparison with the views of ordinary citizens, the more severe the conflict; conversely, the more moderate the views of leaders and activists in comparison with other citizens, the less severe the conflict is likely to be.

3. The patterns of cleavage. The more conflicts accumulate along the same lines of cleavage, the more severe they are likely to be; conversely, the more conflicts intersect along different lines of cleavage, the less severe they are.

4. The political institutions.
   a. Political institutions and processes are likely to intensify conflicts if they require the groups involved to negotiate but do not provide any acceptable way by which leaders can terminate negotiations and arrive at a decision.
   b. Political institutions and processes are likely to intensify conflicts if they make it possible for leaders to make decisions without engaging in negotiations to obtain the consent of the persons, groups, or parties involved.

c. Political institutions and processes are most likely to reduce the intensity of conflicts if they embody widespread agreement on procedures, *both* for negotiating in order to gain consent and for terminating the negotiations and arriving at a decision.

These propositions are summarized in Table 23.1.

24 CROSSCUTTING CLEAVAGES AND LOW POLARIZATION

Although Americans tend to agree on a great many questions, there are some over which they have disagreed through the whole course of American history. Certain types of issues have recurred as subjects of conflict: the nature and extent of democratic processes, foreign policy, the role of the government in the regulation and control of the economy, the place of black Americans in the society.

Yet these issues do not ordinarily polarize Americans into two exclusive and antagonistic camps. Nor do they fragment Americans into a multiplicity of hostile groups incapable of cooperation. Indeed, the pattern of disagreements in political attitudes and loyalties may itself actually inhibit polarization or fragmentation, while it encourages conciliation. In particular, two characteristics of the pattern of cleavages stimulate efforts toward conciliation and compromise and weaken pressures toward polarization and fragmentation.

First, differences in political attitudes, actions, and loyalties are not highly related to differences in region, social standing, occupation, and other socioeconomic characteristics. Of course there often is *some* relation; but it is usually rather weak. People in the same region, in the same status group, or in the same occupation do not tend to form distinct unified political blocs. Consequently, *polarization of politics along social, economic, or regional lines is held in check.*

Second, differences in political attitudes and loyalties are not highly interrelated among themselves. Two people who hold the same attitudes on one question frequently hold different attitudes on other questions. To overstate the point, every ally is sometimes an enemy and every enemy is sometimes an ally. Consequently, *polarization of politics along ideological lines is held in check.*

REGIONAL DIFFERENCES

Consider geography: American politics has often been described as a conflict between different sections or regions. And it is true, of course, that with respect to the place of the Afro-American in American life the split between North and South has been persistent and sometimes bitter. As we shall see in the next chapter, from 1850 to about 1877 the bundle of issues associated with slavery polarized American politics to an unprecedented degree.

With this single exception, however, regional conflicts have never polarized Americans into distinct camps. Like the other major sources of conflict in American politics, the importance of regional factors varies greatly from one issue to another; although powerful on any issue touching the role of blacks in American life, regional differences are only moderately important on other issues and even negligible on a great many questions. Moreover, regionalism in politics is probably declining. Finally, regional conflicts follow a pattern of crosscutting cleavages, not polarization.

In Congress

Evidence for these propositions is readily available from the arena where regional conflicts might be expected to show up most clearly, the halls of Congress.

Southern Democrats have displayed more unity in the way they vote in Congress than any other regional group. Yet even Southern regionalism is quite limited. The distinctive voting pattern of Southern Democrats tended to be confined to a few issues, mainly those involving blacks.[1] From 1937 onward, it is true, a majority of Southern Democrats allied themselves on a number of occasions with a majority of Northern Republicans in voting against a majority of Northern Democrats. This conservative coalition was particularly noticeable during John F. Kennedy's presidency when it defeated a number of his legislative proposals. Yet even during this period, the coalition appeared on only 28 percent of the votes in the House and Senate in 1961, 14 percent in 1962, and 17 percent in 1963.[2] But aside from Southern Democrats, it is difficult to find any persistent regional patterns in congressional voting.

---

1. See Raymond E. Wolfinger and Joan Heifetz, "Safe Seats, Seniority, and Power in Congress," *American Political Science Review,* 59 (June 1965), 337–349; H. Douglas Price, "Are Southern Democrats Different?" in *Politics and Social Life: An Introduction to Political Behavior,* Nelson W. Polsby, R. A. Dentler, and Paul A. Smith (Boston: Houghton Mifflin, 1963), pp. 740–756; Julius Turner, *Party and Constituency: Pressure on Congress* (Baltimore: Johns Hopkins Press, 1951), p. 130 fn. See also the conclusion of V. O. Key, Jr., on examining Senate roll calls for seven Senate sessions from 1933 through 1945: ". . . it is primarily on the race issue that the South presents a united front against the rest of the United States" (*Politics, Parties, and Pressure Groups,* 3rd. ed. [New York: Thomas Y. Crowell, 1952], p. 265); and also V. O. Key, Jr., *Southern Politics* (New York: Knopf, 1949), chs. 16 and 17.

2. *Congressional Quarterly Weekly Report* (April 17, 1964), p. 737.

Table 24.1
Attitudes Toward Busing
of School Children

	National	Region			
		East	Midwest	South	West
Favor	35%	36%	30%	37%	35%
Oppose	65	64	70	63	65
	100%	100%	100%	100%	100%

Source: *Gallup Opinion Index*, Report No. 113, November, 1974. The choice was: "I favor (oppose) busing school children to achieve better racial balance in schools." The question posed an either/or choice, therefore a category for "no opinion" is not listed in the table.

Table 24.2
Attitudes Toward
Speeding up Integration

	National	Region			
		East	Midwest	South	West
Should	38%	45%	35%	29%	43%
Should not	62	55	65	71	57
	100%	100%	100%	100%	100%

Source: *Gallup Opinion Index*, Report No. 65, November, 1970. The choice was: "Racial integration *should/should not* be speeded up."

In the Population at Large

In the population at large, it is difficult nowadays to discover distinctive regional clusters of attitudes. Attitudes change, of course, and regional differences in attitudes are probably in decline. The South, long the most easily distinguishable region in the country, has in recent decades lost a good deal of distinctiveness in attitudes toward public policies. Even on sensitive racial questions differences between the South and other regions of the country have been diminishing—partly because the possibility of integration brings out similar attitudes in both North and South. In 1974, for example, majorities opposed to busing schoolchildren were overwhelming in all regions and scarcely greater in the South than in the West and Midwest (Table 24.1). Although more Southern whites than Northern whites were opposed to speeding the pace of school integration, a 1970 report indicated that the proportion of Southern whites was not vastly higher than in the Midwest (Table 24.2). In actual fact, schools in the South were more integrated by 1971 than in the rest of the country.[3] On other matters, the

3. In the eleven southern states of Alabama, Arkansas, Florida, Georgia, Louisiana, Mississippi, North Carolina, South Carolina, Tennessee, Texas, and Virginia, "the percentage of black pupils in majority-white schools—those with 50 or more percent white children—rose from 18.4 percent in the 1968–69 school year to 39.1 percent in the 1970–71 school year. . . . For the nation as a whole the comparable figure rose from 23.4 percent in 1968–69 to 33.1 percent in the present school year.

"The percentage of black pupils attending all-black schools dropped from 68 percent in the 1968–69 school year to 14.1 percent in the 1970–71 school year. . . . Nationally the percentage of black pupils in fully segregated schools dropped from 39.1 percent two years ago to 14 percent today, marginally below the Southern figure. But the rate of decrease was far slower in the North than it was in the South" (*New York Times*, June 6, 1971, pp. 1, 37).

Table 24.3
Attitudes Toward Five
Different Problems

	National	Region			
		East	Midwest	South	West
Reduction of social programs[a]					
Favor	34%	32%	36%	39%	29%
Oppose	66	68	64	61	71
Firearms Registration[b]					
Favor	72	83	68	67	69
Oppose	28	17	32	33	31
Unconditional amnesty[c]					
Favor	41	50	36	39	41
Oppose	59	50	64	61	59
Death Penalty[d]					
Favor	64	63	63	66	63
Oppose	36	37	37	34	37
Federal Campaign Financing[e]					
Favor	71	72	72	68	74
Oppose	29	28	28	32	26

Source: *Gallup Opinion Index,* Report No. 113, November, 1974. The choices were: (a) "The federal government should/should not reduce spending for social programs such as health, education and welfare"; (b) "Registration of all firearms should/should not be required"; (c) "I favor/oppose unconditional amnesty (a pardon) for Vietnam draft evaders and deserters"; (d) "I favor/oppose the death penalty for persons convicted of murder"; (e) "I favor/oppose having the federal government provide, a fixed amount of money for the election campaigns of all candidates for the Senate and the House, while prohibiting contributions from other sources."

South is not, despite its reputation, significantly more 'conservative' on most questions than the rest of the country (Table 24.3)—and perhaps never has been.[4]

The Midwest was once thought to be the stronghold of isolationism. It may once have been. Yet opinion surveys over almost three decades have not revealed large differences between the opinions of Midwesterners and the rest of the country on international affairs.[5] A 1956 survey measuring attitudes "toward American involvement in foreign affairs" was very revealing (Table 24.4). Respondents were asked whether they agreed or disagreed with the following statements. The answers were then distributed along an attitude measurement scale:

"This country would be better off if we just stayed home and did not concern ourselves with problems in other parts of the world."

4. It is worth recalling that during the period of unrest from the 1870s to about 1896, the South seemed to be more 'radical' than the rest of the country. See Hannah G. Roach, "Sectionalism in Congress (1870 to 1890)," *American Political Science Review,* 19 (August 1925), 500–526; and C. Vann Woodward, *The Burden of Southern History* (New York: Vintage Books, 1960), pp. 149 ff.

5. Since this statement runs contrary to a widespread impression you may wish to look at some surveys. During the two years preceding the entry of the United States into World War II, surveys showed that opinion in the East Central and West Central states was only slightly more 'isolationist' than in the other regions outside the South: the South was consistently less 'isolationist' and more 'interventionist.' See the surveys reported in Hadley Cantril, *Public Opinion 1935–1946* (Princeton, N.J.: Princeton University Press, 1951), pp. 966–978. After America's entry into the war, opinion in favor of joining a world organization was as high in the Midwest as elsewhere, and may have been higher than in some other regions (*Ibid.,* No. 7, p. 906; No. 35, p. 910).

Support for foreign involvement	Midwest	Northeast	Far West	South
High	53%	59%	58%	56%
Medium	27	25	24	26
Low	20	16	18	18
	100%	100%	100%	100%
Number	372	469	177	398

Source: V. O. Key, *Public Opinion and American Democracy* (New York: Knopf, 1961), pp. 107, 562.

	National	East	Region Midwest	South	West
Should reduce spending for military and defense[a]	55%	59%	56%	52%	54%
Should re-establish relations with Cuba[a]	63	68	64	55	67
Mistake sending troops to Vietnam[b]	60	64	59	57	59
President should be required to get Congressional approval for commitment of armed forces abroad[c]	80	80	84	76	80
Should not give up U.N. membership[d]	75	74	76	72	76

[a] October, 1974
[b] January, 1973
[c] November, 1973
[d] February, 1974

Sources: *Gallup Opinion Index,* Report No. 113, November, 1974; Report No. 92, February, 1973; Report No. 102, December, 1973; Report No. 117, March, 1975.

"The United States should give economic help to the poor countries of the world even if they can't pay for it."

"The United States should keep soldiers overseas where they can help countries that are against communism."

"The United States should give help to foreign countries even if they are not as much against communism as we are."

Table 24.5 offers some evidence from surveys made in 1970 on a half dozen issues. The differences among regions on these issues were small.

The reputation of the Midwest as the center of isolationism may have been built upon the conduct of a number of militant isolationists in Congress from midwestern states. Yet a careful study of voting on foreign aid measures from 1939 to 1958 in the House of Representatives showed that midwestern isolationism was confined to the Republican party. Republican members of Congress from the Midwest were more isolationist than those from the East and Pacific coasts. However, Democrats from the Midwest were consistently more internationalist than those from the Southern and Mountain states.[6]

6. Leroy N. Rieselbach, "The Demography of the Congressional Vote on Foreign Aid, 1939–1958," *American Political Science Review,* 58 (September 1964), 577–588, at pp. 582–3; see also Table IV, p. 582.

Factors Reducing Regional Cleavages

How then can we account for the fact that, if we exclude the question of the Afro-American, regional conflict is ordinarily moderate and does not split the country into persistently antagonistic divisions?

Absence of strong regional subcultures. First, outside the Old South, genuinely regional ways of life in sharp contradiction to one another have never developed in the United States. To be sure, there were and still are regional differences—in speech, in manners, in bearing, even to some extent in styles of life; and typically an American has some loyalties, of a sort, to his region. But (always putting the South and the Afro-American to one side) these moderately differing regional cultures have never, as such, constituted much of a threat to one another, at least not in a politically relevant way. The fact that someone from Maine speaks in a fashion that someone from Oklahoma may find puzzling or amusing, or that New Englanders are more formal and less easy-going in their ways than Westerners, hardly constitutes the material for sharp and enduring political controversies. Regional differences in this sense have always been less the source of political conflicts than of superficial and usually good-natured rivalries, a standing opportunity for any speaker to flatter an audience by expounding the virtues of the region, and a justification for the belief, somewhat deceptive but highly prized among Americans, that they are a people of incredible diversity.

Mobility. Second, Americans have never stayed long enough in one place to permit regional loyalties to gain the power they might have if people were more content with life in the old home town. That Americans are a restless people, a nation not only of immigrants but also of migrants, has become a national and international cliché; but it happens to be true. One American in four is now living in a state different from the one in which he was born. Of these migrant Americans, about half have moved from a state next to the present one, and the other half from some more distant state. About one person in seven was born in some other region. And what is true now, we learn from the census, has been true for at least a hundred years. The percentages for 1850 vary only slightly from those for 1950.[7] With an expanding frontier, Americans have always been on the move. In 1850, in the region consisting of Ohio, Indiana, Illinois, Michigan, and Wisconsin, one white resident out of three had been born in some other region; further west in the seven states bounded by Minnesota and North Dakota on the north and by Missouri and Kansas on the south, more than one-half of the native

---

7. *Historical Statistics of the United States, Colonial Times to 1957,* U.S. Department of Commerce, Bureau of the Census (Washington, D.C.: Government Printing Office, 1960).

white population had migrated from other regions; in Arkansas, Louisiana, Oklahoma, and Texas, slightly less than one-half were from outside that region. A century later, the frontier was the Pacific Coast, where more than half of the 1950 population had been born elsewhere—a quarter, in fact, in the Midwest; nearly half the people in the Mountain States came from a different region; even in the South Atlantic states about one white person in seven was not a Southerner by birth.[8]

Internal diversity. Third, within the various regions of the United States there is great diversity. So much so, in fact, that it is exceedingly difficult to decide how to draw regional boundaries: one must choose one set of states for one purpose, another set for a different purpose. The U.S. Census, the Federal Reserve Board, the Department of Agriculture, the student of electoral politics—all use rather different regions. Are there four regions in the United States—or fourteen?

New England and the South are, for historical reasons, the easiest to identify as distinct regions. Yet neither New England nor the South has ever had political unity. Both have been split internally along many different lines of cleavage. Socioeconomic conflicts have been as bitter among white Southerners as anywhere in the United States. Indeed, it is not much of an exaggeration to say that the only question on which the white people of the South have ever been able to unite was on maintaining the subordination of blacks—and even on this question there was generally a dissenting minority. New England, unlike the South, has never had even this incentive to provide it with enduring political unity. As for other regions, they are even more diverse politically.

Socioeconomic nature of regional conflicts. Fourth, what has passed for regional conflict in the past has usually been no more than a special case of socioeconomic conflict. The regional conflicts that occupy attention in history books generally occurred when the occupations or incomes of some people in one section of the country were thought to be threatened in some way by people in another section. Even slavery might be interpreted in this fashion. To some extent, the American economy has always been based upon regional specialization; different regions have somewhat different specialties.[9] Hence the economic needs, opportunities, and goals of some of the people in one region may come into conflict with those of another. When the country was predominantly agricultural, climate and soil influenced the kinds of crops produced; and the availability of markets was affected by loca-

---

8. *Ibid.,* pp. 41, 43, Series C 15–24.
9. See H. S. Perloff, E. J. Dunn, Jr., E. E. Lampard, and R. F. Muth, *Regions, Resources and Economic Growth* (Baltimore: Johns Hopkins Press, 1960).

tion, transportation facilities, and tariffs. All of these factors created opportunities for conflict. But they were in fact socioeconomic conflicts. If regional differences have rarely been great enough to polarize American society along regional lines, what then of socioeconomic differences?

SOCIOECONOMIC DIFFERENCES: OCCUPATIONS

Alas for simplicity, socioeconomic differences in the United States also tend to produce many intersecting lines of cleavage rather than one big dividing line, or even two or three of them.

The way in which citizens make their living, their occupation, their property, their income, all these economic factors have been highly important in shaping the way different citizens appraise the stakes involved in political issues. Because Americans differ in their economic positions, and because differences in economic positions foster differing political views, political controversies can often—though by no means always—be traced to ways in which citizens differ from one another economically. Although economic explanations of American politics do not explain everything, they do explain a good deal.

Yet when we try to explain American politics by looking for economic factors, the resulting divisions are more significant for their variety and complexity than for their simplicity. In fact, one soon makes three discoveries. *First,* socioeconomic differences *do* matter: there is usually some correlation, however weak it may be, between attitudes about politics and differences in social and economic positions. *Second,* however, no matter how Americans are classified, whether in economic categories or any others, the groups invariably turn out to be politically diverse; that is, on most questions any category of Americans is internally divided in its views in somewhat the same way the rest of the population is divided. *Third,* even when individuals or groups agree on one issue, they are likely to be split on another. This always seems to have been the case.

Before the Civil War when most Americans were farmers, differences in crops, markets, problems of transportation and competition, and effects of credit, mortgages, and the supply of currency all helped to produce political conflict. Conflicts over the tariff, national expenditures for canals and roads, banks, the control of the Mississippi—all can be partly explained by economic differences. Yet so far as one can now tell from rather inadequate data, the same economic groups were not always allied. Coalitions both in the electorate and in Congress were somewhat fluid. Even after the Civil War, as industrial capitalism began to displace agriculture in the American economy, the split between businessmen and urban blue-collar workers did not come to dominate politics as it did in a number of European countries and as one might reasonably have expected it would in the United States. (For further discussion, see Chapter 29.) Labor and socialist parties failed to gain much ground. The two major parties remained, as they had been before, conglomerate parties with catch-all programs. It is true that the Republicans and Democrats often seemed to have different centers of gravity. The Republican center of gravity was business; in the Democratic party it was the white South and increasingly the great urban political machines based on the immigrants and the poor. But because businessmen were in a minority, as they always are, the Republicans could not win elections without the support of farmers and even of urban workers. White Southerners were, as had been obvious to their sorrow for generations, also in a minority; hence Democrats, as well, could not win presidential elections without support in the North and West among farmers and urban workers.

In the twentieth century political conflicts have not been fought across any single and constant socioeconomic boundary. For example, it is virtually impossible to find any sizable economic group in the United States whose opinions on political questions are violently at odds with those of the rest of the population. Thus if we classify Americans according to whether the head of the household is in a profession or business, is a clerical worker, a skilled worker, an unskilled worker, or a farmer, we invariably find that whenever Americans in general disagree on some question, then people within each of these occupational groups will also disagree among themselves. This is not to say that opinion is uniform among all occupational groups; it is not, and the differences are of great importance. What is striking, however, is not how much variation there is from one group to another, but how little.

For example, a Gallup survey in 1974 tapped attitudes on a great variety of questions—economic, racial, cultural, and social. A number of these are shown in Table 24.6. It seems clear from the table that attitudes do bear some relation to occupations. Yet what is more emphatically demonstrated is how modest the relationships are. If we interpret polarization to mean, say, that more than two out of three persons in one group hold attitudes in direct conflict with two out of three persons in another group, then what is striking about Table 24.6 is the absence of any significant polarization (with the possible exception of the issue of legal abortion). In fact, on most issues a majority of each occupational group tends to be on the same side.

The similarity of opinion from one group to another, and the differences shown in Table 24.6 *within* occupational groups, mean that political conflict rarely if ever occurs along clear-cut occupational lines. For example, a political leader who favors active government intervention in the economy will draw both supporters and opponents from all occupational groups. A leader cannot therefore appeal exclusively to the

Table 24.6
Attitudes on Ten Public
Issues, by Occupation, 1974

	Professional and Business	Clerical and Sales	Manual Workers	Non-labor force*
a. Busing				
Favor busing schoolchildren to achieve better racial balance in schools	25%	30%	41%	32%
Oppose	75	70	59	68
b. Wage price controls				
Should be put back into effect	58	62	64	72
Should not	42	38	36	28
c. Diplomatic relations with Cuba				
Should be re-established	71	72	61	55
Should not	29	28	39	45
d. Unconditional amnesty (a pardon) for Vietnam draft evaders and deserters				
Favor	46	40	39	38
Oppose	54	60	61	62
e. A 5% surtax on annual family incomes over $15,000 to help pay for programs for the poor and unemployed				
Favor	40	40	45	56
Oppose	60	60	55	44
f. Reduce spending for military and defense purposes				
Should	56	62	55	46
Should not	44	38	45	54
g. Reduce spending for social programs such as health, education and welfare programs				
Should	33	38	30	42
Should not	67	62	70	58
h. Abortions through the third month of pregnancy				
Should continue to be legal	66	56	48	38
Should not	34	44	52	62
i. Equal Rights Amendment for women				
Favor	80	87	77	73
Oppose	20	13	23	27
j. Federal government provide financial aid to parochial schools				
Should	44	48	57	55
Should not	56	52	43	45

* Consists primarily of respondents who are retired, housewives, students, and physically handicapped persons.
Source: *The Gallup Opinion Index*, Report No. 113, November, 1974.

laboring classes without jeopardizing support among business and professional men and farmers. And by the same token, a conservative who opposes government intervention in economic life will gain supporters from a great variety of economic groups, including skilled laborers and farmers.

SOCIAL CLASSES   Paralleling the findings on regional and occupational differences, one's outlook on politics does not seem to vary a great deal in the United States according to one's social and economic class.

Problems of Definition

A problem that presents itself immediately is to define what we mean by *class*. Social scientists have resolved this problem in two ways. One is to assign people among various classes—two, six, or whatever—by relatively objective criteria, such as an individual's level of education, occupation, and income. This is often called an *objective* class or status. The other method is to allow people to assign themselves to a particular class. This is called *subjective* class or status.

Magnitude of social classes

Both methods lead to somewhat uncertain, and sometimes conflicting, results. Social scientists have arrived at substantially different estimates of the working and middle classes using objective criteria, mainly occupation. The chief difference arises over where to put clerical, sales, and service occupations. When service occupations are placed in the working class, then that class comprises around 60 percent of the labor force. If some parts of clerical and sales occupations are also included, then two-thirds or more of the labor force are members of the working class.[10]

When respondents in surveys assign themselves to such class categories as upper, middle, working, and lower, about 60 percent place themselves in the working class and about 40 percent in the middle classes. Only a small percentage put themselves in either the upper or lower classes.[11]

Thus both methods have torpedoed a once-popular theory: that a majority of Americans are, or think of themselves as, middle class. On the contrary, the evidence shows that most Americans work for wages in offices, factories, and elsewhere, and only a minority have occupations as professionals or technicians, or are managers, executives, officials, or owners of their own businesses. The objective class for a majority of Americans, therefore, is the working class. By the subjective standard a substantial majority of Americans also identify themselves as a part of the working class, not the middle class.

What, then, are the consequences?

Findings

Class feelings are moderate. First, class identity seems to be very weak. One adult American out of three, as we have seen, has never identified

10. See Andrew Levison, *Working Class Majority* (New York: Coward, 1974), and Richard F. Hamilton, *Class and Politics in the United States* (New York: John Wiley, 1972), ch. 4, "On the Definition, Dimensions, and Geography of Class."

11. Hamilton, *ibid.,* Table 3.2, "Class Identification 1954–64," p. 101.

with either the middle class or the working class. Even among those who do identify themselves with one or the other, class feelings seem to be lukewarm. It is illuminating, in fact, to look beyond the bare statistics to the kinds of things the respondents say to the interviewers who ask them what "class" they belong to.

Here are some responses given in an early survey (1956) that are probably typical of what one would find today:

> . . . a Nebraska farm housewife on class: "I suppose it would be working class as that is about all we do." A North Carolina gift shop proprietress when asked if she had to make a choice: "That's a new one to me. I just want to say I'm as good as any of them." An Ohio skilled worker when faced by the choice problem: "I wouldn't say." (Why?) "Well, what is the middle class and working class?" A South Carolina housewife: "I think middle class and working class come under the same heading." A Los Angeles housewife: "I can't say. I just wouldn't know." The wife of a New Mexico miner: "I don't quite understand the difference. I guess we work so we must belong to the working class. I don't quite see it." A Pennsylvania steelworker: "When you're in a mill you're workin'." A North Carolina retail grocer had never thought of herself as being of a class: "I think that class talk is just political talk. Here the Republicans are called the rich man's party, and they run a man who came up from just plain people, and the Democrats say they are the little man's party and they run a millionaire." Wirer in California radio factory: "Well I work for a living so I guess I'm in the working class." Retired Ohio worker: (Ever thought of yourself as being in one of these classes?) "Never gave that a thought, missus." A retired hospital orderly said his father had been middle class: "Upper part. My father owned a saloon."[12]

Subjective class is not identical with objective class. To confuse the role of social class even further, there are the persistent discrepancies mentioned above between subjective status—the class with which a voter identifies—and objective status defined by occupation or other measures.[13] The two are not always congruent: some blue-collar workers say they belong to the middle class; a considerable number of white-collar workers say they are in the working class. Altogether, around one out of four Americans gives these kinds of answers. Given the vagueness of class boundaries in the United States, these responses are scarcely surprising. But what is highly significant is that if two people whom an observer would put in the same social class nonetheless put themselves

---

12. V. O. Key, Jr., *Public Opinion and American Democracy* (New York: Knopf, 1961), p. 141 ff.

13. In most countries, the percentages of those who answered "yes" to the question "Do you think you have anything in common with fellow countrymen not of your class?" were considerably higher among middle-class and upper-class respondents than among working-class respondents. See Buchanan and Cantril, *How Nations See Each Other* (Urbana: University of Illinois Press, 1953), Appendix C, Report of Survey Agencies, pp. 125 ff. Among working-class respondents only, the percentage answering "yes" was: United States, 70%; Australia, 70%; Norway, 68%; Great Britain, 60%; France, 58%; Germany (British zone of occupation), 53%; Mexico, 46%; Netherlands, 45%; Italy, 37%; (ibid., pp. 17, 18).

in different social classes, they are likely to make rather different judgments about political matters. A skilled worker who tells you that he or she belongs to the middle class is also likely to look at political questions with the kinds of values, biases, and aspirations that tend to prevail among people with distinctly middle-class occupations—business and professional people, for example. This individual is more likely than other manual workers to vote Republican. A skilled worker who says that he or she belongs to the working class, on the other hand, is likely to consider political choices more nearly from the same viewpoint as other workers. Such a person is more likely to vote Democratic.[14]

Class provides a basis for cleavages: in attitudes. Despite its weakness as a divisive factor, status or social class does of course provide some basis for political cleavages in the United States. "The extensive modern literature on social class and political behavior has shown persistently that individuals of higher status (subjectively or objectively) tend to give 'conservative' responses on questions of economic policy and tend as well to vote Republican; individuals of lower status respond more 'radically' and vote Democratic."[15] The relationship is, however, not very strong. Once again we find that a sizeable proportion of people with higher status are not conservative, whereas a large fraction of voters in the lower status group are. Thus, a 1964 survey found that respondents who identified their interests with the working class were more favorable toward the idea of active federal intervention on key questions than were those who identified themselves with the middle class—and both were markedly more than the self-styled propertied class (Table 24.7).[16] Differences also showed up on the liberal-conservative ideological spectrum (Table 24.8)[17]; but what is even more obvious from Table 24.8 is how modest the ideological differences were between working class and middle class. Only the tiny propertied class stands out very sharply in its conservatism.

---

14. For evidence from the 1964 and 1968 elections, see Gerald Pomper, *Voters' Choice: Varieties of American Electoral Behavior* (New York: Dodd, Mead, 1975), Table 3.2, p. 49.

15. Angus Campbell et al., *The American Voter* (New York: Wiley, 1964), p. 346.

16. The five key issues of public policy were federal aid to education, Medicare, federally subsidized housing, urban renewal, and the government's responsibility to do away with poverty.

17. The ideological spectrum was constructed from responses to five statements that were designed to tap general political perspectives. Depending on the extent to which they agreed or disagreed with the five statements, respondents were classified as "completely conservative," "predominantly conservative," "middle-of-the-road," "predominantly liberal," and "completely liberal." The five statements were: "1. The federal government is interfering too much in state and local matters. 2. The government has gone too far in regulating business and interfering with the free enterprise system. 3. Social problems here in this country could be solved more effectively if the government would only keep its hands off and let people in local communities handle their own problems in their own way. 4. Generally speaking, any able-bodied person who really wants to work in this country can find a job and earn a living. 5. We should rely more on individual initiative and ability and not so much on governmental welfare programs" (Free and Cantril, *Political Beliefs of Americans, A Study of Public Opinion* (New Brunswick, N.J.: Rutgers University Press, 1967) pp. 31–32.

Table 24.7
Attitudes Toward Federal
Action on Five Public
Policy Issues, by Self-
Identified Classes, 1964

Class Identification	Strongly Favorable	Predominantly Favorable	Mixed	Predominantly Against	Strongly Against
Propertied class	20%	20%	34%	12%	14%
Middle class	36	21	24	10	9
Working class	50	24	17	5	4

Source: Free and Cantril, *Political Beliefs of Americans,* p. 216.

Table 24.8
Ideological Attitudes, by
Self-Identified Classes,
1964

Class Identification	Completely or Predominantly Liberal	Middle of Road	Predominantly Conservative	Completely Conservative
Propertied class	4%	33%	18%	45%
Middle class	13	32	20	35
Working class	21	35	20	24

Source: Free and Cantril, *Political Beliefs of Americans,* p. 221.

In voting. As has already been indicated, class differences, like occupational differences, also show up in voting. If we arbitrarily divide the population into working and middle classes by using the objective indicator of manual versus nonmanual occupations, or blue-collar versus white-collar, we would expect to find members of the working class giving more support to the Democratic party than do members of the middle class. And of course they do.

The net impact has been to give a slight class tinge to the two major parties. Thus a 1964 survey found that nearly two out of three Republicans identified their interests with the middle or propertied classes, whereas two out of three Democrats identified their interest with the working class.[18] The two parties, then, tend to have different centers of gravity, and their leaders can generally be counted on to respond somewhat differently to these diverging gravitational pulls.

Yet the influence of class on voting is rather small at best. It varies from one election to another, depending on the kinds of issues that are most striking at the time. In most of the recent presidential elections, it has been difficult to find much of a relationship between a voter's occupation or class identification and how he or she votes. As an influence on voting, class identification is far less important than either one's party identification or one's opinion on issues: and these, in turn, are so weakly related to class that the net impact of class is, in the end, not very great. What is more, the impact of class on voting, on political attitudes, and on party identification appears to be declining.[19]

---

18. Free and Cantril, *Political Beliefs of Americans,* p. 142.

19. Pomper, *Voters' Choice,* p. 62, and Everett Carl Ladd with Charles D. Hadley, *Transformation of the American Party System: Political Coalitions from the New Deal to the 1970s* (New York: W. W. Norton and Co., 1975), pp. 226 ff.

RACIAL, ETHNIC, AND RELIGIOUS DIFFERENCES

It was long thought—and widely hoped—that the United States was truly a melting pot of races, religions, and ethnic groups, all of whose members would rapidly shed their distinctiveness in the process of Americanization. Recently, however, the melting pot has come under severe attack both as ideal and as fact. As an ideal, the melting pot is often seen nowadays as a discreditable process of compulsory homogenization during which successive waves of immigrants were expected to abandon their own cultural heritage and, at great cost to their own identities and sense of self-respect, adapt so far as possible to the predominant culture of the white Anglo-Saxon Protestant American.

However one may evaluate the moral and psychological gains and costs of the melting pot ideal, the extent to which homogenization has occurred is now much more debatable than a few decades ago. For evidence accumulates that earlier announcements of the end of political and social cleavages related to racial, ethnic, and religious differences were premature. Thus a study of the major ethnic groups in New York City a decade ago, concluded:

> Religion and race seem to define the major groups into which American society is evolving as the specifically national aspect of ethnicity (i.e., the specific nation from which one's ancestors came) declines. In our large American cities, four major groups emerge: Catholics, Jews, white Protestants, and Negroes.[20]

Like many other prevailing American social and political ideals, the melting pot tacitly excluded the Afro-American. Today, differences between whites and blacks produce what is almost certainly the most distinguishable political division and very likely the highest degree of polarization existing in American society. Evidence from a 1964 survey, before widespread militancy developed among black activists in the last half of the decade, was conclusive on this point: in attitudes toward government intervention on matters of public policy, the proper extent of government power, a conservative-liberal spectrum, the two major parties, and practically everything else tapped by the survey, differences between blacks and whites outdistanced those of every other category. By comparison, differences according to occupation or class appeared to be of slight importance.[21]

These differences persisted through the following decade of turbulence and beyond. Examining survey data covering the period from 1960 to 1972, one writer concludes:

> On all issues, under any ideological definition, blacks take a liberal position, while whites are substantially more conservative. These differences

20. Nathan Glazer and Daniel Patrick Moynihan, *Beyond the Melting Pot* (Cambridge, Mass.: M.I.T. Press and Harvard University Press, 1963), p. 314.

21. Free and Cantril, *Political Beliefs of Americans*, Appendix F, Tables 1, 2, 3, 9.

Table 24.9
Support for Racial
Integration by Race
and Class, 1964–1972 *

Self-Identification	Black	White	Race Difference
1964			
Working class	91.9%	33.7%	58.2%
Middle class	93.8	31.7	62.1
Class difference	− 1.9	2.0	
1968			
Working class	92.0	29.6	62.4
Middle class	95.0	36.3	58.7
Class difference	− 3.0	− 6.7	
1972			
Working class	90.5	33.4	57.1
Middle class	81.4	44.8	36.6
Class difference	9.1	−11.4	

* Entries are the percentages of each class, within race, that support full integration. Class and race differences result from subtraction by columns or rows. Positive differences show greater support for integration by the working class or by blacks.
Source: Gerald Pomper, *Voters' Choice*, p. 134.

are not only evident on matters related to race, such as means of dealing with urban unrest or aid to minority groups. On the economic issue of government guarantee of jobs, three-fourths of blacks are favorable, compared to only one-quarter of whites. By 1972, some two-thirds of blacks leaned toward withdrawal from Vietnam, while the same position won support from only about two out of five whites.[22]

Since a much higher proportion of blacks than whites are in low-income, working-class occupations, some of these differences can be attributed to class factors rather than race. Yet attitudes on racial integration split the American working class wide open. Doubtless because they are more likely to be directly affected, members of the white working class are even more opposed to integration than the white middle class (Table 24.9).

The extent of political polarization along the white-black plane of cleavage is, however, not typical. Always keeping in mind this important exception, ethnic and religious loyalties are rather like region, occupation, class, and other lines of cleavage: differences among groups do persist, but within any given group there is also a very considerable amount of variation. Ethnic origins and religion, then, continue to have significant impact on American political life long after they should, according to the melting pot theory; yet the impact of ethnic and religious identification is as moderate as that of the other factors discussed earlier. The impact is, indeed, often reduced by the crosscutting effects of these other factors.

Among white ethnic groups, Americans of English, German, and Scandinavian origin have been more 'conservative' than Americans of

22. Pomper, *Voters' Choice*, pp. 131–132.

Table 24.10
Attitudes Toward
Government Intervention
by Ethnic Groups (Whites
Only), Five Issues, 1964

English	30%
German	34
Scandinavian	39
Irish (Catholic)	54
Eastern or Central European	54
Italian	57

Source: Free and Cantril, *Political Beliefs of Americans*, p. 152.

Table 24.11
Political Attitudes, by
Religion, 1968

	Protestant	Catholic	Jewish
For active role of government	33%	37%	55%
For desegregation	36	41	57
For foreign aid	39	42	60

Source: University of Michigan, Survey Research Center, 1968 Election Survey.

Irish, Eastern or Central European, or Italian origins (Table 24.10).[23] In the United States, the major religious categories—Protestants, Catholics, Jews—are as much ethnic as religious. In any case, differences persist in political attitudes and party identifications. As Table 24.11 indicates, in general, Protestants have been the most 'conservative' on national affairs, Jews the most 'liberal.'

The extent to which religious differences cut across 'class' differences is revealed in a very general way by data on voting. In national elections over the past generation, among both manual workers and nonmanual workers, Catholics have voted Democratic in considerably higher proportions than have Protestants. The differences between Catholics and Protestants were least in the elections of 1952 and 1956, when General Eisenhower was the Republican candidate, and, as might be expected, greatest in 1960 when John F. Kennedy, a Catholic, was the Democratic candidate. The biggest discrepancy in 1960, incidentally, was between 'middle-class' (nonmanual occupation) Catholics and Protestants; many Catholics who had moved into nonmanual occupations maintained their traditional loyalties as Democratic voters.

To look at the same data in another way, Protestants split most sharply along class lines in 1936 in the midst of the Great Depression, when Franklin Roosevelt was running for a second term. Catholics split most sharply in 1952 when many middle-class Catholics succumbed to the appeal of Eisenhower; in 1960, on the other hand, Kennedy all but eliminated the appeal of class among Catholics by his appeal as a fellow Catholic.[24]

---

23. See footnote 16 for the five issues of public policy on which the conservative-liberal label was applied.

24. See Table 11, pp. 92–94, in Seymour Martin Lipset, "Religion and Politics in the American Past and Present," in *Religion and Social Conflict*, eds. Robert Lee and Martin Marty (New York: Oxford University Press, 1964).

Thus religion or ethnic identity may either enhance the effects of class and status on voting, as in the case of the blacks or working-class Catholics; or conversely, religion or ethnic identity may depress the significance of class and status by providing a crosscutting split, as in the case of middle-class Catholics and Jews or white working-class Protestants. Moreover, just as the impact of occupation and economic position on voting may vary, depending on the state of the economy, so the impact of religion and ethnic identity is not a constant but a varying factor, depending on current issues and on the candidates themselves.

IDEOLOGIES: DEMOCRACY

Americans are frequently portrayed by foreigners and by themselves as a supremely pragmatic and un-ideological people. This is, at best, a half-truth.

For Americans are a highly ideological people. It is only that one does not ordinarily notice their ideology because they have, to an astounding extent, all agreed on the same ideology.

As we have already seen, perhaps more than any other people in the world, Americans have been united in expressing faith in a democratic ideology, even if they often have not acted on what they claimed to believe. Since their ideology is a source of unity rather than divisiveness, the moment in which to observe Americans as ideologists is not when they talk about domestic politics but when they talk about international politics, and especially about America in relation to the rest of the world. Here we find ordinary Americans looking at political problems in a distinct ideological framework. They tend to interpret the world according to democratic standards. What is democratic is good, what is undemocratic is bad.

IDEOLOGIES: 'LIBERAL' VERSUS 'CONSERVATIVE'

Nonetheless, Americans have often disagreed as to what democracy means, both as an idea and in practice. They have disagreed as to how far democracy and equality should be extended, how widely the advantages enjoyed by elite groups should be distributed throughout the general population, how much equality of opportunity and of power is desirable. The controversy among the Framers between those who wanted an aristocratic republic and those who wanted a democratic republic was just such an ideological cleavage. Further, these two ideological viewpoints have reappeared in various guises ever since the Constitutional Convention. It will do no great harm if, for the moment, we call the one that stresses equality and democracy 'liberalism' and the other 'conservatism.' Most of the time, no doubt, people of wealth, property, and high status have tended to be 'conservative,' while the less well-to-do have tended to be 'liberal.' Moreover, throughout long periods liberals have probably been more numerous in one party while conservatives have been more often drawn to the other. Thus the Federalists, the Whigs, and the Republicans were more attractive to well-to-do conservatives, while the Democratic-Republicans and the Democrats gained the loyalties of the liberals of more modest circumstances.

Of course one must be exceedingly cautious in placing too much confidence in these historical conclusions, for the data with which one could test them properly are almost entirely lacking except for recent years. Fortunately, however, for the most recent period, from the 1930s, survey data have demonstrated beyond any reasonable doubt that voters of higher status tend to be conservative in ideology and are likely to vote Republican, while voters of lower status tend to be more liberal in ideology and are more likely to vote for Democratic candidates.[25]

Conceivably, a three-way relationship between status, ideology, and party might divide Americans into two rather sharply polarized groups. A single division might separate people according to status, ideology, and party, as follows:

	Camp I	Camp II
Class or Status	Upper	Lower
Ideology	Conservative	Liberal
Party	Pro-Republican	Pro-Democratic

But the tendency in this direction is restrained by numerous crosscutting cleavages. Each of the tendencies is important; yet none is strong enough to exert a dominant pull on American political life.

As our discussion of occupations and social class has already shown, status and party are not closely correlated. Likewise, as we saw, in every large occupational or status group, a significant minority hold opinions that diverge ideologically from the prevalent views. A considerable number of manual workers, for example, are as conservative as nonmanual workers, and many nonmanual workers are as liberal as the majority of manual workers. Even the link between ideology and party is not overwhelmingly powerful. Both parties have been supported by conservatives and liberals. Moreover, one relationship often dilutes the purity of another: For example, low-status Republicans are evidently about as likely to be highly liberal on domestic issues as are low-status Democrats.[26]

Since the 1960s, however, the link between party and ideology may have grown somewhat stronger, as college-educated persons in profes-

---

25. "... This triangle of relationships [has been] replicated in dozens of empirical studies. ... Obviously, the facts presented by these relationships cannot be soberly questioned" (Campbell et al., *The American Voter*, p. 203).

26. *Ibid.*, pp. 207–208, including fns. 7 and 8 and Figure 9.1.

sional and other high-status occupations have adopted a more liberal ideology. Where it was once true that high-status Democrats, like high-status Republicans, tended to be conservative, it is now the case that many high-status Democrats are liberal. In fact, as we saw in Chapter 21, the Democrats have recently become something of a 'top stratum–bottom stratum' coalition.[27]

Why Liberalism and Conservatism Do Not Produce a Sharp Split

Why, you might ask at this point, aren't liberalism and conservatism more powerful in stimulating a clear-cut split? There are at least three reasons: the ideologies are vague at best; they consist of several different dimensions; and in any case coherent ideological thinking is highly uncommon among American voters.

Vagueness. Neither liberalism nor conservatism is a clear-cut, thoroughly worked-out statement of principles and programs. They can better be described as a hodgepodge of ideas, ideals, and policies. Because of their generality and vagueness, liberal and conservative ideologies do not provide a clear-cut guide for a citizen who has to decide on a single issue. On concrete questions liberals disagree among themselves, and so do conservatives. For example, many liberals who support welfare measures such as federal aid to education, which unquestionably requires federal expenditures, nonetheless want to cut taxes.

Dimensions. In truth, the terms *liberal* and *conservative,* which we have been using without apology up to this point, cover a wide assortment of views. What we have been calling 'liberalism' is a favorable view of government intervention in economic and social problems to aid citizens who suffer from the effects of an unregulated economy and the unequal distribution of incomes and opportunities. Yet there are other dimensions of 'liberal' and 'conservative' ideologies that often crosscut views on government intervention. Let me suggest several.

1. *Concrete versus abstract.* One of the most interesting findings is that many Americans hold one set of attitudes when they consider *concrete* or specific policies involving government intervention and another set when they are responding at a more general or *abstract* level. Thus in the study cited above in Tables 24.7, 24.8, and 24.10 it was discovered that a preponderant majority of respondents (65 percent) were 'liberal' on the more specific operational spectrum—the dimensions of the degree of government intervention (see footnote 16). But on the ideological spectrum, which tapped general political attitudes (see foot-

---

27. Evidence on this point is presented by Ladd, *Transformations,* and Pomper, *Voters' Choice,* p. 54.

note 17), the largest group, exactly half, were 'conservative'! It turned out that nearly half the ideological conservatives also favored government intervention on concrete issues, while among those most strongly in favor of government intervention on specific matters, slightly more (29 percent) were ideologically 'conservative' than 'liberal' (28 percent), and among those moderately in favor of government intervention, 46 percent were 'conservative' in their general views as compared with only 14 percent who were 'liberal.'[28]

2. *Economic matters versus political and civil liberties.* A person who is concerned about reforming the economic institutions that were created by industrial capitalism need not be particularly concerned about political and civil liberties. These two concerns, which in America are often put together under the label of liberalism, are logically and ideologically distinct. Indeed, the proof, if one were needed, is the classic nineteenth-century English liberal who combined his belief in political liberty with an equally fervent belief in the virtues of a laissez-faire economy. It would serve no good purpose to argue here over the meaning of the terms *liberal* and *conservative.* What is important is to recognize that these loose ideologies comprise several different dimensions; political libertarianism and economic reformism may go hand in hand, but they equally well may not.

It is an exceedingly important fact that, in the United States, people who are in favor of economic reforms are frequently antilibertarian on questions of civil and political rights. Conversely, some citizens who oppose government intervention in the economy nonetheless support government intervention on behalf of civil and political rights. As a good example, we may take the question of racial integration. Do people who believe that the government ought to intervene actively on such matters as federal aid to education, medical care, public housing, urban renewal, unemployment, and the like also believe that the government should intervene in the question of whether white and black children go to the same school? Not necessarily. The study cited above found that 44 percent of those who strongly favored active government intervention on economic matters thought the pace of integration was too fast; 21 percent thought that blacks should have less "influence in government and political matters than they have now." Respondents were also asked whether they agreed or disagreed with the statement, "Most of the organizations pushing for civil rights have been infiltrated by the Communists and are now dominated by Communist trouble-makers." Among those most strongly in favor of government intervention on economic issues, 39 percent agreed with the statement; among those moderately interventionist, just under half agreed.[29]

---

28. Free and Cantril, *Political Beliefs of Americans*, p. 37, Table 3.4; and p. 222, Table 3, Appendix.

29. Free and Cantril, *Political Beliefs of Americans*, pp. 122, 124–125.

Table 24.12
Percent of Liberals
and Conservatives

	Internationalist
Those who qualified on the Operational Spectrum as	
Completely liberal	71%
Predominantly liberal	66
Middle-of-the-road	63
Predominantly conservative	58
Completely conservative	50
Those who qualified on the Ideological Spectrum as	
Completely or predominantly liberal	76%
Middle-of-the-road	71
Predominantly conservative	67
Completely conservative	51
Those who identified themselves as	
Liberal	73%
Middle-of-the-road	69
Conservative	57

Note: Respondents were asked whether they agreed or disagreed with the following statements:
1. The United States should cooperate fully with the United Nations.
2. In deciding on foreign policies, the United States should take into account the views of its allies in order to keep our alliances strong.
3. Since the United States is the most powerful nation in the world, we should go our own way in international matters, not worrying too much about whether other countries agree with us or not.
4. The United States should mind its own business internationally and let other countries get along as best they can on their own.
5. We shouldn't think so much in *international* terms but concentrate more on our own *national* problems and building up our strength and prosperity here at home.
For statements 1 and 2, the internationalist response was represented by agreement; for 3, 4, and 5, by disagreement. In the table, "internationalists" gave the internationalist reponse to at least four of the statements, or three out of four with one "don't know" or two "don't know" responses.
Source: Free and Cantril, *Political Beliefs of Americans,* p. 68

3. *Internationalism versus isolationism.* Historically, the philosophy of liberalism has been associated with an internationalist outlook; conservatives are often more nationalistic than liberals. Among Americans, then, does economic reformism go with internationalism and economic conservatism with isolationism? To some extent, but not entirely. In a 1956 survey the relationship was practically nonexistent.[30] In 1964, however, a somewhat stronger relationship showed up, perhaps because of differences in the questions used (Table 24.12). Yet what is most significant about the data in this table is not the amount of disagreement but the rather high agreement.

It follows, then, that the foreign policies forged after World War II commanded the support of both liberal and conservative voters, and at the same time these policies were opposed by both liberals and conservatives. Or to put the matter in another way, a relatively liberal leader like President Truman could generally count on support for his foreign policies from citizens who opposed his domestic policies, while some citizens who supported his domestic policies were lukewarm or

---

30. Key, *Public Opinion,* p. 158.

hostile to his foreign policies. The same thing held true with a more conservative president like Eisenhower: he drew support for an internationalist foreign policy from liberals who opposed him on domestic issues.

4. *Innovation versus tradition.* There is still another dimension to liberalism and conservatism, or at least so it is commonly supposed. This dimension (or set of dimensions) consists of attitudes toward change, innovation, tradition, custom, conventional morality and so-called 'permissiveness.' Considered along this dimension, we might say that conservatives tend to resist change as undesirable and often unnecessary, while liberals accept it more sympathetically as inevitable and desirable. Drawing upon the writings of political philosophers, Herbert McCloskey has devised a scale for 'conservatism' in this broad sense.[31] Yet curiously enough, in 1956 among the general population there was no significant relationship between this sort of conservatism and the political party with which people identified themselves, even outside the South. Moreover, this species of conservatism seemed to be almost unrelated to the economic policies a voter would support.[32]

That this pattern is an enduring one is suggested by an analysis of the role of 'social issues' in the evaluation of the Democratic and Republican parties and the presidential candidates from 1960–1972. Social issues were defined as the policies of the candidates and parties toward race, poverty, public order and protest, as well as their attitudes toward groups associated with these issues, such as blacks, persons on welfare, young people, and feminists. Although many political commentators assumed that issues like these were strongly helping one party or candidate, the fact was that in all four elections, views on social issues seemed to have little relation to the voters' evaluation of the candidates or parties.[33]

The ideologies of conservatism and liberalism, then, are made up of a number of different dimensions. We have seen that one of these, economic intervention by government, is by no means highly related to four others—general or abstract political views, political and civil liberties, foreign policy, and attitudes toward change. There may be—and very likely are—still other dimensions. Consequently, two people who find themselves close together along one dimension of liberalism–conservatism are likely to find themselves very far apart along another dimension. Thus Americans divide one way on one kind of issue but quite another way on another kind of issue.

---

31. See Herbert McCloskey, "Conservatism and Personality," *American Political Science Review* 52 (March 1958).

32. Campbell et al., *The American Voter*, p. 211.

33. Pomper, *Voters' Choice*, pp. 151–165.

THE LIMITS OF IDEOLOGICAL THINKING

Most Americans (like most people everywhere) simply do not possess an elaborate ideology. It is difficult for political philosophers accustomed to manipulating abstract ideas to realize how slight and fragmentary is the analytical framework most people bring to bear on political problems.[34]

How Ideology is Short-Circuited

A great many people have only weak traces of a liberal or conservative ideological frame of reference with which to judge political issues, candidates, and parties. This does not mean that they are necessarily making foolish or uninformed choices. It does mean that they have to find some basis for judgment other than a liberal or conservative ideology. What seems to happen in a great many cases is that as a voter moves from indecision to decision, he or she bypasses ideology and takes a much more direct route. Somehow ideology is short-circuited. In some cases it is short-circuited by immediate consideration of self-interest or group interest that does not require ideological analysis and that may, in fact, lead to support for policies that a person committed to an ideology would oppose. The fact that the less well-to-do segments of the population favor tax cuts, for example, has very little or nothing to do with their other economic policies: here primitive self-interest short-circuits ideology. Party loyalties also short-circuit ideology. Once voters develop a firm attachment to a party, they can bypass the painful task of appraising policies and candidates according to ideological content. Having concluded long ago that the Democratic party or the Republican party is better for them, for their group, or for the nation, they now support the party's candidates and the party's general policies (so far as these are known to them) without much further thought. Attraction or hostility toward candidates because of their personal qualities also helps to short-circuit the more complex route of ideological thinking.

How Ideology Nonetheless Functions

Are we then to conclude that liberal and conservative ideologies in their various forms and multiple dimensions are unimportant in American politics? Such a conclusion is surely unwarranted, for three reasons: *First,* while the great bulk of the people can often bypass ideological considerations, they cannot always do so. In a complex world, even the connection between self-interest and national policies is often so obscure that it cannot be traced out by an uninformed mind; ideology, however vague it may be, may sometimes help to establish the

---

34. Philip E. Converse, "The Nature of Belief Systems in Mass Politics," in *Ideology and Discontent,* ed. David E. Apter (New York: Free Press of Glencoe, 1964), pp. 206–261.

connection. On international policies in particular, the beliefs of Americans about democracy and political self-determination perhaps serve—however dimly—as guides to some citizens.

Second, some people are much more ideologically minded than others. As might be expected, the more active a person is in political life, the more likely he or she is to think in ideological terms.[35] In all that we have been saying so far, we have been describing ordinary voters, the rank-and-file citizens. But ideologies have always been the special property of political activists. In American political life, as elsewhere, political activists are very much more ideological than the great bulk of the population. Thus liberal–conservative differences that are absent, blurred, confused, or contradictory among ordinary citizens, and particularly among citizens who are least involved in politics, are much sharper among the politically active groups.

The greater importance of ideology among activists and leaders produces a paradox: while activists are in greater agreement than ordinary citizens in their adherence to a democratic and libertarian ideology, they are more divided ideologically on questions of government policy. The explanation for both the greater ideological unity and greater ideological disagreement among the activists and leaders is evidently the same: we noted above that ideological considerations are much more significant among activists than among ordinary citizens. Hence, to the extent that the perspectives of the general overarching American democratic and libertarian ideology are significant among activists, they are united by their common ideology; but to the extent that liberal and conservative ideologies are in the forefront, they are divided by their differing ideological perspectives. And it is these very people, the activists and leaders, who more than any others shape not only policies, party platforms, and nominations but constitutional and political norms. So democratic, liberal, and conservative ideological perspectives do have a significant effect on American political life.

The Growth of Ideological Thinking

Third, the conclusion that ideology is unimportant in American politics is unwarranted because ideological thinking has become more prevalent and is likely to go on increasing. There is good reason to believe that ideological thinking was significantly more widespread in the decade since 1964 than during the preceding decade. Before 1964 a consistent set of 'liberal' attitudes and a consistent set of 'conservative' attitudes were rather rare among the general public; after 1964 liberal and conservative viewpoints grew sharper and more antagonis-

---

35. Key, *Public Opinion,* p. 440; Campbell et al., *The American Voter,* p. 258; Converse, "Nature of Belief Systems," pp. 226–231.

tic.[36] The rise in ideological thinking after 1964 can be attributed to several factors. One is the rising level of conflict from 1964 onward. During the presidency of Dwight D. Eisenhower in the 1950s, political life was comparatively tranquil. Conflict was at a low. It was the period of the 'silent generation' in the colleges, and a mood of 'consensual politics' seemed to prevail, at least on the surface. As we shall see in the next chapter, from 1964 onward that tranquility gave way to hectic unrest. Political passions were inflamed, political attitudes were sharpened and became more conflicting. People who were in favor of more rapid integration, for example, now were also likely to favor more vigorous government intervention in the economy, federal aid to education, medical care, and the like. They were also more likely to give strong support to civil liberties and to be 'dovish' on international affairs.[37] 'Liberals' holding views like these conflicted sharply with 'conservatives' who now tended to hold opposing views on all these issues.

Another factor accounting for the rise in ideological thinking was the spectacular increase in the proportion of voters who had gone to college. As one scholar has observed: "In the electorate that participated in the 1952 election, for example, people whose education was limited to grade school outnumbered people exposed to college education by almost three to one. In 1968, just four presidential elections later, college persons outnumbered grade school persons by almost five to four."[38] Ideological thinking, it was suggested a moment ago, requires a capacity for abstractions and logical consistency that is heightened by education. Political attentiveness and activism also tend to be significantly higher among college-educated citizens.

Thus the political conflicts of the turbulent decade beginning in 1964 coincided with a rapid increase in the average voter's level of education. The combined effect was to increase the prevalence of ideological thinking among the electorate. Although the intensity of conflict temporarily declined after the resignation of President Nixon in 1974, the level of education continued to rise. Thus there is ground for believing that American political life will continue to display more ideological thinking in the future than it did before 1964.

CONSEQUENCES   The pattern of ideological divergencies in the United States is roughly the pattern that ordinarily prevails with respect to geographical, socioeconomic, ethnic, and religious differences. Conflicts do not accumu-

---

36. Norman H. Nie with Kristi Anderson, "Mass Belief Systems Revisited: Political Change and Attitude Structure," *The Journal of Politics*, 36 (August 1974), pp. 540–591.

37. *Ibid.*, Table 1, p. 553; Table 2, p. 562; Table 3, p. 564.

38. Philip E. Converse, "Change in the American Electorate," in Angus Campbell and Philip E. Converse, *The Human Meaning of Social Change* (New York: Russell Sage Foundation, 1972), pp. 263–338, at p. 323.

late along the same lines of cleavage. On the contrary, different conflicts seem to involve rather different splits. As a result, citizens who hold similar views on one issue are likely to hold divergent views on another—or no views at all. How this general pattern bears on the way party coalitions are formed during elections and in Congress is not only complex but rather obscure; it is reasonable to suppose, however, that the general effect is to lessen the severity of any particular electoral and legislative conflict. If you think that among your opponents in today's contest are some potential allies for tomorrow's, you are likely to be conciliatory and unlikely to press extreme demands that could eliminate the possibility of winning recruits from the other side for a new contest another day.

Obviously, unless attitudes are highly polarized, it is impossible to divide a population into two like-minded collections of people. No matter what standard is used for dividing people, within each of any two categories there will be many conflicting views. Given the existence of a two-party system, it follows that in the absence of high polarization, each of the two parties can hope to win only by constructing an electoral coalition made up of people whose views coincide on some questions but diverge on others. This is exactly what happens most of the time in the United States. As long as (1) political attitudes are not polarized, and (2) only two major parties exist, there can be no escape from two parties with diverse followings.

Although we have surveys and election studies for only the past quarter-century, there is substantial reason for thinking that low polarization has been the usual condition of American politics, and that the reasons for low polarization have been about the same in the past as they are now: large socioeconomic groups have generally had diverse political attitudes, and persons who agree on one question disagree on others.

There have been historical fluctuations; undoubtedly the tide of polarization ebbs and flows. But extreme polarization is rare in American politics, and it has never persisted over long periods. Most of the time political life displays the characteristics of moderate conflict that have been examined in the last two chapters. Whether the pattern of crosscutting cleavages and relatively low polarization will prevail in the future depends on the extent to which the American polyarchy is able to deal effectively in the 1970s and 1980s with the issues that began to fragment American cohesion in the 1960s.

SUMMARY   Political conflicts and disagreements in the United States do not ordinarily polarize Americans into two highly antagonistic camps. Nor are Americans fragmented into numerous groups too hostile to act in concert. Two characteristics of the pattern of cleavages stimulate efforts toward conciliation and compromise and weaken pressures toward fragmentation or polarization:

1. Differences in political attitudes, actions, and loyalties are not highly related to

☐ Regional differences, either in Congress or in the population at large. Factors reducing regional cleavages include
  a. The absence of strong regional subcultures
  b. Geographical mobility of Americans
  c. Internal diversity within regions
  d. The socioeconomic nature of regional conflicts
☐ Socioeconomic differences, as reflected by
  a. Occupations
  b. Social classes
  c. Racial, ethnic, and religious differences

2. Differences in political attitudes and loyalties are not highly interrelated among themselves. Consequently, polarization of politics along ideological lines is held in check.

☐ The prevailing democratic ideology tends to unite, not divide Americans
☐ Liberal and conservative ideologies have generally not produced sharp splits because
  a. Both are rather vague
  b. Both contain several different dimensions
  c. The tendency to interpret politics according to complex, internally consistent schemes for understanding and evaluating the world—ideological thinking—is relatively rare
☐ However, there is evidence that ideological thinking has increased among Americans since 1964 as a result of
  a. The decade of intense conflict that began in 1964 and ended with the fall of Richard Nixon in 1974
  b. The rapid rise in the educational level of the voting population

25 PATTERNS OF SEVERE CONFLICT IN AMERICAN POLITICS

It is often supposed, not only by foreigners but by Americans themselves, that except for the Civil War the American political system has managed to avoid severe conflicts. Americans, it is often said, are a moderate people; they display their moderation even in their conflicts, most of all in their political conflicts. How much truth does this view contain?

Not much. The weight of historical evidence offers solid support to the following proposition: from the very first years under the new Constitution, American political life has undergone *about once every generation* a conflict over national politics of *extreme severity*.

THE RECURRENCE OF INTENSE CONFLICT

To suggest the evidence for this proposition, let me review some familiar historical episodes.[1] Before the Constitution had completed its first decade, the Alien and Sedition Acts (1798) threatened the very existence of any organized political opposition by making it possible to jail or deport critics of the federal government. These acts were challenged by the legislatures of Kentucky (1798) and Virginia (1799) in resolutions that hinted for the first time (but definitely not the last) that a state government might deliberately refuse to enforce a federal law which its legislators held to be unconstitutional. The specters raised by the Alien and Sedition Acts on the one side, and by the Kentucky and Virginia resolutions on the other, were temporarily banished

---

1. This section draws heavily on my essay "The American Oppositions: Affirmation and Denial," in Dahl, *Political Oppositions In Western Democracies* (New Haven, Conn.: Yale University Press, 1966).

by Jefferson's election to the presidency, in what he called "the Revolution of 1800."

Within hardly more than another decade, New England Federalists, driven to desperation by the foreign trade embargo policies enforced by the Democratic-Republicans, assembled at Hartford (December, 1814) in a convention that not only adopted a set of resolutions calling for extensive constitutional changes but issued a report asserting among other things that "in cases of deliberate, dangerous, and palpable infraction of the Constitution, affecting the sovereignty of a State and liberties of the people; it is not only the right but the duty of such a State to *interpose* its authority for their protection, in the manner best calculated to secure that end."[2]

Less than twenty years later the United States approached civil war over the tariff. In 1828, the legislature of South Carolina adopted a set of eight resolutions that labeled the newly passed "Tariff of Abominations" (which hit cotton exporters with what seemed to them undue harshness) unconstitutional, oppressive, and unjust. In an accompanying document written by John C. Calhoun the South Carolina legislature espoused the view that in such cases a single state might 'nullify' an unconstitutional law (1828). Four years later when the South Carolinians were still chafing under the protective tariff, a convention called by the state legislature adopted an ordinance that 'nullified' the tariff acts of 1828 and 1832. It prohibited the collection of import duties within the state. And it asserted that the use of force by the federal government could be cause for secession. The state legislature passed laws to enforce the ordinance, to raise a military force, and to appropriate funds for arms. President Jackson thereupon sought and gained from Congress the legal authority to enforce the tariff laws, by military means, if necessary. A compromise tariff was worked out in Congress, South Carolina rescinded her Ordinance of Nullification, and civil war was avoided—or rather postponed for thirty years.

In the 1840s European immigration, chiefly from Ireland and Germany, greatly increased. A nativistic, antiforeign, anti-Catholic, superpatriotic reaction began to set in. In the early 1850s, political tickets consisting of antiforeign candidates appeared in New York, Pennsylvania, and New Jersey. Soon a party began organizing secretly; it called itself the American Party. (Because its members refused to divulge their secrets, their enemies called them Know Nothings.) Although the party showed some promise of replacing the Whig Party, as it turned out, the life of the American Party was brief and unsuccessful, for it was consumed in the struggle over slavery. Had it prospered, the whole course of American history would have been different.

---

2. Richard B. Morris, *Encyclopedia of American History* (New York: Harper, 1953), p. 153.

The middle years of the century were mainly occupied, however, with various aspects of the controversy over slavery, particularly whether slavery should be permitted in the great unsettled areas of the West. This was a question that touched the most sensitive interests of Northerners and Southerners. (How this conflict polarized the country will be examined in Chapter 27.) Finally, as everyone knows, the issue no longer could be contained; and for four terrible years men died of wounds and disease to settle the question—or so it was supposed.

But the issue of slavery was settled only in part by the Civil War: slavery was abolished, to be sure, but the freed blacks were not long permitted to enjoy equal political rights—to say nothing of economic, educational, or social privileges. Ten years after the surrender at Appomattox, the issue of Reconstruction in the election of 1876 brought the country to the verge of another civil war. But as so often happened before and after, the outcome was compromise rather than war—a compromise that began the restoration of white supremacy throughout the South and thus adjourned the whole problem of effective citizenship for blacks until the middle of the present century.

This adjournment allowed economic questions to take over during the last third of the century. Discontented farmers and urban workers formed a pool of recurring opposition to the policies of a national government that responded less and less to their demands than to those of the new men of business, industry, and finance. Out of economic dissatisfaction, radical and reformist movements developed: Socialist Labor, the Greenback Party, the Farmers' Alliance, Populism, the Socialist Party, the IWW ("Wobblies"). The trade union movement also had its turbulent beginnings: the Knights of Labor, the AFL, the railway unions. Strikes, lockouts, and protest meetings frequently led to marked violence.[3]

In the presidential elections of 1896, Democrats and Populists had jointly nominated as their candidate William Jennings Bryan, a man of primitive intellect and beguiling eloquence. In his simple and confused protests against the "domination of Eastern capital," Bryan evoked support among a considerable number of farmers and some urban workers. He was defeated by McKinley after a campaign period of unusually high tension.[4]

---

3. For example, in 1886 during a demonstration near the McCormick Reaper Works in Chicago, six strikers were killed by the police and many more were wounded. The next day two thousand persons attended a protest meeting in Haymarket Square; policemen ordered the meeting to disperse; a bomb was thrown, killing a policeman; in the ensuing battle, seven more policemen and four workers were killed, sixty policemen and fifty workers were wounded. Six men who had addressed the meeting were sentenced to death; four were hanged the following year.

In 1894, Grover Cleveland, the first Democrat elected to the presidency since 1856, then in his second term as president, called out federal troops in order to break a great nationwide strike of railway workers against the Pullman Company.

4. Bryan won 47 percent of the two-party vote and carried twenty-one states. All of them, however, were agricultural states of the South, Midwest, and West.

The 1930s witnessed the Great Depression, mass unemployment, extensive discontent, the election of the third Democratic president since the Civil War, new outbreaks of violence, the rise of quasi-democratic or anti-democratic political movements on both right and left, and extensive changes in national policies—changes that from 1935 onward were fought with increasing bitterness. Driven to extreme measures by a Supreme Court dominated by conservatives who steadily rejected the major items of the New Deal as unconstitutional, President Roosevelt in 1937 even tried to 'pack' the Court. It was his first important move that proved unpopular, and it did not succeed. From about 1937 until the bombing of Pearl Harbor in 1941, political leaders were bitterly divided over the question whether it was better to meet threats of military aggression by 'isolation' or 'intervention.'

Less than thirty years later a new crisis began to develop, one of the most serious in the nation's history. This new test of the political system, beginning about 1964 and ending a decade later, will be discussed in the next chapter.

Whoever supposes, then, that American politics has been nothing more than an ongoing consensus, a sort of national Rotary Club luncheon, has not sufficiently reflected on the regularity of intense conflict, crisis, and violence in American history.

FACTORS INVOLVED IN SEVERE CONFLICTS

Like the massive hurricanes that sweep in from the Atlantic, the brief, violent, and devastating tornadoes of the Middle West, or the earthquakes along the West Coast, great conflicts in American political life are long remembered by the survivors, much discussed, and imperfectly understood. Yet it is possible to discern some elements in the pattern.

If we take as our point of departure a period of moderate conflict that adheres to the pattern described in the last chapter, then the development of a severe conflict is marked by the kinds of shifts suggested in the summary preceding Table 23.1 on page 344. Four factors are involved in intensifying political conflict.

Divergence of Attitudes

Leaders of rival coalitions diverge more and more in their attitudes on key political questions. This growing divergence may come about in a variety of ways:

☐ Older leaders may change their original views. This is probably the least likely development.
☐ Previous issues that would have divided leaders had they been more significant earlier—and perhaps did divide them at times—may become much more urgent than before.

☐ New issues emerge on which the views of leaders had not previously crystallized.

☐ Older leaders may be replaced by newer leaders with different views. For example, the generation of the Revolution and the Constitutional Convention virtually disappeared from active political life after Madison's second term, and a whole new generation—John Quincy Adams, Clay, Calhoun, Jackson, Van Buren, Webster—took its place. This new generation had in turn largely disappeared by the 1850s, when still another generation, that of Lincoln and Douglas, took over.

Even when the views of political leaders are known, it is difficult to speak with confidence about the development of 'public opinion' in a severe conflict. The most reasonable assumption is, however, that the 'public' responds to the divisive issue slowly and in diverse ways. At one extreme many people remain untouched even at the peak of tension (or right up to the time when political conflict turns into organized slaughter from which even the untouched cannot escape—as happened in 1861). Thus a recent examination of "letters from the 1850s and 1860s, which had been preserved by old families in the various attics of a small Ohio community" revealed that "no references to abolition were ever found in any of the letters"![5]

At the other extreme, the most politically active citizens are heavily involved. Indeed, it is mainly the activists who determine the course of the conflict; severe conflict means a growing intensity of conflicting views among the activists; it is they who settle or fail to settle a dispute.

What of the in-between group, the ordinary voters? For the most part they intervene only in one way: by voting. But that one way can be important. Although most voters continue to vote their traditional party loyalties, without regard to the course of a dispute that seems to be polarizing the country, some do change. Ironically, they may change for reasons that have nothing to do with the conflict: a farmer in 1860 might have voted against the Democrats because crops were poor or prices were low and he felt that the Democrats were responsible because they had held the presidency. The perception the ordinary voter has of what is at stake when *he* or *she* votes need not have much to do with what political leaders think is at stake. Nonetheless, political leaders do interpret the election returns; they must perforce interpret an election in terms of their own perspectives, which may not be those of the voter. Hence political leaders often interpret an election as favoring or disapproving this or that policy. As a result their own enthusiasm for one alternative may wax or wane. In politics nothing succeeds like success.

---

5. Converse, "Nature of Belief Systems," in Apter, *Ideology and Discontent*, pp. 206–261, quote on p. 251.

Moreover, whatever the voters may intend, an election has consequences for the balance of power among the contesting groups. One
party, for example, may sweep the Congress and the presidency, while
the other is reduced to a legislative minority. Probably we shall never
know much about what was in the minds of voters when they went to
the polls in 1860. But, as we shall see in Chapter 27, the consequence
of their votes was to reduce the voices for Southern slaveholders to a
clear minority in Congress, and to confront that minority with a president who would not yield on the key issue of whether slavery was to be
allowed in the territories. The message of the election was, then, that
slaveowners were a political minority without enough safe allies in the
rest of the country; that they would remain forever a minority; further-
more, that they would henceforth be a diminishing minority. Thus,
though most voters North and South almost certainly did not intend it,
the indirect consequence of the election was to encourage Southern
leaders to embark on the fatal course that led to secession and civil
war.

High Stakes

In all the conflicts described at the beginning of this chapter, the
stakes were high (or seemed to be high, which amounts to the same
thing) for one side or both. Often a conflict was interpreted by one side
or the other as allowing no satisfactory compromise because gains by
one side entailed losses by the other. This was the case, for example, in
the tariff dispute of 1828 to 1832, discussed earlier in this chapter,
when Southern leaders argued that any protective tariff imposed for the
benefit of Northern industry caused a corresponding loss to Southern
exporters of cotton. In fact, in each of the severe conflicts mentioned
above, leaders on one side—and sometimes on both sides—believed
that the way of life to which they and their constituents were attached
was seriously threatened by the goals pursued by their opponents.
Whether or not their views were 'rational' or even factually correct is
irrelevant: people hate and fight no less if what they believe to be true
happens to be false.

Each of these severe conflicts could also be interpreted as a situation in which leaders of groups whose way of life was supported by the
status quo now saw themselves threatened at the foundations by the
aspirations and policies of other groups whose expanding influence, if
unchecked, would destroy or at the very least seriously impair their stake
in the society. At the outset of a conflict, the 'conservative' groups may
have enjoyed enough influence with national policy-makers—the president, the Congress, and the Supreme Court—to insure their own protection, even if insurance against defeat required vigilance and unremit-
ting struggle. But as these leaders began to believe that their influence

Table 25.1 The Stakes of Conflict: Ways of Life	Spokesmen for the Following Groups or Strata:	Were Perceived by Leaders of the Following Groups or Strata as Threatening Their Way of Life:	Thus Producing Severe Political Conflict and These Crises:
	Small farmers, Southern planters, Democratic-Republicans	New England commercial interests, Federalist 'aristocracy'	1798–9: Alien and Sedition Acts; Va. and Ky. Resolutions
	Northern and Western whites; manufacturers; Western farmers; abolitionists	Southern whites	1828–32: Tariff, So. Car. Nullification 1840–60: Slavery in the territories 1860–77: Civil War and Reconstruction
	Immigrants, Catholics, Irish, Germans	Native Protestants	1850–60: Know-Nothingism
	Farmers and urban laborers	Businessmen, bankers	1880–1900: new parties, Greenback, Socialist, etc.; strikes, violence 1892–6: Populism as major force 1933–7: New Deal
	Southern blacks	Southern whites	1865–75: Reconstruction 1954–present: Integration, civil rights, violence
	Northern blacks	Northern urban whites	1960s–present: Equal opportunities, violence— Harlem, Rochester, Chicago, Los Angeles, etc.

was diminishing and that soon they might be unable to stem the tide, they more and more perceived their opponents as implacable enemies who must be destroyed lest they be destroyers.

How the conflicts described fit this interpretation is shown in Table 25.1.

From Crosscutting to Cumulative Cleavages

As a conflict intensifies, ties which have held the politically active groups together and made it relatively easy for them to negotiate disputes begin to snap; their views have less and less in common. As social and ideological ties begin to snap and crosscutting cleavages diminish, great fractures begin to separate the country, or at any rate the most active and articulate elements in the political life of the country. As we saw in Chapter 23, if there is a single giant fracture, as the issue of slavery in the territories became before the Civil War, then we may speak of a growing polarization of the nation as the country is divided into two ever more hostile camps and as neutrals and moderates begin scrambling to clear out of the no-man's-land between them. If there are several fractures, then we speak of *fragmentation.* In the historic crises in this country, what appears to be polarization was probably accompanied by some fragmentation.

In the next chapter (26) we shall explore a decade of conflict leading to fragmentation, the period from 1964 to 1974. In Chapter 27, we shall examine the polarization that led to the Civil War.

AMERICAN POLITICAL INSTITUTIONS AS MANAGERS OF CONFLICT

How do political institutions—the fourth factor in our model of conflict outlined in Table 23.1—interact with the other three factors? In times of *moderate* conflict, American political institutions encourage compromise, decisions by consensus, and piecemeal changes. But what is the effect of the political institutions when conflict is more intense?

Even in the presence of increasingly severe conflict, the tendency of the political institutions is to handle it along the same lines as moderate conflict. American political institutions encourage political leaders to respond to severe conflicts in several ways:

1. By forming a new political coalition—usually involving a realignment of the major parties—that can overpower the opposition. But this, as we shall see, is a difficult solution.
2. By incremental measures that may not deal with the central issue.
3. By lasting compromises that remove the issue from serious political conflict.

Overpowering the Opposition

A severe conflict is sometimes moderated or even terminated when one political coalition gains enough power to overcome the resistance of its opponents. Instead of compromising, the winning coalition enacts its policies despite the opposition of the defeated coalition. If the opposition fights back, as it is likely to do, it finds itself too weak to prevail. Unable to reverse the main direction of policy imposed by the winning coalition, the opposition may in time accept the major policies enacted by the winners and settle down to bargaining for step-by-step adjustments; thus severe conflict gives way to a period of moderate conflict.

Probably the only effective way in American politics for one coalition significantly to reduce the bargaining power of an enemy coalition is to turn it into a visible and even isolated political minority by defeating it in national elections. However, there are a large number of positions where an embattled minority, unable to win the presidency or a majority in either house of Congress, can dig in and successfully continue to challenge the policies of the majority coalition. These include the Supreme Court, administrative agencies, congressional committees, and state and local governments. Thus a single electoral victory is ordinarily not enough, particularly if the contest is close. The victories of the winning coalition may have to be large, thus visibly demonstrating the weakness of the opposition; and may have to be repeated in a series of presidential and congressional elections, thus demonstrating for all to see that the minority coalition has little chance of regaining its power and must come to terms with the victors.

In at least three instances, severe conflicts seem to have been moderated or terminated in this way:

1. Democratic-Republicans overwhelmed Federalists in the elections of 1800 and continued to do so for a generation. By 1814 when the Federalists at the Hartford Convention talked disunion, their leaders gained little national support. After 1814 Federalism disappeared as an effective political movement, though old Federalist leaders constituted a kind of feeble opposition until they died or despaired.[6]
2. From the midterm elections of 1894 onward, and particularly after the presidential election of 1896 when Republicans overwhelmed the coalition of Democrats and Populists that supported William Jennings Bryan, a severe conflict over economic policies was thereby moderated (and postponed).
3. After 1932 when elections temporarily destroyed the power of the Republican coalition centered on the policies of business, it became possible for most of the New Deal proposals of FDR to be enacted. By the time the Republican opposition was able to regroup, it could no longer *undo* the New Deal except in minor ways. However, it entered into a coalition with Southern Democrats, which by bargaining in Congress impeded or prevented further reforms until the power of both the Republicans and the Southern Democrats was temporarily smashed by the presidential and congressional elections of 1964.

Yet elections are often indecisive; neither Truman's re-election in 1948 nor Kennedy's election in 1960 enabled the victorious president to enact the major policies he and his party had advocated in the campaign, despite the fact that both presidents had Democratic majorities

---

6. Shaw Livermore, Jr., *The Twilight of Federalism, The Disintegration of the Federalist Party, 1815–1830* (Princeton, N.J.: Princeton University Press, 1962).

in Congress. Truman presented to Congress an extensive 'Fair Deal' program involving a number of social reforms. But only a few of these had been enacted when he went out of office.[7] Why are elections so infrequently decisive? Why, people often ask, don't elections settle things one way or the other? Why is it so difficult for a president and Congress ostensibly of the same party to terminate a severe conflict by overriding the objections of their opponents, carrying through their legislative program, and letting the country decide at the next election whether it likes the changes or disapproves of them?

By now it must be clear that American political institutions were never designed to operate in this fashion; nor do they. The pattern of partitioned power, which has been carried about as far in the United States as in any polyarchy in the world, simply prevents elections from being decisive except under the most extraordinary circumstances. Moreover, because Americans predominantly believe in the desirability of partitioning power, and, in particular, approve of the main institutional arrangements that partition power and authority in the United States, there is little support for changes that might make elections more decisive.

Consequently, while a severe conflict is sometimes terminated by an overwhelming victory for one side in a congressional and presidential election, the American political system and American beliefs make this solution somewhat difficult and uncommon.

Incremental Changes

American political institutions are excellently designed for making incremental, or piecemeal, changes. But they also foster delay in coming to grips with questions that threaten severe conflict. It is true that delay may provide precious time during which a seemingly severe problem may change its shape, become more manageable, even disappear. But postponement may also prevent leaders from facing a problem squarely and searching for decisive solutions—solutions that may be forced upon them many years later when they can no longer delay.

Policies of economic reform that go much beyond small piecemeal changes sometimes take decades or even generations to accomplish. The income tax illustrates the point. In 1892 the Democrats won the presidency and sufficient majorities in Congress to pass an income tax law. The Supreme Court, rightly foreseeing that the income tax could be the foundation for redistribution at the expense of the rich, struck it

---

7. Congress passed legislation providing for housing and slum clearance and an expansion of Social Security coverage. It failed to pass Fair Deal proposals for federal aid to education, health insurance, a new Department of Health, Education, and Welfare, repeal of the Taft-Hartley Act, a reorganized farm plan providing production payments to farmers, a fair employment practices commission, and elimination of the poll tax. Most of these proposals have since been enacted, mainly under President Lyndon Johnson.

down as unconstitutional. It required sixteen years and the Sixteenth Amendment to make it possible for Congress to enact an income tax again. The regulation of child labor, as we saw in Chapter 17, was held up for a generation by a Supreme Court unwilling to yield to Congress and the president. In 1948, President Truman, acting on recommendations from his advisory committee on civil rights, recommended federal legislation against lynching, the poll tax, segregation in public transportation, and discrimination in employment. Although limited civil rights legislation was passed in 1957 and 1960, no major legislation on civil rights cleared Congress until 1964, almost two decades after President Truman's recommendations. Passage of American welfare and social security laws has lagged behind the enactment of comparable laws in most European democracies by one to several generations. A national medical care program has been advocated for generations. In 1945, President Truman proposed to Congress a comprehensive medical insurance program for persons of all ages. The first law establishing a national system of medical insurance was not enacted until 1965, and it was restricted to the elderly.

Compromise

The existence of innumerable fortified positions from which an embattled but well-organized minority can fight off and wear down an attack, combined with the absence of any *single* rule for making legitimate decisions on which the political activists are agreed, means that it is difficult to terminate a conflict by the clear-cut victory of one side over another. Hence severe conflicts are sometimes handled by reaching a compromise. Occasionally the result is a long-lasting compromise. Two of the most enduring compromises of this kind in American history involved Afro-Americans. Both sought to eliminate the black presence in the society as a source of severe conflict among whites. Both succeeded in doing so for long periods. Both were at the expense of the blacks. And by present-day standards in all civilized countries, both were unjust. One dealt with the blacks as slaves, the other with blacks as freed slaves.

The first was the Missouri Compromise of 1820. By providing that slavery would be permitted south but not north of latitude 36°30′ across the vast territory acquired in the Louisiana Purchase, it promised to maintain a balance between the numbers of free and slave states and thereby preserve to each side a veto over future national policies. This compromise kept the problem of slavery in the territories and the future of slavery itself within manageable bounds for thirty years. Then the new land acquired as a result of the Mexican war added territories not covered by the old compromise and, as we shall see in Chapter 27, triggered the decade of severe conflict that culminated in the Civil War.

The second great compromise was arrived at in 1877, after the long crisis produced by the contested presidential election of 1876. We shall also return to it in Chapter 27. Briefly, however, the effect of this settlement was to bury Reconstruction and to permit white Southerners to restore white supremacy. Once again the fate of blacks was removed as a source of severe conflict—once again by whites at black expense. This shameful compromise endured for seventy years. The beginning of the end for the Compromise of 1877 was the legislation on civil rights and employment introduced by President Truman. His proposals split the Democratic party and strengthened the coalition of Southern Democrats and Northern Republicans in Congress; hence it was not until the passage of the Civil Rights Acts of 1964 and 1965 that the Compromise of 1877 finally came to an end.

These two experiences say something about the limits of compromise. *First,* there are moral limits; by the standards of the contemporary civilized world, both of our great national compromises went beyond these limits. *Second,* it is obvious that one necessary condition for any such compromise is that the contestants can somehow discover an alternative that vastly reduces the threat from the other side, particularly by eliminating or markedly decreasing the dangers to the way of life defended by one or more contestants. Such a solution may not exist, or —what amounts to much the same thing—it may not be discovered. The Compromises of 1820 and 1877 were possible only because Afro-Americans had no voice in arranging them. If those who might have spoken for the slaves had enjoyed the same veto power over national policies that spokesmen for slaveholders possessed until 1860, the Compromise of 1820 would have been impossible. If the freed blacks had been as influential in 1877 as white Southerners, that compromise too would have been impossible.

A Tentative Conclusion

To make the point once more, the system encourages incremental changes; it discourages comprehensive change. It facilitates the negotiation of moderate conflicts. The consequences of this are twofold and somewhat paradoxical. The system encourages presidents who wish to be decisive to draw on their reservoir of powers that lie outside the control of Congress or Court. As we saw in Chapter 13, in these domains—most visibly in foreign policy—the president is more and more his own master, and the normal processes are more and more displaced by executive decision. Yet side by side with presidential decisiveness in these areas, there are other areas where the system operates to prevent decisive action. Large reforms that in other countries have been enacted in a single session of parliament right after a single election must in the United States await many elections and many sessions of Congress.

But what is the effect of American political institutions on severe conflict? Do they intensify conflict by preventing early, if drastic, changes in policies? Do they prolong and aggravate severe conflict? Although the evidence we have examined in this chapter lends itself to this interpretation, it also allows other arguments. Yet it would be hard to deny that the danger is there.

POSSIBLE CONSEQUENCES OF SEVERE CONFLICT: POLITICAL INTEGRATION, ALIENATION, CIVIL WAR

The Constitutional Convention, we saw, did not decide whether the United States was to be an aristocracy or a polyarchy. That decision was made by the Americans who came after, who affirmed their commitments to a polyarchy rather than to a more aristocratic republic.

The outcome depended upon widespread acceptance among Americans of the desirability of a polyarchy as a system of government for Americans, and on the desirability of certain procedures for arriving at political decisions—procedures, in the case of Americans, largely but not wholly fixed by the Constitution.

Severe and prolonged conflict may cause one or another of the antagonists to reject the system itself. If rejecting the system produces nothing more than apathy, the structure may nonetheless survive. But if rejection leads to revolution or civil war, the structure may be destroyed. The twentieth century has seen this happen with the rise of Mussolini in Italy in the 1920s; Hitler's rise to power in Germany in the early 1930s; and Franco's military overthrow of the Spanish republic between 1935 and 1938. In each of these cases the costs of conflict, rejection, and revolution were staggering.

Each of the conflicts mentioned at the beginning of this chapter and recapitulated in Table 25.1, endangered the solution that Americans had arrived at by about 1800: a polyarchy operating within the institutional and procedural limits set by the Constitution. One of these conflicts led to civil war, and in Chapter 27 we shall try to understand how this came about. The others subsided in time. The fact that they were finally handled peacefully probably made Americans even more attached to their institutions. Yet some alienation, some rejection of the American polyarchy occurred side by side with political integration. In the early years, the victory of the small farmers doubtless sped their political integration and strengthened their loyalty to the republic. Yet the other side of the coin is that many of the defeated New England Federalists rejected it; the importance of their rejection was diminished only by the fact that they were few in numbers. Many of them remained alienated from the more democratic aspects of polyarchy, hostile to the very idea of democracy and wide sharing of power.[8] But they died out and were replaced by a younger generation with more flexible notions.

The conflict between Northerners and Westerners on the one side, and Southern slaveholders on the other, was accompanied in its last stages by an increasing rejection of the American polyarchy by the advocates of slavocracy. The rejection was long lasting: the full political integration of the South into a polyarchy with universal suffrage was retarded for a century after the Civil War by the refusal of Southern whites to concede political equality to black citizens. Only now, and painfully, is that long alienation from democracy crumbling.

The conflict between immigrants and native Protestants never expanded politically beyond the limits of the Know-Nothing Party. Hostilities remained, however, and often had political consequences. For 170 years no person not of Anglo-Saxon Protestant stock was elected president. The parties feared even to nominate presidential candidates of immigrant origins or of the Catholic faith. In 1928 the Catholicism of Democratic candidate Alfred E. Smith was a factor in his defeat. No Catholic was elected president until 1960. Despite all this, the immigrants and their children, who could easily have remained a large politically unintegrated element in the population, were quickly absorbed into the political system and soon came to accept the ideology and institutions of the American polyarchy. Indeed, in few countries in the world have so many people been so fully integrated into a polyarchy in so short a time. Thus the conflict between immigrants and native Protestants never erupted on a nationwide scale; though it persisted, it was contained.

The conflict between labor and capital—to use two vague labels—led to the alienation of one group or the other in many countries. Nearly everywhere in Europe the rapid expansion of the working classes posed a severe problem of political integration. Yet in following another route, the American working classes were politically integrated into the American polyarchy; and in the process their economic antagonists, the business interests, were not permanently alienated. This development took a long time, however, and was often disturbed by sharp conflict. We shall return to it in Chapter 29.

The failure of white Americans to allow equal political, economic, educational, and social opportunities to black Americans produced political apathy, hopelessness, and indifference among many blacks. As we shall see in the next chapter, this mood changed in the mid-1960s to open anger, violence, and rioting. But while black militancy increased, so did alienation. Thus the peaceful political, social, and eco-

8. Alexis de Tocqueville observed that the rich hold a "hearty dislike of the democratic institutions of their country," *Democracy in America,* vol. 1 (New York: Vintage Books, 1955), pp. 186–187.

nomic integration of the black American remains perhaps the greatest internal problem of our time.

Conflicts and rejection of polyarchy ebb and flow in American political life. For a time moderate conflicts prevail. Then the tides of antagonism begin to surge, and political conflict grows more deadly. When by one means or another the antagonisms diminish, the pattern of moderate conflict reappears. But it, too, is impermanent. The high tide of conflict has almost always risen within the span of about one generation.

SUMMARY 1. Although crosscutting cleavages and moderate conflict are the normal pattern of American politics, political life in the United States has undergone a conflict over national policies of extreme severity about once every generation.

2. The development of a severe conflict is marked by the kinds of changes outlined in Table 23.1 on page 345.

□ *Divergence of attitudes:* Leaders of rival coalitions diverge more and more in their attitudes on key political questions. This change may come about as:

Older leaders change their original views.

Previous issues become divisive as they become more urgent than before.

New issues emerge.

Older leaders are replaced by newer leaders with different views.

□ *High stakes.* The outcome of the conflict is increasingly seen as involving very high stakes, perhaps even a way of life, for a large segment of the country.

□ *From crosscutting to cumulative cleavages:* As conflicts accumulate along one or two major splits, the country is increasingly polarized or fragmented into enemy camps.

3. American political institutions tend to handle severe conflicts along the same lines as moderate conflicts. The result may be to aggravate rather than to reduce the conflict. American institutions encourage political leaders to respond to conflicts by:

□ forming a new political coalition that can overpower the opposition. But the institutions, practices, and beliefs in extreme partitioning of power and authority make this rare and difficult.

□ incremental or small-scale changes that postpone comprehensive change. Thus deeper causes of severe conflict may be dealt with too slowly, or not at all.

□ securing long-lasting compromises that remove the issue from serious political conflict. But in some situations, such compromises may be impossible, morally unacceptable, or may sow the seeds of future discontent.

4. Severe conflicts involving extensive polarization or fragmentation may lead to greater political integration and support on the part of some of the contestants, apathy or alienation among others, and, in the extreme case, the possibility of civil war.

26 FRAGMENTATION
AMID SEVERE CONFLICT: 1964–1974

For the greater part of the decade before the bicentennial year 1976, the American polyarchy was rent by political conflict. First the country was torn by the long-standing, familiar unsolved question of race. Then attitudes diverged on another issue, the Vietnam war. This issue cut across all the usual lines of division.

These disagreements generated conflicts that overran the normal political processes. They led not only to unconventional, though perfectly legal, activity but also to violence, riots, takeovers of buildings, illegal wiretapping and surveillance, and even the shooting down of unarmed demonstrators. Two presidents, fearful of provoking violence and disruption by their public appearances, virtually retreated to safe sanctuaries: the White House, military bases, and heavily guarded presidential retreats.

Although the issue of race threatened to polarize the country along racial lines, while the issue of Vietnam divided along ideological lines, these issues did cut across one another to some extent. What was more important, Vietnam cut across social class, region, ethnic group, religion, education, age, and party loyalty. The strength and persistence of these crosscutting cleavages helped to prevent full-scale polarization, but they could not wholly prevent a certain amount of fragmentation of the political parties, the Democratic party in particular. As the Vietnam war receded, the domestic conflict it had brought about also receded, leaving behind a trail of wreckage.

**FROM SURFACE
CONSENSUS
TO INTENSE
CONFLICT**

As Lyndon Johnson swamped Barry Goldwater in the presidential election of 1964, the Democrats also swept the congressional elections. An observer might reasonably have conjectured that 'normal' politics, marked by crosscutting cleavages, low polarization, and moderate conflict, lay ahead. Because Johnson had a liking for compromise and a talent for achieving it that bordered on genius, a politics of consensus seemed in the offing. Johnson was, in fact, able to bring about a significant part of his program of reform, intended to achieve what he was fond of calling the Great Society, thanks to his keen understanding of Congress, his exceptional capacity for persuasion and manipulation, and a larger majority in the House than any Democratic president since Franklin Roosevelt in 1936.

Yet events were moving the United States toward internal conflicts of such great intensity that they would make the politics of compromise and consensus unworkable, undermine his political support, and finally destroy his presidency.

Divergence of Views

In the mid-sixties, Johnson's 'consensus' was torn apart by unrest arising among these groups: blacks in the urban ghettos, students in colleges and universities, and opponents of the Vietnam war.

Unrest among blacks. Chapters 7 and 10 pointed out that severe discrimination against racial minorities had profoundly affected the shape and character of the American polyarchy, and the pattern of its conflicts and compromises. In effect, Americans created a dual political system —polyarchy for whites, hegemony by whites over Southern blacks. In other chapters we have observed some of the political forms of this dual system. In the next chapter, we shall see how it was that after the Civil War, the Reconstruction policy, which might have eliminated the dual system, failed. That failure left unresolved within American society a flat contradiction between racial inequality and the doctrines of freedom, equality, and democracy that constitute the heart of the American public ideology.

In 1964, under the leadership of President Lyndon Johnson, who was from a state (Texas) with a Southern outlook, a bipartisan majority in Congress overcame the bitter and prolonged resistance of Southern congressmen and passed the most far-reaching civil rights legislation since Reconstruction. For the first time in the nation's history a filibuster against civil rights legislation was broken in the Senate. The skillful effort of Southern senators to use this old practice of unlimited debate to delay a vote on the legislation indefinitely—and thus finally to defeat it—which had always succeeded before was overcome after fifty-seven days of debate by a vote of 71–29, four votes more than the two-thirds required under Senate rules.[1]

The following year a Voting Rights Act was passed, again after breaking a Southern filibuster. Among other key provisions, the Civil Rights Act of 1964 and the Voting Rights Act of 1965 protected the rights of Southern blacks to engage in politics.[2] In states where terror and even death had for generations kept blacks from registering and voting, much less running for office, they now began to enter political life. By 1975 in all the eleven states of the old Confederacy there were 1500 black officials, including 76 mayors. White politicians now actively sought black votes. Some who had been in the forefront of opposition to integration and civil rights, like Governor George Wallace of Alabama, changed both their rhetoric and their political strategy in order to gain support from black voters. Thus when President Johnson signed the Civil Rights Act of 1964 on July 6, his action symbolized the beginning of the end for the old dual system of polyarchy for whites and hegemony for blacks.

But the new laws by no means put an end to racial discrimination or to the consequences of past discrimination. In the North, blacks already possessed the political rights and many other civil rights now extended to Southern blacks. Among Northern ghetto blacks, discontent stemmed from other causes: bad housing, police brutality, street crime, discrimination in employment, unsatisfactory schools, discriminatory treatment by banks, merchants, and so on.[3]

In the very month that the Civil Rights Act of 1964 became law, riots broke out in Harlem. They soon followed in Rochester and other cities. In 1965, a riot involving enormous property destruction occurred in the Watts area of Los Angeles; at the same time, disorders also broke out in Chicago. Though some blacks were killed and despite a widespread fear among urban whites, rioters did not take the lives of whites.[4] In 1966, there were riots in Chicago, Cleveland, Jacksonville, Florida, New York City, and South Bend, Indiana. In 1967 disorders erupted in 67 cities, the worst outbreaks in Newark and Detroit. "By the end of August 1967 the American public had been treated to a month's display of looting, arson, and property damage on their television

---

1. The rule has since been changed to require 60 percent of the entire Senate (i.e., 60 votes) to end debate.

2. In 1975, the Voting Rights Act was extended for seven years and broadened to include Spanish-speaking citizens and other 'language minorities.'

3. See, for example, Peter H. Rossi, Richard A. Berk, and Bettye K. Eidson, *The Roots of Urban Discontent* (New York: John Wiley, 1974); Howard Schuman and Shirley Hatchett, *Black Racial Attitudes* (Ann Arbor, Mich.: Survey Research Center, 1974); Jerome H. Skolnick, *The Politics of Protest,* A Staff Report to the National Commission on the Causes and Prevention of Violence (Washington D.C.: Government Printing Office, 1969), Ch. 4.

4. See Richard Maxwell Brown, "Historical Patterns of Violence in America," in Hugh Davis Graham and Ted Robert Gurr, *Violence in America* (Washington: Government Printing Office, 1969), p. 41.

screens, centering mainly around the events of Newark and Detroit."[5] In 1968 great riots—once again brought by television into the living rooms of white Americans—occurred in Washington, Chicago, Baltimore, and Pittsburgh. In March 1968, President Johnson appointed a Commission on the Causes and Prevention of Violence. In April, Dr. Martin Luther King, Jr. was assassinated; a white man was convicted of the crime. At the end of 1969, by one count, there had been over 2400 civil disorders involving blacks since 1962.[6]

Thereafter, rioting in the Northern urban ghettos began to wane. By the early 1970s it virtually disappeared. Many whites doubtless concluded with relief that major grievances of blacks had been alleviated. Yet as we shall see in a moment, blacks were probably more alienated at the end of the decade of turbulence than they had been at the beginning.

Unrest among students. After some years of exceptional calm among students, in the late 1950s political activity began to manifest itself at a few universities, notably at the Berkeley campus of the University of California. There, a student political party, SLATE, sought to end restrictions on students' freedom of speech and off-campus political activity. In 1960, when black students began sitting in at lunch counters to protest segregation, Northern white students also became involved, particularly through two biracial organizations, the Student Nonviolent Coordinating Committee (SNCC) and the Congress of Racial Equality (CORE). White students took over the techniques of protest and direct action used by blacks, such as marches, sit-ins, and picketing. At its convention in Port Huron, Michigan in 1962, a new radical organization, Students for a Democratic Society (SDS), adopted 'participatory democracy' as its goal. This was to be a decentralized system of local democracy in neighborhoods, factories, and schools in which the poor and relatively powerless groups in the society would work to advance their hitherto neglected interests. By the summer of 1964, thousands of students had been recruited by SDS, SNCC and CORE to work with the poor in urban ghettos, Appalachia, and the Southern black belt. A thousand persons, mainly students, came to Mississippi that summer. Their aim was to help Mississippi blacks pursue their right to organize politically and to vote. Three of these volunteers were murdered.

Many white students, particularly those who shared the daily dangers of blacks seeking to destroy the age-old code of white supremacy, and who were shaken by the brutal murder of three fellow volunteers, became political activists, militants, radicals, occasionally even revolutionaries. (In the atmosphere of the 1950s these students might well

5. Rossi, *Roots of Discontent*, p. 4.
6. *Ibid.*, p. 3.

have been politically indifferent.) The Free Speech Movement at Berkeley during the autumn of 1964 organized a series of giant demonstrations and sit-ins protesting restrictions on off-campus political and social action. Though the movement was victorious and the restrictions were removed, the mood of militancy deepened and spread.

Increasingly, this militancy focused on Vietnam. Sharper restrictions on deferments from military service for male students were imposed in 1966. The growing hostility to the war within the colleges and universities intensified. Although from time to time strife occurred over other issues, student protest more and more tended to become a part of the larger antiwar movement. Then in May 1970, during an antiwar demonstration at Kent State University in Ohio, four students were killed by National Guardsmen. Thereafter the site of protest moved beyond the campuses. The antiwar movement, in which students were an important component, concentrated its energies on persuading national political leaders to oppose the war, or on removing them from office.[7]

Unrest over Vietnam. For much of the turbulent decade the war in Vietnam dominated American political life. Until 1965 American military involvement in Indochina had remained comparatively insignificant. A decade earlier, President Eisenhower had dispatched the first American military advisers to help train the South Vietnamese army. When John F. Kennedy assumed office in January 1961, these 'advisers' numbered 900; at the time Johnson took over after Kennedy's assassination in 1963, the American military presence numbered little more than 16,000. A few months before his death Kennedy had said, "In the final analysis, it's their war. They are the ones who have to win or lose it. We can help them, give them equipment, send our men out there as advisers, but they have to win it, the people of Vietnam against the communists."[8] Whether Kennedy would have avoided deeper involvement, as some of his closest advisers suggested in later years, will never be known. In any case, less than a year after Kennedy's death, Lyndon Johnson began his steady escalation of American commitments.

In August 1964, American destroyers in the Gulf of Tonkin off the coast of Vietnam reported attacks by North Vietnamese torpedo boats. Although later investigations were to cast considerable doubt on the reliability of these reports, Johnson ordered the first U.S. air attacks against North Vietnamese bases. On his urging, the Congress approved

---

7. This section has mainly drawn on Skolnick, *Politics of Protest,* and Seymour Martin Lipset and Philip G. Altback, "Student Politics and Higher Education in the United States" in S. M. Lipset, ed., *Student Politics* (New York: Basic Books, 1967).

8. Quoted in *Congress and the Nation,* Vol. 3 (Washington, D.C.: Congressional Quarterly Service, 1973), p. 940. This volume's section on "Vietnam War Policy" (pp. 899–948) contains a number of useful summaries, including a table on U.S. troop levels in Vietnam from 1960–1970 (p. 901), Vietnam war statistics (pp. 935–938), and "Indochina Chronology 1950–1973" (pp. 939–943).

a resolution promising support for "all necessary measures to repel any armed attack against the forces of the United States and to prevent further aggression."[9] The vote in the Senate was 88 to 2; in the House 414 to zero. As it turned out, the Gulf of Tonkin Resolution provided President Johnson with one of his main props for the legality, constitutionality, propriety, and congressional endorsement of his growing military commitment to the government of South Vietnam.

By the end of Johnson's term in 1968 there were 536,000 American troops in Vietnam. The United States and its allies had dropped over 2.6 million tons of bombs on Southeast Asia—more than the tonnage in all of World War II. American aid to South Vietnam amounted to over $1.5 billion a year.

The principal architects of the war, aside from Johnson himself, were a collection of exceptionally talented officials, most of them originally appointed by Kennedy. They have been called "the best and the brightest."[10] These policy-makers were profoundly influenced by memories of the failure to confront Hitler when he began his conquest of small, neighboring countries. Convinced that World War II might have been prevented by an early show of resoluteness, these veterans of a decade of Cold War against the Soviet Union, unreconciled to the Soviet domination of Eastern Europe, were fearful that the Russians might come to dominate Western Europe as well. Sensitive to the uproar caused by the 'loss of China to Communism' in 1949, and emboldened by a widespread perception of the Korean War (1950–1953) as a successful American effort to block Communist aggression, these leaders now saw South Vietnam as a small beleaguered 'ally' in the struggle of 'the free world' against 'Communist aggression.'

At the outset their policies in Vietnam won wide if not necessarily active or enthusiastic support. The Gulf of Tonkin Resolution, as we have just seen, sailed through Congress with only two dissenting votes. Senators who were to become leading opponents of the administration's policies on Vietnam joined in expressing their support for the resolution, to their later regret and embarrassment. In fact, Senator William Fulbright, chairman of the Senate Foreign Relations Committee, who was to become an implacable opponent of the war, was in charge of the resolution on the Senate floor. Asked whether, "if the President decided that it was necessary to use such force as could lead into war, we will give that authority by this resolution?" Fulbright answered, "That is the way I would interpret it."[11] The *New York Times* and the

---

9. The full text of this lamentable abdication of congressional responsibility and authority was even broader. It can be found in *Congress and the Nation*, Vol 2, p. 70.

10. The phrase is the title of the most detailed and informative study of the policy-makers involved in the war and their decisions: David Halberstam, *The Best and the Brightest* (New York: Random House, 1972).

11. Arthur M. Schlesinger, Jr., *The Imperial Presidency* (Boston: Houghton Mifflin, 1973), p. 180.

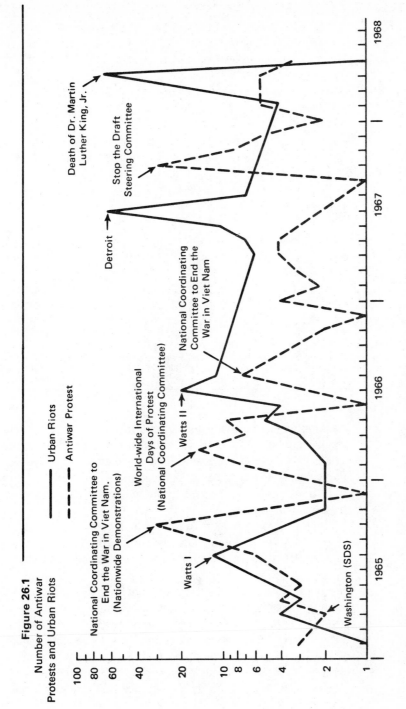

Figure 26.1
Number of Antiwar
Protests and Urban Riots

Urban Riots

Antiwar Protest

Source: Hugh Davis Graham and Ted Robert Gurr, *The History of Violence in America* (New York: Bantam Books, 1969), p. 558.

Figure 26.2
Size of Antiwar
Demonstrations and
Percentage of Antiwar
Sentiment

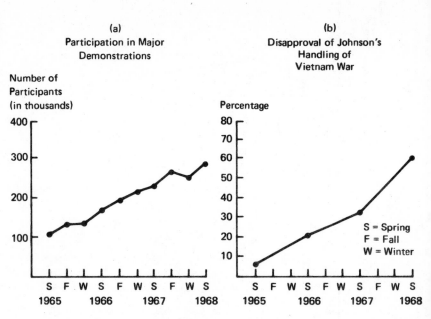

(a)
Participation in Major
Demonstrations

(b)
Disapproval of Johnson's
Handling of
Vietnam War

Source: Jerome H. Skolnick, *The Politics of Protest,* A Staff Report to the National Commission on the Causes and Prevention of Violence (Washington, D.C.: U.S. Government Printing Office, 1969), p. 24.

Washington Post, newspapers of enormous influence that were later to provide crucial support to the antiwar forces in news reports and editorials, initially endorsed American involvement. The public, ordinarily highly responsive to presidential leadership on foreign affairs, and with little to inform it about possible alternatives, was strongly favorable to the president's actions.

Initially, too, Vietnam was a problem to which most Americans gave very little attention. The escalation of American involvement in 1965 and 1966, however, not only focused attention on the war but also stimulated increasing opposition. The bombing of North Vietnam in February 1965, provoked a strong reaction; it marked a major turning point in the evolution of the domestic conflict. In April the first demonstration in Washington was organized by SDS. During the next half-dozen years, antiwar demonstrations were to become a familiar aspect of the American political scene (see Figure 26.1). As military involvement grew, so did the numbers of antiwar demonstrators (Panel [a] of Figure 26.2). Opposition to the war, as evidenced by public opinion polls, also continued to grow (Panel [b] of Figure 26.2). In October 1967, a giant crowd of antiwar protestors, estimated by the police at 55,000 and by others as much larger, assembled in Washington and marched toward the Pentagon. The building was surrounded by federal troops, and other troops were held in reserve throughout the city. But after a brief conflict between troops and demonstrators at the door of the Pentagon, the peace march dissolved. Almost exactly two years later antiwar demonstrations involving an estimated one million persons took place throughout the country.

Never before had so many Americans engaged in unconventional forms of political protest. Certainly never before had the United States fought a war abroad in the face of so much public opposition.

By 1968 the country was divided between 'hawks' who supported the war or wished to prosecute it even more vigorously, and 'doves' who opposed it. On January 30, at the time of the Vietnamese holiday *Tet,* the North Vietnamese began a major offensive that included attacks on almost all of South Vietnam's provincial capitals and uprisings in Saigon itself. Although the White House and the Pentagon said the Tet offensive was a defeat for the enemy,

> In the Pentagon, the Tet offensive performed the curious service of fully revealing the doubters and dissenters to each other in a lightning flash. Nitze [Secretary of the Navy] suddenly spoke out on "the unsoundness of continuing to reinforce weakness".... Warnke [Assistant Secretary for International Security Affairs] thought Tet showed that our military strategy was "foolish to the point of insanity".... In various ways, the Undersecretary of the Army ... the Assistant Secretary of Defense for Manpower, ... the Deputy Assistant Secretary for Far Eastern Affairs ... and other influential civilians expressed their strong belief that the Administration's Vietnam policy was at a dead end.[12]

From the time of the Tet offensive onward, a majority of Americans were convinced that the United States had made a mistake in sending troops to fight in Vietnam (Figure 26.3). This did not mean, however, that a majority of Americans now favored immediate withdrawal of American troops. Without a clearer lead from the president, opinion remained divided. A survey in September 1968, showed about 48 percent taking a dovish position and 43 percent a hawkish position. The doves wanted the war to be wound down; most were not yet in favor of immediate withdrawal of American troops. The hawks wanted the war to go on until the North Vietnamese were defeated or accepted peace on American terms—which, from the perspective of North Vietnam, amounted to the same thing. A substantial proportion of hawks wanted

---

12. Townsend Hoopes, *The Limits of Intervention, An Inside Account of How the Johnson Policy of Escalation in Vietnam was Reversed* (New York: David McKay, 1969), pp. 147–8.

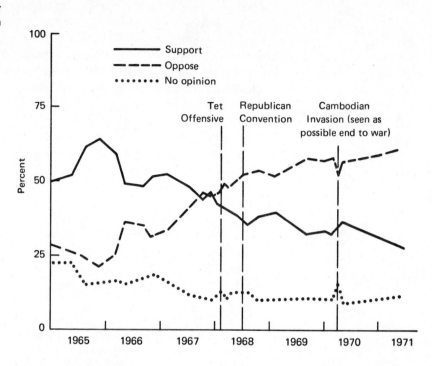

Figure 26.3
Trends in Support for
the War in Vietnam

Source: John E. Mueller, *War, Presidents, and Public Opinion* (New York: John Wiley, 1973), p. 56.

a further increase in American military support; a quarter of the population were ready to go all out to win the war, and 8 percent were ready to use nuclear weapons "to bomb North Vietnam into the Stone Age," as one of their leading spokesmen put it (Table 26.1).

High Stakes, No Satisfactory Compromise

To hawks and doves the dispute over Vietnam was no ordinary political matter on which an artful compromise would be acceptable to both sides. For one thing, the war had gained in visibility and impact. From 1965 onward, more Americans mentioned Vietnam as the most important problem facing the nation than any other problem. In Washington and among political leaders throughout the country, in the mass media, in academic and intellectual circles, and among political activists, Vietnam was the dominant question—the magnet to which all political discussion was drawn.

It will probably be difficult for later generations to understand the

Table 26.1 Attitudes toward the Vietnam War, 1968	Suppose the Vietnam war is not over by the time the next president takes office. If you had to choose one, which one of the following courses would you favor his following in Vietnam?* (Options apparently presented in reverse of order shown)	
	Get out of Vietnam altogether	13%
	Withdraw United States troops gradually but keep supplying the South Vietnamese militarily	18
	Pull United States troops back to the cities and let the South Vietnamese do more of the fighting until Communists make peace	17
	Keep military pressure on until the Communists make peace	17
	Pour in troops and bombs to win war with conventional weapons	18
	Use nuclear weapons and win the war once and for all	8
	No opinion	9

* September 1968.

Source: Mueller, *War, Presidents, and Public Opinion*, p. 91.

intensity of the passions aroused by Vietnam. Why, they may well wonder, with the benefit of hindsight, did the stakes seem so high?

High personal stakes for some. To begin with, some Americans had a direct personal stake in the war. They were not many. There were of course the troops in Vietnam and their families at home. At a greater distance psychologically and physically were those in military service outside Vietnam. From 1964–1972, a total of nearly 9 million persons served in the military.[13] There were also the potential draftees and their families.

To some, the prospect or actuality of service sharpened opposition to the war. Certainly the threat of the draft helped crystallize opposition among college students—even though, as it turned out, most college students who tried to avoid military service were able to do so. To others, who justified their sacrifice on patriotic grounds, the sight of young men demonstrating their opposition to the war by burning their draft cards was offensive and provocative. Yet military service itself seemed not to have a definite effect one way or another. A survey in 1968 showed negligible differences in attitudes toward the war by respondents with a family member in service in Vietnam, in service but not in Vietnam, or with no family member in service. Respondents with family members in service were, if anything, slightly more hawkish than the others.[14]

Because many of the demonstrators were students and opposition to the war was strongest in the best-known colleges and universities, it was often assumed that the youth of America were opposed to the war: according to their critics, out of pure self-interest. In fact, however, this

13. *Congress and the Nation*, Vol. 3, p. 936.

14. John E. Mueller, *War, Presidents, and Public Opinion* (New York: John Wiley, 1973), p. 150.

was not so: young people consistently gave more support to the war than older people.[15]

Because draftees, volunteers, and casualties came disproportionately from the ranks of the blacks, the poor, and the working people one might have expected greater opposition among these groups. Moreover, they were adversely affected in another way. To avoid arousing deeper opposition to the war, President Johnson had deliberately decided neither to raise taxes nor to curtail the Great Society programs he had helped inaugurate. The huge deficits that were the result of this decision set off a spiral of inflation that the country was to grapple with for years to come. Inflation was particularly hard on the poor. And war expenditures, which by 1969 approached $30 billion a year, used up resources that might have yielded tax reductions or larger sums for health, education, housing, and urban redevelopment. Meanwhile, as we have seen, the cities were burning. Senator Fulbright, now a leader of the antiwar forces, told the American Bar Association in 1967, "Abroad we are engaged in a savage and unsuccessful war against poor people in a small and backward nation. At home—largely because of the neglect resulting from twenty-five years of preoccupation with foreign involvement—our cities are exploding in violent protest against generations of social injustice."[16]

As a consequence, working people might conceivably have turned against the war more readily than people who were better off. Yet this was not the case either. In their attitudes toward the war, manual workers were not markedly different from white-collar workers or professional and business people. Because they sometimes displayed hostility to antiwar demonstrators, 'hardhats' came to be perceived as prowar, especially among antiwar activists. But survey evidence does not confirm that view.[17] To be sure, blacks were less supportive than whites. Their comparative lack of enthusiasm may have been generated in some measure by an awareness of how much of the actual fighting was being done by black soldiers. Some blacks also asserted, however, and with considerable justice, that if the Vietnamese were white their country would not have been subjected to so much devastation by Americans. Among some blacks, then, the war stimulated feelings of injustice that went beyond individual and even group interests to a certain degree of sympathetic identification with those they saw as fellow victims of racial prejudice.

Since the better-educated and better-off strata of Americans were less likely to suffer directly from the hardships caused by the war, it is plausible that these groups would have been correspondingly more

---

15. Mueller, *War, Presidents, and Public Opinion*, p. 137, and Milton J. Rosenberg, Sidney Verba, and Philip Converse, *Vietnam and the Silent Majority; The Dove's Guide* (New York: Harper and Row, 1970), pp. 65 ff.

16. Quoted in Skolnick, *The Politics of Protest*, pp. 40–41.

17. See Mueller, *War, Presidents, and Public Opinion*, p. 135.

supportive. Yet because articulate public opposition to the war was led mainly by educated white persons from the middle and upper social and economic strata, and because opposition was very strong in the 'prestige' colleges and universities, it would also have been a reasonable guess that these strata were more opposed to the war. The fact is, that in surveys taken at the time, college-educated respondents gave somewhat more support for the war than respondents with a high-school education, and both groups were more favorable than those with only a grade-school education. However, a substantial part of the difference is attributable to the fact that the less well-educated are also less likely when interviewed to express an opinion at all—in this case, either in support for or in opposition to the war.[18]

To the president, members of Congress, and perhaps some other political leaders, the desire to gain or retain prestige and public office provided a kind of self-interest that doubtless influenced their public positions toward the war. In the earlier years of the war, it was politically risky to challenge the president, the prevailing ideology, and majority views by opposing the war. As support for the war declined, however, a politician might rationally decide that he would gain support by taking a dovish position and lose it by being a hawk.

Moreover, Johnson (and later, Nixon) had committed themselves so fully to securing the independence of South Vietnam that to 'bug out' or 'cut and run' as Johnson contemptuously referred to withdrawal, would be to confess that their past policies were a failure. Vanity and the possibility of adverse political consequences thus provided high personal stakes for pursuing the war.

If congressmen are not famous for bucking the president on foreign affairs when he has public opinion behind him, members of the Executive Branch were not conspicuously more courageous. Few chose to incur Johnson's well-known wrath by contesting his policies, and many convinced themselves that his policies were right or that, even if they were wrong, dutiful silence was the loyal and patriotic course to follow.[19] But as we shall see, as the war went on more and more public

18. See the data and discussion in Mueller, *War, Presidents, and Public Opinion*, pp. 123ff, and in Rosenberg, Verba, and Converse, *Vietnam and the Silent Majority*, pp. 55ff.

19. Thus Townsend Hoopes would later write of the Secretary of Defense: "McNamara himself seemed to me, during that summer and early fall [1967] increasingly tired and depressed. Always a man of incredible physical and mental resilience, he now appeared to stay thin and tired. He also seemed increasingly alone in the cavernous Pentagon. It was the aloneness of a man in deep doubts, a man whose intelligence and integrity forced him to accept the realization that, in the major decisions of the war, rigorous logical and quantification analysis had conspicuously failed. They had failed because of Ho Chi Minh's 'irrational' determination that North Vietnamese, by reason of their readiness to die in great numbers, could in fact outlast U.S. firepower. But owing to his strict conception of loyalty to the President, McNamara found it officially necessary to deny all doubt and, by his silence, to discourage doubt in his professional associates and subordinates." (*The Limits of Intervention*, pp. 84–91.) It is only fair to add that on August 25, 1967, McNamara finally expressed his doubts publicly in testimony before a Senate Committee without having cleared his statement with the White House. In November, in a stunning surprise, the President nominated McNamara to be president of the World Bank and thereby brought about his departure from the Cabinet.

figures opposed the president's policies, sometimes in circumstances requiring considerable courage and integrity.

Yet if narrow self-interest, or group interest, sometimes played a part, it would be hard to account for the intensity and scope of the conflict primarily on these grounds. For what was also at issue were fundamentally diverging beliefs about the nature and consequences of the war.

Compromise Becomes Difficult

As we saw in Chapter 24, most Americans do not seem to be strongly influenced in their political judgments by elaborate, comprehensive, carefully worked out political ideas, belief systems, or ideologies. But Vietnam was a small country remote from the experience and knowledge of Americans. Most citizens were unable to perceive how the war affected them in any direct, concrete, long-range way. Judgments about the war, then, required a rather complex 'cognitive chart,' an understanding of the best course to take. Mapping out such a course required some understanding of intentions, means, causes, consequences, values, costs and gains. For charting such a course, direct experience could provide precious little guidance.

Without a cognitive map and sense of direction that makes complex international issues understandable, a great many Americans tend to be guided by sources they trust, mainly the president and other public figures. In the case of Vietnam, the president was thus able to gain support by evoking familiar moral and political perspectives: loyalty to the country in time of war; the need to support allies in their hour of peril; the threat of communist aggression; not giving in to bullies; demonstrating to friend and foe that we keep our word; fear that defeat in Vietnam inevitably meant further losses and thus decay in American strength everywhere (the domino theory), and so on. Lacking trustworthy sources for forming alternative views, most citizens responded by supporting the president. Often they assumed that he must have special information unknown to them and not publicly reported.

It is not surprising that if critical alternative views were to develop at all, they would develop first among intellectuals, academics, and students in the colleges and universities. These are people with access to alternative information, perspectives and interpretations, who are in the habit of constructing complex cognitive maps, and who have considerable confidence in their capacity to work their way through intellectually difficult territory. In this case, their confidence was steadily reinforced as the war produced mounting evidence that the administration's confident predictions were regularly refuted by events. Rarely have events so quickly discredited the views of the 'practical' people in public office and confirmed 'unrealistic' views coming from 'eggheads' and 'impractical idealists.'

Initially, as we have seen, the antiwar movement was largely concentrated in the colleges and universities and was expressed mainly in demonstrations of protest on and off the campus. Yet it is doubtful that many Americans changed their views because of these antiwar demonstrations. Indeed, there is strong evidence that throughout the war massive majorities remained hostile to the protesters, whose unconventional actions only persuaded the bystanders that protesting the war in this fashion was indeed unpatriotic.[20]

Other events, however, did gradually undermine confidence in the administration's policies. For one thing, the public was increasingly exposed to the arguments by critics of the war whose loyalty and respectability could not be lightly dismissed. Although in 1966 only a handful of senators and representatives expressed open opposition, by the end of 1967 a number of prominent members of Congress had gone over to the antiwar side. In November of that year, Senator Eugene McCarthy of Minnesota, a leading opponent of the war, entered the race for the Democratic nomination for President. His campaign immediately insured a national forum for his views. Events lent him further support: In early 1968, the Tet offensive dramatically called into question the credibility of the administration. On March 12, McCarthy won 42 percent of the vote in the Democratic presidential primary in New Hampshire; in comparison with Johnson's 49 percent, this was widely seen as a stunning moral victory. Senator Robert Kennedy, a brother of the late president, a popular figure among traditionally Democratic voters, and an increasingly vigorous critic of the war, entered the presidential race on March 16. On March 31, President Johnson announced that he would not seek re-election. In effect, the chief apologist for the war had declared his inability to win the election and to govern the country.

Meanwhile, leading newspapers like the *New York Times* and the *Washington Post* had joined the antiwar forces. War correspondents filed column upon column of stories belying the administration's claims. Nightly television newsfilm revealed the grimness of the war and often the doubts of those who broadcast the reports. After a visit to Vietnam in February, 1968, Walter Cronkite, one of the most popular and respected television news reporters, said that we were in a military stalemate and that the only acceptable way out lay through negotiations with the communists.

Thus the administration's onetime monopoly on authoritative and trustworthy beliefs about the war had been shattered. It had become legitimate, respectable, and even patriotic to oppose the war.

Even so, the intensity of the domestic conflict over the war might have abated if the President could have found an acceptable compro-

20. Rosenberg, Verba, and Converse, *Vietnam and the Silent Majority*, pp. 44–45.

mise between his own position and that of his opponents. But the strength and single-mindedness of the North Vietnamese allowed no room for any solution to the war other than a defeat for the United States. Increasingly the alternatives seemed to be either to escalate the war even further as the Joint Chiefs of Staff recommended, or else to begin, somehow, the painful process of winding it down. The first, it was now clear, would provoke a sharp and probably even violent response from the antiwar movement. What is more, following the Tet offensive a number of influential members of the Executive Branch began to express their own reservations about that course of action. Three days after the New Hampshire primary, Johnson met with Dean Acheson

> whom he held in highest regard as a brilliant mind, a courageous and distinguished former Secretary of State, and the toughest of the Cold Warriors. . . . Acheson told the president he was being led down a garden path by the JCS [Joint Chiefs of Staff], that what [General] Westmoreland was attempting in Vietnam was simply not possible—without the application of totally unlimited resources "and maybe five years". He told the president that his recent speeches were quite unrealistic and believed by no one, either at home or abroad. He added the judgment that the country was no longer supporting the war.[21]

The insiders soon gained an exceptionally influential and courageous ally in the new Secretary of Defense. Within a few months after his confirmation as McNamara's successor, Clark Clifford, a man of enormous stature in knowledgeable Washington circles, had swung around to "a firm conviction that the Administration's policy in Vietnam was indefensible."[22] He soon proceeded to make his views known.

Yet negotiations on any terms acceptable to the North Vietnamese were sure to lead to a scaling down of the American involvement, a weakening of South Vietnam's precarious position, and quite possibly a collapse. In that event, the whole war would be revealed as a tragic and costly mistake, and a colossal error of judgment by President Johnson. Although Johnson halted further escalation and called for negotiations, he left office without ever having clearly accepted the fact that the war aims he had so often proclaimed could not be achieved. Between the disaster of further escalation and the total defeat of the objectives to which Johnson had publicly committed himself and the country, there was—as events were to show—simply no satisfactory compromise. A gifted man who had made his political career out of the art of compromise was caught in a conflict abroad and at home that

---

21. Hoopes, *The Limits of Intervention*, p. 200. Hoopes provides an excellent insider's account of the change. See especially pp. 218–221.

22. *Ibid.*, pp. 204–205.

could not be terminated by "giving a little here and taking a little there."

LIMITS ON POLARIZATION

War that did not produce victory and could not be ended in the foreseeable future except by defeat was a wholly new experience. The United States had always been on the winning side (the War of 1812 had long been only a vague and irrelevant memory). Hawks were frustrated by what they often referred to as Johnson's no-win strategy. Their anger surfaced in harsh attacks on the president and harsher attacks on the antiwar movement. For their part, the antiwar forces were frustrated by their clear inability, after years of effort, to bring about a significant change in the policies of the administration. The main targets of their anger were therefore Johnson and his principal advisors. Some also attacked a source of frustration they vaguely called 'the system.'

These disagreements were of exceptional intensity and involved antagonists whose aims were totally incompatible. Frustration and anger deepened their mutual hostility. Compounded by urban riots and unrest on the campuses, some sober observers feared that the country was approaching disintegration or civil war. The fact was, however, that while frustration, anger and discontent were high, polarization was rather incomplete. At least three factors put limits on the polarizing tendencies: *First,* a substantial proportion of the population and the political leadership were neither extreme hawks nor extreme doves. *Second,* the conflict over Vietnam cut across and was restrained by a great variety of other differences. Its effect was thus not polarization but political fragmentation. *Third,* although the actions of the administration intensified the domestic conflict, other political actions helped to moderate it.

The Muddled Middle

The judgment that Dean Acheson conveyed to President Johnson in March 1968 was doubtless right: the country no longer supported the war. It was proving to be the longest war in American history and the end was not yet in sight. From the Tet offensive onward, Americans who thought it was a mistake to have sent troops to fight in Vietnam outnumbered those who didn't; a small percentage was still unsure. By mid-1968, a clear majority thought it had been a mistake. The proportion continued to grow. Yet even when a majority had concluded that the war was a mistake, there was no majority for bringing it to a quick and decisive end, either by escalating American military attacks without limit, as extreme hawks advocated, or by rapidly withdrawing

American military support, as extreme doves advocated. A substantial number of Americans were unwilling to accept either alternative. They hoped for peace negotiations, or a weakening of North Vietnam's resolve, or some other elusive solution that might allow the United States to exit gradually, gracefully, and "with honor." Even those who said they wanted the war to end quickly did not always want American withdrawal; some wanted to end it quickly by an all-out attack in North Vietnam.

It would be wrong to suppose that most people had clear notions about how to end the war. Although only a dwindling minority favored further escalation, many others were waiting for the president to find an acceptable solution. As events were to show, once President Nixon adopted a policy of gradual withdrawal he readily crystallized a large majority in favor of definite but not hasty withdrawal.[23]

Crosscutting Cleavages

We have already seen how opinions about Vietnam cut across a variety of other cleavages, interests, opinions, and characteristics. It is no great exaggeration to say that the sum total of Americans who favored the war, like the aggregate who opposed it, could agree about few other public issues. Both groups would tend to fall apart as soon as other issues emerged or the war issue became less pressing.

Scholars who have attempted to find a pattern in the distribution of opinions for and against the Vietnam war have not had much success. For there seem to be no sharp patterns: except for minor variations, differences over the war seemed to occur without much relation to age, education, sex, occupation, income, socioeconomic status, region, self-interest or political party.[24]

The effect of the bitter conflict over Vietnam, then, was not to polarize Americans into two antagonistic camps, each united on a common set of beliefs and policies. The effect was instead to fragment the existing national coalitions. Of these, the most important were the two political parties. Throughout Johnson's last year in office, the Democratic party in particular contained both the principal advocates

23. The conflicting, contradictory, and changing views of Americans from May 1964 to May 1971, are reflected in answers to the surveys reported in Mueller, *War, Presidents, and Public Opinion*, Table 4.5, "Support for Withdrawal from Vietnam," pp. 81–98.

24. For reasons we have already discussed, blacks were more opposed to the war than whites. Whites who identified strongly with their nationality group ('ethnics') may have been more hawkish than the white population as a whole. Jews appear to have been somewhat more dovish than Protestants or Catholics. Students in Ivy League and 'prestige' universities were more dovish than students elsewhere. 'Left intellectuals' (Mueller) were more opposed than the general population; like the Ivy League students, however, they were miniscule in number though of very considerable visibility. Under Johnson, respondents who identified themselves as Democrats gave somewhat more support than Republicans; under Nixon it was the other way around. For these findings and conjectures on sources of support and opposition, see Mueller, *ibid.*, Ch. 5 and Rosenberg, Verba, and Converse, *Vietnam and the Silent Majority*, Ch. 3.

of the war and its major opponents, such as Senators William Fulbright and Eugene McCarthy. By the time of the 1968 elections, the Democrats were fragmented as they had not been in half a century or more.

THE POLITICAL INSTITUTIONS AND THE CONFLICT OVER VIETNAM

Decisions Without Consent

As we have seen, President Johnson placed great stress on government by 'consensus.' Short of that, he paid his respects to the principle of majority rule. As long as public opinion was fairly solidly behind him, he was fond of quoting public opinion polls to demonstrate that a majority of the country supported him on the war.

Although he was technically correct, three flaws in his position would soon become clear. *First,* support for the war was, as we have seen, fragile. Much of the support depended on the prospect of an early and satisfactory end to American involvement, and on the absence of well-known and highly regarded opponents of the war who could lend respectability and credibility to antiwar sentiments. As respectable opposition began to make itself heard, and it became obvious that the war might not end either soon or satisfactorily, Johnson's majority slowly crumbled. (Journalists gleefully called attention to the fact that the president no longer quoted the public opinion polls.)

Second, the opposition was intensely angry and growing more visible. Located in influential segments of the society whose bitterness and hostility were bound to be costly to the administration, it could not be ignored or dismissed. As opposition to the war intensified and support declined, Johnson's claim to be carrying out policies that had the backing of 'the American people' became transparently false. At home and abroad, Vietnam was increasingly seen as 'Mr. Johnson's war,' a war he kept going for his own reasons and not because the country supported it.

Finally, Johnson was less and less willing to seek consent for his war policies through customary constitutional and political processes. In the longest war in American history, neither Johnson (nor, for that matter, any other president) ever asked Congress for a declaration of war—in spite of the unambiguous words of the Constitution: "The Congress shall have power . . . to declare war" (Article I, Sec. 8). After the Gulf of Tonkin Resolution, which many members of Congress later concluded they had been tricked into approving through misleading information, the president never again sought the specific approval of Congress for his policies. For its part, as we shall see, the Congress continued to vote war appropriations and failed to take any definite stand on ending the war.

What is more, the processes of informal consultation with congressional and other leaders, which provide an alternative to more cumbersome and formal procedures for gaining consent, also languished. Even within the Executive Branch consultation dwindled as Johnson, and later Nixon, withdrew into an ever-smaller circle of advisors whose members could usually be counted on to voice support for the president's view.

Foregoing the traditional, constitutional, and political processes for gaining consent, Johnson and Nixon drew upon and further enlarged the discretionary power of the presidency. Thus both presidents, and Congress as well, contributed to the rapid growth of the imperial presidency.[25]

Political Action

The politics of protest. Many opponents of the war had at first assumed that their public opposition and the arguments of their leaders would persuade the president and his advisors to alter their war policies. White, middle-class, educated Americans have tended to believe that the government responds to their demands, especially if these are vigorously made. The government may not necessarily grant all they want, but at least will yield enough to produce satisfactory compromise. In the case of Vietnam, as we have seen, President Johnson could discover no compromise that would both achieve his goals in Vietnam and reduce American involvement in the war. A large number of white, middle-class, educated opponents of the war therefore found themselves in the unaccustomed situation of confronting a government whose policies they could not alter by the usual methods.

In these circumstances, many turned to the unconventional politics of protest and confrontation. In the antiwar movement, working 'within the system' through Congress, parties, and elections often came to be contrasted unfavorably with working 'outside the system' through the politics of protest and confrontation, even though most protest actions were in fact perfectly legal, regularly upheld by the courts, and in that sense quite within the system.

Working outside the system, however, tended to have an adverse effect on public opinion:

> The depth of antipathy of most Americans to any political dissent that goes beyond the confines of conventional debate is clearly revealed in a Survey Research Center study conducted in 1968. Respondents were asked to evaluate a wide range of political leaders and groups on a feeling scale, ranging from extremely negative to highly positive. Reactions toward 'Vietnam war protesters' were by a substantial amount the most negative in the set. . . . But one can go further. Sixty-three percent of those believing the war was a mistake viewed protesters negatively, *and even of the*

---

25. See Chapter 13, above.

group favoring complete withdrawal from Vietnam, 53 percent put the pro-testers on the negative side of the scale. Plainly, opposition to the war and opposition to active protest against it [went] together for a significant part of the population.[26]

Thus it is hard to say whether the politics of protest made converts or instead simply provided a way by which the feelings of those who were strongly opposed to the war could be publicly expressed. On balance, the politics of protest probably did far less to influence American opinion against the war than the Tet offensive and the public's weariness of waging a war without end. Nonetheless, it is altogether possible that the antiwar movement may have contributed something to Johnson's sense that he could no longer govern the country, and hence to his resignation. For by 1967 he could hardly appear in public without creating a demonstration against him, and thus he chose to make fewer and fewer public appearances around the country. Probably, too, the emotion and solidarity of demonstrations helped to maintain the spirits of many opponents of the war through the interminable years it continued.

Congressional politics. Individual members of Congress provided some leadership in opposing the war; and Congress became an important national forum for criticism, particularly during the hearings held by the Senate Foreign Relations Committee under the chairmanship of Senator Fulbright. Hearings, debates, and appearances around the country of leading congressional critics of the administration's war policies gave wide exposure to opposition views. These congressional activities probably influenced a good many opinions.

As a lawmaking body, however, Congress did almost nothing to bring about the cessation of hostilities.[27] In 1966, for example, the Senate turned down an amendment to repeal the Gulf of Tonkin resolution by a vote of 92 to 5. The Congress did not repeal it until the end of 1970, well after President Nixon had stated that the resolution was unnecessary because his constitutional powers as commander-in-chief were a sufficient basis for waging the war. Although the Congress occasionally made ineffectual and mainly symbolic gestures, it steadily turned down measures with real teeth, such as amendments to appropriations bills that would have prohibited the spending of military funds

---

26. Rosenberg, Verba, and Converse, *Vietnam and the Silent Majority*, p. 45. (Italics in original). Mueller arrives at a similar conclusion in *War, Presidents, and Public Opinion*, p. 164.

27. "From the mid-1960s through the signing of the cease-fire agreement, 94 roll calls had been taken on the question of limiting or halting American involvement in the Indochina war. Antiwar amendments were attached to bills dealing with defense procurement, foreign aid, defense appropriations and military sales, among others. But no matter what the package, Congressmen against the war were unable to muster enough strength to send an explicit policy directive to the president." *Congress and the Nation*, Vol. 3, p. 853. The roll calls are described on pp. 944–945.

in Southeast Asia. In fact, Congress regularly passed all war appropriations by substantial margins.

Indeed, as late as September, 1970, the Senate voted down a strong antiwar measure sponsored by Senator Hatfield, an Oregon Republican, and Senator McGovern of South Dakota, who because of his leadership in the fight against the war was to become the Democratic presidential candidate in 1972. Their proposal would have cut the number of American troops in Vietnam. It required that after April 1971, military appropriations could not be spent in Vietnam except to withdraw all remaining troops by the end of 1971. The proposal was defeated 39 to 55. Not until 1971, when public opinion was already solidly against the war and President Nixon had begun large-scale withdrawals of American troops, did Congress begin to express its collective will more strenuously to bring about an end to the American military presence in Vietnam. Even in 1971, however, the Congress continued to defeat attempts to cut off funds for the war as of the end of that year.

Although one ought not to underestimate the effect of these various congressional debates on public attitudes toward the war and on the administration's halting and episodic steps toward negotiating with North Vietnam, the fact is that all the major decisions—whether escalation, de-escalation, bombing halts or bombing resumptions, entering into negotiations or breaking off negotiations, cease-fires or a peace agreement—were made by the president, not by the Congress. In controlling the conduct of the war, the imperial presidency was at its peak; Congress was at its nadir.

Electoral politics. As we have seen, President Johnson faced growing unpopularity, mounting opposition to his war policies, and widespread distrust: "What sets the Johnson Administration apart from its predecessors," two newsmen wrote, "is merely that the dissemination of half-truths and untruths has become a matter of day-to-day routine."[28] His inability to make public appearances without setting off a demonstration, and Senator Eugene McCarthy's surprising showing in the New Hampshire primaries—in essence a defeat for the president—resulted in Johnson's announcement at the conclusion of a nationally televised address on the night of March 31, 1968, that "I shall not seek, and I will not accept, the nomination of my party for another term as your president."

The nomination was soon contested by three candidates—Senators Eugene McCarthy and Robert Kennedy, both opponents of the war,

---

28. Quoted in *Congress and the Nation*, Vol. 2, p. 640. "The credibility gap" of the Johnson administration is discussed at length, pp. 640–644.

and Vice-President Hubert Humphrey, who though he sought to placate the doves in the party was unwilling to break openly with his and Johnson's past policies. After Robert Kennedy's assassination in June, the contest narrowed to Humphrey, who was backed by Johnson, organized labor, the South, and the Democratic organizations in the larger states, and McCarthy, who had built an enthusiastic organization of youthful supporters, won a number of important primaries, and accumulated a substantial minority of convention delegates.

The national convention in August brought into plain view the split within the Democratic Party that had been engendered by the war. From the streets of Chicago, scenes of antiwar demonstrations, confrontation with the Chicago police, violence, and brutality were shown to millions of television viewers watching the convention proceedings. In the convention hall itself, the Humphrey majority overrode the minority's attempt to gain adoption of a plank in the Democratic platform calling for an immediate halt to all bombing of North Vietnam, and negotiations to withdraw American troops and establish a coalition government with the communists. Winning the nomination on the first ballot, Humphrey faced the coming election as the candidate of a party deeply divided by the bitter dispute over the war. Although he never overcame the fragmentation within the ranks of his party, in late September he promised if elected to end the bombing in Vietnam. President Johnson did exactly that a month later. As a result, many antiwar Democrats finally gave their support to Humphrey.

Meanwhile, the Republicans nominated Richard Nixon, and George C. Wallace, a Southern Democrat with a following in both parties, entered the race as a third-party candidate. In the election, Nixon won 43.4 percent of the popular vote, Humphrey 42.7 percent, and Wallace 13.5 percent. Nixon gained a majority of votes in the electoral college and thus the presidency.

Instead of dissociating himself from 'Mr. Johnson's war' and bringing it to a speedy end, as many persons had expected, Nixon soon found himself in much the same position as his predecessor. Unable to end the war on terms that would ensure the principal war aim—an independent South Vietnam capable of survival—and reluctant to settle for less, Nixon sought to compromise by gradually reducing troops levels in Vietnam at the same time that heavy bombing continued. In April 1970, he authorized the invasion of Cambodia in order, he asserted, to protect the remaining American troops in Vietnam. The Cambodian invasion touched off nationwide demonstrations against the war, a large antiwar gathering in Washington, and increasing opposition in Congress. (It also helped set in motion a series of actions and reactions that a few years later led to a victory of the communist forces [the Khmer Rouge] in Cambodia.)

As the 1972 elections approached, the antiwar forces turned to the candidacy of Senator McGovern, long a critic of the war. He created a coalition of followers unprecedented in the history of the Democratic party: youthful veterans of Senator McCarthy's campaign four years earlier; young people who were awakened to their first political activity by his appeal; protesters from the '60s who had grown tired of the apparent futility of the politics of protest and confrontation; adherents of emerging cultural trends and values that were deviant from the dominant culture; and a few old-line Democrats. What he could not do, however, was to overcome the fragmentation that the war and other events of the 1960s had created within the Democratic party. He was unable to put together the core of the old Democratic coalition, i.e., urban workers, unions, blacks, the South, the Democratic big-city organizations. In particular, many labor leaders who were accustomed to the 'old politics' were alienated by youthful representatives of 'new politics' with whom they had little in common and who did little to cultivate their support. Events were to show that these disgruntled representatives of the 'old politics' were more in tune with the electorate than McGovern's 'new politics' coalition.

Nixon adroitly diluted McGovern's standing as the peace candidate by entering into negotiations with North Vietnam for a peace settlement. A week before the election, Secretary of State Henry Kissinger, saying he believed that "peace is at hand," announced that the United States and North Vietnam had substantially agreed on a nine-point peace settlement. Nixon emphasized a similar note in his final campaign speeches: in a harsher tone he also asserted that he would not be rushed into a peace treaty by the election.

With McGovern's antiwar position undermined by the President's actions and a large part of the older Democratic coalition alienated by the style of the Democratic convention, the candidate, and his campaign, the leader of the antiwar movement, who reflected much of what had been demanded in the politics of protest throughout the '60s, went down to a crushing defeat. Nixon gained the largest share of the two-party vote won by any candidate since the Civil War.

Although American involvement in Vietnam was not yet over, the end was at hand. In December 1972, with North Vietnam continuing to insist on demands the administration thought unacceptable, Nixon unleashed the heaviest bombing of North Vietnam in the history of the war, and for the first time mined North Vietnam's major harbors. Domestic and world reactions were strongly hostile. Talks were resumed, and on January 27, 1973, a cease-fire agreement was signed that would, in President Nixon's words, "end the war and bring peace with honor in Vietnam and Southeast Asia."

Two years later that 'peace with honor,' gained at enormous cost—

human, social, economic, political, ecological—was in shambles. Under North Vietnamese attack, South Vietnam collapsed almost overnight.

The collapse furnished the final evidence that American involvement in Vietnam had been a complete failure. One might have thought that this now inescapable conclusion of failure for a policy that had dominated American political life for nearly a decade would engender a vast angry public response. But one would have been wrong. The American reaction to the collapse of South Vietnam and the final victory of North Vietnam was largely one of apathy and relief.

In two years Vietnam had become virtually a dead issue. Watergate, impeachment, inflation, and recession had pushed it to one side. The 'new left' had long since disintegrated. The 'new politics' had pretty much merged into the 'old politics.' Nixon had resigned. For most people, the period of protest and confrontation had become a lifeless historical episode.

CONSEQUENCES OF THE CONFLICTS

The three sources of unrest described earlier—the urban ghettos, the colleges and universities, and the Vietnam war—produced a decade of severe conflicts. We have explored some of the factors that prevented these conflicts from fully polarizing the country. Because of these factors, the country probably was never very close to civil war. Nonetheless, together with Watergate and impeachment, this protracted period of intense conflict left some marks on the country that persisted as the conflicts themselves waned.

Political Alienation

One legacy of the turbulent decade was a substantial decline in the confidence and trust Americans, particularly middle-class whites, expressed in their government. Correspondingly, there was an increase in expressions of distrust, cynicism, and powerlessness. This change was described in some detail in Chapter 10.

Racial Attitudes

Although political alienation increased among both blacks and whites, in certain respects their views diverged more sharply at the end of the decade of turbulence and conflict than at the beginning.

Among whites. Whites expressed less support for racial discrimination and more for integration, civil rights, and generally for ending all forms of racial discrimination. Opposition to discriminatory treatment of racial minorities was particularly strong among young persons who had attended college, and these constituted a rapidly increasing proportion of citizens.

On the other hand, substantial majorities of whites believed that the actions of blacks to bring about changes had been mostly violent and had hurt their cause. They were, no doubt, thinking of the riots. Yet unlike most previous riots involving blacks, during the ghetto riots of the 1960s whites almost entirely stayed out of the fracas. In a 1968 survey of white attitudes in fifteen cities, only 5 percent thought that whites should do some counterrioting of their own; 93 percent said the riots should be left to the authorities. They also made a distinction between short-run and long-run solutions to the problem of rioting. Forty-seven percent thought the most important thing their city government could do to keep a disturbance like the one in Detroit from breaking out in their own city was to have stronger police control; one out of three thought the most important thing was improving the conditions of blacks. But when asked about the next five to ten years, a majority said the best thing to do about the problem of riots was to try harder to improve the condition of blacks. Only 17 percent saw tighter police control as the solution.[29]

Among blacks. When the rioting drew to an end, many whites concluded that blacks were now much more content with their position than they had been a few years before. And there is some evidence to suggest that during the first half of the 1960s, blacks did think their situation was improving, gained hope about future changes, and believed most whites wanted to be helpful. But there is also strong evidence that during the latter part of the 1960s, the number substantially increased who felt that while their lot had greatly improved, progress was much too slow. The assassination of Dr. Martin Luther King in 1968 may have been something of a turning point. In any case, the late '60s saw a significant increase in the proportion of alienated blacks—and the increase was greatest in precisely the segment of the population in which opposition to racial discrimination was greatest among whites: the young and educated.

Unlike whites, blacks saw their actions in behalf of their rights as having been mainly peaceful. And unlike whites, more than three out of four blacks thought these actions had helped, not hurt, their cause. In Detroit, the percentage of blacks who believed that most white people in Detroit wanted to see blacks get a better break actually fell from 43 percent in 1968 to 28 percent in 1971, while the percentage who said that whites wanted to keep blacks down had risen from 23 percent in 1968 to 41 percent in 1971. Indeed, black responses to a whole series

29. Angus Campbell, *White Attitudes Toward Black People* (Ann Arbor, Mich.: Institute for Social Research, 1971), Tables 2–5, p. 29; 2–10, p. 32; 2–12, p. 34; pp. 54–67; and Ch. 7, pp. 127–154.

	1968	1971
Best way to gain rights[a]		
Laws and persuasion	33.6%	41.0%
Nonviolent protest	60.0	47.4
Violence	6.4	11.4
If laws, persuasion, nonviolent protest don't work, use violence?[b]		
Yes	23.5%	44.4%
No	76.6	55.7

[a] As you see it, what's the best way for Negroes to try to gain their rights—use laws and persuasion, use nonviolent protest, or be ready to use violence?

[b] (Asked of those *not* saying violence to question above.) If [laws and persuasion/nonviolent protest] don't work, then do you think Negroes should be ready to use violence?

Source: Howard Schuman and Shirley Hatchett, *Black Racial Attitudes* (Ann Arbor, Mich.: Institute for Social Research, 1974), Table 1, Qu. 8 and 9, p. 8.

of questions showed an increased distrust of whites.[30] The percentage of blacks in the Detroit survey who thought that the riots in 1967 had made more whites favor equal rights for blacks had declined from 58 percent in 1968 to 43 percent in 1971; yet they still outnumbered those who thought that the riots had reduced white support (24 percent in 1971 as against 9 percent in 1968). Ninety percent of the blacks still believed that laws, persuasion, and nonviolence were the best way to gain their rights. Yet among those who opposed violence, 44 percent now said that if these means did not work, then blacks should be ready to use violence—almost double the percentage in 1968 (Table 26.2).

Break-up of Party Coalitions

Although other causes may also have contributed, the decade of turbulence sped the disintegration of the two major parties. The proportion of Americans who identified with either the Republicans or Democrats continued to decline. Republicans, already a small minority, declined even more. But the Democrats, who began the decade with the old Rooseveltian coalition more or less intact, were shattered. These changes are described in more detail in Chapter 21.

Unsolved Problems

The end of the Vietnam war banished a major cause of unrest. But it did not end the causes of possible future unrest stemming from the unsolved problems of American society. The war itself solved no problems; it created new ones. An unprecedented rate of inflation resulted in the United States, which thereby contributed to worldwide inflation. Drastic measures to reduce inflation in turn produced a rate of unem-

30. *Ibid.*, pp. 138–139, and Howard Schuman and Shirley Hatchett, *Black Racial Attitudes* (Ann Arbor, Mich.: Institute for Social Research, 1974), Table 1, pp. 5–10.

ployment that had not been seen in the United States since the Great Depression of the 1930s.

By absorbing the energies and attention of the country's leaders, policy-makers, critics, and oppositions, the Vietnam war stifled political creativity. By introducing a massive crosscutting cleavage, and by fragmenting the parties and embittering political life, it prevented the development of governing coalitions that might have vigorously attacked the country's major problems.

Thus the turbulent political conflicts of the 1964–1974 decade did not solve the major problems at home that were likely to create new conflicts. Indeed, the major source of discontent and alienation among middle-class whites, the war in Vietnam, culminated in a total failure of American objectives.

The intense conflicts of the decade did not, however, lead to polarization and the likelihood of civil war. Instead they produced political fragmentation. Although both parties were weakened, the Democrats were most deeply shattered by their disputes. As a result, some realignment in support for the parties was occurring.

After Nixon's fall, the intensity of national conflicts rapidly declined. For a time, at least, the more usual pattern of American politics —crosscutting cleavages with moderate conflict—reasserted itself.

SUMMARY 1. Beginning in 1964, some of the signs of increasing severity in political conflicts (shown in Table 23.1) began to appear in American political life:

☐ A growing *divergence of political views and attitudes* was revealed by
   a. Unrest among blacks, particularly in northern urban ghettos.
   b. Unrest among college students.
   c. Unrest over the Vietnam war.
☐ The dispute over Vietnam, which came to dominate political life, proved increasingly to be a *conflict with high stakes* and *no grounds for a satisfactory compromise* between supporters and opponents of American involvement.

2. The conflict over Vietnam, though intense, did not lead to polarization because:

☐ A substantial proportion of the population and the political leadership did not hold clear-cut views either in support of, or in opposition to continued American involvement in the war.
☐ The conflict *cut across,* and to some extent was restrained by, a great variety of other differences. Thus the conflict tended to *fragment* political coalitions, not to *polarize* the country into two cohesive and antagonistic camps.

3. The political institutions contributed to the process of fragmentation:

☐ Presidents Johnson and Nixon made *decisions without* seeking *consent* for war policies through the customary constitutional and political processes.

☐ Political action included

    a. Protest actions, which seem to have made fewer converts than enemies.

    b. Congressional passivity, which contributed to the growth of the imperial presidency and to presidential decision-making without congressional consent.

    c. Electoral politics, which intensified the fragmentation of the Democratic party.

4. Consequences of the decade of unrest and intense conflict were:

☐ A significant decline in the confidence and trust of Americans in their government, particularly among middle-class whites.

☐ Greater polarization of attitudes along racial lines, as a result of

    a. Some increase in support for integration and racial tolerance among whites, which however was more than offset by

    b. Increased political alienation among blacks.

☐ Break-up of the party coalitions, particularly the Democratic party.

☐ A failure to deal successfully with the problems that might give rise to future conflicts.

27 POLITICAL POLARIZATION AND CIVIL WAR

In the disputes that thrust this country into civil war, American experience offers a compelling and tragic illustration of severe conflict. It is the course of this conflict, the greatest failure in the history of American polyarchy, that we examine in this chapter.

Whether any polyarchy could have arrived at a peaceful solution to any issue as monumental as slavery had become in the United States, no one can say with confidence. What we do know—what no American can forget—is that the American political system was unequal to the task of negotiating a peaceful settlement to the problem of slavery. Violence was substituted for politics. Yet even civil war, the supreme mark of political failure, did not solve the issue, which now became the question of whether the freed slaves were to acquire full and effective citizenship.

The Civil War did not answer this question. Nor did the postwar Reconstruction policy. The unresolved issue was passed down from one generation to the next, until it exploded for all the world to see, a century after the outbreak of the Civil War.

SYMPTOMS OF RISING CONFLICT

In Chapter 25 we saw how the Missouri Compromise in 1820 enabled political leaders from North and South to avoid the issue of slavery in the territories for a generation. That compromise solution did not apply, however, to the lands that were acquired from Mexico in the late 1840s as a result of the Mexican War. Confronted by the problem of providing government for these new territories, the aging politician and master of the art of compromise, Senator Henry Clay of Kentucky, joined with a new senator from Illinois, Stephen A. Douglas, and engineered a new compromise solution. The Compromise of 1850 provided that the people of California, New Mexico, and Utah could themselves decide the question of slavery. This was 'popular sovereignty.' It was to become the program on which Douglas would seek to win the presidency.

In 1854, when the vast unorganized remnants of the Louisiana purchase were given territorial government, Douglas piloted through Congress another compromise on the same basis. But under pressure from Southerners to put slavery on an equal footing, the venerable Missouri Compromise was repealed outright. At its national convention in Cincinnati in 1856, the Democratic party proclaimed popular sovereignty as its official doctrine. Many of the delegates no doubt believed that they had found a formula that would not only enable the Democratic party to win the presidency that year but once again to push the dangerous question of slavery off the agenda of national politics, as the Missouri Compromise had done.

They were right about winning the election. They were profoundly wrong about the conflict over slavery. In May, 1856, John Brown and a small party of antislavery Kansans massacred five proslavery men in the Pottawatomie region of Kansas. Over the next few years, violence frequently broke out between pro- and antislavery forces in what came to be popularly called 'bleeding Kansas.' At almost the same time as the Pottawatomie massacre, Senator Charles Sumner of Massachusetts delivered a vehement attack on slavery in the Senate. His speech contained a degree of personal invective. Shortly afterward a Southern congressman entered the Senate and beat Sumner repeatedly over the head with a heavy cane. In both houses of Congress there were other outbursts of violence involving antagonisms over slavery. In the course of a debate about Kansas in 1858, proceedings in the House became riotous. On other occasions, too, the House and Senate verged on open physical violence.[1]

At a time when intemperate language was commonplace, public figures frequently invoked threats of secession, disruption of the Union, violence, and civil war. In letters, in the press, even in Congress, the more radical Southerners began to speak of secession as the only alternative if the North could not be brought to terms. As the election of 1860 approached, Southerners frequently reiterated the threat that the

---

1. For historical details this chapter relies heavily on Roy Nichols' exceptionally important study of the Democratic Party from 1856–1860, *The Disruption of American Democracy* (New York: Macmillan, 1948); and his *The Stakes of Power, 1845–1877* (New York: Hill & Wang, 1961); C. Vann Woodward, *Reunion and Reaction: The Compromise of 1877 and the End of Reconstruction* (Boston: Little, Brown, 1951); *The Burden of Southern History* (New York: New American Library, 1969); *The Strange Career of Jim Crow* (New York: Oxford University Press, 1957); and "Seeds of Failure in Radical Race Policy," *Proceedings of the American Philosophical Society*, 110, no. 1 (February 1966), 1–9.

South would secede if a Republican were elected president. Senator William Seward of New York stoked the fires of controversy by his statement in Rochester in October, 1858: "It is an irrepressible conflict between opposing and enduring forces, and it means that the United States must and will, sooner or later, become either entirely a slave-holding nation or entirely a free-labor nation." Just one year later, John Brown staged his futile raid at Harpers Ferry in a vain, poorly-organized, and half-insane attempt to free the slaves of Virginia. On the heels of the news of Harpers Ferry, the legislature of Alabama met and authorized the governor to call a state convention if a Republican should be elected president in 1860. In the summer of 1860, a number of conservative South Carolina Democrats, hitherto opposed to the 'fire-eaters' who advocated secession, declared that if the Republicans were to win the election in November, South Carolina would secede. If this was Southern bluster and bravado, in November the bluff was called. It was not a bluff. On December 20, 1860, the state of South Carolina seceded from the Union. Within six months, ten other Southern states had followed. Lincoln, backed by a substantial share of articulate Northern opinion, refused to permit the Southern states to secede and thereby dismember the Union. The result was civil war.

'Explanations' of the 'causes' of the Civil War abound. Yet in the best of circumstances—under laboratory conditions—causal analysis is not easy. Causal interpretations of complex, multifaceted historical events are particularly uncertain and vulnerable. It would therefore be absurd in this brief chapter to introduce another causal theory about the origins of the Civil War. All the following analysis is intended to show is that the events of 1850–61 closely conform to the expected pattern indicated by the summary in Table 23.1. Conditions that encourage moderation gave way to conditions that would be expected to produce a more severe conflict. Never before or since in American history has the pattern of moderate conflict with crosscutting divisions been so fully transformed into the pattern of severe conflict and polarization.

First Condition: Divergence of Views

During the course of the 1850s, events and new perspectives posed the issue of slavery in the territories in such a way that compromise became increasingly difficult. As the decade wore on, the issue of slavery was more and more bound up with a second major question—union or secession.

The slavery issue. At the start of the decade, there was an exact balance in the Senate between the slave states and free states. Slavery already existed in fifteen Southern states and it was prohibited in fifteen Northern states. The balance in the Senate could be maintained or disrupted by what happened in the Western territories. Should slavery be protected in the territories, or prohibited? If it were protected, would there not be, in due course, more slave states than free states? If it were prohibited in the territories, could there ever again be an additional slave state? Would not the South become an ever-smaller minority in the nation, and in the Senate, finally perhaps too small to prevent the free states from abolishing slavery by constitutional amendment and, if need be, by coercion?

In principle, the policies adhered to by the federal government on slavery required an answer to a single question applied to three different regions. The question was this: Should slavery be prohibited or protected? The regions were these: the existing free states of the North and Northwest, the slave states of the South, and the territories of the West.

Revolutionary opposition: abolition. Consider the alternatives. An abolitionist would prohibit slavery in all three regions. His position demanded a revolution in Southern life and institutions. If enough Americans had supported the abolitionist position in 1800, the attempt to perpetuate slavery and the tragedies caused by that discredited institution might never have occurred. Although we shall never know how many Americans held the abolitionist position before the Civil War, the membership of the Anti-Slavery Society amounted to only 3 or 4 percent of the adult population outside the South.[2] Discrimination against blacks was commonplace in the North; Northerners who were prepared to accept blacks as their equal were evidently a minority, and probably a very small minority.[3] It is clear that until the outbreak of war the abolitionists remained a tiny opposition whose views were widely thought to be extreme—as revolutionary views generally are.

Radical opposition: prohibit slavery outside the South. A less revolutionary position, though in the perspectives of the 1850s a radical one nonetheless, was taken by Lincoln, Seward, and the Republican party. Like all the other major protagonists to the great controversies of the 1850s, with the exception of the abolitionists, Lincoln and most leading Republicans assumed that although the free states would continue to prohibit slavery, slavery might be left intact in the South. In fact, as the

2. Philip Converse, "The Nature of Belief Systems," in David E. Apter, *Ideology and Discontent* (New York: Free Press, 1964), p. 250. "This figure is for 1840, and it undoubtedly advanced further in the next decade or two, although one deduces that the expansion of membership slowed down after 1840. Our estimates do not take into account, however, the standard inflation of membership (intentional or unintentional) that seems to characterize movements of this sort" (p. 260, fn. 46).

3. "The fact was that the constituency on which the Republican congressmen relied in the North lived in a race-conscious, segregated society devoted to the doctrine of white supremacy and Negro inferiority . . . 94 percent of the Northern Negroes in 1860 lived in states that denied them the ballot, and the 6 percent who lived in the five states that permitted them to vote were often disenfranchised by ruse." C. Vann Woodward, *American Counterpoint* (Boston: Little, Brown, 1971) pp. 163–164.

price of Union, the South might even be given additional guarantees that its peculiar institution would be protected from the abolitionists. In this view, the institution was so deeply rooted in the South that it could not be abolished in the near future; hence Southern slavery would be protected until such time as the South itself would peacefully yield it up. What was immediately at stake, however, was not slavery in the South or the prohibition of slavery in the North; it was the question of whether slavery was to be permitted in any of the Western territories.

As early as 1846, David Wilmot, a Democrat from Pennsylvania, had introduced a resolution that would have barred slavery in all the territories. Although the Wilmot Proviso was never adopted, it became a rallying point for a number of Northern congressmen. The view of Lincoln and some of his fellow Republicans was essentially that of the Wilmot Proviso: the federal government should prohibit slavery through-out the length and breadth of the territories; hence it would be all but certain that when these territories finally came into the Union, they would enter as free states, not slave states. Lincoln and Seward were willing to compromise on many points in order to reassure the South-ern slavocracy—compromises often thought to be serious blemishes on Lincoln's overblown reputation as the Great Emancipator. But on this issue they never budged. And the frantic efforts to forge another great compromise during the tense months as the year 1860 closed and the new year began all failed because neither Lincoln nor the leaders of the South would alter their positions on the crucial issue of slavery in the territories.

Limited opposition: local option. The policy of 'popular sovereignty' em-bodied in the famous Compromises of 1850 and 1854 provided better grounds for compromise in the early 1850s than was offered by the Wilmot Proviso.

However, this solution, pushed by Senator Douglas, suffered from two disadvantages common to compromise proposals in times of pro-found controversy. First, it was ambiguous, since it did not specify clearly *when* the people of a territory were to decide about slavery. (Opponents of slavery favored an early decision; those who spoke for the slavocracy wanted it as late as possible, preferably when the terri-tory was ready for admission as a state. Presumably, both were oper-ating on the assumption that slave owners would move into a territory much more slowly than free farmers.) Second, and more important, popular sovereignty became increasingly less acceptable to the major antagonists. Lincoln, Seward, and a sizeable number of other leaders rejected popular sovereignty because they favored the total exclusion of slavery in the territories.

Table 27.1
Principal Positions on the
Question of Slavery,
1850–61

Stand on Slavery	Free States	Type of Action Proposed for		Adherents and Proposals
		Territories	Southern States	
Revolutionary opposition	Prohibit	Prohibit	Prohibit	Abolitionists
Radical opposition	Prohibit	Prohibit	Protect	Wilmot Proviso, Lincoln, Seward, Republicans
Limited opposition	Prohibit	Protect or prohibit: People decide	Protect	Advocates of Popular Sovereignty: Clay, Douglas—Compromise of 1850, 1854, Cincinnati Platform of Democratic Party
Limited defense	Prohibit	Protect *and* prohibit: Congress decides		Advocates of extending Missouri Compromise; Crittenden
Radical defense	Prohibit	Protect	Protect	Taney/Dred Scott Decision, Calhoun, Constitutional Democrats, Breckenridge

Radical defense: protect slavery in the territories. Spokesmen for Southern slaveholders also found local option more and more unacceptable. Many of them came to espouse a view that was, in its own way, as radical a break with the past as Lincoln's policy. This was the view that only the people of a *state* had the power to prohibit slavery. Hence the federal government had no constitutional power to prohibit slavery in the territories, nor did the people of the territories, until (or just prior to) their admission as a state. It was the duty of the federal government, then, to protect the rights of slaveholders throughout all the territories. Between this position and Lincoln's, there was no room for compromise.

Although numerous minor variations on these main themes can be detected, they did not change the alternatives in any significant way. The five principal alternatives are summarized in Table 27.1.

The secession issue. As the decade wore on, the question of slavery in the territories (and with it the ultimate future of slavery in the South) more and more required an answer to a second question: Was the Union to be preserved at all costs, or was secession a permissible solution? Is one particular combination of human beings into a single polity more right than any other combination? If so, why? If one of the main ends of a democracy is to secure the consent of all citizens, should not citizens who no longer consent to the basic principles of their government be allowed to depart in peace? Why must the integrity of the Union not be broken by secession? Although the Civil War settled the matter by establishing the principle that secession from the United States is impermissible, the questions themselves are among the most troublesome in the whole domain of political theory.

Lincoln's answer, as everyone knows, was a profound commitment to the Union. In part, his view reflected the nationalism that forms a vital underpinning for the modern nation-state all over the world. It is a nonrational and almost unanalyzable dedication. Nationalists may disagree about boundaries; but they do not doubt that once the nation has been defined, the nation must be preserved. In addition, there was also Lincoln's deep commitment to the importance of the American polyarchy, founded on principles of liberty and equality, as an example for all mankind. If the South should secede, then the greatest living evidence for the proposition that a polyarchy could survive the challenge of dissident minorities would no longer serve as "proof of the impossible." "If the minority will not acquiesce, the majority must, or the government must cease," Lincoln said in his First Inaugural Address. ". . . If a minority in such case will secede rather than acquiesce, they make a precedent which in turn will divide and ruin them. . . . Rejecting the majority principle, anarchy or despotism in some form is all that is left." As he said at Gettysburg, the Civil War was a testing of whether any nation conceived in liberty and dedicated to the proposition that all men are created equal could long endure.

Nearly every one of the groups listed in Table 27.1 contained both Unionists and those who advocated or accepted secession. Some abolitionists who despaired of developing a free society as long as the South was in the Union were not unhappy at the prospect of a separation. There were even Republicans who took this pragmatic view of the matter and did not share Lincoln's passionate belief that the Union must be preserved. At the other extreme, some Southerners who advocated radical defense of slavery were, throughout most of the decade, opposed to secession; many of these fell in line only during the last months before Fort Sumter. In the election of 1860 the Constitutional Union party, which had only two planks—support for the Constitution and loyalty to the Union—gained much of its support from Southern Whigs. Its presidential candidate, Senator John Bell of Tennessee, together with the pro-Union candidate of the Democratic party, Senator Douglas, carried eight of the fifteen slave states against Breckenridge, the candidate of the secessionist Democrats. In the fourteen slave states where presidential electors were chosen by the voters (characteristically, the outdated practice of choosing electors in the state legislature still existed in South Carolina), Breckenridge received only 570,000 votes to his opponent's 705,000.

Table 27.2
Slavery and
Secession, 1850–61

| Stand on Slavery | Stand on Secession | |
	Pro-Union	Pro-Secession
Revolutionary opposition	Most Abolitionists, Radical Republicans	Some Abolitionists
Radical opposition	Lincoln, Seward, most Republicans	Some Republicans
Limited opposition	Clay, Douglas	—
Limited defense	Crittenden, Buchanan	—
Radical defense	Taney/Dred Scott	Calhoun, Jefferson Davis

If we put the two dimensions of policy together—slavery and secession—a new pattern emerges (Table 27.2).

Among those who helped form public opinion, discussed and debated the alternatives, and made the decisions, the events of the 1850s thinned out the center and pushed leaders more and more toward the upper left and lower right corners of Table 27.2. The presidential election of 1860, in which no advocate of any of the principal positions won a majority of popular votes, provided the final polarizing thrust that gave Lincoln and the Republicans in Congress enough control to insure that their views would prevail, and encouraged Southern leaders to unite around the view that only secession would protect slavery in the South. Between these two radically opposed alternatives, it proved impossible to find any compromise.

Second Condition:
High Stakes and No Acceptable Compromise

By the spring of 1861, leaders had exhausted the major possibilities of compromise between the two radical positions. No compromise could be acceptable so long as Republicans and Southerners held to their positions. Yet neither would yield; for in the 1850s the issue of slavery was converted into a zero-sum contest with no mutual benefits, in which the stakes were different ways of life.

In the perspectives of the principal contestants, either slavery had to be prohibited in all the territories or it had to be allowed in all the territories. And the stakes in the contest (if we interpret them as the contestants claimed to see them) had come to be nothing less than this: a society based on slavery or a society based on free farmers and free labor.

Southern stakes. These alternatives were most sharply visible in the perspectives of Southern leaders. From the Constitutional Convention onward, it was clear that the South could maintain slavery only under a Constitution that insured protection for the rights of slaveholders in the Southern states. The South had, in fact, gained such a Constitution in 1787, and the South could maintain it as long as slave states had enough power to veto a change in the Constitution. If the time were to come, however, when the growth of population and the increase in the number of free states permitted the North and West to override the opposition of the South and to alter the Constitution, then the institution of slavery, and with it the whole structure of the planter society, would be imperiled.

This was the shape of the future that Southern leaders perceived. More and more vehemently, they insisted that every solution not guaranteeing a full opportunity for slaveholders to implant their institutions in the territories would lead to the destruction of their society. Hence not only were the Wilmot Proviso and the Republican commitment to free territories intolerable, but even popular sovereignty. Quite possibly even an outright constitutional guaranty would not insure that slavery would in fact be exported to the Western territories. If not, then surely the only solution was secession. If slavery *could* be introduced in the West, however, then another solution might be acceptable to Southerners: this was nothing less than the principle announced in 1857 by Chief Justice Roger Taney in the Dred Scott case: Congress has no power to prohibit slavery in the territories.

Northern stakes. The alternatives may have seemed less stark in the free states than in the South. Nonetheless, from 1856 onwards, Northern politicians who were unwilling to commit themselves to halting the expansion of slavery by federal legislation were to an increasing degree challenged and defeated by opponents who were prepared to put a definite and permanent end to the spread of slavery beyond its existing boundaries. Not only were individuals voted out; whole parties were defeated. The Whigs disintegrated; the Democrats split; the Republicans surged.

The evidence suggests, then, that even if the perspectives for the future were not so grim in the North as in the South, among Northerners a variety of views helped to crystallize the belief that the territories should be preserved exclusively for free farmers. Among these precipitating factors was a loathing for slavery that went far beyond the abolitionists. Many people who were not ready to accept blacks as their equals nor willing to bear the costs of abolishing slavery where it was already entrenched were, like Lincoln, sickened by all proposals, even those in the name of compromise, that would let slavery expand one inch beyond its existing limits. Then, too, the states of the North and

Northwest were still populated predominantly by farmers—free farmers —some of whom had themselves wrested land out of the wilderness; of the others many, perhaps most, must have shared the deeply ingrained expectation, then well over a century old, that the great rich lands to the west were open to them, their neighbors, their sons, or other white farmers like themselves. The spread of slavery would violate that interest, destroy that dream. (It is relevant as a symbol that the first act of the Republicans after secession began was to admit Kansas as a free state.) There were also economic issues on which the veto of the Southern slaveholders prevented solutions favored by many Northerners: the admission of Kansas, a protective tariff, federal expenditures for internal improvements, railroads to the West. Early in 1861, as soon as enough Southern states had seceded to make the Republicans a majority in Congress, Republicans together with a handful of Northern Democrats rushed bills through Congress that admitted Kansas, raised the tariff, and by ending a mail subsidy for steamships to the Pacific Coast eased the way for the construction of a railroad to California.[4] Within a few years, other major policies were enacted that the South had long opposed: the Homestead Law, land grants for agricultural colleges, subsidies for two transcontinental railroads, a contract labor law permitting agents to contract abroad for labor, and, under the pressure of war, even an income tax.

Thus slavery in the territories was no narrow issue. In the waning years of the 1850s, it was interpreted by more and more leaders (and presumably by many involved citizens) as a matter that posed two alternative ways of life, two kinds of society.

Third Condition:
Decline of Crosscutting Cleavages

In the course of the 1850s, the issue of slavery in the territories was like a wall rising between neighbors. At the beginning of the decade the wall could still be climbed; but as it grew higher, it became more and more impassable to traffic of all kinds. A pattern of crosscutting cleavages which had prevailed through the Compromise of 1854 was transformed into a pattern of nonoverlapping or cumulative splits. The ties between North and South snapped, one by one:

☐ Several major religious groups had already split into separate Northern and Southern churches over the issue of slavery:
1844: the Methodist Episcopal Church
1845: the Baptist Church

---

4. Nichols, *Disruption of American Democracy*, pp. 476ff.

Table 27.3
Election of 1860:
Percentage of Votes Won,
by Major Regions

	North and West	South	Total
Lincoln	98.6%	1.4%	100%
Douglas	88	12	100
Breckenridge	33	67	100
Bell	13	87	100

Source: Computed from data in Walter Dean Burnham, *Presidential Ballots, 1836–1892* (Baltimore: Johns Hopkins Press, 1955), pp. 78, 246.

☐ The political parties fell apart or split:
  1850–56: disintegration of the Whigs
  1854–60: formation and rise of the Republican party as a sectional party with no Southern wing
☐ The Democrats split in 1860:
  Northern Democrats nominate Douglas
  Southern Democrats nominate Breckenridge
☐ The Federal Union split:
  1860, December: South Carolina secedes
  1861, January: Florida, Alabama, Mississippi, Georgia, and Louisiana follow
      February: Texas
      April: Virginia
      May: Arkansas, Tennessee, North Carolina

To be sure, total polarization was never reached. But it was enough.

From fragmentation. Between 1850 and 1860, the Whig party, one of the two national parties that had leaders and constituents in both North and South, disintegrated into a weak rump party in the South, and thereafter vanished.

Between 1854 and 1860, a new party took the place of the Whigs. The Republican party was exclusively a Northern and Western party. If we discount the Federalists in their declining years, for the first time in the history of American parties one of the two major parties did not spread across both sides of the Mason and Dixon line. In the election of 1860, Lincoln won only 1.4 percent of the total vote in the fifteen slave states (Table 27.3). In ten slave states Lincoln did not gain so much as a single vote!

In 1860, the Democratic party, which for more than sixty years had been the great nationwide party, whose leaders had worked with unflagging zeal to knit the sections together, split apart on the issue of slavery in the territories. One wing, the Constitutional Democrats (Breckenridge) became a predominantly Southern party. The other, Douglas's party, barely retained any Southern following at all in the

Table 27.4
Election of 1860:
Votes Won

	Number of Votes (000)	Percentage of Total
Republicans: Lincoln	1,866	40
Democrats: Douglas	1,383	30
Constitutional Democrats: Breckenridge	848	18
Constitutional Union: Bell	593	12
Total	4,690	100%

Source: Burnham, *Presidential Ballots*, p. 246.

elections of 1860 (Table 27.3). Southern Whigs and other unionists organized a new party, the Constitutional Union party (Bell); its platform was "The Constitution of the Country, the Union of the States, and the enforcement of the laws." But it, too, proved to be a sectional party.

Thus in 1860, for the first (and, so far, last) time in American history, four, not two, major parties sought the presidency. No party came close to winning a majority of popular votes (Table 27.4) and each was wholly or almost wholly a sectional party (Table 27.3).

To polarization. Congress, hitherto the forum of compromise, became in the late 1850s a battleground where almost every issue split the membership into the same two camps. In 1858–9, Congress had lengthy deadlocks on almost every issue: the admission of Kansas, transcontinental railroads, rivers and harbors appropriations, a homestead bill, the tariff. Deadlock and conflict so much dominated the session that the Congress was not even able to agree on the annual appropriation for the Post Office, and at the end of the session, the Post Office Department was left without funds. In the Congress that met in the winter of 1859–60, no party had a majority in the House; it took two months and more than forty ballots simply to elect a speaker. During all this time the legislative business of the House was at a complete standstill.

In the preceding decade (1840s and early 1850s), political leaders who might have quarreled over slavery agreed on so many other key questions that they were impelled toward a compromise on slavery. In Congress, and, it seems, in the country, attitudes on both sides of the Mason-Dixon line were not so distinct as to prevent coalition, agreement, mutual concession, and compromise on many issues. An opponent on one issue was not necessarily an opponent on all issues. By the late 1850s, however, the chances were that a Northerner and a Southerner not only disagreed about slavery; they disagreed about a great many other key questions as well. The political leaders of the country were increasingly polarized into two opposing sides. More and more, then, one's enemies today would be one's enemies tomorrow and the day after. The North-South fracture split the country not only on slavery in the territories and the admission of Kansas, but as we noted above on the tariff, government aid for roads, harbors, and other internal improvements, the need for and the route of transcontinental railways, federal land grants for educational institutions, homestead laws, banking laws, constitutional theory, and ideological views on aristocracy and democracy. By the spring of 1860, a year before Fort Sumter, a Senator from South Carolina privately observed: "There are no relations, not absolutely indispensable in the conduct of the joint business, between the North and South in either House. No two nations on earth are or ever were more distinctly separate and hostile than we are here."[5]

Limits of polarization. It would be easy, nonetheless, to exaggerate the point. Among political leaders the split was never total. As to the views of the people themselves, one cannot be certain how much they ever became polarized. Then as now the views of ordinary citizens must have been more fragmented, less coherent, less clearly formed than the views of those whose daily lives were wrapped up in the great public controversies. To many citizens, perhaps to most (though one cannot be sure), the issues of slavery probably seemed more remote, less distinct, perhaps even less important than the preoccupations of daily life.

Perhaps the North-South division was weakest on the very issue that moved to the forefront in 1860–1: union or secession. Not all those who supported or were willing to go along with secession were Southerners; and by no means all Southerners supported secession. Without question the secessionists were a minority in the nation. Very likely they were a minority even in the South. Of the four candidates in the presidential election of 1860, none advocated outright and immediate secession. Three were flatly opposed to secession. Although Breckenridge was the candidate of the secessionists, he said he did not favor it as a solution. Breckenridge won only 18 percent of the national vote (Table 27.4) and he won considerably less than a majority—38 percent—of the votes in the South. In fact, Breckenridge received absolute majorities in only eight of the fifteen slave states. Moreover, it appears that even in these states a considerable number of his supporters were opponents of secession who were loyal Southern Democrats, supporting, as they thought, the candidate of their party. Later, in voting on candidates for the conventions called in the seven states that seceded before Fort Sumter fell, the issue of union or secession was made clearer. In these elections many of the counties that had voted *for* Breckenridge voted *against* secessionists in favor of union candidates. Support for secession was concentrated most heavily in the counties with large numbers

---

5. Nichols, *The Stakes of Power*, p. 287.

of slaves, where the vote was about 7 to 3 for secessionist candidates. In counties where slaves were few, the proportions were reversed: voters supported pro-union candidates by about 2 to 1.[6] Even in the states that led the movement to secede, the secessionists barely outnumbered their unionist opponents; in Mississippi in the election of candidates for the convention that was to vote on secession, the ratio of votes cast for secession versus cooperation was 4 to 3; in Alabama, 9 to 7; in Georgia, 5 to 4. As late as March, North Carolina voted decisively against secession.[7] Tennessee and Arkansas did not vote to secede until after the outbreak of war. Four other slave states remained in the Union: Maryland, Delaware, Kentucky, Missouri; and West Virginia split off from Virginia rather than secede.

Triumph of a minority. Thus it is probably no exaggeration to say that it was a small minority of slaveholders who, together with their retainers, followers, and political representatives, engineered secession and thereby precipitated civil war.[8] It seems altogether possible that if a plebiscite had been held during the week before Fort Sumter, and perhaps after, it would have revealed the secessionists to be a minority in the South. Yet with skill, energy, and luck, secessionist leaders gained control in seven states in the deep South, and in the end brought four additional but more reluctant slave states along.

Fourth Condition:
Negotiation without Decision?

How, if at all, did the operation of American political institutions affect the course of the controversy over slavery?

That the institutions and the ways of thinking about them provided powerful inducements for negotiation and compromise on the issue of slavery is hardly open to question. In the first half of the century, the issue which was to tear the country apart during the second half was handled by one compromise after another: 1820, 1850, 1854. The forces of the system that resisted change continued to operate until May of 1861. During the final year of peace, or cold war, there were frantic and unceasing efforts toward compromise. A number of initiatives were taken: the Conference Convention; the Crittenden Compromise; the Committee of Thirty-three in the House; the Committee of Thirteen in the Senate; proposals by Senator Toombs, Jefferson Davis, Stephen Douglas, and countless other political leaders; even a constitutional

---

6. Lipset, "The Emergence of the One-Party South," in *Political Man* (Garden City, N.Y.: Doubleday, 1960), pp. 344–356. Table II, p. 349.

7. See Nichols, *Disruption of American Democracy,* pp. 418, 435, 499.

8. See Burnham's comment, "... it was probably a rather small minority which engineered secession in a good many Southern states," *Presidential Ballots, 1863–1892* (Baltimore: Johns Hopkins Press, 1955), p. 83.

amendment proposed by the House and backed by Seward and Lincoln which would have preserved slavery in the states where it already existed. (The amendment, incidentally, passed both House and Senate as—height of irony—the *Thirteenth* Amendment, but it was never ratified.)

By 1860, however, events were too advanced for these compromises. Did the political institutions encourage compromise too much and too long? Did they inhibit political leaders and citizens from squarely confronting the alternatives?

It is impossible to provide a confident answer. Human rationality has distinct limits. Because history has unfolded its answer to us, we can now discern those who in 1820 already divined correctly the shape of the future. But wrong guesses about 1860 could not be proved wrong in 1820.

The Southern veto. Nonetheless, it seems clear that the political institutions provided both Southerners and Northerners with sound reasons for believing that slaveholders—or the political representatives of the South—could prevent enactment of national laws directed to the peaceful abolition of slavery. So long as the South was in the Union, then, the alternatives were either revolution or some sort of compromise, because no decision on slavery could be reached without the assent of the South.

The power of the South was protected by federalism and the Constitution, for slavery could not be abolished in Southern states except by amending the Constitution. The power of the South was further protected by the Senate, where numbers of states counted, not numbers of people. The South might also seek protection from the Supreme Court, as it did in the case of Dred Scott.[9] The South gained further political advantage, as it was to do for the century following the Civil War,

---

9. *Dred Scott* v. *Sandford,* 19 How. 393 (1857). The Court, incidentally, has never been more knowingly and deliberately a political and legislative body than in that case. One of the justices, Catron, kept his old friend, incoming President James Buchanan, closely informed of what was happening; Buchanan was thus able to compose his Inaugural Address in the confident expectation that Taney and four other members of the Court would relieve Buchanan of the need for making a statement on the controversial matter of slavery in the territories. On March 4, Buchanan announced in his Inaugural Address that the forthcoming decision of the Court had made the question of slavery in the territories "happily, a matter of but little practical importance." Rather insincerely, since he knew what the decision was to be, he also pledged: "To their decision, in common with all good citizens I shall cheerfully submit, whatever this may be." Within a few days, the Supreme Court, as Buchanan expected, announced its decision. A bare majority of five members of the Court—four of whom were Southerners—declared the Missouri Compromise unconstitutional; four, all Southerners, declared that Congress could not prohibit slavery in the territories. Although their lack of foresight is scarcely credible, Buchanan and Taney evidently believed that the Dred Scott decision would actually solve the most burning issue of contemporary politics by judicial declaration. Never has the fragile basis of the Court's power over political questions been made so obvious. (For these details, see Nichols, *Disruption of American Democracy,* pp. 60–73.)

by the long continuity in leadership that enhanced the influence of her politicians.[10]

The political parties. Finally, the very merits of the political parties as instruments for settling moderate conflict may have disabled them during severe conflicts. The parties, both Democratic and Whig, were a nonideological conglomeration. They were nationwide, with crosscutting splits, eager for compromise on an issue that their leaders accurately foresaw would, if inflamed, destroy them. The small parties, like the Free-Soilers, who tried to pose the issue of slavery, clearly were crushed by the giants. For many years, the efforts of the parties succeeded; they were able to compromise the issue and thereby keep the peace. In 1836 they had even pushed through a 'gag rule' in the House, which prevented it from taking up "petitions, memorials, resolutions, propositions or papers relating in any way or to any extent whatsoever to the subject of slavery or the abolition of slavery."[11] This rule, or others even stricter, endured until 1844. By these and other means the oldest, largest, and most clearly national party—the American Democracy as it called itself—managed to maintain a compromise between Northern and Southern wings until 1860.

Yet the following hypothesis is defensible: If the American system had been based more fully on the principle of majority rule at the national level, and if the parties had been more concerned with ideological issues, they might have presented a clearer picture of the alternatives much earlier than they did. Southern slaveholders would have seen quite early that slavery was subject to a decision by the representatives of a majority of voters. As a distinct minority in the nation, their bargaining power would not have been amplified as it was by the innumerable devices of the American Constitution that reinforce minorities against majorities.

If slavery had been ended earlier, without disrupting the country, the gains would have been incalculable. A problem would have been solved while it was still manageable in the ways of peace. But would a political system less responsive to minority power only have led to secession earlier, when the Republic was still young? If the Republic had split earlier, what would have been the fate of Southern and Northern

---

10. "The control of the federal government by the South during the [1850s] had been almost complete. While the presidents were of Northern origin they had been nominated by national conventions dominated by Southern leaders. The Cabinets had generally had four of the seven members from the South. In Congress the most important committees were chaired by Southerners. At one time the President pro tempore of the Senate and the chairmen of the Foreign Relations, Finance, and Judiciary committees were experienced representatives from the South. When the Democrats were in control, the Speakers of the House were Southern. Five of the nine members of the Supreme Court were from that section. These men controlled both legislation and the fortunes of statesmen. . . ." Nichols, *The Stakes of Power,* p. 76.

11. Morris, *Encyclopedia of American History,* p. 179.

blacks? Compared with what actually transpired, would their lot have been worse—or better?

This much seems clear: the political institutions encouraged compromises that preserved a system based on slavery for so long in the South that this peculiar but deeply entrenched way of life was not likely to be revolutionized by peaceful negotiations.

CHANGE, COMPROMISE, RECONCILIATION

Only the immediate question was settled by Civil War: slavery was forever barred not only in the territories but in the old slave states as well.

Unimpeded by the political opposition of the Southern slavocracy, the Republican coalition of North and West carried through a program of comprehensive changes that insured the expansion of industry, commerce, and free farming. I have already mentioned the main items. Instead of a Thirteenth Amendment that would have preserved slavery, another Thirteenth Amendment abolished it. Instead of the policies of economic laissez-faire that the slavocracy had demanded (side by side with a rigid and detailed governmental intervention to protect slavery), the Republicans substituted the doctrine that the federal government would provide assistance for business, industry, and farming: the protective tariff; homesteads; land subsidies for agricultural colleges; transcontinental railways and other internal improvements; and national banks. When the defeated South came back into the Union, it had to accept the comprehensive alteration in government policy and economic institutions that historians later named the Second American Revolution.

Yet the revolution in the South that might have liberated the freed slaves, a revolution sought by some abolitionists and Radical Republicans, was never carried out. The only hope for black Americans to commence their march to full equality depended upon the prospects for a social, economic, and political revolution. But the freed black was provided with neither education nor land nor civil rights.

The Prospects for Revolution:
Change in the South

How could the domination of politics by a small white oligarchy be ended? For this was the central pattern of political life in the South in the pre–Civil War period. As in many developing nations of the world today, one hopeful possibility lay in land reform. If a large body of prosperous, independent, free farmers (as in the North) could be created by redistributing land holdings, then political power might come to rest with coalitions of free farmers, white and black, and the dominance of the great landowner might be destroyed. Education and civil rights would also be required. In time, the system would be able to sustain itself without protection from the outside.

It was some such strategy that a few Radical Republicans such as Thaddeus Stevens seem to have had in mind during Reconstruction. Even if hesitantly and from a variety of motives, the Radical Republicans in Congress took steps to reorganize the Southern economy, society, and polity. In 1866 they passed the Southern Homestead Act. Although it was weak and never implemented, it provided that in five Southern states where federal lands remained, all public lands (constituting one-third of the total area of these five states) were reserved exclusively for homesteaders. Like many whites, most blacks needed education. This was a major aim of Reconstruction government in creating public school systems in the Southern states. Above all, blacks needed political influence, which first of all meant the ballot. Neither the Civil Rights Act of 1866 nor the Fourteenth Amendment, which the Southern states were required to accept before being readmitted to Congress, gave blacks the right to vote. However, the Military Reconstruction Act of 1867 organized the South into five military districts and instructed the commanding general of each to register black voters and to protect their right to vote by stationing soldiers at polls and registration places. By the end of 1867, 703,000 blacks (and only 627,000 whites) had been registered.

The Revolution that Failed

Yet the revolution so boldly envisioned by a few was never completed. As we have seen during the present century, it is extraordinarily difficult for outsiders to impose a lasting revolution on a country. Without support from people inside a country, policies imposed entirely from outside are likely to produce only shallow changes.

By blacks? Freed slaves could not make a revolution unaided. They were a black minority amidst a national and even a regional majority of whites. In its awful destruction of racial pride and solidarity, slavery left its scars.[12] If there was to be a revolution after the Civil War, it had to be made by white citizens for black citizens. But the North was too irresolute, too infirm, and too divided in its aims to persist in the revolutionary reconstruction of Southern institutions that might have really

---

12. A lively debate goes on among historians as to whether American slavery was the most—or least—inhuman in the Western hemisphere. The most devastating interpretation is by Stanley M. Elkins, *Slavery* (New York: Grosset's Universal Library, 1959–1963). See also Kenneth M. Stampp, *The Peculiar Institution* (New York: Vintage Books, 1956). For a different interpretation, see Marvin Harris, *Patterns of Race in the Americas* (New York: Walker & Co., 1964).

An authoritative study that will probably be the major scholarly work on the subject for years to come is Eugene D. Genovese, *Roll, Jordan, Roll, the World the Slaves Made* (New York: Pantheon Books, 1974). A quantitative approach by economic historians that argues against many conventional interpretations is Robert William Fogel and Stanley L. Engerman, *Time on the Cross, The Economics of American Negro Slavery* (Boston: Little, Brown, 1974).

liberated the freed slaves. The white South and its traditional leaders were much more easily mobilized to resist that revolution.

By whites? Whether many Northern citizens, or even Northern leaders, ever eagerly embraced the idea of making a revolution in Southern society remains uncertain. There is strong evidence that few Northerners who supported Reconstruction in the South were ready to accept Northern blacks as their equals.[13] After the Civil War, as before, Northerners remained notably unenthusiastic about extending civil rights to the blacks in their midst. Except for Minnesota and Iowa—neither of which had many blacks—no Northern state in the postwar period voluntarily granted the vote to blacks; efforts to do so were steadily defeated. As the obstacles to Reconstruction in the South became more evident, support dwindled in the North. The reforming spirit flagged. "One is driven by the evidence," a leading historian has written, "to the conclusion that the radicals committed the country to a guarantee of equality that popular convictions were not prepared to sustain."[14] The erstwhile Radical leaders also wearied. Men like Charles A. Dana, editor of the influential *New York Sun* and once a Radical, used his newspaper to proclaim throughout Grant's second term: "No force bill! No Negro domination!" Poets and popular writers with longtime antislavery credentials like William Cullen Bryant, editor of the *New York Evening Post,* James Russell Lowell, and Robert Ingersoll all foreswore Radicalism and Reconstruction. Edwin L. Godkin in the columns of the *Nation* (a journal that had been in the vanguard in opposing the subjugation of blacks) now steadily attacked the notion that the evils of the South could be cured by outsiders.[15]

Neither the people nor their leaders were prepared to commit themselves to the long, persistent, and often disagreeable tasks of reconstructing an alien society—nor, for that matter, of reconstructing their own. The old and often decent impulse to compromise and conciliate was strong. Equality for the Afro-American had little appeal for white citizens other than the weak attraction of abstract justice. Also, for a time, radical politicians saw the alluring prospect of a Republican South founded upon black votes. But a policy of reconciliation (at the expense of the black) made a strong appeal not only to the spirit of compromise so deeply ingrained in Americans, but to history, tradition, identity, race, and economic interest, North and South. Revolution was tiresome. In any case, by 1876 all the signs showed that the revolution was failing.

---

13. See C. Vann Woodward, "Seeds of Failure in Radical Race Policy." *Proceedings of the American Philosophical Society,* 110, No. 1 (February, 1966).

14. Woodward, *The Burden of Southern History,* p. 83. See also his comments at pp. 79–83, 90–93.

15. Paul H. Buck, *The Road to Reunion, 1865–1900* (New York: Vintage Books, 1959), p. 101.

Restoration of white supremacy. In the defeated states where blacks were a minority, whites used a mixture of votes and intimidation to restore their control. In states like Mississippi where blacks were a majority, whites needed to administer an even stronger dose of intimidation and Ku Klux Klan terror in order to win elections. In one state after another, Reconstruction governments that fully protected the rights of black voters in the old slave states were displaced by 'conservative' governments: Tennessee in 1869, Virginia and North Carolina in 1870, Georgia in 1872, Alabama and Arkansas in 1874, Mississippi in 1876. By the time of the elections of 1876, Republican governments controlled only three Southern states, South Carolina, Louisiana, and Florida. Two sets of actions symbolized what was happening and foreshadowed the full restoration of white supremacy: First, in a series of decisions the Supreme Court held as unconstitutional the laws passed by Congress intended to protect the right of free slaves under the amendments to the Constitution enacted after the Civil War. Instead, the Court began to draw on one of these amendments, the Fourteenth, to protect business enterprise from government regulation.[16] Second, in July, 1876, Southern congressmen won enough support among their Northern colleagues to gut the Southern Homestead Act of 1866: land reform, half-hearted at best, was ended.

Return to Subugation: The Compromise of 1877

In November, 1876, the presidential contest led to a disputed outcome in which both candidates, backed by their parties, claimed victory. The bitter and inflamatory dispute went on through the fall of 1876 and the winter of 1877 and was finally settled by a compromise only a few days before the date for the new president's inaugural (March 4). This compromise permitted the Republican candidate to take office and marked the end of Reconstruction in the South.

The most eminent historian of that episode has summed it up:

> The Compromise of 1877 marked the abandonment of force and a return to the traditional ways of expediency and concession. The compromise laid the political foundation for reunion. It established a new sectional truce that proved more enduring than any previous one and provided a settlement for an issue that had troubled American politics for more than a generation. It wrote an end to Reconstruction and recognized a new regime in the South. More profoundly than Constitutional amendments and wordy statutes it shaped the future of four million freedmen and their progeny for generations to come. It preserved one part of the fruits of the 'Second American Revolution'—the pragmatic and economic part—at the expense of the other part—the idealistic and humanitarian part. . . .
>
> The Compromise of 1877 did not restore the old order to the South,

---

16. In *The Slaughter House Cases* (1873); *United States* v. *Reese* (1876); *United States* v. *Cruikshank* (1876). See the discussion of some of these cases in chapter 18, above.

nor did it restore the South to parity with other sections. It did assure the dominant whites political autonomy and nonintervention in matters of race policy and promised them a share in the blessings of the new economic order. So long as the Conservative Redeemers held control they scotched any tendency of the South to combine forces with the internal enemies of the new economy—laborites, Western agrarians, reformers. Under the regime of the Redeemers the South became a bulwark instead of a menace to the new order.[17]

After the compromise, troops were withdrawn in the states where they still remained. All serious efforts at Reconstruction ceased. The attempt to create an independent group of free farmers of both races failed utterly:

> The split-up of the plantation did not result in a land-owning, independent and sturdy yeomanry. A system of tenancy, in which the laborer worked assigned tracts and shared the produce with the owner, developed and became permanent. . . .
> The abounding poverty depressed the tenant into a status approximating peonage. Lacking sufficient savings to live through a season of growing crops without borrowing, he discovered that credit was an expensive luxury. Banking facilities in rural areas fell sadly short of the demand. Even where they existed, the only security the tenant had to offer the bank was a lien placed on his share of the anticipated crop. The village merchant with whom he traded for food, clothing, and other supplies perforce became his banker, giving credit in return for a crop lien. By 1880 approximately three-fourths of the agricultural classes in the South were chronic debtors, and the merchants through their control of credit were the dominant factor in the new economic structure.[18]

White supremacy was restored and the South became the one-party region it remained for almost a century. White Southerners not only abhorred the Republican party as responsible for inflicting civil war on their soil, freeing the slaves, and attempting to push through the policies of Reconstruction; they also saw that whites could unite to maintain white supremacy in a single party, whereas they would be dangerously weakened if they divided into two competing and conflicting parties.

The Supreme Court of the United States, as it must do sooner or later, adhered to the terms of the compromise: it undertook the long and sordid process of whittling down the meaning of the Fourteenth and Fifteenth Amendments—and converting the Fourteenth into a protection for business enterprise against state regulation. As the Court and federal government stood aside, blacks were, in time, disfranchised throughout the South. In 1896 in *Plessy* v. *Ferguson* the Court held that the Constitution did not forbid the states to segregate the races if separate but equal facilities were provided. Thus it finally wrapped the Con-

---

17. Woodward, *Reunion and Reaction*, pp. 245–246.
18. Buck, *The Road to Reunion*, pp. 151, 152.

stitution around the doctrine of segregation, popularly known as "Jim Crow."

"Capitulation to racism," now became complete. During the years that followed *Plessy* v. *Ferguson* a new wave of segregationism fastened the yoke of Jim Crow and black disfranchisement firmly upon the South. It was a system into which most white (and many black) Southerners were to be so thoroughly indoctrinated by overwhelming social pressure backed by violence that they perceived it as a precious and unalterable way of life to be protected against all change and all interference. Not until after the middle of the present century did this way of life—surely one of the greatest throwbacks to the past in our century—finally come under attack from outside and from within so powerful and so persistent that the hallowed ways began to yield, at last, to new ways. For the first time in the nation's history, treatment of blacks might someday be reconciled with the democratic promises of American polyarchy.

SUMMARY The developments leading to the Civil War conform in the main to the model of extreme conflict summarized on page 344 and discussed in Chapter 25:

1. In the course of the 1850s two issues came to the forefront: slavery and secession. Views diverged so widely on these two issues that compromise became increasingly difficult.

2. The conflict over these issues came to be increasingly perceived by the contestants as a zero-sum contest with high stakes involving, indeed, alternative and irreconcilable ways of life.

3. The pattern of crosscutting cleavages that had prevailed until about 1854 was transformed into a pattern of cumulative cleavages. The effect was initially to fragment political parties and other institutions of reconciliation and finally to polarize the contestants into two camps. However, even by the outbreak of the Civil War polarization of attitudes was far from complete, particularly among the general public. Secession was engineered by a small minority of slaveholders and their retainers, followers, and political representatives.

4. Negotiations could no longer produce acceptable solutions. The existence of what was in effect a veto in the hands of Southern leaders on decisions about slavery, the diversity within the parties and their inability to act unitedly, and the extreme partitioning of political authority all made elimination of slavery through ordinary political processes virtually impossible throughout the whole period from 1787 to the Civil War.

Yet despite enormous human cost, the Civil War did not lead to equal political rights for the freed slaves, much less equal opportunities for Afro-Americans generally. The revolutionary change in Southern landholding patterns that might have created a body of prosperous, independent free farmers, black and white, was not carried through. Freed slaves could not bring about changes unaided, and Northern whites finally proved unwilling to enforce changes over the opposition of Southern whites. The Compromise of 1877 permitted the restoration of white supremacy in the South.

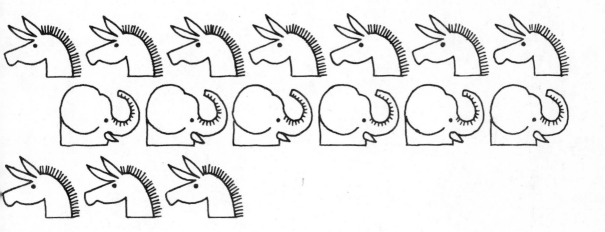

PART FIVE

REFLECTIONS ON POLITICAL ACTION

28 INFLUENCING THE CONDUCT OF GOVERNMENT: AN OVERVIEW

Whether one is aware of it or not, the daily life and the long-run opportunities and handicaps of each citizen are powerfully shaped by the actions and inactions of American governments. If you doubt it, perform any one of the following mental experiments: imagine that the American governments abolish public education; triple the tax rate; equalize incomes; abolish police and judiciary; prohibit divorce on any grounds; repeal all laws having to do with property; prohibit strikes and trade unions; nationalize all private businesses; suppress all political parties except one; sell all highways to private owners; make it a criminal offense to go to church. It is true that these are extreme possibilities; but that these are *possible* emphasizes what American governments actually do by showing what they *might* do.

American governments, then, like most other governments exercise great influence over the lives of their citizens. Only governments can legally punish a citizen who refuses to send his children to school, to treat them humanely, to allow them to receive blood transfusions, if necessary. Only governments can lawfully seize a citizen's property without consent and compel payment of taxes. Governments have the legal authority to coerce; they can fine, imprison, or even kill citizens who disobey their rules. American governments add to their legal powers a very large measure of legitimacy. Most citizens feel that it is not only dangerous to disobey the laws but also wrong to do so. Armed with legality and acceptability, American governments can and do acquire vast resources. They can and do use these resources not only to punish but also to reward. They allocate jobs, salaries, grants, contracts, payments, and other benefits in infinite variety. Cash expenditures by the federal government alone amount to about 20 percent of the gross national product, state and local expenditures, more than 10 percent; thus government spending is equal to about one-third of the gross national product.[1]

Because governments are extraordinarily influential, they are inevitably the objects of influence. To influence the conduct of government is to influence the way it uses its ability to allocate rewards, penalties, and power itself. It is easy to see, then, why few things are fought over with more persistence, vigor, and bloodshed than the conduct of government. But how, specifically, can and do Americans influence the conduct of their governments? This is the question that will concern us in this chapter and the next. To answer it will require, first, drawing together a number of matters that have already been treated in previous chapters.

PROSPECTS FOR SUCCESS

All societies regulate the ways in which people may attempt to influence the government. Only in a state of nature as described by Thomas Hobbes in Chapter 1 is everything permissible; and a state of nature in which everything is permissible would surely be as unbearable as Hobbes insisted it must be.

Like other systems, polyarchies regulate attempts to influence government. Thus they try to rule out efforts to gain influence and power over government officials by coercion, violence, and corruption. More than other systems, they also try to disperse influence widely to their citizens by means of the vote, elections, freedom of speech, press, and assembly, the right of opponents to criticize the conduct of government, the right to organize political parties, and in other ways.

Even so, it is obvious that citizens do not enjoy perfectly equal chances of getting the government to follow their wishes. Why not?

Four Key Factors

At least four kinds of factors affect the chances that a citizen or a group of citizens can secure favorable action from the government. These are: one's own situation, the situation of one's allies, the situations of one's opponents or potential opponents, and the amount of change one seeks.

Own situation. If you reflect on the chances of personally influencing government, you will readily see that the chances depend on your own

1. See "Federal Cash Expenditures as a Percentage of Gross National Product, 1869–1964," in D. J. Ott and A. F. Ott, *Federal Budget Policy* (Washington, D.C.: The Brookings Institution, 1965), p. 42, Figure VI. For state and local expenditures, see Maxwell, *Financing State and Local Governments* (Washington, D.C.: The Brookings Institution, 1965), p. 22.

situation, that is, on your political resources, political skills, and incentives.

Allies and opponents. Because no one is alone in a political system, chances of success will also depend upon the situation of your allies and opponents. All that has been said about resources, skills, and incentives applies equally to them. Allies may enable you to multiply resources and skills and, hence, improve your chances of success. Conversely, the greater the resources, skills, and incentives of your opponents, the worse your prospects are. Indeed, one of the characteristics of political systems is the frequency of *mutual escalation:* if you and your allies begin to invest your skills and resources in order to change the conduct of government, your political activity activates your opponents. They, too, mobilize their skills and resources; they seek allies. In response, you now mobilize more skills and resources and search for additional allies. Yet your reaction once again provokes your opponents to respond.

Fortunately, legal limits and accepted norms vastly reduce the likelihood that mutual escalation will finally proceed to the level of violence, although that possibility is never wholly out of the question—as the American Civil War illustrates. Another restraint on mutual escalation results from its *anticipation.* If you are quite sure your opponents will respond by escalating, you may decide that the potential gain from political action is not worth the cost. People sometimes think that politics is a cheap game to buy into, but it can be a costly game to win. This is one reason why many people with sizeable resources choose to remain aloof from politics or confine their actions to some specific aspect of the conduct of government that they care most about— schools, taxes, foreign policy, civil liberties, racial integration, agricultural subsidies, or one of a thousand other possibilities.

Amount of change required. In addition to the resources, skills, and incentives of you, your allies, and your opponents, the chances of gaining a favorable action from the government depend on still another factor: *how much change* you require in the behavior of other people in order for the government to do what you want it to do. The greater the amount of change required, the less your chances of success—other things being equal, of course.

How do we determine or measure the amount of change required? If there were time to explore it here, the concept would prove to be highly complex and multidimensional. But it is convenient, and sufficient for the purpose of this chapter, to think of the amount of change required as having two dimensions: the *number of persons* who must change their minds, and the *costs* to each person involved in changing his or her mind. Obviously, chances of success are much better if it is necessary to persuade only one key member of a congressional committee rather than all the members; winning over a majority of only one committee rather than a majority of a whole chamber; or influencing 10 percent of the electorate rather than 51 percent, etc. In Southern states, a Republican candidate for Congress or state office would ordinarily have to change the minds of many more voters than his or her Democratic opponent in order to win. In presidential elections, the two major parties each begin with a hard core of millions of supporters; to win, a candidate needs to change the minds of only a minority of the electorate. But third-party candidates, who begin with only a tiny hard core of support, might have to change the minds of one-third or more of the electorate in order to win.

As we all know, changing one's mind may be very easy or extraordinarily difficult. You find it easier to change your mind when you see only small differences between the alternatives than when you see large differences; thus if you are a Republican it is ordinarily easier for you to switch to another Republican when your preferred candidate fails to gain the Republican nomination than it is to switch to the Democratic candidate. It is easier to change your mind on matters you consider unimportant than on important matters. It is easier to change recently acquired or superficial views than to give up long-standing, deeply rooted views. It is easier to change consciously held opinions than unconscious attitudes, easier to change your opinions than your personality, loyalties, identifications—in short, yourself.

If you want to get other people to change their views, it appears that the greater the amount of change in other people's behavior you require for success, the more resources and skills you will need to use, the greater your incentives will have to be, and the more you need allies. Also, the more change you require, the easier it will be for your opponents to block the change. Conversely, the less the amount of change in other people you require, the less resources and skills you need, the lower your incentives need be, and the less you may have to depend on allies. These elements are summarized in Figure 28.1.

INEQUALITIES IN INFLUENCE
The fact is, of course, that resources, skills, and incentives—the key ingredients shown in Figure 28.1—are not distributed equally.[2] As a consequence, citizens by no means exert equal influence over their government.

From the opening chapters onward, we have seen that the existence of inequalities poses a persistent obstacle to the attainment of democracy. In polyarchies, the political institutions are intended to dis-

2. See the discussion in Chapter 5, pp. 37–39.

Figure 28.1
Successful Efforts to
Influence Government

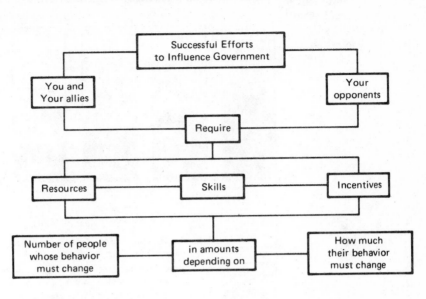

perse influence widely. As compared with hegemonic regimes, they surely do. Yet polyarchies are very far from attaining the degree of political equality envisioned in democratic ideals.

In the United States, as has been pointed out many times in this book, race has always been a major source of social, economic, and political inequality.[3] Racial inequality has been so massive and visible throughout American history that it has hardly been denied even by mythmakers who would have us believe that Americans have achieved a perfect (or almost perfect) democracy. Yet national mythology has often obscured the general existence of the political inequality that results from social and economic inequalities.

In Chapter 24 we saw that among Americans differences in socioeconomic levels and status—as measured, for example, by education, income, and occupation—do not seem to exert a strong influence on the way they vote or on the policies and programs they support. Where these differences do count, and count for a great deal, is in their influence on political participation: *Those who are better off participate more, and by participating more they exercise more influence on government officials. Those who are worse off participate less, and because they participate less they exercise less influence on government officials than those who are better off.*

---

3. See Chapter 7.

Figure 28.2
Amount of Political
Participation by Upper,
Middle and Lower-Status
Groups

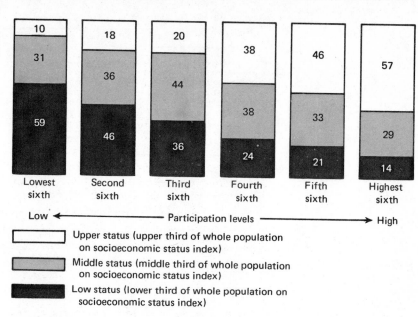

Low ◄──────── Participation levels ────────► High

Upper status (upper third of whole population on socioeconomic status index)

Middle status (middle third of whole population on socioeconomic status index)

Low status (lower third of whole population on socioeconomic status index)

Source: Sidney Verba and Norman H. Nie, *Participation in America: Political Democracy and Social Equality* (New York: Harper & Row, 1972), p. 131.

Findings on Political Inequality

The evidence on this point is powerful and convincing. Americans of higher social and economic status, whether measured by education, income, or occupation, participate more in political life than do citizens of lower social and economic status. Indeed, of all the factors that social scientists have used to account for differences in political participation, *differences in social and economic status are the most important.*

Some results from one of the most careful studies of participation are shown in Figure 28.2. In this study, each individual in the sample was given an overall participation score based on twelve types of political activity. The sample was then divided into six groups according to each person's level of participation. Each of the six groups was in turn divided into three equal-sized strata according to an index of social and economic status based on education, family income, and occupation of head of household. As we can see from the figure, of the persons who participated least, 59 percent are of low status and only 10 percent of upper status. At the other extreme, among those who are politically most active, only 14 percent are of low status while 57 percent are of upper status.[4]

4. Sidney Verba and Norman H. Nie, *Participation in America, Political Democracy and Social Equality* (New York: Harper & Row, 1972), Figure 8.3, p. 131.

What is more, it must come as a shock to many Americans to learn that the effects on political participation of these differences in social and economic status appear to be greater in the United States than in other democracies. In one comparison, only in India were the differences in participation greater![5]

The study also confirms that participation does make a difference. Officials are much more likely to concur with the views of the more active than of the less active. In fact, it was found that the degree to which officials concurred with views of citizens was directly related to the amount that citizens participated. The consequence, then, is that government officials respond more to upper-status citizens than to lower-status citizens.[6]

Solutions to the Problem of Political Inequality

How can these inequalities in influence be reduced? To begin with, it seems clear that a full solution would require reductions in the social and economic inequalities themselves. I shall return to this point in the last chapter. It is useful here to call attention to one major obstacle to this solution: If governmental action is required in order to reduce inequalities—in education and income, for example—such action is unlikely to be forthcoming as long as officials are more responsive to the citizens who are better off and might suffer from that change than to the citizens who are worse off and would gain from it.

From another perspective, however, political inequality is a special and acute case of how citizens can make the government more responsive to their wants. If the key ingredients in influence are political resources, skills, and incentives, then to attain greater political equality, and thus move toward greater democracy, a greater diffusion of these factors is required among American citizens. One key political resource is *organization*. In the next chapter some alternative strategies are examined that citizens can adopt for organizing themselves to bring about changes in government policies.

The second major factor, skills, requires knowledge of how the political system operates, and how changes are best brought about. This book is intended to provide such knowledge, of course. In the remainder of this chapter I want to add a few general observations bearing on this factor.

As to the third ingredient, incentives to participate in politics arise from psychological factors that are to some extent independent of both skills and resources. Some people enjoy interacting with others, for example, while some do not. Some people develop an early liking for political campaigns, while others never do. Yet incentives also interact

---

5. *Ibid.,* Table 20.1, p. 340.
6. *Ibid.,* Chapter 20, pp. 334ff.

with skills and resources. Incentives to participate in political life often lead to the acquisition of skills and a willingness to use one's resources of time, energy, and money in the pursuit of political ends. Political success in turn heightens the incentives to political participation. Unfortunately, failure depresses the incentives to participate, and as we shall see in the last chapter, the cycle of defeat and nonparticipation is not easy to overcome.

THE KEY GOVERNMENTAL ACTOR In a concrete sense governments are made up of officials. To influence the conduct of government one must sooner or later influence the conduct of officials. Far and away the most important government official is the president. The president's extraordinary influence follows from the president's extraordinary resources, skills, and incentives.

As we have already seen, among the president's resources, unmatched by any other official, are:

☐ Preeminence in legal authority, the duties, privileges and powers which by law and Constitution no one else can legally perform: the veto, the need for the president's signature on laws, the right to act as commander-in-chief of the armed forces.
☐ The exceptional legitimacy, respect, and deference endowed on the office during the course of its historical evolution.
☐ Widespread popularity.
☐ Command of public attention, and thus the influence on the content of the mass media.
☐ Influence over appointments and promotions to key posts in the national government.
☐ Unparalleled access to expertness, knowledge, secret information.
☐ Influence over the executive and administrative agencies of the national government, and hence the way they allocate rewards and punishments.

Not only does the president have exceptional resources. Any person who wins that office is likely to have acquired exceptional political skills before moving into the White House, skills that will be further refined by the manifold challenges of the presidency. Then, too, the president has stronger incentives than most people for using skills and resources as effectively as possible, for few people can see more clearly than the occupant in the White House how much hangs on successes and failures.

Because the presidency is the repository of more influence than any other office, the president becomes the most important object of political influence. All politically active groups tend to gravitate toward the White House. It is difficult and often impossible for any group to affect the conduct of the national government over continued and active presidential opposition. Even with presidential support, a group may fail to secure favorable action from the government. Without it, their chances are much worse. Those who most need the president's aid are those who seek the greatest changes, who advocate comprehensive alterations, innovations, or radical departures from existing policies. But even for conservatives, it is comforting to have an ally in the White House who can be counted on to oppose attempts to change the status quo. The presidential veto is a powerful instrument for preventing change.

How then does a group gain presidential support? Most commonly, by supporting the president. Probably the most effective way to gain the president's support is to be in on the process of choosing the person who will become president: by helping someone to be nominated, elected, or reelected. One may win the support of the president by giving support in other ways: by supporting presidential policies, for example, particularly when they are in trouble. Allies may also win the president's gratitude and future support by refraining from criticizing policies they disagree with: in the mettle of politics, silence can be golden. Groups may cultivate the president's friendship or the friendship of the president's friends and associates. They may even seek to win over the president by persuasion. Rational persuasion—or at any rate semirational persuasion—may be more important in winning the chief executive over to proposed policies than is commonly supposed. Failing these and other friendly ways of winning presidential support, one may turn to the public, the citizenry, the voters, in the hopes that if one can write the handwriting on the wall in letters large enough, the president will read it.

OTHER ACTORS   **Congress**

Even if a group has access to the president, it may also need to influence the Congress or some part of Congress. A group that lacks presidential backing may need to cultivate support in Congress all the more. The techniques that are used to win presidential support are also used to acquire support among senators and representatives. But senators and representatives are ordinarily closer and more accessible; it is easier to approach one's representative in Congress than to gain a hearing from the president.

While an individual or a group that seeks comprehensive change in government policies must turn toward the White House for leadership, groups with less ambitious goals may gain all they seek with little more than the cooperation of a handful of members of Congress. They may use Congress to kill or amend a hostile measure advanced by the president. Strategically placed support in Congress may be enough to provide the marginal changes in existing policies that a group considers critical: a loophole opened up, an appropriation increased or cut, and so on. One's senator or representative can also serve as an ambassador to one of the administrative agencies. Most do.

Lobbies. A persistent organization may—and sooner or later probably will—establish a Washington representative to lobby for its interests in Congress. Former senators and representatives—retired, usually, by the voters—are available. Between 1946 and 1965, twenty former senators and seventy-six former representatives registered themselves as lobbyists under the Federal Regulation of Lobbying Act passed in 1946.[7] In 1973, nearly 800 groups reported a total of $9.5 million for lobbying in Congress; unreported lobbying would doubtless swell the totals to figures considerably larger.[8]

Administrative Agencies

With or without the aid of lobbyists, groups also seek to gain their ends directly through the administrative agencies themselves. The relationships between agencies and private groups are sometimes antagonistic; occasionally, on the other hand, the private group may virtually capture the government agency. For example, the Maritime Administration, which is responsible for allocating government subsidies to the shipping industry, often acts as hardly more than a pressure group *for* the shipping industry *within* the government. Far from being an agressive regulatory agency, it is ordinarily the captive of the industry it is supposed to regulate. Leading officials of the Maritime Administration frequently leave their posts to join the industry. The shipping lobby is also influential in Congress. The coziness of these relationships is suggested by some congressional hearings in 1971 before the House Merchant Marine and Fisheries Committee. The election campaigns of the chairman of the committee had been heavily financed by shipping interests. Before his appointment in 1971, the committee's general counsel had been for more than a decade president of the industry's lobbying organization. The current president of the industry organization, who was now testifying before the committee, had previously been Undersecretary of Labor for labor-management relations, where he was the key official in negotiating maritime labor disputes.[9]

---

7. *Congress and the Nation, A Review of Government and Politics*, vol. 1 (Washington, D.C.: Congressional Quarterly, 1965), pp. 1572–1576.

8. *Washington Lobby*, 2nd ed. (Washington, D.C.: Congressional Quarterly, 1974), pp. 18, 37, 43.

9. *Ibid.*, p. 31.

Supreme Court

An individual or a group may also turn to the Supreme Court for help. Sometimes the Court will extend the protection of the Constitution to an otherwise defenseless person. However, for reasons already explored in Chapter 18, a group in outright opposition to the dominant national coalition of the day is unlikely in the long run to secure striking success in the Court. Even such an opposition group may nonetheless win delaying actions—and sometimes the delay can go on for a very long time, as in the defeat by business interests of child-labor legislation. A group stands a better chance of winning the Court's support and protection if the national coalition is divided, or if the group itself represents one segment of the national coalition. Occasionally, the Court may support a neglected group that stands outside the national coalition. The Court is an awkward, uncertain, unreliable, and rarely used instrument for bringing about major changes in national policies. It is better for veto than for positive innovation. Yet as we have seen, it was neither the president nor the Congress but the Supreme Court, responding not to outside pressures but to the sense of justice and ideological commitments of the justices themselves, that launched the United States on the road to integration and the extension of civil rights to minorities. It was the Court, as we have seen, that altered the existing balance of political power among cities, suburbs, small towns, and rural areas by forcing the states to reapportion their legislatures. In both these cases, however, the action of the Court was directed to state governments. Particularly in the case of civil rights, the Court's action was not effective until the Executive Branch, and ultimately Congress, backed it up with new and positive policies to replace those struck down by the Court.

State and Local Governments

The state and local governments are in many ways duplicates of the national government on a local scale. Individuals and organizations may succeed in achieving at these lower levels what they could not gain at the national level. They may even use the states to defy the national government. Within the state itself, the same process goes on. Groups who lack influence with city governments may turn to the state legislature. Urban groups unable to gain what they want at the state level may concentrate on the city administration, and city administrations themselves may bypass the state government and acquire allies, funds, and legal backing in Washington.

THE GREAT NUMBER OF CHECKPOINTS   When one looks at American political institutions in their entirety and compares them with institutions in other polyarchies, what stands out is the extraordinary variety of opportunities these institutions provide for an organized minority to block, modify, or delay a policy which the minority opposes. Consequently, it is a rarity for any coalition to carry out its policies without having to bargain, negotiate, and compromise with its opponents. Often, indeed, it wins a victory in one institution only to suffer defeat in another.

The president, the House, and the Senate are separate institutions. Each reposes on a separate and different system of elections with different terms of office and different electorates. Groups weighty in a presidential election may be much weaker in House and Senate elections. The policies of a particular group or coalition may be supported in one institution and opposed in another. In many areas of policy, each of these major institutions has a veto over the others. Each has a reservoir of legal, constitutional, and actual power.

Neither the executive, the House, nor the Senate is unified. A group may be strong in one executive agency, weak in another; strong in a particular House or Senate committee, weak elsewhere. A group may have individual advocates and opponents located at various places in the executive agencies, the regulatory commissions, the House, the Senate, the standing committees, or a conference committee.

The political parties themselves are coalitions. Nominations are not centrally controlled. National party leaders have limited resources for influencing their members in Congress. A minority may be defeated at the presidential nominating convention, yet retain its strength in state and local party organizations. It cannot be pushed aside.

Again and again in the history of the Supreme Court, a minority coalition that could not win the presidency or majorities in Congress has preserved a majority within the Supreme Court to fight a rear-guard delaying action. Chief Justice John Marshall fought Thomas Jefferson on judicial review. In the Dred Scott case, Chief Justice Taney, fearing what future majorities might do, fought to preserve dead or dying Court majorities. Embattled minorities entrenched in the Court knocked out the income tax in 1894, child-labor laws in 1918 and 1922, and New Deal reforms from 1935 to 1937. In its decision on school integration in 1954, the Court pronounced policy that could not possibly have passed through Congress at that time. Even if they rarely win their wars in the Congress, minorities well represented on the Court can win some impressive battles.

When minorities lose in national politics, they still may win in the states. Although defeated in the Civil War, the white South nonetheless forced the North to concede white supremacy, thanks in considerable measure to the institutions of federalism. In the North, trade unions and advocates of factory reform, abolition of child labor, workmen's compensation, shorter hours, and protection of women workers won in the state legislatures what they could not win nationally without the agreement of president, Congress, and Court. The principle holds even within the states, where legislative, executive, and judicial institutions follow the pattern of the national government, though often with greater fragmentation. Local governments provide still other checkpoints.

In constitutional theory there is no hierarchy of legitimate authorites. Fact conforms with theory: The president is no mere agent of the Congress; Congress is not subordinate to the president; neither the federal government nor a state is subordinate to the other on all matters. These are facts of political life, facts doubly resistant to change because fact corresponds to constitutional doctrine and American ideology.

The institutions, then, offer organized minorities innumerable arenas in which to fight, perhaps to defeat, or at least to damage an opposing coalition. Consequently, the institutions place a high premium on the strategies of compromise and conciliation—on a search for agreement. They retard and delay change until there is wide support. They render comprehensive change unlikely. They foster piecemeal adjustments. They generate politicians who learn how to deal gently with opponents, who struggle endlessly in building and holding coalitions together, who doubt the possibilities of great change, and who seek compromises.

SOME POLITICAL AXIOMS   What conclusions can be drawn from this somewhat general and abstract discussion? Some axioms—most of them rather obvious—suggested by the discussion follow:

☐ Other things being equal, the more resources you have—time, energy, money and so on—the more likely you are to influence the conduct of government.
☐ Other things are rarely equal, however, and if you have less of one resource than someone else, you may nonetheless gain greater influence because you have other resources. Though you have less money, you may have more time, more energy, greater popularity, or stronger ethnic ties.
☐ Even if you are weak in resources, you may gain allies and thereby increase the total resources, skills, and incentives mobilized for your policies.
☐ Probably no resource is uniformly most effective in American politics. A variety of resources therefore is generally a greater political asset than a very large amount of only one kind of resource.
☐ It is easier to block a change than to bring change about.
☐ Thus, it is generally easier to maintain old programs than to initiate new government policies.

☐ Modifying a law is easier than changing the attitudes that give rise to a law.

☐ Piecemeal changes stand a better chance than comprehensive changes.

☐ The less a proposal appears to deviate from prevailing ideas and ideology, the better its chance of success. If your opponents succeed in portraying your proposal as un-American, they have won more than half the battle.

☐ You have more chance of gaining favorable action if you need to influence only one segment of government rather than several. The greater the number of obstacles on the course, the better the chance that you will fall on your face.

☐ Hence, supporters of the existing state of affairs usually need fewer resources, less skill, and lower political incentives to *prevent* changes than opponents of the status quo need in order to *make* changes. Reformers and radicals, then, require more resources, skills, and incentives than conservatives. Revolutionaries require the most.

These observations are valid in a general way, but one must be cautious in drawing further conclusions that would be invalid. People who benefit most from the way things are and thus have the greatest resources of wealth, income, and social standing are likely to support the existing state of affairs most strongly. Thus, it might appear that conservatives who defend the status quo would always be in an impregnable position. Not only is this conclusion historically incorrect; it does not follow from what we have said. For those who benefit most from the status quo are often fewer in *numbers* than those who expect to benefit by a change. Moreover, well-to-do defenders of the way things are may be more out of touch with other citizens and hence lack political skills and popularity. Critics of the present state of affairs may greatly outnumber defenders; by combining and organizing they may mobilize greater total resources. They may possess greater skills. They may even have stronger incentives and a greater willingness to use what resources they have to bring about change.

So if the opponents of change often win a great many skirmishes, persistent and untiring critics of the status quo sometimes win the big battles.

SUMMARY   1. In general, prospects for success in influencing the government depend upon one's own resources, skills, and incentives, those of one's allies, and the amount of change required in the behavior of others. The amount of change includes both the number of persons who must change their behavior and the costs each person incurs by changing.

2. In the American polyarchy the key governmental actor is the president.

3. But gaining the support of the president is often not enough to secure the policy you want. Thus you may need to turn to the other important actors: Congress, the administrative agencies, the Supreme Court, state and local governments.

4. Perhaps the most distinctive general condition bearing on the problem of influencing the government, a characteristic not shared by all other polyarchies, is the existence of a great number of checkpoints that offer organized minorities innumerable arenas in which to fight and perhaps to defeat an opposing coalition.

5. These observations reinforce the following conclusions:

☐ The tendency for influence on government to be distributed unequally is strong.
☐ It is often possible, however, to compensate for weaknesses in some resources (e.g., money) by strength in others (e.g., numbers or energy).
☐ At any given time, supporters of the status quo are likely to exercise greater influence in proportion to their numbers than advocates of change.
☐ Those who seek incremental or piecemeal changes stand a better chance of succeeding in the American polyarchy than those who seek comprehensive change.

29 ORGANIZING TO INFLUENCE THE GOVERNMENT

To influence the conduct of the government in a significant way, citizens nearly always need an organization of some sort. Organizations are important for anyone who wishes to influence government, but they are particularly crucial for those who lack great individual resources. By banding together and pooling their small resources, including their votes, citizens who would be politically ineffectual if they were to act alone can sometimes gain influence by acting jointly. In this way, organization can be a resource that helps members of a group to compensate for their lack of individual resources.

Many citizens, however, do not participate in political organizations of any kind. As with other types of participation, so with organizations: people who are better off participate more in organizations than people who are worse off.

What then is the effect of organizations on political inequality? The study of American political participation cited in the last chapter concludes that "one may have to answer in terms of actuality and potentiality." In practice, organizations increase political inequality "for the simple reason that those who come from advantaged groups are more likely to be organizationally active." This, the authors argue, is not inevitable. In other polyarchies, better organization among disadvantaged groups reduces the differences in political influence and thus strengthens political equality. "Therefore organizations remain an important 'potential' source for reducing the participation gap between the socially advantaged and disadvantaged."[1]

This chapter examines five different organizational strategies open to a group wanting to change the conduct of the American national government. One of those is to organize a revolutionary movement in order to overthrow the government by force. This strategy is unlikely to be acceptable to many Americans in the foreseeable future, and therefore has scant chance of success. Each of the four more acceptable and successful strategies, as we shall see, has advantages and disadvantages.

RISE UP AGAINST THE GOVERNMENT?

In a polyarchy that was the fruit of a revolution, one should hardly forget Lincoln's sentences quoted earlier in this book: "This country, with its institutions, belongs to the people who inhabit it. Whenever they shall grow weary of the existing government, they can exercise their constitutional right of amending it, or their revolutionary right to dismember or overthrow it."

Our group of citizens, then, would need to make a crucial preliminary judgment: Should they choose to exercise "their revolutionary right to dismember or overthrow" the American polyarchy? Or, alternatively, should they use the peaceful processes that are available, or potentially available, in a polyarchy?

After the United States entered into its latest cycle of severe political conflict in the mid-1960s, fragmentation, antagonism, and alienation increased. As the crises in American society intensified, there was, not surprisingly, a corresponding increase in the advocacy of revolution as a way out.

By the end of the decade, in fact, the term *revolution* had become so fashionable that even President Nixon could safely use it to refer to his programs. As often happens when serious terms become modish, what the term *revolution* gained in popularity it lost in meaning. To some people revolution evidently had no specific political content: it meant speeding up cultural and attitudinal changes—about race, poverty, war, sex, drugs, or life-styles. To others it simply meant bringing about comprehensive changes in government policies, mainly by legal means: for example, eliminating poverty, unemployment, and inflation. To some it meant the use of what had once been thought of as unconventional ways to achieve specific changes, such as mass marches or civil disobedience. To a few the term meant little more than a justification for random violence—'trashing,' killing 'the pigs,' hurling Molotov cock-

---

1. Sidney Verba and Norman H. Nie, *Participation in America: Political Democracy and Social Equality* (New York: Harper and Row, 1972), p. 208. Membership and activity rates in sixteen types of organizations, from labor unions to school fraternities, are shown in Table 2.2, p. 42.

tails. To a few others, it meant a political strategy aimed at bringing down the government by force and replacing it with another kind of regime, headed by different leaders, with different aims and policies.

Revolution in this strict sense—overthrowing the existing government by force and replacing it with a new and different type of regime—offers, as Lincoln pointed out, a genuine political alternative to achieving changes by means of the processes available in a polyarchy. In my view, it is an alternative with such scant prospects of succeeding in the United States that I find it difficult to weigh with the seriousness its advocates, who are sometimes deeply committed and self-sacrificing persons, would insist is appropriate. Since 1787 there has probably never been a time when some Americans have not advocated overthrowing the existing government by force, somehow, and replacing it by a new and better regime. Probably their numbers have waxed during periods of severe conflict and waned during the lengthier intervals of moderate conflict and crosscutting cleavages. These revolutionaries have always been a tiny minority of the population, powerless to do much more than bring down upon themselves the often crushing weight of social, economic, and physical penalties, both legal and illegal. In the United States it has been the fate of revolutionaries—using the term still in its strict sense—to be well-supplied with incentives, but inept, pitifully weak in all political resources, and lacking wholly what is most needed by revolutionaries to overcome their scant resources: allies who are powerful either because of sheer numbers, superior organization, or for other reasons.

The operation of the American polyarchy in the 1960s was, if not exactly typical in this respect, at least familiar. Like their predecessors, active revolutionaries were a tiny proportion of the adult population, even among young people, where they were assumed to be most numerous. As usual, violence by or attributed to revolutionaries alienated more persons than it won over.[2] And as usual, social economic, and political penalties, legal and illegal, decimated the ranks of revolution-

2. The preceding propositions are supported by a substantial amount of data. "Researchers have agreed since 1968 that only about 19 percent of the students are alienated or politically radical, and of these perhaps one-third have revolutionary views," S. M. Lipset, "Youth and Politics," in R. K. Merton and Robert Nisbet, *Contemporary Social Problems* (New York: Harcourt Brace Jovanovich, 1971), p. 755.

Based on interviews with 4,000 young people, Daniel Yankelovich found that 87 percent of the students agreed with the statement that the "American system of representative democracy can respond effectively to the needs of the people," Daniel Yankelovich, Inc., *Generations Apart* (Columbia Broadcasting System, 1969), p. 24.

Among the population at large, revolutionary sympathies are so scarce that they hardly show up in national surveys. Even nonrevolutionary but simply new and unconventional attitudes are often confined to an astoundingly small percentage of the population. Thus in 1968, "those who opposed Vietnam and were sympathetic to Vietnam war protestors make up less than 3 percent of the electorate—even if we add comparable blacks to the group—and law and order were not unpopular with the 97 percent," Philip Converse et al., "Continuity and Change in American Politics: Parties and Issues in the 1968 Election," *American Political Science Review* 63 (December 1969), p. 1088.

aries, discouraged many, confused others, and caused a few leaders to rethink questions of strategy and tactics.[3]

The political revolutionary, in the narrow sense used here, faces a dilemma in a long-established polyarchy where the people tend to adhere to a democratic ideology. If revolutionaries could win a majority of the people to their program, it will be said, they would have no need to overthrow the government by force. They could gain office by elections. If they are unable to gain enough support among the people to accomplish their program through the processes of polyarchy, they suffer not only from a shortage of political resources but also from lack of acceptability to other citizens. On that moral basis can these modern advocates of aristocracy justify their claim to rule over a preponderant majority unwilling to support them?

In fact, in every polyarchy where widespread suffrage and the other main institutions of polyarchy have been in existence for a generation or more, the polyarchy has so far proved invulnerable to being overturned by strictly internal forces. Experience shows that long-established polyarchies are extremely tough and resilient and have a remarkable capacity for riding out severe crises.

A prolonged failure to cope satisfactorily with issues that a large proportion of citizens regarded as urgent could, of course, so undermine the legitimacy of polyarchy as to generate widespread support for some alternative to polyarchy. Well-established polyarchies may be sturdy but they are surely not invulnerable.

FOUR STRATEGIES FOR INFLUENCING THE GOVERNMENT

If one concludes for the reasons set out above that revolution in the strict sense is not a serious alternative in the American polyarchy, the question of effective organization remains unanswered. To simplify, let us put to one side for the moment matters of *tactics*—whether in a given situation to support a particular candidate, to appeal to friends and neighbors at the local level, to engage in mass demonstrations in Washington, or whatever. Tactics aside, a political movement that rejects the path of revolution, and seeks to use the processes constitutionally available or potentially available in the American polyarchy, has open to it, roughly speaking, four strategies:

1. A particular interest can organize a separate political party of its own.
2. The particular interest can form a new coalition party by combining

---

3. Thus in 1971, Huey Newton, a leader of the Black Panthers, a self-styled revolutionary organization, announced that henceforth the Panthers would avoid violence and cultivate the support of religious and other groups within the black community.

with another group or interest that has similar, overlapping, but not identical objectives.

3. Although it remains neutral between the two major parties, the special interest can act as a pressure group to secure favorable legislation and the nomination and election of sympathetic candidates.

4. By entering into one of the existing parties, the particular interest can become an element in a major party coalition; it can then use its bargaining power to gain influence within the party.

Each of these alternatives has its own inner logic, its special advantages and disadvantages. Perhaps this is why all four strategies have been tried so often. The first strategy has been tried by Free Soilers, Socialists, Greenbackers, Communists, Prohibitionists, Single Taxers, America Firsters, Vegetarians, and the Church of God party, among others. The first strategy enables a movement to maintain its ideological purity and avoid compromising its goals. Yet the usual price is political isolation and defeat. The second strategy helps a movement break out of its isolation; but in doing so the movement may lose at least some of its purity and still fail to become a major party. The second strategy was that of the Populists, until they went all the way in 1896 and backed the Democratic candidate, Bryan. It was also the strategy of Progressive movements in 1924 and 1948. The third strategy may yield high payoff if the goals of the movement are narrow and group-oriented. But as a price, the movement must do nothing to alienate the major parties. This is the strategy of most pressure groups; in some states and localities it has also been the strategy of third parties, like the Liberal party in New York. The fourth strategy may yield a movement more influential over a greater range of goals than the third strategy, with a better chance of winning elections than the second strategy. The price, however, is a willingness to negotiate, to bargain, to compromise in order to form a winning coalition, and to run the risk of turning members of the other party into opponents. This is the strategy that some labor unions have adopted at the state level, like the United Automobile Workers in Michigan. It was also the strategy the Populists were moving toward when they supported Bryan in 1896.

Weighing the advantages and disadvantages of the four alternatives is a recurrent task in American politics. Few choices are so important to the destiny of a political movement. It is instructive, therefore, to examine the experience of a movement that has had to face these four alternatives.

A CASE HISTORY For two reasons, the experience of the American labor movement provides an excellent case history. *First,* when the labor movement began to grow in the late nineteenth century, workers had few political resources. The history of the labor movement, then, illustrates how a group of people, each of whom was politically powerless standing alone, gained influence by means of *organization*. Like workers elsewhere, American workers typically had brutally long hours and little leisure. In the steel industry, they worked twelve hours a day, seven days a week, twenty-four hours steadily on the day that workers on the night shift became the day shift. They had virtually no economic resources, no savings, no protection against unemployment, ill-health, accidents, or loss of support in old age. Politics, economic life, the society, the very culture itself were all deeply permeated by the influence of businessmen and the goals and values of business enterprise.

The political influence of workers was weak; but they had at least three resources. Unlike their counterparts in European countries, most American workers had the vote and full legal rights to participate in the political system. Even immigrants usually became citizens. They had numbers. If they were organized, they might make their votes count. And they had the capacity to withhold their labor from their employers by joint action: to go on strike. However, legal guarantees for the right to strike were still primitive. Here was one area where political influence might help to change the law.

To gain influence in politics, then, very nearly required workers to lift themselves up by their own bootstraps. To make use of what meager resources they had—their votes, their numbers, and their capacity to strike—they needed organizations. This meant, first of all, trade unions. As the American trade union movement developed it had to face the question of how to use its resources to gain influence in politics.

Second, the experience of the trade union movement is particularly instructive because from its earliest years down to the present day the labor movement has debated the pros and cons of the various strategies. The debate over alternatives is not yet ended; perhaps it never will be. The reader may well ask: Has the American labor movement made the right choice of political strategies?

Rise of the Labor Movement

Not only in the Western world but throughout much of the globe, industrialization has gone hand in hand with the growth of cities and the rapid expansion of the urban working classes. A nation of traders and farmers, as Britain still remained in the eighteenth century, was already well on the road to becoming a nation of urban employers and urban workers before the end of the nineteenth century. The United States began as a nation of farmers and, as a result, Americans have not yet wholly given up a romantic assessment of the virtures of rural life. Yet the country was nonetheless destined to become a nation of urban workers, white-collar employees, technicians, and business people.

The Civil War not only stimulated the growth of Northern industry but liberated economic development from the dead hand of Southern slavocracy. In the last half of the nineteenth century, the proportion of Americans employed in commerce and industry rose steadily as the proportion in farming declined. By 1880, farmers and farm workers outnumbered nonfarm workers. By 1930, the urban population exceeded the rural population. Between 1910 and 1920, the absolute number of farmers reached its peak and thereafter the total number of farmers steadily declined. By the 1970s, the farm population was less than 5 percent of the total population.

The workers who were employed in urban industries represented a new class. It was all too obvious that they were not farmers, even if they might once have been farmers, farm laborers, or peasants who had come to the cities from an American or European countryside. They were not middle class. They were not, at least to any great extent, property owners. They were definitely not employers. Nor were they shopkeepers. Huddled in the cities, often living in miserable slums, they constituted a new and separate interest in society, a social and economic class.

In the nineteenth century, not only Karl Marx but many other observers took for granted that the relative expansion of the industrial working classes would continue more or less indefinitely. A few observers like the German socialist critic of Marx, Eduard Bernstein, foresaw that industry and commerce might also expand the size of the white-collar classes. Bernstein, it turned out, was closer to the truth than Marx. The proportion of blue-collar workers, the authentic 'working class,' would rise less rapidly than the proportion of those employed in white-collar occupations. Between 1910 and 1920 this trend showed up markedly in the most advanced industrial nation, the United States. The full political significance of the development, however, is far clearer in retrospect than it was to most observers at the time. In the mid-1950s, white-collar groups began to outnumber the historic blue-collar working class.

Labor Organizations Gain Against Violent Opposition

In the United States, as in the north European countries, labor-management conflicts were often harsh and brutal. "Violence in labor disputes," a leading student of the subject has said, "is more common in the United States than in any other industrial nation."[4] Not only was

---

4. Philip Taft, "Violence in American Labor Disputes," *The Annals of the American Academy of Political and Social Science*, 364 (March 1966), 127–140, especially p. 128.

violence more common; in the United States labor conflicts took on a ferocity seldom equaled in Europe. An authority on both the French and American labor movements has remarked that "American workers had to fight bloodier battles than the French for the right of unions to exist and to function."[5] Nonetheless, despite occasional setbacks and fierce opposition from employers, union membership grew from 447,000 in 1897 to over 2 million in 1904.[6]

Government and employers frequently formed a coalition against workers. State governments, and on occasion even the federal government, were brought into industrial disputes. In the strike of the American Railway Union against the Pullman Company in 1894, U.S. Attorney General Richard Olney, who had formerly been a railroad lawyer, sought an injunction in federal court against Eugene V. Debs and other strike leaders on the ground that the strike interfered with the mails and interstate commerce and violated the Sherman Antitrust law. The federal court issued a sweeping order against the strike leaders. When the U.S. marshal claimed that he was unable to enforce the court order, Olney persuaded President Cleveland to send federal troops to Chicago, although neither the mayor of Chicago nor the liberal governer of Illinois, John Peter Altgeld, had requested federal help and both protested against the presence of the troops. Extensive rioting erupted. The strike failed. "It was not the soldiers that ended the strike," Debs concluded ". . . it was simply the United States courts." Debs was sentenced to six months in jail for contempt of court, and three other strike leaders to three months.[7] Later, Debs was to run five times as candidate for president on the Socialist ticket. It is altogether likely—and fitting—that Debs became a Socialist while he was serving his prison sentence.[8]

THE FIRST STRATEGY: TRIAL AND REJECTION   In Europe the labor movements usually adopted the first and second strategies: formation of a separate and independent labor or socialist party that would ultimately become one of the major governing parties and help to bring about extensive reforms. The American labor movement deliberately and with full awareness that it was deviating from the path of European labor chose a different route. It explicitly and self-consciously rejected the first and second strategies. For many decades it favored the third strategy, political neutrality. Then from the time of the New Deal onward, the fourth alternative has more and more be-

---

5. Val R. Lorwin, "Reflections on the History of the French and American Labor Movement," *Journal of Economic History,* 17 (March 1957), 37.

6. Philip Taft, *Organized Labor in American History* (New York: Harper & Row, 1964), p. 162.

7. See *ibid.,* pp. 148–158, for a description of the strike, and the statement by Debs.

8. On Deb's conversion to socialism, see Ira Kipnis, *The American Socialist Movement, 1897–1912* (New York: Columbia University Press, 1952), p. 47.

come the policy of key labor unions and the unofficial policy of the AFL-CIO, the merged superfederation of the American Federation of Labor and the Congress of Industrial Organizations.

Trial

Surprising as it may seem, the first authentic party of the urban working classes was born not in Europe but in the United States. Called the Working Men's party, it was organized in Philadelphia in 1828 and lasted about three years.[9] After the Civil War, a number of American socialists affiliated themselves with the First International, a mainly European association of workers. Socialist parties multiplied with what now seems a bewildering profusion of names, programs, and ideologies. In every presidential election since 1892, voters in most states have had an opportunity to vote for socialist candidates for the presidency. But the socialist vote never went beyond 6 percent of the total votes cast (1912), and finally all but died out.

Rejection

Why did the first strategy, adopted by labor movements in many European polyarchies, fail in the United States?

Different levels of conflict? It was not for lack of conflict over capitalism, the role of government, and the power of labor and business in society and the economy. As we have already seen, the relations between workers and employers frequently displayed the most visible symbol of severe conflict—violence. Moreover, two more of the principal conditions of severe conflict were also present: *conflicting views* on matters involving *high stakes.*

In the conflicts between labor and business, the stakes, as we noted above, have never been insignificant and often they have been high. Who is entitled to control decisions on wages, working conditions, and personnel? According to what standards? How and by what standards are prices and employment to be regulated? How shall incomes be distributed? Who is to be protected and who harmed by government intervention? Whose freedom is to be expanded or reduced? These are the weightier if not always visible stakes involved in disputes over the role of labor unions, regulation of business, antitrust action, the forms and incidence of taxes, welfare measures, and monetary, fiscal, tariff, and agricultural policies.

At times, important blocs of national leaders have diverged widely on these issues: in the 1890s, certainly, and again in the 1930s. From all the evidence at hand, both decades were periods of severe conflict. During both periods there was a sharp divergence of views; and during

---

9. Taft, *Organized Labor In American History*, pp. 15–20.

both periods the stakes were high. (To repeat a point made earlier, the leaders involved obviously *thought* the stakes were high, and for our purposes that is all that matters.)

Yet the conflict was never successfully pressed by a distinct labor party nor a party bearing a classic socialist ideology and program. The political conflicts occurred between and within parties that were conglomerate coalitions. And these coalitions lacked ideologies as distinctly different as European socialism was from European liberalism or conservatism.

No doubt the absence of a labor party with a socialist ideology and program as a major competitor of the other parties helped to keep down the size of the stakes involved in American politics. The absence of a powerful socialist party also meant that political views did not diverge so sharply as in the north European polyarchies. Yet it is worth noting that European socialist parties gradually abandoned much of the distinctively socialist ideology they had begun with. They turned to piecemeal reform. They grew less enthusiastic about the classic socialist solution: nationalization of industry. They became, or tried hard to become, conglomerate catch-all parties uniting urban labor with rural labor, white-collar workers, farmers, fishermen, and government employees.

The United States did not, then, avoid sharp and sometimes severe conflicts over economic issues. Yet it did skip a transitional stage that was universal among the northern European polyarchies and quite possibly essential to their success in winning over business and labor to polyarchic institutions and a common set of constitutional procedures. Why did the United States and Europe diverge? Why did labor-socialist parties fail to thrive in the United States?

Economic growth? One part of the answer is perhaps to be found in the fact that while the stakes were high in the United States, the contest was not 'zero-sum.' An expanding economy created an ever-available surplus to be distributed.[10] Gross national product and personal consumption grew faster than population; from 1839 to 1959 they increased at the rate of about 1.6 percent a year per capita. These seemingly modest rates of incremental change amounted to a doubling about every forty years, a fivefold increase in a century. Working-class hostilities were vastly weakened by rising living standards; it took major depressions, as in 1893–4 and the Great Depression after 1929 to deepen hostilities to a point where the working class could be mobilized to support extensive reforms.

Yet the European economies were also expanding. And it is often argued with persuasive evidence that revolutionary movements prosper

10. David Potter, *People of Plenty* (Chicago: University of Chicago Press, 1957).

most when improving conditions stimulate hope and confidence. Hence to call on the expanding American economy to explain the inability of a labor-socialist party to grow in the United States is not a wholly satisfactory explanation. Was it then because the fruits of economic growth came earlier in the United States than in Europe? Possibly, but there were other differences.

To what extent is the explanation, or a part of it, to be found in the other two sets of factors described in Chapter 23 that influence the course of political conflict? These are the pattern of cleavage and the political institutions.

Cleavages. It seems clear that a pattern of crosscutting cleavages was never fully displaced by a pattern of divisions accumulating along a single fracture. One cannot be dead sure that the crosscutting cleavages were greater in the United States than in the European democracies, but there is an impressive amount of evidence suggesting that they were, and that in any event neither workers nor business people were sharply cut off from one another or from the rest of American society.

Three factors helped to maintain a pattern of crosscutting splits even during times of considerable stress. One of these was the extraordinary consensus among Americans on a number of basic ideological issues. In Europe, the socialist parties often battled for polyarchy against their 'bourgeois' opponents; it was the socialists, often, who fought for parliamentary government, cabinet responsibility, and an equal and universal suffrage. In Norway and Sweden, for example, in the early stages, socialist and middle-class parties fought more over democracy than over socialism. In the United States this ideological, institutional, and constitutional conflict had been pretty well settled before the urban laboring population began to expand. The American labor movement of the 1880s and 1890s did not have to fight for polyarchy; the institutions of polyarchy were already here and a democratic ideology widely accepted. To be sure, the constitutional structure was at stake in the Civil War, but it was never again seriously contested. The labor movement joined in the broad consensus on democratic ideas and the institutions of polyarchy that have been such a pronounced aspect of American life. What is more, the labor movement never mounted a strong opposition even to the traditions of private property and competitive self-advancement.

Another factor that helped to maintain crosscutting was the fact that in comparison with Europe, other cleavages were stronger than class. The 'solidarity of the working classes' predicted by Marx was weakened in the United States by ethnic differences, language, religion, and region. In many cities where the socialist parties drew most of their strength from the foreign born, the very parties that most strongly stressed the importance of working-class solidarity had to establish separate branches to accommodate their different and sometimes unfriendly ethnic groups. Differences like these inhibited the growth of the class consciousness that had developed in countries with less ethnic and religious diversity, such as Sweden, France, Germany, and Britain.

Finally, the course of American economic development doomed both blue-collar labor and business people, like all other economic interests, to remain minorities. Until 1880, urban workers were outnumbered by farmers. Yet when the number of farmers began to decline, the number of white-collar workers rose. Hence a party that drew its support exclusively or even mainly from blue-collar workers could not hope to win majorities in national elections. Business people were equally condemned to minority status. Owners and executives of business firms were bound to be outnumbered by their employees. Hence they too could not hope to win majorities in national elections with a party that appealed only to business interests.

Impact of federalism. The political institutions also offered a powerful and quite possibly a decisive resistance to the creation of a successful labor-socialist party or even a labor-farmer coalition. First of all, the institutions of federalism made it risky for the labor movement to identify itself exclusively with a single party. For in a federal system many of the specific aims of labor could be achieved more quickly through state action than by federal laws. A separate party which ran candidates against those of the major parties would antagonize state legislators otherwise responsive to demands made on them by workingmen's organizations. A leading student of American labor history has written:

> Only a state legislature could compel defaulting employers to pay wages earned, impose safety rules on hazardous occupations, and define minimum sanitary standards in work places. The state legislatures prescribed standards for schooling, voting, and minimum age for working, the employment of women, and limitations of hours of labor in certain occupations. . . . Promotion of an independent labor party would have necessitated the severance of relations with many members of the legislatures, who, assured of organized labor's political hostility, would have been more reluctant to support the bills labor annually or biennially presented to the legislatures.[11]

Thus the strategies of the American labor movement were shaped, during its formative years, by the political realities of the federal system.

Impact of winner-take-all elections. Second, there was the sobering matter of the election system, the effects of which we have already ex-

---

11. Philip Taft. "Labor History and the Labor Issues of Today," *Proceedings of the American Philosophical Society*, 106 (August 1962), 306. See also Taft, "On the Origins of Business Unionism," *Industrial and Labor Relations Review*, 17 (October 1963), 20–38.

plored. In no country in Europe did the labor-socialist parties ever manage to gain a majority of popular votes. But they did obtain the introduction of systems of proportional representation, which reduced or eliminated the multiplier effect of the winner-take-all system. In the United States, not only in national but also in state elections, the single-member district and the winner-take-all system had depressing consequences for a third party trying to make its way against the two existing giants. The evidence of American experience was clear enough to anyone who cared to examine it: for a third party to cross the magic threshold to major party status was a discouraging, and probably hopeless task.

It is true that in Britain, which was also a two-party country, the Labor party in the 1920s became the main opposition party. Though it never acquired an absolute majority of popular votes in subsequent elections, thanks to the winner-take-all system it has gained a majority of seats in the House of Commons on a number of occasions. However, by the time the experience of the British Labor party became available as an example to encourage the advocates of a separate labor party in the United States, that strategy had long since been firmly rejected by the American labor movement.

Impact of already existing parties. In any event, another aspect of American political life greatly reduced the relevance of British experience with the Labor party. This was the fact that the urban workers had already been won over to the two existing parties before the American labor movement itself developed.

As the number of urban workers multiplied rapidly after the Civil War, there were already on the scene two major parties accustomed to assimilating workers into their organizations. In Europe, in Britain, in the Scandinavian countries and elsewhere the urban workers faced existing parties—Liberals, Conservatives, and the like—that were run by members of the middle classes and the aristocracy. These middle-class parties had little or no grass-roots organization extending down to the wards and precincts. They lacked the kind of organization that was created for American parties during Jefferson's presidency, perfected during Jackson's, and adopted as a matter of course by the newly organized Republican party in the late 1850s. In Europe the middle-class and aristocratic parties could ignore the urban workers, for workers were deprived of the vote.[12] But in the United States, where

---

12. In Britain, a substantial proportion of urban working-class householders were enfranchised in 1867–8; further reforms enlarged the franchise in 1884; virtually universal male suffrage came in 1918. It has been estimated that "perhaps one in twelve males could vote before 1832, one in seven thereafter, one in three after 1868, and three in five after 1884." Allen Potter, "Great Britain: Opposition with a Capital 'O'," in Dahl, *Political Oppositions in Western Democracies* (New Haven, Conn.: Yale University Press, 1966), p. 3. The dates for universal manhood suffrage in some other European countries were: Norway, 1898; Sweden, 1909; Denmark, 1901; The Netherlands, 1917; Belgium, 1919; France, 1848; Italy, 1912.

the working classes had enjoyed the franchise from the early decades of the nineteenth century, to ignore these potential voters would have been political stupidity; and party politicians were not that inept. The urban 'machines' of the Democratic party were particularly adept at using primitive social welfare devices to gain the votes and often the permanent loyalties of immigrants. Thus, unlike Europe, in the United States there was no vacuum into which a labor party could rush.

The Democratic and Republican parties not only had the advantages of organization; they also profited from the built-in reluctance to change established party loyalties. A successful labor party would need more than a program or an ideological appeal to workers; to be successful a labor party would first have to break down well-established attachments to one of the existing parties. There was nothing peculiar to the mentality of a worker that prevented him from incurring emotional ties to the Democratic or the Republican party.

A realistic appraisal of the American political scene, then, would lead to the conclusion that the two major parties could not be thrust aside by a labor party organized by the labor movement.

THE SECOND STRATEGY: TRIALS AND POLITICAL DEFEATS

There was, however, another possibility: a coalition party drawing its strength from both farmers and urban workers. This strategy was doubly tempting, for, oddly enough, the farmers of South and West were much more responsive than labor itself to new parties that advocated labor-socialist programs. Even the Socialist party, although organized and led mainly by urban socialists, gained more electoral support in the agricultural states than in the industrial states. In 1912 at the high-water mark of the Socialist vote, their candidate for president, Eugene V. Debs, received 5.9 percent of the national vote. The highest percentage he won in any state was 16.6 percent which he won in—of all states—Oklahoma. The five other states in which Debs won more than 10 percent of the vote were Nevada, Montana, Washington, California, and Idaho—none at this time a highly industrial state.

The greatest success for the strategy of a farmer-labor coalition— and the most consequential failure—was achieved by the Populists in the 1890s. As we have seen, the period from 1892 to 1896 marked a series of critical elections in which party loyalties were realigned for the following three decades. The defeat of Bryan in 1896 amounted to a profound defeat not only for Populism but for the prospects of a new third party that would unite farmers with labor in a powerful national coalition.

Even though industrial labor and farmers constituted a shrinking proportion of the electorate, proponents of the farmer-labor strategy did not wholly die out. Both farmers and urban wage earners were hurt by the economic turbulence of the usual cycle of inflation and depression that followed the First World War. In 1920 a combination of socialists, trade unionists, and liberals organized a Farmer-Labor party that nominated a presidential slate; however it gained only 265,000 votes—less than a third of the perennial Socialist party total and barely more than the Prohibition party.

Although "the Farmer-Labor Party did not attract many top labor or agricultural leaders,"[13] during the next few years a far more serious effort was launched, mainly on the initiative of trade union leaders, chiefly those in the railway unions. Their instrument, the Committee for Progressive Political Action, nominated Senator Robert M. LaFollette, a nationally known Progressive Republican, as their presidential candidate. As his vice-presidential running mate the Committee selected a well-known progressive Democrat from Montana, Burton K. Wheeler. Despite the fact that the American Federation of Labor had not sponsored the Committee for Progressive Political Action nor proposed the nomination of a third-party slate, in a departure from standing policy the executive board of the AFL publicly endorsed the election of LaFollette and Wheeler.[14]

LaFollette and Wheeler carried only LaFollette's home state of Wisconsin, but they did get 4.8 million votes, or 16 percent of the total, and they ran second in eleven states. As in the past, the Progressive candidates won their biggest share of the votes in rural, not industrial, states. In 1925 the Committee for Progressive Political Action was dissolved.[15]

In 1948, a group of liberals and communists organized the Progressive party and nominated as its presidential candidate a well-known New Dealer, the one-time secretary of agriculture and former vice-president, Henry Wallace. The Progressive party was a sad caricature of the authentic farmer-labor parties that had preceded it. The national labor movements opposed it. The AFL maintained its traditional policy of neutrality, though in fact its leaders were hostile. The head of the CIO's political organization announced that it had been "the policy of the CIO Political Action Committee not to support a third party." The CIO Executive Board decided by a vote of 33–11 that "it was politically unwise to inject a third party into the political scene of 1948."[16] In late August, the CIO Executive Board endorsed the Democratic presidential slate of Truman and Barkley. Deprived of trade-union support and leadership, the Progressive party and Wallace's candidacy became little more than an instrument of the Communist party. In the election of 1948, Wallace was crushed; not only did he fail to carry a single state but he actually

13. Taft, *Organized Labor in American History*, p. 384.
14. *Ibid.*, p. 387.
15. *Ibid.*, p. 388.
16. *Ibid.*, p. 612.

won fewer votes than the States' Rights party, a dissenting Southern group on the right.

With the passage of time, the prospects for a separate farmer-labor party have been dimmed by changes in the labor force. In 1964 less than one person out of four in the total United States working force was a member of a trade union; only four persons out of ten in the working force were farmers, farm laborers, or blue-collar workers. No party that attended exclusively or even primarily to the interests of blue-collar workers and farmers, and ignored the claims of service and white-collar workers, could hope to become a majority party.

THE THIRD AND FOURTH STRATEGIES

It was not from want of trial, then, that the first two strategies were rejected. Nor was it from any failure to consider the pros and cons of each alternative. For decades, in fact, socialists and others who advocated comprehensive social and economic reforms and an independent labor or farmer-labor party put their case before the annual meetings of the AFL. The discussions were highly sophisticated; it is doubtful whether working-class leaders in any other country more thoroughly canvassed the consequences of the various alternatives. The first leader of the AFL, Samuel Gompers, a social radical in his native England in his youth, knew the arguments for third-party action; he heard them again and again, but he rejected them as inapplicable to the American scene.

The Traditional Strategy of the AFL: Neutrality and Local Autonomy

At the first conventions of the AFL in the late 1880s and the 1890s, the question was argued out and a position adopted from which the AFL has never deviated:[17] it rejected an independent party of workers and instead chose to be neutral as between the major parties, to endorse candidates favorable to the labor movement, and to secure favorable legislative and administrative action by pressure-group activities.[18] As the controversy over Populism approached its peak in 1895, the annual convention of the AFL declared that "party politics, whether they be democratic, republican, socialist, populistic, prohibition or any other, should have no place in the convention."[19]

The AFL adopted one more position of some importance: it permitted complete autonomy on political matters to the constituent unions and to state and local federations. These departed more frequently than

17. Even in 1924 the AFL endorsed LaFollette and Wheeler by *name* and made clear that it did not endorse any *party* as such.

18. Taft, *Organized Labor in American History*, pp. 230ff., and *passim*. See also Taft, *The AFL in the Age of Gompers* (New York: Harper & Brothers, 1957), pp. 289–301.

19. Taft, *Organized Labor in American History*, p. 232.

the parent body from the practice of political neutrality, but even they were politically neutral more often than not.

Although leaders of the labor movement consistently found the Democratic party more sympathetic to their demands than the Republicans,[20] so long as the Republicans were the dominant party in the North, where trade unionism, industrialization, and urbanism were strongest, while the strength of the Democrats lay in the least industrialized region, the South, the Democratic party did not appear to be a particularly good risk for the labor movement.

As we have seen, however, the critical presidential elections from 1928 to 1936 saw a realignment of party loyalties. This time the balance in national support tilted decisively toward the Democrats. Urban workers, North, South, and West, flocked to Democratic candidates and identified themselves as Democrats. Though it was by no means a labor party or even a farmer-labor party, the Democratic party was nonetheless highly dependent on and highly responsive to urban labor in general and to organized labor in particular.

Challenges to the Traditional Strategy

Organized labor made great gains under the New Deal. The National Labor Relations Act guaranteed the right of workers to join unions. For the first time, the powers of the national government were now definitely on the side of unionism, not against it. From 1935 to 1941 trade union membership expanded from 3.6 million to over 10 million. Unemployment insurance, old-age annuities, and other New Deal measures gave benefits to blue-collar workers. Then in 1947, a Republican Congress passed the Taft-Hartley Act over President Truman's veto; this act banned the closed shop, allowed employers to sue unions for broken contracts, and imposed other restraints on unions. Perhaps the most offensive provision to the labor movement was Section 14b, which dealt with the closed shop and the union shop, both highly prized among various unions. The closed shop—where union membership is a condition for obtaining a job—was banned outright by 14b. The union shop—where union membership is a condition for holding a job— was not banned directly; but 13b permitted states to outlaw the union shop if they chose. The Democrats pledged themselves to repeal the Taft-Hartley Act.

Support for Democrats. With Democratic leaders more friendly to labor than the Republicans, the AFL-CIO became more and more deeply involved in partisan politics despite its formal neutrality. It established a Committee on Political Education (COPE) to press for policies favor-

---

20. For the period from 1900 to ,920, see *ibid.*, pp. 241–245, 372–382.

able to labor, promote the registration of voters, and support specific candidates. Its financial support for candidates—usually Democrats—was impressive. Sometimes, as in 1960, and even more so in 1964, a substantial part of all expenditures for Democratic candidates came from organized labor.[21]

Support by Democrats. In pursuing its traditional strategy, the AFL-CIO also lobbied in Congress, not only for bills directly bearing on unionism, but also to promote Medicare, federal aid to education, civil rights, and other measures. In terms of reported expenditures, the AFL-CIO is generally among the half-dozen largest lobbyists in Congress. Individual unions also lobby heavily. In 1973 the United Automobile Workers reported expenditures of over $460,000.[22] Legislation supported by the AFL-CIO has frequently been backed by a majority of Democrats and opposed by a majority of Republicans. Thus the labor movement has often found that even in pursuing the third strategy, acting as a pressure group in Congress, it is more dependent on Democrats than Republicans.

An unofficial part of the Democratic party. More and more, then, in spite of its official policy of neutrality, the labor movement has become one of the major coalition partners in the Democratic party. In fact, the CIO (which was separate from the AFL until 1955) began life under the sponsorship of the New Deal and rejected the notion that the labor movement must necessarily remain outside the Democratic party. In 1944 the CIO Political Action Committee openly worked for the Democratic presidential ticket of Franklin Roosevelt and Harry Truman. In 1948, the CIO Executive Board officially endorsed Harry Truman for president. In a number of industrial states and cities, the main leaders of organized labor became deeply involved in Democratic party politics —nominations, campaign finances, elections, and policies. One opinion poll after another revealed that trade union members were among the staunchest Democratic voters in the North. In 1964 the labor movement was offered a choice between a Democratic presidential candidate, Lyndon Johnson, who supported most of its goals, including the repeal of Section 14b of the Taft-Hartley Act, or an avowedly conservative Republican, Barry Goldwater, who opposed practically all of the existing laws and new legislation that the labor movement most ardently supported. In this instance the general board of the AFL-CIO rejected

---

21. Herbert E. Alexander, *Financing the 1960 Election* (Princeton, N.J.: Citizens' Research Foundation, 1962), p. 42; and *Financing the 1964 Election* (Princeton, N.J.: Citizens' Research Foundation, 1966), p. 40, Table 4 and p. 64; *The New York Times,* December 3, 1965, p. 39 M.
Also, Herbert E. Alexander and Harold B. Meyers, "The Switch in Campaign Giving," *Fortune* (November, 1965), 216.
22. Congressional Quarterly, *The Washington Lobby,* 2nd ed. (Washington, D.C.: Congressional Quarterly Service, 1974), p. 38.

neutrality and publicly endorsed the election of President Johnson and Vice-President Humphrey.

Return to formal neutrality? Despite its endorsement of Democratic candidates in 1964 and its unofficial involvement with the Democratic party, however, the AFL-CIO did not officially reject its classic position. The labor movement may have embraced the Democratic party—but it did not endorse the party. Nonetheless, that possibility was weighed by leaders of the AFL-CIO. In 1965, in fulfillment of his campaign promises President Johnson sought to persuade Congress to repeal Section 14b of the Taft-Hartley Act. The Republican majority leader in the Senate, Senator Everett Dirksen of Illinois, mounted a filibuster that contributed mightily to the defeat of the repeal measure. President Johnson thereupon pledged that he would again fight for repeal in 1966. The president of the AFL-CIO, George Meany, announced to his fellow unionists that "If they [the Republican leaders] are going to conduct their business on the basis of absolute bias against the organized trade-union movement . . . then I think labor, itself, is going to take a new look at this entire question of our relationship with the political parties."[23] However, after President Johnson failed again in 1966 to persuade the Democratic majority in Congress to unite behind the repeal of 14b, Meany's ardor for the Democrats cooled. The AFL-CIO did not, after all, "take a new look at . . . our relationship with the political parties." In 1972, few of the candidates supported by the AFL-CIO as delegates to the Democratic national convention were selected. Meany's influence at the convention was less than it had been in decades. As a result, the Executive Council of the AFL-CIO decided not to support either of the presidential candidates that year. In 1975, still smarting under the wounds inflicted at the 1972 convention, the Executive Council under Meany's leadership voted unanimously to take no part in the selection of delegates to the Democratic National Convention in 1976. For the time being, then, the Executive Council had rejected the fourth strategy and reverted to the third. A number of member unions, however, continued to work actively within the Democratic party.

Thus after three-quarters of a century, the American labor movement remained undecided as between the third and fourth strategies.

AN APPRAISAL OF THE FOUR STRATEGIES

Every group, every organization, every movement that seeks changes in government policies faces the same alternatives as the labor movement. Weighing the pros and cons of alternative strategies is no easy task. Those who are strong advocates of an ideology are drawn toward the

---

23. Political memo from COPE, November 29, 1965.

first or second strategy; those who are more interested in concrete gains lean toward the third or fourth. A strong desire to maintain the purity of its aim beckons a movement toward independent political action; a strong desire to be effective beckons a movement toward negotiation and coalition. Idealism cries: Reject compromises! Realism asks: Of what value is ideological purity when it leads merely to political futility?

Difficulties and Failures
of the First Strategy

If success is measured by the ability to win elections, then historically the first strategy—forming a separate party—has been the least successful. The history of the first strategy is, in plain fact, a record of very nearly total failure. Why this is so should by now be self-evident. The first strategy is likely to appeal most to a movement committed to goals that are unacceptable to either of the two major parties. Yet, if the goals of the movement are unacceptable to either of the existing parties, is there not good reason to think that these goals will also be unacceptable to the followers of the major parties and hence to most voters? If one goal of a political movement is to win elections, the first strategy will work only if at least one of the two major parties has fallen down badly on its prime job: finding out what appeals to voters and acting accordingly.

The one clear historical instance of atrophy among the existing parties and the emergence of a new major party is furnished by the birth of the Republican party; the newborn Republican organization rapidly acquired the support of dissident Whigs and Democrats throughout the North and West. Yet this example remains the only case in which a third party has attracted enough support from discontented followers of the major parties to develop into a major party in its own right.

Doctrine of the hidden majority. If this is so, why does the first strategy have any appeal at all? Partly, no doubt, because its advocates ignore the historical regularities in American politics; partly because a movement with goals unacceptable to the major parties may simply have no other alternative open to it; and partly, one suspects, because of faith in the 'doctrine of the hidden majority.' The doctrine of the hidden majority, which is sometimes propounded by movements on both the extreme right and the extreme left, is the belief that a majority of like-minded citizens already exists waiting only to be mobilized, since the two major parties are for some reason ignoring and frustrating that latent majority. Belief in the doctrine of the hidden majority is not always confined to people on the most extreme fringes. In 1964 Barry Goldwater seems to have assumed the validity of the doctrine and to

Figure 29.1
The Vicious Cycle of
Political Alienation

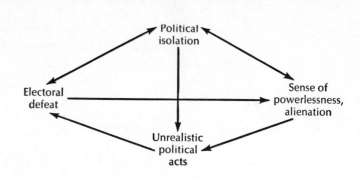

have fashioned his campaign accordingly with disastrous results.[24]
Many of the Democratic Convention delegates working for the nomination of Senator McGovern in 1972 appear to have shared a similar belief.

The vicious cycle of political alienation. Choice of the first strategy by a movement that is already divorced from the main currents of American opinion may establish a vicious cycle of political alienation (Figure 29.1). Defeat, political isolation, and powerlessness reinforce a sense of political alienation and lack of realism in the movement, while alienation and lack of realism in turn increase the likelihood that the movement will be badly defeated in elections and will remain politically isolated and powerless.

Difficulties and Failures
of the Second Strategy

According to the second strategy, a particular interest joins with another interest pursuing similar but not identical objectives. This approach has been, at least in national politics, no more successful than the first. The second strategy has some of the appeal of the first, for it enables a group to adhere to most of its goals even though it enters into a coalition with one or two other groups with slightly divergent (but in the main overlapping or crosscutting) goals. The strategy reached its zenith of success in the Populist party; but the needed majority was not forthcoming. Neither 'labor' nor 'farmers' constituted a

---

24. Cf. Converse et al., "Electoral Myth and Reality: The 1964 Election." See also, however, the statement by William C. Baum, "On Electoral Myth and Reality," both in *American Political Science Review,* 59 (September 1965), 693.

unified body of like-minded citizens, and the combination of the two groups created an even more diversified coalition. Bryan and the Populists gained a good deal of support in some farming areas, especially in the South and West. But they lost badly in others and failed to win urban labor. If the American citizen body was already highly diverse in the 1890s, it is probably even more so today.

Doctrine of the pure and simple coalition. Just as the appeal of the first strategy may lie in the doctrine of the hidden majority, so the appeal of the second may be drawn from the 'doctrine of the pure and simple coalition.' This belief contends that it is possible to form a majority coalition that is *pure,* in the sense that the coalition partners do not need to modify their goals in order to create or maintain a coalition, and that is *simple,* in the sense that it can be formed from only two or three groups, each of which is internally unified. Hence the appeal of a pure and simple coalition of workers and farmers; of the civil rights movement and the peace movement; of conservatives and property owners.

Yet if the interpretation set out in Chapter 24 is roughly correct, the doctrine of the pure and simple coalition must also be largely mythical. For where are these two or three internally like-minded groups that can combine to form a majority? Blue-collar workers are a minority of the working force, and a declining minority at that. Trade union members are an even smaller minority—a fifth to a quarter of the employed population. The white-collar groups constitute a complex of occupational minorities, from clerical workers to professional people and employers. Professional men and women are a small minority of the working force; doctors are a minority of professionals; psychiatrists, a minority of doctors. The poor are a minority, but so are the rich; the middle-income levels are only a statistical category, not a like-minded group. Blacks are a minority and so are white Southerners. Southerners, white and black, are a minority of the whole nation. Jews and Catholics are minorities; the Protestant 'majority' is largely a fiction, for it is an assortment of minorities as different as Southern Baptists, Lutherans, Episcopalians, and Quakers. What is more, none of the categories just mentioned are, in fact, collections of like-minded people—blue-collar workers, trade union members, white-collar workers, professionals, doctors, psychiatrists, the poor, the rich, the middle-income strata, blacks, white Southerners, Northerners, Jews, Catholics, Protestants, Democrats, Republicans, liberals, conservatives. No major category of the population defined by a single standard, whether occupation, income, religion, ethnic group, region, or any other, consists altogether of like-minded voters.

Limits and Possibilities
of the Third Strategy

The third strategy—that of acting as a pressure group—offers a fair chance of success for any interest smaller than a majority, provided that the members of the group agree on relatively narrow or specific goals that do not run sharply counter to widely prevailing beliefs. For limited purposes a pressure group can be highly successful. Farm organizations, representing at most a small and diminishing minority, have used it with enormous success. So, in varying degrees, have literally thousands of other organizations, representing or claiming to represent trade unionists, veterans, business people, industrialists, taxpayers, bankers, oil companies, copper importers, doctors, women's clubs, nature lovers, stream pollutionists, conservationists, foreign policy groups, old people.

But a movement that seeks something more than its own group interests may conclude that as a pure pressure group it will exert too limited an influence over the policies of the American republic. If a movement also has a numerous following of prospective voters, like the labor movement, it may find the fourth strategy more reasonable than the third.

Limits and Possibilities
of the Fourth Strategy

Is the fourth strategy—entering into the Democratic or Republican party—perhaps the 'best' all around strategy? Not necessarily. A very small and well-organized group without many votes behind it may retain more influence as an independent pressure group. A large group whose members are divided among people loyal to both parties would run the risk of splitting its following if it adopted the fourth strategy. A group with narrow goals more or less acceptable to both parties may succeed better as a pressure group. A group whose goals diverge widely from those supported by both parties could not find a home in either party.

Thus each strategy has its advantages and disadvantages. Since enthusiasts tend to believe that they can have the advantages of a strategy without its disadvantages, a choice among the four strategies is often a somewhat irrational process ruled more by hope and faith than by hard-headed analysis.

FOUR FACTORS RELEVANT TO CHOOSING A STRATEGY It is probably impossible, and in any case not very useful, to lay down a set of hard and fast rules according to which one strategy or the other would always be the most 'rational' in the American political system. Instead, let me try to draw the discussion together by pinpointing four factors that seem relevant in choosing among strategies (Table 29.1).

Table 29.1
Four Factors Relevant to the Choice of Political Strategies by a Group

A. GOALS		Goals of the group are:	
1. Breadth	1a. Oriented to NARROW objectives	1b. Oriented to COMPRE-HENSIVE objectives	
2. Acceptability	2a. ACCEPTABLE to at least one of the major parties	2b. UNACCEPTABLE to either major party	
B. MEMBERS		Members of the group are:	
3. Number	3a. FEW in number	3b. NUMEROUS	
4. Unity	4a. UNIFIED in political outlook	4b. DIVERSE in political outlook	

Table 29.2
Appropriate Strategies for Four Kinds of Groups

Thus if a group's Goals are:	Members are:	An appropriate strategy would be to:
I. Comprehensive, acceptable to neither party	Few, unified	Form an independent party.
II. Comprehensive, acceptable to neither party	Numerous, diverse	Form a new coalition party.
III. Narrow, acceptable to both parties	Few, diverse or unified	Form a pressure group.
IV. Comprehensive, acceptable to one party	Numerous, diverse	Form a coalition with an existing party.

Theoretically, these factors can be combined in a number of different ways. For many combinations it might be difficult or impossible to say that one strategy is more 'rational' than another. For others, however, one strategy does seem more appropriate than the others. Table 29.2 shows four types of groups for which a particular strategy seems appropriate.

Why is it that every strategy seems to have certain disadvantages? The main source of trouble is an apparently inescapable fact: *In the United States, any group of people with virtually the same views on political questions, with the same political loyalties and identifications, is certain to be a minority.* Whether the group is microscopic or relatively numerous, it will be a minority of the total body of citizens, even a minority of voters, and a rather small minority at that. To make the same point in another way, every grouping of American citizens large enough to constitute a majority of voters is necessarily a rather diverse collection of individuals and groups who may agree on some matters but are sure to disagree on others. No group of like-minded citizens can ever win a national election merely by mobilizing themselves and others who think exactly the way they do. To win national elections, even to win influence over national policies, every group must participate somehow in the politics of coalition building. To be sure, it can pursue its own goals, and it must engage in conflict. But it must also conciliate, compromise, negotiate, bargain—and in the process often forego its lesser goals for its greater objectives. In this sense, no single group *can* win national elections—only a diverse combination of groups can.

Some people, particularly if they happen to be highly confident of their own political virtue, the rightness of their own goals, and the evils of compromise, finds this a most repugnant interpretation of American political life. Either this interpretation is false, they say, and the strict, undiminished pursuit of the goals held by the group, the movement, the cause will one day culminate in political success unstained by compromise, or if the view is true, then politics is a dirty and evil business.

This, I think, is too narrow, too inhuman a view of political life. For it seems obvious that, in a polyarchy, freedom and diversity inevitably lead toward conflict. Yet conflict does not lead inevitably to morally unacceptable compromises, nor to fragmentation, polarization, repression, or civil war. For among a people guided, even in their conflicts, by a talent for conciliation and a commitment to the principles and institutions of a polyarchy, both freedom and diversity can flourish.

SUMMARY 1. A group of American citizens who wish to bring about changes in the conduct of the government have the option of adopting a revolutionary strategy; that is, they can try to overthrow the government by force and replace it with a different kind of regime, presumably not a polyarchy. In long-established polyarchies where the people tend to adhere to a democratic ideology, as in the United States, this strategy has regularly failed. However, chances for success might rise in the face of a prolonged failure to cope satisfactorily with issues that a large proportion of citizens regard as urgent.

2. If a group rejects the revolutionary option and chooses to use the processes available in the American polyarchy, it has open to it four general strategies:

☐ A particular interest can organize a political party of its own.
☐ The particular interest can form a new coalition party by combining with another group or movement that has similar, overlapping, but not identical objectives.
☐ Although it remains neutral between the two major parties, the special interest can act as a pressure group to secure favorable legislation and the nomination and election of sympathetic candidates.
☐ By entering into one of the existing parties, the particular interest can become an element in a major party coalition.

3. An examination of the choice among these strategies made by the American labor movement reveals that unlike labor movements in many European countries, the American labor movement rejected the first strategy. An explanation for the difference is found mainly in:

☐ The pattern of crosscutting cleavages in the United States.
☐ The operation of American political institutions, particularly federalism, the winner-take-all system of elections, and the existence of two well-organized national parties before the American labor movement itself developed.

4. The labor movement also experienced severe difficulties with the second strategy: efforts to form a labor-farmer coalition proved unsuccessful.

5. The AFL adopted the third strategy. It came out against an independent labor party and opted for neutrality toward the two major parties and for seeking political goals by pressure group activities. It did, however, permit complete autonomy on political matters to the member unions and to state and local federations. But, under the impact of the New Deal and the development of goals more in line with the policies of Democrats than Republicans, the AFL-CIO has often found political neutrality difficult and has in fact, if not officially, become a part of the Democratic coalition.

6. An appraisal of the experience of the labor movement suggests that none of the four strategies is in all cases the one best. Which strategy is best depends upon at least four factors:

☐ The breadth of a group's goals.
☐ The acceptability of their goals to the major political parties.
☐ The size of their following.
☐ The similarity or diversity of their following.

7. Each of the four strategies may be the most appropriate for a different combination of these factors (Table 29.2).

8. The main reason that every political strategy has some drawbacks is that in the United States any group of people with virtually the same views on political questions, and with the same political loyalties and identifications, is certain to be a minority.

30 THE UNCOMPLETED AGENDA OF THE AMERICAN POLYARCHY

In 1787 the Framers of the Constitution, we saw, left an uncompleted agenda for Americans to finish. The constitutional system they prescribed could have foundered completely, as constitutions have done so often since in so many countries. Or the constitution they proposed could have been adapted to government by a narrow elite, an oligarchy, or a meritocracy. Or it could, as we now know, help form the framework of a polyarchy based on a broad adult suffrage.

The Framers themselves did not, nor could they, close off the options. The political system did move, with astounding speed, toward polyarchy, rather than toward the narrow oligarchy that was still to prevail in Britain for some generations or toward the breakdown of the new constitutional order and the rise of dictatorship that was to happen in France within one generation. But this development depended on circumstances and events mainly, though not wholly, beyond the capacity of the Framers to influence.

Today's uncompleted agenda contains matters that were, in a larger sense, on the agenda as far back as 1787. I have in mind the audacious attempt to develop a political system that would achieve a satisfactory level of political equality and consent. How satisfactory we judge the performance of the American polyarchy to be, when it is measured against these standards, forms the subject of this final chapter.

**DESCRIPTION,
EXPLANATION,
AND APPRAISAL**
With such a task we move to matters where my own biases, values, and subjective perceptions are certain to play a larger part than they have had, I hope, on the rest of this book.

To be sure, it would be claiming too much to insist that all the descriptions and explanations set forth up to now have the same degree of objective validity as, say, a biologist's description and explanation of the performance of a frog's circulatory system. One critical test for objectivity is whether other well-trained observers concur. Over a very considerable domain biologists agree on their descriptions and explanations. It is on the frontiers of theory, data, and research that they begin to diverge. Although I would not claim to have achieved the biologists' level of objectivity throughout, that is what I have aimed for in all the details, descriptions, and explanations in Parts Two, Three, and Four of this book. In Part Five, particularly the preceding chapter, my assessment of complex alternatives was, I have no doubt, more subjective and more debatable.

When we turn to the task of *appraising* a system as vast and complex as the American polyarchy, as we do briefly and incompletely in this chapter, objectivity is likely to be even harder to achieve. Appraisal requires standards of judgment or values; it requires a comparison of actual performance, or what is believed to be actual performance, with the standards; and it requires a judgment on the significance or meaning of the discrepancy between actual performance and standards. The very process of evaluation insures that one person's appraisal will contain judgments with which other observers can disagree. These differences in judgments cannot be resolved easily, or perhaps cannot be resolved at all.

Nonetheless, appraising a political system need not be, as is sometimes thought, a purely arbitrary decision to which objectivity and data are irrelevant. Standards of performance may be subjective in their ultimate grounds, as many modern philosophers have contended. Yet choosing appropriate and relevant standards for judging the American polyarchy need not be *wholly* arbitrary, if only because history, tradition, and public ideology give us some guidelines. Moreover, once standards of performance have been chosen—arbitrarily or not—comparing the actual performance with the standards need not, and obviously should not, be wholly a subjective exercise; for unless it is intended as pure daydreaming, such a comparison requires and depends on data about actual performance.

**CONSENT AND
POLITICAL EQUALITY
AS STANDARDS**
Among the standards most clearly available and relevant for judging the performance of the American polyarchy are the historic goals that have for so long been central to American public values: political equal-

Figure 30.1
The Cycle of Defeat

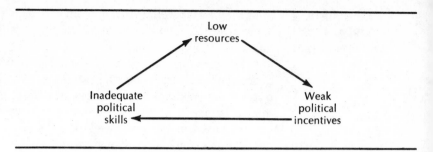

ity and consent. In Chapter 3, I suggested that continuing consent (as against once-and-for-all consent) combined with political equality would require that full citizens must have unimpaired opportunities:

1. to figure out, discover, and formulate their goals or preferences: to find out what they really want;
2. by acting individually or in concert to indicate their goals or preferences to fellow citizens and to the government; and
3. to have their preferences weighted equally in the conduct of the government—that is, weighted with no discrimination because of *what* they want or *who* they happen to be.

So our question now is: How well does the American polyarchy measure up to these standards? To the extent that it falls short—and thus falls short of democracy—what can we do about it?

PERFORMANCE: INEQUALITIES

No political system, to my knowledge, has ever attained anything like full political equality among all the adults within its boundaries—or even among all its citizens. The persistence of political inequalities is the basis for the pessimistic appraisal of democracy and polyarchy advanced by the political theorists discussed in Chapter 5.

Differences in political influence, as we have seen, arise from differences in political resources, skills, and incentives. Although skills and incentives are to some extent independent of resources, as we saw in Chapter 28 they do tend to run together in the United States. Hence there is a self-fulfilling prophecy about political influence: political weakness leads to continued political weakness, and strength to continued strength. Where a long history of inequality creates a group with few resources—wealth, income, status, education, official position—the prospects of successful political action are so meager that incentives to act politically are low: as a consequence, political skills are not acquired. So the cycle tends to be perpetuated (Figure 30.1). Conversely,

Figure 30.2
The Cycle of Success

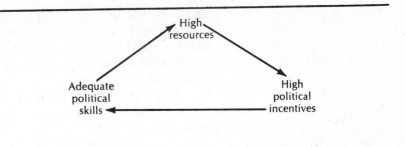

groups with large resources are likely to have both their incentives and their skills reinforced by success (Figure 30.2).

In my view, inequalities in political resources are at the root of many of the most serious problems of the American polyarchy. Certainly the gap between democracy and polyarchy in the United States cannot be narrowed very much without reducing the amount of inequality among Americans in their access to political resources.

Let me call your attention again to three kinds of disparities among Americans that lead to gross inequalities in political resources and thus to gross inequality in political influence. (These disparities were discussed in Chapter 7.)

Traditional Institutionalized Inequalities

In Chapter 7, I emphasized that one of the distinctive characteristics of the American polyarchy is its long history of discrimination against certain racial minorities: not only Afro-Americans, but also American Indians, Chicanos, and Orientals. A few racial minorities, most notably Japanese-Americans, have in recent years substantially overcome these inequalities and appear to have attained full political equality. There has undoubtedly been more progress since the mid-1950s with respect to the others than during the whole prior history of this country. Nevertheless, traditional and institutionalized inequalities have left some minorities with such limited political resources, skills, and incentives that it is impossible for them to achieve equality solely by lifting themselves up by their own bootstraps, as many white Americans evidently feel they should. For traditional institutionalized inequalities tend to create all the conditions needed for the self-fulfilling prophecy mentioned above.

Inequalities in Wealth and Income

Many of the founding fathers of this republic assumed, as had earlier political theorists from Aristotle to Locke and Rousseau, that a democratic polity could be attained only if the society could avoid extremes of wealth and poverty. For they believed that extreme differences in wealth and income would produce extreme differences in power, extreme class conflict, extreme hostility, fear, and resentment, and a high probability of rule by either an oligarchy of the wealthy or a dictatorship of the poor.

In the United States, the distribution of income is highly unequal both before and after taxes and government assistance. Recent studies have shown that:

☐ The poorest 20 percent of American families receive only about 2 percent of the family income. The poorest 40 percent receive only about 12 percent of the family income.

☐ At the other end of the scale, the top 20 percent receive about 50 percent of the income. The top 5 percent get about 24 percent of the income, and the top 1 percent about 11 percent.

☐ Differences in income among Americans are not declining. In fact, the best evidence indicates that differences in income may be increasing.

☐ Despite a widely held belief to the contrary, taxes do not change the distribution of income very much. One study shows that the sum total of all federal, state, and local taxes bears more heavily on the very poor than on any other income group.

☐ Some redistribution takes place as a result of the sum total of what economists call 'transfer payments,' or government payments of benefits to individuals. These include Social Security benefits, welfare payments, veterans' pensions and disability benefits, workmen's compensation, and the like. Transfer payments like these comprise a substantial part of the income of the very poor and of people over the age of 65. Except for the very poor and the aged, however, transfer payments are a small proportion of family incomes. Consequently they do not have much effect on income inequality.

☐ Wealth is highly concentrated. In 1969, the richest 4 percent of American adults owned 35 percent of the country's private wealth. The richest 1 percent owned 21 percent. Indeed, 8 percent of the private wealth of the United States is owned by only 70,000 persons—about one-tenth of 1 percent of the adult population.[1]

1. The figures on income distribution and the effects of transfer payments are mainly from Benjamin A. Okner, "Individual Taxes and the Distribution of Income" in James D. Smith, ed., *The Personal Distribution of Income and Wealth* (New York: National Bureau of Economic Research, 1975), pp. 45–74. Okner includes only income and employee payroll taxes. For the effect of *all* federal, state, and local taxes, see Roger A. Herriot and Herman P. Miller, "Who Paid Taxes in 1968?" presented at a meeting of the National Statistical Conference Board, March 18, 1971, and published in *Conference Board Record* (May 1971) under the title "The Taxes We Pay." The figures on the distribution of personal wealth (net worth) are from James D. Smith, Stephen D. Franklin and Douglas A. Wion, "The Distribution of Financial Assets," Washington, D.C.: The Urban Institute, Working Paper 1208–2, September 22, 1973. For evidence that inequality in income distribution has increased, see Martin Schnitzer, *Income Distribution, A Comparative Study of the United States, Sweden, West Germany, East Germany, the United Kingdom, and Japan* (New York: Praeger Publishers, 1974), p. 40.

It is true that polyarchies have existed in spite of great inequalities in wealth and income. After all, the American polyarchy has managed to survive in the midst of the inequalities I have just described. Yet the survival of polyarchy is one thing; attaining democracy is another. Inequalities in wealth and income generate a large gap between ideal democracy and the actual performance of political institutions. This is why Jefferson and Madison, like political theorists from Aristotle to Rousseau, held that economic inequalities would seriously hamper democratic institutions and might finally undermine them.

The reasons are all but self-evident. Where wide differences exist in access to economic resources, there are bound also to be great differences in resources for influencing the government—that is, in political resources. Economic resources are often directly convertible into political resources. This is plainly the case with spending for political campaigns, for example, or buying television time, or advertising, or bribing officials, or bringing economic pressures to bear on an official. But economic resources are also indirectly convertible into political resources. For example, economic advantages increase one's chances of getting an education, gaining higher status, having more available time for politics, and so on. Economic advantages also help in providing psychological resources such as confidence and optimism, which strengthen both the incentives to participation in politics and the willingness to acquire political skills.

As with traditional institutionalized inequalities based on race, the self-fulfilling prophecy about influence tends to operate also on the basis of economic inequality. Poverty often leads to a cycle of powerlessness that feeds upon itself; the advantages of wealth and income help produce a self-sustaining cycle of successful influence (Figure 30.3).

Inequalities in Education

It has always been a central assumption of democratic philosophers and advocates that a satisfactory achievement of democratic goals would require that opportunities for education be widely available and utilized among the vast body of citizens. Modern social science confirms this traditional view. In study after study social scientists have found a relatively high correlation between education and a variety of factors on which political influence depends: political participation in its various forms, organization memberships, political knowledge, confidence, etc. Probably no other single factor shows up so steadily in so many different studies as being so highly related to political effectiveness.

In a more general sense, it is obvious that education tends to enhance the three basic opportunities used here as standards of political equality and active consent: opportunities for discovering what one wants, for communicating to others what one wants, and for acting

Figure 30.3
How Economic and
Political Inequalities
Tend to Reinforce
One Another

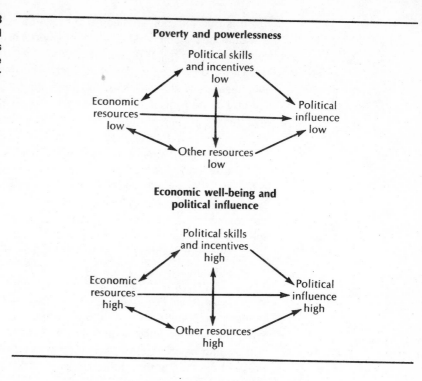

Figure 30.3
How Economic and Political Inequalities Tend to Reinforce One Another

effectively to insure that these wants are taken into account equally with those of others when government decisions are to be made. Looking at the matter in a different way, it is again obvious that by providing knowledge and skills and ways of acquiring new knowledge and skills, education facilitates the acquisition of resources useful in gaining influence. It also helps one to develop the special skills that are particularly relevant to political life—skills in the arts of communication and organization, for example. Education also tends to be associated with and probably contributes to the development of the kinds of incentives that make it more likely that an individual will direct his or her energies toward political action and will persist in political action over comparatively long periods.

Education, then, has a powerful channeling or screening function. Thus a person with only an elementary-school education is very much less likely to be highly involved in politics than a person who has gone to college. In every polyarchy, consequently, and more so in the United States than in some, elected officials are rarely recruited from the ranks of blue-collar workers; full-time politics is distinctly a monopoly of the white-collar groups.

Until recently, the United States led most other countries in the distribution of educational opportunities to its citizens. In recent decades the differences have diminished between the United States and other countries with a comparatively high level of per capita income. For many reasons, including inequalities of the kinds discussed earlier, many Americans are wretchedly educated. As a consequence, they are severely disadvantaged in politics. Decisions in the American polyarchy are likely to be made, therefore, without taking their preferences into account, certainly not as fully as the standard of political equality implies—and without their active consent.

Solutions

Anyone who thinks that the problem of political inequality can be easily solved is, in my view, living in a dream world. There are people who claim to have instant solutions: all you need to do is to add some simple and easily available factor and you get equality. At best such people are hopelessly utopian. At worst, they are, without quite saying so, ready to sell the democratic ideal down the river. What they promise is to reduce *social* and *economic* inequalities by creating a government run by a benevolent elite. For some nations, such a solution may very well be the best available; and lucky is the country where once it gains power, the elite proves to be truly benevolent! But rule by an aristocracy, even in modern dress, is not what Americans have ever wanted. Nor is it, in my view the best to which we can reasonably aspire. Moreover, as I indicated in Chapter 3, it seems more than likely that a ruling elite, however benevolent its stated purpose, would soon become corrupted by its power. We have already seen how the powers of the imperial presidency helped to weaken the self-restraint of one such elite under President Nixon. Luckily for the United States, a peaceful, constitutional solution proved to be available.

So I do not pretend that solutions are easy. Nor is it my purpose to set out specific policies. To formulate concrete policies intended for more or less immediate application would go far beyond the limits of this book.

It is difficult, and frequently impossible, to predict accurately what all the important consequences of a policy will be. And there is probably no desirable policy that does not have some undesirable consequences. Weighing the relative advantages and disadvantages—the trade-offs, as policy makers often say today—nearly always involves judgments that cannot be entirely supported by explicit reasons. Policy-making is not yet close to being a science, and may never be. Nevertheless, there are three general lines of action that might be taken to reduce the political inequalities arising out of social, economic, and educational inequalities in the United States.

1. *Redistributive policies. First,* some inequalities can be directly reduced by government action. Inequalities in income, wealth, and education will probably yield more readily to direct government action than will racial inequalities.

The distribution of wealth and income is not inevitable or fixed by nature. The way net incomes are distributed depends partly on the policies of federal, state, and local governments with respect to taxes and transfer payments. The federal income tax is somewhat progressive; social security, property, and sales taxes are regressive. One result of tax policy (and other factors) is that, as we noted earlier, the distribution of income is highly unequal in the United States, more so than in several other polyarchies where governments have sought to reduce inequalities, such as Norway, Britain, and Australia.[2]

To bring about government action on these matters, Americans will have to change their priorities. How much do we value democracy and political equality in comparison with the opportunity to gain wealth and riches? To Jefferson and Madison, as to most of the Framers, this question was already solved. A nation of farmers, it appeared to them, would provide enough social and economic equality to guarantee a high degree of political equality. But when that agrarian society disappeared, Americans failed to insist on the priority of democracy over material gain. We cannot now move much closer toward democracy until we reverse that failure and give a higher priority to democratic goals.

In effect, then, we need to choose the kind of society we want to have. If we want to give priority to democracy, and therefore to political equality, the solution seems to me fairly clear. We shall have to use taxes and transfer payments to reduce some of the inequalities in wealth, income, and educational opportunities that now contribute to the great inequality among Americans in their influence over government.

2. *Floors and ceilings on the use of political resources.* Another alternative is to try to minimize the effects of social and economic inequalities on political influence. This solution requires that everyone have certain minimum political resources and that no one exceeds certain maximum levels. One kind of floor and ceiling is provided by the ballot box: every citizen has one vote, and no one is supposed to have more than one. The fundamental rights of citizenship in the Bill of Rights also

---

2. Bruce Russett, *World Handbook of Political and Social Indicators* (New Haven, Conn.: Yale University Press, 1964), Tables 71, 72, pp. 245, 247; and Schnitzer, *Income Distribution.*

provide a floor—though not always a ceiling. Redistribution policies would of course bring floors and ceilings on available resources closer together. But even without changing the distribution of wealth and income, it would be possible to reduce political inequalities by setting floors and ceilings on the *use* of wealth and income for political influence.

An example is furnished by the Campaign Finance Reform Act of 1974, which was stimulated by the disclosures after the Watergate episode and enacted after Nixon's resignation. This act provides for government financing of presidential campaigns and partial financing for presidential primaries. Spending limits of $10 million are set for candidates in the primaries and $20 million for presidential nominees during the election campaign. Limits are also set on spending by congressional candidates in both the primaries and the election campaign. The act limits contributions in each election to $1,000 by an individual contributor and $5,000 by an organization. It creates a full-time independent election commission with its own civil enforcement powers to enforce the law.[3]

Earlier federal laws on campaign expenditures were rather easily evaded. Experience will undoubtedly show weaknesses in the new legislation. Some parts may even prove to be unconstitutional. Nonetheless, as long as great differences in wealth and income exist among Americans, laws establishing floors and ceilings on the use of economic resources provide one way of reducing inequalities in influence on the conduct of government.

3. *Organization and coalition.* To break out of the cycle of defeat is particularly difficult if a group is a small minority, weak in economic resources, and lacks even the potential resource of large numbers— a resource, as we saw in Chapter 29, of great historical importance to labor movements. With activity and skill, however, a minority may be able to organize its numbers so as to maximize its impact: for example, to win local elections and to count heavily enough in nominations and elections for state and local offices so that minority views and leaders gain influence. In this respect, the increasing dispersion of the black population throughout the country is both an advantage and a disadvantage for the black minority: blacks have become a smaller minority in the South but they have become larger minorities elsewhere. Meanwhile, too, the Civil Rights Acts of 1964 and 1965 opened up the possibility, for the first time since Reconstruction, of large numbers of blacks gaining entry into the South's political system. As a result, since 1965

---

3. For an account of the 1974 federal law and provisions of various state laws, see *Dollar Politics, The Issue of Campaign Spending*, Vol. 2 (Washington, D.C.: Congressional Quarterly Service, 1974), 29–39.

	*South	Non-South	Total	Change 1971–1974
Total	1370	1621	2991	1134
Congress				
Senators	0	1	1	0
Representatives	2	14	16	3
State				
State executives	0	3	3	1
Senators	5	35	40	4
Representatives	49	147	196	34
County				
Commissioners, supervisors, council members	119	81	200	114
Other county officials	32	10	42	8
City				
Mayors	53	55	108 }	
Vice mayors, mayor *pro tem*	39	23	62 }	89
Council members, commissioners	583	497	1080	427
Others	37	73	110	59
Law enforcement				
Judges, magistrates	24	148	172	24
Chiefs of police, constables, marshals	93	18	111	53
Justices of the peace	40	8	48	9
Others	6	3	9	2
Education				
State and college boards	2	22	24	15
Local school board members	285	482	767	312
Others	1	1	2	**

*"South" includes Alabama, Arkansas, Florida, Georgia, Kentucky, Louisiana, Mississippi, North Carolina, South Carolina, Texas, and Virginia.
** Category not listed in 1971
Source: *National Roster of Black Elected Officials*, Vol. 4 (Washington, D.C.: The Joint Center for Political Studies, 1974), April 1974, pp. xix, xxi.

Southern blacks have gradually been bringing an end to the South's old dual system of a polyarchy for whites who collectively exercised hegemony over blacks. And in the North the awakening of the ghettos and the increasing proportion of blacks in the general population, especially in the central cities, have given blacks an increasing political voice, particularly within the Democratic party. Though still underrepresented in political life, by 1974 there were 2,991 black elected officials in the United States (Table 30.1).

Partly in response to the example set by blacks, other minorities—ethnic, economic, and cultural—have also undertaken to organize them selves to protect and advance their interests. Although fragmented into many different organizations, the women's movement—the 'majority minority,'—has also begun to have an influence on government and thereby on traditional discriminatory practices against women.

Although organization is usually necessary if a group is to influence the government, for those weak in resources it is not sufficient. As the last chapter makes clear, particular interests must also ordinarily enter into coalitions with other interests. Like the labor movement, any organized interest must seek to discover allies among groups with overlapping but not necessarily identical interests. For example, in 1973 the Congressional Black Caucus, which consists of all the black members of Congress, decided to "form coalitions, even with those traditionally regarded as enemies of black people, to promote the interests of black Americans."[4] Although many people might view this as a cynical sell-out to 'the system', it represents a realistic assessment of how a minority without vast political resources might move in order to influence government policies on matters important to the group.

Political purists will find such a coalition strategy unacceptable. But the price of maintaining political purity is almost certain to be political ineffectiveness.

PERFORMANCE: DECISIONS WITHOUT CONSENT

Political inequality directly impairs political consent. Citizens who are unable to participate effectively in influencing the conduct of the government do not give their consent to its policies.

Yet even if political resources were more equally distributed among citizens *outside* the government, government officials might gain so much influence over decisions, and so much independence from popular control, that they could make decisions without the informed and active consent of the citizens.

The Framers intended to prevent this from happening; they intended to insure consent mainly in two ways. *First,* the system of partitioned power was expected to insure that no official could gain very much power in relation to other officials. *Second,* the president and Congress, the main policy-makers, would hold office only by virtue of their direct or indirect election by the people, and so would be accountable to the people, or to a majority among them.

We have seen how the Framers' design failed to prevent the rise of the imperial presidency, how crucial decisions came to be made by the president without adhering to constitutional processes for gaining congressional consent, and how one president, Richard Nixon, was checked on the very threshold of organizing the vast resources of the presidency into a national political machine. We have also seen that although some of the causes of the imperial presidency were transitory, and may have vanished as a result of the impeachment process and the resignation of Richard Nixon, other causes endure.

Central to the problem of the presidency, and thus to the constitu-

---

4. *New York Times,* October 1, 1973.

tional system, are the demands Americans make on a president. The power and prestige we seem eager to bestow upon the Chief Executive have created an office that could be properly filled only by a person of extraordinary talent and exceptional moral character. Most men who attained the presidency have fallen far short of these exalted requirements. They have been neither greatly talented nor have they had unusually high moral standards. There is no reason to think that future presidents will be different from those of the past. Almost certainly the office will continue to be held by men, and someday, no doubt, by women, who are not greater in their moral and intellectual capacities than other citizens. Yet unless and until we alter the presidency, they will hold an office of incomparable power for good and evil. And, being all too human, sometimes they will do great evil.

To paper over the gap between high expectations and cruel reality, a great many Americans hold firmly to the belief that the White House transforms its occupant: it makes a silk purse out of a sow's ear. The transformation, alas, is largely in the eye of the beholder, who passionately wishes to see, and so manages to see, majesty and divinity where there are only the ordinary (or sometimes extraordinary) shortcomings of a mere mortal being. There is no solid evidence, as far as I know, for hoping that the highly imperfect person who reaches the presidency will, in the conventional and ever hopeful phrase, "rise to the office." To be sure, the office may sometimes bring out the best in its holder. But it may, and often does, also bring out the worst. It may, and probably often does, do both.

What we need to confront, then, is an unpleasantness that the Framers understood and that later Americans in their longing for a superhuman greatness in the presidency have too often forgotten. Because the worst that the office may bring out in the person who holds it may be injurious to the life of a republic, and nowadays a danger to the world, the president must not be allowed to obtain too much discretionary power. If we had assumed all along that the president was likely to use discretion badly if given half a chance, would we ever have allowed the institution to evolve into the plebiscitary monarchy it seemed on the way to becoming? I think not.

Here again, solutions will be very hard to come by. A steady search for workable solutions ought surely to occupy a very high place on the agenda of our public life. The danger is that with the immediate crisis of the imperial presidency behind us, we shall ignore the problem.

The sort of unbalanced political system represented by the presidency of Richard Nixon did not, as we have seen, develop by itself. It developed with the support—sometimes active, sometimes passive—of Congress, the Supreme Court, the political parties, the major political figures of the country, the newspapers and commentators, intellectuals, lawyers, political scientists—and the electorate. In this sense, the country gave its uninformed consent to a political system in which the government could frequently make crucial decisions without the consent of the people. Thus, even though events have made the presidency the element most urgently in need of reform, the greater, more enduring, challenge is to refashion a government that would rest upon the informed and active consent of the people.

ACKNOWLEDGMENTS

The following copyrighted material is reprinted by permission of copyright holders and publishers:

Quotations in Chapters 3 and 12 from *Abraham Lincoln, The War Years* by Carl Sandburg, copyright © 1939. Reprinted by permission of Harcourt Brace Jovanovich, Inc.

Quotations in Chapters 10 and 19 from *Democracy in America* by Alexis de Tocqueville, translated by Reeve/Bowen/Bradley, copyright © 1945 by Alfred A. Knopf, Inc. Reprinted by permission of the publisher.

Quotations in Chapter 12 from *President and Congress* by Wilfred E. Binkley, copyright © 1937, 1947 by Wilfred E. Binkley. Reprinted by permission of Alfred A. Knopf, Inc.

Quotations in Chapter 12 from *His Majesty's Opposition 1714–1830* by Archibald S. Foord, copyright © 1964. Reprinted by permission of the Clarendon Press, Oxford.

Figure 15.3 from *Mass Politics* by Erik Allart and Stein Rokkan, copyright © 1970 by The Free Press. Reprinted by permission of The Macmillan Company.

Footnote table in Chapter 19 from *The Civic Culture: Political Attitudes and Democracy in Five Nations* by Gabriel A. Almond and Sidney Verba, copyright © 1963 by Princeton University Press. Reprinted by permission of Princeton University Press.

Tables 19.10 and 19.11 from unpublished survey data gathered by Sidney Verba and Gabriel A. Almond. Reprinted by permission of authors.

Table 21.1 from *Third Parties in Presidential Elections* by Daniel A. Mazmanian, copyright © 1974 by the Brookings Institution, Washington, D.C.

Quotations in Chapter 24 and Table 24.4 from *Public Opinion and American Democracy* by V. O. Key, Jr., copyright © 1961 by V. O. Key, Jr. Reprinted by permission of Alfred A. Knopf, Inc.

Table 26.2 from *Black Racial Attitudes* by Howard Schuman and Shirley Hatchett, copyright © 1974 by the Institute for Social Research of the University of Michigan.

Tables 27.3 and 27.4 from *Presidential Ballots, 1836–1892* by Walter Dean Burnham, copyright © 1955 by The Johns Hopkins Press.

Figure 28.2 from *Participation in America: Political Democracy and Social Equality* by Sidney Verba and Norman H. Nie, copyright © 1972 by Harper & Row and reprinted by permission.

Figures and tables from *Gallup Opinion Index*, Numbers 65, 92, 102, 108, 109, 111, 113, 117, 120, and Surveys on Watergate, April 1973–1974. Reprinted by permission of publisher.

INDEX

Printed in U.S.A.